Accounting Principles ACCT 210, Volume 1 - SDSU

SOUTH DAKOTA STATE UNIVERSITY

create.mheducation.com

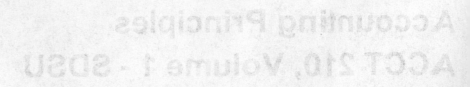

ISBN-13: 9781307661330

ISBN-10: 1307661335

Contents

1 Accounting in Business

Chapter Preview

ACCOUNTING USES	ETHICS AND ACCOUNTING	TRANSACTION ANALYSIS	FINANCIAL STATEMENTS
C1 Purpose of accounting	**C2** Ethics	**A1** Accounting equation and its components	**P2** Income statement
Accounting users	Generally accepted accounting principles	Expanded accounting equation	Statement of owner's equity
Opportunities in accounting	Business types	**P1** Transaction analysis—Illustrated	Balance sheet
AI and data analytics			Statement of cash flows
			A2 Financial analysis
NTK 1-1	NTK 1-2	NTK 1-3, 1-4	NTK 1-5

***Chapter Preview** is organized by "blocks" of key content and learning objectives followed by **Need-to-Know (NTK)** guided examples (with video)*

***Learning Objectives** are classified as conceptual, analytical, or procedural*

Learning Objectives

CONCEPTUAL

C1 Explain the importance of accounting and identify its users.

C2 Describe the importance of ethics and GAAP.

ANALYTICAL

A1 Define and interpret the accounting equation and each of its components.

A2 Compute and interpret return on assets.

PROCEDURAL

P1 Analyze business transactions using the accounting equation.

P2 Identify and prepare basic financial statements and explain how they interrelate.

Decision Feature launches each chapter showing the relevance of accounting for a real entrepreneur; Entrepreneurial Decision assignment returns to this feature with a mini-case

By the Numbers

"Learn from others' failures"—**REED HASTINGS**

netflix
STRANGER THINGS

Gabriel Aponte/Stringer/Getty Images

SAN JOSE, CA—Reed Hastings recalls he got the idea for **Netflix (Netflix.com)** after paying a $40 late fee on the movie *Apollo 13.* "I was embarrassed . . . and it got me thinking that there's a big market out there," says Reed. While Netflix started out delivering movies and shows by mail, Reed's college coursework convinced him that Internet streaming was the future. Today, Netflix's video-streaming service accounts for 40% of Internet traffic in the evening hours.

While some of Netflix's success is attributed to a good business idea, much of it is a result of execution. In the early stages, Netflix invested heavily in accounting and data analytics systems. These systems track everything from detailed sales information to how long a customer watches a show. "Being an entrepreneur is about patience and persistence, not the quick buck," claims Reed.

Accounting and data analytics help Netflix make key decisions. For example, Netflix spent $140 million for one season of *The Crown,* which was the most expensive show ever produced. Using sales data and analytics on viewing habits, Netflix predicted the show would be a hit and generate additional sales.

Netflix's accounting analytics also enable it to target customers with personalized content suggestions. Some estimate that this accounting-driven strategy to customer retention adds an additional $1 billion in revenue each year.

While accounting analytics have contributed to success for Netflix, Reed insists business is fun: "For some people, high school graduation is the peak . . . but I find running a company to be a lot more fun and exciting."

Sources: *Netflix website*, January 2021; *Quartz*, August 2017 and February 2017; *Inc.com*, December 2005

IMPORTANCE OF ACCOUNTING

C1 Explain the importance of accounting and identify its users.

Why is accounting so popular on campus? Why are there so many openings for accounting jobs? Why is accounting so important to companies? The answer is that we live in an information age in which accounting information impacts us all.

Accounting is an information and measurement system that identifies, records, and communicates an organization's business activities. Exhibit 1.1 shows these accounting functions.

EXHIBIT 1.1 Accounting Functions

Identifying
Recording
Communicating
Select transactions and events
Examples are Apple's sale of iPhones and TicketMaster's receipt of ticket money.
Input, measure, and log
Examples are dated logs of transactions measured in dollars.
Prepare, analyze, and interpret
Examples are reports that we analyze and interpret.

Our most common contact with accounting is through credit checks, checking accounts, tax forms, and payroll. These experiences focus on **recordkeeping,** or **bookkeeping,** which is the recording of transactions and events. This is just one part of accounting. Accounting also includes analysis and interpretation of information.

Users of Accounting Information

Accounting is called the *language of business* because it communicates data that help people make better decisions. People using accounting information are divided into two groups: *external users* and *internal users*. **Financial accounting** focuses on the needs of external users, and **managerial accounting** focuses on the needs of internal users.

External Users **External users** of accounting information do *not* directly run the organization and have limited access to its accounting information. These users get accounting information from general-purpose financial statements. Following is a partial list of external users and decisions they make with accounting information.

Point: The largest accounting firms are EY, KPMG, PwC, and Deloitte.

- *Lenders* (creditors) loan money or other resources to an organization. Banks, savings and loans, and mortgage companies are lenders. Lenders use information to assess if an organization will repay its loans.
- *Shareholders* (*investors*) are the owners of a corporation. They use accounting reports to decide whether to buy, hold, or sell stock.
- *External* (independent) *auditors* examine financial statements to verify that they are prepared according to generally accepted accounting principles.
- *Nonmanagerial* and *nonexecutive employees* and *labor unions* use external information to bargain for better wages.
- *Regulators* have legal authority over certain activities of organizations. For example, the Internal Revenue Service (IRS) requires accounting reports for computing taxes.
- *Voters* and *government officials* use information to evaluate government performance.
- *Contributors* to nonprofits use information to evaluate the use and impact of donations.
- *Suppliers* use information to analyze a customer before extending credit.
- *Customers* use financial reports to assess the stability of potential suppliers.

Internal Users **Internal users** of accounting information directly manage the organization. Internal reports are designed for the unique needs of managerial or executive employees, such as the chief executive officer (CEO). Following is a partial list of internal users and decisions they make with accounting information.

- *Purchasing managers* need to know what, when, and how much to purchase.
- *Human resource managers* need information about employees' payroll, benefits, and performance.
- *Production managers* use information to monitor costs and ensure quality.
- *Distribution managers* need reports for timely and accurate delivery of products and services.
- *Marketing managers* use reports to target consumers, set prices, and monitor consumer needs.
- *Service managers* use reports to provide better service to customers.
- *Research and development managers* use information on projected costs and revenues of innovations.

Opportunities in Accounting

Accounting has four areas of opportunities: financial, managerial, taxation, and accounting-related. Exhibit 1.2 lists selected opportunities in each area.

Exhibit 1.3 shows that the majority of opportunities are in *private accounting,* which are employees working for businesses. *Public accounting* involves accounting services such as auditing, taxation, and advisory services. Opportunities also exist in government and not-for-profit agencies, including business regulation and law enforcement.

EXHIBIT 1.2

Accounting Opportunities

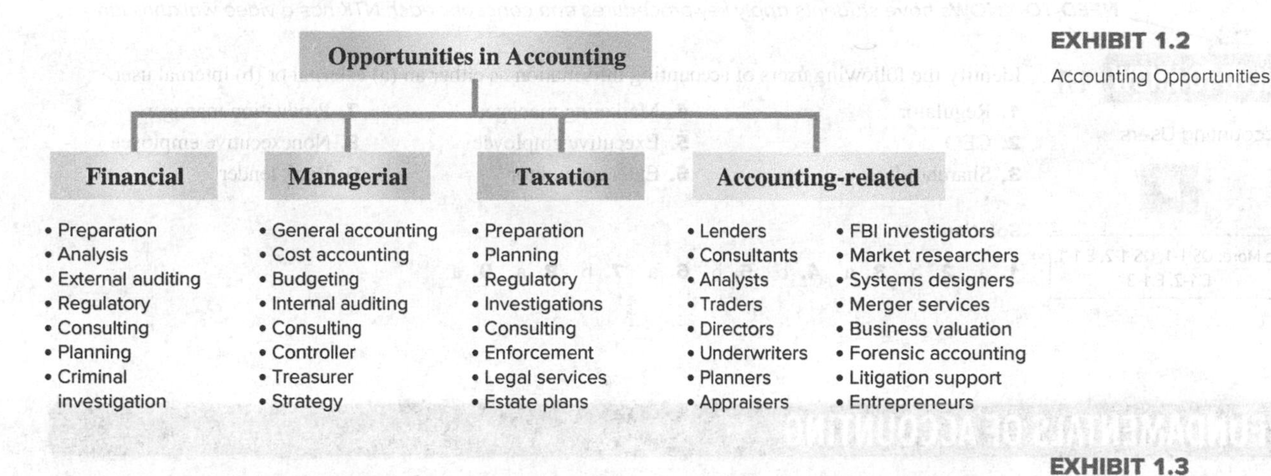

EXHIBIT 1.3

Accounting Jobs by Area

Private accounting 54%
Government and not-for-profit 22%
Public accounting 24%

Accounting specialists are highly regarded, and their professional standing is often denoted by a certificate. Certified public accountants (CPAs) must meet education and experience requirements, pass an exam, and be ethical. Many accounting specialists hold certificates in addition to or instead of the CPA. Two of the most common are the certificate in management accounting (CMA) and the certified internal auditor (CIA). Employers want specialists with designations such as certified bookkeeper (CB), certified payroll professional (CPP), certified fraud examiner (CFE), and certified forensic accountant (CrFA).

Accounting specialists are in demand. Exhibit 1.4 reports average annual salaries for several accounting positions. Salaries vary based on location, company size, and other factors.

EXHIBIT 1.4

Accounting Salaries

Public Accounting	Salary
Partner	$245,000
Manager (6–8 years)	112,000
Senior (3–5 years)	90,000
Junior (0–2 years)	62,500

Private Accounting	Salary
CFO	$290,000
Controller/Treasurer	180,000
Manager (6–8 years)	98,500
Senior (3–5 years)	81,500
Junior (0–2 years)	60,000

Recordkeeping	Salary
Full-charge bookkeeper	$60,500
Accounts manager	58,000
Payroll manager	59,500
Accounting clerk (0–2 years)	39,500

Artificial Intelligence in Accounting Some estimate that artificial intelligence (AI) could replace 40% of today's workforce in the next decade. Repetitive tasks such as entering invoice and transaction data will be done by AI and software. This trend toward more AI integration bodes well for those with accounting knowledge. Accountants will be needed to help develop advanced AI systems and to analyze reports and graphics created by AI systems. Because employers recognize these valuable skills, accounting is consistently ranked among the top professions in terms of both future demand and future earnings.

Data Analytics and Visualization in Accounting Data analytics and data visualization are among the top skills sought by employers. **Data analytics** is a process of analyzing data to identify meaningful relations and trends. **Data visualization** is a graphical presentation of data to help people understand their significance. In accounting, data analytics and visualization help individuals make informed business decisions. **Dr Pepper Snapple Group** uses data analytics and visualization to send accounting information to its sales route staff via an app in real time. Staff then make data-driven decisions on what sales and promotions to offer retailers. **Tableau Dashboard Activities** in Connect offer the opportunity to begin developing such skills.

NEED-TO-KNOWs have students apply key procedures and concepts; each NTK has a video walkthrough

NEED-TO-KNOW 1-1

Accounting Users

C1

Do More: QS 1-1, QS 1-2, E 1-1, E 1-2, E 1-3

Identify the following users of accounting information as either an (a) external or (b) internal user.

1. Regulator	**4.** Marketing manager	**7.** Production manager
2. CEO	**5.** Executive employee	**8.** Nonexecutive employee
3. Shareholder	**6.** External auditor	**9.** Bank lender

Solution

1. a **2.** b **3.** a **4.** b **5.** b **6.** a **7.** b **8.** a **9.** a

FUNDAMENTALS OF ACCOUNTING

C2

Describe the importance of ethics and GAAP.

Ethics—A Key Concept

For information to be useful, it must be trusted. This demands ethics in accounting. **Ethics** are beliefs that separate right from wrong. They are accepted standards of good and bad behavior.

Accountants face ethical choices as they prepare financial reports. These choices can affect the salaries and bonuses paid to workers. They even can affect the success of products and services. Misleading information can lead to a bad decision that harms workers and the business. There is an old saying: *Good ethics are good business.* Exhibit 1.5 gives a three-step process for making ethical decisions.

EXHIBIT 1.5

Ethical Decision Making

1. Identify ethical concerns

Use ethics to recognize an ethical concern.

2. Analyze options

Consider all consequences.

3. Make ethical decision

Choose best option after weighing all consequences.

Fraud Triangle: Ethics under Attack The fraud triangle shows *three* factors that push a person to commit fraud.

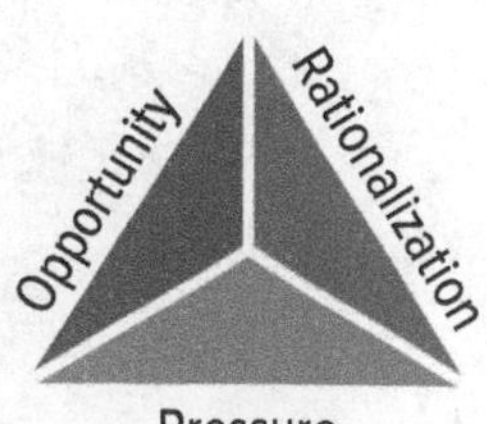

- **Opportunity.** A person must be able to commit fraud with a low risk of getting caught.
- **Pressure,** or incentive. A person must feel pressure or have incentive to commit fraud.
- **Rationalization,** or attitude. A person justifies fraud or does not see its criminal nature.

The key to stopping fraud is to focus on prevention. It is less expensive and more effective to prevent fraud from happening than it is to detect it.

To help prevent fraud, companies set up internal controls. **Internal controls** are procedures to protect assets, ensure reliable accounting, promote efficiency, and uphold company policies. Examples are good records, physical controls (locks), and independent reviews. **Auditors** verify the effectiveness of internal controls.

Generally Accepted Accounting Principles

Financial accounting is governed by concepts and rules known as **generally accepted accounting principles (GAAP).** GAAP wants information to have *relevance* and *faithful representation.* Relevant information affects decisions of users. Faithful representation means information accurately reflects the business results.

The **Financial Accounting Standards Board (FASB)** is given the task of setting GAAP from the **Securities and Exchange Commission (SEC).** The SEC is a U.S. government agency that oversees proper use of GAAP by companies that sell stock and debt to the public. An **audit** examines whether financial statements are prepared using GAAP.

International Standards Our global economy demands comparability in accounting reports. The **International Accounting Standards Board (IASB)** issues **International Financial Reporting Standards (IFRS)** that identify preferred accounting practices. These standards are similar to, but sometimes different from, U.S. GAAP. The FASB and IASB are working to reduce differences between U.S. GAAP and IFRS.

Conceptual Framework

The FASB **conceptual framework** in Exhibit 1.6 consists of the following.

- **Objectives**—to provide information useful to investors, creditors, and others.
- **Qualitative characteristics**—to require information that has *relevance* and *faithful representation.*
- **Elements**—to define items in financial statements.
- **Recognition and measurement**—to set criteria for an item to be recognized as an element; and how to measure it.

EXHIBIT 1.6

Conceptual Framework

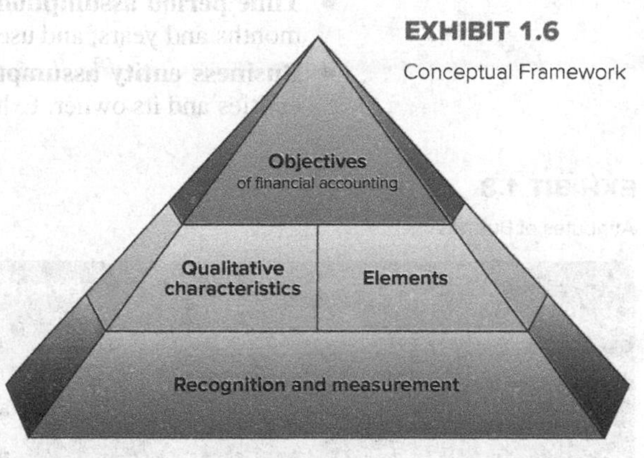

Principles, Assumptions, and Constraint There are two types of accounting principles (and assumptions). *General principles* are the assumptions, concepts, and guidelines for preparing financial statements; these are shown in purple font in Exhibit 1.7, along with key assumptions in red font. *Specific principles* are detailed rules used in reporting business transactions and events; they are described as we encounter them.

EXHIBIT 1.7

Building Blocks for GAAP

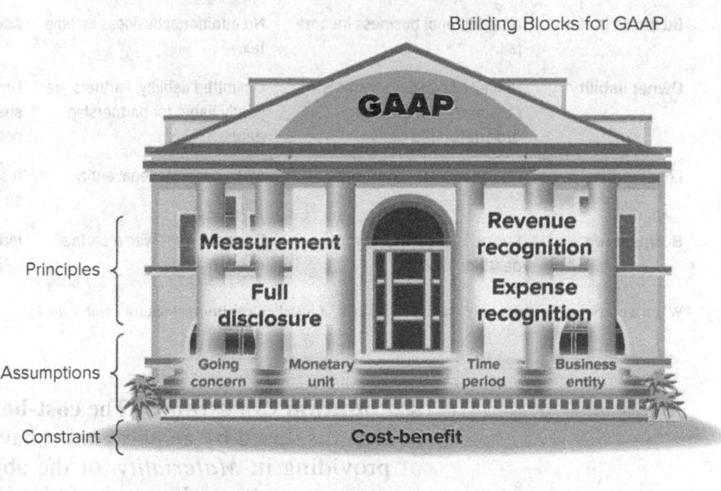

Accounting Principles There are four general principles.

- **Measurement principle (cost principle)** Accounting information is based on actual cost. Cost is measured on a cash or equal-to-cash basis. This means if cash is given for a service, its cost is measured by the cash paid. If something besides cash is exchanged (such as a car traded for a truck), cost is measured as the cash value of what is given up or received. Information based on cost is considered objective. *Objectivity* means that information is supported by independent, unbiased evidence. Later chapters cover adjustments to market and introduce *fair value.*
- **Revenue recognition principle** Revenue is recognized (1) when goods or services are provided to customers and (2) at the amount expected to be received from the customer. Revenue (sales) is the amount received from selling products and services. The amount received is usually in cash, but it also can be a customer's promise to pay at a future date, called credit sales. (To *recognize* means to record it.)
- **Expense recognition principle (matching principle)** A company records the expenses it incurred to generate the revenue reported. An example is rent costs of office space.

Point: A company pays $500 for equipment. The cost principle requires it be recorded at $500. It makes no difference if the owner thinks this equipment is worth $700.

Example: A lawn service bills a customer $800 on June 1 for two months of mowing (June and July). The customer pays the bill on July 1. When is revenue recorded? *Answer:* It is recorded over time as it is earned; record $400 revenue for June and $400 for July.

Example: Credit cards are used to pay $200 in gas for a lawn service during June and July. The cards are paid in August. When is expense recorded? *Answer:* If revenue is earned over time, record $100 expense in June and $100 in July.

- **Full disclosure principle** A company reports the details behind financial statements that would impact users' decisions. Those disclosures are often in footnotes to the statements.

Accounting Assumptions There are four accounting assumptions.

- **Going-concern assumption** Accounting information presumes that the business will continue operating instead of being closed or sold. This means, for example, that property is reported at cost instead of liquidation value.
- **Monetary unit assumption** Transactions and events are expressed in monetary, or money, units. Examples of monetary units are the U.S. dollar and the Mexican peso.
- **Time period assumption** The life of a company can be divided into time periods, such as months and years, and useful reports can be prepared for those periods.
- **Business entity assumption** A business is accounted for separately from other business entities and its owner. Exhibit 1.8 describes four common business entities.

EXHIBIT 1.8

Attributes of Businesses

	Sole Proprietorship	Partnership	Corporation	Limited Liability Company (LLC)
Number of owners	1 owner; easy to set up.	2 or more, called *partners;* easy to set up.	1 or more, called *shareholders;* can get many investors by selling **stock** or **shares** of corporate ownership.*	1 or more, called *members*.
Business taxation	No additional business income tax.	No additional business income tax.	Additional corporate income tax.	No additional business income tax.
Owner liability	Unlimited liability. Owner is personally liable for **proprietorship** debts.	Unlimited liability. Partners are jointly liable for partnership debts.	Limited liability. Owners, called **shareholders** (or **stockholders**), are not liable for corporate acts and debts.	Limited liability. Owners, called **members,** are not personally liable for LLC debts.
Legal entity	*Not* a separate legal entity.	*Not* a separate legal entity.	A separate entity with the same rights and responsibilities as a person.	A separate entity with the same rights and responsibilities as a person.
Business life	Business ends with owner death or choice.	Business ends with a partner death or choice.	Indefinite.	Indefinite.

*When a corporation issues only one class of stock, it is called **common stock** (or *capital stock*).

Accounting Constraint The **cost-benefit constraint, or cost constraint,** says that information disclosed by an entity must have benefits to the user that are greater than the costs of providing it. *Materiality,* or the ability of information to influence decisions, is also sometimes mentioned as a constraint. *Conservatism* and *industry practices* are sometimes listed as well.

***Decision Ethics** boxes are role-playing exercises that stress ethics in accounting*

Decision Ethics

Entrepreneur You and a friend develop a new design for ice skates that improves speed but increases risk of injury. You plan to form a business to manufacture and sell the skates. You and your friend want to minimize taxes, but your big concern is potential lawsuits from customers who might be injured on these skates. What form of organization do you set up? ■ *Answer:* You should probably form an LLC. An LLC helps protect *personal* property from lawsuits directed at the business. Also, an LLC is not subject to an additional business income tax. You also must examine the ethics of starting a business where injuries are expected.

Part 1: Identify the accounting principle or assumption that best reflects each situation.

1. AAA Painting performs services for a customer. AAA records revenue this period even though the customer is not billed until next period.
2. Ming Studios purchases camera equipment for $12,000 cash. The owner thinks the equipment is worth $18,000. The equipment is recorded at $12,000.
3. Alfonso owns Consulting LLC. Alfonso keeps personal expenses separate from LLC expenses.

NEED-TO-KNOW 1-2

Accounting Guidance
C2

Solution

1. Revenue recognition principle 2. Measurement principle 3. Business entity assumption

Part 2: Recommend a business entity type in each situation.

a. An entrepreneur is deciding between a sole proprietorship and an LLC. Two goals are to pay no additional business income tax and to have limited liability.
b. An entrepreneur is deciding between a partnership and a corporation. Two goals are the ability to add many investors by selling shares of ownership and a business with an indefinite life.

Do More: QS 1-3, QS 1-4, QS 1-5, QS 1-6, E 1-4, E 1-5, E 1-6, E 1-7, E 1-8

Solution

a. LLC b. Corporation

BUSINESS TRANSACTIONS AND ACCOUNTING

Accounting shows two basic aspects of a company: what it owns and what it owes. *Assets* are resources a company owns or controls. The claims on a company's assets—what it owes—are separated into owner (equity) and nonowner (liability) claims. Together, liabilities and equity are the source of funds to acquire assets.

A1

Define and interpret the accounting equation and each of its components.

Assets **Assets** are resources a company owns or controls. These resources are expected to yield future benefits. Examples are web servers for an online services company, musical instruments for a rock band, and land for a vegetable grower. Assets include cash, supplies, equipment, land, and accounts receivable. A *receivable* is an asset that promises a future inflow of resources. A company that provides a service or product on credit has an account receivable from that customer.

Point: "On credit" and "on account" mean cash is received or paid at a future date.

Liabilities **Liabilities** are creditors' claims on assets. These claims are obligations to provide assets, products, or services to others. A *payable* is a liability that promises a future outflow of resources. Examples are wages payable to workers, accounts payable to suppliers, notes (loans) payable to banks, and taxes payable.

Equity **Equity** is the owner's claim on assets and is equal to assets minus liabilities. Equity is also called *net assets* or *residual equity*.

Accounting Equation

The relation of assets, liabilities, and equity is shown in the following **accounting equation. The accounting equation applies to all transactions and events, to all companies and organizations, and to all points in time.**

Assets = Liabilities + Equity

Point: This equation can be rearranged. Example: Assets − Liabilities = Equity

Equity has four parts as shown in the **expanded accounting equation.**

Assets = Liabilities + Owner, Capital − Owner, Withdrawals + Revenues − Expenses
(The last four terms, Owner, Capital through Expenses, are bracketed together as **Equity**.)

We see that equity increases from owner investments and from revenues. It decreases from owner withdrawals and from expenses. These four parts of equity follow.

Owner investments are inflows of cash and other net assets from owner contributions, which increase equity.

Owner withdrawals are outflows of cash and other assets to owners for personal use, which reduce equity.

Revenues increase equity (via net income) from sales of products and services to customers; examples are sales of products, consulting services provided, facilities rented to others, and commissions from services.

− Expenses

Expenses decrease equity (via net income) from costs of providing products and services to customers; examples are costs of employee time, use of supplies, advertising, utilities, and insurance fees.

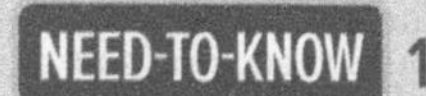

1-3

Accounting Equation

A1

Part 1: Use the *accounting equation* to compute the missing financial statement amounts.

Company	Assets	Liabilities	Equity
Bose	$150	$ 30	$ (a)
Vogue	$ (b)	$100	$300

Solution

a. $120 **b.** $400

Part 2: Use the *expanded accounting equation* to compute the missing financial statement amounts.

Company	Assets	Liabilities	Owner, Capital	Owner, Withdrawals	Revenues	Expenses
Tesla	$200	$ 80	$100	$ 5	$ (a)	$40
YouTube	$400	$160	$220	$ (b)	$120	$90

Do More: QS 1-7, QS 1-8, E 1-9, E 1-10, E 1-11

Solution

a. $65 **b.** $10

Transaction Analysis

P1 Analyze business transactions using the accounting equation.

Business activities are described in terms of transactions and events. **External transactions** are exchanges of value between two entities, which cause changes in the accounting equation. An example is the sale of the *AppleCare Protection Plan* by **Apple**. **Internal transactions** are exchanges within an entity, which may or may not affect the accounting equation. An example is **Target**'s use of its supplies, which are reported as expenses when used. **Events** are happenings that affect the accounting equation *and* are reliably measured. They include business events such as changes in the market value of certain assets and liabilities and natural events such as fires that destroy assets and create losses.

This section uses the accounting equation to analyze 11 transactions and events of FastForward, a start-up consulting (service) business, in its first month of operations. **Remember that after each transaction and event, assets always equal liabilities plus equity.**

Transaction 1: Investment by Owner On December 1, Chas Taylor forms a consulting business named FastForward and it is set up as a proprietorship. FastForward evaluates the performance of footwear and accessories. Taylor owns and manages the business, which will publish online reviews and consult with clubs, athletes, and others who purchase **Nike** and **Adidas** products.

Real companies are in bold magenta

Taylor invests $30,000 cash in the new company and deposits the cash in a bank account opened under the name of FastForward. After this transaction, cash (an asset) and equity each equals $30,000. Equity is increased by the owner's investment, which is included in that column and titled C. Taylor, Capital. The effect of this transaction on FastForward is shown in the accounting equation as follows (we label the equity entries).

	Assets	=	Liabilities	+	Equity
	Cash	=			C. Taylor, Capital
(1)	+$30,000	=			+$30,000 Owner investment

Transaction 2: Purchase Supplies for Cash FastForward uses $2,500 of its cash to buy supplies of Nike and Adidas footwear for performance testing over the next few months. This transaction is an exchange of cash, an asset, for another kind of asset, supplies. It simply changes the form of assets from cash to supplies. The decrease in cash is exactly equal to the increase in supplies. The supplies of footwear are assets because of the expected future benefits from performance tests.

	Assets			=	Liabilities	+	Equity
	Cash	+	Supplies	=			C. Taylor, Capital
Old Bal.	$30,000			=			$30,000
(2)	−2,500	+	$2,500				
New Bal.	$27,500	+	$ 2,500	=			$30,000
	$30,000						$30,000

Transaction 3: Purchase Equipment for Cash FastForward spends $26,000 to acquire equipment for testing footwear. Like Transaction 2, Transaction 3 is an exchange of one asset, cash, for another asset, equipment. The equipment is an asset because of its expected future benefits from testing footwear. This purchase changes the makeup of assets but does not change the asset total. The accounting equation remains in balance.

	Assets					=	Liabilities	+	Equity
	Cash	+	Supplies	+	Equipment	=			C. Taylor, Capital
Old Bal.	$27,500	+	$2,500			=			$30,000
(3)	−26,000			+	$26,000				
New Bal.	$ 1,500	+	$2,500	+	$ 26,000	=			$30,000
			$30,000						$30,000

Transaction 4: Purchase Supplies on Credit Taylor decides more supplies of footwear and accessories are needed. These additional supplies cost $7,100, but FastForward has only $1,500 in cash. Taylor arranges to purchase them on credit from CalTech Supply

Point: Supplies bought "on credit" are received now and then cash is paid for them later.

Point: Accounts payable are amounts owed to others for items purchased on credit.

Company. Thus, FastForward acquires supplies in exchange for a promise to pay for them later. This purchase increases assets by $7,100 in supplies, and liabilities (called *accounts payable* to CalTech Supply) increase by the same amount.

	Assets					=	Liabilities	+	Equity
	Cash	+	Supplies	+	Equipment	=	Accounts Payable	+	C. Taylor, Capital
Old Bal.	$1,500	+	$2,500	+	$26,000	=			$30,000
(4)		+	7,100				+$7,100		
New Bal.	$1,500	+	$9,600	+	$26,000	=	$7,100	+	$30,000
			$37,100					$37,100	

Transaction 5: Provide Services for Cash

FastForward plans to earn revenues by selling online ad space and consulting with clients about footwear and accessories. In its first job, FastForward provides consulting services and immediately collects $4,200 cash. The accounting equation reflects this increase in cash of $4,200 and in equity of $4,200. This increase in equity is shown in the far right column under Revenues because the cash received is earned by providing consulting services.

	Assets					=	Liabilities	+	Equity		
	Cash	+	Supplies	+	Equipment	=	Accounts Payable	+	C. Taylor, Capital	+	Revenues
Old Bal.	$1,500	+	$9,600	+	$26,000	=	$7,100	+	$30,000		
(5)	+4,200									+	$4,200 Consulting
New Bal.	$5,700	+	$9,600	+	$26,000	=	$7,100	+	$30,000	+	$ 4,200
			$41,300						$41,300		

Transactions 6 and 7: Payment of Expenses in Cash

FastForward pays $1,000 to rent facilities for the month of December. The rental payment is shown in the following accounting equation as Transaction 6. FastForward also pays the biweekly $700 salary of the company's only employee. This is shown in the accounting equation as Transaction 7. Both Transactions 6 and 7 are December expenses for FastForward. The costs of both rent and salary are expenses, not assets, because their benefits are used in December (they have no future benefits after December). The accounting equation shows that both transactions reduce cash and equity. The far right column shows these decreases as Expenses.

Point: Expense recognition principle requires that expenses are recognized when the revenue they help generate is recorded.

Expenses decrease equity.

	Assets					=	Liabilities	+	Equity				
	Cash	+	Supplies	+	Equipment	=	Accounts Payable	+	C. Taylor, Capital	+	Revenues	−	Expenses
Old Bal.	$5,700	+	$9,600	+	$26,000	=	$7,100	+	$30,000	+	$4,200		
(6)	−1,000											−	$1,000 Rent
Bal.	4,700	+	9,600	+	26,000	=	7,100	+	30,000	+	4,200	−	1,000
(7)	− 700											−	700 Salaries
New Bal.	$4,000	+	$9,600	+	$26,000	=	$7,100	+	$30,000	+	$4,200	−	$ 1,700
			$39,600						$39,600				

Transaction 8: Provide Services and Facilities for Credit FastForward provides consulting services of $1,600 and rents its test facilities for an additional $300 to Adidas on credit. Adidas is billed for the $1,900 total. This transaction creates a new asset, called *accounts receivable,* from Adidas. Accounts receivable is increased instead of cash because the payment has not yet been received. Equity is increased from the two revenue components shown in the Revenues column of the accounting equation.

Point: Accounts receivable are amounts owed by customers for services or items sold on credit.

Point: Transaction 8, like 5, records revenue when work is performed, not necessarily when cash is received.

	Assets								=	Liabilities	+	Equity					
	Cash	+	Accounts Receivable	+	Supplies	+	Equipment		=	Accounts Payable	+	C. Taylor, Capital	+	Revenues		−	Expenses
Old Bal.	$4,000			+	$9,600	+	$26,000		=	$7,100	+	$30,000	+	$4,200		−	$1,700
(8)		+	$1,900										+	1,600	Consulting		
													+	300	Rental		
New Bal.	$4,000	+	$ 1,900	+	$9,600	+	$26,000		=	$7,100	+	$30,000	+	$6,100		−	$1,700
	$41,500											$41,500					

Transaction 9: Receipt of Cash from Accounts Receivable The client in Transaction 8 (Adidas) pays $1,900 to FastForward 10 days after it is billed for consulting services. Transaction 9 does not change the total amount of assets and does not affect liabilities or equity. It converts the receivable (an asset) to cash (another asset). It does not create new revenue. Revenue was recognized when FastForward performed the services in Transaction 8, not when the cash is collected.

Point: Transaction 9 involved no added client work, so no added revenue is recorded.

Point: Receipt of cash is not always a revenue.

	Assets							=	Liabilities	+	Equity				
	Cash	+	Accounts Receivable	+	Supplies	+	Equipment	=	Accounts Payable	+	C. Taylor, Capital	+	Revenues	−	Expenses
Old Bal.	$4,000	+	$1,900	+	$9,600	+	$26,000	=	$7,100	+	$30,000	+	$6,100	−	$1,700
(9)	+1,900	−	1,900												
New Bal.	$5,900	+	$ 0	+	$9,600	+	$26,000	=	$7,100	+	$30,000	+	$6,100	−	$1,700
	$41,500										$41,500				

Transaction 10: Payment of Accounts Payable FastForward pays CalTech Supply $900 cash as partial payment for its earlier $7,100 purchase of supplies (Transaction 4), leaving $6,200 unpaid. This transaction decreases FastForward's cash by $900 and decreases its liability to CalTech Supply by $900. Equity does not change. This event does not create an expense even though cash flows out of FastForward (instead the expense is recorded when FastForward uses these supplies).

	Assets							=	Liabilities	+	Equity				
	Cash	+	Accounts Receivable	+	Supplies	+	Equipment	=	Accounts Payable	+	C. Taylor, Capital	+	Revenues	−	Expenses
Old Bal.	$5,900	+	$ 0	+	$9,600	+	$26,000	=	$7,100	+	$30,000	+	$6,100	−	$1,700
(10)	−900								−900						
New Bal.	$5,000	+	$ 0	+	$9,600	+	$26,000	=	$6,200	+	$30,000	+	$6,100	−	$1,700
	$40,600										$40,600				

Transaction 11: Withdrawal of Cash by Owner The owner of FastForward withdraws $200 cash for personal use. Withdrawals (decreases in equity) are not reported as expenses because they do not help earn revenue. Because withdrawals are not expenses, they are not used in computing net income.

Withdrawals decrease equity.

	Assets				= Liabilities +	Equity			
	Cash	+ Accounts Receivable	+ Supplies	+ Equipment	= Accounts Payable	+ C. Taylor, Capital	− C. Taylor, Withdrawals	+ Revenues	− Expenses
Old Bal.	$5,000	+ $ 0	+ $9,600	+ $26,000	= $6,200	+ $30,000		+ $6,100	− $1,700
(11)	−200						− $200 Owner Withdrawals		
New Bal.	$4,800	+ $ 0	+ $9,600	+ $26,000	= $6,200	+ $30,000	− $200	+ $6,100	− $1,700
	$40,400				$40,400				

EXHIBIT 1.9

Summary of Transactions Using the Accounting Equation

Summary of Transactions

Exhibit 1.9 shows the effects of these 11 transactions of FastForward using the accounting equation. Assets equal liabilities plus equity after each transaction.

	Assets				= Liabilities +	Equity			
	Cash	+ Accounts Receivable	+ Supplies	+ Equipment	= Accounts Payable	+ C. Taylor, Capital	− C. Taylor, Withdrawals	+ Revenues	− Expenses
(1)	$30,000				=	$30,000			
(2)	− 2,500		+ $2,500						
Bal.	27,500		+ 2,500		=	30,000			
(3)	−26,000			+ $26,000					
Bal.	1,500		+ 2,500	+ 26,000	=	30,000			
(4)			+ 7,100		= +$7,100				
Bal.	1,500		+ 9,600	+ 26,000	= 7,100	+ 30,000			
(5)	+ 4,200							+ $4,200	
Bal.	5,700		+ 9,600	+ 26,000	= 7,100	+ 30,000		+ 4,200	
(6)	− 1,000								− $1,000
Bal.	4,700		+ 9,600	+ 26,000	= 7,100	+ 30,000		+ 4,200	− 1,000
(7)	− 700								− 700
Bal.	4,000		+ 9,600	+ 26,000	= 7,100	+ 30,000		+ 4,200	− 1,700
(8)		+ $1,900						+ 1,600	
								+ 300	
Bal.	4,000	+ 1,900	+ 9,600	+ 26,000	= 7,100	+ 30,000		6,100	− 1,700
(9)	+ 1,900	− 1,900							
Bal.	5,900	+ 0	+ 9,600	+ 26,000	= 7,100	+ 30,000		+ 6,100	− 1,700
(10)	− 900				− 900				
Bal.	5,000	+ 0	+ 9,600	+ 26,000	= 6,200	+ 30,000		+ 6,100	− 1,700
(11)	− 200						− $200		
Bal.	$ 4,800	+ $ 0	+ $ 9,600	+ $ 26,000	= $ 6,200	+ $ 30,000	− $200	+ $6,100	− $ 1,700

Larry W. Smith/EPA-EFE/Shutterstock

Decision Insight

Measurement and Recognition Revenues for the **Kansas City Chiefs, Los Angeles Rams, Green Bay Packers,** and other professional sports teams include ticket sales, television broadcasts, concessions, and advertising. Revenues from ticket sales are earned when the team plays each game. Advance ticket sales are not revenues; instead, they are a liability until the team plays the game for which the ticket was sold. At that point, the liability is removed and revenues are reported. ■

NEED-TO-KNOW 1-4

Transaction Analysis
P1

Do More: QS 1-10, QS 1-11, E 1-12, E 1-13, E 1-14, E 1-15

Assume Tata Company began operations on January 1 and completed the following transactions during its first month of operations. Show the effects of each transaction in a table like Exhibit 1.9.

Jan. 1 Jamsetji Tata invested $4,000 cash in Tata Company.
5 The company purchased $2,000 of equipment on credit.
14 The company provided $540 of services for a client on credit.
21 The company paid $250 cash for an employee's salary.

Solution

	Assets			=	Liabilities	+	Equity						
	Cash	+	Accounts Receivable	+	Equipment	=	Accounts Payable	+	J. Tata, Capital	−	J. Tata, Withdrawals	+	Revenues	−	Expenses
Jan. 1	$4,000					=			$4,000						
Jan. 5				+	$2,000		+$2,000								
Bal.	4,000			+	2,000	=	2,000	+	4,000						
Jan. 14		+	$540									+	$540		
Bal.	4,000	+	540	+	2,000	=	2,000	+	4,000			+	540		
Jan. 21	−250													−	$250
Bal.	3,750	+	540	+	2,000	=	2,000	+	4,000			+	540	−	250
			$6,290								$6,290				

FINANCIAL STATEMENTS

P2 Identify and prepare basic financial statements and explain how they interrelate.

Financial statements are prepared in the order below using the 11 transactions of FastForward. (These statements are *unadjusted*—we explain this in Chapters 2 and 3.) The four financial statements and their purposes follow.

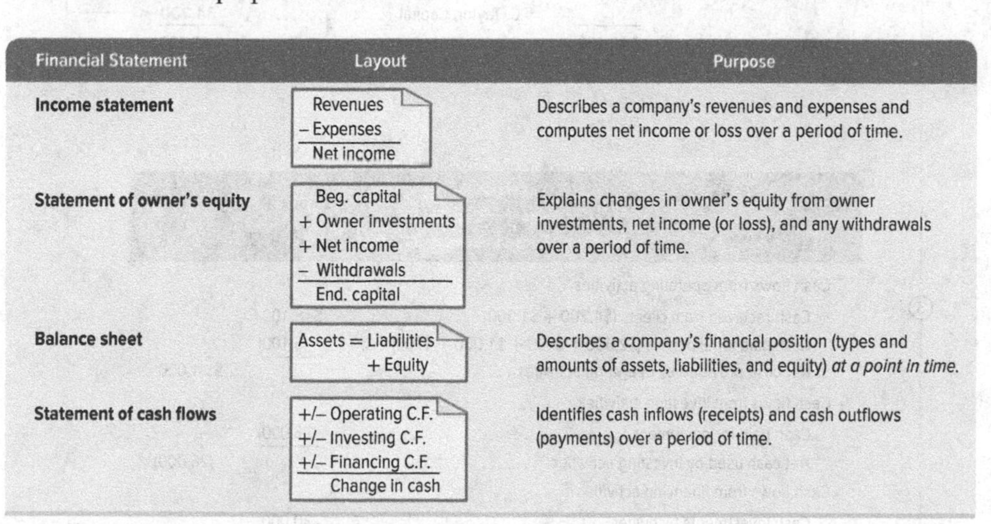

Financial Statement	Layout	Purpose
Income statement	Revenues − Expenses Net income	Describes a company's revenues and expenses and computes net income or loss over a period of time.
Statement of owner's equity	Beg. capital + Owner investments + Net income − Withdrawals End. capital	Explains changes in owner's equity from owner investments, net income (or loss), and any withdrawals over a period of time.
Balance sheet	Assets = Liabilities + Equity	Describes a company's financial position (types and amounts of assets, liabilities, and equity) *at a point in time*.
Statement of cash flows	+/− Operating C.F. +/− Investing C.F. +/− Financing C.F. Change in cash	Identifies cash inflows (receipts) and cash outflows (payments) over a period of time.

Income Statement

FastForward's income statement for December is shown at the top of Exhibit 1.10. Information about revenues and expenses is taken from the Equity columns of Exhibit 1.9. Revenues are reported first on the income statement. They include consulting revenues of $5,800 from Transactions 5 and 8 and rental revenue of $300 from Transaction 8. Expenses are reported after

EXHIBIT 1.10

Financial Statements and Their Links

Point: A statement's heading identifies the company, the statement title, and the date or time period.

Point: Arrow lines show how the statements are linked.
① Net income is used to compute owner capital.
② Owner capital is used to prepare the balance sheet.
③ Cash from the balance sheet is used to reconcile the statement of cash flows.

Point: The income statement, the statement of owner's equity, and the statement of cash flows are prepared for a *period* of time. The balance sheet is prepared as of a *point* in time.

Point: A single ruled line means an addition or subtraction. Final totals are double underlined. Negative amounts may or may not be in parentheses.

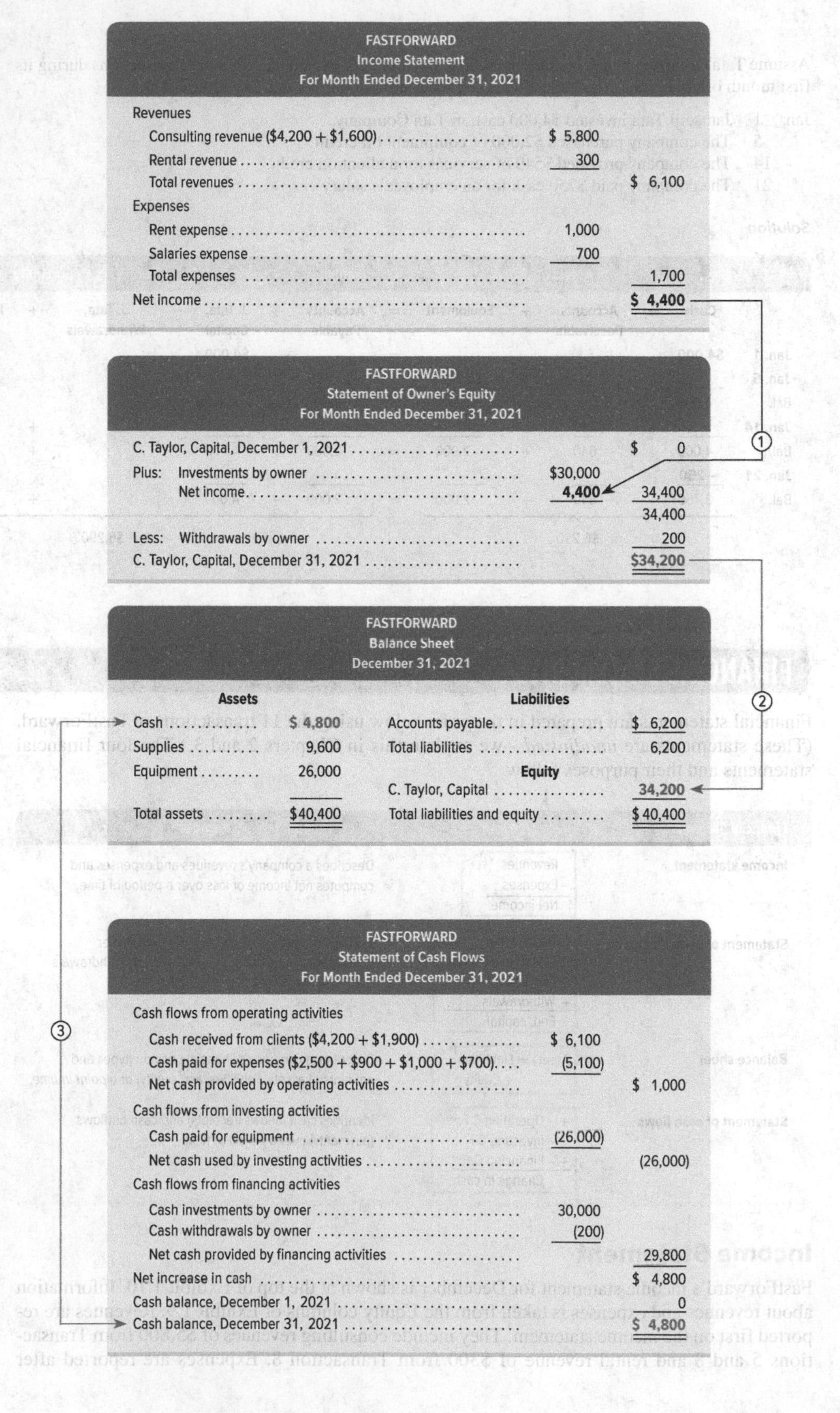

FASTFORWARD
Income Statement
For Month Ended December 31, 2021

Revenues		
Consulting revenue ($4,200 + $1,600)	$ 5,800	
Rental revenue	300	
Total revenues		$ 6,100
Expenses		
Rent expense	1,000	
Salaries expense	700	
Total expenses		1,700
Net income		$ 4,400

FASTFORWARD
Statement of Owner's Equity
For Month Ended December 31, 2021

C. Taylor, Capital, December 1, 2021		$ 0
Plus: Investments by owner	$30,000	
Net income	4,400	34,400
		34,400
Less: Withdrawals by owner		200
C. Taylor, Capital, December 31, 2021		$34,200

FASTFORWARD
Balance Sheet
December 31, 2021

Assets		**Liabilities**	
Cash	$ 4,800	Accounts payable	$ 6,200
Supplies	9,600	Total liabilities	6,200
Equipment	26,000	**Equity**	
		C. Taylor, Capital	34,200
Total assets	$40,400	Total liabilities and equity	$40,400

FASTFORWARD
Statement of Cash Flows
For Month Ended December 31, 2021

Cash flows from operating activities		
Cash received from clients ($4,200 + $1,900)	$ 6,100	
Cash paid for expenses ($2,500 + $900 + $1,000 + $700)	(5,100)	
Net cash provided by operating activities		$ 1,000
Cash flows from investing activities		
Cash paid for equipment	(26,000)	
Net cash used by investing activities		(26,000)
Cash flows from financing activities		
Cash investments by owner	30,000	
Cash withdrawals by owner	(200)	
Net cash provided by financing activities		29,800
Net increase in cash		$ 4,800
Cash balance, December 1, 2021		0
Cash balance, December 31, 2021		$ 4,800

revenues. Rent and salary expenses are from Transactions 6 and 7. Expenses are the costs to generate the revenues reported. **Net income** occurs when revenues exceed expenses. A **net loss** occurs when expenses exceed revenues. Net income (or loss) is shown at the bottom of the statement and is the amount reported in December. Owner investments and withdrawals are *not* part of income.

Key ***terms*** *are in bold and defined again in the* ***glossary***

Point: Net income is sometimes called *earnings* or *profit.*

Statement of Owner's Equity

The statement of owner's equity reports how equity changes over the reporting period. This statement shows beginning capital, events that increase it (owner investments and net income), and events that decrease it (withdrawals and net loss). Ending capital is computed in this statement and is carried over and reported on the balance sheet. FastForward's statement of owner's equity is the second report in Exhibit 1.10. The beginning balance is measured as of the start of business on December 1. It is zero because FastForward did not exist before then. An existing business reports a beginning balance equal to the prior period's ending balance (such as from November 30). FastForward's statement shows the $4,400 of net income for the period, which links the statement to the statement of owner's equity (see line ①). The statement also reports the $200 cash withdrawal and FastForward's end-of-period capital balance.

teekid/iStockphoto.com

Balance Sheet

FastForward's balance sheet is the third report in Exhibit 1.10. This statement shows FastForward's financial position at the end of the business day on December 31. The left side of the balance sheet lists FastForward's assets: cash, supplies, and equipment. The upper right side of the balance sheet shows that FastForward owes $6,200 to creditors. Any other liabilities (such as a bank loan) would be listed here. The equity balance is $34,200. Line ② shows the link between the ending balance of the statement of owner's equity and the equity balance on the balance sheet. (This presentation of the balance sheet is called the *account form:* assets on the left and liabilities and equity on the right. Another presentation is the *report form:* assets on top, followed by liabilities and then equity at the bottom. Both are acceptable.) As always, the accounting equation balances: Assets of $40,400 = Liabilities of $6,200 + Equity of $34,200.

Statement of Cash Flows

FastForward's statement of cash flows is the final report in Exhibit 1.10. The first section reports cash flows from *operating activities*. It shows the $6,100 cash received from clients and the $5,100 cash paid for supplies, rent, and employee salaries. Outflows are in parentheses to denote subtraction. Net cash provided by operating activities for December is $1,000. The second section reports *investing activities,* which involve buying and selling assets such as land and equipment that are held for *long-term use* (typically more than one year). The only investing activity is the $26,000 purchase of equipment. The third section shows cash flows from *financing activities,* which include *long-term* borrowing and repaying of cash from lenders and the cash investments from, and withdrawals by, the owner. FastForward reports $30,000 from the owner's initial investment and a $200 cash withdrawal. The net cash effect of all financing transactions is a $29,800 cash inflow. The final part of the statement shows an increased cash balance of $4,800. The ending balance is also $4,800 as it started with no cash—see line ③.

Point: Payment for supplies is an operating activity because supplies are expected to be used up in short-term operations (typically less than one year).

Point: Investing activities refer to long-term asset investments by the company, *not* to owner investments.

Decision Insight

Big Data The SEC keeps an online database called **EDGAR** (**sec.gov/edgar**) that has accounting information for thousands of companies, such as **Columbia Sportswear**, that issue stock to the public. The annual report filing for most publicly traded U.S. companies is known as Form 10-K, and the quarterly filing is Form 10-Q. Information services such as **Finance.Yahoo.com** offer online data and analysis. ■

Greg Epperson/Shutterstock

NEED-TO-KNOW 1-5

Financial Statements

P2

Prepare the (a) income statement, (b) statement of owner's equity, and (c) balance sheet for Accel using the following information from its current year ended December 31.

Cash	$17,000	B. Accel, Capital, Dec. 31, prior year	$58,000
Accounts receivable	5,000	Withdrawals	12,500
Equipment	27,000	Revenues	41,000
Land	30,000	Wages expense	21,000
Accounts payable	7,500	Rent expense	7,000
Wages payable	13,000	Owner investments	0

Solution

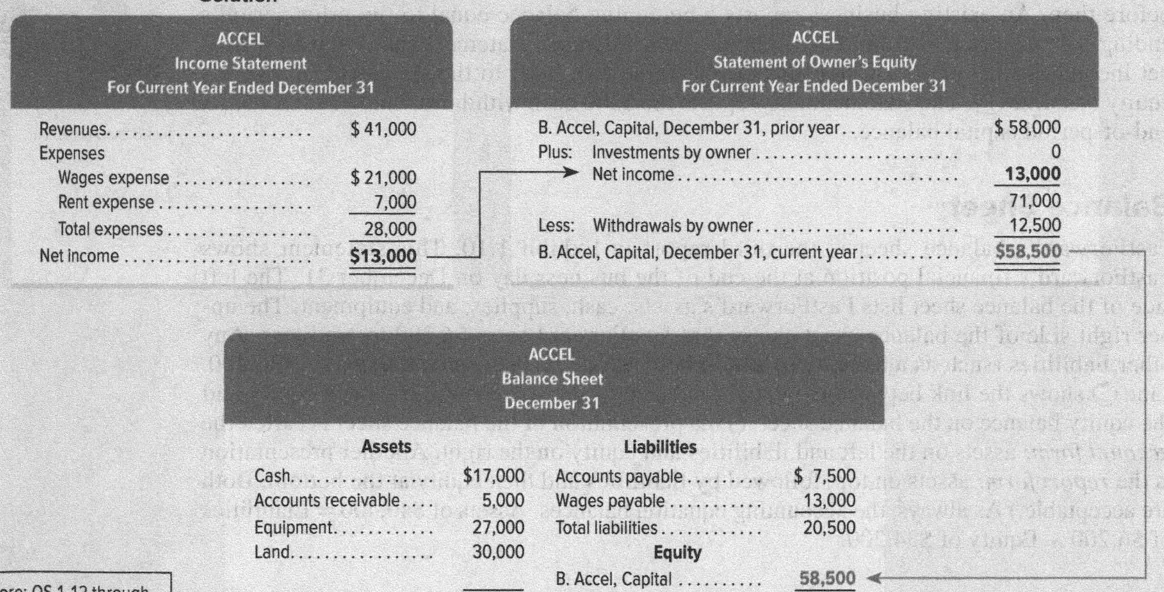

ACCEL
Income Statement
For Current Year Ended December 31

Revenues		$ 41,000
Expenses		
Wages expense	$ 21,000	
Rent expense	7,000	
Total expenses		28,000
Net income		**$13,000**

ACCEL
Statement of Owner's Equity
For Current Year Ended December 31

B. Accel, Capital, December 31, prior year	$ 58,000
Plus: Investments by owner	0
Net income	13,000
	71,000
Less: Withdrawals by owner	12,500
B. Accel, Capital, December 31, current year	**$58,500**

ACCEL
Balance Sheet
December 31

Assets		**Liabilities**	
Cash	$17,000	Accounts payable	$ 7,500
Accounts receivable	5,000	Wages payable	13,000
Equipment	27,000	Total liabilities	20,500
Land	30,000	**Equity**	
		B. Accel, Capital	58,500
Total assets	$79,000	Total liabilities and equity	$79,000

Do More: QS 1-12 through QS 1-19, E 1-16 through E 1-24

***Decision Analysis** (at the end of each chapter) covers ratios for decision making using real company data. Instructors can skip this section and cover all ratios in Chapter 17*

Decision Analysis  Return on Assets

A2

Compute and interpret return on assets.

We organize financial statement analysis into four areas: (1) liquidity and efficiency, (2) solvency, (3) profitability, and (4) market prospects—Chapter 17 has a ratio listing with definitions and groupings by area. When analyzing ratios, we use a company's prior year ratios and competitor ratios to evaluate performance.

This chapter presents a profitability measure: return on assets. Return on assets helps evaluate if management is effectively using assets to generate net income. **Return on assets (ROA),** also called *return on investment* (*ROI*), is defined in Exhibit 1.11.

EXHIBIT 1.11

Return on Assets

$$\textbf{Return on assets} = \frac{\textbf{Net income}}{\textbf{Average total assets}}$$

Net income is from the annual income statement, and average total assets is computed by adding the beginning and ending amounts for that same period and dividing by 2. **Nike** reports total net income of $4,029 million for the current year. At the beginning of the current year its total assets are $22,536 million, and at the end of the current year assets total $23,717 million. Nike's return on assets for the current year is

$$\text{Return on assets} = \frac{\$4{,}029 \text{ million}}{(\$22{,}536 \text{ million} + \$23{,}717 \text{ million})/2} = 17.4\%$$

Is a 17.4% return on assets good or bad for Nike? To help answer this question, we compare (benchmark) Nike's return with its prior performance and the return of its competitor, **Under Armour** (see Exhibit 1.12). Nike shows a pattern of positive returns that reflects effective use of assets. Nike has outperformed Under Armour in each of the last three years. Under Armour had a negative ROA in the previous two years due to net losses.

EXHIBIT 1.12

Nike and Under Armour Returns

Return on Assets	Current Year	1 Year Ago	2 Years Ago
Nike..................	17.4%	8.4%	19.0%
Under Armour..........	2.0%	(1.1)%	(1.3)%

***Decision Maker** requires critical thinking to make decisions*

Decision Maker

Business Owner You own a winter ski resort that earns a 21% return on its assets. An opportunity to purchase a winter ski equipment manufacturer is offered to you. This manufacturer earns a 14% return on its assets. The industry return for competitors of this manufacturer is 9%. Do you purchase this manufacturer? ■ *Answer:* The 14% return on assets for the manufacturer exceeds the 9% industry return. This is positive for a potential purchase. Also, this purchase is an opportunity to spread your risk over two businesses. Still, you should hesitate to purchase a business whose 14% return is lower than your current 21% return. You might better direct efforts to increase investment in your resort if it can earn more than the 14% alternative.

***Comprehensive Need-to-Know** is a review of key chapter content*

NEED-TO-KNOW 1-6

COMPREHENSIVE

Transaction Analysis, Statement Preparation, and Return on Assets

Jasmine Worthy started a haircutting business called Expressions. The following events occurred during its first month of business.

a. Dec. 1 Worthy invested $3,000 cash and $15,000 of equipment in Expressions.
b. Dec. 2 Expressions paid $600 cash for furniture for the shop.
c. Dec. 3 Expressions paid $500 cash to rent space in a strip mall for December.
d. Dec. 4 Purchased $1,200 of equipment on credit (recorded as accounts payable).
e. Dec. 15 Expressions opened for business on December 5. Cash received from haircutting services in the first week and a half of business (ended December 15) was $825.
f. Dec. 16 Expressions provided $100 of haircutting services on credit.
g. Dec. 17 Expressions received a $100 check for services previously rendered on credit.
h. Dec. 18 Expressions paid $125 cash to an assistant for hours worked for the grand opening.
i. Dec. 31 Cash received from services provided during the second half of December was $930.
j. Dec. 31 Expressions paid $400 cash toward the accounts payable from December 4.
k. Dec. 31 Worthy made a $900 cash withdrawal from Expressions for personal use.

Required

1. Show the effects of each transaction in a table like Exhibit 1.9.
2. Prepare an income statement for December.
3. Prepare a statement of owner's equity for December.
4. Prepare a balance sheet as of December 31.
5. Prepare a statement of cash flows for December.
6. Determine the return on assets ratio for December.

SOLUTION

1.

	Assets				= Liabilities +	Equity			
	Cash	+ Accounts Receivable	+ Furniture	+ Equipment	= Accounts Payable	+ J. Worthy, Capital	− J. Worthy, Withdrawals	+ Revenues	− Expenses
a.	$3,000			$15,000		$18,000			
b.	− 600		+ $600						
Bal.	2,400		+ 600	+ 15,000	=	18,000			
c.	− 500								− $500
Bal.	1,900		+ 600	+ 15,000	=	18,000			− 500
d.				+ 1,200	+$1,200				
Bal.	1,900		+ 600	+ 16,200	= 1,200	+ 18,000			− 500
e.	+ 825							+ $ 825	
Bal.	2,725		+ 600	+ 16,200	= 1,200	+ 18,000		+ 825	− 500
f.		+ $100						+ 100	
Bal.	2,725	+ 100	+ 600	+ 16,200	= 1,200	+ 18,000		+ 925	− 500
g.	+ 100	− 100							
Bal.	2,825	+ 0	+ 600	+ 16,200	= 1,200	+ 18,000		+ 925	− 500
h.	− 125								− 125
Bal.	2,700	+ 0	+ 600	+ 16,200	= 1,200	+ 18,000		+ 925	− 625
i.	+ 930							+ 930	
Bal.	3,630	+ 0	+ 600	+ 16,200	= 1,200	+ 18,000		+ 1,855	− 625
j.	− 400				− 400				
Bal.	3,230	+ 0	+ 600	+ 16,200	= 800	+ 18,000		+ 1,855	− 625
k.	− 900						− $900		
Bal.	$ 2,330	+ 0	+ $ 600	+ $ 16,200	= $ 800	+ $ 18,000	− $ 900	+ $1,855	− $625

2.

EXPRESSIONS
Income Statement
For Month Ended December 31

Revenues		
Services revenue		$ 1,855
Expenses		
Rent expense	$500	
Wages expense	125	
Total expenses		625
Net income		$1,230

3.

EXPRESSIONS
Statement of Owner's Equity
For Month Ended December 31

J. Worthy, Capital, December 1*		$ 0
Plus: Investments by owner	$18,000	
Net income	1,230	19,230
		19,230
Less: Withdrawals by owner		900
J. Worthy, Capital, December 31 ...		$18,330

*If Expressions had existed before December 1, the beginning capital balance would equal the prior period's ending balance.

4.

EXPRESSIONS
Balance Sheet
December 31

Assets		**Liabilities**	
Cash	$ 2,330	Accounts payable	$ 800
Furniture	600	**Equity**	
Equipment	16,200	J. Worthy, Capital	18,330
Total assets	$19,130	Total liabilities and equity	$19,130

5.

EXPRESSIONS Statement of Cash Flows For Month Ended December 31		
Cash flows from operating activities		
Cash received from customers	$1,855	
Cash paid for expenditures ($500 + $125 + $400)	(1,025)	
Net cash provided by operating activities		$ 830
Cash flows from investing activities		
Cash paid for furniture	(600)	
Net cash used by investing activities		(600)
Cash flows from financing activities		
Cash investments by owner	3,000	
Cash withdrawals by owner	(900)	
Net cash provided by financing activities		2,100
Net increase in cash		$2,330
Cash balance, December 1		0
Cash balance, December 31		$2,330

6. $\text{Return on assets} = \frac{\text{Net income}}{\text{Average assets}} = \frac{\$1,230}{(\$18,000^* + \$19,130)/2} = \frac{\$1,230}{\$18,565} = \mathbf{6.63\%}$

*Uses the initial $18,000 investment as the beginning balance for the *start-up period only*.

Summary: Cheat Sheet

ACCOUNTING USES

External users: Do not directly run the organization and have limited access to its accounting information. Examples are lenders, shareholders, external auditors, nonexecutive employees, labor unions, regulators, voters, donors, suppliers, and customers.

Internal users: Directly manage organization operations. Examples are the CEO and other executives, research and development managers, purchasing managers, production managers, and other managerial-level employees.

Private accounting: Accounting employees working for businesses.

Public accounting: Offering audit, tax, and advisory services to others.

ETHICS AND ACCOUNTING

Fraud triangle: Three factors that push a person to commit fraud.

- **Opportunity:** Must be able to commit fraud with a low risk of getting caught.
- **Pressure,** or incentive: Must feel pressure or have incentive to commit fraud.
- **Rationalization,** or attitude: Justifies fraud or does not see its criminal nature.

Common business entities:

	Sole Proprietorship	Partnership
Number of owners	1 owner; easy to set up.	2 or more, called *partners*; easy to set up.
Business taxation	No additional business income tax.	No additional business income tax.
Owner liability	Unlimited liability. Owner is personally liable for proprietorship debts.	Unlimited liability. Partners are jointly liable for partnership debts.
Legal entity	*Not* a separate legal entity.	*Not* a separate legal entity.
Business life	Business ends with owner death or choice.	Business ends with a partner death or choice.

	Corporation	Limited Liability Company (LLC)
Number of owners	1 or more, called *shareholders;* can get many investors by selling **stock** or **shares** of corporate ownership.	1 or more, called *members*.
Business taxation	Additional corporate income tax.	No additional business income tax.
Owner liability	Limited liability. Owners, called **shareholders** (or **stockholders**), are not liable for corporate acts and debts.	Limited liability. Owners, called **members**, are not personally liable for LLC debts.
Legal entity	A separate entity with the same rights and responsibilities as a person.	A separate entity with the same rights and responsibilities as a person.
Business life	Indefinite.	Indefinite.

TRANSACTION ANALYSIS

Assets: Resources a company owns or controls that are expected to yield future benefits.

Liabilities: Creditors' claims on assets. These are obligations to provide assets, products, or services to others.

Equity: Owner claim on assets. It consists of:

+ Owner, Capital	**Owner investments** are inflows of cash and other net assets from owner contributions, which increase equity.
− Owner, Withdrawals	**Owner withdrawals** are outflows of cash and other assets to owners for personal use, which reduce equity.
+ Revenues	**Revenues** increase equity (via net income) from sales of products and services to customers; examples are sales of products, consulting services provided, facilities rented to others, and commissions from services.
− Expenses	**Expenses** decrease equity (via net income) from costs of providing products and services to customers; examples are costs of employee time, use of supplies, advertising, utilities, and insurance fees.

Accounting equation: Applies to all transactions and events, to all companies and organizations, and to all points in time.

Assets = Liabilities + Equity

Expanded accounting equation:

Assets = Liabilities + Owner, Capital − Owner, Withdrawals + Revenues − Expenses (the last four terms together = Equity)

Summary of transactions:

Financial effects of the following transactions are shown in the table using the expanded accounting equation.

Transaction 1: Investment by owner
Transaction 2: Purchase supplies for cash
Transaction 3: Purchase equipment for cash
Transaction 4: Purchase supplies on credit
Transaction 5: Provide services for cash
Transactions 6 and 7: Payment of expenses in cash
Transaction 8: Provide services and facilities for credit
Transaction 9: Receipt of cash from accounts receivable
Transaction 10: Payment of accounts payable
Transaction 11: Withdrawal of cash by owner

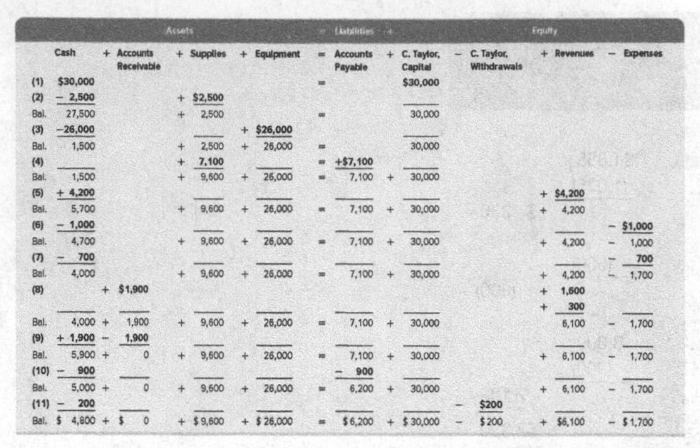

	Assets				= Liabilities +	Equity			
	Cash	+ Accounts Receivable	+ Supplies	+ Equipment	= Accounts Payable	+ C. Taylor, Capital	− C. Taylor, Withdrawals	+ Revenues	− Expenses
(1)	$30,000				=	$30,000			
(2)	− 2,500		+ $2,500						
Bal.	27,500		+ 2,500		=	30,000			
(3)	−26,000			+ $26,000					
Bal.	1,500		+ 2,500	+ 26,000	=	30,000			
(4)			+ 7,100		= +$7,100				
Bal.	1,500		+ 9,600	+ 26,000	= 7,100	+ 30,000			
(5)	+ 4,200							+ $4,200	
Bal.	5,700		+ 9,600	+ 26,000	= 7,100	+ 30,000		+ 4,200	
(6)	− 1,000								− $1,000
Bal.	4,700		+ 9,600	+ 26,000	= 7,100	+ 30,000		+ 4,200	− 1,000
(7)	− 700								− 700
Bal.	4,000		+ 9,600	+ 26,000	= 7,100	+ 30,000		+ 4,200	− 1,700
(8)		+ $1,900						+ 1,600	
								+ 300	
Bal.	4,000	+ 1,900	+ 9,600	+ 26,000	= 7,100	+ 30,000		6,100	− 1,700
(9)	+ 1,900	− 1,900							
Bal.	5,900	+ 0	+ 9,600	+ 26,000	= 7,100	+ 30,000		+ 6,100	− 1,700
(10)	− 900				− 900				
Bal.	5,000	+ 0	+ 9,600	+ 26,000	= 6,200	+ 30,000		+ 6,100	− 1,700
(11)	− 200						− $200		
Bal.	$ 4,800	+ $ 0	+ $ 9,600	+ $ 26,000	= $6,200	+ $ 30,000	− $200	+ $6,100	− $ 1,700

FINANCIAL STATEMENTS

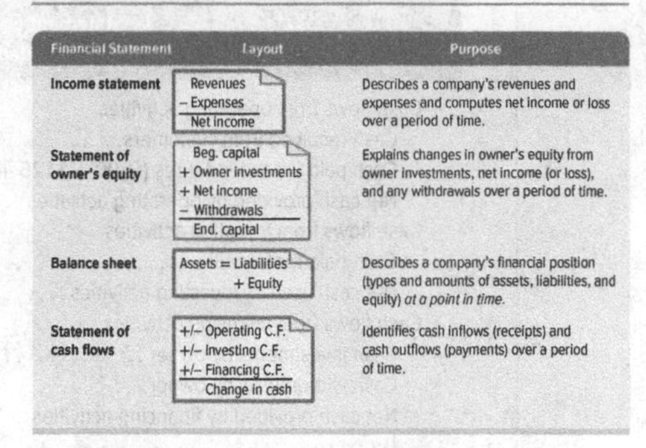

Financial Statement	Layout	Purpose
Income statement	Revenues − Expenses Net income	Describes a company's revenues and expenses and computes net income or loss over a period of time.
Statement of owner's equity	Beg. capital + Owner investments + Net income − Withdrawals End. capital	Explains changes in owner's equity from owner investments, net income (or loss), and any withdrawals over a period of time.
Balance sheet	Assets = Liabilities + Equity	Describes a company's financial position (types and amounts of assets, liabilities, and equity) *at a point in time.*
Statement of cash flows	+/− Operating C.F. +/− Investing C.F. +/− Financing C.F. Change in cash	Identifies cash inflows (receipts) and cash outflows (payments) over a period of time.

Key Terms conclude each chapter (a complete glossary is available in Connect)

Key Terms

Accounting (3)
Accounting equation (9)
Assets (9)
Audit (7)
Auditors (6)
Balance sheet (15)
Bookkeeping (3)
Business entity assumption (8)
Common stock (8)
Conceptual framework (7)
Corporation (8)
Cost constraint (8)
Cost principle (7)
Cost-benefit constraint (8)
Data analytics (5)
Data visualization (5)
Equity (9)
Ethics (6)
Events (10)
Expanded accounting equation (10)
Expense recognition principle (7)
Expenses (10)
External transactions (10)
External users (4)
Financial accounting (4)
Financial Accounting Standards Board (FASB) (7)
Full disclosure principle (8)
Generally accepted accounting principles (GAAP) (6)
Going-concern assumption (8)
Income statement (15)
Internal controls (6)
Internal transactions (10)
Internal users (4)
International Accounting Standards Board (IASB) (7)
International Financial Reporting Standards (IFRS) (7)
Liabilities (9)
Limited liability company (LLC) (8)
Managerial accounting (4)
Matching principle (7)
Measurement principle (7)
Members (8)
Monetary unit assumption (8)
Net income (17)
Net loss (17)
Owner, Capital (24)
Owner, Withdrawals (24)
Owner investments (10)
Partnership (8)
Proprietorship (8)
Recordkeeping (3)
Return on assets (ROA) (19)
Revenue recognition principle (7)
Revenues (10)
Securities and Exchange Commission (SEC) (7)
Shareholders (8)
Shares (8)
Sole proprietorship (21)
Statement of cash flows (15)
Statement of owner's equity (15)
Stock (8)
Stockholders (8)
Time period assumption (8)

Multiple Choice Quiz

1. A building is offered for sale at $500,000 but is currently assessed at $400,000. The purchaser of the building believes the building is worth $475,000, but ultimately purchases the building for $450,000. The purchaser records the building at:

a. $50,000. **c.** $450,000. **e.** $500,000.
b. $400,000. **d.** $475,000.

2. On December 30 of the current year, **KPMG** signs a $150,000 contract to provide accounting services to one of its clients in *the next year*. KPMG has a December 31 year-end. Which accounting principle or assumption requires KPMG to record the accounting services revenue from this client in *the next year* and not in the current year?

a. Business entity assumption
b. Revenue recognition principle
c. Monetary unit assumption
d. Cost principle
e. Going-concern assumption

3. If the assets of a company increase by $100,000 during the year and its liabilities increase by $35,000 during the same year, then the change in equity of the company during the year must have been a(n):

a. Increase of $135,000. **c.** Decrease of $65,000.
b. Decrease of $135,000. **d.** Increase of $65,000.

4. **Brunswick** borrows $50,000 cash from Third National Bank. How does this transaction affect the accounting equation for Brunswick?

a. Assets increase by $50,000; liabilities increase by $50,000; no effect on equity.

b. Assets increase by $50,000; no effect on liabilities; equity increases by $50,000.
c. Assets increase by $50,000; liabilities decrease by $50,000; no effect on equity.
d. No effect on assets; liabilities increase by $50,000; equity increases by $50,000.
e. No effect on assets; liabilities increase by $50,000; equity decreases by $50,000.

5. **Geek Squad** performs services for a customer and bills the customer for $500. How would Geek Squad record this transaction?
   a. Accounts receivable increase by $500; revenues increase by $500.
   b. Cash increases by $500; revenues increase by $500.
   c. Accounts receivable increase by $500; revenues decrease by $500.
   d. Accounts receivable increase by $500; accounts payable increase by $500.
   e. Accounts payable increase by $500; revenues increase by $500.

ANSWERS TO MULTIPLE CHOICE QUIZ

1. c; $450,000 is the actual cost incurred.
2. b; revenue is recorded when services are provided.
3. d;

Assets	=	Liabilities	+	Equity
+$100,000	=	+$35,000	+	?

Change in equity = $100,000 − $35,000 = $65,000

4. a
5. a

Select Quick Study and Exercise assignments feature Guided Example videos, called "Hints" in Connect. Hints use different numbers, and instructors can turn this feature on or off.

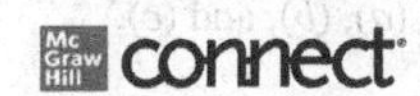

QUICK STUDY

QS 1-1
Understanding accounting
C1

Choose the term or phrase below that best completes each statement.

a. Accounting
b. Identifying
c. Recording
d. Communicating
e. Governmental
f. Artificial intelligence
g. Language of business
h. Recordkeeping (bookkeeping)

1. ______ helps accountants by performing repetitive tasks such as entering invoice data.
2. ______ requires that we input, measure, and log transactions and events.
3. ______ is the recording of transactions and events, either manually or electronically.

QS 1-2
Identifying accounting users
C1

Identify the following users as either External users or Internal users.

a. Customers
b. Suppliers
c. External auditors
d. Business press
e. Managers
f. District attorney
g. Shareholders
h. Lenders
i. Controllers
j. FBI and IRS
k. Consumer group
l. Voters

QS 1-3
Applying the fraud triangle
C2

Identify the fraud triangle risk factor (Opportunity, Pressure, or Rationalization) in each situation.

1. The business has no cameras or security devices at its warehouse.
2. Managers are expected to grow business or be fired.
3. A worker sees other employees regularly take inventory for personal use.
4. No one matches the cash in the register to receipts when shifts end.
5. Officers are told to report rising income or risk layoffs.
6. A worker feels that fellow employees are not honest.

QS 1-4
Identifying principles, assumptions, and constraints
C2

Identify each of the following as an accounting Principle, Assumption, or Constraint.

1. Full disclosure
2. Time period
3. Going-concern
4. Revenue recognition

QS 1-5
Identifying attributes of businesses
C2

Complete the following table with either a *yes* or *no* regarding the attributes of a sole proprietorship, partnership, corporation, and limited liability company (LLC).

Attribute Present	Sole Proprietorship	Partnership	Corporation	LLC
1. Business taxed	____	____	____	____
2. Limited liability	____	____	____	____
3. Legal entity	____	____	____	____

QS 1-6
Identifying accounting principles and assumptions
C2

Identify the accounting principle or assumption that best explains each situation.

1. In December of this year, Chavez Landscaping received a customer's order and cash prepayment to install sod at a house that would not be ready for installation until March of *next year*. Chavez should record the revenue from the customer order in March of *next year,* not in December of this year.
2. If $51,000 cash is paid to buy land, the land is reported on the buyer's balance sheet at $51,000.
3. Mike Derr owns both Sailing Passions and Dockside Digs. In preparing financial statements for Dockside Digs, Mike makes sure that the expense transactions of Sailing Passions are kept separate from Dockside Digs's transactions and financial statements.

QS 1-7
Applying the accounting equation A1

a. Total assets of Charter Company equal $700,000 and its equity is $420,000. What is the amount of its liabilities?

b. Total assets of Martin Marine equal $500,000 and its liabilities and equity amounts are equal to each other. What is the amount of its liabilities? What is the amount of its equity?

QS 1-8
Applying the accounting equation
A1

1. Use the accounting equation to compute the missing financial statement amounts (*a*), (*b*), and (*c*).

	A	B		C		D
1	Company	Assets	=	Liabilities	+	Equity
2	1	$ 75,000		$ (a)		$ 40,000
3	2	(b)		25,000		70,000
4	3	85,000		20,000		(c)

2. Use the expanded accounting equation to compute the missing financial statement amounts (*a*) and (*b*).

	A	B	C	D	E	F	G
1-2	Company	Assets	Liabilities	Owner, Capital	Owner, Withdrawals	Revenues	Expenses
3	1	$ 40,000	$ 16,000	$ 20,000	$ 0	(a)	$ 8,000
4	2	$ 80,000	$ 32,000	$ 44,000	(b)	$ 24,000	$ 18,000

QS 1-9
Determining effects of transactions on equity
P1

Determine whether each of the following transactions increases or decreases equity.

a. Owner invested cash in the company.
b. Incurred maintenance expenses.
c. Performed services for a client.
d. Incurred employee wage expenses.

QS 1-10
Identifying effects of transactions using accounting equation—revenues and expenses
P1

Create a table similar to Exhibit 1.9. Then use additions and subtractions to show the dollar effects of each transaction on individual items of the accounting equation.

Assets			=	Liabilities	+			Equity				
Cash	+	Accounts Receivable	=	Accounts Payable	+	Owner, Capital	−	Owner, Withdrawals	+	Revenues	−	Expenses

a. The company completed consulting work for a client and immediately collected $5,500 cash.
b. The company completed commission work for a client and sent a bill for $4,000 to be received within 30 days.
c. The company paid an assistant $1,400 cash as wages for the period.
d. The company collected $1,000 cash as a partial payment for the amount owed by the client in transaction *b*.
e. The company paid $700 cash for this period's cleaning services.

QS 1-11
Identifying effects of transactions using accounting equation—assets and liabilities
P1

Create a table similar to Exhibit 1.9. Then use additions and subtractions to show the dollar effects of each transaction on individual items of the accounting equation.

Assets								=	Liabilities	+	Equity						
Cash	+	Supplies	+	Equipment	+	Land		=	Accounts Payable	+	Owner, Capital	−	Owner, Withdrawals	+	Revenues	−	Expenses

a. The owner invested $15,000 cash in the company.
b. The company purchased supplies for $500 cash.
c. The owner invested $10,000 of equipment in the company.
d. The company purchased $200 of additional supplies on credit.
e. The company purchased land for $9,000 cash.

QS 1-12
Identifying items with financial statements
P2

Indicate in which financial statement each item would most likely appear: income statement, balance sheet, or statement of cash flows.

a. Assets
b. Cash from operating activities
c. Equipment
d. Expenses
e. Liabilities
f. Net decrease (or increase) in cash
g. Revenues
h. Total liabilities and equity

QS 1-13
Identifying income and equity accounts
P2

Classify each of the following items as revenues, expenses, or withdrawals.

1. Utilities expense
2. Service revenue
3. Wages expense
4. Owner withdrawals
5. Rent expense
6. Rental revenue
7. Insurance expense
8. Consulting revenue

QS 1-14
Identifying assets, liabilities, and equity **P2**

Classify each of the following items as assets, liabilities, or equity.

1. Land
2. Wages payable
3. Equipment
4. Accounts payable
5. Accounts receivable
6. Supplies

QS 1-15
Preparing an income statement
P2

On December 31, Hawkin's records show the following accounts. Use this information to prepare a December income statement for Hawkin.

Cash	$ 5,100	Accounts payable	$ 6,000	Wages expense	$8,000
Accounts receivable	600	Hawkin, Capital, December 1	10,900	Rent expense	1,500
Supplies	2,000	Hawkin, Withdrawals	1,000	Utilities expense	700
Equipment	14,000	Services revenue	16,000		

QS 1-16
Preparing a statement of owner's equity **P2**

Use the information in QS 1-15 to prepare a statement of owner's equity for Hawkin for the month ended December 31. *Hint:* Net income is $5,800 and owner investments are $0 for the period.

QS 1-17
Preparing a balance sheet **P2**

Use the information in QS 1-15 to prepare a December 31 balance sheet for Hawkin. *Hint:* Hawkin, Capital, December 31, equals $15,700.

QS 1-18
Preparing a statement of cash flows
P2

Use the following information to prepare a statement of cash flows for Studio One for the month ended December 31. The cash balance at the start of December 1 was $1,000.

Cash withdrawals by owner	$ 2,000	Cash paid for equipment.	$ 3,000
Cash received from customers.	23,500	Cash paid for truck	22,000
Cash investments by owner	11,000	Cash paid for expenditures. . . .	6,000

QS 1-19
Classifying items on the statement of cash flows
P2

Identify the following cash flows as reported under either operating activities, investing activities, or financing activities.

1. Cash purchase of equipment
2. Cash paid for land
3. Cash paid for advertising
4. Cash paid for wages
5. Cash paid on account payable to supplier
6. Cash received from clients
7. Cash paid for rent
8. Cash investment by owner

QS 1-20
Interpreting return on assets
A2

Return on assets for Deutsche Auto for each of the last three years follows. Over the three-year period shown, did the company's return on assets improve or worsen?

	Current Year	1 Year Ago	2 Years Ago
Return on assets	13.5%	11.2%	8.9%

QS 1-21
Computing and interpreting return on assets
A2

Home Demo reports the following results. (a) Compute Home Demo's return on assets. (b) Is Home Demo's return on assets better than the 11% return of Lows Hardware (a competitor)?

Sales.	$95 billion	Net income	$8 billion	Average total assets	$42 billion

*Select Exercises and Quick Studies have Guided Example videos, called "Hints" in **Connect**. Hints use different numbers, and instructors can turn this feature on or off.*

EXERCISES

Exercise 1-1
Classifying activities reflected in the accounting system C1

Classify the following activities as part of the Identifying, Recording, or Communicating aspects of accounting.

1. Analyzing and interpreting reports.
2. Presenting financial information.
3. Keeping a log of service costs.
4. Measuring the costs of a product.
5. Preparing financial statements.
6. Acquiring knowledge of revenue transactions.
7. Observing transactions and events.
8. Registering cash sales of products sold.

Exercise 1-2
Identifying accounting users and uses
C1

Part A. Identify the following questions as most likely to be asked by an Internal user or an External user of accounting information.

1. Which inventory items are out of stock?
2. Should we make a five-year loan to that business?
3. What are the costs of our product's ingredients?
4. Should we buy, hold, or sell a company's stock?
5. Should we spend additional money for redesign of our product?
6. Which firm reports the highest sales and income?
7. What are the costs of our service to customers?

Part B. Identify the following users as either an Internal user or an External user.

1. Research and development executive
2. Human resources executive
3. Politician
4. Shareholder
5. Distribution manager
6. Creditor
7. Production supervisor
8. Purchasing manager

Exercise 1-3
Describing accounting responsibilities
C1

Determine whether each of the following accounting duties mainly involves financial accounting, managerial accounting, or tax accounting.

1. Internal auditing.
2. External auditing.
3. Cost accounting.
4. Budgeting.
5. Enforcing tax laws.
6. Planning transactions to minimize taxes.
7. Preparing external financial statements.
8. Analyzing external financial reports.

Exercise 1-4
Learning the language of business
C1 C2

Match each of the descriptions with the term or phrase it best reflects.

A. Audit **C.** Ethics **E.** SEC **G.** Net income
B. GAAP **D.** FASB **F.** Public accountants **H.** IASB

1. An assessment of whether financial statements follow GAAP.
2. Amount a business earns in excess of all expenses and costs associated with its sales and revenues.
3. A group that sets accounting principles in the United States.
4. Accounting professionals who provide services to many clients.
5. Principles that determine whether an action is right or wrong.

Exercise 1-5
Identifying ethical terminology
C2

Match each of the descriptions with the term or phrase it best reflects.

A. Ethics **C.** Prevention **E.** Audit
B. Fraud triangle **D.** Internal controls

1. Examines whether financial statements are prepared using GAAP.
2. Procedures set up to protect company property and equipment, ensure reliable accounting, promote efficiency, and encourage adherence to policies.
3. A less expensive and more effective means to stop fraud.
4. Three factors push a person to commit fraud: opportunity, pressure, and rationalization.
5. Beliefs that distinguish right from wrong.

Exercise 1-6
Distinguishing business organizations
C2

Determine whether each description best refers to a sole proprietorship, partnership, corporation, or limited liability company (LLC).

a. Micah and Nancy own Financial Services, which pays a business income tax. Micah and Nancy do not have personal responsibility for the debts of Financial Services.
b. Riley and Kay own Speedy Packages, a courier service. Both are personally liable for the debts of the business.
c. IBC Services does not have separate legal existence apart from the one person who owns it.
d. Trent Company is owned by Trent Malone, who is personally liable for the company's debts.
e. Ownership of Zander Company is divided into 1,000 shares of stock. The company pays a business income tax.
f. Physio Products does not pay a business income tax and has one owner. The owner has unlimited liability for business debt.
g. AJ Company pays a business income tax and has two owners.
h. Jeffy Auto is a separate legal entity from its owner, but it does not pay a business income tax.

Exercise 1-7
Identifying accounting principles and assumptions
C2

Identify the accounting principle or assumption that best reflects each situation.

a. A company reports details behind financial statements that would impact users' decisions.
b. Financial statements reflect the assumption that the business continues operating.
c. A company records the expenses incurred to generate the revenues reported.
d. Each business is accounted for separately from its owner or owners.
e. Revenue is recorded when products and services are delivered.
f. Information is based on actual costs incurred in transactions.

Exercise 1-8
Applying measurement principle and revenue recognition principle
C2

a. Byrde Co. purchased a truck. The seller asked for $11,000, but Byrde paid only $10,000 after negotiation. The owner of Byrde Co. believes he got a great deal and the truck is really worth $15,000. What amount does Byrde record on its financial statements for the truck?

b. Snell Co. performs services for a client in May and bills the client $1,000. In June, the client makes a partial payment of $300 cash. In July, the remaining $700 cash is paid. Determine the monthly revenue recorded in May, June, and July applying revenue recognition principle.

Exercise 1-9
Using the accounting equation
A1

Determine the missing amount from each of the separate situations *a*, *b*, and *c* below.

	A		B		C
1	Assets	=	Liabilities	+	Equity
2	$ *(a)*		$ 20,000		$ 45,000
3	100,000		34,000		*(b)*
4	154,000		*(c)*		40,000

Exercise 1-10
Using the accounting equation
A1

Check (c) Beg. equity, $60,000

Answer the following questions. *Hint:* Use the accounting equation.

a. At the beginning of the year, Addison Company's assets are $300,000 and its equity is $100,000. During the year, assets increase $80,000 and liabilities increase $50,000. What is the equity at year-end?

b. Office Store Co. has assets equal to $123,000 and liabilities equal to $47,000 at year-end. What is the equity for Office Store Co. at year-end?

c. At the beginning of the year, Quaker Company's liabilities equal $70,000. During the year, assets increase by $60,000, and at year-end assets equal $190,000. Liabilities decrease $5,000 during the year. What are the beginning and ending amounts of equity?

Exercise 1-11
Determining effect of transactions on accounting equation
A1

Answer the following questions. *Hint:* Use the accounting equation.

a. On January 1, Lumia Company's liabilities are $60,000 and its equity is $40,000. On January 3, Lumia purchases and installs solar panel assets costing $10,000. For the panels, Lumia pays $4,000 cash and promises to pay the remaining $6,000 in six months. What is the total of Lumia's assets after the solar panel purchase?

b. On March 1, ABX Company's assets are $100,000 and its liabilities are $30,000. On March 5, ABX is fined $15,000 for failing emission standards. ABX immediately pays the fine in cash. After the fine is paid, what is the amount of equity for ABX?

c. On August 1, Lola Company's assets are $30,000 and its liabilities are $10,000. On August 4, Lola issues a sustainability report. On August 5, ownership invests $3,000 cash and $7,000 of equipment in Lola. After the investment, what is the amount of equity for Lola?

Exercise 1-12
Analysis using the accounting equation
P1

Zen began a new consulting firm on January 5. Following is a financial summary, including balances, for each of the company's first five transactions (using the accounting equation form).

	Assets							=	Liabilities	+	Equity		
Transaction	Cash	+	Accounts Receivable	+	Supplies	+	Equipment	=	Accounts Payable	+	Zen, Capital	+	Revenues
____ 1.	$40,000	+	$ 0	+	$ 0	+	$ 0	=	$ 0	+	$40,000	+	$ 0
____ 2.	38,000	+	0	+	3,000	+	0	=	1,000	+	40,000	+	0
____ 3.	30,000	+	0	+	3,000	+	8,000	=	1,000	+	40,000	+	0
____ 4.	30,000	+	6,000	+	3,000	+	8,000	=	1,000	+	40,000	+	6,000
____ 5.	31,000	+	6,000	+	3,000	+	8,000	=	1,000	+	40,000	+	7,000

Identify the explanation from *a* through *j* that best describes each transaction *1* through *5*.

a. The company purchased equipment for $8,000 cash.
b. The company received $40,000 cash from a bank loan.
c. The owner invested $1,000 cash in the business.
d. The owner invested $40,000 cash in the business.
e. The company purchased supplies for $3,000 by paying $2,000 cash and putting $1,000 on credit.
f. The company billed a customer $6,000 for services provided.

g. The company purchased equipment worth $8,000 on credit.
h. The company provided services for $1,000 cash.
i. The company sold supplies for $3,000 and received $2,000 cash and $1,000 on credit.
j. The company provided services for $6,000 cash.

Exercise 1-13
Identifying effects of transactions on the accounting equation
P1

The following table shows the effects of transactions *1* through *5* on the assets, liabilities, and equity of Mulan's Boutique.

	Assets				=	Liabilities +	Equity	
	Cash	+ Accounts Receivable	+ Supplies	+ Land	=	Accounts Payable	+ Mulan, Capital	+ Revenues
	$21,000	+ $ 0	+ $3,000	+ $19,000	=	$ 0	+ $43,000	+ $ 0
___ 1.	−4,000			+ 4,000				
___ 2.			+ 1,000			+1,000		
___ 3.		+ 1,900						+ 1,900
___ 4.	−1,000					−1,000		
___ 5.	+1,900	− 1,900						
	$17,900	+ $ 0	+ $4,000	+ $23,000	=	$ 0	+ $43,000	+ $1,900

Identify the explanation from *a* through *j* that best describes each transaction *1* through *5*.

a. The company purchased $1,000 of supplies on credit.
b. The company collected $1,900 cash from an account receivable.
c. The company sold land for $4,000 cash.
d. The company paid $1,000 cash for land.
e. The company purchased supplies for $1,000 cash.
f. The company purchased land for $4,000 cash.
g. The company billed a client $1,900 for services provided.
h. The company paid $1,000 cash toward an account payable.
i. The owner invested $1,900 cash in the business.
j. The company sold supplies for $1,900 on credit.

Exercise 1-14
Identifying effects of transactions on the accounting equation
P1

For each transaction *a* through *f*, identify its impact on the accounting equation (select from *1* through *5* below).

1. Decreases an asset and decreases equity.
2. Increases an asset and increases a liability.
3. Decreases an asset and decreases a liability.
4. Increases an asset and decreases an asset.
5. Increases an asset and increases equity.

a. The company pays cash toward an account payable.
b. The company purchases equipment on credit.
c. The owner invests cash in the business.
d. The company pays workers for wages earned.
e. The company purchases supplies for cash.
f. The company provides services for cash.

Exercise 1-15
Identifying effects of transactions using the accounting equation
P1

Ming Chen started a business and had the following transactions in June. Create the following table similar to Exhibit 1.9 and use additions and subtractions to show the dollar effects of the transactions on individual items of the accounting equation. Show new balances after each transaction.

Assets			=	Liabilities +	Equity			
Cash	+ Accounts Receivable	+ Equipment	=	Accounts Payable	+ M. Chen, Capital	− M. Chen, Withdrawals	+ Revenues	− Expenses

Check Ending balances: Cash, $46,000; Expenses, $4,500

a. Owner invested $60,000 cash in the company along with $15,000 of equipment.
b. The company paid $1,500 cash for rent of office space for the month.
c. The company purchased $10,000 of additional equipment on credit (payment due within 30 days).
d. The company completed work for a client and immediately collected $2,500 cash.

[continued on next page]

[continued from previous page]

e. The company completed work for a client and sent a bill for $8,000 to be received within 30 days.
f. The company purchased additional equipment for $6,000 cash.
g. The company paid an assistant $3,000 cash as wages for the month.
h. The company collected $5,000 cash as a partial payment for the amount owed by the client in transaction *e*.
i. The company paid $10,000 cash to settle the liability created in transaction *c*.
j. The owner withdrew $1,000 cash from the company for personal use.

Exercise 1-16
Computing net income using accounting equation
P2

Shep Company's records show the following information for the current year.

	Beginning of Year	End of Year
Total assets	$50,000	$80,000
Total liabilities	$22,000	$35,000

Determine net income (loss) for each of the following separate situations.

a. Additional owner investments of $3,000 were contributed, and withdrawals of $7,000 were made during the current year.
b. Additional owner investments of $15,000 were contributed, and no withdrawals were made during the current year.
c. No additional owner investments were contributed, and withdrawals of $12,000 were made during the current year.

Exercise 1-17
Reporting cash flows and determining effects
P2

For each transaction, (*a*) determine whether the transaction appears on the statement of cash flows under cash flows from operating activities, cash flows from investing activities, or cash flows from financing activities and (*b*) indicate whether the transaction is a cash outflow or cash inflow.

1. Cash received from client for performing services.
2. Cash investment from the owner.
3. Cash paid for this month's rent.
4. Cash paid for equipment.
5. Cash paid for employee wages.
6. Cash paid to settle long-term loan.

Exercise 1-18
Preparing an income statement
P2

On December 1, Jasmin Ernst organized Ernst Consulting. On December 3, the owner contributed $84,000 in assets to launch the business. On December 31, the company's records show the following items and amounts. Use this information to prepare a December income statement for the business.

Cash	$11,360	Cash withdrawals by owner	$ 2,000
Accounts receivable	14,000	Consulting revenue	14,000
Office supplies	3,250	Rent expense	3,550
Office equipment	18,000	Salaries expense	7,000
Land	46,000	Telephone expense	760
Accounts payable	8,500	Miscellaneous expenses	580
Owner investments	84,000		

Check Net income, $2,110

Exercise 1-19
Preparing a statement of owner's equity **P2**

Use the information in Exercise 1-18 to prepare a December statement of owner's equity for Ernst Consulting. *Hint:* J. Ernst, Capital, on December 1 was $0.

Exercise 1-20
Preparing a balance sheet **P2**

Use the information in Exercise 1-18 to prepare a December 31 balance sheet for Ernst Consulting. *Hint:* The solution to Exercise 1-19 can help.

Exercise 1-21
Preparing a statement of cash flows
P2

Use the information in Exercise 1-18 to prepare a December statement of cash flows for Ernst Consulting. Assume the following additional information.

a. The owner's initial investment consists of $38,000 cash and $46,000 in land.
b. The company's $18,000 equipment purchase is paid in cash.
c. Cash paid to employees is $1,750. (The accounts payable balance of $8,500 consists of the $3,250 office supplies purchase and $5,250 in employee salaries yet to be paid.)
d. The company's rent expense, telephone expense, and miscellaneous expenses are paid in cash.
e. No cash has yet been collected on the $14,000 consulting revenue earned.

Check Net increase in cash, $11,360

Exercise 1-22
Preparing consecutive statements of owner's equity
P2

Jarvis began operations on January 1, Year 1. Jarvis made an owner investment of $10,000 early in Year 1. There have been no additional owner investments. In its first two years of operations, it reported the following at its December 31 year-end. Prepare the statement of owner's equity for (*a*) Year 1 and (*b*) Year 2.

	Year 1	Year 2
Net income	$30,000	$50,000
Jarvis, Withdrawals	$ 8,000	$14,000

Exercise 1-23
Linking the income statement and statement of owner's equity
P2

Terrell Co. reported the following data at the end of its first year of operations on December 31. (*a*) Prepare its year-end income statement. (*b*) Prepare its year-end statement of owner's equity using net income calculated in part *a*. *Hint:* Terrell, Capital, on January 1 was $0.

Equipment	$18,000	Terrell, Withdrawals	$ 5,000	Salaries expense	$37,000
Accounts payable	7,000	Services revenue	48,000	Advertising expense	3,000
Owner investments	22,000	Rent revenue	9,000	Utilities expense	1,000

Exercise 1-24
Linking the statement of owner's equity and balance sheet
P2

Mahomes Co. reported the following data at the end of its first year of operations on December 31. (*a*) Prepare its year-end statement of owner's equity. (*b*) Prepare its year-end balance sheet using owner's capital calculated in part *a*. *Hint:* Mahomes, Capital, on January 1 was $0.

Cash	$6,000	Land	$34,000	Mahomes, Withdrawals	$22,000
Accounts receivable	7,000	Accounts payable	3,000	Net income	60,000
Equipment	9,000	Owner investments	15,000		

Exercise 1-25
Analyzing return on assets
A2

Swiss Group reports net income of $40,000 for the year. At the beginning of the year, Swiss Group had $200,000 in assets. By the end of the year, assets had grown to $300,000. What is Swiss Group's return on assets for the current year? Did Swiss Group perform better or worse than its competitors if competitors average an 11% return on assets?

Mc Graw Hill connect

***Problem Set B,** located at the end of **Problem Set A,** is provided for each problem to reinforce the learning process*

PROBLEM SET A

Problem 1-1A
Identifying effects of transactions on financial statements
P1

Identify how each of the following separate transactions *1* through *10* affects financial statements. For increases, place a "+" *and* the dollar amount in the column or columns. For decreases, place a "−" *and* the dollar amount in the column or columns. Some cells may contain both an increase (+) and a decrease (−) along with dollar amounts. The first transaction is completed as an example.

Required

a. For the balance sheet, identify how each transaction affects total assets, total liabilities, and total equity. For the income statement, identify how each transaction affects net income.
b. For the statement of cash flows, identify how each transaction affects cash flows from operating activities, cash flows from investing activities, and cash flows from financing activities.

[continued on next page]

[continued from previous page]

		a.				b.		
		Balance Sheet			Income Statement	Statement of Cash Flows		
	Transaction	Total Assets	Total Liab.	Total Equity	Net Income	Operating Activities	Investing Activities	Financing Activities
1	Owner invests $900 cash in business	+900		+900				+900
2	Receives $700 cash for services provided							
3	Pays $500 cash for employee wages							
4	Buys $100 of equipment on credit							
5	Purchases $200 of supplies on credit							
6	Buys equipment for $300 cash							
7	Pays $200 on accounts payable							
8	Provides $400 of services on credit							
9	Owner withdraws $50 cash							
10	Collects $400 cash on accounts receivable							

Problem 1-2A
Computing missing information using accounting knowledge
A1

The following financial statement information is from five separate companies.

	Company A	Company B	Company C	Company D	Company E
Beginning of year					
Assets	$55,000	$34,000	$24,000	$60,000	$119,000
Liabilities	24,500	21,500	9,000	40,000	?
End of year					
Assets	58,000	40,000	?	85,000	113,000
Liabilities	?	26,500	29,000	24,000	70,000
Changes during the year					
Owner investments	6,000	1,400	9,750	?	6,500
Net income (loss)	8,500	?	8,000	14,000	20,000
Owner withdrawals	3,500	2,000	5,875	0	11,000

Required

1. Answer the following questions about Company A.
   a. What is the amount of equity at the beginning of the year?
   b. What is the amount of equity at the end of the year?
   c. What is the amount of liabilities at the end of the year?
2. Answer the following questions about Company B.
   a. What is the amount of equity at the beginning of the year?
   b. What is the amount of equity at the end of the year?
   c. What is net income for the year?
3. Compute the amount of assets for Company C at the end of the year.
4. Compute the amount of owner investments for Company D during the year.
5. Compute the amount of liabilities for Company E at the beginning of the year.

Check (1b) $41,500

(2c) $1,600

(3) $55,875

Problem 1-3A
Preparing an income statement
P2

As of December 31 of the current year, Armani Company's records show the following.

Cash	$10,000	Armani, Withdrawals	$13,000
Accounts receivable	9,000	Consulting revenue	33,000
Supplies	7,000	Rental revenue	22,000
Equipment	4,000	Salaries expense	20,000
Accounts payable	11,000	Rent expense	12,000
Armani, Capital, Dec. 31, prior year	16,000	Selling and administrative expenses	8,000
Armani, Capital, Dec. 31, current year	19,000		

Required

Prepare the income statement for Armani Company for the current year ended December 31.

Check Net income, $15,000

Problem 1-4A
Preparing a statement of owner's equity P2

Use the information in Problem 1-3A to prepare the statement of owner's equity for Armani Company for the current year ended December 31. *Hint:* The owner invested $1,000 cash during the year.

Problem 1-5A
Preparing a balance sheet
P2

Use the information in Problem 1-3A to prepare the current year-end balance sheet for Armani Company.

Problem 1-6A
Preparing a statement of cash flows
P2

Following is selected financial information of Kia Company for the current year ended December 31.

Cash used by investing activities	$(2,000)	Cash from operating activities	$6,000
Net increase in cash	1,200	Cash, December 31, prior year	2,300
Cash used by financing activities	(2,800)		

Required

Prepare the statement of cash flows for Kia Company for the current year ended December 31.

Check Cash balance, Dec. 31, current year, $3,500

Problem 1-7A
Analyzing transactions and preparing financial statements
P1 P2

Gabi Gram started The Gram Co., a new business that began operations on May 1. The Gram Co. completed the following transactions during its first month of operations.

May 1 G. Gram invested $40,000 cash in the company.
1 The company rented a furnished office and paid $2,200 cash for May's rent.
3 The company purchased $1,890 of equipment on credit.
5 The company paid $750 cash for this month's cleaning services.
8 The company provided consulting services for a client and immediately collected $5,400 cash.
12 The company provided $2,500 of consulting services for a client on credit.
15 The company paid $750 cash for an assistant's salary for the first half of this month.
20 The company received $2,500 cash payment for the services provided on May 12.
22 The company provided $3,200 of consulting services on credit.
25 The company received $3,200 cash payment for the services provided on May 22.
26 The company paid $1,890 cash for the equipment purchased on May 3.
27 The company purchased $80 of equipment on credit.
28 The company paid $750 cash for an assistant's salary for the second half of this month.
30 The company paid $300 cash for this month's telephone bill.
30 The company paid $280 cash for this month's utilities.
31 G. Gram withdrew $1,400 cash from the company for personal use.

[continued on next page]

[continued from previous page]

Required

Check (1) Ending balances: Cash, $42,780; Expenses, $5,030

1. Create the following table similar to Exhibit 1.9. Enter the effects of each transaction on the accounts of the accounting equation by recording dollar increases and decreases in the appropriate columns. Determine the final total for each account and verify that the equation is in balance.

	Assets					=	Liabilities	+	Equity						
Date	Cash	+	Accounts Receivable	+	Equipment	=	Accounts Payable	+	G. Gram, Capital	−	G. Gram, Withdrawals	+	Revenues	−	Expenses

(2) Net income, $6,070; Total assets, $44,750

2. Prepare the income statement and the statement of owner's equity for the month of May, and the balance sheet as of May 31.

3. Prepare the statement of cash flows for the month of May.

Problem 1-8A
Analyzing effects of transactions
P1 P2

Lita Lopez started Biz Consulting, a new business, and completed the following transactions during its first year of operations.

a. Lita Lopez invested $70,000 cash and equipment valued at $10,000 in the company.
b. The company purchased a building for $40,000 cash.
c. The company purchased equipment for $15,000 cash.
d. The company purchased $1,200 of supplies and $1,700 of equipment on credit.
e. The company paid $500 cash for advertising expenses.
f. The company completed a financial plan for a client and billed that client $2,800 for the service.
g. The company designed a financial plan for another client and immediately collected a $4,000 cash fee.
h. L. Lopez withdrew $3,275 cash from the company for personal use.
i. The company received $1,800 cash as partial payment from the client described in transaction *f*.
j. The company made a partial payment of $700 cash on the equipment purchased in transaction *d*.
k. The company paid $1,800 cash for the secretary's wages for this period.

Required

Check (1) Ending balances: Cash, $14,525; Expenses, $2,300; Accounts Payable, $2,200

1. Create the following table similar to Exhibit 1.9. Use additions and subtractions within the table to show the dollar effects of each transaction on individual items of the accounting equation. Show new balances after each transaction.

Assets									=	Liabilities	+	Equity						
Cash	+	Accounts Receivable	+	Supplies	+	Equipment	+	Building	=	Accounts Payable	+	L. Lopez, Capital	−	L. Lopez, Withdrawals	+	Revenues	−	Expenses

(2) Net income, $4,500

2. Determine the company's net income.

Problem 1-9A
Analyzing transactions and preparing financial statements
P1 P2

Sanyu Sony started a new business and completed these transactions during December.

Dec. 1 Sanyu Sony transferred $65,000 cash from a personal savings account to a checking account in the name of Sony Electric.
2 The company paid $1,000 cash for the December rent.
3 The company purchased $13,000 of electrical equipment by paying $4,800 cash and agreeing to pay the $8,200 balance in 30 days.
5 The company purchased supplies by paying $800 cash.
6 The company completed electrical work and immediately collected $1,200 cash for these services.
8 The company purchased $2,530 of office equipment on credit.
15 The company completed electrical work on credit in the amount of $5,000.
18 The company purchased $350 of supplies on credit.
20 The company paid $2,530 cash for the office equipment purchased on December 8.
24 The company billed a client $900 for electrical work completed; the balance is due in 30 days.
28 The company received $5,000 cash for the work completed on December 15.
29 The company paid the assistant's salary of $1,400 cash for this month.
30 The company paid $540 cash for this month's utility bill.
31 Sanyu Sony withdrew $950 cash from the company for personal use.

Required

1. Create the following table similar to Exhibit 1.9. Use additions and subtractions within the table to show the dollar effects of each transaction on individual items of the accounting equation. Show new balances after each transaction.

	Assets					= Liabilities +	Equity			
Date	Cash +	Accounts Receivable +	Supplies +	Office Equipment +	Electrical Equipment =	Accounts Payable +	S. Sony, Capital −	S. Sony, Withdrawals +	Revenues −	Expenses

2. Prepare the income statement and the statement of owner's equity for the current month, and the balance sheet as of the end of the month.
3. Prepare the statement of cash flows for the current month.

Analysis Component

4. Assume that the owner investment transaction on December 1 was $49,000 cash instead of $65,000 and that Sony Electric obtained another $16,000 in cash by borrowing it from a bank. Compute the dollar effect of this change on the month-end amounts for (*a*) total assets, (*b*) total liabilities, and (*c*) total equity.

Check (1) Ending balances: Cash, $59,180; Accounts Payable, $8,550

(2) Net income, $4,160; Total assets, $76,760

Problem 1-10A
Determining expenses, liabilities, equity, and return on assets
A1 A2

Kyzera manufactures, markets, and sells cellular telephones. The average total assets for Kyzera is $250,000. In its most recent year, Kyzera reported net income of $65,000 on revenues of $475,000.

Required

1. What is Kyzera's return on assets?
2. Does return on assets seem satisfactory for Kyzera given that its competitors average a 12% return on assets?
3. What are total expenses for Kyzera in its most recent year?
4. What is the average total amount of liabilities plus equity for Kyzera?

Check (3) $410,000

(4) $250,000

Problem 1-11A
Computing and interpreting return on assets
A2

Coca-Cola and **PepsiCo** both produce and market beverages that are direct competitors. Key financial figures for these businesses for a recent year follow.

Key Figures ($ millions)	Coca-Cola	PepsiCo
Sales	$46,542	$66,504
Net income	8,634	6,462
Average assets	76,448	70,518

Required

1. Compute return on assets for (*a*) Coca-Cola and (*b*) PepsiCo.
2. Which company is more successful in its total amount of sales to consumers?
3. Which company is more successful in returning net income from its assets invested?

Check (1*a*) 11.3%; (1*b*) 9.2%

PROBLEM SET B

Problem 1-1B
Identifying effects of transactions on financial statements
P1

Identify how each of the following separate transactions *1* through *10* affects financial statements. For increases, place a "+" *and* the dollar amount in the column or columns. For decreases, place a "−" *and* the dollar amount in the column or columns. Some cells may contain both an increase (+) and a decrease (−) along with dollar amounts. The first transaction is completed as an example.

Required

a. For the balance sheet, identify how each transaction affects total assets, total liabilities, and total equity. For the income statement, identify how each transaction affects net income.
b. For the statement of cash flows, identify how each transaction affects cash flows from operating activities, cash flows from investing activities, and cash flows from financing activities.

[continued on next page]

[continued from previous page]

		a.				b.		
		Balance Sheet			Income Statement	Statement of Cash Flows		
	Transaction	Total Assets	Total Liab.	Total Equity	Net Income	Operating Activities	Investing Activities	Financing Activities
1	Owner invests $800 cash in business	+800		+800				+800
2	Purchases $100 of supplies on credit							
3	Buys equipment for $400 cash							
4	Provides services for $900 cash							
5	Pays $400 cash for rent incurred							
6	Buys $200 of equipment on credit							
7	Pays $300 cash for wages incurred							
8	Owner withdraws $50 cash							
9	Provides $600 of services on credit							
10	Collects $600 cash on accounts receivable							

Problem 1-2B
Computing missing information using accounting knowledge
A1

The following financial statement information is from five separate companies.

	Company V	Company W	Company X	Company Y	Company Z
Beginning of year					
Assets..............	$54,000	$ 80,000	$141,500	$92,500	$144,000
Liabilities.............	25,000	60,000	68,500	51,500	?
End of year					
Assets..............	59,000	100,000	186,500	?	170,000
Liabilities.............	36,000	?	65,800	42,000	42,000
Changes during the year					
Owner investments	5,000	20,000	?	48,100	60,000
Net income (or loss)	?	40,000	18,500	24,000	32,000
Owner withdrawals	5,500	2,000	0	20,000	8,000

Required

1. Answer the following questions about Company V.
   a. What is the amount of equity at the beginning of the year?
   b. What is the amount of equity at the end of the year?
   c. What is the net income or loss for the year?

Check (1*b*) $23,000

2. Answer the following questions about Company W.
   a. What is the amount of equity at the beginning of the year?
   b. What is the amount of equity at the end of the year?
   c. What is the amount of liabilities at the end of the year?

(2c) $22,000

3. Compute the amount of owner investments for Company X during the year.

4. Compute the amount of assets for Company Y at the end of the year.

(4) $135,100

5. Compute the amount of liabilities for Company Z at the beginning of the year.

Problem 1-3B
Preparing an income statement
P2

As of December 31 of the current year, Audi Company's records show the following.

Cash	$2,000	Audi, Withdrawals	$2,600
Accounts receivable	1,800	Consulting revenue	6,600
Supplies	1,200	Rental revenue	4,400
Equipment	1,000	Salaries expense	4,000
Accounts payable	3,600	Rent expense	2,400
Audi, Capital, Dec. 31, prior year	1,900	Selling and administrative expenses	1,600
Audi, Capital, Dec. 31, current year	2,400		

Required

Prepare the income statement for Audi Company for the current year ended December 31.

Check Net income, $3,000

Problem 1-4B
Preparing a statement of owner's equity P2

Use the information in Problem 1-3B to prepare the statement of owner's equity for Audi Company for the current year ended December 31. *Hint:* The owner invested $100 cash during the year.

Problem 1-5B
Preparing a balance sheet P2

Use the information in Problem 1-3B to prepare the current year-end balance sheet for Audi Company.

Problem 1-6B
Preparing a statement of cash flows
P2

Selected financial information of Banji Company for the current year ended December 31 follows.

Cash from investing activities	$1,600	Cash used by operating activities	$(3,000)
Net increase in cash	400	Cash, December 31, prior year	1,300
Cash from financing activities	1,800		

Required

Prepare the statement of cash flows for Banji Company for the current year ended December 31.

Problem 1-7B
Analyzing transactions and preparing financial statements
P1 P2

Nina Niko launched a new business, Niko's Maintenance Co., that began operations on June 1. The following transactions were completed by the company during that first month.

June 1 Nina Niko invested $130,000 cash in the company.
2 The company rented a furnished office and paid $6,000 cash for June's rent.
4 The company purchased $2,400 of equipment on credit.
6 The company paid $1,150 cash for this month's advertising of the opening of the business.
8 The company completed maintenance services for a customer and immediately collected $850 cash.
14 The company completed $7,500 of maintenance services for City Center on credit.
16 The company paid $800 cash for an assistant's salary for the first half of the month.
20 The company received $7,500 cash payment for services completed for City Center on June 14.
21 The company completed $7,900 of maintenance services for Paula's Beauty Shop on credit.
24 The company completed $675 of maintenance services for Build-It Coop on credit.
25 The company received $7,900 cash payment from Paula's Beauty Shop for the work completed on June 21.
26 The company made payment of $2,400 cash for equipment purchased on June 4.
28 The company paid $800 cash for an assistant's salary for the second half of this month.
29 Nina Niko withdrew $4,000 cash from the company for personal use.
30 The company paid $150 cash for this month's telephone bill.
30 The company paid $890 cash for this month's utilities.

[continued on next page]

[continued from previous page]

Required

Check (1) Ending balances: Cash, $130,060; Expenses, $9,790

1. Create the following table similar to Exhibit 1.9. Enter the effects of each transaction on the accounts of the accounting equation by recording dollar increases and decreases in the appropriate columns. Determine the final total for each account and verify that the equation is in balance.

	Assets					=	Liabilities	+	Equity						
Date	Cash	+	Accounts Receivable	+	Equipment	=	Accounts Payable	+	N. Niko, Capital	−	N. Niko, Withdrawals	+	Revenues	−	Expenses

(2) Net income, $7,135; Total assets, $133,135

2. Prepare the income statement and the statement of owner's equity for the month of June, and the balance sheet as of June 30.

3. Prepare the statement of cash flows for the month of June.

Problem 1-8B
Analyzing effects of transactions
P1 P2

Neva Nadal started a new business, Nadal Computing, and completed the following transactions during its first year of operations.

a. Neva Nadal invested $90,000 cash and equipment valued at $10,000 in the company.
b. The company purchased a building for $50,000 cash.
c. The company purchased equipment for $25,000 cash.
d. The company purchased $1,200 of supplies and $1,700 of equipment on credit.
e. The company paid $750 cash for advertising expenses.
f. The company completed a financial plan for a client and billed that client $2,800 for the service.
g. The company designed a financial plan for another client and immediately collected a $4,000 cash fee.
h. Neva Nadal withdrew $11,500 cash from the company for personal use.
i. The company received $1,800 cash from the client described in transaction *f*.
j. The company made a payment of $700 cash on the equipment purchased in transaction *d*.
k. The company paid $2,500 cash for the secretary's wages.

Required

Check (1) Ending balances: Cash, $5,350; Expenses, $3,250; Accounts Payable, $2,200

1. Create the following table similar to Exhibit 1.9. Use additions and subtractions within the table to show the dollar effects of each transaction on individual items of the accounting equation. Show new balances after each transaction.

Assets									=	Liabilities	+	Equity						
Cash	+	Accounts Receivable	+	Supplies	+	Equipment	+	Building	=	Accounts Payable	+	N. Nadal, Capital	−	N. Nadal, Withdrawals	+	Revenues	−	Expenses

(2) Net income, $3,550

2. Determine the company's net income.

Problem 1-9B
Analyzing transactions and preparing financial statements
P1 P2

Rivera Roofing Company, owned by Reyna Rivera, began operations in July and completed these transactions during that first month of operations.

July 1 Reyna Rivera invested $80,000 cash in the company.
2 The company paid $700 cash for the July rent.
3 The company purchased roofing equipment for $5,000 by paying $1,000 cash and agreeing to pay the $4,000 balance in 30 days.
6 The company purchased supplies for $600 cash.
8 The company completed work for a customer and immediately collected $7,600 cash for the work.
10 The company purchased $2,300 of office equipment on credit.
15 The company completed work for a customer on credit in the amount of $8,200.
17 The company purchased $3,100 of supplies on credit.
23 The company paid $2,300 cash for the office equipment purchased on July 10.
25 The company billed a customer $5,000 for work completed; the balance is due in 30 days.

28 The company received $8,200 cash for the work completed on July 15.
30 The company paid an assistant's salary of $1,560 cash for this month.
31 The company paid $295 cash for this month's utility bill.
31 Reyna Rivera withdrew $1,800 cash from the company for personal use.

Required

1. Create the following table similar to Exhibit 1.9. Use additions and subtractions within the table to show the dollar effects of each transaction on individual items of the accounting equation. Show new balances after each transaction.

Check (1) Ending balances: Cash, $87,545; Accounts Payable, $7,100

	Assets					= Liabilities +	Equity			
Date	Cash +	Accounts Receivable +	Supplies +	Office Equipment +	Roofing Equipment =	Accounts Payable +	R. Rivera, Capital −	R. Rivera, Withdrawals +	Revenues −	Expenses

2. Prepare the income statement and the statement of owner's equity for the month of July, and the balance sheet as of July 31.

(2) Net income, $18,245; Total assets, $103,545

3. Prepare the statement of cash flows for the month of July.

Analysis Component

4. Assume that the $5,000 purchase of roofing equipment on July 3 was financed from an owner investment of another $5,000 cash in the business (instead of the purchase conditions described in the transaction above). Compute the dollar effect of this change on the month-end amounts for (*a*) total assets, (*b*) total liabilities, and (*c*) total equity.

Problem 1-10B
Determining expenses, liabilities, equity, and return on assets
A1 A2

Ski-Doo Company manufactures, markets, and sells snowmobiles and snowmobile equipment and accessories. The average total assets for Ski-Doo is $3,000,000. In its most recent year, Ski-Doo reported net income of $201,000 on revenues of $1,400,000.

Required

1. What is Ski-Doo Company's return on assets?
2. Does return on assets seem satisfactory for Ski-Doo given that its competitors average a 9.5% return on assets?
3. What are the total expenses for Ski-Doo Company in its most recent year?
4. What is the average total amount of liabilities plus equity for Ski-Doo Company?

Check (3) $1,199,000
(4) $3,000,000

Problem 1-11B
Computing and interpreting return on assets
A2

AT&T and Verizon produce and market telecommunications products and are competitors. Key financial figures for these businesses for a recent year follow.

Key Figures ($ millions)	AT&T	Verizon
Sales	$126,723	$110,875
Net income	4,184	10,198
Average assets	269,868	225,233

Required

1. Compute return on assets for (*a*) AT&T and (*b*) Verizon.
2. Which company is more successful in the total amount of sales to consumers?
3. Which company is more successful in returning net income from its assets invested?

Check (1*a*) 1.6%; (1*b*) 4.5%

Analysis Component

4. Write a one-paragraph memorandum explaining which company you would invest your money in and why. (Limit your explanation to the information provided.)

Serial Problem starts here and follows the same company throughout the text. It is available in Connect.

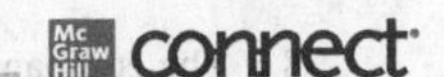

SERIAL PROBLEM

Business Solutions

P1

Alexander Image/Shutterstock

SP 1 On October 1, 2021, Santana Rey launched a computer services company, **Business Solutions**, that is organized as a proprietorship and provides consulting services, computer system installations, and custom program development.

Required

Create a table like Exhibit 1.9 using these headings: Cash; Accounts Receivable; Computer Supplies; Computer System; Office Equipment; Accounts Payable; S. Rey, Capital; S. Rey, Withdrawals; Revenues; and Expenses. Use additions and subtractions within the table to show the dollar effects for each of the following transactions on the individual items of the accounting equation. Show new balances after each transaction.

Oct.	1	S. Rey invested $45,000 cash, a $20,000 computer system, and $8,000 of office equipment in the company.
	3	The company purchased $1,420 of computer supplies on credit.
	6	The company billed Easy Leasing $4,800 for services performed in installing a new web server.
	8	The company paid $1,420 cash for the computer supplies purchased on credit on October 3.
	10	The company hired a part-time assistant.
	12	The company billed Easy Leasing another $1,400 for services performed.
	15	The company received $4,800 cash from Easy Leasing as partial payment toward its account.
	17	The company paid $805 cash to repair its computer equipment.
	20	The company paid $1,728 cash for advertisements published on Facebook.
	22	The company received $1,400 cash from Easy Leasing toward its account.
	28	The company billed IFM Company $5,208 for services performed.
	31	The company paid $875 cash for the assistant's wages for this month.
	31	S. Rey withdrew $3,600 cash from the company for personal use.

Check Ending balances: Cash, $42,772; Revenues, $11,408; Expenses, $3,408

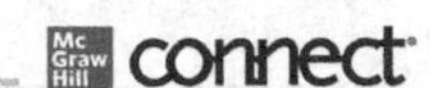

TABLEAU DASHBOARD ACTIVITIES

Tableau Dashboard Activities expose students to accounting analytics using visual displays. These assignments (1) do not require instructors to know Tableau, (2) are accessible to introductory students, (3) do not require Tableau software, and (4) run in **Connect**. All are auto-gradable. Chapter 1 analytics assignments follow.

Tableau DA 1-1 Quick Study, Applying the accounting equation, **A1**—similar to QS 1-7.

Tableau DA 1-2 Exercise, Applying the accounting equation and identifying balance sheet accounts, **A1, P2**—similar to QS 1-8 and Exercise 1-9.

Tableau DA 1-3 Mini-Case, Preparing an income statement, **A1, P2**—similar to QS 1-15 and Exercise 1-18.

*Accounting Analysis (AA) assignments refine analysis and critical thinking skills and are **auto-gradable** in Connect. They can be assigned for each chapter or as a group for a financial statement analysis project.*

Accounting Analysis connect

COMPANY ANALYSIS

A1 A2

AA 1-1 Key financial figures for **Apple**'s two most recent fiscal years follow.

$ millions	Current Year	Prior Year
Liabilities + Equity	$338,516	$365,725
Net income	55,256	59,531
Revenues	260,174	265,595

Required

1. What is the total amount of assets invested in Apple in the current year?
2. What is Apple's return on assets for the current year?
3. How much are total expenses for Apple for the current year?
4. Is Apple's current year return on assets better or worse than competitors' average return of 10%?

AA 1-2 Key comparative figures for both **Apple** and **Google** follow.

COMPARATIVE ANALYSIS
A1 A2

	Apple		Google	
$ millions	Current Year	Prior Year	Current Year	Prior Year
Liabilities + Equity	$338,516	$365,725	$275,909	$232,792
Net income	55,256	59,531	34,343	30,736
Revenues	260,174	265,595	161,857	136,819

Required

1. What is the total amount of assets invested for the current year in (*a*) Apple and (*b*) Google?
2. What is the current year return on assets for (*a*) Apple and (*b*) Google?
3. How much are current year expenses for (*a*) Apple and (*b*) Google?
4. Is the current year return on assets better than the 10% return of competitors for (*a*) Apple and (*b*) Google?
5. Relying only on return on assets, would we invest in Google or Apple?

Note: Reference to **Google** throughout the text refers to **Alphabet Inc.**, as Google is a wholly owned subsidiary of Alphabet.

AA 1-3 **Samsung** is a leading global manufacturer that competes with **Apple** and **Google**. Key financial figures for Samsung follow.

EXTENDED ANALYSIS
A1 A2

	Samsung		Apple	Google
$ millions	Current Year	Prior Year	Current Year	Current Year
Average assets..........	$296,845	$282,723	$352,121	$254,351
Net income.............	18,653	38,049	55,256	34,343
Revenues	197,691	209,163	260,174	161,857

Required

1. What is the return on assets for Samsung in the (*a*) current year and (*b*) prior year?
2. Does Samsung's return on assets exhibit a favorable or unfavorable change?
3. Is Samsung's current year return on assets better or worse than that for (*a*) Apple and (*b*) Google?

Discussion Questions

1. What is the purpose of accounting in society?
2. Technology is increasingly used to process accounting data. Why then must we study and understand accounting?
3. Identify four kinds of external users and describe how they use accounting information.
4. What are at least three questions business owners and managers might be able to answer by looking at accounting information?
5. Identify three actual businesses that offer services and three actual businesses that offer products.
6. Describe the internal role of accounting for organizations.
7. Identify three types of services typically offered by accounting professionals.
8. What type of accounting information might be useful to the marketing managers of a business?
9. Why is accounting described as a service activity?
10. What are some accounting-related professions?
11. How do ethics rules affect auditors' choice of clients?
12. What work do tax accounting professionals perform in addition to preparing tax returns?
13. What does the concept of *objectivity* imply for information reported in financial statements?
14. A business reports its own office stationery on the balance sheet at its $400 cost, although it cannot be sold for more than $10 as scrap paper. Which accounting principle and/or assumption justifies this treatment?
15. Why is the revenue recognition principle needed? What does it demand?
16. Describe the four basic forms of business organization and their key attributes.

17. Define (*a*) *assets*, (*b*) *liabilities*, (*c*) *equity*, and (*d*) *net assets*.
18. What events or transactions change equity?
19. Identify the two main categories of accounting principles.
20. What do accountants mean by the term *revenue?*
21. Define *net income* and explain its computation.
22. Identify the four basic financial statements of a business.
23. What information is reported in an income statement?
24. Give two examples of expenses a business might incur.
25. What is the purpose of the statement of owner's equity?
26. What information is reported in a balance sheet?
27. The statement of cash flows reports on what major activities?
28. Define and explain return on assets.

Beyond the Numbers (BTN) assignments refine communication, conceptual, analysis, and research skills and can help develop an active learning environment.

Beyond the Numbers

ETHICS CHALLENGE

C2

BTN 1-1 Tana Thorne works in a public accounting firm and hopes to eventually be a partner. The management of Allnet Company invites Thorne to prepare a bid to audit Allnet's financial statements. In discussing the audit fee, Allnet's management suggests a fee range in which the amount depends on the reported profit of Allnet. The higher its profit, the higher will be the audit fee paid to Thorne's firm.

Required

1. Identify the parties potentially affected by this audit and the fee plan proposed.
2. What are the ethical factors in this situation? Explain.
3. Would you recommend that Thorne accept this audit fee arrangement? Why or why not?
4. Describe some ethical considerations guiding your recommendation.

COMMUNICATING IN PRACTICE

C1 C2

APPLE

BTN 1-2 Refer to **Apple**'s financial statements in Appendix A. Assume that the owners, sometime during their first five years of business, desire to expand their computer product services to meet business demand regarding computing services. They eventually decide to meet with their banker to discuss a loan to allow Apple to expand and offer computing services.

Required

1. Prepare a half-page report outlining the information you would request from the owners if you were the loan officer.
2. Indicate whether the information you request and your loan decision are affected by the form of business organization for Apple.

TEAMWORK IN ACTION

C1

BTN 1-3 Teamwork is important in today's business world. Successful teams schedule convenient meetings, maintain regular communications, and cooperate with and support their members. This assignment aims to establish support/learning teams, initiate discussions, and set meeting times.

Required

1. Form teams and open a team discussion to determine a regular time and place for your team to meet between each scheduled class meeting. Notify your instructor via a memorandum or e-mail message as to when and where your team will hold regularly scheduled meetings.
2. Develop a list of telephone numbers, LinkedIn pages, and/or e-mail addresses of your teammates.

BTN 1-4 Refer to this chapter's opening feature about **Netflix**. Assume that the owner decides to open a new company with an innovative mobile app devoted to microblogging for accountants and those learning accounting. This new company will be called **AccountApp**.

ENTREPRENEURIAL DECISION

A1 A2

Required

1. AccountApp obtains a $500,000 loan, and the owner contributes $250,000 in total from his own savings in exchange for ownership of the new company.
   a. What is the new company's total amount of liabilities plus equity?
   b. What is the new company's total amount of assets?
2. If the new company earns $80,250 in net income in the first year of operation, compute its return on assets (assume average assets equal $750,000). Assess its performance if competitors average a 10% return.

Check (2) 10.7%

2 Analyzing and Recording Transactions

Chapter Preview

SYSTEM OF ACCOUNTS	DEBITS AND CREDITS	RECORDING TRANSACTIONS	FINANCIAL REPORTING
C1 Source documents	**C2** T-account	**A1** Journalizing and posting	**P1** Trial balance preparation and use
Types of accounts	Debits and credits	Processing transactions—Examples	Financial statement preparation
General ledger	Normal balance		**A2** Debt ratio
NTK 2-1	**NTK 2-2**	**NTK 2-3**	**NTK 2-4**

Learning Objectives

CONCEPTUAL

C1 Describe an account and its use in recording transactions.

C2 Define *debits* and *credits* and explain double-entry accounting.

ANALYTICAL

A1 Analyze and record transactions and their impact on financial statements.

A2 Compute the debt ratio and describe its use in analyzing financial condition.

PROCEDURAL

P1 Prepare financial statements from a trial balance.

Stitch in Time

"Drive loyalty and relevance for customers"
—KATRINA LAKE

SAN FRANCISCO—Katrina Lake planned to pursue a health care career until she came up with a business idea as part of a class project. "I looked at people like [Google founders] Larry Page and Sergey Brin," recalls Katrina, "It took me a while to think that this was a path that was available to me." Katrina believed in her idea and launched her business, **Stitch Fix** (**Stitchfix.com**). Stitch Fix is an online subscription service that sends stylish clothes to customers' homes.

Katrina's business has taken off. Stitch Fix already has over 2 million customers, and the company recently began offering its stock for sale to the public (ticker: SFIX), which makes Katrina the youngest woman ever to take a company public. Admits Katrina, "We've been underestimated before."

Katrina explains that accounting is one key to her success. In the early stages of her business, Katrina set up an accounting system to track sales and expenses. She also made sure her financial reports were top quality to attract investors. Katrina asserts that reliable numbers cause "people [investors] to pay more attention."

Katrina is among the best at using accounting analytics to predict customer preferences. Much of what drives Stitch Fix's success is its algorithm that recommends clothing to customers. This drives additional sales and further subscription revenue. Katrina says that her use of accounting analytics is "what makes this company special!"

Dia Dipasupil/Getty Images

Sources: *Stitch Fix website*, January 2021; *CNN*, July 2018; *Time.com*, May 2018

BASIS OF FINANCIAL STATEMENTS

C1 Describe an account and its use in recording transactions.

Business transactions and events are the starting points of financial statements. The process to go from transactions and events to financial statements includes the following.

- Identify each transaction and event from source documents.
- Analyze each transaction and event using the accounting equation.
- Record relevant transactions and events in a journal.
- Post journal information to ledger accounts.
- Prepare and analyze the trial balance and financial statements.

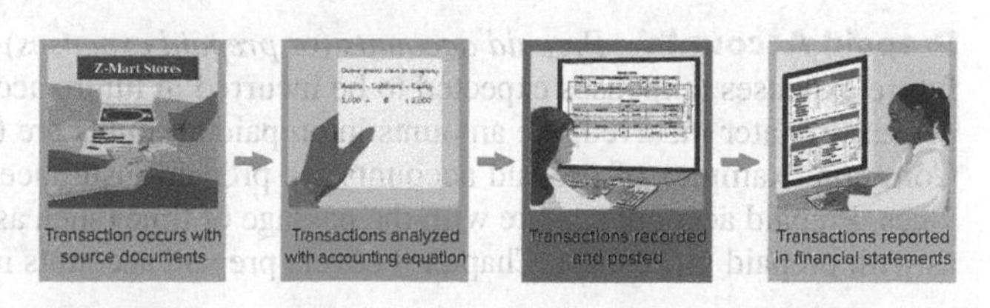

Source Documents

Source documents identify and describe transactions and events entering the accounting system. They can be in hard copy or electronic form. Examples are sales receipts, checks, purchase orders, bills from suppliers, payroll records, and bank statements. For example, cash registers record each sale on a tape or electronic file. This record is a source document for recording sales in the accounting system. Source documents are objective and reliable evidence about transactions and events and their amounts.

Point: Accounting records also are called *accounting books* or *the books*.

"Account" Underlying Financial Statements

An **account** is a record of increases and decreases in a specific asset, liability, equity, revenue, or expense. The **general ledger,** or simply **ledger,** is a record of all accounts and their balances. The ledger is often in electronic form. While most companies' ledgers have similar accounts, a

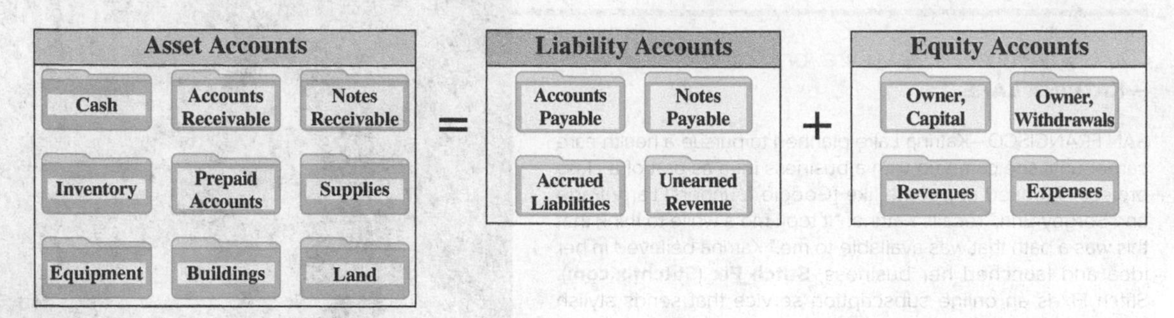

EXHIBIT 2.1

Accounts Organized by the Accounting Equation

company often uses one or more unique accounts to match its type of operations. Exhibit 2.1 shows common asset, liability, and equity accounts.

Asset Accounts Assets are resources owned or controlled by a company. Resources have expected future benefits. Most accounting systems include (at a minimum) separate accounts for the assets described here.

Cash A *Cash* account shows a company's cash balance. All increases and decreases in cash are recorded in the Cash account. It includes money and any funds that a bank accepts for deposit (coins, checks, money orders, and checking account balances).

Accounts Receivable *Accounts receivable* are held by a seller and are promises of payment from customers to sellers. Accounts receivable are increased by *credit sales* or *sales on credit* (or *on account*). They are decreased by customer payments. We record all increases and decreases in receivables in the Accounts Receivable account. When there are multiple customers, separate records are kept for each, titled Accounts Receivable—'Customer Name'.

Notes Receivable A *note receivable,* or promissory note, is a written promise of another entity to pay a specific sum of money on a specified future date to the holder of the note; the holder has an asset recorded in a Notes Receivable account. It is different than accounts receivable because it comes from a *formal contract called a promissory note.* Notes receivable usually require interest, whereas accounts receivable do not.

Prepaid Accounts *Prepaid accounts* (or *prepaid expenses*) are assets from prepayments of future expenses (expenses expected to be incurred in future accounting periods). When the expenses are later incurred, the amounts in prepaid accounts are transferred to expense accounts. Common examples of prepaid accounts are prepaid insurance, prepaid rent, and prepaid services. Prepaid accounts expire with the passage of time (such as with rent) or through use (such as with prepaid gift cards). Chapter 3 covers prepaid accounts in detail.

Supplies Accounts *Supplies* are assets until they are used. When they are used up, their costs are reported as expenses. Unused supplies are recorded in a Supplies asset account. Supplies often are grouped by purpose—for example, office supplies and store supplies.

Equipment Accounts *Equipment* is an asset. Its cost is allocated over time to expense, called *depreciation.* Equipment often is grouped by its purpose—for example, office equipment and store equipment.

Buildings Accounts *Buildings* such as stores, offices, warehouses, and factories are assets. Cost of buildings is allocated over time to expense, called *depreciation.* When several buildings are owned, separate accounts are sometimes kept for each of them.

Land The cost of *land* is recorded in a Land account. The cost of buildings located on the land is separately recorded in building accounts.

Decision Insight

Women Entrepreneurs "Do-goodr" Jasmine Crowe (in photo), the founder and CEO of **Goodr**, works to reduce food waste and combat hunger. The Center for Women's Business Research reports women-owned businesses (1) total more than 11 million and employ nearly 20 million workers, (2) generate $2.5 trillion in annual sales and tend to embrace technology, and (3) are philanthropic—70% of owners volunteer at least once per month. ■

Jasmine Crowe, Founder and CEO of Goodr

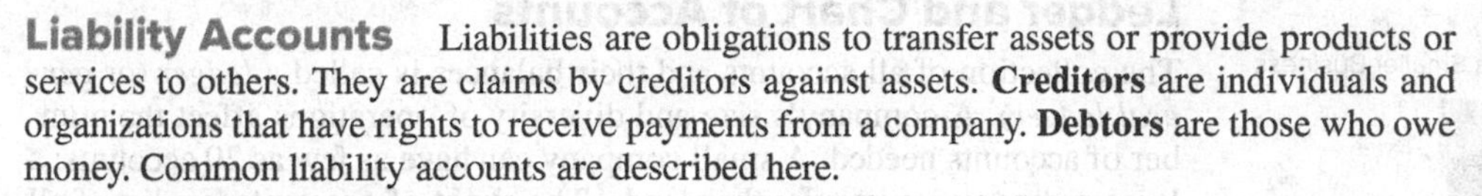

Liability Accounts Liabilities are obligations to transfer assets or provide products or services to others. They are claims by creditors against assets. **Creditors** are individuals and organizations that have rights to receive payments from a company. **Debtors** are those who owe money. Common liability accounts are described here.

Accounts Payable *Accounts payable* are promises to pay later. Payables can come from purchases *on credit* or *on account* of merchandise-for-resale, supplies, equipment, and services. We record all increases and decreases in payables in the Accounts Payable account. When there are multiple suppliers, separate records are kept for each, titled Accounts Payable—'Supplier Name'.

Notes Payable A *note payable* is a written promissory note to pay a future amount. Notes payable are different than accounts payable because they come from a *formal contract called a promissory note* and usually require interest.

Unearned Revenue Accounts **Unearned revenue** is a liability that is recorded when customers pay in advance for products or services. Examples of unearned revenue include magazine subscriptions collected in advance by a publisher, rent collected in advance by a landlord, and season ticket sales by sports teams. The seller would record these in liability accounts such as Unearned Subscriptions and Unearned Rent. When products and services are later delivered, unearned revenue is transferred to revenue.

Point: Two words that almost always identify liability accounts: "payable," meaning liabilities that must be paid, and "unearned," meaning liabilities that must be fulfilled.

Accrued Liabilities *Accrued liabilities* are amounts owed that are not yet paid. Examples are wages payable, taxes payable, and interest payable. These often are recorded in separate liability accounts by the same title.

Equity Accounts The owner's claim on a company's assets is called *equity,* or *owner's equity.* Equity is the owner's *residual interest* in the assets of a business after subtracting liabilities. Equity is impacted by four types of accounts, as shown in Exhibit 2.2.

EXHIBIT 2.2

Equity Accounts

Owner Capital When an owner invests in a company, it increases both assets and equity. The increase to equity is recorded in the account titled **Owner, Capital**, where the owner's name is inserted in place of 'Owner.' *C. Taylor, Capital* is used for FastForward. Owner investments are not revenues of the business.

Owner Withdrawals When an owner withdraws assets for personal use, it decreases both company assets and total equity. The decrease to equity is recorded in an account titled **Owner, Withdrawals.** *C. Taylor, Withdrawals* is used for FastForward. Withdrawals are not expenses of the business; they are simply the opposite of owner investments.

Revenue Accounts Sales of products and services to customers are recorded in revenue accounts, which increase equity. Examples of revenue accounts are Sales, Commissions Revenue, Professional Fees Revenue, Rent Revenue, and Interest Revenue. **Revenues always increase equity.** Account titles can differ: Product sales are called *net sales* at Apple, *revenues* at Google, and *revenue* at Samsung. *Revenues* or *fees* is commonly used with service businesses, and *net sales* or *sales* is used with product businesses.

Expense Accounts Costs of providing products and services are recorded in expense accounts, which decrease equity. Examples of expense accounts are Advertising Expense, Salaries Expense, Rent Expense, Utilities Expense, and Insurance Expense. **Expenses always decrease equity.** A variety of revenues and expenses are in the *chart of accounts* at the end of this book.

EXHIBIT 2.3

Typical Chart of Accounts for a Smaller Business

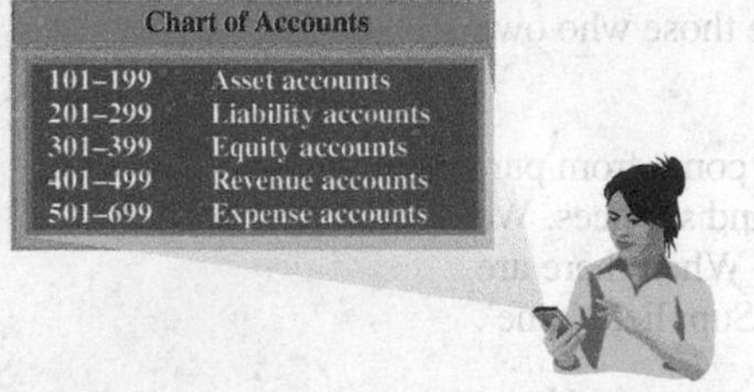

Chart of Accounts	
101–199	Asset accounts
201–299	Liability accounts
301–399	Equity accounts
401–499	Revenue accounts
501–699	Expense accounts

Ledger and Chart of Accounts

The collection of all accounts and their balances is called a *ledger* (or *general ledger*). A company's size and diversity of operations affect the number of accounts needed. A small company can have as few as 20 accounts; a large company can require thousands. The **chart of accounts** is a list of all ledger accounts with an identification number assigned to each account. Exhibit 2.3 shows a common numbering system of accounts for a smaller business.

These account numbers have a three-digit code that is useful in recordkeeping. In this example, the first digit of asset accounts is a 1, the first digit of liability accounts is a 2, and so on. The second and third digits relate to the accounts' subcategories. Exhibit 2.4 shows a partial chart of accounts for FastForward.

EXHIBIT 2.4

Partial Chart of Accounts for FastForward

Chart of Accounts											
Assets		**Liabilities**		**Equity**							
						Revenues		**Expenses**	
101	Cash	201	Accounts payable	301	C. Taylor, Capital	403	Consulting revenue	622	Salaries expense
106	Accounts receivable	236	Unearned consulting revenue	302	C. Taylor, Withdrawals	406	Rental revenue	637	Insurance expense
126	Supplies							640	Rent expense
128	Prepaid insurance							652	Supplies expense
167	Equipment							690	Utilities expense

Sam Wasson/Getty Images

Decision Insight

Unearned Revenue Many professional sports teams have over $100 million in advance ticket sales in *Unearned Revenue*. When a team plays its home games, it settles this liability to its ticket holders and then transfers the amount earned to *Ticket Revenue*. Teams such as the **Seattle Storm**, **Minnesota Lynx**, and **L.A. Sparks** of the Women's National Basketball Association have unearned revenue. ■

NEED-TO-KNOW 2-1

Classifying Accounts

C1

Classify each of the following accounts as either an asset (A), liability (L), or equity (EQ) account.

1. Prepaid Rent	**5.** Accounts Receivable	**9.** Land
2. Owner, Capital	**6.** Equipment	**10.** Prepaid Insurance
3. Note Receivable	**7.** Interest Payable	**11.** Wages Payable
4. Accounts Payable	**8.** Unearned Revenue	**12.** Rent Payable

Solution

1. A **2.** EQ **3.** A **4.** L **5.** A **6.** A **7.** L **8.** L **9.** A **10.** A **11.** L **12.** L

Do More: QS 2-1, QS 2-2, QS 2-3, E 2-1, E 2-2, E 2-3, E 2-4

DOUBLE-ENTRY ACCOUNTING

Debits and Credits

C2 Define *debits* and *credits* and explain double-entry accounting.

A **T-account** represents a ledger account and is used to show the effects of transactions. Its name comes from its shape like the letter **T**. The layout of a T-account is shown in Exhibit 2.5.

The left side of an account is called the **debit** side, or *Dr.* The right side is called the **credit** side, or *Cr.* To enter amounts on the left side of an account is to *debit* the account. To enter amounts on the right side is to *credit* the account. The term *debit* or *credit,* by itself, does not mean increase or decrease. Whether a debit or a credit is an increase or decrease depends on the account.

EXHIBIT 2.5

The T-Account

Account Title	
(Left side) *Debit*	(Right side) *Credit*

Point: *Debit* and *credit* are accounting directions for left and right.

The difference between total debits and total credits for an account, including any beginning balance, is the **account balance.** When total debits exceed total credits, the account has a *debit balance*. It has a *credit balance* when total credits exceed total debits. When total debits equal total credits, the account has a *zero balance*.

Double-Entry System

Double-entry accounting demands the accounting equation remain in balance, which means that for each transaction:

- **At least two accounts are involved, with at least one debit and one credit.**
- **Total amount debited must equal total amount credited.**

This means total debits must equal total credits for all entries, and total debit account balances in the ledger must equal total credit account balances. The system for recording debits and credits follows the accounting equation—see Exhibit 2.6.

EXHIBIT 2.6

Debits and Credits in the Accounting Equation

Assets		=	Liabilities		+	Equity	
Debit for increases	Credit for decreases		Debit for decreases	Credit for increases		Debit for decreases	Credit for increases
+	–		–	+		–	+
Normal				Normal			Normal

Net increases or decreases on one side have equal net effects on the other side. For example, a net increase in assets must include an equal net increase on the liabilities and equity side. Some transactions affect only one side of the equation, such as acquiring a land asset by giving up a cash asset, but their net effect on this one side is zero.

The left side is the *normal balance* side for assets; the right side is the *normal balance* side for liabilities and equity. This matches their layout in the accounting equation, where assets are on the left side and liabilities and equity are on the right.

Point: Assets are on the left-hand side of the equation and thus increase on the left. Liabilities and equity are on the right-hand side of the equation and thus increase on the right.

Equity increases from revenues and owner investments, and it decreases from expenses and owner withdrawals. We see this by expanding the accounting equation to include debits and credits in double-entry form, as shown in Exhibit 2.7.

EXHIBIT 2.7

Debit and Credit Effects for Component Accounts

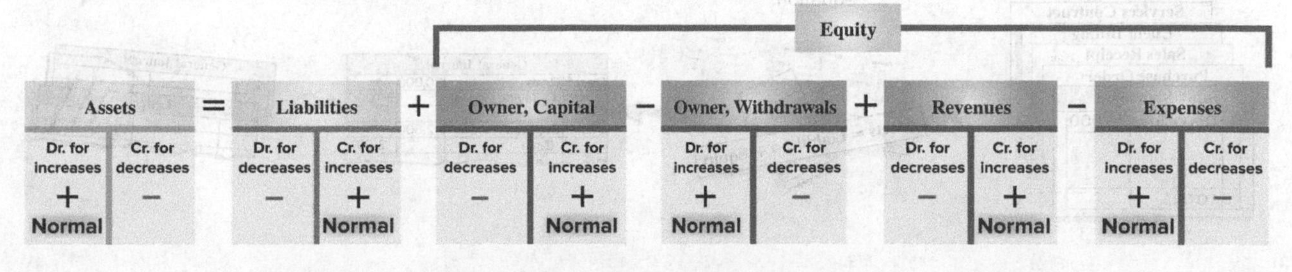

Increases (credits) to owner's capital and revenues *increase* equity; increases (debits) to withdrawals and expenses *decrease* equity. The normal balance of each account is the side where *increases* are recorded.

Point: **DrEAD** means debit (**Dr**) is the normal balance side for **E**xpense, **A**sset, and **D**rawing accounts; credit the others.

The T-account for FastForward's Cash account, reflecting its first 11 transactions (from Exhibit 1.9), is shown in Exhibit 2.8. The total increases (debits) in its Cash account are $36,100, and the total decreases (credits) are $31,300. Total debits exceed total credits by $4,800, resulting in its ending debit balance of $4,800.

EXHIBIT 2.8

Computing the Balance for a T-Account

Cash			
Receive investment by owner	30,000	Purchase of supplies	2,500
Consulting services revenue earned	4,200	Purchase of equipment	26,000
Collection of account receivable	1,900	Payment of rent	1,000
		Payment of salary	700
		Payment of account payable	900
		Withdrawal by owner	200
Balance	4,800		

36,100 (total debits) 31,300 (total credits) Balance: 36,100 − 31,300

Point: The ending balance is on the side with the larger dollar amount.

NEED-TO-KNOW 2-2

Normal Account Balance

C2

Do More: QS 2-4, QS 2-5, QS 2-6, QS 2-7, E 2-5

Identify the normal balance (debit [Dr] or credit [Cr]) for each of the following accounts.

1. Prepaid Rent
2. Owner, Capital
3. Note Receivable
4. Accounts Payable
5. Accounts Receivable
6. Equipment
7. Interest Payable
8. Unearned Revenue
9. Land
10. Prepaid Insurance
11. Owner, Withdrawals
12. Utilities Expense

Solution

1. Dr. **2.** Cr. **3.** Dr. **4.** Cr. **5.** Dr. **6.** Dr. **7.** Cr. **8.** Cr. **9.** Dr. **10.** Dr. **11.** Dr. **12.** Dr.

ANALYZING AND PROCESSING TRANSACTIONS

This section covers analyzing, recording, and posting transactions.

A1

Analyze and record transactions and their impact on financial statements.

Journalizing and Posting Transactions

The four steps of processing transactions are shown in Exhibit 2.9. Steps 1 and 2—transaction analysis and the accounting equation—already were covered. This section focuses on steps 3 and 4. Step 3 is to record each transaction chronologically in a journal. A **journal** is a complete record of each transaction in one place. It also shows debits and credits for each transaction. Recording transactions in a journal is called **journalizing.** Step 4 is to transfer (or *post*) entries from the journal to the ledger. Transferring journal entry information to the ledger is called **posting.**

EXHIBIT 2.9

Steps in Processing Transactions

Step 1: Identify transactions and source documents. **Step 2:** Analyze transactions using the accounting equation. **Step 3:** Record journal entry. **Step 4:** Post entry to ledger.

Services Contract
Client Billing
Sales Receipt
Purchase Order
Bank Statement
1 Deposit 30,000
TOTAL

Assets = Liabilities + Equity

General Journal			
Dec. 1	Cash	30,000	
	C. Taylor, Capital		30,000
Dec. 2	Supplies	2,500	
	Cash		2,500

General Journal
Ledger

Journalizing Transactions Journalizing transactions requires an understanding of a journal. While companies can use various journals, every company uses a **general journal.** It can be used to record any transaction. Exhibit 2.10 shows how the first two transactions of FastForward are recorded in a general journal.

To record entries in a general journal, apply these steps; refer to Exhibit 2.10.

ⓐ Date the transaction on the first line of each journal entry.

ⓑ Enter titles of accounts debited and then enter amounts in the Debit column on the same line. Account titles are taken from the chart of accounts.

ⓒ Enter titles of accounts credited and then enter amounts in the Credit column on the same line. Account titles are from the chart of accounts and are indented to separate them from debited accounts.

ⓓ Enter a brief explanation of the transaction on the line below the entry.

EXHIBIT 2.10

Partial General Journal

General Journal

Date	Account Titles and Explanation	PR	Debit	Credit
2021 ⓐ Dec. 1	ⓑ Cash		30,000	
	ⓒ C. Taylor, Capital			30,000
	Receive investment by owner. ⓓ			
Dec. 2	Supplies		2,500	
	Cash			2,500
	Purchase supplies for cash.			

When a transaction is first recorded, the **posting reference (PR) column** is left blank (in a manual system). Later, when posting entries to the ledger, the identification numbers of the individual ledger accounts are entered in the PR column.

Balance Column Account T-accounts are simple and show how the accounting process works. However, actual accounting systems need more structure and therefore use a different formatting of T-accounts, called **balance column accounts,** shown in Exhibit 2.11.

EXHIBIT 2.11

Cash Account in Balance Column Format

General Ledger

Cash				Account No. 101	
Date	Explanation	PR	Debit	Credit	Balance
2021					
Dec. 1		G1	30,000		30,000
Dec. 2		G1		2,500	27,500
Dec. 3		G1		26,000	1,500
Dec. 10		G1	4,200		5,700

The balance column account format is similar to a T-account in having columns for debits and credits. It is different in including transaction date and explanation columns. It also has a column where the balance of the account after each entry is recorded. FastForward's Cash account in Exhibit 2.11 is debited on December 1 for the $30,000 owner investment, yielding a $30,000 debit balance. The account is credited on December 2 for $2,500, yielding a $27,500 debit balance. On December 3, it is credited for $26,000, and its debit balance is reduced to $1,500. The Cash account is debited for $4,200 on December 10, and its debit balance increases to $5,700; and so on.

The heading of the Balance column does not show whether it is a debit or credit balance. Instead, an account is assumed to have a *normal balance*. Unusual events can sometimes temporarily create an abnormal balance. An *abnormal balance* is a balance on the side where decreases are recorded. For example, a customer might mistakenly overpay a bill.

Posting Journal Entries Step 4 of processing transactions is to post journal entries to ledger accounts. All entries are posted to the ledger before financial statements are prepared so that account balances are up-to-date. When entries are posted to the ledger, the debits in journal entries are transferred into ledger accounts as debits, and credits are transferred into ledger

Point: Posting is automatic with accounting software.

Point: The fundamental concepts of a manual system are identical to those of a computerized information system.

accounts as credits. Exhibit 2.12 shows *four parts to* ***posting*** *a journal entry.* Ⓐ Identify the ledger account(s) that is debited in the entry. In the ledger, enter the entry date, the journal and page in its PR column, the debit amount, and the new balance of the ledger account. (*G* shows it came from the general journal.) Ⓑ Enter the ledger account number in the PR column of the journal. Parts Ⓒ and Ⓓ repeat the first two steps for credit entries and amounts. The posting process creates a link between the ledger and the journal entry. This link is a useful cross-reference for tracing an amount from one record to another.

EXHIBIT 2.12

Posting an Entry to the Ledger

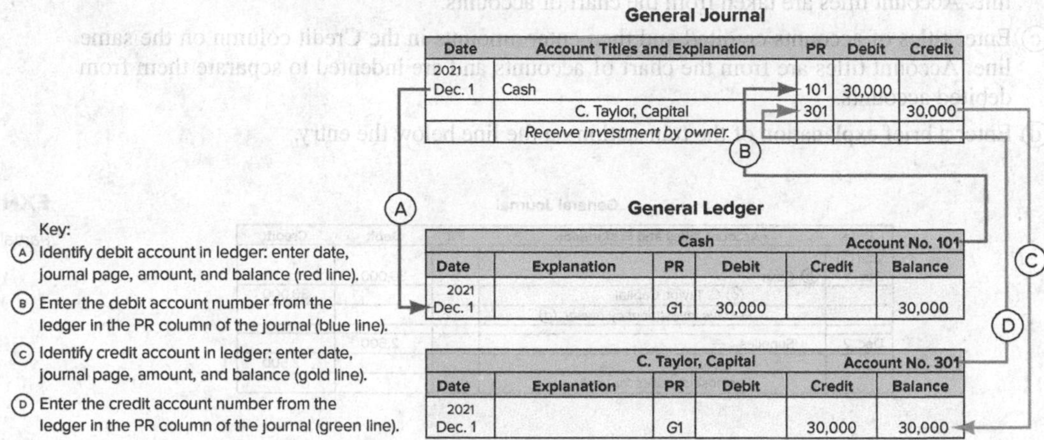

Ekaphon maneechot/Shutterstock

Analytics Insight

Blockchain Ledger Blockchain, the technology used to authenticate and track Bitcoin transactions, could radically change accounting systems. This technology unlocks the potential for a new type of ledger that is constantly verified, and one that cannot be changed without others noticing. Blockchain presents a unique opportunity for those with accounting knowledge, as they are highly desired to help build, implement, maintain, and audit this new technology. ■

Processing Transactions—An Example

We use FastForward to show how double-entry accounting is used in analyzing and processing transactions. Analysis of each transaction follows the four steps of Exhibit 2.9.

Step 1 Identify transactions and source documents.

Step 2 Analyze the transaction using the accounting equation.

Step 3 Record the journal entry.

Step 4 Post the entry (for simplicity, we use T-accounts as ledger accounts).

Point: In Need-to-Know 2-5, we show how to use balance column accounts for the ledger.

Study each transaction before moving to the next. The first 11 transactions are from Chapter 1, and we analyze five additional December transactions of FastForward (numbered 12 through 16).

1. Receive Investment by Owner

1 IDENTIFY FastForward receives $30,000 cash from Chas Taylor as an owner investment.

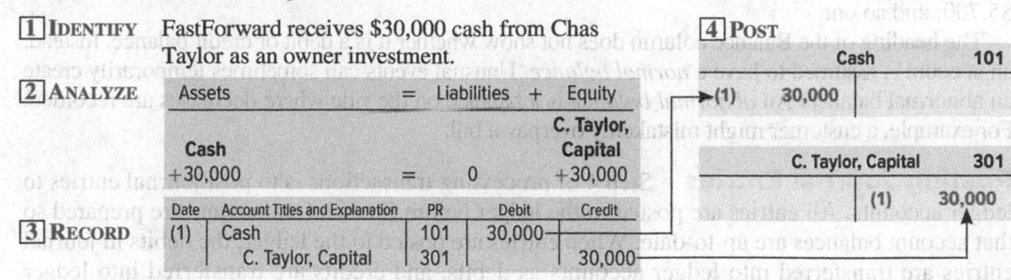

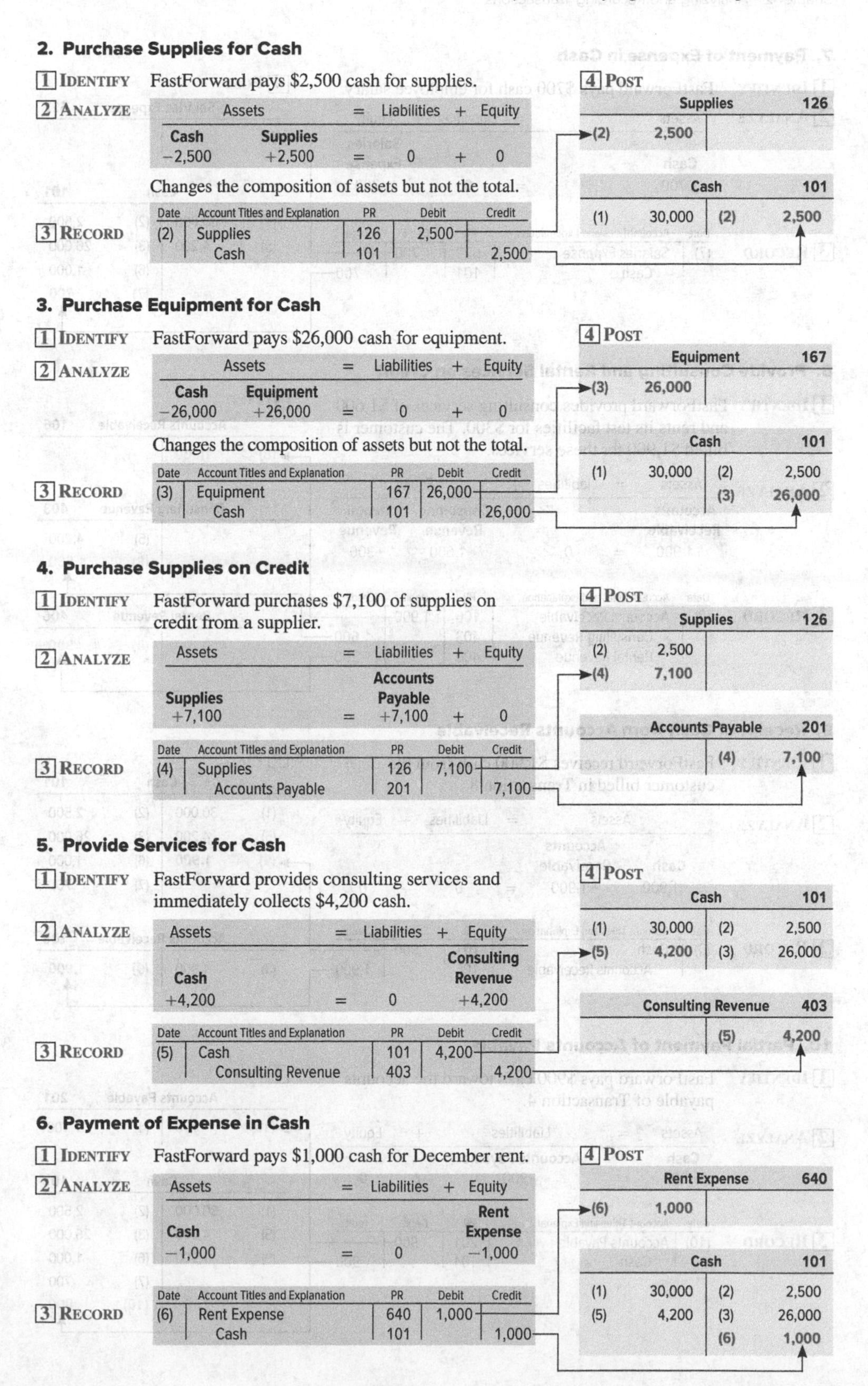

2. Purchase Supplies for Cash

1 IDENTIFY FastForward pays $2,500 cash for supplies.

2 ANALYZE

Assets		=	Liabilities	+	Equity
Cash	Supplies				
−2,500	+2,500	=	0	+	0

Changes the composition of assets but not the total.

3 RECORD

Date	Account Titles and Explanation	PR	Debit	Credit
(2)	Supplies	126	2,500	
	Cash	101		2,500

4 POST

Supplies			126
(2)	2,500		

Cash			101
(1)	30,000	(2)	2,500

3. Purchase Equipment for Cash

1 IDENTIFY FastForward pays $26,000 cash for equipment.

2 ANALYZE

Assets		=	Liabilities	+	Equity
Cash	Equipment				
−26,000	+26,000	=	0	+	0

Changes the composition of assets but not the total.

3 RECORD

Date	Account Titles and Explanation	PR	Debit	Credit
(3)	Equipment	167	26,000	
	Cash	101		26,000

4 POST

Equipment			167
(3)	26,000		

Cash			101
(1)	30,000	(2)	2,500
		(3)	26,000

4. Purchase Supplies on Credit

1 IDENTIFY FastForward purchases $7,100 of supplies on credit from a supplier.

2 ANALYZE

Assets	=	Liabilities	+	Equity
Supplies		Accounts Payable		
+7,100	=	+7,100	+	0

3 RECORD

Date	Account Titles and Explanation	PR	Debit	Credit
(4)	Supplies	126	7,100	
	Accounts Payable	201		7,100

4 POST

Supplies			126
(2)	2,500		
(4)	7,100		

Accounts Payable			201
		(4)	7,100

5. Provide Services for Cash

1 IDENTIFY FastForward provides consulting services and immediately collects $4,200 cash.

2 ANALYZE

Assets	=	Liabilities	+	Equity
Cash				Consulting Revenue
+4,200	=	0		+4,200

3 RECORD

Date	Account Titles and Explanation	PR	Debit	Credit
(5)	Cash	101	4,200	
	Consulting Revenue	403		4,200

4 POST

Cash			101
(1)	30,000	(2)	2,500
(5)	4,200	(3)	26,000

Consulting Revenue			403
		(5)	4,200

6. Payment of Expense in Cash

1 IDENTIFY FastForward pays $1,000 cash for December rent.

2 ANALYZE

Assets	=	Liabilities	+	Equity
Cash				Rent Expense
−1,000	=	0		−1,000

3 RECORD

Date	Account Titles and Explanation	PR	Debit	Credit
(6)	Rent Expense	640	1,000	
	Cash	101		1,000

4 POST

Rent Expense			640
(6)	1,000		

Cash			101
(1)	30,000	(2)	2,500
(5)	4,200	(3)	26,000
		(6)	1,000

Point: *Salary* usually refers to compensation of a fixed amount for a given time period. *Wages* is compensation based on time worked.

7. Payment of Expense in Cash

1 IDENTIFY FastForward pays $700 cash for employee salary.

2 ANALYZE

Assets	=	Liabilities	+	Equity
Cash				Salaries Expense
−700	=	0		−700

3 RECORD

Date	Account Titles and Explanation	PR	Debit	Credit
(7)	Salaries Expense	622	700	
	Cash	101		700

4 POST

Salaries Expense			622
(7)	700		

Cash			101
(1)	30,000	(2)	2,500
(5)	4,200	(3)	26,000
		(6)	1,000
		(7)	700

Point: Revenue is recognized when products and services are provided, not necessarily when the customer pays.

8. Provide Consulting and Rental Services on Credit

1 IDENTIFY FastForward provides consulting services of $1,600 and rents its test facilities for $300. The customer is billed $1,900 for these services.

2 ANALYZE

Assets	=	Liabilities	+	Equity	
Accounts Receivable				Consulting Revenue	Rental Revenue
+1,900	=	0		+1,600	+300

Point: Transaction 8 is a compound journal entry, which is an entry that affects three or more accounts.

3 RECORD

Date	Account Titles and Explanation	PR	Debit	Credit
(8)	Accounts Receivable	106	1,900	
	Consulting Revenue	403		1,600
	Rental Revenue	406		300

4 POST

Accounts Receivable			106
(8)	1,900		

Consulting Revenue			403
		(5)	4,200
		(8)	1,600

Rental Revenue			406
		(8)	300

9. Receipt of Cash from Accounts Receivable

1 IDENTIFY FastForward receives $1,900 cash from the customer billed in Transaction 8.

2 ANALYZE

Assets		=	Liabilities	+	Equity
Cash	Accounts Receivable				
+1,900	−1,900	=	0	+	0

3 RECORD

Date	Account Titles and Explanation	PR	Debit	Credit
(9)	Cash	101	1,900	
	Accounts Receivable	106		1,900

4 POST

Cash			101
(1)	30,000	(2)	2,500
(5)	4,200	(3)	26,000
(9)	1,900	(6)	1,000
		(7)	700

Accounts Receivable			106
(8)	1,900	(9)	1,900

10. Partial Payment of Accounts Payable

1 IDENTIFY FastForward pays $900 cash toward the accounts payable of Transaction 4.

2 ANALYZE

Assets	=	Liabilities	+	Equity
Cash		Accounts Payable		
−900	=	−900	+	0

3 RECORD

Date	Account Titles and Explanation	PR	Debit	Credit
(10)	Accounts Payable	201	900	
	Cash	101		900

4 POST

Accounts Payable			201
(10)	900	(4)	7,100

Cash			101
(1)	30,000	(2)	2,500
(5)	4,200	(3)	26,000
(9)	1,900	(6)	1,000
		(7)	700
		(10)	900

11. Withdrawal of Cash by Owner

1 IDENTIFY C. Taylor withdraws $200 cash from FastForward for personal use.

2 ANALYZE

Assets	=	Liabilities	+	Equity
Cash				C. Taylor, Withdrawals
−200	=	0		−200

3 RECORD

Date	Account Titles and Explanation	PR	Debit	Credit
(11)	C. Taylor, Withdrawals	302	200	
	Cash	101		200

4 POST

C. Taylor, Withdrawals			302
(11)	200		

Cash			101
(1)	30,000	(2)	2,500
(5)	4,200	(3)	26,000
(9)	1,900	(6)	1,000
		(7)	700
		(10)	900
		(11)	200

Point: Withdrawals always decrease equity.

12. Receipt of Cash for Future Services

1 IDENTIFY FastForward receives $3,000 cash in advance of providing consulting services to a customer.

2 ANALYZE

Assets	=	Liabilities	+	Equity
Cash		Unearned Consulting Revenue		
+3,000	=	+3,000	+	0

Accepting $3,000 cash requires FastForward to perform future services and is a liability. No revenue is recorded until services are provided.

3 RECORD

Date	Account Titles and Explanation	PR	Debit	Credit
(12)	Cash	101	3,000	
	Unearned Consulting Revenue	236		3,000

4 POST

Cash			101
(1)	30,000	(2)	2,500
(5)	4,200	(3)	26,000
(9)	1,900	(6)	1,000
(12)	3,000	(7)	700
		(10)	900
		(11)	200

Unearned Consulting Revenue			236
		(12)	3,000

Point: "Unearned" accounts are liabilities that must be fulfilled.

13. Pay Cash for Future Insurance Coverage

1 IDENTIFY FastForward pays $2,400 cash (insurance premium) for a 24-month insurance policy. Coverage begins on December 1.

2 ANALYZE

Assets		=	Liabilities	+	Equity
Cash	Prepaid Insurance				
−2,400	+2,400	=	0	+	0

Changes the composition of assets from cash to prepaid insurance. Expense is recorded as insurance coverage expires.

3 RECORD

Date	Account Titles and Explanation	PR	Debit	Credit
(13)	Prepaid Insurance	128	2,400	
	Cash	101		2,400

4 POST

Prepaid Insurance			128
(13)	2,400		

Cash			101
(1)	30,000	(2)	2,500
(5)	4,200	(3)	26,000
(9)	1,900	(6)	1,000
(12)	3,000	(7)	700
		(10)	900
		(11)	200
		(13)	2,400

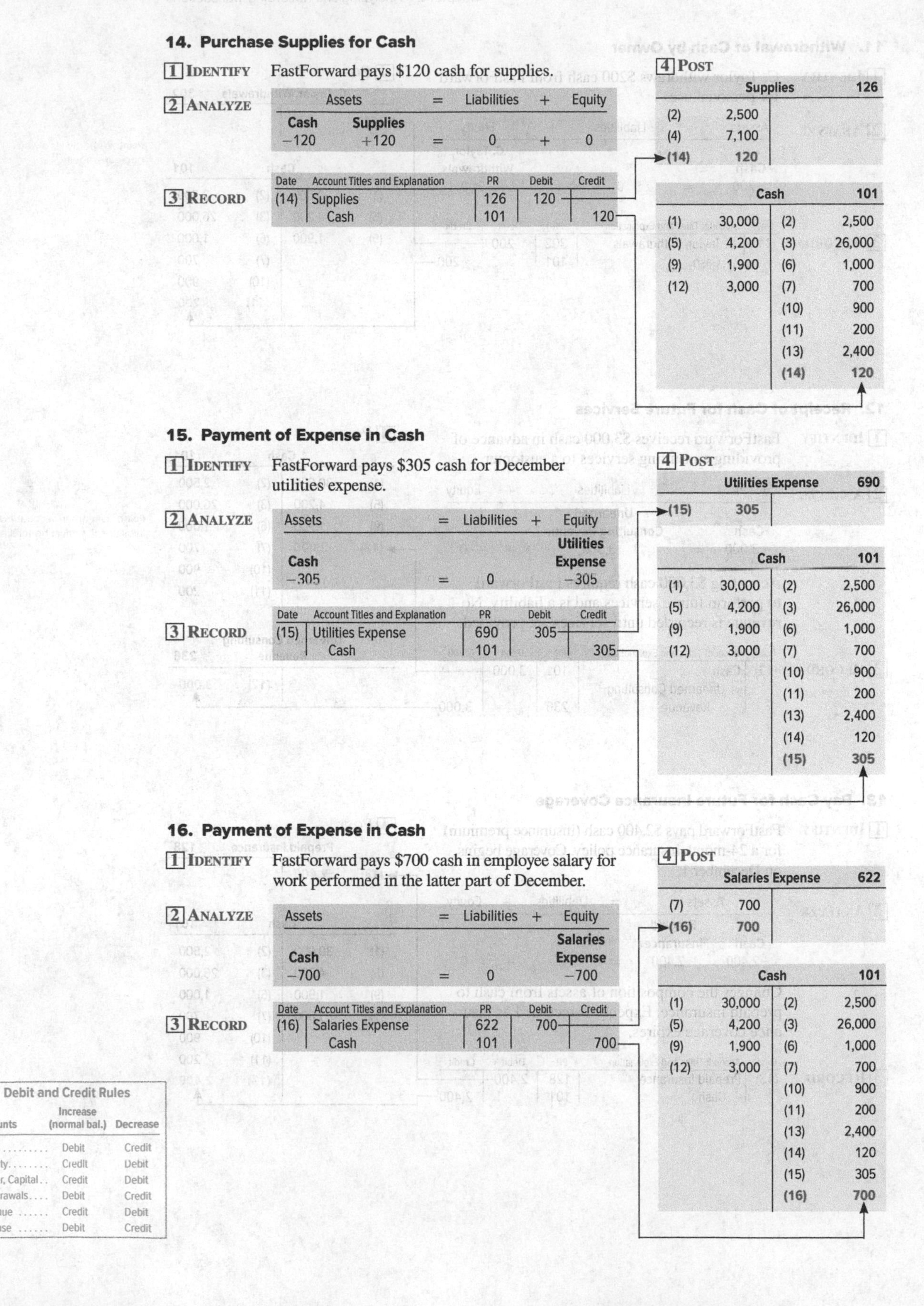
14. Purchase Supplies for Cash
1 IDENTIFY FastForward pays $120 cash for supplies.
2 ANALYZE
Assets = Liabilities + Equity
Cash Supplies
−120 +120 = 0 + 0
3 RECORD
Date Account Titles and Explanation PR Debit Credit
(14) Supplies 126 120
Cash 101 120
4 POST
Supplies 126
(2) 2,500
(4) 7,100
(14) 120
Cash 101
(1) 30,000 (2) 2,500
(5) 4,200 (3) 26,000
(9) 1,900 (6) 1,000
(12) 3,000 (7) 700
(10) 900
(11) 200
(13) 2,400
(14) 120
15. Payment of Expense in Cash
1 IDENTIFY FastForward pays $305 cash for December utilities expense.
2 ANALYZE
Assets = Liabilities + Equity
Cash Utilities Expense
−305 = 0 −305
3 RECORD
Date Account Titles and Explanation PR Debit Credit
(15) Utilities Expense 690 305
Cash 101 305
4 POST
Utilities Expense 690
(15) 305
Cash 101
(1) 30,000 (2) 2,500
(5) 4,200 (3) 26,000
(9) 1,900 (6) 1,000
(12) 3,000 (7) 700
(10) 900
(11) 200
(13) 2,400
(14) 120
(15) 305
16. Payment of Expense in Cash
1 IDENTIFY FastForward pays $700 cash in employee salary for work performed in the latter part of December.
2 ANALYZE
Assets = Liabilities + Equity
Cash Salaries Expense
−700 = 0 −700
3 RECORD
Date Account Titles and Explanation PR Debit Credit
(16) Salaries Expense 622 700
Cash 101 700
4 POST
Salaries Expense 622
(7) 700
(16) 700
Cash 101
(1) 30,000 (2) 2,500
(5) 4,200 (3) 26,000
(9) 1,900 (6) 1,000
(12) 3,000 (7) 700
(10) 900
(11) 200
(13) 2,400
(14) 120
(15) 305
(16) 700
Debit and Credit Rules
Accounts Increase (normal bal.) Decrease
Asset Debit Credit
Liability Credit Debit
Owner, Capital Credit Debit
Withdrawals Debit Credit
Revenue Credit Debit
Expense Debit Credit

Summarizing Transactions in a Ledger

Exhibit 2.13 shows the ledger accounts (in T-account form) of FastForward after all 16 transactions are recorded and posted and the balances computed. The accounts are grouped into three columns following the accounting equation: assets, liabilities, and equity.

- Totals for the three columns obey the accounting equation:
  - Assets equal **$42,395** ($4,275 + $0 + $9,720 + $2,400 + $26,000).
  - Liabilities equal **$9,200** ($6,200 + $3,000).
  - Equity equals **$33,195** ($30,000 − $200 + $5,800 + $300 − $1,400 − $1,000 − $305).

  The accounting equation: $42,395 = $9,200 + $33,195.
- Owner capital, withdrawals, revenue, and expense accounts reflect transactions that change equity.
- Revenue and expense account balances are reported in the income statement.

EXHIBIT 2.13

Ledger for FastForward (in T-Account Form)

General Ledger

Assets = Liabilities + Equity

Assets

Cash			101
(1)	30,000	(2)	2,500
(5)	4,200	(3)	26,000
(9)	1,900	(6)	1,000
(12)	3,000	(7)	700
		(10)	900
		(11)	200
		(13)	2,400
		(14)	120
		(15)	305
		(16)	700
Balance	**4,275**		

Accounts Receivable			106
(8)	1,900	(9)	1,900
Balance	**0**		

Supplies			126
(2)	2,500		
(4)	7,100		
(14)	120		
Balance	**9,720**		

Prepaid Insurance			128
(13)	**2,400**		

Equipment			167
(3)	**26,000**		

Liabilities

Accounts Payable			201
(10)	900	(4)	7,100
		Balance	**6,200**

Unearned Consulting Revenue			236
		(12)	**3,000**

Equity

C. Taylor, Capital			301
		(1)	**30,000**

C. Taylor, Withdrawals			302
(11)	**200**		

Consulting Revenue			403
		(5)	4,200
		(8)	1,600
		Balance	**5,800**

Rental Revenue			406
		(8)	**300**

Salaries Expense			622
(7)	700		
(16)	700		
Balance	**1,400**		

Rent Expense			640
(6)	**1,000**		

Utilities Expense			690
(15)	**305**		

Accounts in this white area are on the income statement.

$42,395 = **$9,200** + **$33,195**

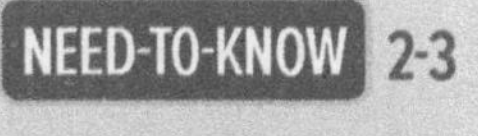

Recording Transactions

A1

Tata Company began operations on January 1 and completed the following transactions. For each transaction, (a) analyze the transaction using the accounting equation, (b) record the journal entry, and (c) post the entry using T-accounts as ledger accounts.

Jan. 1 Jamsetji Tata invested $4,000 cash in the Tata Company.
5 Tata Company purchased $2,000 of equipment on credit.
14 Tata Company provided $540 of services for a client on credit.

Solution

Jan. 1 Receive Investment by Owner

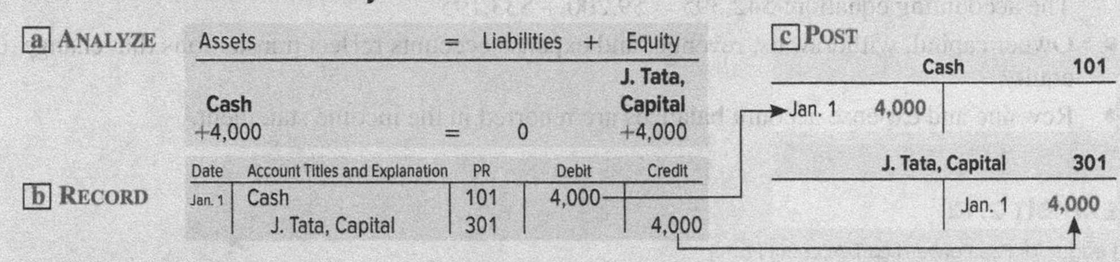

Jan. 5 Purchase Equipment on Credit

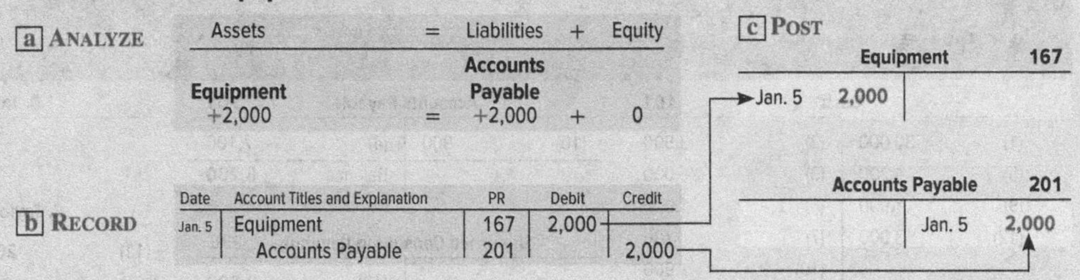

Jan. 14 Provide Services on Credit

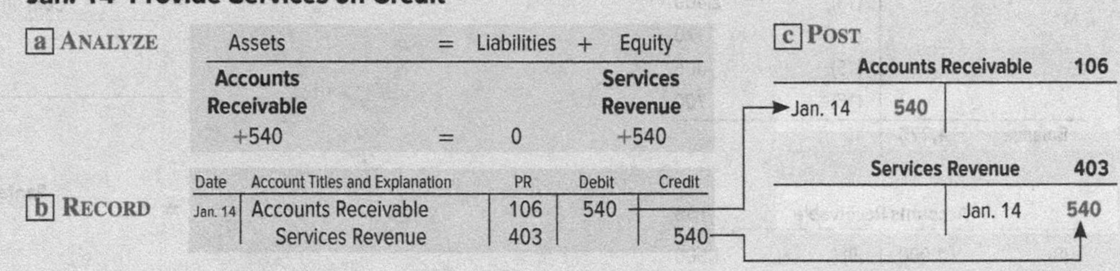

Do More: QS 2-8 through QS 2-11, E 2-6 through E 2-11, E 2-13, E 2-15 through E 2-19

TRIAL BALANCE AND FINANCIAL STATEMENTS

P1 Prepare financial statements from a trial balance.

A **trial balance** is a list of all ledger accounts and their balances at a point in time. It is *not* a financial statement but a tool for checking equality of debits and credits in the ledger. Exhibit 2.14 shows the trial balance for FastForward after its 16 entries are posted to the ledger. (This is an *unadjusted* trial balance. Chapter 3 explains adjustments.)

Preparing a Trial Balance

Preparing a trial balance has three steps.

1. List each account title and its amount (from the ledger) in the trial balance.
2. Compute the total of debit balances and the total of credit balances.
3. Verify (*prove*) total debit balances equal total credit balances.

The total of debit balances equals the total of credit balances for the trial balance in Exhibit 2.14. Equality of these two totals does not guarantee that no errors were made. For example, the column totals will be equal when a debit or credit of a correct amount is made to a wrong account. Another error not identified with a trial balance is when equal debits and credits of an incorrect amount are entered.

EXHIBIT 2.14

Trial Balance (Unadjusted)

FASTFORWARD Trial Balance December 31, 2021	Debit	Credit
Cash	$ 4,275	
Accounts receivable	0	
Supplies	9,720	
Prepaid insurance	2,400	
Equipment	26,000	
Accounts payable		$ 6,200
Unearned consulting revenue		3,000
C. Taylor, Capital		30,000
C. Taylor, Withdrawals	200	
Consulting revenue		5,800
Rental revenue		300
Salaries expense	1,400	
Rent expense	1,000	
Utilities expense	305	
Totals	$45,300	$45,300

Example: If a credit to Unearned Revenue was incorrectly posted to the Revenue ledger account, would the ledger still balance? *Answer:* The ledger would balance, but liabilities would be understated, equity would be overstated, and income would be overstated.

Searching for Errors If the trial balance does not balance (when its columns are not equal), the error(s) must be found and corrected. An efficient way to search for an error is to check the journalizing, posting, and trial balance preparation in *reverse order.* Step 1 is to verify that the trial balance columns are correctly added. If step 1 does not find the error, step 2 is to verify that account balances are accurately entered from the ledger. Step 3 is to see whether a debit (or credit) balance is mistakenly listed in the trial balance as a credit (or debit). A clue to this error is when the difference between total debits and total credits equals twice the amount of the incorrect account balance. Step 4 is to recompute each account balance in the ledger. Step 5 is to verify that each journal entry is properly posted. Step 6 is to verify that the original journal entry has equal debits and credits. At this point, the errors should be uncovered.

Financial Statements Prepared from Trial Balance

Financial Statements across Time How financial statements are linked in time is shown in Exhibit 2.15. A balance sheet reports an organization's financial position at a *point in time.* The income statement, statement of owner's equity, and statement of cash flows report financial performance over a *period of time*. The three statements in the middle column of Exhibit 2.15 explain how financial position changes from the beginning to the end of a reporting period.

A one-year (annual) reporting period is common, as are semiannual, quarterly, and monthly periods. The one-year reporting period is called the *accounting,* or *fiscal, year.* Businesses whose accounting year begins on January 1 and ends on December 31 are called *calendar-year* companies.

EXHIBIT 2.15

Links between Financial Statements across Time

Beginning Balance Sheet			
Cash	$30,000	Liabilities	$ 0
Other assets	0	Equity	30,000
Total assets	$30,000	Total	$30,000

Point in time

Statement of Cash Flows

Statement of Owner's Equity

Income Statement	
Revenues	$6,100
Expenses	2,705
Net income	$3,395

Period of time

Ending Balance Sheet			
Cash	$ 4,275	Liabilities	$ 9,200
Other assets	38,120	Equity	33,195
Total assets	$42,395	Total	$42,395

Point in time

Financial Statement Preparation This section shows how to prepare *financial statements* from the trial balance. (These are *unadjusted statements*. Chapter 3 explains adjustments.) We prepare these statements in the following order.

❶ **Income Statement** An income statement reports revenues earned minus expenses incurred over a period of time. FastForward's income statement for December is shown at the top right side of Exhibit 2.16. Information about revenues and expenses is taken from the trial balance on the left side. Net income of $3,395 is the *bottom line* for the income statement. Owner investments and withdrawals are *not* part of income.

Point: An income statement also is called an *earnings statement,* a *statement of operations,* or a *P&L* (profit and loss) *statement.* A balance sheet also is called a *statement of financial position.*

❷ Statement of Owner's Equity The statement of owner's equity reports how equity changes over the reporting period. FastForward's statement of owner's equity is the second report in Exhibit 2.16. It shows the $30,000 owner investment, the $3,395 of net income, the $200 withdrawal, and the $33,195 end-of-period capital balance. (The beginning balance in the statement of owner's equity is rarely zero, except in the first period of operations. The beginning balance in January 2022 is $33,195, which is December 2021's ending balance.)

❸ Balance Sheet The balance sheet reports the financial position of a company at a point in time. FastForward's balance sheet is the third report in Exhibit 2.16. This statement shows financial condition at the close of business on December 31. The left side of the balance sheet lists its assets: cash, supplies, prepaid insurance, and equipment. The liabilities section of the balance sheet shows that it owes $6,200 to creditors and $3,000 in services to customers who paid in advance. The equity section shows an ending capital balance of $33,195. See the link between the ending balance of the statement of owner's equity and the owner capital balance. (This presentation of the balance sheet is called the *account form:* assets on the left and liabilities and equity on the right. Another presentation is the *report form:* assets on top, followed by liabilities and then equity. Either presentation is acceptable.)

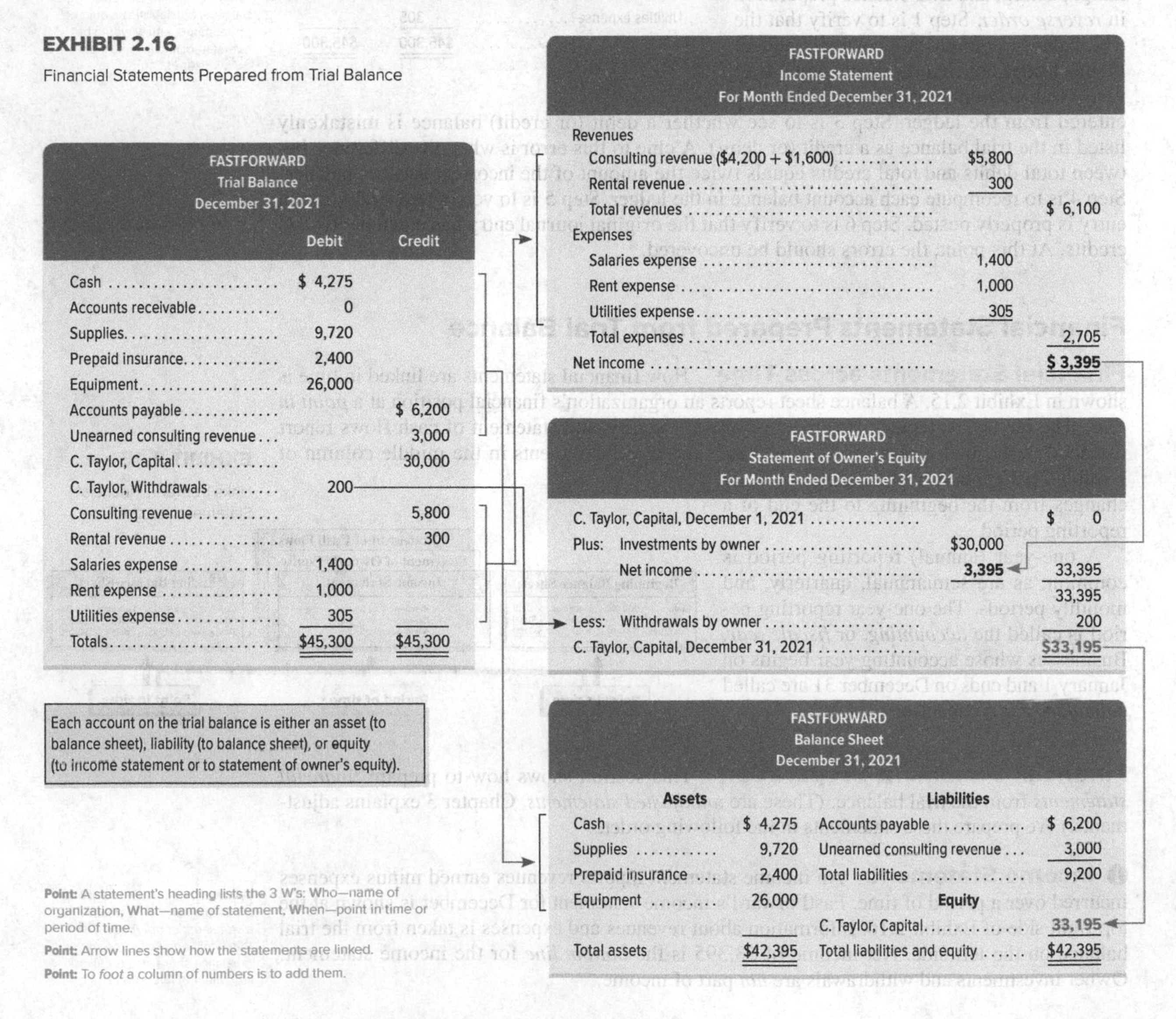

EXHIBIT 2.16

Financial Statements Prepared from Trial Balance

FASTFORWARD
Trial Balance
December 31, 2021

	Debit	Credit
Cash	$ 4,275	
Accounts receivable	0	
Supplies	9,720	
Prepaid insurance	2,400	
Equipment	26,000	
Accounts payable		$ 6,200
Unearned consulting revenue		3,000
C. Taylor, Capital		30,000
C. Taylor, Withdrawals	200	
Consulting revenue		5,800
Rental revenue		300
Salaries expense	1,400	
Rent expense	1,000	
Utilities expense	305	
Totals	$45,300	$45,300

Each account on the trial balance is either an asset (to balance sheet), liability (to balance sheet), or equity (to income statement or to statement of owner's equity).

FASTFORWARD
Income Statement
For Month Ended December 31, 2021

Revenues		
Consulting revenue ($4,200 + $1,600)	$5,800	
Rental revenue	300	
Total revenues		$ 6,100
Expenses		
Salaries expense	1,400	
Rent expense	1,000	
Utilities expense	305	
Total expenses		2,705
Net income		$ 3,395

FASTFORWARD
Statement of Owner's Equity
For Month Ended December 31, 2021

C. Taylor, Capital, December 1, 2021		$ 0
Plus: Investments by owner	$30,000	
Net income	3,395	33,395
		33,395
Less: Withdrawals by owner		200
C. Taylor, Capital, December 31, 2021		$33,195

FASTFORWARD
Balance Sheet
December 31, 2021

Assets		Liabilities	
Cash	$ 4,275	Accounts payable	$ 6,200
Supplies	9,720	Unearned consulting revenue	3,000
Prepaid insurance	2,400	Total liabilities	9,200
Equipment	26,000	**Equity**	
		C. Taylor, Capital	33,195
Total assets	$42,395	Total liabilities and equity	$42,395

Point: A statement's heading lists the 3 W's: Who—name of organization, What—name of statement, When—point in time or period of time.

Point: Arrow lines show how the statements are linked.

Point: To *foot* a column of numbers is to add them.

Presentation Issues Dollar signs are not used in journals and ledgers. They do appear in financial statements and other reports such as trial balances. We usually put dollar signs beside only the first and last numbers in a column.

Ethical Risk

marekuliasz/Shutterstock

Accounting Quality Recording valid and accurate transactions enhances the quality of financial statements. Roughly 30% of employees in IT report observing misconduct such as falsifying accounting data. They also report increased incidences of such misconduct in recent years. Source: KPMG. ■

NEED-TO-KNOW 2-4

Preparing Trial Balance

P1

Prepare a trial balance for Accel using the following information from its current year ended December 31.

Accounts payable	$ 7,500	Land	$30,000
Wages payable	13,000	Equipment	27,000
Rent expense	7,000	Wages expense	21,000
Cash	17,000	Accounts receivable	5,000
Services revenue	41,000	B. Accel, Capital	58,000
B. Accel, Withdrawals	12,500		

Solution

ACCEL
Trial Balance
December 31

	Debit	Credit
Cash	$ 17,000	
Accounts receivable	5,000	
Equipment	27,000	
Land	30,000	
Accounts payable		$ 7,500
Wages payable		13,000
B. Accel, Capital		58,000
B. Accel, Withdrawals	12,500	
Services revenue		41,000
Rent expense	7,000	
Wages expense	21,000	
Totals	$119,500	$119,500

Do More: QS 2-12 through QS 2-17, E 2-12, E 2-14, E 2-20 through E 2-28

Debt Ratio — Decision Analysis

A2 Compute the debt ratio and describe its use in analyzing financial condition.

It is important to assess a company's risk of failing to pay its debts. Companies finance their assets with either liabilities or equity. A company that finances a relatively large portion of its assets with liabilities is said to have higher *financial leverage*. Higher financial leverage means greater risk because liabilities must be repaid and often require regular interest payments (equity financing does not). One measure of the risk associated with liabilities is the **debt ratio,** as defined in Exhibit 2.17.

EXHIBIT 2.17

Debt Ratio

$$\textbf{Debt ratio} = \frac{\textbf{Total liabilities}}{\textbf{Total assets}}$$

Costco's total liabilities, total assets, and debt ratio for the past three years are shown in Exhibit 2.18. Costco's debt ratio ranges from a low of 0.66 to a high of 0.70. Its ratio exceeds **Walmart**'s in each of the last three years, suggesting a slightly higher-than-average risk from financial leverage. So, is financial leverage good or bad for Costco? The answer: If Costco is making more money with this debt than it is paying the lenders, then it is successfully borrowing money to make more money. A company's use of debt can turn unprofitable quickly if its return from that money drops below the rate it is paying lenders.

EXHIBIT 2.18

Computation and Analysis of Debt Ratio

Company ($ millions)		Current Year	1 Year Ago	2 Years Ago
Costco	Total liabilities.	$29,816	$27,727	$25,268
	Total assets.	$45,400	$40,830	$36,347
	Debt ratio.	**0.66**	**0.68**	**0.70**
Walmart	Debt ratio	0.64	0.60	0.59

Decision Maker

Investor You consider buying stock in **Converse**. As part of your analysis, you compute the company's debt ratio for 2019, 2020, and 2021 as 0.35, 0.74, and 0.94, respectively. Based on the debt ratio, is Converse a low-risk investment? Has the risk of buying Converse stock changed over this period? (The industry debt ratio averages 0.40.) ■ *Answer:* The debt ratio suggests that Converse's stock is of higher risk than normal and that this risk is rising. The average industry ratio of 0.40 supports this conclusion. The 2021 debt ratio for Converse is twice the industry norm. Also, a debt ratio approaching 1.0 indicates little to no equity.

NEED-TO-KNOW 2-5

COMPREHENSIVE

Journalizing and Posting Transactions, Statement Preparation, and Debt Ratio

Jasmine Worthy started a haircutting business called Expressions. The following events occurred during its first month.

Dec.	1	Worthy invested $3,000 cash and $15,000 of equipment in Expressions.
	2	Expressions paid $600 cash for furniture for the shop.
	3	Expressions paid $500 cash to rent space in a strip mall for December.
	4	Expressions purchased $1,200 of equipment on credit (recorded as accounts payable).
	15	Expressions opened for business on December 5. Cash received from haircutting services in the first week and a half of business (ended December 15) was $825.
	16	Expressions provided $100 of haircutting services on credit.
	17	Expressions received a $100 check for services previously rendered on credit.
	18	Expressions paid $125 to an assistant for hours worked for the grand opening.
	31	Cash received from services provided during the second half of December was $930.
	31	Expressions paid $400 cash toward the account payable from December 4.
	31	Worthy made a $900 cash withdrawal from the company for personal use.

Required

1. Prepare general journal entries for the transactions. Account numbers are taken from the *Chart of Accounts* near the end of the text.
2. Post the journal entries from part 1 to ledger accounts.
3. Prepare a trial balance as of December 31.
4. Prepare an income statement for December.
5. Prepare a statement of owner's equity for December.
6. Prepare a balance sheet as of December 31.
7. Determine the debt ratio as of December 31.

Extended Analysis

8. In the coming months, Expressions will have new business transactions. Identify which accounts are debited and which are credited for the following transactions.
   a. Purchase supplies with cash.
   b. Purchase supplies on credit.
   c. Pay cash for future insurance coverage.
   d. Receive cash for services to be provided in the future.

SOLUTION

1. General journal entries.

General Journal				
Date	Account Titles and Explanation	PR	Debit	Credit
Dec. 1	Cash	101	3,000	
	Equipment	165	15,000	
	J. Worthy, Capital	301		18,000
	Owner investment.			
2	Furniture	161	600	
	Cash	101		600
	Purchased furniture for cash.			
3	Rent Expense	640	500	
	Cash	101		500
	Paid rent for December.			
4	Equipment	165	1,200	
	Accounts Payable	201		1,200
	Purchased equipment on credit.			
15	Cash	101	825	
	Services Revenue	403		825
	Cash receipts from first half of December.			
16	Accounts Receivable	102	100	
	Services Revenue	403		100
	Record revenue for services provided on credit.			

General Journal				
Date	Account Titles and Explanation	PR	Debit	Credit
17	Cash	101	100	
	Accounts Receivable	102		100
	Record cash received as payment on credit.			
18	Wages Expense	623	125	
	Cash	101		125
	Paid wages to assistant.			
31	Cash	101	930	
	Services Revenue	403		930
	Cash receipts from second half of December.			
31	Accounts Payable	201	400	
	Cash	101		400
	Paid cash toward accounts payable.			
31	J. Worthy, Withdrawals	302	900	
	Cash	101		900
	Cash withdrawal by owner.			

2. Post journal entries from part 1 to the ledger accounts (in balance column format).

General Ledger

Cash — Account No. 101

Date	PR	Debit	Credit	Balance
Dec. 1	G1	3,000		3,000
2	G1		600	2,400
3	G1		500	1,900
15	G1	825		2,725
17	G1	100		2,825
18	G1		125	2,700
31	G1	930		3,630
31	G1		400	3,230
31	G1		900	2,330

Accounts Receivable — Account No. 102

Date	PR	Debit	Credit	Balance
Dec. 16	G1	100		100
17	G1		100	0

Furniture — Account No. 161

Date	PR	Debit	Credit	Balance
Dec. 2	G1	600		600

Equipment — Account No. 165

Date	PR	Debit	Credit	Balance
Dec. 1	G1	15,000		15,000
4	G1	1,200		16,200

Accounts Payable — Account No. 201

Date	PR	Debit	Credit	Balance
Dec. 4	G1		1,200	1,200
31	G1	400		800

J. Worthy, Capital — Account No. 301

Date	PR	Debit	Credit	Balance
Dec. 1	G1		18,000	18,000

J. Worthy, Withdrawals — Account No. 302

Date	PR	Debit	Credit	Balance
Dec. 31	G1	900		900

Services Revenue — Account No. 403

Date	PR	Debit	Credit	Balance
Dec. 15	G1		825	825
16	G1		100	925
31	G1		930	1,855

Wages Expense — Account No. 623

Date	PR	Debit	Credit	Balance
Dec. 18	G1	125		125

Rent Expense — Account No. 640

Date	PR	Debit	Credit	Balance
Dec. 3	G1	500		500

[continued on next page]

[continued from previous page]

3. Prepare a trial balance from the ledger—see how it feeds the financial statements.

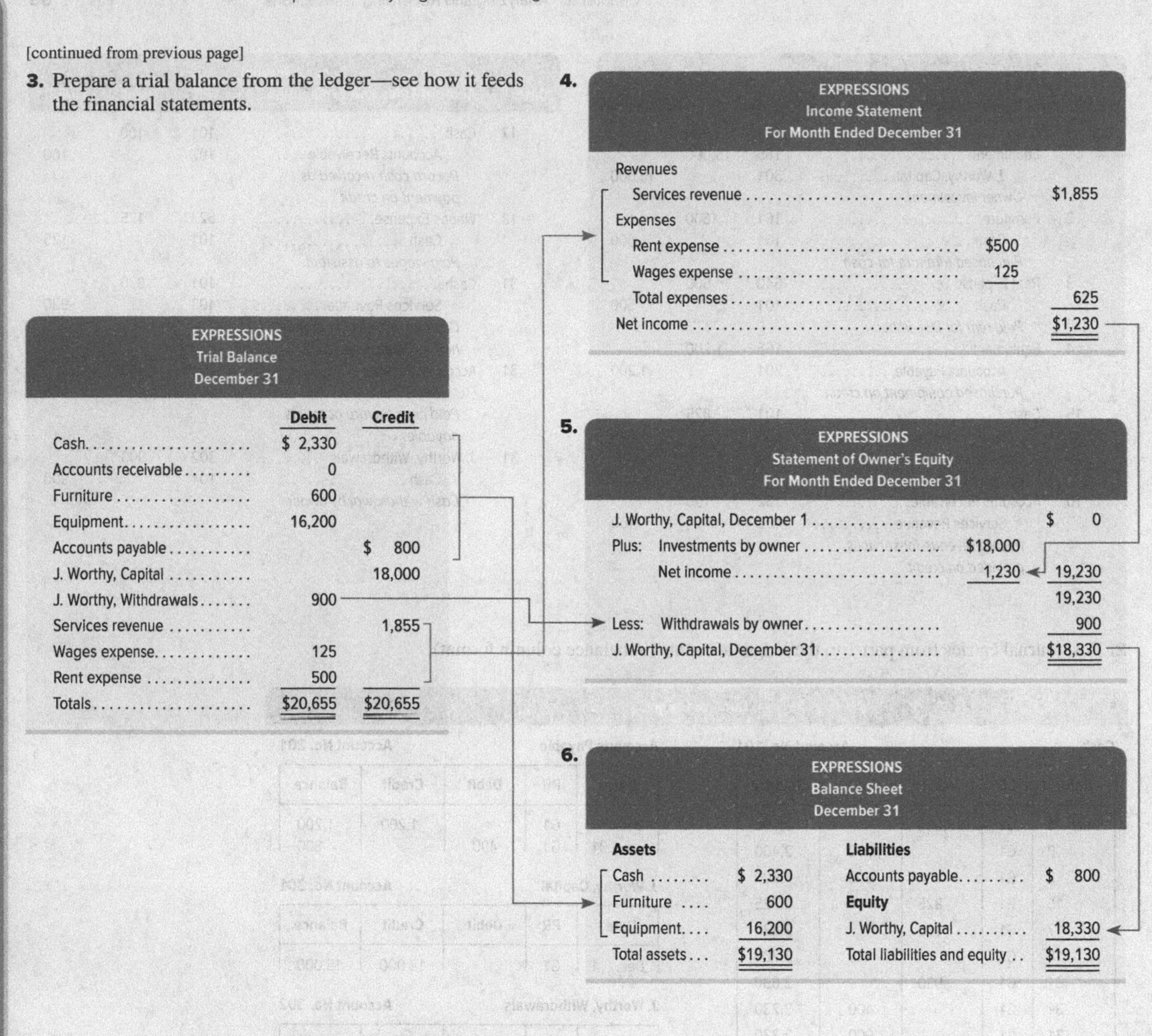

EXPRESSIONS
Trial Balance
December 31

	Debit	Credit
Cash	$ 2,330	
Accounts receivable	0	
Furniture	600	
Equipment	16,200	
Accounts payable		$ 800
J. Worthy, Capital		18,000
J. Worthy, Withdrawals	900	
Services revenue		1,855
Wages expense	125	
Rent expense	500	
Totals	$20,655	$20,655

4.

EXPRESSIONS
Income Statement
For Month Ended December 31

Revenues		
Services revenue		$1,855
Expenses		
Rent expense	$500	
Wages expense	125	
Total expenses		625
Net income		$1,230

5.

EXPRESSIONS
Statement of Owner's Equity
For Month Ended December 31

J. Worthy, Capital, December 1		$ 0
Plus: Investments by owner	$18,000	
Net income	1,230	19,230
		19,230
Less: Withdrawals by owner		900
J. Worthy, Capital, December 31		$18,330

6.

EXPRESSIONS
Balance Sheet
December 31

Assets		Liabilities	
Cash	$ 2,330	Accounts payable	$ 800
Furniture	600	**Equity**	
Equipment	16,200	J. Worthy, Capital	18,330
Total assets	$19,130	Total liabilities and equity	$19,130

7. Debt ratio $= \frac{\text{Total liabilities}}{\text{Total assets}} = \frac{\$800}{\$19,130} = \underline{\underline{4.18\%}}$

8a. Supplies *debited*
Cash *credited*

8b. Supplies *debited*
Accounts Payable *credited*

8c. Prepaid Insurance *debited*
Cash *credited*

8d. Cash *debited*
Unearned Revenue *credited*

Summary: Cheat Sheet

SYSTEM OF ACCOUNTS

Asset Accounts

Cash: A company's cash balance.

Accounts receivable: Held by a seller; promises of payment from customers to sellers. Accounts receivable are increased by credit sales; often phrased as sales *on account* or *on credit*.

Notes receivable: Held by a lender; a borrower's written promise to pay the lender a specific sum of money on a specified future date.

Prepaid accounts (or **expenses**): Assets that arise from prepayment of future expenses. Examples are prepaid insurance and prepaid rent.

More assets: Supplies, equipment, buildings, and land.

Liability Accounts

Accounts payable: Held by a buyer; a buyer's promise to pay a seller later for goods or services received. More generally, payables arise from purchases of merchandise for resale, supplies, services, and other items.

Notes payable: Held by a borrower; a written promissory note to pay a future amount at a future date.

Unearned revenue: A liability to be settled in the future when a company delivers its products or services. When a customer pays in advance for products or services, the seller records this receipt as unearned revenue.

Accrued liabilities: Amounts owed that are not yet paid. Examples are wages payable, taxes payable, and interest payable.

Equity Accounts

Owner capital: When an owner invests in a company, the company increases both assets and equity.

Owner withdrawals: When an owner withdraws assets for personal use, it decreases both company assets and total equity.

Revenue: Amounts received from sales of products and services. Revenue increases equity.

Expenses: Costs of providing products and services. Expenses decrease equity.

DEBITS AND CREDITS

Debit: Left side of an account is called the **debit** side, or Dr.

Credit: Right side of an account is called the **credit** side, or Cr.

Double-entry accounting transaction rules:

- At least two accounts are involved, with at least one debit and one credit.
- Total amount debited must equal total amount credited.

Debits and credits in accounting equation:

Assets		=	Liabilities		+	Owner, Capital		−	Owner, Withdrawals		+	Revenues		−	Expenses	
Dr. for increases	Cr. for decreases		Dr. for decreases	Cr. for increases		Dr. for decreases	Cr. for increases		Dr. for increases	Cr. for decreases		Dr. for decreases	Cr. for increases		Dr. for increases	Cr. for decreases
+	−		−	+		−	+		+	−		−	+		+	−
Normal				Normal			Normal		Normal				Normal		Normal	

(Owner, Capital − Owner, Withdrawals + Revenues − Expenses = Equity)

Net increases or decreases on one side have equal net effects on the other side.
Left side is the normal balance side for assets.
Right side is the normal balance side for liabilities and equity.

RECORDING TRANSACTIONS

Receive owner investment:

Date	Account Titles and Explanation	PR	Debit	Credit
(1)	Cash	101	30,000	
	C. Taylor, Capital	301		30,000

Purchase supplies for cash:

Date	Account Titles and Explanation	PR	Debit	Credit
(2)	Supplies	126	2,500	
	Cash	101		2,500

Purchase equipment for cash:

Date	Account Titles and Explanation	PR	Debit	Credit
(3)	Equipment	167	26,000	
	Cash	101		26,000

Purchase supplies on credit:

Date	Account Titles and Explanation	PR	Debit	Credit
(4)	Supplies	126	7,100	
	Accounts Payable	201		7,100

Provide services for cash:

Date	Account Titles and Explanation	PR	Debit	Credit
(5)	Cash	101	4,200	
	Consulting Revenue	403		4,200

Payment of expenses in cash:

Date	Account Titles and Explanation	PR	Debit	Credit
(6)	Rent Expense	640	1,000	
	Cash	101		1,000

Date	Account Titles and Explanation	PR	Debit	Credit
(7)	Salaries Expense	622	700	
	Cash	101		700

Date	Account Titles and Explanation	PR	Debit	Credit
(15)	Utilities Expense	690	305	
	Cash	101		305

Provide consulting and rental services on credit:

Date	Account Titles and Explanation	PR	Debit	Credit
(8)	Accounts Receivable	106	1,900	
	Consulting Revenue	403		1,600
	Rental Revenue	406		300

Receipt of cash from receivable:

Date	Account Titles and Explanation	PR	Debit	Credit
(9)	Cash	101	1,900	
	Accounts Receivable	106		1,900

Partial payment of accounts payable:

Date	Account Titles and Explanation	PR	Debit	Credit
(10)	Accounts Payable	201	900	
	Cash	101		900

Withdrawal of cash by owner:

Date	Account Titles and Explanation	PR	Debit	Credit
(11)	C. Taylor, Withdrawals	302	200	
	Cash	101		200

Receipt of cash for future services:

Date	Account Titles and Explanation	PR	Debit	Credit
(12)	Cash	101	3,000	
	Unearned Consulting Revenue	236		3,000

Pay cash for future insurance coverage:

Date	Account Titles and Explanation	PR	Debit	Credit
(13)	Prepaid Insurance	128	2,400	
	Cash	101		2,400

FINANCIAL STATEMENTS

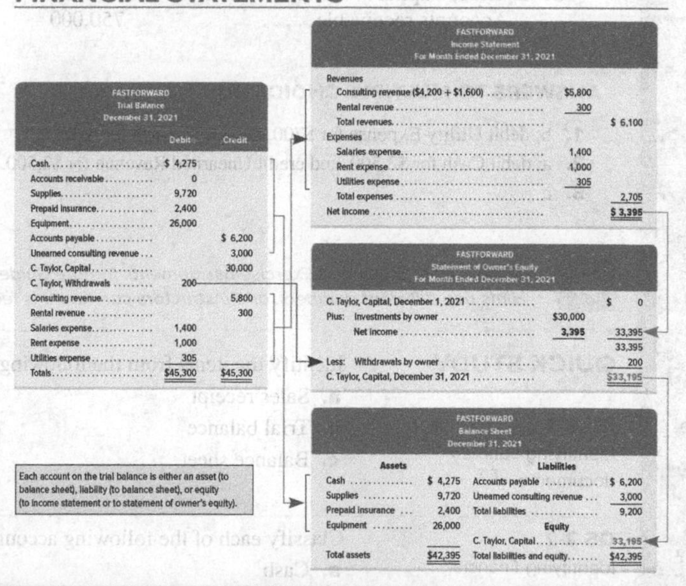

FASTFORWARD
Trial Balance
December 31, 2021

	Debit	Credit
Cash	$ 4,275	
Accounts receivable	0	
Supplies	9,720	
Prepaid insurance	2,400	
Equipment	26,000	
Accounts payable		$ 6,200
Unearned consulting revenue		3,000
C. Taylor, Capital		30,000
C. Taylor, Withdrawals	200	
Consulting revenue		5,800
Rental revenue		300
Salaries expense	1,400	
Rent expense	1,000	
Utilities expense	305	
Totals	$45,300	$45,300

FASTFORWARD
Income Statement
For Month Ended December 31, 2021

Revenues		
Consulting revenue ($4,200 + $1,600)	$5,800	
Rental revenue	300	
Total revenues		$ 6,100
Expenses		
Salaries expense	1,400	
Rent expense	1,000	
Utilities expense	305	
Total expenses		2,705
Net income		$ 3,395

FASTFORWARD
Statement of Owner's Equity
For Month Ended December 31, 2021

C. Taylor, Capital, December 1, 2021		$ 0
Plus: Investments by owner	$30,000	
Net income	3,395	33,395
		33,395
Less: Withdrawals by owner		200
C. Taylor, Capital, December 31, 2021		$33,195

FASTFORWARD
Balance Sheet
December 31, 2021

Assets		Liabilities	
Cash	$ 4,275	Accounts payable	$ 6,200
Supplies	9,720	Unearned consulting revenue	3,000
Prepaid insurance	2,400	Total liabilities	9,200
Equipment	26,000	**Equity**	
		C. Taylor, Capital	33,195
Total assets	$42,395	Total liabilities and equity	$42,395

Each account on the trial balance is either an asset (to balance sheet), liability (to balance sheet), or equity (to income statement or to statement of owner's equity).

Key Terms

Account (45)
Account balance (49)
Balance column account (51)
Chart of accounts (48)
Compound journal entry (54)
Credit (49)
Creditors (47)
Debit (49)
Debt ratio (61)
Debtors (47)
Double-entry accounting (49)
General journal (51)
General ledger (45)
Journal (50)
Journalizing (50)
Ledger (45)
Posting (50)
Posting reference (PR) column (51)
Source documents (45)
T-account (49)
Trial balance (58)
Unearned revenue (47)

Multiple Choice Quiz

1. Amalia Company received its utility bill for the current period of $700 and immediately paid it. Its journal entry to record this transaction includes a

a. Credit to Utility Expense for $700.
b. Debit to Utility Expense for $700.
c. Debit to Accounts Payable for $700.
d. Debit to Cash for $700.
e. Credit to Accounts Receivable for $700.

2. On May 1, Ruby Lawn Service collected $2,500 cash from a customer in advance of five months of lawn service. Ruby's journal entry to record this transaction includes a

a. Credit to Unearned Revenue for $2,500.
b. Debit to Services Revenue for $2,500.
c. Credit to Cash for $2,500.
d. Debit to Unearned Revenue for $2,500.
e. Credit to Accounts Payable for $2,500.

3. Liang Shue contributed $250,000 cash and land worth $500,000 to open his new business, Shue Consulting. Which of the following journal entries does Shue Consulting make to record this transaction?

		Debit	Credit
a.	Cash	750,000	
	L. Shue, Capital		750,000
b.	L. Shue, Capital	750,000	
	Accounts receivable		750,000
c.	Cash	250,000	
	Land	500,000	
	L. Shue, Capital		750,000
d.	L. Shue, Capital	750,000	
	Cash		250,000
	Land		500,000

4. A trial balance prepared at year-end shows total credits exceed total debits by $765. This discrepancy could have been caused by

a. An error in the general journal where a $765 increase in Accounts Payable was recorded as a $765 decrease in Accounts Payable.
b. The ledger balance for Accounts Payable of $7,650 being entered in the trial balance as $765.
c. A general journal error where a $765 increase in Accounts Receivable was recorded as a $765 increase in Cash.
d. The ledger balance of $850 in Accounts Receivable was entered in the trial balance as $85.
e. An error in recording a $765 increase in Cash as a credit.

5. Bon Company has total assets of $1,000,000, liabilities of $400,000, and equity of $600,000. What is its debt ratio?

a. 250%
b. 167%
c. 67%
d. 150%
e. 40%

ANSWERS TO MULTIPLE CHOICE QUIZ

1. b; debit Utility Expense for $700, and credit Cash for $700.
2. a; debit Cash for $2,500, and credit Unearned Revenue for $2,500.
3. c
4. d
5. e; Debt ratio = $400,000/$1,000,000 = 40%

Select Quick Study and Exercise assignments feature Guided Example videos, called "Hints" in Connect. Hints use different numbers, and instructors can turn this feature on or off.

QUICK STUDY

QS 2-1
Identifying source documents C1

Identify the items from the following list that are likely to serve as source documents.

a. Sales receipt
b. Trial balance
c. Balance sheet
d. Prepaid insurance account
e. Invoice from supplier
f. Company revenue account
g. Income statement
h. Bank statement
i. Telephone bill

QS 2-2
Identifying financial statement accounts C1

Classify each of the following accounts as an Asset, Liability, or Equity account.

a. Cash
b. Prepaid Rent
c. Office Supplies
d. Prepaid Insurance
e. Office Equipment
f. Notes Payable
g. Accounts Payable
h. Unearned Rent Revenue
i. Notes Receivable

QS 2-3
Reading a chart of accounts C1

A chart of accounts is a list of all ledger accounts and an identification number for each. One example of a chart of accounts is near the end of the book on pages CA and CA-1. Using that chart, identify the following accounts as either an Asset, Liability, Equity, Revenue, or Expense account, along with its identification number.

a. Advertising Expense
b. Rent Revenue
c. Rent Receivable
d. Machinery
e. Accounts Payable
f. Furniture
g. Notes Payable
h. Prepaid Insurance
i. Utilities Expense

QS 2-4
Identifying normal balance
C2

Identify the normal balance (debit or credit) for each of the following accounts.

a. Rideshare Revenue
b. Office Supplies
c. Cash
d. Wages Expense
e. Accounts Receivable
f. Prepaid Rent
g. Wages Payable
h. Building
i. Unearned Revenue

QS 2-5
Linking debit or credit with normal balance C2

Indicate whether a debit or credit *decreases* the normal balance of each of the following accounts.

a. Interest Payable
b. Accounts Receivable
c. Prepaid Insurance
d. Buildings
e. Accounts Payable
f. Land

QS 2-6
Analyzing debit or credit by account
C2

Identify whether a debit or credit results in the indicated change for each of the following accounts.

a. To increase Land
b. To decrease Cash
c. To increase Consulting Revenue
d. To increase Salaries Expense
e. To decrease Unearned Revenue
f. To decrease Prepaid Rent
g. To increase Notes Payable
h. To decrease Accounts Receivable
i. To increase Accounts Payable
j. To increase Store Equipment

QS 2-7
Computing T-account balance
C2

Determine the ending balance of each of the following T-accounts.

a.

Cash	
100	50
300	60
20	

b.

Accounts Payable	
2,000	8,000
2,700	

c.

Supplies	
10,000	3,800
1,100	

d.

Accounts Receivable	
600	150
	150
	150
	100

e.

Wages Payable	
	700
700	

f.

Cash	
11,000	4,500
800	6,000
100	1,300

QS 2-8
Analyzing transactions and preparing journal entries
A1

For each transaction, (1) analyze the transaction using the accounting equation, (2) record the transaction in journal entry form, and (3) post the entry using T-accounts to represent ledger accounts. Use the following partial chart of accounts—account numbers in parentheses: Cash (101); Accounts Receivable (106); Office Supplies (124); Trucks (153); Equipment (167); Accounts Payable (201); Unearned Landscaping Revenue (236); D. Tyler, Capital (301); D. Tyler, Withdrawals (302); Landscaping Revenue (403); Wages Expense (601); and Landscaping Expense (696).

a. On May 15, DeShawn Tyler opens a landscaping company called Elegant Lawns by investing $7,000 in cash along with equipment having a $3,000 value.
b. On May 21, Elegant Lawns purchases office supplies on credit for $500.
c. On May 25, Elegant Lawns receives $4,000 cash for performing landscaping services.
d. On May 30, Elegant Lawns receives $1,000 cash in advance of providing landscaping services to a customer.

QS 2-9
Preparing journal entries
A1

Prepare general journal entries for the following transactions of Green Energy Company. Use the following partial chart of accounts: Cash; Accounts Receivable; Supplies; Accounts Payable; Consulting Revenue; and Utilities Expense.

May 1	The company provided $2,000 of sustainability consulting services on credit to a customer.
3	The company purchased $300 of energy-efficient supplies on credit.
9	The company collected $500 cash as partial payment of the May 1 consulting revenue.
20	The company paid $300 cash toward the payable for energy-efficient supplies.
31	The company paid $100 cash for May's renewable energy utilities.

QS 2-10
Analyzing transactions using accounting equation
A1

Analyze each transaction in QS 2-9 by showing its effects on the accounting equation—specifically, identify the accounts and amounts (including + or −) for each transaction.

QS 2-11
Preparing compound journal entries **A1**

Prepare compound journal entries for each transaction.

a. The owner, J. Cruz, invests $6,500 cash and $3,500 of equipment in the company.
b. The company acquires $2,000 of supplies by paying $500 cash and putting $1,500 on credit (accounts payable).

QS 2-12
Identifying a posting error
P1

A trial balance has total debits of $20,000 and total credits of $24,500. Which one of the following errors would create this imbalance?

a. A $2,250 debit to Utilities Expense in a journal entry was incorrectly posted to the ledger as a $2,250 credit, leaving the Utilities Expense account with a $3,000 debit balance.
b. A $4,500 debit to Salaries Expense in a journal entry was incorrectly posted to the ledger as a $4,500 credit, leaving the Salaries Expense account with a $750 debit balance.
c. A $2,250 credit to Consulting Revenue in a journal entry was incorrectly posted to the ledger as a $2,250 debit, leaving the Consulting Revenue account with a $6,300 credit balance.
d. A $2,250 debit posting to Accounts Receivable was posted mistakenly to Land.
e. A $4,500 debit posting to Equipment was posted mistakenly to Cash.
f. An entry debiting Cash and crediting Accounts Payable for $4,500 was mistakenly not posted.

QS 2-13
Classifying accounts in financial statements
P1

Indicate the financial statement on which each of the following items appears: income statement, statement of owner's equity, or balance sheet.

a. Services Revenue
b. Interest Payable
c. Accounts Receivable
d. Salaries Expense
e. Equipment
f. Prepaid Insurance
g. Buildings
h. Rental Revenue
i. Unearned Revenue
j. Office Supplies
k. Interest Expense
l. Insurance Expense

QS 2-14
Preparing a trial balance
P1

Lawson Consulting had the following accounts and amounts on December 31. Prepare a December 31 trial balance.

Cash	$5,000	Accounts payable	$ 3,000	Services revenue	$12,000
Accounts receivable	4,500	I. Lawson, Capital	10,500	Rent expense	2,000
Equipment	6,500	I. Lawson, Withdrawals	1,500	Wages expense	6,000

QS 2-15
Preparing an income statement **P1**

Use the information in QS 2-14 to prepare a December income statement for Lawson Consulting. The company began operations on December 1.

QS 2-16
Preparing a statement of owner's equity **P1**

Use the information in QS 2-14 to prepare a December statement of owner's equity for Lawson Consulting. The I. Lawson, Capital account balance at December 1 was $0. *Hint:* Net income for December is $4,000 and the owner invested $10,500 cash in the company on December 2.

QS 2-17
Preparing a balance sheet
P1

Use the information in QS 2-14 to prepare a December 31 balance sheet for Lawson Consulting. *Hint:* The ending I. Lawson, Capital account balance as of December 31 is $13,000.

QS 2-18
Interpreting debt ratio
A2

The debt ratio for Deutsche Auto for each of the last three years follows. Over this three-year period, did the company's risk from financial leverage increase or decrease?

	Current Year	1 Year Ago	2 Years Ago
Debt ratio	61%	45%	37%

QS 2-19
Computing and using the debt ratio A2

Home Demo reports the following: Total liabilities = $38,633 million and Total assets = $42,966 million. (a) Compute Home Demo's debt ratio. (b) Assuming Lows Hardware (a competitor) has a debt ratio of 60.0%, which company has higher risk from financial leverage?

connect

EXERCISES

Exercise 2-1
Steps in analyzing and recording transactions C1

Order the following steps in the accounting process that focus on analyzing and recording transactions.

a. Prepare and analyze the trial balance.
b. Analyze each transaction from source documents.
c. Record relevant transactions in a journal.
d. Post journal information to ledger accounts.

Exercise 2-2
Identifying source documents from accounting processes C1

Identify the source document for NDX Company in each of the following accounting processes.

a. A customer purchases merchandise with a credit card. NDX uses the electronic sales receipt to record transaction details in its accounting system.
b. NDX purchases goods and receives a bill from the supplier. Details from the bill are captured and entered in the accounting database, which is stored in the cloud.
c. An NDX employee receives a bank statement each month on her company e-mail. The statement is used to record bank fees incurred for that month.

Exercise 2-3
Identifying and classifying accounts C1

Identify the item that best completes each of the descriptions below.

1. Asset **2.** Equity **3.** Account **4.** Liability **5.** Three

a. Balance sheet accounts are arranged into ______ general categories.
b. The owner's claim on a company's assets is called ______.
c. Accounts Payable and Notes Payable are examples of ______ accounts.
d. Accounts Receivable, Prepaid Accounts, Supplies, and Land are examples of ______ accounts.
e. A(n) ______ is a record of increases and decreases in a specific asset, liability, equity, revenue, or expense item.

Exercise 2-4
Identifying a ledger and chart of accounts C1

Identify the item that best completes each of the descriptions below.

1. Chart **2.** General ledger **3.** Journal **4.** Account **5.** Source document

a. A(n) ______ of accounts is a list of all accounts a company uses, not including account balances.
b. The ______ is a record containing all accounts used by a company, including account balances.
c. A(n) ______ describes transactions entering an accounting system, such as a purchase order.
d. Increases and decreases in a specific asset, liability, equity, revenue, or expense are recorded in a(n) ______.
e. A(n) ______ has a complete record of every transaction recorded.

Exercise 2-5
Identifying type and normal balances of accounts C2

For each of the following, (1) identify the account as an asset, liability, equity, revenue, or expense; (2) identify the normal balance of the account; and (3) enter *debit* or *credit* to identify the kind of entry that would increase the account balance.

a. Land
b. Cash
c. Legal Expense
d. Prepaid Insurance
e. Accounts Receivable
f. Tour Service Revenue
g. Unearned Revenue
h. Services Revenue
i. Equipment
j. Notes Payable

Exercise 2-6
Analyzing effects of a compound entry A1

Groro Co. bills a client $62,000 for services provided and agrees to accept the following three items in full payment: (1) $10,000 cash, (2) $80,000 of equipment, and (3) $28,000 note payable owed on the equipment. For this transaction, (*a*) analyze the transaction using the accounting equation, (*b*) record the transaction in journal entry form, and (*c*) post the entry using T-accounts to represent ledger accounts. Use the following partial chart of accounts—account numbers in parentheses: Cash (101); Supplies (124); Equipment (167); Accounts Payable (201); Note Payable (245); and Services Revenue (403).

Exercise 2-7
Analyzing account entries and balances
A1

Use the information in each of the following separate cases to calculate the unknown amount.

a. Corentine Co. had $152,000 of accounts payable on September 30 and $132,500 on October 31. Total purchases on credit during October were $281,000. Determine how much cash was paid on accounts payable during October.

b. On September 30, Valerian Co. had a $102,500 balance in Accounts Receivable. During October, the company collected $102,890 from its credit customers. The October 31 balance in Accounts Receivable was $89,000. Determine the amount of sales on credit that occurred in October.

c. During October, Alameda Company had $102,500 of cash receipts and $103,150 of cash disbursements. The October 31 Cash balance was $18,600. Determine how much cash the company had at the close of business on September 30.

Exercise 2-8
Preparing journal entries
A1

Prepare general journal entries for the following transactions of Sustain Company.

June	1	T. James, owner, invested $11,000 cash in Sustain Company.
	2	The company purchased $4,000 of furniture made from reclaimed wood on credit.
	3	The company paid $600 cash for a 12-month prepaid insurance policy on the reclaimed furniture.
	4	The company billed a customer $3,000 for sustainability services provided.
	12	The company paid $4,000 cash toward the payable from the June 2 furniture purchase.
	20	The company collected $3,000 cash for services billed on June 4.
	21	T. James invested an additional $10,000 cash in Sustain Company.
	30	The company received $5,000 cash in advance of providing sustainability services to a customer.

Exercise 2-9
Preparing general journal entries
A1

Prepare general journal entries for the following transactions of a new company called Pose-for-Pics. Use the following partial chart of accounts: Cash; Supplies; Prepaid Insurance; Equipment; M. Harris, Capital; Services Revenue; and Utilities Expense.

Aug.	1	M. Harris, the owner, invested $6,500 cash and $33,500 of photography equipment in the company.
	2	The company paid $2,100 cash for an insurance policy covering the next 24 months.
	5	The company purchased supplies for $880 cash.
	20	The company received $3,331 cash from taking photos for customers.
	31	The company paid $675 cash for August utilities.

Exercise 2-10
Recording transactions in balance column accounts
A1

Open a ledger account for Cash in balance column format. Post general journal entries that impact cash from Exercise 2-9 to the ledger account for Cash, and enter the balance after each posting.

Exercise 2-11
Analyzing transactions using accounting equation A1

Analyze each transaction in Exercise 2-9 by showing its effects on the accounting equation—specifically, identify the accounts and amounts (including + or −) for each transaction.

Exercise 2-12
Preparing T-accounts (ledger) and a trial balance
P1

Use the information in Exercise 2-9 to open these T-accounts: Cash; Supplies; Prepaid Insurance; Equipment; M. Harris, Capital; Services Revenue; and Utilities Expense. (1) Post the general journal entries to these T-accounts (which will serve as the ledger). (2) Prepare the August 31 trial balance.

Exercise 2-13
Recording effects of transactions in T-accounts
A1

For the following transactions of Spade Company, (1) prepare general journal entries and (2) post entries to T-accounts and calculate the ending balance of each T-account. Use the following accounts: Cash; Accounts Receivable; Supplies; Equipment; Accounts Payable; K. Spade, Capital; K. Spade, Withdrawals; Services Revenue; and Rent Expense.

a. K. Spade, owner, invested $100,750 cash in the company.
b. The company purchased supplies for $1,250 cash.
c. The company purchased $10,050 of equipment on credit.
d. The company received $15,500 cash for services provided to a customer.
e. The company paid $10,050 cash to settle the payable for the equipment purchased in transaction *c*.
f. The company billed a customer $2,700 for services provided.
g. The company paid $1,225 cash for the monthly rent.
h. The company collected $1,125 cash as partial payment for the account receivable created in transaction *f*.
i. K. Spade withdrew $10,000 cash from the company for personal use.

Check Cash ending balance, $94,850

Exercise 2-14
Preparing a trial balance
P1

After recording the transactions of Exercise 2-13 in T-accounts and calculating the balance of each account, prepare a trial balance. Use May 31 as its report date.

Exercise 2-15
Analyzing and journalizing transactions involving cash payments
A1

1. Prepare general journal entries for the following transactions of Valdez Services.
   - **a.** The company paid $2,000 cash for payment on a 6-month-old account payable for office supplies.
   - **b.** The company paid $1,200 cash for the just-completed two-week salary of the receptionist.
   - **c.** The company paid $39,000 cash for equipment purchased.
   - **d.** The company paid $800 cash for this month's utilities.
   - **e.** The owner, B. Valdez, withdrew $4,500 cash from the company for personal use.
2. Transactions *a, c,* and *e* did not result in an expense. Match each transaction (*a, c,* and *e*) with one of the following reasons for not recording an expense.
   - ______ This transaction is a distribution of cash to the owner. Even though equity decreased, that decrease did not occur in the process of providing goods or services to customers.
   - ______ This transaction decreased cash in settlement of a previously existing liability (equity did not change). Supplies expense is recorded when assets are used, not necessarily when cash is paid.
   - ______ This transaction involves the purchase of an asset. The form of the company's assets changed, but total assets did not (and neither did equity).

Exercise 2-16
Analyzing and journalizing transactions involving receipt of cash
A1

1. Prepare general journal entries for the following transactions of Valdez Services.
   - **a.** B. Valdez invested $20,000 cash in the company.
   - **b.** The company provided services to a client and immediately received $900 cash.
   - **c.** The company received $10,000 cash from a client in advance for services to be provided next year.
   - **d.** The company received $3,500 cash from a client in partial payment of accounts receivable.
2. Transactions *a, c,* and *d* did not yield revenue. Match each transaction (*a, c,* and *d*) with one of the following reasons for not recording revenue.
   - ______ This transaction changed the form of an asset from a receivable to cash. Total assets were not increased (revenue was recognized when the services were originally provided).
   - ______ This transaction brought in cash, but this is an owner investment.
   - ______ This transaction brought in cash, but it created a liability to provide services to the client in the next year.

Exercise 2-17
Entering transactions into T-accounts
A1

Fill in each of the following T-accounts for Belle Co.'s seven transactions listed here. The T-accounts represent Belle Co.'s general ledger. Code each entry with transaction numbers *1* through *7* (in order) for reference.

1. D. Belle created a new business and invested $6,000 cash, $7,600 of equipment, and $12,000 in web servers.
2. The company paid $4,800 cash in advance for prepaid insurance coverage.
3. The company purchased $900 of supplies on credit.
4. The company paid $800 cash for selling expenses.
5. The company received $4,500 cash for services provided.
6. The company paid $900 cash toward accounts payable.
7. The company paid $3,400 cash for equipment.

Cash	Supplies	Prepaid Insurance
Equipment	Web Servers	Accounts Payable
D. Belle, Capital	Services Revenue	Selling Expenses

Exercise 2-18
Preparing general journal entries A1

Use information from Exercise 2-17 to prepare the general journal entries for Belle Co.'s first seven transactions.

Exercise 2-19
Identifying transactions from T-accounts
A1

Chase Company posted transactions (*a* through *f*) in the following T-accounts in December, its first month of operations. Prepare the six journal entries from which the postings were made.

Cash		Supplies		Accounts Payable	
a. 6,000	b. 2,000	b. 2,000		f. 1,000	d. 1,500
c. 5,000	e. 3,000	d. 1,500			
	f. 1,000				

Chase, Capital		Services Revenue		Rent Expense	
	a. 6,000		c. 5,000	e. 3,000	

Exercise 2-20
Preparing a trial balance from T-accounts **P1**

Use the T-accounts in Exercise 2-19 from Chase Company's first month of operations to prepare its December 31 trial balance.

Exercise 2-21
Preparing a trial balance from data with a missing value
P1

Prepare a December 31 trial balance for Jindal Co. using the following information and fill in the missing amount for Equipment (assume all data are correct).

Cash	$ 8,000	Equipment	$_?_	Wages expense	$12,000
Accounts payable.......	4,000	Jindal, Withdrawals	500	Accounts receivable......	1,000
Services revenue	20,000	Jindal, Capital.............	16,500	Unearned revenue.......	2,000
Rent expense	3,000				

Exercise 2-22
Identifying effects of posting errors on the trial balance
P1

Posting errors are identified in the following table. In column (1), enter the amount of the difference between the two trial balance columns (debit and credit) due to the error. In column (2), identify the trial balance column (debit or credit) with the larger amount if they are not equal. In column (3), identify the account(s) affected by the error. In column (4), indicate the amount by which the account(s) in column (3) is under- or overstated. Item (a) is completed as an example.

	Description of Posting Error	(1) Difference between Debit and Credit Columns	(2) Column with the Larger Total	(3) Identify Account(s) Incorrectly Stated	(4) Amount That Account(s) Is Over- or Understated
a.	$3,600 debit to Rent Expense is posted as a $1,340 debit.	$2,260	Credit	Rent Expense	Rent Expense understated $2,260
b.	$6,500 credit to Cash is posted twice as two credits to Cash.				
c.	$2,050 debit to Prepaid Insurance is posted as a debit to Insurance Expense.				
d.	$38,000 debit to Machinery is posted as a debit to Accounts Payable.				
e.	$5,850 credit to Services Revenue is posted as a $585 credit.				
f.	$1,390 debit to Store Supplies is not posted.				

Exercise 2-23
Analyzing a trial balance error
P1

You are told the column totals in a trial balance are not equal. After careful analysis, you discover only one error. Specifically, a correctly journalized credit purchase of an automobile for $18,950 is posted from the journal to the ledger with an $18,950 debit to Automobiles and another $18,950 debit to Accounts Payable. The Automobiles account has a debit balance of $37,100 on the trial balance. (1) Answer each of the following questions and (2) compute the dollar amount of any misstatement for parts *a* through *d*.

a. Is the Debit column total of the trial balance overstated, understated, or correctly stated?

b. Is the Credit column total of the trial balance overstated, understated, or correctly stated?

c. Is the Automobiles account balance overstated, understated, or correctly stated in the trial balance?
d. Is the Accounts Payable account balance overstated, understated, or correctly stated in the trial balance?
e. If the Debit column total of the trial balance is $200,000 before correcting the error, what is the total of the Credit column before correction?

Exercise 2-24
Computing net income
P1

A company had the following assets and liabilities at the beginning and end of this year.

	Assets	Liabilities
Beginning of the year	$ 60,000	$20,000
End of the year	105,000	36,000

Determine net income or net loss for the business during the year for each of the following *separate* cases.
a. Owner made no investments in the business, and no withdrawals were made during the year.
b. Owner made no investments in the business but did withdraw $15,000 during the year.
c. Owner made no withdrawals during the year, but the owner did invest an additional $55,000 cash.
d. Owner withdrew $15,000 during the year, but the owner did invest an additional $35,000 cash near year-end.

Exercise 2-25
Preparing an income statement
P1

Carmen Camry operates a consulting firm called Help Today, which began operations on December 1. On December 31, the company's records show the following selected accounts and amounts for the month of December. Use this information to prepare a December income statement for the business.

Cash	$25,360	Accounts payable	$ 10,500	Salaries expense	$5,600
Accounts receivable	22,360	C. Camry, Capital	102,000	Telephone expense	860
Office supplies	5,250	C. Camry, Withdrawals	6,000	Miscellaneous expenses	520
Office equipment	20,000	Consulting revenue	27,000		
Land	44,000	Rent expense	9,550		

Check Net income, $10,470

Exercise 2-26
Preparing a statement of owner's equity
P1

Use the information in Exercise 2-25 to prepare a December statement of owner's equity for Help Today. The C. Camry, Capital account balance at December 1 was $0, and the owner invested $102,000 in the company on December 2. *Hint:* Net income for December is $10,470.

Exercise 2-27
Preparing a balance sheet
P1

Use the information in Exercise 2-25 to prepare a December 31 balance sheet for Help Today. *Hint:* The ending C. Camry, Capital account balance as of December 31 is $106,470.

Exercise 2-28
Analyzing changes in a company's equity
P1

Compute the missing amount for each of the following separate companies in columns B through E.

	A	B	C	D	E
1		CBS	ABC	CNN	NBC
2	Equity, beginning of year	$ 0	$ 0	$ 0	$ 0
3	Owner investments during the year	110,000	?	87,000	210,000
4	Owner withdrawals during the year	?	(47,000)	(10,000)	(55,000)
5	Net income (loss) for the year	22,000	90,000	(4,000)	?
6	Equity, end of year	104,000	85,000	?	110,000

Exercise 2-29
Calculating and interpreting the debt ratio
A2

Company	Expenses	Total Assets	Net Income	Total Liabilities
DreamWorks	$22,000	$ 40,000	$19,000	$30,000
Pixar	67,000	150,000	27,000	147,000
Universal	12,000	68,000	5,000	17,000

a. Compute the debt ratio for each of the three companies.
b. Which company has the most financial leverage?

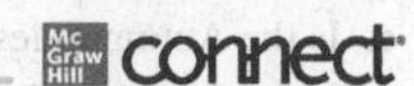

PROBLEM SET A

Problem 2-1A
Preparing and posting journal entries; preparing a trial balance
P1 A1

Karla Tanner opened a web consulting business called Linkworks and completed the following transactions in its first month of operations.

Apr.	1	Tanner invested $80,000 cash along with office equipment valued at $26,000 in the company.
	2	The company prepaid $9,000 cash for 12 months' rent for office space. *Hint:* Debit Prepaid Rent for $9,000.
	3	The company made credit purchases for $8,000 in office equipment and $3,600 in office supplies. Payment is due within 10 days.
	6	The company completed services for a client and immediately received $4,000 cash.
	9	The company completed a $6,000 project for a client, who must pay within 30 days.
	13	The company paid $11,600 cash to settle the account payable created on April 3.
	19	The company paid $2,400 cash for the premium on a 12-month prepaid insurance policy. *Hint:* Debit Prepaid Insurance for $2,400.
	22	The company received $4,400 cash as partial payment for the work completed on April 9.
	25	The company completed work for another client for $2,890 on credit.
	28	Tanner withdrew $5,500 cash from the company for personal use.
	29	The company purchased $600 of additional office supplies on credit.
	30	The company paid $435 cash for this month's utility bill.

Required

1. Prepare general journal entries to record these transactions (use account titles listed in part 2).
2. Open the following ledger accounts—their account numbers are in parentheses (use the balance column format): Cash (101); Accounts Receivable (106); Office Supplies (124); Prepaid Insurance (128); Prepaid Rent (131); Office Equipment (163); Accounts Payable (201); K. Tanner, Capital (301); K. Tanner, Withdrawals (302); Services Revenue (403); and Utilities Expense (690). Post journal entries from part 1 to the ledger accounts and enter the balance after each posting.
3. Prepare a trial balance as of April 30.

Check (2) Ending balances: Cash, $59,465; Accounts Receivable, $4,490; Accounts Payable, $600

(3) Total debits, $119,490

Problem 2-2A
Preparing and posting journal entries; preparing a trial balance
P1 A1

Aracel Engineering completed the following transactions in the month of June.

a. J. Aracel, the owner, invested $100,000 cash, office equipment with a value of $5,000, and $60,000 of drafting equipment to launch the company.
b. The company purchased land worth $49,000 for an office by paying $6,300 cash and signing a note payable for $42,700.
c. The company purchased a portable building with $55,000 cash and moved it onto the land acquired in *b*.
d. The company paid $3,000 cash for the premium on an 18-month insurance policy.
e. The company provided services to a client and collected $6,200 cash.
f. The company purchased $20,000 of additional drafting equipment by paying $9,500 cash and signing a note payable for $10,500.
g. The company completed $14,000 of services for a client. This amount is to be received in 30 days.
h. The company purchased $1,150 of additional office equipment on credit.
i. The company completed $22,000 of services for a customer on credit.
j. The company purchased $1,333 of TV advertising on credit.
k. The company collected $7,000 cash in partial payment from the client described in transaction *g*.
l. The company paid $1,200 cash for employee wages.
m. The company paid $1,150 cash to settle the account payable created in transaction *h*.
n. The company paid $925 cash for repairs.
o. J. Aracel withdrew $9,480 cash from the company for personal use.
p. The company paid $1,200 cash for employee wages.
q. The company paid $2,500 cash for advertisements on the web during June.

Required

1. Prepare general journal entries to record these transactions (use the account titles listed in part 2).
2. Open the following ledger accounts—their account numbers are in parentheses (use the balance column format): Cash (101); Accounts Receivable (106); Prepaid Insurance (108); Office Equipment (163); Drafting Equipment (164); Building (170); Land (172); Accounts Payable (201); Notes Payable (250); J. Aracel, Capital (301); J. Aracel, Withdrawals (302); Services Revenue (403); Wages Expense (601); Advertising Expense (603); and Repairs Expense (604). Post the journal entries from part 1 to the accounts and enter the balance after each posting.
3. Prepare a trial balance as of the end of June.

Check (2) Ending balances: Cash, $22,945; Accounts Receivable, $29,000; Accounts Payable, $1,333

(3) Trial balance totals, $261,733

Problem 2-3A
Preparing and posting journal entries; preparing a trial balance
P1 A1

Denzel Brooks opened a web consulting business called Venture Consultants and completed the following transactions in March.

Mar. 1 Brooks invested $150,000 cash along with $22,000 in office equipment in the company.
2 The company prepaid $6,000 cash for six months' rent for an office. *Hint:* Debit Prepaid Rent for $6,000.
3 The company made credit purchases of office equipment for $3,000 and office supplies for $1,200. Payment is due within 10 days.
6 The company completed services for a client and immediately received $4,000 cash.
9 The company completed a $7,500 project on credit for a client, who must pay within 30 days.
12 The company paid $4,200 cash to settle the account payable created on March 3.
19 The company paid $5,000 cash for the premium on a 12-month insurance policy. *Hint:* Debit Prepaid Insurance for $5,000.
22 The company received $3,500 cash as partial payment for the work completed on March 9.
25 The company completed work for another client for $3,820 on credit.
29 Brooks withdrew $5,100 cash from the company for personal use.
30 The company purchased $600 of additional office supplies on credit.
31 The company paid $500 cash for this month's utility bill.

Required

1. Prepare general journal entries to record these transactions (use the account titles listed in part 2).
2. Open the following ledger accounts—their account numbers are in parentheses (use the balance column format): Cash (101); Accounts Receivable (106); Office Supplies (124); Prepaid Insurance (128); Prepaid Rent (131); Office Equipment (163); Accounts Payable (201); D. Brooks, Capital (301); D. Brooks, Withdrawals (302); Services Revenue (403); and Utilities Expense (690). Post the journal entries from part 1 to the ledger accounts and enter the balance after each posting.
3. Prepare a trial balance as of the end of March.

Check (2) Ending balances: Cash, $136,700; Accounts Receivable, $7,820; Accounts Payable, $600

(3) Total debits, $187,920

Problem 2-4A
Recording transactions; posting to ledger; preparing a trial balance
P1 A1

Business transactions completed by Hannah Venedict during the month of September are as follows.

a. Venedict invested $60,000 cash along with office equipment valued at $25,000 in a new business named HV Consulting.
b. The company purchased land valued at $40,000 and a building valued at $160,000. The purchase is paid with $30,000 cash and a note payable for $170,000.
c. The company purchased $2,000 of office supplies on credit.
d. Venedict invested an automobile in the company. The automobile has a value of $16,500.
e. The company purchased $5,600 of additional office equipment on credit.
f. The company paid $1,800 cash salary to an assistant.
g. The company provided services to a client and collected $8,000 cash.
h. The company paid $635 cash for this month's utilities.
i. The company paid $2,000 cash to settle the account payable created in transaction *c*.
j. The company purchased $20,300 of new office equipment by paying $20,300 cash.
k. The company completed $6,250 of services on credit for a client, who must pay within 30 days.
l. The company paid $1,800 cash salary to an assistant.
m. The company received $4,000 cash in partial payment on the receivable created in transaction *k*.
n. Venedict withdrew $2,800 cash from the company for personal use.

Required

1. Prepare general journal entries to record these transactions (use account titles listed in part 2).
2. Open the following ledger accounts—their account numbers are in parentheses (use the balance column format): Cash (101); Accounts Receivable (106); Office Supplies (108); Office Equipment (163); Automobiles (164); Building (170); Land (172); Accounts Payable (201); Notes Payable (250); H. Venedict, Capital (301); H. Venedict, Withdrawals (302); Consulting Revenue (403); Salaries Expense (601); and Utilities Expense (602). Post the journal entries from part 1 to the ledger accounts and enter the balance after each posting.
3. Prepare a trial balance as of the end of September.

Check (2) Ending balances: Cash, $12,665; Office Equipment, $50,900

(3) Trial balance totals, $291,350

Problem 2-5A
Computing net income from equity analysis, preparing a balance sheet, and computing the debt ratio
P1 A2

The accounting records of Nettle Distribution show the following assets and liabilities as of December 31 for Year 1 and Year 2.

December 31	Year 1	Year 2	December 31	Year 1	Year 2
Cash	$ 64,300	$ 15,640	Building	$ 0	$80,000
Accounts receivable	26,240	19,100	Land	0	60,000
Office supplies	3,160	1,960	Accounts payable	3,500	33,500
Office equipment	44,000	44,000	Note payable	0	40,000
Trucks	148,000	157,000			

Required

1. Prepare balance sheets for the business as of December 31 for Year 1 and for Year 2. *Hint:* Report only total equity on the balance sheet and remember that total equity equals the difference between assets and liabilities.
2. Compute net income for Year 2 by comparing total equity amounts for these two years and using the following information: During Year 2, the owner invested $35,000 additional cash in the business and withdrew $19,000 cash for personal use.
3. Compute the Year 2 year-end debt ratio.

Check (2) Net income, $6,000

(3) Debt ratio, 19.5%

Problem 2-6A
Analyzing account balances and reconstructing transactions
P1 A1

Yi Min started an engineering firm called Min Engineering. He began operations and completed seven transactions in May, which included his initial investment of $18,000 cash. After those seven transactions, the ledger included the following accounts with normal balances.

Cash	$37,600	Office equipment	$12,900	Y. Min, Withdrawals	$ 3,370
Office supplies	890	Accounts payable	12,900	Services revenue	36,000
Prepaid insurance	4,600	Y. Min, Capital	18,000	Rent expense	7,540

Required

1. Prepare a trial balance for this business as of the end of May.
2. The following seven transactions produced the account balances shown above.
   a. Y. Min invested $18,000 cash in the business.
   b. Paid $7,540 cash for monthly rent expense for May.
   c. Paid $4,600 cash in advance for the annual insurance premium beginning the next period.
   d. Purchased office supplies for $890 cash.
   e. Purchased $12,900 of office equipment on credit (with accounts payable).
   f. Received $36,000 cash for services provided in May.
   g. Y. Min withdrew $3,370 cash from the company for personal use.

   Prepare a Cash T-account, enter the cash effects (if any) of each transaction, and compute the ending Cash balance. Code each entry in the T-account with one of the transaction codes *a* through *g*.

Check (1) Trial balance totals, $66,900
(2) Ending Cash balance, $37,600

Problem 2-7A
Preparing an income statement, statement of owner's equity, and balance sheet
P1

Angela Lopez owns and manages a consulting firm called Metrix, which began operations on December 1. On December 31, Metrix shows the following selected accounts and amounts for the month of December.

Cash	$8,000	Accounts payable	$ 1,300	Rental revenue	$ 500
Accounts receivable	3,500	Notes payable	2,400	Salaries expense	3,000
Notes receivable	2,500	Unearned revenue	300	Rent expense	2,000
Office supplies	1,500	A. Lopez, Capital	11,600	Advertising expense	400
Prepaid insurance	1,000	A. Lopez, Withdrawals	2,000	Utilities expense	200
Equipment	4,000	Consulting revenue	12,000		

Required

1. Prepare a December income statement for the business.
2. Prepare a December statement of owner's equity. The A. Lopez, Capital account balance at December 1 was $0, and the owner invested $11,600 cash in the company on December 2.
3. Prepare a December 31 balance sheet. *Hint:* Use the A. Lopez, Capital account balance calculated in part 2.

PROBLEM SET B

Problem 2-1B
Preparing and posting journal entries; preparing a trial balance
P1 A1

Humble Management Services opened for business and completed these transactions in September.

Sep. 1 H. Humble, the owner, invested $38,000 cash along with office equipment valued at $15,000 in the company.
2 The company prepaid $9,000 cash for 12 months' rent for office space. *Hint:* Debit Prepaid Rent for $9,000.
4 The company made credit purchases for $8,000 in office equipment and $2,400 in office supplies. Payment is due within 10 days.
8 The company completed work for a client and immediately received $3,280 cash.
12 The company completed a $15,400 project for a client, who must pay within 30 days.
13 The company paid $10,400 cash to settle the payable created on September 4.
19 The company paid $1,900 cash for the premium on an 18-month insurance prepaid policy. *Hint:* Debit Prepaid Insurance for $1,900.
22 The company received $7,700 cash as partial payment for the work completed on September 12.
24 The company completed work for another client for $2,100 on credit.
28 H. Humble withdrew $5,300 cash from the company for personal use.
29 The company purchased $550 of additional office supplies on credit.
30 The company paid $860 cash for this month's utility bill.

Required

1. Prepare general journal entries to record these transactions (use account titles listed in part 2).
2. Open the following ledger accounts—their account numbers are in parentheses (use the balance column format): Cash (101); Accounts Receivable (106); Office Supplies (124); Prepaid Insurance (128); Prepaid Rent (131); Office Equipment (163); Accounts Payable (201); H. Humble, Capital (301); H. Humble, Withdrawals (302); Services Revenue (403); and Utilities Expense (690). Post journal entries from part 1 to the ledger accounts and enter the balance after each posting.
3. Prepare a trial balance as of the end of September.

Check (2) Ending balances: Cash, $21,520; Accounts Receivable, $9,800; Accounts Payable, $550

(3) Total debits, $74,330

Problem 2-2B
Preparing and posting journal entries; preparing a trial balance
P1 A1

At the beginning of April, Bernadette Grechus launched a custom computer solutions company called Softworks. The company had the following transactions during April.

a. B. Grechus invested $65,000 cash, office equipment with a value of $5,750, and $30,000 of computer equipment in the company.
b. The company purchased land worth $22,000 for an office by paying $5,000 cash and signing a note payable for $17,000.
c. The company purchased a portable building with $34,500 cash and moved it onto the land acquired in *b.*
d. The company paid $5,000 cash for the premium on a two-year insurance policy.
e. The company provided services to a client and immediately collected $4,600 cash.
f. The company purchased $4,500 of additional computer equipment by paying $800 cash and signing a note payable for $3,700.
g. The company completed $4,250 of services for a client. This amount is to be received within 30 days.
h. The company purchased $950 of additional office equipment on credit.
i. The company completed $10,200 of services for a customer on credit.
j. The company purchased $580 of TV advertising on credit.
k. The company collected $5,100 cash in partial payment from the client described in transaction *i.*
l. The company paid $1,800 cash for employee wages.
m. The company paid $950 cash to settle the payable created in transaction *h.*
n. The company paid $608 cash for repairs.

[continued on next page]

[continued from previous page]

o. B. Grechus withdrew $6,230 cash from the company for personal use.
p. The company paid $1,800 cash for employee wages.
q. The company paid $750 cash for advertisements on the web during April.

Required

1. Prepare general journal entries to record these transactions (use account titles listed in part 2).

2. Open the following ledger accounts—their account numbers are in parentheses (use the balance column format): Cash (101); Accounts Receivable (106); Prepaid Insurance (108); Office Equipment (163); Computer Equipment (164); Building (170); Land (172); Accounts Payable (201); Notes Payable (250); B. Grechus, Capital (301); B. Grechus, Withdrawals (302); Services Revenue (403); Wages Expense (601); Advertising Expense (603); and Repairs Expense (604). Post the journal entries from part 1 to the accounts and enter the balance after each posting.

3. Prepare a trial balance as of the end of April.

Check (2) Ending balances: Cash, $17,262; Accounts Receivable, $9,350; Accounts Payable, $580

(3) Trial balance totals, $141,080

Problem 2-3B
Preparing and posting journal entries; preparing a trial balance
P1 A1

Zucker Management Services opened for business and completed these transactions in November.

Nov. 1 M. Zucker, the owner, invested $30,000 cash along with $15,000 of office equipment in the company.
2 The company prepaid $4,500 cash for six months' rent for an office. *Hint:* Debit Prepaid Rent for $4,500.
4 The company made credit purchases of office equipment for $2,500 and office supplies for $600. Payment is due within 10 days.
8 The company completed work for a client and immediately received $3,400 cash.
12 The company completed a $10,200 project on credit for a client, who must pay within 30 days.
13 The company paid $3,100 cash to settle the payable created on November 4.
19 The company paid $1,800 cash for the premium on a 24-month insurance policy.
22 The company received $5,200 cash as partial payment for the work completed on November 12.
24 The company completed work for another client for $1,750 on credit.
28 M. Zucker withdrew $5,300 cash from the company for personal use.
29 The company purchased $249 of additional office supplies on credit.
30 The company paid $831 cash for this month's utility bill.

Required

1. Prepare general journal entries to record these transactions (use account titles listed in part 2).

2. Open the following ledger accounts—their account numbers are in parentheses (use the balance column format): Cash (101); Accounts Receivable (106); Office Supplies (124); Prepaid Insurance (128); Prepaid Rent (131); Office Equipment (163); Accounts Payable (201); M. Zucker, Capital (301); M. Zucker, Withdrawals (302); Services Revenue (403); and Utilities Expense (690). Post the journal entries from part 1 to the ledger accounts and enter the balance after each posting.

3. Prepare a trial balance as of the end of November.

Check (2) Ending balances: Cash, $23,069; Accounts Receivable, $6,750; Accounts Payble, $249

(3) Total debits, $60,599

Problem 2-4B
Recording transactions; posting to ledger; preparing a trial balance
P1 A1

Nuncio Consulting completed the following transactions during June.

a. A. Nuncio, the owner, invested $35,000 cash along with office equipment valued at $11,000 in the new company.
b. The company purchased land valued at $7,500 and a building valued at $40,000. The purchase is paid with $15,000 cash and a note payable for $32,500.
c. The company purchased $500 of office supplies on credit.
d. A. Nuncio invested an automobile in the company. The automobile has a value of $8,000.
e. The company purchased $1,200 of additional office equipment on credit.
f. The company paid $1,000 cash salary to an assistant.
g. The company provided services to a client and collected $3,200 cash.
h. The company paid $540 cash for this month's utilities.
i. The company paid $500 cash to settle the payable created in transaction *c*.
j. The company purchased $3,400 of new office equipment by paying $3,400 cash.
k. The company completed $4,200 of services on credit for a client, who must pay within 30 days.
l. The company paid $1,000 cash salary to an assistant.
m. The company received $2,200 cash in partial payment on the receivable created in transaction *k*.
n. A. Nuncio withdrew $1,100 cash from the company for personal use.

Required

1. Prepare general journal entries to record these transactions (use account titles listed in part 2).
2. Open the following ledger accounts—their account numbers are in parentheses (use the balance column format): Cash (101); Accounts Receivable (106); Office Supplies (108); Office Equipment (163); Automobiles (164); Building (170); Land (172); Accounts Payable (201); Notes Payable (250); A. Nuncio, Capital (301); A. Nuncio, Withdrawals (302); Consulting Revenue (403); Salaries Expense (601); and Utilities Expense (602). Post the journal entries from part 1 to the ledger accounts and enter the balance after each posting.
3. Prepare a trial balance as of the end of June.

Check (2) Ending balances: Cash, $17,860; Office Equipment, $15,600

(3) Trial balance totals, $95,100

Problem 2-5B
Computing net income from equity analysis, preparing a balance sheet, and computing the debt ratio

P1 A2

The accounting records of Tama Co. show the following assets and liabilities as of December 31 for Year 1 and for Year 2.

December 31	Year 1	Year 2	December 31	Year 1	Year 2
Cash	$30,000	$ 5,000	Building	$ 0	$250,000
Accounts receivable	35,000	25,000	Land	0	50,000
Office supplies	8,000	13,500	Accounts payable	4,000	12,000
Office equipment	40,000	40,000	Note payable	0	250,000
Machinery	28,000	28,500			

Required

1. Prepare balance sheets for the business as of December 31 for Year 1 and Year 2. *Hint:* Report only total equity on the balance sheet and remember that total equity equals the difference between assets and liabilities.
2. Compute net income for Year 2 by comparing total equity amounts for these two years and using the following information: During Year 2, the owner invested $5,000 additional cash in the business and withdrew $3,000 cash for personal use.
3. Compute the Year 2 debt ratio.

Check (2) Net income, $11,000

(3) Debt ratio, 63.6%

Problem 2-6B
Analyzing account balances and reconstructing transactions

P1 A1

Roshaun Gould started a web consulting firm called Gould Solutions. He began operations and completed seven transactions in April that resulted in the following accounts, which all have normal balances.

Cash	$20,000	Office equipment	$12,250	R. Gould, Withdrawals	$ 5,200
Office supplies	750	Accounts payable	12,250	Consulting revenue	20,400
Prepaid rent	1,800	R. Gould, Capital	15,000	Miscellaneous expenses	7,650

Required

1. Prepare a trial balance for this business as of the end of April.
2. The following seven transactions produced the account balances shown above.
   a. Gould invested $15,000 cash in the business.
   b. Paid $1,800 cash in advance for next month's rent expense.
   c. Paid $7,650 cash for miscellaneous expenses.
   d. Purchased office supplies for $750 cash.
   e. Purchased $12,250 of office equipment on credit (with accounts payable).
   f. Received $20,400 cash for consulting services provided in April.
   g. Gould withdrew $5,200 cash from the company for personal use.

   Prepare a Cash T-account, enter the cash effects (if any) of each transaction, and compute the ending Cash balance. Code each entry in the T-account with one of the transaction codes *a* through *g*.

Check (1) Trial balance totals, $47,650
(2) Ending Cash balance, $20,000

Problem 2-7B
Preparing an income statement, statement of owner's equity, and balance sheet

P1

Victoria Rivera owns and manages a consulting firm called Prisek, which began operations on July 1. On July 31, the company's records show the following selected accounts and amounts for the month of July.

Cash	$24,000	Accounts payable	$ 3,900	Rental revenue	$1,500
Accounts receivable	10,500	Notes payable	7,200	Salaries expense	9,000
Notes receivable	7,500	Unearned revenue	900	Rent expense	6,000
Office supplies	4,500	V. Rivera, Capital	34,800	Advertising expense	1,200
Prepaid insurance	3,000	V. Rivera, Withdrawals	6,000	Utilities expense	600
Equipment	12,000	Consulting revenue	36,000		

[continued on next page]

[continued from previous page]

Required

1. Prepare a July income statement for the business.
2. Prepare a July statement of owner's equity. The V. Rivera, Capital account balance at July 1 was $0, and the owner invested $34,800 cash in the company on July 2.
3. Prepare a July 31 balance sheet. *Hint:* Use the V. Rivera, Capital account balance calculated in part 2.

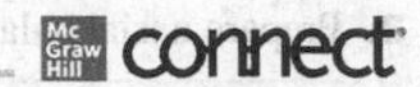

SERIAL PROBLEM

Business Solutions

P1 A1

Serial problem started in Chapter 1. If the Chapter 1 segment was not completed, the problem can begin at this point. It is available in ***Connect*** *with an algorithmic option.*

Alexander Image/Shutterstock

SP 2 On October 1, 2021, Santana Rey launched a computer services company called **Business Solutions**, which provides consulting services, computer system installations, and custom program development. The company's initial chart of accounts follows.

Account	No.	Account	No.
Cash	101	S. Rey, Capital	301
Accounts Receivable	106	S. Rey, Withdrawals	302
Computer Supplies	126	Computer Services Revenue	403
Prepaid Insurance	128	Wages Expense	623
Prepaid Rent	131	Advertising Expense	655
Office Equipment	163	Mileage Expense	676
Computer Equipment	167	Miscellaneous Expenses	677
Accounts Payable	201	Repairs Expense—Computer	684

Required

1. Prepare journal entries to record each of the following transactions for Business Solutions.

Oct. 1 S. Rey invested $45,000 cash, a $20,000 computer system, and $8,000 of office equipment in the company.
2 The company paid $3,300 cash for four months' rent. *Hint:* Debit Prepaid Rent for $3,300.
3 The company purchased $1,420 of computer supplies on credit from Harris Office Products.
5 The company paid $2,220 cash for one year's premium on a property and liability insurance policy. *Hint:* Debit Prepaid Insurance for $2,220.
6 The company billed Easy Leasing $4,800 for services performed in installing a new web server.
8 The company paid $1,420 cash for the computer supplies purchased from Harris Office Products on October 3.
10 The company hired Lyn Addie as a part-time assistant.
12 The company billed Easy Leasing another $1,400 for services performed.
15 The company received $4,800 cash from Easy Leasing as partial payment on its account.
17 The company paid $805 cash to repair computer equipment that was damaged when moving it.
20 The company paid $1,728 cash for advertisements.
22 The company received $1,400 cash from Easy Leasing on its account.
28 The company billed IFM Company $5,208 for services performed.
31 The company paid $875 cash for Lyn Addie's wages for seven days' work.
31 S. Rey withdrew $3,600 cash from the company for personal use.

Nov. 1 The company paid $320 cash for mileage expenses.
2 The company received $4,633 cash from Liu Corporation for computer services performed.
5 The company purchased computer supplies for $1,125 cash from Harris Office Products.
8 The company billed Gomez Co. $5,668 for services performed.
13 The company agreed to perform future services for Alex's Engineering Co. No work has yet been performed.
18 The company received $2,208 cash from IFM Company as partial payment of the October 28 bill.
22 The company paid $250 cash for miscellaneous expenses. *Hint:* Debit Miscellaneous Expenses for $250.
24 The company completed work and sent a bill for $3,950 to Alex's Engineering Co.
25 The company sent another bill to IFM Company for the past-due amount of $3,000.

28 The company paid $384 cash for mileage expenses.
30 The company paid $1,750 cash for Lyn Addie's wages for 14 days' work.
30 S. Rey withdrew $2,000 cash from the company for personal use.

2. Open ledger accounts (in balance column format) and post the journal entries from part 1 to them.
3. Prepare a trial balance as of the end of November.

Check (2) Cash, Nov. 30 bal., $38,264
(3) Trial bal. totals, $98,659

Mc Graw Hill **connect**

TABLEAU DASHBOARD ACTIVITIES

Tableau Dashboard Activities expose students to accounting analytics using visual displays. These assignments (1) do not require instructors to know Tableau, (2) are accessible to introductory students, (3) do not require Tableau software, and (4) run in **Connect**. All are auto-gradable.

Tableau DA 2-1 Quick Study, Identifying normal balance, **C2**—similar to QS 2-4 and 2-5.

Tableau DA 2-2 Exercise, Preparing an income statement, **P1**—similar to QS 2-15.

Tableau DA 2-3 Mini-Case, Preparing an income statement, statement of owner's equity, and balance sheet, **P1**—similar to Exercises 2-25, 2-26, and 2-27.

GENERAL LEDGER

General Ledger (GL) Assignments expose students to general ledger software similar to that in practice. **GL** is part of **Connect**, and **GL** assignments are auto-gradable and have algorithmic options. For the following **GL** assignments, we prepare journal entries and identify the financial statement impacts of each entry. Financial statements are automatically generated based on the journal entries recorded—this feature can be turned off.

GL 2-1 Based on FastForward
GL 2-2 Based on Exercise 2-13
GL 2-3 Based on Exercise 2-16
GL 2-4 Based on Problem 2-1A

For the following **GL** assignments, we record journal entries, create financial statements, and assess the impact of each transaction on financial statements.

GL 2-5 Based on Problem 2-2A
GL 2-6 Based on Problem 2-3A
GL 2-7 Based on Problem 2-4A
GL 2-8 Based on the Serial Problem SP 2

Accounting Analysis

Mc Graw Hill **connect**

COMPANY ANALYSIS A2

AA 2-1 Refer to **Apple**'s financial statements in Appendix A for the following questions.

Required

1. What amount of total liabilities does Apple report for each of the fiscal years ended (*a*) September 28, 2019, and (*b*) September 29, 2018?
2. What amount of total assets does it report for each of the fiscal years ended (*a*) September 28, 2019, and (*b*) September 29, 2018?
3. Compute its debt ratio for each of the fiscal years ended (*a*) September 28, 2019, and (*b*) September 29, 2018. (Report ratio in percent and round it to one decimal.)
4. In which fiscal year did it employ more financial leverage: the year ending September 28, 2019, or September 29, 2018? Explain.

COMPARATIVE ANALYSIS A2

AA 2-2 Key comparative figures for **Apple** and **Google** follow.

	Apple		Google	
$ millions	Current Year	Prior Year	Current Year	Prior Year
Total liabilities	$248,028	$258,578	$ 74,467	$ 55,164
Total assets	338,516	365,725	275,909	232,792

1. What is the debt ratio for Apple in the current year and for the prior year?
2. What is the debt ratio for Google in the current year and for the prior year?
3. Which of the two companies has the higher degree of financial leverage in the current year?

EXTENDED ANALYSIS
A2

AA 2-3 Key comparative figures for **Apple**, **Google**, and **Samsung** follow.

	Samsung		Apple	Google
$ millions	Current Year	Prior Year	Current Year	Current Year
Total liabilities..........	$ 76,952	$ 78,599	$248,028	$ 74,467
Total assets............	302,511	291,179	338,516	275,909

Required

1. Compute Samsung's debt ratio for the current year and prior year.
2. Did Samsung's financial leverage increase or decrease in the current year?
3. Looking at the current year debt ratio, is Samsung a more risky or less risky investment than (*a*) Apple and (*b*) Google?

Discussion Questions

1. Provide the names of two (*a*) asset accounts, (*b*) liability accounts, and (*c*) equity accounts.
2. What is the difference between a note payable and an account payable?
3. Discuss the steps in processing business transactions.
4. What kinds of transactions can be recorded in a general journal?
5. Are debits or credits typically listed first in general journal entries? Are the debits or the credits indented?
6. Should a transaction be recorded first in a journal or the ledger? Why?
7. If assets are valuable resources and asset accounts have debit balances, why do expense accounts also have debit balances?
8. Why does the recordkeeper prepare a trial balance?
9. If an incorrect amount is journalized and posted to the accounts, how should the error be corrected?
10. Identify the four financial statements of a business.
11. What information is reported in a balance sheet?
12. What information is reported in an income statement?
13. Why does the user of an income statement need to know the time period that it covers?
14. Define (*a*) *assets*, (*b*) *liabilities*, and (*c*) *equity*.
15. Which financial statement is sometimes called the *statement of financial position?*

Beyond the Numbers

ETHICS CHALLENGE
C1

BTN 2-1 Assume that you are a cashier and your manager requires that you immediately enter each sale when it occurs. Recently, lunch hour traffic has increased and the assistant manager asks you to avoid delays by taking customers' cash and making change without entering sales. The assistant manager says she will add up cash and enter sales after lunch. She says that, in this way, customers will be happy and the register record will always match the cash amount when the manager arrives at three o'clock.

The advantages to the process proposed by the assistant manager include improved customer service, fewer delays, and less work for you. The disadvantage is that the assistant manager could steal cash by simply recording less sales than the cash received and then pocketing the excess cash. You decide to reject her suggestion without the manager's approval and to confront her on the ethics of her suggestion.

Required

Propose and evaluate two other courses of action you might consider, and explain why.

COMMUNICATING IN PRACTICE
P1

BTN 2-2 Lila Corentine is an aspiring entrepreneur and your friend. She is having difficulty understanding the purposes of financial statements and how they fit together across time.

Required

Write a one-page memorandum to Corentine explaining the purposes of the four financial statements and how they are linked across time.

TAKING IT TO THE NET

P1

BTN 2-3 Access EDGAR online (sec.gov/edgar) and locate the 2018 10-K report of **Amazon.com** (ticker: AMZN) filed on February 1, 2019. Review its financial statements reported for years ended 2018, 2017, and 2016 to answer the following questions.

Required

1. What are the amounts of Amazon's net income or net loss reported for each of these three years?
2. Do Amazon's operating activities provide cash or use cash for each of these three years? *Hint:* See the statement of cash flows.
3. If Amazon has 2018 net income of $10,073 million and 2018 operating cash flows of $30,723 million, how is it possible that its cash balance at December 31, 2018, increases by only $10,317 million relative to its balance at December 31, 2017?

TEAMWORK IN ACTION

C1 C2 A1

BTN 2-4 The expanded accounting equation consists of assets, liabilities, owner capital, withdrawals, revenues, and expenses. It can be used to reveal insights into changes in a company's financial position.

Required

1. Form *learning teams* of six (or more) members. Each team member must select one of the six components, and each team must have at least one expert on each component: (*a*) assets, (*b*) liabilities, (*c*) owner capital, (*d*) withdrawals, (*e*) revenues, and (*f*) expenses.
2. Form *expert teams* of individuals who selected the same component in part 1. Expert teams are to draft a report that each expert will present to his or her learning team addressing the following:
   - **a.** Identify for its component the (i) increase and decrease sides of the account and (ii) normal balance side of the account.
   - **b.** Describe a transaction, with amounts, that increases its component.
   - **c.** Using the transaction and amounts in (*b*), verify the equality of the accounting equation and then explain any effects on the income statement and statement of cash flows.
   - **d.** Describe a transaction, with amounts, that decreases its component.
   - **e.** Using the transaction and amounts in (*d*), verify the equality of the accounting equation and then explain any effects on the income statement and statement of cash flows.
3. Each expert should return to his/her learning team. In rotation, each member presents his/her expert team's report to the learning team. Team discussion is encouraged.

ENTREPRENEURIAL DECISION

P1 A2

BTN 2-5 Assume that Katrina Lake of **Stitch Fix** plans to expand her business to accommodate more product lines. She is considering financing expansion in one of two ways: (1) contributing more of her own funds to the business or (2) borrowing the funds from a bank.

Required

Identify at least two issues that Katrina should consider when trying to decide on the method for financing the expansion.

ENTREPRENEURIAL DECISION

P1 A2

BTN 2-6 Angel Martin is a young entrepreneur who operates Martin Music Services, offering singing lessons and instruction on musical instruments. Martin wishes to expand but needs a $30,000 loan. The bank requests that Martin prepare a balance sheet and key financial ratios. Martin has not kept formal records but is able to provide the following accounts and their amounts as of December 31.

Cash	$ 3,600	Accounts receivable	$ 9,600	Prepaid insurance	$ 1,500
Prepaid rent	9,400	Store supplies	6,600	Equipment	50,000
Accounts payable	2,200	Unearned lesson fees	15,600	Total equity*	62,900
Annual net income	40,000				

*The total equity amount reflects all owner investments, withdrawals, revenues, and expenses as of December 31.

Required

1. Prepare a balance sheet as of December 31 for Martin Music Services. (Report only the total equity amount on the balance sheet.)
2. Compute Martin's debt ratio and its return on assets (the latter ratio is defined in Chapter 1). Assume average assets equal its ending balance.
3. Do you believe the prospects of a $30,000 bank loan are good? Why or why not?

3 Adjusting Accounts for Financial Statements

Chapter Preview

DEFERRAL OF EXPENSE	DEFERRAL OF REVENUE	ACCRUED EXPENSE	ACCRUED REVENUE	REPORTING
C1 Timing Accrual vs. cash 3-Step process **P1** Framework Examples	**P2** Framework Examples	**P3** Framework Examples	**P4** Framework Examples Summary	**P5** Adjusted trial balance Financial statements **A1** Profit margin
NTK 3-1	**NTK 3-2**	**NTK 3-3**	**NTK 3-4**	**NTK 3-5**

Learning Objectives

CONCEPTUAL

C1 Explain the importance of periodic reporting and the role of accrual accounting.

ANALYTICAL

A1 Compute and analyze profit margin.

PROCEDURAL

P1 Prepare adjusting entries for deferral of expenses.

P2 Prepare adjusting entries for deferral of revenues.

P3 Prepare adjusting entries for accrued expenses.

P4 Prepare adjusting entries for accrued revenues.

P5 Prepare financial statements from an adjusted trial balance.

P6 *Appendix 3A*—Explain the alternatives in accounting for prepaids.

Leading the Way

"Whatever you dream, you can do"

—Emily Núñez Cavness

DENVER—Emily Núñez Cavness co-founded **Sword & Plough** (**SwordandPlough.com**) while deployed in Afghanistan. "It was not the usual startup location," recalls Emily as she describes a Skype meeting interrupted by mortar fire. Emily and her sister Betsy recycle military surplus materials to create totes, handbags, backpacks, and accessories. The sisters reuse materials that "would otherwise be burned or buried."

Emily and Betsy have already recycled 30,000 pounds of materials. They stress their success is in part due to the accounting system. "We were able to pinpoint some immediate problems to solve," explains Emily. They describe how moving from a cash to an accrual system gave more timely information. Emily insists the information "didn't just stay stored on my iPhone, or scrap piece of paper—we took action!"

Accounting adjustments that increased the value of revenue and expense data were used to better set prices and manage costs. Accounting analytics helped Emily and Betsy with business decisions and overall idea development. "We took the idea seriously," exclaims Emily, "and today . . . [it is] a powerful reality."

Bart Young/Invision for Intuit/AP Images

"It has been challenging," admits Emily. "I want Sword & Plough to be a leader in the field of social entrepreneurship." Hoo-ah!

Sources: *Sword & Plough website*, January 2021; *ABC News*, August 2014; *Military Times*, September 2015; *NationSwell*, January 2016; *HuffPost*, October 2017; *Facebook*, 2019

TIMING AND REPORTING

The Accounting Period

C1 Explain the importance of periodic reporting and the role of accrual accounting.

The value of information is linked to its timeliness. Useful information must reach decision makers frequently. To provide timely information, accounting systems prepare reports at regular intervals. The **time period assumption** presumes that an organization's activities can be divided into specific time periods such as a month, a three-month quarter, a six-month interval, or a year. Exhibit 3.1 shows various **accounting,** or *reporting,* **periods.** Most organizations use a year as their primary accounting period. Reports covering a one-year period are known as **annual financial statements.** Many organizations also prepare **interim financial statements** covering one, three, or six months of activity.

EXHIBIT 3.1

Accounting Periods

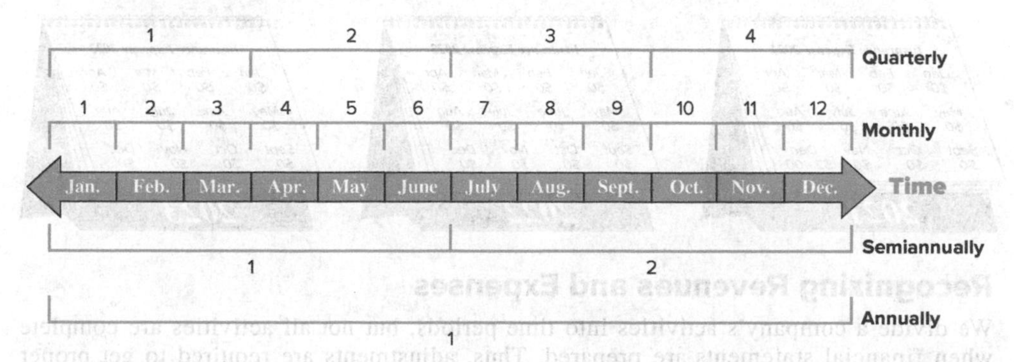

The annual reporting period is not always a calendar year ending on December 31. An organization can use a **fiscal year** consisting of any 12 consecutive months or 52 weeks. For example, **Gap**'s fiscal year consistently ends the final week of January or the first week of February each year.

Companies with little seasonal variation in sales often use the calendar year as their fiscal year. **Netflix** uses calendar-year reporting. Companies that have seasonal variations in sales often use a **natural business year** end, which is when sales are at their lowest level for the year. The natural business year for retailers such as **Target** and **Nordstrom** ends around January 31, after the holidays.

Accrual Basis versus Cash Basis

After external transactions and events are recorded, several accounts require adjustments before their balances appear in financial statements. This is needed because internal transactions and events are not yet recorded.

- **Accrual basis accounting** records revenues when services and products are delivered and records expenses when incurred (matched with revenues).
- **Cash basis accounting** records revenues when cash is received and records expenses when cash is paid. Cash basis income is cash receipts minus cash payments.

Most agree that accrual accounting better reflects business performance than cash basis accounting. Accrual accounting also increases the *comparability* of financial statements from period to period.

Accrual Basis To compare these two systems, let's consider FastForward's Prepaid Insurance account. FastForward paid $2,400 for 24 months of insurance coverage that began on December 1, 2021. Accrual accounting requires that $100 of insurance expense be reported each month, from December 2021 through November 2023. (This means expenses are $100 in 2021, $1,200 in 2022, and $1,100 in 2023.) Exhibit 3.2 shows this allocation of insurance cost across the three years. Any unexpired premium is reported as a Prepaid Insurance asset on the accrual basis balance sheet.

EXHIBIT 3.2

Accrual Accounting

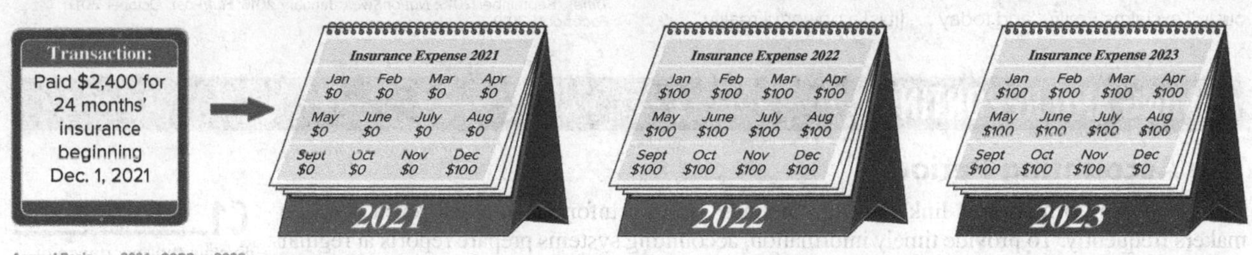

Accrual Basis	2021	2022	2023
Insurance expense .	$100	$1,200	$1,100

Cash Basis A *cash basis* income statement for December 2021 reports insurance expense of $2,400, as shown in Exhibit 3.3. The cash basis income statements for years 2022 and 2023 report no insurance expense. The cash basis balance sheet never reports a prepaid insurance asset because it is immediately expensed. Also, cash basis income for 2021–2023 does not match the cost of insurance with the insurance benefits received for those years.

EXHIBIT 3.3

Cash Accounting

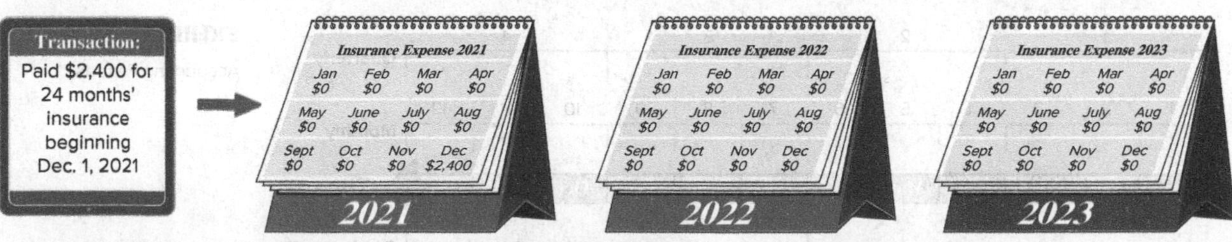

Cash Basis	2021	2022	2023
Insurance expense . . .	$2,400	$0	$0

Recognizing Revenues and Expenses

We divide a company's activities into time periods, but not all activities are complete when financial statements are prepared. Thus, adjustments are required to get proper account balances.

We use two principles in the adjusting process: revenue recognition and expense recognition.

- **Revenue recognition principle** requires that revenue be recorded when goods or services are provided to customers and at an amount expected to be received from customers. Adjustments ensure revenue is recognized (reported) in the time period when those services and products are provided.
- **Expense recognition** (or **matching**) **principle** requires that expenses be recorded in the same accounting period as the revenues that are recognized as a result of those expenses.

Framework for Adjustments

Four types of adjustments exist for transactions and events that extend over more than one period.

Deferral of expense | Deferral of revenue | Accrued expense | Accrued revenue

Adjustments are made using a 3-step process, as shown in Exhibit 3.4.

EXHIBIT 3.4

Three-Step Process for Adjusting Entries

Step 1: **Determine what the current account balance *equals.***

Step 2: **Determine what the current account balance *should equal.***

Step 3: **Record an adjusting entry to get from step 1 to step 2.**

Each **adjusting entry** made at the end of an accounting period reflects a transaction or event that is not yet recorded. An adjusting entry affects one or more income statement accounts *and* one or more balance sheet accounts (but never the Cash account).

DEFERRAL OF EXPENSE

P1 Prepare adjusting entries for deferral of expenses.

Prepaid expenses, or *deferred expenses,* are assets *paid for* in advance of receiving their benefits. When these assets are used, those advance payments become expenses.

Framework Adjusting entries for prepaid expenses increase expenses and decrease assets, as shown in the T-accounts of Exhibit 3.5. This adjustment shows the using up of prepaid expenses. To demonstrate accounting for prepaid expenses, we look at prepaid insurance, supplies, and depreciation. In each case we decrease an asset (balance sheet) account and increase an expense (income statement) account.

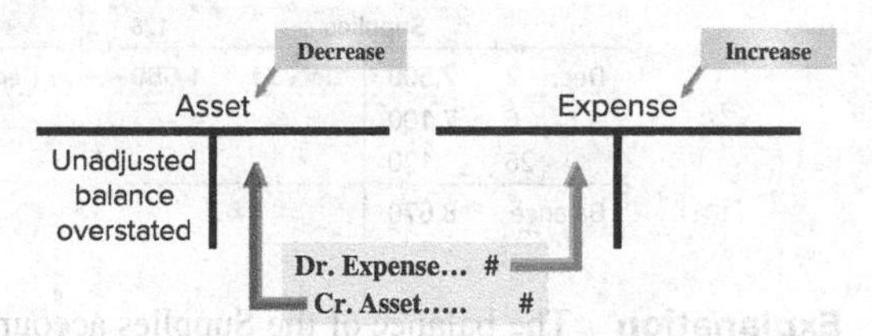

EXHIBIT 3.5

Adjusting for Prepaid Expenses (decrease an asset and increase expense)

Prepaid Insurance

Prepaid insurance expires with time. We use our three-step process.

Step 1: We determine that the current balance of FastForward's prepaid insurance is equal to its $2,400 payment for 24 months of insurance benefits that began on December 1, 2021.

Step 2: The benefits of the insurance expire over time and a portion of the Prepaid Insurance asset becomes expense. For FastForward, one month's insurance coverage expires by December 31, 2021. This expense is $100, or 1/24 of $2,400, which leaves $2,300.

Step 3: The adjusting entry to record this expense and reduce the asset, along with T-account postings, follows.

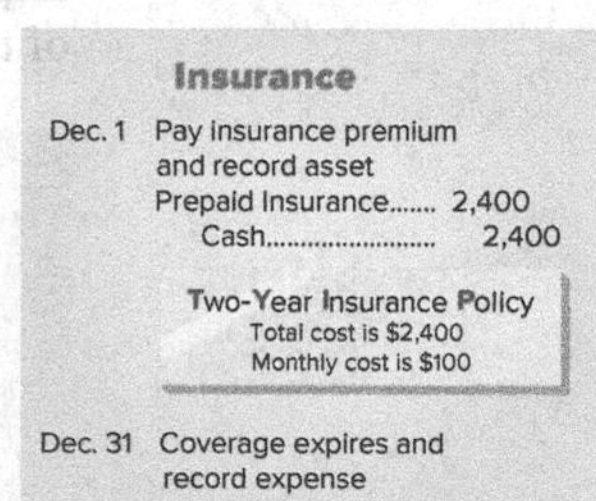

Insurance
Dec. 1 Pay insurance premium and record asset
Prepaid Insurance....... 2,400
Cash........................ 2,400
Two-Year Insurance Policy
Total cost is $2,400
Monthly cost is $100
Dec. 31 Coverage expires and record expense

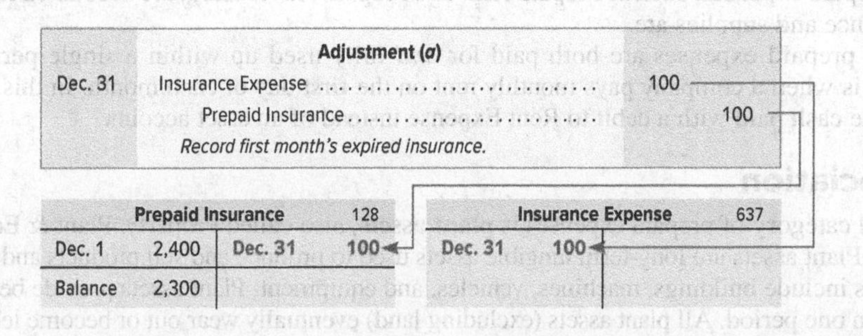

Adjustment (*a*)

Dec. 31	Insurance Expense	100	
	Prepaid Insurance		100
	Record first month's expired insurance.		

Prepaid Insurance			128
Dec. 1	2,400	Dec. 31	100
Balance	2,300		

Insurance Expense			637
Dec. 31	100		

Assets = Liabilities + Equity
−100 −100

Explanation After adjusting and posting, the $100 balance in Insurance Expense and the $2,300 balance in Prepaid Insurance are ready for reporting in financial statements. The following highlights the adjustment for prepaid insurance.

Before Adjustment	Adjustment	After Adjustment
Prepaid Insurance = $2,400	**Deduct $100 from Prepaid Insurance Add $100 to Insurance Expense**	**Prepaid Insurance = $2,300**
Reports $2,400 policy for 24 months' coverage.	Record current month's $100 insurance expense and $100 reduction in prepaid.	Reports $2,300 in coverage for remaining 23 months.

Supplies

We count supplies at period-end and make an adjusting entry.

Supplies
Dec. 2,6,26 Purchase supplies and record asset
Dec. 31 Physical count
Dec. 31 Record expense

Step 1: FastForward purchased $9,720 of supplies in December, some of which were used during that same month. When financial statements are prepared at December 31, the cost of supplies used during December is expensed.

Step 2: When FastForward computes (physically counts) its remaining unused supplies at December 31, it finds $8,670 of supplies remaining of the $9,720 total supplies. The $1,050 difference between these two amounts is December's supplies expense.

Step 3: The adjusting entry to record this expense and reduce the Supplies asset account, along with T-account postings, follows.

Assets = Liabilities + Equity
−1,050 −1,050

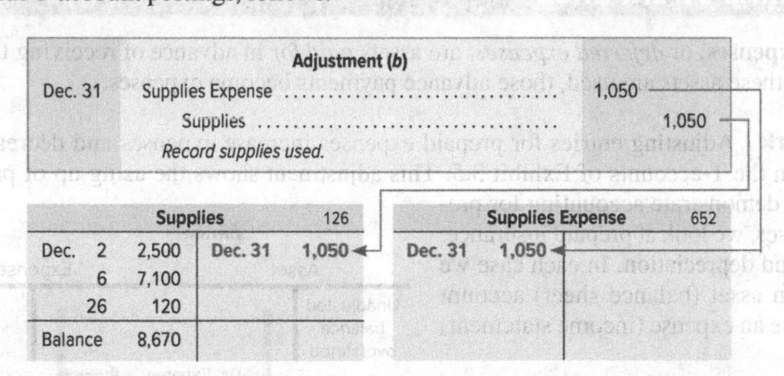

Adjustment (b)

Dec. 31	Supplies Expense	1,050	
	Supplies		1,050
	Record supplies used.		

Supplies 126

Dec. 2	2,500	Dec. 31	1,050
6	7,100		
26	120		
Balance	8,670		

Supplies Expense 652

Dec. 31	1,050		

Explanation The balance of the Supplies account is $8,670 after posting—equaling the cost of the remaining supplies. The following highlights the adjustment for supplies.

Before Adjustment	Adjustment	After Adjustment
Supplies = $9,720	**Deduct $1,050 from Supplies Add $1,050 to Supplies Expense**	**Supplies = $8,670**
Reports $9,720 in supplies.	Record $1,050 in supplies used and $1,050 as supplies expense.	Reports $8,670 in supplies.

Other Prepaid Expenses

Other prepaid expenses, such as Prepaid Rent and Prepaid Advertising, are accounted for exactly as insurance and supplies are.

Some prepaid expenses are both paid for *and* fully used up within a single period. One example is when a company pays monthly rent on the first day of each month. In this case, we record the cash paid with a debit to Rent Expense instead of an asset account.

Depreciation

A special category of prepaid expenses is **plant assets,** also called Property, Plant & Equipment (PP&E). Plant assets are long-term tangible assets used to produce and sell products and services. Examples include buildings, machines, vehicles, and equipment. Plant assets provide benefits for more than one period. All plant assets (excluding land) eventually wear out or become less useful.

The costs of plant assets are gradually reported as expenses in the income statement over the assets' useful lives (benefit periods). **Depreciation** is the allocation of the costs of these assets over their expected useful lives, but it does not necessarily measure decline in market value. Depreciation expense is recorded with an adjusting entry similar to that for other prepaid expenses.

Point: An asset's expected value at the end of its useful life is called *salvage value*.

Step 1: FastForward purchased equipment for $26,000 in early December to use in earning revenue. This equipment's cost must be depreciated.

Step 2: The equipment is expected to have a useful life (benefit period) of five years and to be worth about $8,000 at the end of five years. This means the *net* cost of this equipment over its useful life is $18,000 ($26,000 − $8,000). FastForward depreciates it using **straight-line depreciation,** which allocates equal amounts of the asset's net cost to depreciation during its useful life. Dividing the $18,000 net cost by the 60 months (5 years) in the asset's useful life gives a monthly cost of $300 ($18,000/60).

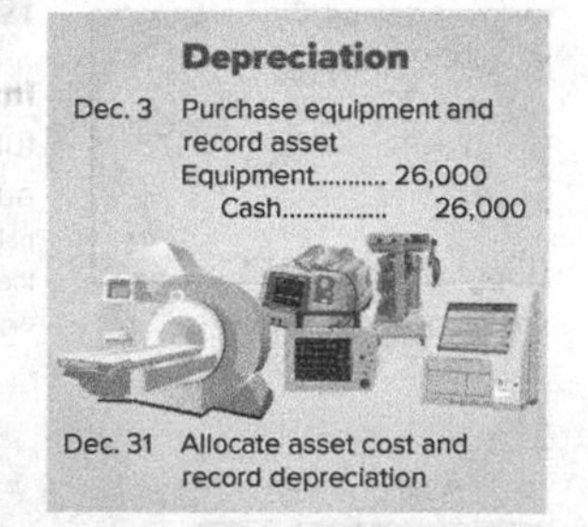

Depreciation
Dec. 3 Purchase equipment and record asset
Equipment.......... 26,000
Cash.................. 26,000
Dec. 31 Allocate asset cost and record depreciation

Step 3: The adjusting entry to record monthly depreciation expense, along with T-account postings, follows.

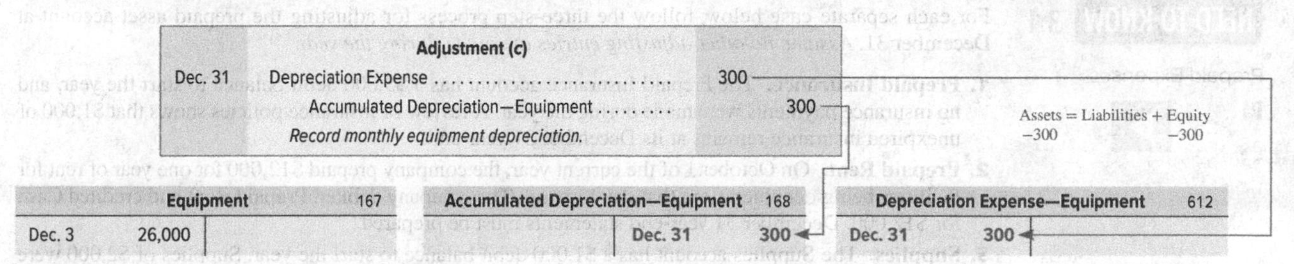

Explanation After posting the adjustment, the Equipment account ($26,000) minus its Accumulated Depreciation ($300) account equals the $25,700 net cost. The $300 balance in the Depreciation Expense account is reported in the December income statement. The following highlights the adjustment for depreciation.

Before Adjustment	Adjustment	After Adjustment
Equipment, net = $26,000	**Deduct $300 from Equipment, net** **Add $300 to Depreciation Expense**	**Equipment, net = $25,700**
Reports $26,000 in equipment.	Record $300 in depreciation and $300 as accumulated depreciation.	Reports $25,700 in equipment, net of accumulated depreciation.

Accumulated Depreciation is a separate contra account and has a normal credit balance. A **contra account** is an account linked with another account, it has an opposite normal balance, and it is reported as a subtraction from that other account's balance. FastForward's contra account of Accumulated Depreciation—Equipment is subtracted from the Equipment account in the balance sheet.

The Accumulated Depreciation contra account includes total depreciation expense for all prior periods for which the asset was used. To demonstrate, on February 28, 2022, after three months of adjusting entries, the Equipment and Accumulated Depreciation accounts appear as in Exhibit 3.6. The $900 balance in the Accumulated Depreciation account is subtracted from its related $26,000 asset cost. The difference ($25,100) between these two balances is called **book value,** or *net amount,* which is the asset's costs minus its accumulated depreciation.

EXHIBIT 3.6

Accounts after 3 Months of Depreciation

Equipment			167
Dec. 3	26,000		

Accumulated Depreciation—Equipment			168
		Dec. 31	300
		Jan. 31	300
		Feb. 28	300
		Balance	**900**

These account balances are reported in the assets section of the February 28 balance sheet. Exhibit 3.7 shows two ways to report plant assets.

EXHIBIT 3.7

Reporting Equipment and Accumulated Depreciation

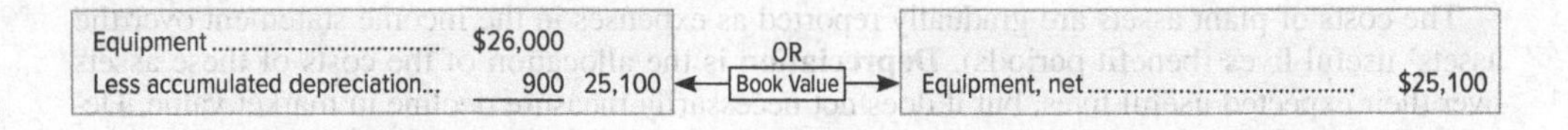

Equipment	$26,000		OR		
Less accumulated depreciation	900	25,100	← Book Value →	Equipment, net	$25,100

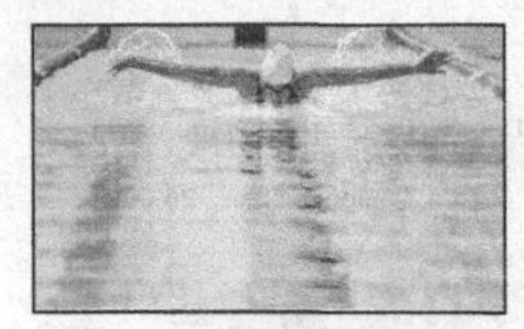

Caia Image/Image Source

Decision Maker

Investor A publisher signs an Olympic athlete to write a book. The company pays the athlete $500,000 to sign plus future book royalties. A note to the company's financial statements says, "prepaid expenses include $500,000 in author signing fees to be matched against future expected sales." How does this affect your analysis? ■ *Answer:* Prepaid expenses are assets paid for in advance of receiving their benefits–they are expensed as they are used up. As an investor, you are concerned about the risk of future book sales. The riskier the likelihood of future book sales is, the more likely your analysis is to treat the $500,000, or a portion of it, as an expense, not a prepaid expense (asset).

NEED-TO-KNOW 3-1

Prepaid Expenses

P1

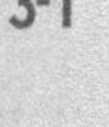

For each separate case below, follow the three-step process for adjusting the prepaid asset account at December 31. *Assume no other adjusting entries are made during the year.*

1. **Prepaid Insurance.** The Prepaid Insurance account has a $5,000 debit balance to start the year, and no insurance payments were made during the year. A review of insurance policies shows that $1,000 of unexpired insurance remains at its December 31 year-end.
2. **Prepaid Rent.** On October 1 of the current year, the company prepaid $12,000 for one year of rent for facilities being occupied from that day forward. The company debited Prepaid Rent and credited Cash for $12,000. December 31 year-end statements must be prepared.
3. **Supplies.** The Supplies account has a $1,000 debit balance to start the year. Supplies of $2,000 were purchased during the current year and debited to the Supplies account. A December 31 physical count shows $500 of supplies remaining.
4. **Accumulated Depreciation.** The company has only one plant asset (equipment) that it purchased at the start of this year. That asset had cost $38,000, had an estimated life of 10 years, and is expected to be valued at $8,000 at the end of the 10-year life. December 31 year-end statements must be prepared.

Solution

1. Step 1: Prepaid Insurance equals $5,000 (before adjustment)
   Step 2: Prepaid Insurance should equal $1,000 (the unexpired part)
   Step 3: Adjusting entry to get from step 1 to step 2

Dec. 31	Insurance Expense	4,000	
	Prepaid Insurance		4,000
	Record expired insurance coverage ($5,000 – $1,000).		

2. Step 1: Prepaid Rent equals $12,000 (before adjustment)
   Step 2: Prepaid Rent should equal $9,000 (the unexpired part)*
   Step 3: Adjusting entry to get from step 1 to step 2

Dec. 31	Rent Expense	3,000	
	Prepaid Rent		3,000
	*Record expired prepaid rent. *$12,000 – $3,000 = $9,000, where $3,000 is from: ($12,000/12 months) × 3 months*		

3. Step 1: Supplies equal $3,000 (from $1,000 + $2,000; before adjustment)
   Step 2: Supplies should equal $500 (what's left)
   Step 3: Adjusting entry to get from step 1 to step 2*

Dec. 31	Supplies Expense	2,500	
	Supplies		2,500
	*Record supplies used. *$1,000 + $2,000 purchased – $500 remaining = **$ 2,500** supplies used*		

4. Step 1: Accumulated Depreciation equals $0 (before adjustment)
   Step 2: Accumulated Depreciation should equal $3,000 (after current-period depreciation of $3,000)*
   Step 3: Adjusting entry to get from step 1 to step 2

Dec. 31	Depreciation Expense—Equipment	3,000	
	Accumulated Depreciation—Equipment.		3,000
	*Record depreciation for period. *($38,000 – $8,000)/10 years*		

Do More: QS 3-5, QS 3-6, QS 3-7, QS 3-8, QS 3-9

DEFERRAL OF REVENUE

P2 Prepare adjusting entries for deferral of revenues.

Unearned revenue is cash received in advance of providing products and services. Unearned revenues, or *deferred revenues,* are liabilities. When cash is accepted, an obligation to provide products or services is accepted. We *defer,* or postpone, reporting amounts received as revenues until the product or service is provided.

Framework As products or services are provided, the liability decreases and the unearned revenues become revenues. Adjusting entries for unearned revenue decrease the unearned revenue (balance sheet) account and increase the revenue (income statement) account, as shown in Exhibit 3.8.

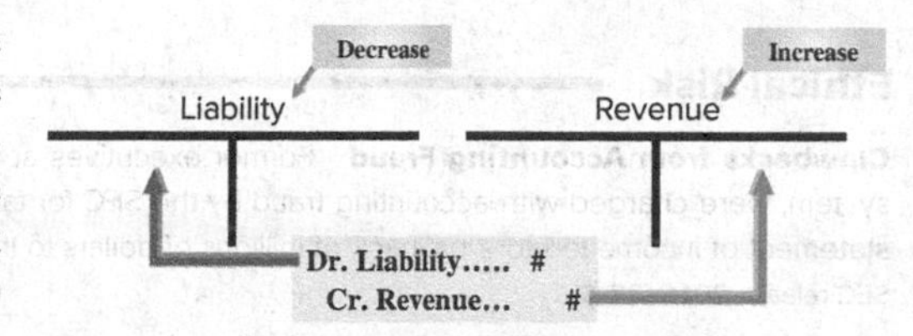

EXHIBIT 3.8 Adjusting for Unearned Revenues (decrease a liability and increase revenue)

Unearned revenues are common in sporting and concert events. When the **Boston Celtics** receive cash from advance ticket sales, they record it in an unearned revenue account called *Deferred Game Revenues.* The Celtics record revenue as games are played.

Unearned Consulting Revenue

FastForward has unearned revenues. The company agreed on December 26 to provide consulting services to a client for 60 days for a fixed fee of $3,000.

Step 1: On December 26, the client paid the 60-day fee in advance, covering the period December 27 to February 24. The entry to record the cash received in advance is

Dec. 26	Cash	3,000	
	Unearned Consulting Revenue..............		3,000
	Received advance payment for services over the next 60 days.		

Assets = Liabilities + Equity
+3,000 +3,000

This advance payment increases cash and creates a liability to do consulting work over the next 60 days (5 days this year and 55 days next year).

Step 2: As time passes, FastForward earns this payment through consulting. By December 31, it has provided five days' service and earned 5/60 of the $3,000 unearned revenue. This amounts to $250 ($3,000 × 5/60). The *revenue recognition principle* requires that $250 of unearned revenue be reported as revenue on the December income statement.

Step 3: The adjusting entry to reduce the liability account and recognize revenue, along with T-account postings, follows.

Unearned Revenues
Dec. 26 Cash received in advance and record liability
Thanks for cash in advance. I'll work now through Feb. 24
Dec. 31 Provided 5 days of services and record revenue

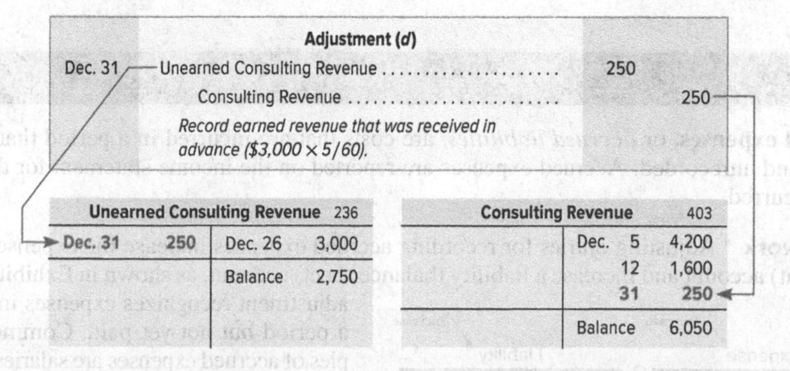

Adjustment (*d*)

Dec. 31	Unearned Consulting Revenue	250	
	Consulting Revenue		250
	Record earned revenue that was received in advance ($3,000 × 5/60).		

Assets = Liabilities + Equity
−250 +250

Unearned Consulting Revenue 236			
Dec. 31	250	Dec. 26	3,000
		Balance	2,750

Consulting Revenue 403			
		Dec. 5	4,200
		12	1,600
		31	250
		Balance	6,050

Explanation The adjusting entry transfers $250 from unearned revenue (a liability account) to a revenue account. The following highlights the adjustment for unearned revenue.

Before Adjustment	Adjustment	After Adjustment
Unearned Consulting Revenue = $3,000	**Deduct $250 from Unearned Consulting Revenue Add $250 to Consulting Revenue**	**Unearned Consulting Revenue = $2,750**
Reports $3,000 in unearned revenue for consulting services promised for 60 days ($50 per day).	Record 5 days of earned consulting revenue, which is 5/60 of unearned amount.	Reports $2,750 in unearned revenue for consulting services owed over next 55 days (55 days × $50 = $2,750).

LifeJourneys/iStock/Getty Images

Ethical Risk

Clawbacks from Accounting Fraud Former executives at **Saba Software**, a cloud-based talent management system, were charged with accounting fraud by the SEC for falsifying revenue to boost income. This alleged overstatement of income led to a payback of millions of dollars to the company by the former CEO and former CFO. See SEC release 2015–28. ■

NEED-TO-KNOW 3-2

Unearned Revenues

P2

For each separate case below, follow the three-step process for adjusting the unearned revenue liability account at December 31. *Assume no other adjusting entries are made during the year.*

a. Unearned Rent Revenue. The company collected $24,000 rent in advance on September 1, debiting Cash and crediting Unearned Rent Revenue. The tenant was paying 12 months' rent in advance and moved in on September 1.

b. Unearned Services Revenue. The company charges $100 per month to spray a house for insects. A customer paid $600 on November 1 in advance for six treatments, which was recorded with a debit to Cash and a credit to Unearned Services Revenue. At year-end, the company has applied two treatments for the customer.

Solution

a. Step 1: Unearned Rent Revenue equals $24,000 (before adjustment)

Step 2: Unearned Rent Revenue should equal $16,000 (current-period earned revenue is $8,000*)

Step 3: Adjusting entry to get from step 1 to step 2

Dec. 31	Unearned Rent Revenue	8,000	
	Rent Revenue		8,000
	*Record earned portion of rent received in advance. *($24,000/12 months) × 4 months' rental usage*		

b. Step 1: Unearned Services Revenue equals $600 (before adjustment)

Step 2: Unearned Services Revenue should equal $400 (current-period earned revenue is $200*)

Step 3: Adjusting entry to get from step 1 to step 2

Dec. 31	Unearned Services Revenue	200	
	Services Revenue		200
	*Record earned portion of revenue received in advance. *$100 × 2 treatments = Services revenue*		

Do More: QS 3-10, QS 3-11, QS 3-12

ACCRUED EXPENSE

P3

Prepare adjusting entries for accrued expenses.

Accrued expenses, or *accrued liabilities,* are costs that are incurred in a period that are both unpaid and unrecorded. Accrued expenses are reported on the income statement for the period when incurred.

Framework Adjusting entries for recording accrued expenses increase the expense (income statement) account and increase a liability (balance sheet) account, as shown in Exhibit 3.9. This adjustment recognizes expenses incurred in a period but not yet paid. Common examples of accrued expenses are salaries, interest, rent, and taxes. We use salaries and interest to show how to adjust accounts for accrued expenses.

EXHIBIT 3.9

Adjusting for Accrued Expenses (increase a liability and increase expense)

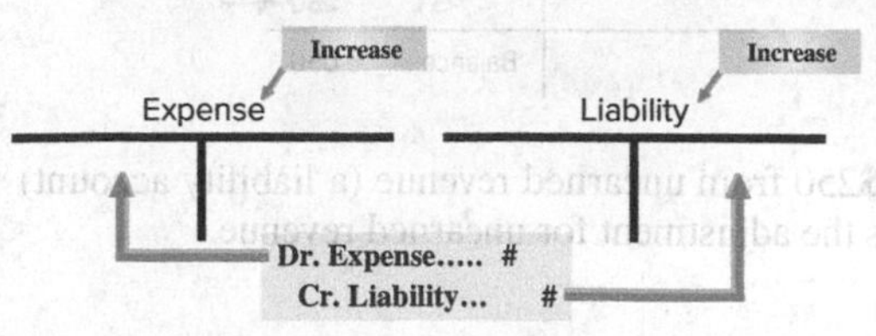

Accrued Salaries Expense

FastForward's employee earns $70 per day, or $350 for a five-day workweek beginning on Monday and ending on Friday.

Step 1: Its employee is paid every two weeks on Friday. On December 12 and 26, the wages are paid, recorded in the journal, and posted to the ledger.

Step 2: The calendar in Exhibit 3.10 shows three working days after the December 26 payday (29, 30, and 31). This means the employee has earned three days' salary by the close of business on Wednesday, December 31, but this salary cost has not been paid or recorded. FastForward must report the added expense and liability for unpaid salary from December 29, 30, and 31.

EXHIBIT 3.10

Salary Accrual and Paydays

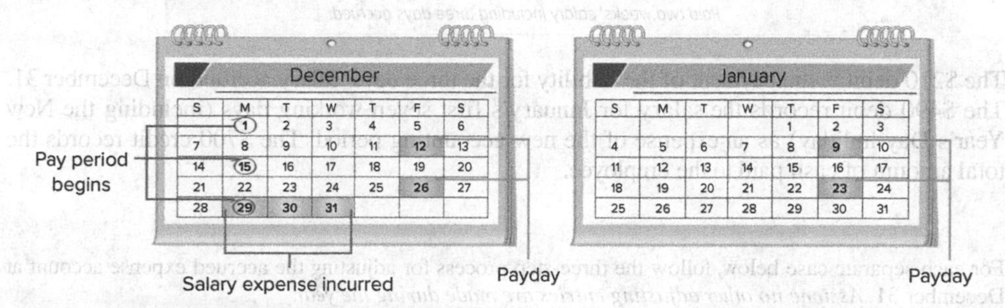

Step 3: The adjusting entry for accrued salaries, along with T-account postings, follows.

Adjustment (e)

Dec. 31	Salaries Expense	210	
	Salaries Payable		210
	Record three days' accrued salary (3 × $70).		

Assets = Liabilities + Equity
+210 −210

Salaries Expense	622		Salaries Payable	209
Dec. 12	700		Dec. 31	210
26	700			
31	210			
Balance	1,610			

Explanation Salaries expense of $1,610 is reported on the December income statement, and $210 of salaries payable (liability) is reported in the balance sheet. The following highlights the adjustment for salaries incurred.

Before Adjustment	Adjustment	After Adjustment
Salaries Payable = $0	**Add $210 to Salaries Payable** **Add $210 to Salaries Expense**	**Salaries Payable = $210**
Reports $0 from employee salaries incurred but not yet paid in cash.	Record 3 days' salaries owed, but not yet paid, at $70 per day.	Reports $210 salaries payable to employee but not yet paid.

Accrued Interest Expense

Companies accrue interest expense on notes payable (loans) and other long-term liabilities at the end of a period. Interest expense is incurred as time passes. Unless interest is paid on the last day of an accounting period, we need to adjust for interest expense incurred but not yet paid. This means we must accrue interest cost from the most recent payment date up to the end of the period. The formula for computing accrued interest is

Principal amount owed × Annual interest rate × Fraction of year since last payment

If a company has a $6,000 loan from a bank at 5% annual interest, then 30 days' accrued interest expense is $25—computed as $6,000 × 0.05 × 30/360. The adjusting entry debits Interest Expense for $25 and credits Interest Payable for $25.

Ghing/Shutterstock

Point: Interest computations use a 360-day year, called the ***bankers' rule.***

Future Cash Payment of Accrued Expenses

Accrued expenses at the end of one accounting period result in *cash payment* in a *future period(s)*. Recall that FastForward recorded accrued salaries of $210. On January 9, the first payday of the next period, the following entry settles the accrued liability (salaries payable) and records salaries expense for seven days of work in January.

Assets = Liabilities + Equity
−700 −210 −490

Jan. 9	Salaries Payable (3 days at $70 per day)	210	
	Salaries Expense (7 days at $70 per day)	490	
	Cash		700
	Paid two weeks' salary including three days accrued.		

The $210 debit is the payment of the liability for the three days' salary accrued on December 31. The $490 debit records the salary for January's first seven working days (including the New Year's Day holiday) as an expense of the new accounting period. The $700 credit records the total amount of cash paid to the employee.

NEED-TO-KNOW 3-3

Accrued Expenses

P3

For each separate case below, follow the three-step process for adjusting the accrued expense account at December 31. *Assume no other adjusting entries are made during the year.*

a. Salaries Payable. At year-end, salaries expense of $5,000 has been incurred by the company but is not yet paid to employees.

b. Interest Payable. At its December 31 year-end, the company holds a mortgage payable that has incurred $1,000 in annual interest that is neither recorded nor paid. The company will pay the interest on January 3 of the next year.

Solution

a. Step 1: Salaries Payable equals $0 (before adjustment)
Step 2: Salaries Payable should equal $5,000 (not yet recorded)
Step 3: Adjusting entry to get from step 1 to step 2

Dec. 31	Salaries Expense	5,000	
	Salaries Payable		5,000
	Record accrued salaries expense.		

b. Step 1: Interest Payable equals $0 (before adjustment)
Step 2: Interest Payable should equal $1,000 (not yet recorded)
Step 3: Adjusting entry to get from step 1 to step 2

Dec. 31	Interest Expense	1,000	
	Interest Payable		1,000
	Record interest incurred but not yet paid.		

Do More: QS 3-13, QS 3-14, E 3-6, E 3-7, E 3-8

ACCRUED REVENUE

P4

Prepare adjusting entries for accrued revenues.

Accrued revenues are revenues earned in a period that are both unrecorded and not yet received in cash (or other assets). An example is a technician who bills customers after the job is done. If one-third of a job is complete by the end of a period, then the technician must record one-third of the expected billing as revenue in that period—even though there is no billing or collection. Accrued revenues are also called ***accrued assets.***

EXHIBIT 3.11

Adjusting for Accrued Revenues (increase an asset and increase revenue)

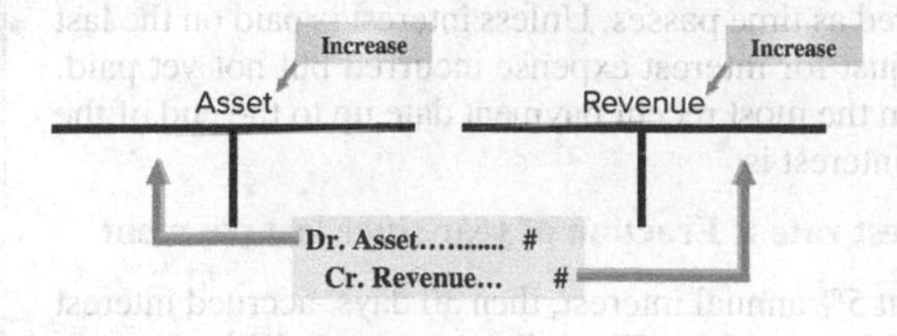

Framework The adjusting entries for accrued revenues increase a revenue (income statement) account and increase an asset (balance sheet) account, as shown in Exhibit 3.11. Accrued revenues usually come from services, products, interest, and rent. We use services and interest to show how to adjust for accrued revenues.

Accrued Services Revenue

Accrued revenues are recorded when adjusting entries are made at the end of the accounting period. These accrued revenues are earned but unrecorded because either the buyer has not yet paid or the seller has not yet billed the buyer. FastForward provides an example.

Step 1: In the second week of December, FastForward agreed to provide 30 days of consulting services to a fitness club for a fixed fee of $2,700 (or $90 per day). FastForward will provide services from December 12 through January 10, or 30 days of service. The club agrees to pay FastForward $2,700 on January 10 when the service is complete.

Step 2: At December 31, 20 days of services have already been provided. Because the contracted services have not yet been entirely provided, FastForward has neither billed the club nor recorded the services already provided. Still, FastForward has earned two-thirds of the 30-day fee, or $1,800 ($2,700 × 20/30). The *revenue recognition principle* requires FastForward to report the $1,800 on the December income statement. The balance sheet reports that the club owes FastForward $1,800.

Step 3: The adjusting entry for accrued services, along with T-account postings, follows.

Accrued Revenues

Dec. 31 Record revenue and receivable for services provided but unbilled

Pay me when I'm done

Jan. 10 Receive cash and reduce receivable

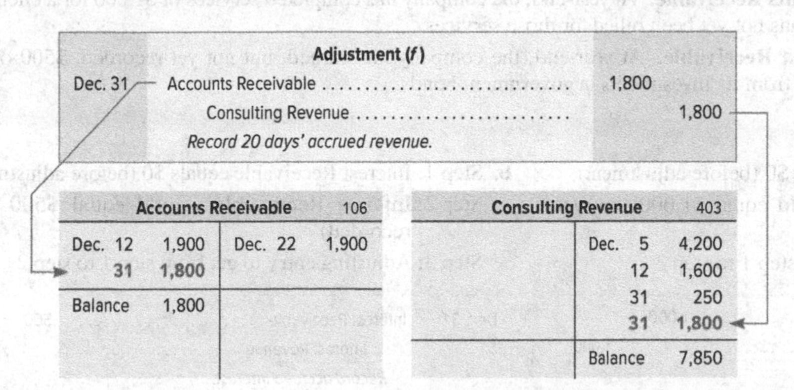

Adjustment (*f*)

		Debit	Credit
Dec. 31	Accounts Receivable	1,800	
	Consulting Revenue		1,800
	Record 20 days' accrued revenue.		

Accounts Receivable 106

Dec. 12	1,900	Dec. 22	1,900
31	**1,800**		
Balance	1,800		

Consulting Revenue 403

		Dec. 5	4,200
		12	1,600
		31	250
		31	**1,800**
		Balance	7,850

Assets = Liabilities + Equity
+1,800 +1,800

Explanation Accounts receivable are reported on the balance sheet at $1,800, and the $7,850 total of consulting revenue is reported on the income statement. The following highlights the adjustment for accrued revenue.

Before Adjustment	Adjustment	After Adjustment
Accounts Receivable = $0	**Add $1,800 to Accounts Receivable** **Add $1,800 to Consulting Revenue**	**Accounts Receivable = $1,800**
Reports $0 from revenue earned but not yet received in cash.	Record 20 days of earned revenue, which is 20/30 of total contract.	Reports $1,800 in accounts receivable from services provided.

Accrued Interest Revenue

If a company is holding notes receivable that produce interest revenue, we must adjust the accounts to record any earned and yet uncollected interest revenue. The adjusting entry is similar to the one for accruing services revenue. Specifically, debit Interest Receivable (asset) and credit Interest Revenue.

Future Cash Receipt of Accrued Revenues

Accrued revenues at the end of one accounting period result in *cash receipts* in a *future period(s)*. Recall that FastForward made an adjusting entry for $1,800 to record 20 days' accrued revenue earned from its consulting contract. When FastForward receives $2,700 cash on January 10 for the entire contract amount, it makes the following entry to remove the accrued asset (accounts receivable) and record revenue earned in January. The $2,700 debit is the cash received. The $1,800 credit is the removal of the receivable, and the $900 credit is revenue earned in January.

Assets	=	Liabilities	+	Equity
+2,700				+900
−1,800				

Jan. 10	Cash	2,700	
	Accounts Receivable (20 days at $90 per day)		1,800
	Consulting Revenue (10 days at $90 per day)		900
	Received cash for accrued asset and recorded earned consulting revenue for January.		

Wit Olszewski/Shutterstock

Analytics Insight

We Accept Bitcoin **Microsoft, Subway, Expedia,** and others accept Bitcoin as a form of payment. Bitcoin is a digital currency that can be bought and sold. In recent years, one Bitcoin has been worth between $500 and $20,000. Companies accepting Bitcoin must ensure their accounting system properly accounts for rapid changes in Bitcoin value when setting a sales price. ■

NEED-TO-KNOW 3-4

Accrued Revenues

P4

For each separate case below, follow the three-step process for adjusting the accrued revenue account at December 31. *Assume no other adjusting entries are made during the year.*

a. Accounts Receivable. At year-end, the company has completed services of $1,000 for a client, but the client has not yet been billed for those services.

b. Interest Receivable. At year-end, the company has earned, but not yet recorded, $500 of interest earned from its investments in government bonds.

Solution

a. Step 1: Accounts Receivable equals $0 (before adjustment)

Step 2: Accounts Receivable should equal $1,000 (not yet recorded)

Step 3: Adjusting entry to get from step 1 to step 2

Dec. 31	Accounts Receivable	1,000	
	Services Revenue		1,000
	Record accrued revenue.		

b. Step 1: Interest Receivable equals $0 (before adjustment)

Step 2: Interest Receivable should equal $500 (not yet recorded)

Step 3: Adjusting entry to get from step 1 to step 2

Dec. 31	Interest Receivable	500	
	Interest Revenue		500
	Record accrued interest.		

Do More: QS 3-3, QS 3-15, QS 3-16, E 3-9 through E 3-13

Links to Financial Statements

Exhibit 3.12 summarizes the four adjustments. Each adjusting entry affects one or more income statement (revenue or expense) accounts *and* one or more balance sheet (asset or liability) accounts, but never the Cash account.

EXHIBIT 3.12

Summary of Adjustments

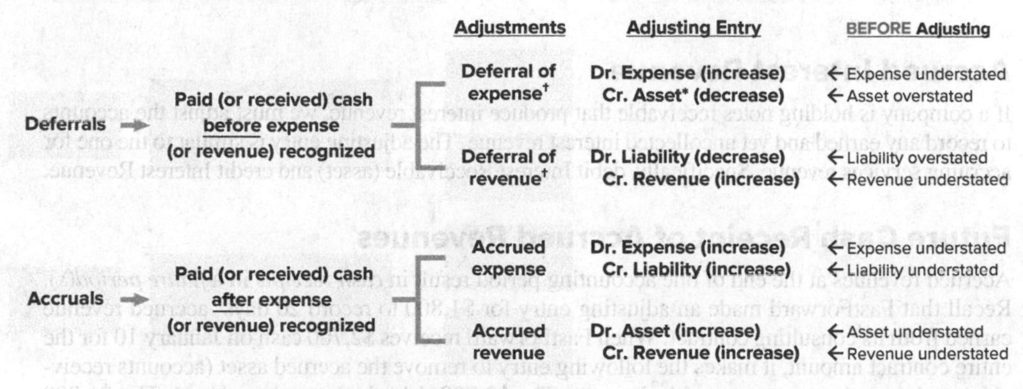

		Adjustments	Adjusting Entry	BEFORE Adjusting
Deferrals →	Paid (or received) cash before expense (or revenue) recognized	Deferral of expense†	Dr. Expense (increase) Cr. Asset* (decrease)	← Expense understated ← Asset overstated
		Deferral of revenue†	Dr. Liability (decrease) Cr. Revenue (increase)	← Liability overstated ← Revenue understated
Accruals →	Paid (or received) cash after expense (or revenue) recognized	Accrued expense	Dr. Expense (increase) Cr. Liability (increase)	← Expense understated ← Liability understated
		Accrued revenue	Dr. Asset (increase) Cr. Revenue (increase)	← Asset understated ← Revenue understated

*For depreciation, the credit is to Accumulated Depreciation (contra asset).

†Exhibit assumes that deferred expenses are initially recorded as assets and that deferred revenues are initially recorded as liabilities.

Decision Ethics

Financial Officer At year-end, the president instructs you, the financial officer, not to record accrued expenses until next year because they will not be paid until then. The president also directs you to record in current year sales a recent purchase order from a customer that requires merchandise to be delivered two weeks after the year-end. Your company would report a net income instead of a net loss if you follow these instructions. What do you do? ■ *Answer:* Omitting accrued expenses and recognizing revenue early mislead financial statement users. One action is to explain to the president what is required. If the president persists, you might talk to lawyers and any auditors involved.

TRIAL BALANCE AND FINANCIAL STATEMENTS

Adjusted Trial Balance

P5 Prepare financial statements from an adjusted trial balance.

An **unadjusted trial balance** is a list of accounts and balances *before* adjustments are recorded. An **adjusted trial balance** is a list of accounts and balances *after* adjusting entries have been recorded and posted to the ledger.

Exhibit 3.13 shows both the unadjusted and the adjusted trial balances for FastForward at December 31, 2021. The order of accounts in the trial balance usually matches the order in the chart of accounts. Several new accounts usually arise from adjusting entries.

Each adjustment (see middle columns) has a letter that links it to an adjusting entry explained earlier. Each amount in the Adjusted Trial Balance columns is computed by taking that account's amount from the Unadjusted Trial Balance columns and adding or subtracting any adjustment(s). To demonstrate, Supplies has a $9,720 Dr. balance in the unadjusted columns. Subtracting the $1,050 Cr. amount shown in the Adjustments columns equals an adjusted $8,670 Dr. balance for Supplies. An account can have more than one adjustment, such as for Consulting Revenue. Also, some accounts might not require adjustment for this period, such as Accounts Payable.

EXHIBIT 3.13

Unadjusted and Adjusted Trial Balances

FASTFORWARD
Trial Balances
December 31, 2021

Acct. No.	Account Title	Unadjusted Trial Balance Dr.	Unadjusted Trial Balance Cr.	Adjustments Dr.	Adjustments Cr.	Adjusted Trial Balance Dr.	Adjusted Trial Balance Cr.
101	Cash	$ 4,275				$ 4,275	
106	Accounts receivable	0		(f) $1,800		1,800	
126	Supplies	9,720			(b) $1,050	8,670	
128	Prepaid insurance	2,400			(a) 100	2,300	
167	Equipment	26,000				26,000	
168	Accumulated depreciation—Equip.		$ 0		(c) 300		$ 300
201	Accounts payable		6,200				6,200
209	Salaries payable		0		(e) 210		210
236	Unearned consulting revenue		3,000	(d) 250			2,750
301	C. Taylor, Capital		30,000				30,000
302	C. Taylor, Withdrawals	200				200	
403	Consulting revenue		5,800		(d) 250 (f) 1,800		7,850
406	Rental revenue		300				300
612	Depreciation expense—Equip.	0		(c) 300		300	
622	Salaries expense	1,400		(e) 210		1,610	
637	Insurance expense	0		(a) 100		100	
640	Rent expense	1,000				1,000	
652	Supplies expense	0		(b) 1,050		1,050	
690	Utilities expense	305				305	
	Totals	$45,300	$45,300	$3,710	$3,710	$47,610	$47,610

Preparing Financial Statements

We can prepare financial statements directly from information in the *adjusted* trial balance. Exhibit 3.14 shows how revenue and expense balances are transferred from the adjusted trial balance to the income statement (red lines). The net income and withdrawals amounts are then used to prepare the statement of owner's equity (brown lines). Asset and liability balances are then transferred to the balance sheet (blue lines). The ending capital is computed in the statement of owner's equity and transferred to the balance sheet (green line).

EXHIBIT 3.14
Preparing Financial Statements

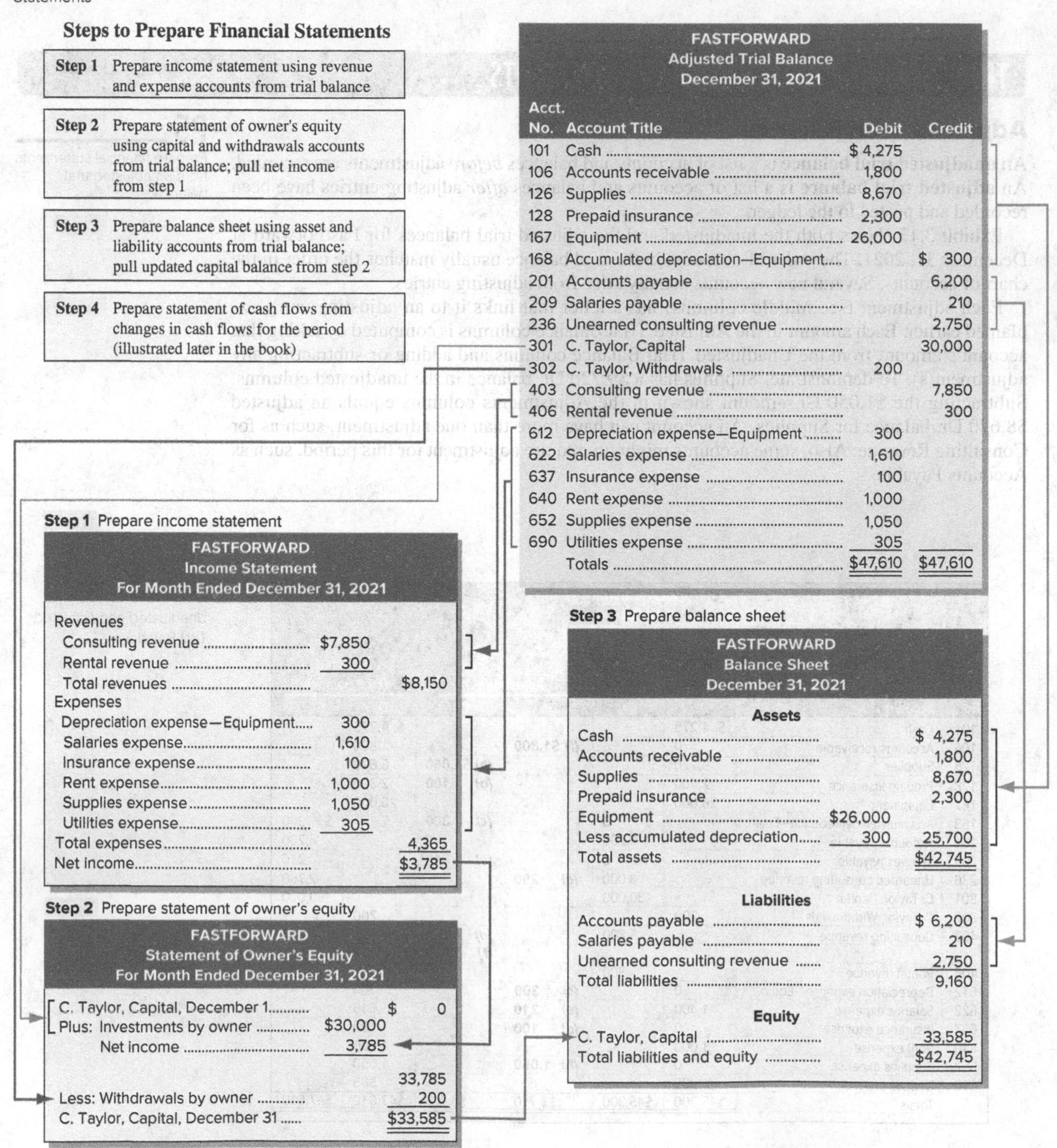

Steps to Prepare Financial Statements

Step 1 Prepare income statement using revenue and expense accounts from trial balance

Step 2 Prepare statement of owner's equity using capital and withdrawals accounts from trial balance; pull net income from step 1

Step 3 Prepare balance sheet using asset and liability accounts from trial balance; pull updated capital balance from step 2

Step 4 Prepare statement of cash flows from changes in cash flows for the period (illustrated later in the book)

FASTFORWARD
Adjusted Trial Balance
December 31, 2021

Acct. No.	Account Title	Debit	Credit
101	Cash	$ 4,275	
106	Accounts receivable	1,800	
126	Supplies	8,670	
128	Prepaid insurance	2,300	
167	Equipment	26,000	
168	Accumulated depreciation—Equipment		$ 300
201	Accounts payable		6,200
209	Salaries payable		210
236	Unearned consulting revenue		2,750
301	C. Taylor, Capital		30,000
302	C. Taylor, Withdrawals	200	
403	Consulting revenue		7,850
406	Rental revenue		300
612	Depreciation expense—Equipment	300	
622	Salaries expense	1,610	
637	Insurance expense	100	
640	Rent expense	1,000	
652	Supplies expense	1,050	
690	Utilities expense	305	
	Totals	$47,610	$47,610

Step 1 Prepare income statement

FASTFORWARD
Income Statement
For Month Ended December 31, 2021

Revenues		
Consulting revenue	$7,850	
Rental revenue	300	
Total revenues		$8,150
Expenses		
Depreciation expense—Equipment	300	
Salaries expense	1,610	
Insurance expense	100	
Rent expense	1,000	
Supplies expense	1,050	
Utilities expense	305	
Total expenses		4,365
Net income		$3,785

Step 2 Prepare statement of owner's equity

FASTFORWARD
Statement of Owner's Equity
For Month Ended December 31, 2021

C. Taylor, Capital, December 1		$ 0
Plus: Investments by owner	$30,000	
Net income	3,785	
		33,785
Less: Withdrawals by owner		200
C. Taylor, Capital, December 31		$33,585

Step 3 Prepare balance sheet

FASTFORWARD
Balance Sheet
December 31, 2021

Assets		
Cash		$ 4,275
Accounts receivable		1,800
Supplies		8,670
Prepaid insurance		2,300
Equipment	$26,000	
Less accumulated depreciation	300	25,700
Total assets		$42,745
Liabilities		
Accounts payable		$ 6,200
Salaries payable		210
Unearned consulting revenue		2,750
Total liabilities		9,160
Equity		
C. Taylor, Capital		33,585
Total liabilities and equity		$42,745

We prepare financial statements in the following order: (1) income statement, (2) statement of owner's equity, and (3) balance sheet. This order makes sense because the balance sheet uses information from the statement of owner's equity, which in turn uses information from the income statement. The statement of cash flows is usually the final statement prepared.

Point: Each trial balance amount is used in only *one* financial statement.

NEED-TO-KNOW 3-5

Preparing Financial Statements from a Trial Balance

P5

Use the following adjusted trial balance of Magic Company to prepare its December 31 year-end (1) income statement, (2) statement of owner's equity, and (3) balance sheet (unclassified). The Magic, Capital account balance was $75,000 on December 31 of the *prior year*.

MAGIC COMPANY
Adjusted Trial Balance
December 31

Account Title	Debit	Credit
Cash	$ 13,000	
Accounts receivable	17,000	
Land	85,000	
Accounts payable		$ 12,000
Long-term notes payable		33,000
Magic, Capital		75,000
Magic, Withdrawals	20,000	
Services revenue		79,000
Salaries expense	56,000	
Supplies expense	8,000	
Totals	$199,000	$199,000

Solution

Step 1

MAGIC COMPANY
Income Statement
For Year Ended December 31

Revenues		
Services revenue		$79,000
Expenses		
Salaries expense	$56,000	
Supplies expense	8,000	
Total expenses		64,000
Net income		$15,000

Step 2

MAGIC COMPANY
Statement of Owner's Equity
For Year Ended December 31

Magic, Capital, December 31, prior year-end	$75,000
Add: Investments by owner	0
Net income	15,000
	90,000
Less: Withdrawals by owner	20,000
Magic, Capital, December 31 current year-end	$70,000

Step 3

MAGIC COMPANY
Balance Sheet
December 31

Assets	
Cash	$ 13,000
Accounts receivable	17,000
Land	85,000
Total assets	$115,000
Liabilities	
Accounts payable	$ 12,000
Long-term notes payable	33,000
Total liabilities	45,000
Equity	
Magic, Capital	70,000
Total liabilities and equity	$115,000

Do More: QS 3-18, QS 3-19, E 3-15, E 3-16, E 3-17, P 3-4

Decision Analysis  Profit Margin

A1 Compute and analyze profit margin.

A useful measure of a company's operating results is the ratio of its net income to net sales. This ratio is called **profit margin,** or *return on sales,* and is computed as in Exhibit 3.15. This ratio shows the percent of profit in each dollar of sales.

EXHIBIT 3.15

Profit Margin

$$\textbf{Profit margin} = \frac{\textbf{Net income}}{\textbf{Net sales}}$$

Visa's profit margins are shown in Exhibit 3.16. Visa's profit margin is superior to **Mastercard**'s in each of the last three years. For Mastercard to improve its profit margin, it must either reduce expenses or increase revenues at a relatively greater amount than expenses.

EXHIBIT 3.16

Computation and Analysis Using Profit Margin.

Company	Figure ($ millions)	Current Year	1 Year Ago	2 Years Ago
Visa	Net income	$12,080	$10,301	$ 6,699
	Net sales	$22,977	$20,609	$18,358
	Profit margin	**53%**	**50%**	**36%**
Mastercard	Profit margin	48%	39%	31%

Decision Maker

CFO Your health care equipment company consistently reports a 9% profit margin, which is similar to that of competitors. The treasurer argues that profit margin can be increased to 20% if the company cuts marketing expenses. Do you cut those expenses? ■ *Answer:* Cutting those expenses increases profit margin in the short run. However, over the long run, cutting such expenses can hurt current and future sales. You must explain that the company can cut the "fat" (expenses that do not create sales) but should be careful if cutting those that create sales.

NEED-TO-KNOW 3-6

COMPREHENSIVE 1

Preparing Year-End Accounting Adjustments

The following information relates to Fanning's Electronics on December 31.

a. The company's weekly payroll is $8,750, paid each Friday for a five-day workweek. Assume December 31 falls on a Monday, but the employees will not be paid their wages until Friday, January 4 of next year.

b. At the beginning of the current year, the company purchased equipment that cost $20,000. Its useful life is predicted to be five years, at which time the equipment is expected to be worthless (zero salvage value).

c. On October 1, the company agreed to work on a new housing development. The company is paid $120,000 on October 1 in advance of future installation of similar alarm systems in 24 new homes. That amount was credited to the Unearned Revenue account. Between October 1 and December 31, work on 20 homes was completed.

d. On September 1, the company purchased a 12-month insurance policy for $1,800. The transaction was recorded with an $1,800 debit to Prepaid Insurance.

e. On December 29, the company completed $7,000 in services that have not been billed or recorded as of December 31.

Required

1. Prepare any necessary adjusting entries on December 31 of the current year related to transactions and events *a* through *e*.

2. Prepare T-accounts for the accounts affected by adjusting entries, and post the adjusting entries. Determine the adjusted balances for the Prepaid Insurance, Unearned Revenue, and Services Revenue accounts.

3. Complete the following table and determine the amounts and effects of each adjusting entry on the current year income statement and the year-end balance sheet. Use up (down) arrows to indicate an increase (decrease) in the four "Effect on" columns.

Entry	Amount in the Entry	Effect on Net Income	Effect on Total Assets	Effect on Total Liabilities	Effect on Total Equity

SOLUTION

1. Adjusting journal entries.

Date	Account	Debit	Credit
(a) Dec. 31	Wages Expense	1,750	
	Wages Payable		1,750
	Accrue wages ($8,750 × 1/5).		
(b) Dec. 31	Depreciation Expense—Equipment	4,000	
	Accumulated Depreciation—Equipment		4,000
	Record depreciation ($20,000/5 years = $4,000 per year).		
(c) Dec. 31	Unearned Revenue	100,000	
	Services Revenue		100,000
	Record revenue earned ($120,000 × 20/24).		
(d) Dec. 31	Insurance Expense	600	
	Prepaid Insurance		600
	Adjust for expired insurance ($1,800 × 4/12).		
(e) Dec. 31	Accounts Receivable	7,000	
	Services Revenue		7,000
	Record accrued revenue.		

2. T-accounts for adjusting journal entries *a* through *e*.

Accounts Receivable

Debit	Credit
(e) 7,000	

Wages Payable

Debit	Credit
	(a) 1,750

Wages Expense

Debit	Credit
(a) 1,750	

Prepaid Insurance

Debit	Credit
Unadj. Bal. 1,800	
	(d) 600
Adj. Bal. 1,200	

Unearned Revenue

Debit	Credit
	Unadj. Bal. 120,000
(c) 100,000	
	Adj. Bal. 20,000

Insurance Expense

Debit	Credit
(d) 600	

Accumulated Depreciation—Equipment

Debit	Credit
	(b) 4,000

Services Revenue

Debit	Credit
	(c) 100,000
	(e) 7,000
	Adj. Bal. 107,000

Depreciation Expense—Equipment

Debit	Credit
(b) 4,000	

3. Financial statement effects of adjusting journal entries.

Entry	Amount in the Entry	Effect on Net Income	Effect on Total Assets	Effect on Total Liabilities	Effect on Total Equity
a	$ 1,750	$ 1,750 ↓	No effect	$ 1,750 ↑	$ 1,750 ↓
b	4,000	4,000 ↓	$4,000 ↓	No effect	4,000 ↓
c	100,000	100,000 ↑	No effect	$100,000 ↓	100,000 ↑
d	600	600 ↓	$ 600 ↓	No effect	600 ↓
e	7,000	7,000 ↑	$7,000 ↑	No effect	7,000 ↑

NEED-TO-KNOW 3-7

COMPREHENSIVE 2

Preparing Financial Statements from Adjusted Account Balances

Use the following year-end adjusted trial balance to answer questions 1–3.

CHOI COMPANY
Adjusted Trial Balance
December 31

	Debit	Credit
Cash	$ 3,050	
Accounts receivable	400	
Prepaid insurance	910	
Equipment	217,200	
Accumulated depreciation—Equipment		$ 29,100
Interest payable		4,480
Unearned revenue		460
Long-term notes payable		150,000
M. Choi, Capital		40,340
M. Choi, Withdrawals	21,000	
Services revenue		57,500
Wages expense	25,000	
Utilities expense	1,900	
Insurance expense	3,450	
Depreciation expense—Equipment	5,970	
Interest expense	3,000	
Totals	$281,880	$281,880

1. Prepare the annual income statement from the adjusted trial balance of Choi Company. *Answer follows:*

CHOI COMPANY
Income Statement
For Year Ended December 31

Revenues		
Services revenue		$57,500
Expenses		
Wages expense	$25,000	
Utilities expense	1,900	
Insurance expense	3,450	
Depreciation expense—Equipment	5,970	
Interest expense	3,000	
Total expenses		39,320
Net income		$18,180

2. Prepare a statement of owner's equity from the adjusted trial balance of Choi Company. The beginning-year capital balance was $30,340, and the owner invested $10,000 in the company in the current year. *Answer follows:*

CHOI COMPANY
Statement of Owner's Equity
For Year Ended December 31

M. Choi, Capital, December 31, prior year-end		$30,340
Plus: Investments by owner	$10,000	
Net income	18,180	28,180
		58,520
Less: Withdrawals by owner		21,000
M. Choi, Capital, December 31, current year-end		$37,520

3. Prepare a balance sheet (unclassified) from the adjusted trial balance of Choi Company. *Answer follows:*

CHOI COMPANY
Balance Sheet
December 31

Assets		
Cash		$ 3,050
Accounts receivable		400
Prepaid insurance		910
Equipment	$217,200	
Less accumulated depreciation	29,100	188,100
Total assets		$192,460
Liabilities		
Interest payable		$ 4,480
Unearned revenue		460
Long-term notes payable		150,000
Total liabilities		154,940
Equity		
M. Choi, Capital		37,520
Total liabilities and equity		$192,460

APPENDIX

Alternative Accounting for Prepayments 3A

P6 Explain the alternatives in accounting for prepaids.

This appendix explains alternative accounting for deferred expenses and deferred revenues.

RECORDING PREPAYMENT OF EXPENSES IN EXPENSE ACCOUNTS

An alternative method is to record *all* prepaid expenses with debits to expense accounts. If any prepaids remain unused or unexpired at the end of an accounting period, then adjusting entries transfer the cost of the unused portions from expense accounts to prepaid expense (asset) accounts. The financial statements are identical under either method, but the adjusting entries are different. To demonstrate the differences between these two methods, let's look at FastForward's cash payment on December 1 for 24 months of insurance coverage beginning on December 1. FastForward recorded that payment with a debit to an asset account, but it could have recorded a debit to an expense account. These alternatives are shown in Exhibit 3A.1.

EXHIBIT 3A.1 Alternative Initial Entries for Prepaid Expenses

Payment Recorded as Asset			
Dec. 1	Prepaid Insurance	2,400	
	Cash..............		2,400

Payment Recorded as Expense			
Dec. 1	Insurance Expense	2,400	
	Cash		2,400

At the end of its accounting period on December 31, insurance protection for one month has expired. This means $100 ($2,400/24) of insurance coverage expired and is an expense for December. The adjusting entry depends on how the original payment was recorded. This is shown in Exhibit 3A.2.

EXHIBIT 3A.2 Adjusting Entry for Prepaid Expenses for the Two Alternatives

Payment Recorded as Asset			
Dec. 31	Insurance Expense	100	
	Prepaid Insurance		100

Payment Recorded as Expense			
Dec. 31	Prepaid Insurance	2,300	
	Insurance Expense ..		2,300

When the entries are posted, we see in Exhibit 3A.3 that the two methods give identical ending balances.

EXHIBIT 3A.3 Account Balances under Two Alternatives for Recording Prepaid Expenses

Payment Recorded as Asset

Prepaid Insurance			128
Dec. 1	2,400	Dec. 31	100
Balance	2,300		

Insurance Expense			637
Dec. 31	100		

Payment Recorded as Expense

Prepaid Insurance			128
Dec. 31	2,300		

Insurance Expense			637
Dec. 1	2,400	Dec. 31	2,300
Balance	100		

RECORDING PREPAYMENT OF REVENUES IN REVENUE ACCOUNTS

An alternative method is to record *all* unearned revenues with credits to revenue accounts. If any revenues are unearned at the end of an accounting period, then adjusting entries transfer the unearned portions from revenue accounts to unearned revenue (liability) accounts. The adjusting entries are different for these two alternatives, but the financial statements are identical. To demonstrate the differences between these two methods, let's look at FastForward's December 26 receipt of $3,000 for consulting services covering the period December 27 to February 24. FastForward recorded this transaction with a credit to a liability account. The alternative is to record it with a credit to a revenue account, as shown in Exhibit 3A.4.

EXHIBIT 3A.4 Alternative Initial Entries for Unearned Revenues

Receipt Recorded as Liability			
Dec. 26	Cash	3,000	
	Unearned Consulting Revenue ...		3,000

Receipt Recorded as Revenue			
Dec. 26	Cash	3,000	
	Consulting Revenue ..		3,000

By the end of its accounting period on December 31, FastForward has earned $250 of this revenue. This means $250 of the liability has been satisfied. Depending on how the initial receipt is recorded, the adjusting entry is as shown in Exhibit 3A.5.

EXHIBIT 3A.5
Adjusting Entry for Unearned Revenues for the Two Alternatives

Receipt Recorded as Liability				Receipt Recorded as Revenue			
Dec. 31	Unearned Consulting Revenue	250		Dec. 31	Consulting Revenue	2,750	
	Consulting Revenue		250		Unearned Consulting Revenue		2,750

After entries are posted, the two alternatives give identical ending balances, as shown in Exhibit 3A.6.

EXHIBIT 3A.6
Account Balances under Two Alternatives for Recording Unearned Revenues

Receipt Recorded as Liability

Unearned Consulting Revenue		236	
Dec. 31	250	Dec. 26	3,000
		Balance	**2,750**

Consulting Revenue		403	
		Dec. 31	**250**

Receipt Recorded as Revenue

Unearned Consulting Revenue		236	
		Dec. 31	**2,750**

Consulting Revenue		403	
Dec. 31	2,750	Dec. 26	3,000
		Balance	**250**

Summary: Cheat Sheet

DEFERRAL OF EXPENSE

Prepaid expenses: Assets paid for in advance of receiving their benefits. When these assets are used, the advance payments become expenses.

Prepaid insurance expires:

Insurance Expense	100	
Prepaid Insurance		100

Supplies are used up:

Supplies Expense	1,050	
Supplies		1,050

Accumulated depreciation: A separate contra account. A **contra account** is an account linked with another account. It has an opposite normal balance and is a subtraction from that other account's balance.

Depreciation of assets:

Depreciation Expense	300	
Accumulated Depreciation—Equipment		300

DEFERRAL OF REVENUE

Unearned revenue: Cash received in advance of providing products and services. When cash is accepted, the company has a liability to provide products or services.

Record unearned revenue (cash received in advance):

Cash	3,000	
Unearned Consulting Revenue		3,000

Reduce unearned revenue (products or services are provided):

Unearned Consulting Revenue	250	
Consulting Revenue		250

ACCRUED EXPENSE

Accrued expenses: Costs incurred in a period that are both unpaid and unrecorded. They are reported on the income statement for the period when incurred.

Salaries expense owed but not yet paid:

Salaries Expense	210	
Salaries Payable		210

Accrued interest formula:

Principal amount owed × Annual interest rate × Fraction of year since last payment

Payment of accrued expenses:

Salaries Payable (3 days at $70 per day)	210	
Salaries Expense (7 days at $70 per day)	490	
Cash		700

ACCRUED REVENUE

Accrued revenues: Revenues earned in a period that are both unrecorded and not yet received in cash.

Revenue earned but not received in cash:

Accounts Receivable	1,800	
Consulting Revenue		1,800

Receipt of accrued revenue:

Cash	2,700	
Accounts Receivable (20 days at $90 per day)		1,800
Consulting Revenue (10 days at $90 per day)		900

REPORTING AND ANALYSIS

Unadjusted trial balance: A list of ledger accounts and balances *before* adjustments are recorded.

Adjusted trial balance: A list of accounts and balances *after* adjusting entries have been recorded and posted to the ledger.

Preparing financial statements from adjusted trial balance:

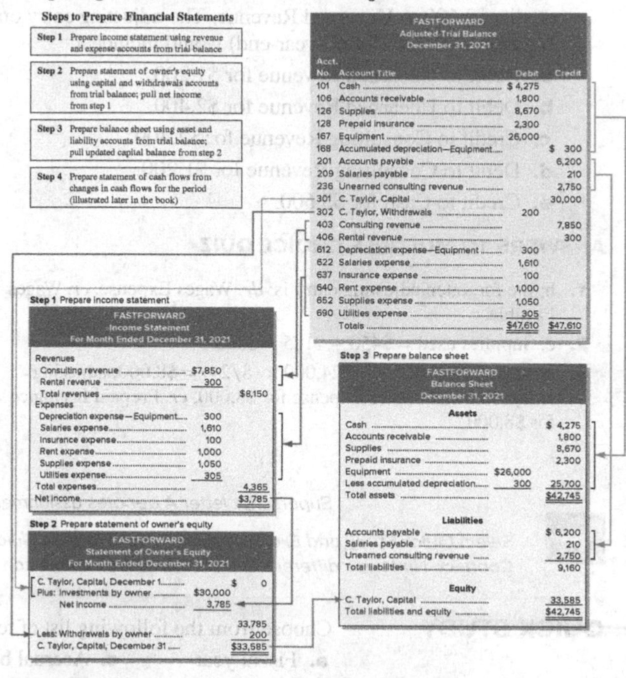

Steps to Prepare Financial Statements

Step 1 Prepare income statement using revenue and expense accounts from trial balance

Step 2 Prepare statement of owner's equity using capital and withdrawals accounts from trial balance; pull net income from step 1

Step 3 Prepare balance sheet using asset and liability accounts from trial balance; pull updated capital balance from step 2

Step 4 Prepare statement of cash flows from changes in cash flows for the period (illustrated later in the book)

FASTFORWARD
Adjusted Trial Balance
December 31, 2021

Acct. No.	Account Title	Debit	Credit
101	Cash	$ 4,275	
106	Accounts receivable	1,800	
126	Supplies	8,670	
128	Prepaid insurance	2,300	
167	Equipment	26,000	
168	Accumulated depreciation—Equipment		$ 300
201	Accounts payable		6,200
209	Salaries payable		210
236	Unearned consulting revenue		2,750
301	C. Taylor, Capital		30,000
302	C. Taylor, Withdrawals	200	
403	Consulting revenue		7,850
406	Rental revenue		300
612	Depreciation expense—Equipment	300	
622	Salaries expense	1,610	
637	Insurance expense	100	
640	Rent expense	1,000	
652	Supplies expense	1,050	
690	Utilities expense	305	
	Totals	$47,610	$47,610

Step 1 Prepare income statement

FASTFORWARD
Income Statement
For Month Ended December 31, 2021

Revenues		
Consulting revenue	$7,850	
Rental revenue	300	
Total revenues		$8,150
Expenses		
Depreciation expense—Equipment	300	
Salaries expense	1,610	
Insurance expense	100	
Rent expense	1,000	
Supplies expense	1,050	
Utilities expense	305	
Total expenses		4,365
Net income		$3,785

Step 2 Prepare statement of owner's equity

FASTFORWARD
Statement of Owner's Equity
For Month Ended December 31, 2021

C. Taylor, Capital, December 1		$ 0
Plus: Investments by owner	$30,000	
Net income	3,785	
		33,785
Less: Withdrawals by owner		200
C. Taylor, Capital, December 31		$33,585

Step 3 Prepare balance sheet

FASTFORWARD
Balance Sheet
December 31, 2021

Assets		
Cash		$ 4,275
Accounts receivable		1,800
Supplies		8,670
Prepaid insurance		2,300
Equipment	$26,000	
Less accumulated depreciation	300	25,700
Total assets		$42,745
Liabilities		
Accounts payable		$ 6,200
Salaries payable		210
Unearned consulting revenue		2,750
Total liabilities		9,160
Equity		
C. Taylor, Capital		33,585
Total liabilities and equity		$42,745

Key Terms

Accounting period (85)
Accrual basis accounting (86)
Accrued expenses (95)
Accrued revenues (94)
Accumulated depreciation (89)
Adjusted trial balance (97)
Adjusting entry (87)
Annual financial statements (85)
Book value (89)
Cash basis accounting (86)
Contra account (89)
Depreciation (89)
Expense recognition (or matching) **principle** (86)
Fiscal year (85)
Interim financial statements (85)
Natural business year (85)
Plant assets (88)
Prepaid expenses (87)
Profit margin (100)
Revenue recognition principle (86)
Straight-line depreciation (89)
Time period assumption (85)
Unadjusted trial balance (97)
Unearned revenue (91)

Multiple Choice Quiz

1. A company forgot to record accrued and unpaid employee wages of $350,000 at period-end. This oversight would

a. Understate net income by $350,000.
b. Overstate net income by $350,000.
c. Have no effect on net income.
d. Overstate assets by $350,000.
e. Understate assets by $350,000.

2. Prior to recording adjusting entries, the Supplies account has a $450 debit balance. A physical count of supplies shows $125 of unused supplies still available. The required adjusting entry is

a. Debit Supplies $125; credit Supplies Expense $125.
b. Debit Supplies $325; credit Supplies Expense $325.
c. Debit Supplies Expense $325; credit Supplies $325.
d. Debit Supplies Expense $325; credit Supplies $125.
e. Debit Supplies Expense $125; credit Supplies $125.

3. On May 1 of the current year, a two-year insurance policy was purchased for $24,000 with coverage to begin immediately. What is the amount of insurance expense that appears on the company's income statement for the current year ended December 31?

a. $4,000 **b.** $8,000 **c.** $12,000 **d.** $20,000 **e.** $24,000

4. On November 1, Stockton Co. receives $3,600 cash from Hans Co. for consulting services to be provided evenly over the period November 1 to April 30—at which time Stockton credits $3,600 to Unearned Revenue. The adjusting entry on December 31 (Stockton's year-end) would include a

a. Debit to Unearned Revenue for $1,200.
b. Debit to Unearned Revenue for $2,400.
c. Credit to Consulting Revenue for $2,400.
d. Debit to Consulting Revenue for $1,200.
e. Credit to Cash for $3,600.

5. If a company had $15,000 in net income for the year, and its sales were $300,000 for the same year, what is its profit margin?

a. 20% **b.** 2,000% **c.** $285,000 **d.** $315,000 **e.** 5%

ANSWERS TO MULTIPLE CHOICE QUIZ

1. b; the forgotten adjusting entry is: *dr.* Wages Expense, *cr.* Wages Payable.
2. c; Supplies used = $450 − $125 = $325
3. b; Insurance expense = $24,000 × (8/24) = $8,000; adjusting entry is: *dr.* Insurance Expense for $8,000, *cr.* Prepaid Insurance for $8,000.
4. a; Consulting Revenue earned = $3,600 × (2/6) = $1,200; adjusting entry is: *dr.* Unearned Revenue for $1,200, *cr.* Consulting Revenue for $1,200.
5. e; Profit margin = $15,000/$300,000 = 5%

Superscript letter A denotes assignments based on Appendix 3A.

Select Quick Study and Exercise assignments feature Guided Example videos, called "Hints" in Connect. Hints use different numbers, and instructors can turn this feature on or off.

QUICK STUDY

QS 3-1
Periodic reporting
C1

Choose from the following list of terms and phrases to best complete the statements below.

a. Fiscal year **b.** Timeliness **c.** Accrual basis accounting **d.** Annual financial statements **e.** Cash basis accounting **f.** Time period assumption

1. _____ presumes that an organization's activities can be divided into specific time periods.
2. Financial reports covering a one-year period are known as _____.
3. A(n) _____ consists of any 12 consecutive months.
4. _____ records revenues when services are provided and records expenses when incurred.
5. The value of information is often linked to its _____.

QS 3-2
Computing accrual and cash income
C1

In its first year of operations, Roma Company reports the following. Compute Roma's first-year net income under the cash basis *and* the accrual basis of accounting.

- Earned revenues of $45,000 ($37,000 cash received from customers).
- Incurred expenses of $25,500 ($20,250 cash paid toward them).
- Prepaid $6,750 cash for costs that will not be expensed until next year.

QS 3-3
Identifying accounting adjustments
P1 P2 P3 P4

Classify the following adjusting entries as involving prepaid expenses, unearned revenues, accrued expenses, or accrued revenues.

a. To record revenue earned that was previously received as cash in advance.
b. To record wages expense incurred but not yet paid or recorded.
c. To record revenue earned but not yet billed or recorded.
d. To record expiration of prepaid insurance.
e. To record annual depreciation expense.

QS 3-4
Concepts of adjusting entries
P1 P2 P3 P4

At the end of its annual accounting period, the company must make three adjusting entries. For each of these adjusting entries, indicate the account to be debited and the account to be credited.

a. Accrue salaries expense.
b. Adjust the Unearned Revenue account to recognize earned services revenue.
c. Record services revenue earned for which cash will be received the following period.

QS 3-5
Prepaid (deferred) expenses adjustments
P1

For each separate case below, follow the three-step process for adjusting the prepaid asset account at December 31. Step 1: Determine what the current account balance equals. Step 2: Determine what the current account balance should equal. Step 3: Record the December 31 adjusting entry to get from step 1 to step 2. *Assume no other adjusting entries are made during the year.*

a. Prepaid Insurance. The Prepaid Insurance account has a $4,700 debit balance to start the year. A review of insurance policies shows that $900 of unexpired insurance remains at year-end.

b. Prepaid Insurance. The Prepaid Insurance account has a $5,890 debit balance at the start of the year. A review of insurance policies shows $1,040 of insurance has expired by year-end.

c. Prepaid Rent. On September 1 of the current year, the company prepaid $24,000 for two years of rent for facilities being occupied that day. The company debited Prepaid Rent and credited Cash for $24,000.

QS 3-6
Prepaid (deferred) expenses adjustments
P1

For each separate case below, follow the three-step process for adjusting the Supplies asset account at December 31. Step 1: Determine what the current account balance equals. Step 2: Determine what the current account balance should equal. Step 3: Record the December 31 adjusting entry to get from step 1 to step 2. *Assume no other adjusting entries are made during the year.*

a. Supplies. The Supplies account has a $300 debit balance to start the year. No supplies were purchased during the current year. A December 31 physical count shows $110 of supplies remaining.

b. Supplies. The Supplies account has an $800 debit balance to start the year. Supplies of $2,100 were purchased during the current year and debited to the Supplies account. A December 31 physical count shows $650 of supplies remaining.

c. Supplies. The Supplies account has a $4,000 debit balance to start the year. During the current year, supplies of $9,400 were purchased and debited to the Supplies account. The inventory of supplies available at December 31 totaled $2,660.

QS 3-7
Adjusting prepaid (deferred) expenses
P1

For each separate case, record the necessary adjusting entry.

a. On July 1, Lopez Company paid $1,200 for six months of insurance coverage. No adjustments have been made to the Prepaid Insurance account, and it is now December 31. Prepare the year-end adjusting entry to reflect expiration of the insurance as of December 31.

b. Zim Company has a Supplies account balance of $5,000 at the beginning of the year. During the year, it purchases $2,000 of supplies. As of December 31, a physical count of supplies shows $800 of supplies available. Prepare the adjusting journal entry to correctly report the balance of the Supplies account and the Supplies Expense account as of December 31.

QS 3-8
Accumulated depreciation calculations and adjustments
P1

For each separate case below, follow the three-step process for adjusting the Accumulated Depreciation account at December 31. Step 1: Determine what the current account balance equals. Step 2: Determine what the current account balance should equal. Step 3: Record the December 31 adjusting entry to get from step 1 to step 2. *Assume no other adjusting entries are made during the year.*

a. Accumulated Depreciation. The Krug Company's Accumulated Depreciation account has a $13,500 balance to start the year. A review of depreciation schedules reveals that $14,600 of depreciation expense must be recorded for the year.

b. Accumulated Depreciation. The company has only one plant asset (truck) that it purchased at the start of this year. That asset had cost $44,000, had an estimated life of five years, and is expected to have zero value at the end of the five years.

c. Accumulated Depreciation. The company has only one plant asset (equipment) that it purchased at the start of this year. That asset had cost $32,000, had an estimated life of seven years, and is expected to be valued at $4,000 at the end of the seven years.

QS 3-9
Adjusting for depreciation
P1

For each separate case, record an adjusting entry (if necessary).

a. Barga Company purchases $20,000 of equipment on January 1. The equipment is expected to last five years and be worth $2,000 at the end of that time. Prepare the entry to record one year's depreciation expense of $3,600 for the equipment as of December 31.

b. Welch Company purchases $10,000 of land on January 1. The land is expected to last forever. What depreciation adjustment, if any, should be made with respect to the Land account as of December 31?

QS 3-10
Unearned (deferred) revenues adjustments
P2

For each separate case below, follow the three-step process for adjusting the unearned revenue liability account at December 31. Step 1: Determine what the current account balance equals. Step 2: Determine what the current account balance should equal. Step 3: Record the December 31 adjusting entry to get from step 1 to step 2. *Assume no other adjusting entries are made during the year.*

a. Unearned Rent Revenue. The Krug Company collected $6,000 rent in advance on November 1, debiting Cash and crediting Unearned Rent Revenue. The tenant was paying 12 months' rent in advance and occupancy began November 1.

[continued on next page]

[continued from previous page]

b. Unearned Services Revenue. The company charges $75 per insect treatment. A customer paid $300 on October 1 in advance for four treatments, which was recorded with a debit to Cash and a credit to Unearned Services Revenue. At year-end, the company has applied three treatments for the customer.

c. Unearned Rent Revenue. On September 1, a client paid the company $24,000 cash for six months of rent in advance and took occupancy immediately. The company recorded the cash as Unearned Rent Revenue.

QS 3-11
Adjusting for unearned (deferred) revenues
P2

For each separate case, record the necessary adjusting entry.

a. Tao Co. receives $10,000 cash in advance for four months of evenly planned legal services beginning on October 1. Tao records it by debiting Cash and crediting Unearned Revenue both for $10,000. It is now December 31, and Tao has provided legal services as planned. What adjusting entry should Tao make to account for the work performed from October 1 through December 31?

b. Caden started a new publication called *Contest News*. Its subscribers pay $24 to receive 12 monthly issues. With every new subscriber, Caden debits Cash and credits Unearned Subscription Revenue for the amounts received. The company has 100 new subscribers as of July 1. It sends *Contest News* to each of these subscribers every month from July through December. Assuming no changes in subscribers, prepare the year-end journal entry that Caden must make as of December 31 to adjust the Subscription Revenue account and the Unearned Subscription Revenue account.

QS 3-12
Adjusting for unearned (deferred) revenues
P2

For each separate case, record an adjusting entry (if necessary).

a. Lonzo Co. receives $3,000 cash in advance for six months of recycling services on September 1 and records it by debiting Cash and crediting Unearned Revenue for $3,000. Lonzo provides recycling services monthly as promised. Prepare the December 31 year-end adjusting entry that Lonzo records for the work performed from September 1 through December 31.

b. On October 20, **Milwaukee Bucks** sold a 10-game ticket package for $200 and recorded Unearned Revenue. By December 31, 4 of the 10 games had been played. Record the December 31 year-end adjusting entry that the Bucks record for the 40% of revenue earned on the $200 ticket package.

QS 3-13
Accrued expenses adjustments
P3

For each separate case below, follow the three-step process for adjusting the accrued expense account at December 31. Step 1: Determine what the current account balance equals. Step 2: Determine what the current account balance should equal. Step 3: Record the December 31 adjusting entry to get from step 1 to step 2. *Assume no other adjusting entries are made during the year.*

a. Salaries Payable. At year-end, salaries expense of $15,500 has been incurred by the company but is not yet paid to employees.

b. Interest Payable. At its December 31 year-end, the company owes $250 of interest on a loan. That interest will not be paid until sometime in January of the next year.

c. Interest Payable. At its December 31 year-end, the company holds a mortgage payable that has incurred $875 in annual interest that is neither recorded nor paid. The company intends to pay the interest on January 7 of the next year.

QS 3-14
Accruing salaries
P3

Molly Mocha employs one college student every summer in her coffee shop. The student works the five weekdays and is paid on the following Monday. (For example, a student who works Monday through Friday, June 1 through June 5, is paid for that work on Monday, June 8.) The coffee shop makes an adjusting entry each month to show salaries earned but unpaid at month-end.

The student works the last week of July, which is Monday, July 28, through Friday, August 1. If the student earns $100 per day, what adjusting entry must the coffee shop make on July 31 to correctly record accrued salaries expense for July?

QS 3-15
Accrued revenues adjustments
P4

For each separate case below, follow the three-step process for adjusting the accrued revenue account at December 31. Step 1: Determine what the current account balance equals. Step 2: Determine what the current account balance should equal. Step 3: Record the December 31 adjusting entry to get from step 1 to step 2. *Assume no other adjusting entries are made during the year.*

a. Accounts Receivable. At year-end, the L. Cole Company has completed services of $19,000 for a client, but the client has not yet been billed for those services.

b. Interest Receivable. At year-end, the company has earned, but not yet recorded, $390 of interest earned from its investments in government bonds.

c. Accounts Receivable. A painting company bills customers when jobs are complete. The work for one job is now complete. The customer has not yet been billed for the $1,300 of work.

QS 3-16
Recording and analyzing adjusting entries
P1 P2 P3 P4

For the entries below, identify the account to be debited and the account to be credited. Indicate which of the accounts is the income statement account and which is the balance sheet account.

a. Entry to record services revenue earned that was previously received as cash in advance.
b. Entry to record wage expenses incurred but not yet paid or recorded.
c. Entry to record services revenue earned but not yet billed or recorded.
d. Entry to record expiration of prepaid insurance.
e. Entry to record annual depreciation expense.

QS 3-17
Determining effects of adjusting entries
P1 P3

In making adjusting entries at the end of its accounting period, Chao Consulting mistakenly forgot to record:

1. $3,200 of insurance coverage that had expired (this $3,200 cost had been initially debited to the Prepaid Insurance account).
2. $2,000 of accrued salaries expense.

As a result of these two oversights, the financial statements for the reporting period will [choose one]:

a. Understate assets by $3,200.
b. Understate expenses by $5,200.
c. Understate net income by $2,000.
d. Overstate liabilities by $2,000.

QS 3-18
Preparing an adjusted trial balance
P5

Following are unadjusted balances along with year-end adjustments for Quinlan Company. Complete the adjusted trial balance by entering the adjusted balance for each of the following accounts.

		Unadjusted Trial Balance		Adjustments		Adjusted Trial Balance	
No.	**Account Title**	**Dr.**	**Cr.**	**Dr.**	**Cr.**	**Dr.**	**Cr.**
101	Cash	$8,000					
106	Accounts receivable	2,000		$4,000			
126	Supplies	4,500			$2,500		
209	Salaries payable		$ 0		400		
301	J. Quinlan, Capital		9,000				
403	Consulting revenue		11,000		4,000		
622	Salaries expense	5,500		400			
652	Supplies expense	0		2,500			

QS 3-19
Preparing financial statements
P5

The adjusted trial balance for Happ Company follows. Use the adjusted trial balance to prepare the December 31 year-end (*a*) income statement, (*b*) statement of owner's equity, and (*c*) balance sheet. The E. Happ, Capital account balance was $65,500 on December 31 of the *prior year*, and there were no owner investments in the current year.

Adjusted Trial Balance December 31		
Account Title	**Dr.**	**Cr.**
Cash	$ 7,000	
Accounts receivable	27,200	
Trucks	42,000	
Accumulated depreciation—Trucks		$ 17,500
Land	32,000	
Accounts payable		15,000
Salaries payable		4,200
Unearned revenue		3,600
E. Happ, Capital		65,500
E. Happ, Withdrawals	15,400	
Plumbing revenue		84,000
Depreciation expense—Trucks	6,500	
Salaries expense	46,700	
Rent expense	13,000	
Totals	$189,800	$189,800

Check Net income, $17,800

QS 3-20
Computing and analyzing profit margin **A1**

Gomez Company reported net income of $48,025 and net sales of $425,000 for the current year. (*a*) Compute Gomez's profit margin. (*b*) Assuming Cruz (a competitor) has a profit margin of 15%, which company is generating more profit on each dollar of sales?

QS 3-21^A
Preparing adjusting entries **P6**

Garcia Company had the following selected transactions during the year.

Jan. 1 The company paid $6,000 cash for 12 months of insurance coverage beginning immediately.
Aug. 1 The company received $2,400 cash in advance for 6 months of contracted services beginning on August 1 and ending on January 31.
Dec. 31 The company prepared any necessary year-end adjusting entries related to insurance coverage and services performed.

a. Record journal entries for these transactions assuming Garcia follows the usual practice of recording a prepayment of an expense in an asset account *and* recording a prepayment of revenue received in a liability account.
b. Record journal entries for these transactions assuming Garcia follows the alternative practice of recording a prepayment of an expense in an expense account *and* recording a prepayment of revenue received in a revenue account.

QS 3-22^A
Preparing adjusting entries **P6**

Cal Consulting follows the practice that prepayments are debited to expense when paid, and unearned revenues are credited to revenue when cash is received. Given this company's accounting practices, which one of the following applies to the preparation of adjusting entries at the end of its first accounting period?

a. Unearned revenue (on which cash was received in advance earlier in the period) is recorded with a debit to Consulting Revenue of $500 and a credit to Unearned Revenue of $500.
b. Unpaid salaries of $400 are recorded with a debit to Prepaid Salaries of $400 and a credit to Salaries Expense of $400.
c. Office supplies purchased for the period were $1,000. The cost of unused office supplies of $650 is recorded with a debit to Supplies Expense of $650 and a credit to Office Supplies of $650.
d. Earned but unbilled (and unrecorded) consulting revenue for the period was $1,200, which is recorded with a debit to Unearned Revenue of $1,200 and a credit to Consulting Revenue of $1,200.

Mc Graw Hill connect

EXERCISES

Exercise 3-1
Determining assets and expenses for accrual and cash accounting
C1

On March 1, Year 1, a company paid an $18,000 premium on a 36-month insurance policy for coverage beginning on that date. Refer to that policy and fill in the blanks in the following table.

Balance Sheet: Prepaid Insurance			Income Statement: Insurance Expense		
	Accrual Basis	Cash Basis		Accrual Basis	Cash Basis
Dec. 31, Year 1	$____	$____	Year 1	$____	$____
Dec. 31, Year 2	____	____	Year 2	____	____
Dec. 31, Year 3	____	____	Year 3	____	____
Dec. 31, Year 4	____	____	Year 4	____	____
			Total	$____	$____

Exercise 3-2
Determining when to recognize revenue **C1**

For each of the following separate situations, determine how much revenue is recognized in December (using accrual basis accounting).

a. On December 7, **Oklahoma City Thunder** sold a $90 ticket to a basketball game to be played in March.
b. **Tesla** sold and delivered a $58,000 car on December 25. The customer will not pay until February.
c. **Deloitte** signs a contract on December 1 to provide 40 days of advisory services with receipt of $10,000 due at the end of the contract. On December 31, 75% of the services have been completed.

Exercise 3-3
Determining when to recognize expenses
C1

For each of the following separate situations, determine the amount of expense each company should recognize in December (using accrual basis accounting).

a. **Chipotle** has monthly wages expense of $3,200 that has been incurred but not paid as of December 31.
b. **United Airlines** purchases a 24-month insurance policy for $48,000 on December 1 for immediate coverage.
c. On December 15, **Pfizer** prepays $20,000 for hotel rooms for its January sales meeting.

Exercise 3-4
Classifying adjusting entries
P1 P2 P3 P4

For journal entries *1* through *6*, identify the explanation that most closely describes it.

A. To record this period's depreciation expense.
B. To record accrued salaries expense.
C. To record this period's use of a prepaid expense.
D. To record accrued interest revenue.
E. To record accrued interest expense.
F. To record the earning of previously unearned income.

		Debit	Credit
____ 1.	Interest Expense	2,208	
	Interest Payable		2,208
____ 2.	Insurance Expense	3,180	
	Prepaid Insurance		3,180
____ 3.	Unearned Revenue	19,250	
	Services Revenue		19,250
____ 4.	Interest Receivable	3,300	
	Interest Revenue		3,300
____ 5.	Depreciation Expense	38,217	
	Accumulated Depreciation		38,217
____ 6.	Salaries Expense	13,280	
	Salaries Payable		13,280

Exercise 3-5
Determining cost flows through accounts
P1

Determine the missing amounts in each of these four separate situations *a* through *d*.

	a	b	c	d
Supplies available—prior year-end	$ 400	$1,200	$1,260	?
Supplies purchased during current year	2,800	6,500	?	$3,000
Supplies available—current year-end	650	?	1,350	700
Supplies expense for current year	?	1,200	8,400	4,588

Exercise 3-6
Preparing adjusting entries
P1 P2 P3

Prepare adjusting journal entries for the year ended December 31 for each separate situation. Entries can draw from the following partial chart of accounts: Cash; Accounts Receivable; Supplies; Prepaid Insurance; Prepaid Rent; Equipment; Accumulated Depreciation—Equipment; Wages Payable; Unearned Revenue; Services Revenue; Wages Expense; Supplies Expense; Insurance Expense; Rent Expense; and Depreciation Expense—Equipment.

a. Depreciation on the company's equipment for the year is computed to be $18,000.

b. The Prepaid Insurance account had a $6,000 debit balance at December 31 before adjusting for the costs of any expired coverage. An analysis of the company's insurance policies showed that $1,100 of unexpired insurance coverage remains.

c. The Supplies account had a $700 debit balance at the beginning of the year, and $3,480 of supplies were purchased during the year. The December 31 physical count showed $300 of supplies available.

Check (c) Dr. Supplies Expense, $3,880

d. Two-thirds of the work related to $15,000 of cash received in advance was performed this period.

e. The Prepaid Rent account had a $6,800 debit balance at December 31 before adjusting for the costs of expired prepaid rent. An analysis of the rental agreement showed that $5,800 of prepaid rent had expired.

(e) Dr. Rent Expense, $5,800

f. Wage expenses of $3,200 have been incurred but are not paid as of December 31.

Exercise 3-7
Adjusting and paying accrued wages
P3

Pablo Management has five employees, each of whom earns $250 per day. They are paid on Fridays for work completed Monday through Friday of the same week. Near year-end, the five employees worked Monday, December 31, and Wednesday, Thursday, and Friday, January 2, 3, and 4. New Year's Day (January 1) was an unpaid holiday.

a. Prepare the December 31 year-end adjusting entry for wages expense.

b. Prepare the journal entry to record payment of the employees' wages on Friday, January 4.

Exercise 3-8
Adjusting and paying accrued expenses
P3

The following three *separate* situations require adjusting journal entries to prepare financial statements as of April 30. For each situation, present both:

- The April 30 adjusting entry.
- The subsequent entry during May to record payment of the accrued expenses.

Entries can draw from the following partial chart of accounts: Cash; Accounts Receivable; Salaries Payable; Interest Payable; Legal Services Payable; Unearned Revenue; Services Revenue; Salaries Expense; Interest Expense; Legal Services Expense; and Depreciation Expense.

a. On April 1, the company hired an attorney for April for a flat fee of $3,500. Payment for April legal services was made by the company on May 12.

[continued on next page]

[continued from previous page]

Check (*b*) May 20, Dr. Interest Expense, $6,000

b. As of April 30, $3,000 of interest expense has accrued on a note payable. The full interest payment of $9,000 on the note is due on May 20.

c. Total weekly salaries expense for all employees is $10,000. This amount is paid at the end of the day on Friday of each five-day workweek. April 30 falls on a Tuesday, which means that the employees had worked two days since the last payday. The next payday is May 3.

Exercise 3-9
Preparing adjusting entries
P1 P3 P4

For each of the following separate cases, prepare adjusting entries required of financial statements for the year ended December 31. Entries can draw from the following partial chart of accounts: Cash; Interest Receivable; Supplies; Prepaid Insurance; Equipment; Accumulated Depreciation—Equipment; Wages Payable; Interest Payable; Unearned Revenue; Interest Revenue; Wages Expense; Supplies Expense; Insurance Expense; Interest Expense; and Depreciation Expense—Equipment.

a. Wages of $8,000 are earned by workers but not paid as of December 31.

b. Depreciation on the company's equipment for the year is $18,000.

c. The Supplies account had a $240 debit balance at the beginning of the year. During the year, $5,200 of supplies are purchased. A physical count of supplies at December 31 shows $440 of supplies available.

d. The Prepaid Insurance account had a $4,000 balance at the beginning of the year. An analysis of insurance policies shows that $1,200 of unexpired insurance benefits remain at December 31.

e. The company has earned (but not recorded) $1,050 of interest revenue for the year ended December 31. The interest payment will be received 10 days after the year-end on January 10.

f. The company has a bank loan and has incurred (but not recorded) interest expense of $2,500 for the year ended December 31. The company will pay the interest five days after the year-end on January 5.

Check (*d*) Dr. Insurance Expense, $2,800

(*e*) Cr. Interest Revenue, $1,050

Exercise 3-10
Analyzing adjusting entries using accounting equation
P1 P3 P4

Analyze each adjusting entry in Exercise 3-9 by showing its effects on the accounting equation—specifically, identify the accounts and amounts (including + or −) for each transaction or event.

Exercise 3-11
Preparing adjusting entries—accrued revenues and expenses
P3 P4

Prepare year-end adjusting journal entries for M&R Company as of December 31 for each of the following separate cases. Entries can draw from the following partial chart of accounts: Cash; Accounts Receivable; Interest Receivable; Equipment; Wages Payable; Salary Payable; Interest Payable; Lawn Services Payable; Unearned Revenue; Services Revenue; Interest Revenue; Wages Expense; Salary Expense; Supplies Expense; Lawn Services Expense; and Interest Expense.

a. M&R Company provided $2,000 in services to customers in December, which are not yet recorded. Those customers are expected to pay the company in January following the company's year-end.

b. Wage expenses of $1,000 have been incurred but are not paid as of December 31.

c. M&R Company has a $5,000 bank loan and has incurred (but not recorded) 8% interest expense of $400 for the year ended December 31. The company will pay the $400 interest in cash on January 2 following the company's year-end.

d. M&R Company hired a firm that provided lawn services during December for $500. M&R will pay for December lawn services on January 15 following the company's year-end.

e. M&R Company has earned $200 in interest revenue from investments for the year ended December 31. The interest revenue will be received on January 15 following the company's year-end.

f. Salary expenses of $900 have been earned by supervisors but not paid as of December 31.

Exercise 3-12
Analyzing adjusting entries using accounting equation
P3 P4

Analyze each adjusting entry in Exercise 3-11 by showing its effects on the accounting equation—specifically, identify the accounts and amounts (including + or −) for each transaction or event.

Exercise 3-13
Preparing adjusting entries
P1 P2 P3 P4

For each of the following separate cases, prepare the required December 31 year-end adjusting entries.

a. Depreciation on the company's wind turbine equipment for the year is $5,000.

b. The Prepaid Insurance account for the solar panels had a $2,000 debit balance at December 31 before adjusting for the costs of any expired coverage. Analysis of prepaid insurance shows that $600 of unexpired insurance coverage remains at year-end.

c. The company received $3,000 cash in advance for sustainability consulting work. As of December 31, one-third of the sustainability consulting work had been performed.

d. As of December 31, $1,200 in wages expense for the organic produce workers has been incurred but not yet paid.

e. As of December 31, the company has earned, but not yet recorded, $400 of interest revenue from investments in socially responsible bonds. The interest revenue is expected to be received on January 12.

Exercise 3-14
Analyzing effects of adjusting entries on financial statements
P5

For each of the separate cases in Exercise 3-13, determine the financial statement impact of each required year-end adjusting entry. Fill in the table below by indicating the amount and direction (+ or −) of the effect.

Adjusting Entry	Net Income	Total Assets	Total Liabilities	Total Equity
a.				
b.				
c.				
d.				
e.				

Exercise 3-15
Analyzing and preparing adjusting entries
P5

Following are two income statements for Alexis Co. for the year ended December 31. The left number column is prepared before adjusting entries are recorded, and the right column is prepared after adjusting entries. Analyze the statements and prepare the seven adjusting entries *a* through *g* that likely were recorded. *Hint:* The entry for *a* refers to revenue that has been earned but not yet billed. No adjusting entry involves cash.

Income Statements
For Year Ended December 31

	Unadjusted	Adjustments	Adjusted
Revenues			
Services revenue	$18,000	a.	$25,000
Commissions revenue	36,500		36,500
Total revenues	54,500		61,500
Expenses			
Depreciation expense—Computers	0	b.	1,600
Depreciation expense—Office furniture	0	c.	1,850
Salaries expense	13,500	d.	15,750
Insurance expense	0	e.	1,400
Rent expense	3,800		3,800
Office supplies expense	0	f.	580
Advertising expense	2,500		2,500
Utilities expense	1,245	g.	1,335
Total expenses	21,045		28,815
Net income	$33,455		$32,685

Exercise 3-16
Preparing an adjusted trial balance
P5

Stark Company has the following adjusted accounts with normal balances at its December 31 year-end. Prepare an adjusted trial balance for Stark Company at December 31.

Notes payable	$11,000	Accumulated depreciation—Buildings	$15,000
Prepaid insurance	2,500	Accounts receivable	4,000
Interest expense	500	Utilities expense	1,300
Accounts payable	1,500	Interest payable	100
Wages payable	400	Unearned revenue	800
Cash	10,000	Supplies expense	200
Wages expense	7,500	Buildings	40,000
Insurance expense	1,800	Stark, Withdrawals	3,000
Stark, Capital	24,800	Depreciation expense—Buildings	2,000
Services revenue	20,000	Supplies	800

Exercise 3-17
Preparing financial statements
P5

Use the adjusted accounts for Stark Company from Exercise 3-16 to prepare the (1) income statement and (2) statement of owner's equity for the year ended December 31 and (3) balance sheet at December 31. The Stark, Capital account balance was $24,800 on December 31 of the *prior year*, and there were no owner investments in the current year.

Exercise 3-18
Computing and interpreting profit margin
A1

Use the following information to compute profit margin for each separate company *a* through *e*. Which of the five companies is the most profitable according to the profit margin ratio? Interpret the profit margin ratio for company *c*.

	Net Income	Net Sales		Net Income	Net Sales
a.	$ 4,361	$ 44,500	d.	$65,646	$1,458,800
b.	97,706	398,800	e.	80,132	435,500
c.	111,281	257,000			

Exercise 3-19[A]
Adjusting for prepaids recorded as expenses and unearned revenues recorded as revenues
P6

Ricardo Construction began operations on December 1. In setting up its accounting procedures, the company decided to debit expense accounts when it prepays its expenses and to credit revenue accounts when customers pay for services in advance. Prepare journal entries for items *a* through *d* and the adjusting entries as of its December 31 period-end for items *e* through *g*. Entries can draw from the following partial chart of accounts: Cash; Accounts Receivable; Interest Receivable; Supplies; Prepaid Insurance; Unearned Remodeling Revenue; Remodeling Revenue; Supplies Expense; Insurance Expense; and Interest Expense.

a. Supplies are purchased on December 1 for $2,000 cash.
b. The company prepaid its insurance premiums for $1,540 cash on December 2.
c. On December 15, the company receives an advance payment of $13,000 cash from a customer for remodeling work.
d. On December 28, the company receives $3,700 cash from another customer for remodeling work to be performed in January.
e. A physical count on December 31 indicates that the company has $1,840 of supplies available.
f. An analysis of insurance policies in effect on December 31 shows that $340 of insurance coverage had expired.
g. As of December 31, only one remodeling project has been worked on and completed. The $5,570 price for this project had been received in advance and recorded as Remodeling Revenue.

Check (*f*) Cr. Insurance Expense, $1,200

(*g*) Dr. Remodeling Revenue, $11,130

Exercise 3-20[A]
Recording and reporting revenues received in advance
P6

Costanza Company experienced the following events and transactions in July. The company has the following partial chart of accounts: Cash; Accounts Receivable; Unearned Revenue; and Services Revenue.

July	1	Received $3,000 cash in advance of performing work for Vivian Solana.
	6	Received $7,500 cash in advance of performing work for Iris Haru.
	12	Completed the job for Solana.
	18	Received $8,500 cash in advance of performing work for Amina Jordan.
	31	(a) Completed the job for Haru. (b) None of the work for Jordan has been performed.

a. Prepare journal entries (including any adjusting entries as of the July 31 month-end) to record these events using the procedure of initially crediting the Unearned Revenue account when payment is received from a customer in advance of performing services.
b. Prepare journal entries (including any adjusting entries as of the July 31 month-end) to record these events using the alternative procedure of initially crediting the Services Revenue account when payment is received from a customer in advance of performing services.
c. Under each method, determine the amount of Services Revenue reported on the income statement for July and the amount of Unearned Revenue reported on the balance sheet as of July 31.

connect

PROBLEM SET A

Problem 3-1A
Identifying adjusting entries with explanations

P1 P2 P3 P4

For journal entries *1* through *12*, indicate the explanation that most closely describes it. You can use explanations more than once.

A. To record receipt of unearned revenue.
B. To record this period's earning of prior unearned revenue.
C. To record payment of an accrued expense.
D. To record receipt of an accrued revenue.
E. To record an accrued expense.
F. To record an accrued revenue.
G. To record this period's use of a prepaid expense.
H. To record payment of a prepaid expense.
I. To record this period's depreciation expense.

	Account	Debit	Credit
1.	Interest Expense	1,000	
	Interest Payable		1,000
2.	Depreciation Expense	4,000	
	Accumulated Depreciation		4,000
3.	Unearned Revenue	3,000	
	Services Revenue		3,000
4.	Insurance Expense	4,200	
	Prepaid Insurance		4,200
5.	Salaries Payable	1,400	
	Cash		1,400
6.	Prepaid Rent	4,500	
	Cash		4,500
7.	Salaries Expense	6,000	
	Salaries Payable		6,000
8.	Interest Receivable	5,000	
	Interest Revenue		5,000
9.	Cash	9,000	
	Accounts Receivable (from consulting)		9,000
10.	Cash	7,500	
	Unearned Revenue		7,500
11.	Cash	2,000	
	Interest Receivable		2,000
12.	Rent Expense	2,000	
	Prepaid Rent		2,000

Problem 3-2A
Preparing adjusting and subsequent journal entries

P1 P2 P3 P4

Arnez Company's annual accounting period ends on December 31. The following information concerns the adjusting entries to be recorded as of that date. Entries can draw from the following partial chart of accounts: Cash; Accounts Receivable; Office Supplies; Prepaid Insurance; Building; Accumulated Depreciation—Building; Salaries Payable; Unearned Revenue; Rent Revenue; Salaries Expense; Office Supplies Expense; Insurance Expense; and Depreciation Expense—Building.

a. The Office Supplies account started the year with a $4,000 balance. During the year, the company purchased supplies for $13,400, which was added to the Office Supplies account. The inventory of supplies available at December 31 totaled $2,554.

b. The Prepaid Insurance account had a $20,000 debit balance at December 31 before adjusting for the costs of any expired coverage for the year. An analysis of prepaid insurance shows that $12,880 of unexpired insurance coverage remains at year-end.

c. The company has 15 employees, who earn a total of $1,960 in salaries each working day. They are paid each Monday for their work in the five-day workweek ending on the previous Friday. Assume that December 31 is a Tuesday, and all 15 employees worked the first two days of that week. Because New Year's Day is a paid holiday, they will be paid salaries for five full days on Monday, January 6 of next year.

d. The company purchased a building at the beginning of this year. It cost $960,000 and is expected to have a $45,000 salvage value at the end of its predicted 30-year life. Annual depreciation is $30,500.

e. Since the company is not large enough to occupy the entire building it owns, it rented space to a tenant at $3,000 per month, starting on November 1. The rent was paid on time on November 1, and the amount received was credited to Rent Revenue. However, the tenant has not paid the December rent. The company has worked out an agreement with the tenant, who has promised to pay both December and January rent in full on January 15.

f. On November 1, the company rented space to another tenant for $2,800 per month. The tenant paid five months' rent in advance on that date. The payment was recorded with a credit to the Unearned Revenue account.

Required

1. Use the information to prepare adjusting entries as of December 31.
2. Prepare journal entries to record the first subsequent cash transaction in January of the next year for parts *c* and *e*.

Check (1*b*) Dr. Insurance Expense, $7,120
(1*d*) Dr. Depreciation Expense, $30,500

Problem 3-3A
Preparing adjusting entries, adjusted trial balance, and financial statements
P1 P2 P3 P4 P5

Wells Technical Institute (WTI), a school owned by Tristana Wells, provides training to individuals who pay tuition directly to the school. WTI also offers training to groups in off-site locations. Its unadjusted trial balance as of December 31 follows, along with descriptions of items *a* through *h* that require adjusting entries on December 31.

Additional Information

a. An analysis of WTI's insurance policies shows that $2,400 of coverage has expired.
b. An inventory count shows that teaching supplies costing $2,800 are available at year-end.
c. Annual depreciation on the equipment is $13,200.
d. Annual depreciation on the professional library is $7,200.
e. On September 1, WTI agreed to do five training courses for a client for $2,500 each. Two courses will start immediately and finish before the end of the year. Three courses will not begin until next year. The client paid $12,500 cash in advance for all five training courses on September 1, and WTI credited Unearned Revenue.
f. On October 15, WTI agreed to teach a four-month class (beginning immediately) for an executive with payment due at the end of the class. At December 31, $7,500 of the tuition revenue has been earned by WTI.
g. WTI's two employees are paid weekly. As of the end of the year, two days' salaries have accrued at the rate of $100 per day for each employee.
h. The balance in the Prepaid Rent account represents rent for December.

WELLS TECHNICAL INSTITUTE
Unadjusted Trial Balance
December 31

	Debit	Credit
Cash	$ 34,000	
Accounts receivable	0	
Teaching supplies	8,000	
Prepaid insurance	12,000	
Prepaid rent	3,000	
Professional library	35,000	
Accumulated depreciation—Professional library		$ 10,000
Equipment	80,000	
Accumulated depreciation—Equipment		15,000
Accounts payable		26,000
Salaries payable		0
Unearned revenue		12,500
T. Wells, Capital		90,000
T. Wells, Withdrawals	50,000	
Tuition revenue		123,900
Training revenue		40,000
Depreciation expense—Professional library	0	
Depreciation expense—Equipment	0	
Salaries expense	50,000	
Insurance expense	0	
Rent expense	33,000	
Teaching supplies expense	0	
Advertising expense	6,000	
Utilities expense	6,400	
Totals	$317,400	$317,400

Required

1. Prepare T-accounts (representing the ledger) with balances from the unadjusted trial balance.
2. Prepare the necessary adjusting journal entries for items *a* through *h* and post them to the T-accounts. Assume that adjusting entries are made only at year-end.
3. Update balances in the T-accounts for the adjusting entries and prepare an adjusted trial balance.
4. Prepare Wells Technical Institute's income statement and statement of owner's equity for the year and prepare its balance sheet as of December 31. The T. Wells, Capital account balance was $90,000 on December 31 of the *prior year*, and there were no owner investments in the current year.

Check (2e) Cr. Training Revenue, $5,000
(2f) Cr. Tuition Revenue, $7,500
(3) Adj. trial balance totals, $345,700
(4) Net income, $49,600

Problem 3-4A
Preparing financial statements from the adjusted trial balance
P5

The adjusted trial balance for Chiara Company as of December 31 follows.

	Debit	Credit
Cash	$ 30,000	
Accounts receivable	52,000	
Interest receivable	18,000	
Notes receivable (due in 90 days)	168,000	
Office supplies	16,000	
Automobiles	168,000	
Accumulated depreciation—Automobiles		$ 50,000
Equipment	138,000	
Accumulated depreciation—Equipment		18,000
Land	78,000	
Accounts payable		96,000
Interest payable		20,000
Salaries payable		19,000
Unearned revenue		30,000
Long-term notes payable		138,000
R. Chiara, Capital		255,800
R. Chiara, Withdrawals	46,000	
Services revenue		484,000
Interest revenue		24,000
Depreciation expense—Automobiles	26,000	
Depreciation expense—Equipment	18,000	
Salaries expense	188,000	
Wages expense	40,000	
Interest expense	32,000	
Office supplies expense	34,000	
Advertising expense	58,000	
Repairs expense—Automobiles	24,800	
Totals	$1,134,800	$1,134,800

Required

Use the information in the adjusted trial balance to prepare (*a*) the income statement for the year ended December 31; (*b*) the statement of owner's equity for the year ended December 31 [*Note:* R. Chiara, Capital at December 31 of the *prior year* was $255,800, and there were no owner investments in the current year.]; and (*c*) the balance sheet as of December 31.

Check Total assets, $600,000

Problem 3-5A[A]
Recording prepaid expenses and unearned revenues
P6

Gomez Co. had the following transactions in the last two months of its year ended December 31. Entries can draw from the following partial chart of accounts: Cash; Prepaid Insurance; Prepaid Advertising; Prepaid Consulting; Unearned Revenue; Services Revenue; Insurance Expense; Advertising Expense; and Consulting Expense.

Nov. 1 Paid $1,800 cash for future advertising.
1 Paid $2,460 cash for 12 months of insurance through October 31 of the next year.
30 Received $3,600 cash for future services to be provided to a customer.
Dec. 1 Paid $3,000 cash for consulting to be received over the next three months.
15 Received $7,950 cash for future services to be provided to a customer.
31 Of the advertising paid for on November 1, $1,200 worth is not yet used.
31 A portion of the insurance paid for on November 1 has expired. No adjustment was made in November to Prepaid Insurance.
31 Services worth $1,500 are not yet provided to the customer who paid on November 30.
31 One-third of the consulting paid for on December 1 has been received.
31 The company has performed $3,300 of services that the customer paid for on December 15.

Required

1. Prepare entries for these transactions under the method that initially records prepaid expenses as assets and records unearned revenues as liabilities. Also prepare adjusting entries at the end of the year.
2. Prepare entries for these transactions under the method that initially records prepaid expenses as expenses and records unearned revenues as revenues. Also prepare adjusting entries at the end of the year.

PROBLEM SET B

Problem 3-1B
Identifying adjusting entries with explanations
P1 P2 P3 P4

For journal entries *1* through *12,* indicate the explanation that most closely describes it. You can use explanations more than once.

A. To record payment of a prepaid expense.
B. To record this period's use of a prepaid expense.
C. To record this period's depreciation expense.
D. To record receipt of unearned revenue.
E. To record this period's earning of prior unearned revenue.
F. To record an accrued expense.
G. To record payment of an accrued expense.
H. To record an accrued revenue.
I. To record receipt of accrued revenue.

		Debit	Credit
1.	Interest Receivable	3,500	
	Interest Revenue		3,500
2.	Salaries Payable	9,000	
	Cash		9,000
3.	Depreciation Expense	8,000	
	Accumulated Depreciation		8,000
4.	Cash	9,000	
	Unearned Revenue		9,000
5.	Insurance Expense	4,000	
	Prepaid Insurance		4,000
6.	Interest Expense	5,000	
	Interest Payable		5,000
7.	Cash	1,500	
	Accounts Receivable (from services)		1,500
8.	Salaries Expense	7,000	
	Salaries Payable		7,000
9.	Cash	1,000	
	Interest Receivable		1,000
10.	Prepaid Rent	3,000	
	Cash		3,000
11.	Rent Expense	7,500	
	Prepaid Rent		7,500
12.	Unearned Revenue	6,000	
	Services Revenue		6,000

Problem 3-2B
Preparing adjusting and subsequent journal entries
P1 P2 P3 P4

Natsu Company's annual accounting period ends on October 31. The following information concerns the adjusting entries that need to be recorded as of that date. Entries can draw from the following partial chart of accounts: Cash; Accounts Receivable; Office Supplies; Prepaid Insurance; Building; Accumulated Depreciation—Building; Salaries Payable; Unearned Revenue; Rent Revenue; Salaries Expense; Office Supplies Expense; Insurance Expense; and Depreciation Expense—Building.

a. The Office Supplies account started the fiscal year with a $600 balance. During the fiscal year, the company purchased supplies for $4,570, which was added to the Office Supplies account. The supplies available at October 31 totaled $800.

b. The Prepaid Insurance account had a $12,000 debit balance at October 31 before adjusting for the costs of any expired coverage for the fiscal year. An analysis of prepaid insurance shows that $7,270 of unexpired insurance coverage remains at October 31.

c. The company has four employees, who earn a total of $1,000 for each workday. They are paid each Monday for their work in the five-day workweek ending on the previous Friday. Assume that October 31 is a Monday, and all four employees worked the first day of that week. They will be paid salaries for five full days on Monday, November 7 of the next fiscal year.

d. The company purchased a building at the beginning of this fiscal year that cost $175,000 and is expected to have a $40,000 salvage value at the end of its predicted 25-year life. Annual depreciation is $5,400.

e. Because the company does not occupy the entire building it owns, it rented space to a tenant at $1,000 per month, starting on September 1. The rent was paid on time on September 1, and the amount received was credited to the Rent Revenue account. However, the October rent has not been paid. The company has worked out an agreement with the tenant, who has promised to pay both October and November rent in full on November 15.

f. On September 1, the company rented space to another tenant for $725 per month. The tenant paid five months' rent in advance on that date. The payment was recorded with a credit to Unearned Revenue.

Required

1. Use the information to prepare adjusting entries as of October 31.

2. Prepare journal entries to record the first subsequent cash transaction in November for parts *c* and *e*.

Check (1*b*) Dr. Insurance Expense, $4,730
(1*d*) Dr. Depreciation Expense, $5,400

Problem 3-3B
Preparing adjusting entries, adjusted trial balance, and financial statements
P1 P2 P3 P4 P5

Following is the unadjusted trial balance for Alonzo Institute as of December 31. The Institute provides one-on-one training to individuals who pay tuition directly to the business and offers extension training to groups in off-site locations. Shown after the trial balance are items *a* through *h* that require adjusting entries as of December 31.

ALONZO INSTITUTE Unadjusted Trial Balance December 31		
	Debit	**Credit**
Cash	$ 60,000	
Accounts receivable	0	
Teaching supplies	70,000	
Prepaid insurance	19,000	
Prepaid rent	3,800	
Professional library	12,000	
Accumulated depreciation—Professional library		$ 2,500
Equipment	40,000	
Accumulated depreciation—Equipment		20,000
Accounts payable		11,200
Salaries payable		0
Unearned revenue		28,600
C. Alonzo, Capital		71,500
C. Alonzo, Withdrawals	20,000	
Tuition revenue		129,200
Training revenue		68,000
Depreciation expense—Professional library	0	
Depreciation expense—Equipment	0	
Salaries expense	44,200	
Insurance expense	0	
Rent expense	29,600	
Teaching supplies expense	0	
Advertising expense	19,000	
Utilities expense	13,400	
Totals	$331,000	$331,000

Additional Information

a. An analysis of the Institute's insurance policies shows that $9,500 of coverage has expired.

b. An inventory count shows that teaching supplies costing $20,000 are available at year-end.

c. Annual depreciation on the equipment is $5,000.

d. Annual depreciation on the professional library is $2,400.

e. On November 1, the Institute agreed to do a special two-month training course (starting immediately) for a client. The contract calls for a $14,300 monthly fee, and the client paid the two months' training fees in advance. When the cash was received, the Unearned Revenue account was credited.

f. On October 15, the Institute agreed to teach a four-month class (beginning immediately) to an executive with payment due at the end of the class. At December 31, $5,750 of the tuition revenue has been earned by the Institute.

g. The Institute's only employee is paid weekly. As of the end of the year, three days' salaries have accrued at the rate of $150 per day.

h. The balance in the Prepaid Rent account represents rent for December.

Required

1. Prepare T-accounts (representing the ledger) with balances from the unadjusted trial balance.

2. Prepare the necessary adjusting journal entries for items *a* through *h* and post them to the T-accounts. Assume that adjusting entries are made only at year-end.

3. Update balances in the T-accounts for the adjusting entries and prepare an adjusted trial balance.

4. Prepare the company's income statement and statement of owner's equity for the year, and prepare its balance sheet as of December 31. The C. Alonzo, Capital account balance was $71,500 on December 31 of the *prior year*, and there were no owner investments in the current year.

Check (2e) Cr. Training Revenue, $28,600
(2f) Cr. Tuition Revenue, $5,750
(3) Adj. trial balance totals, $344,600
(4) Net income, $54,200

Problem 3-4B
Preparing financial statements from adjusted trial balance
P5

The adjusted trial balance for Speedy Courier as of December 31 follows.

	Debit	Credit
Cash	$ 58,000	
Accounts receivable	120,000	
Interest receivable	7,000	
Notes receivable (due in 90 days)	210,000	
Office supplies	22,000	
Trucks	134,000	
Accumulated depreciation—Trucks		$ 58,000
Equipment	270,000	
Accumulated depreciation—Equipment		200,000
Land	100,000	
Accounts payable		134,000
Interest payable		20,000
Salaries payable		28,000
Unearned revenue		120,000
Long-term notes payable		200,000
L. Garcia, Capital		125,000
L. Garcia, Withdrawals	50,000	
Services revenue		611,800
Interest revenue		34,000
Depreciation expense—Trucks	29,000	
Depreciation expense—Equipment	48,000	
Salaries expense	74,000	
Wages expense	300,000	
Interest expense	15,000	
Office supplies expense	31,000	
Advertising expense	27,200	
Repairs expense—Trucks	35,600	
Totals	$1,530,800	$1,530,800

Required

Use the information in the adjusted trial balance to prepare (*a*) the income statement for the year ended December 31; (*b*) the statement of owner's equity for the year ended December 31 [*Note:* L. Garcia, Capital at Dec. 31 of the *prior year* was $125,000, and there were no owner investments in the current year.]; and (*c*) the balance sheet as of December 31.

Check Total assets, $663,000

Problem 3-5B[A]
Recording prepaid expenses and unearned revenues
P6

Tremor Co. had the following transactions in the last two months of its fiscal year ended May 31. Entries can draw from the following partial chart of accounts: Cash; Prepaid Insurance; Prepaid Advertising; Prepaid Consulting; Unearned Revenue; Services Revenue; Insurance Expense; Advertising Expense; and Consulting Expense.

Apr.	1	Paid $2,450 cash to an accounting firm for future consulting services.
	1	Paid $3,600 cash for 12 months of insurance through March 31 of the next year.
	30	Received $8,500 cash for future services to be provided to a customer.
May	1	Paid $4,450 cash for future advertising.
	23	Received $10,450 cash for future services to be provided to a customer.
	31	Of the consulting paid for on April 1, $2,000 worth has been performed.
	31	A portion of the insurance paid for on April 1 has expired. No adjustment was made in April to Prepaid Insurance.
	31	Services worth $4,600 are not yet provided to the customer who paid on April 30.
	31	Of the advertising paid for on May 1, $2,050 worth is not yet used.
	31	The company has performed $5,500 of services that the customer paid for on May 23.

Required

1. Prepare entries for these transactions under the method that initially records prepaid expenses and unearned revenues in balance sheet accounts. Also prepare adjusting entries at its May 31 fiscal year-end.
2. Prepare entries for these transactions under the method that initially records prepaid expenses and unearned revenues in income statement accounts. Also prepare adjusting entries at its May 31 fiscal year-end.

Analysis Component

3. Explain why the alternative sets of entries in parts 1 and 2 do not result in different financial statement amounts.

connect

SERIAL PROBLEM

Business Solutions

P1 P2 P3 P4 P5

*Serial problem began in Chapter 1. If previous chapter segments were not completed, the serial problem can begin at this point. It is available in **Connect** with an algorithmic option.*

SP 3 After the success of the company's first two months, Santana Rey continues to operate **Business Solutions**. (Transactions for the first two months are described in the Chapter 2 serial problem.) The November 30, 2021, unadjusted trial balance of Business Solutions (reflecting its transactions for October and November of 2021) follows.

Alexander Image/Shutterstock

No.	Account Title	Debit	Credit
101	Cash	$38,264	
106	Accounts receivable	12,618	
126	Computer supplies	2,545	
128	Prepaid insurance	2,220	
131	Prepaid rent	3,300	
163	Office equipment	8,000	
164	Accumulated depreciation—Office equipment		$ 0
167	Computer equipment	20,000	
168	Accumulated depreciation—Computer equipment		0
201	Accounts payable		0
210	Wages payable		0
236	Unearned computer services revenue		0
301	S. Rey, Capital		73,000
302	S. Rey, Withdrawals	5,600	
403	Computer services revenue		25,659
612	Depreciation expense—Office equipment	0	
613	Depreciation expense—Computer equipment	0	
623	Wages expense	2,625	
637	Insurance expense	0	
640	Rent expense	0	
652	Computer supplies expense	0	
655	Advertising expense	1,728	
676	Mileage expense	704	
677	Miscellaneous expenses	250	
684	Repairs expense—Computer	805	
	Totals	$98,659	$98,659

Business Solutions had the following transactions and events in December 2021.

Dec.	2	Paid $1,025 cash to Hillside Mall for Business Solutions's share of mall advertising costs.
	3	Paid $500 cash for minor repairs to the company's computer.
	4	Received $3,950 cash from Alex's Engineering Co. for the receivable from November.
	10	Paid cash to Lyn Addie for six days of work at the rate of $125 per day.
	14	Notified by Alex's Engineering Co. that Business Solutions's bid of $7,000 on a proposed project has been accepted. Alex's paid a $1,500 cash advance to Business Solutions.
	15	Purchased $1,100 of computer supplies on credit from Harris Office Products.
	16	Sent a reminder to Gomez Co. to pay the fee for services recorded on November 8.
	20	Completed a project for Liu Corporation and received $5,625 cash.
	22–26	Took the week off for the holidays.
	28	Received $3,000 cash from Gomez Co. on its receivable.
	29	Reimbursed S. Rey for business automobile mileage (600 miles at $0.32 per mile).
	31	S. Rey withdrew $1,500 cash from the company for personal use.

The following additional facts are collected for use in making adjusting entries prior to preparing financial statements for the company's first three months.

a. The December 31 inventory count of computer supplies shows $580 still available.

b. Three months have expired since the 12-month insurance premium was paid in advance.

c. As of December 31, Lyn Addie has not been paid for four days of work at $125 per day.

d. The computer system, acquired on October 1, is expected to have a four-year life with no salvage value.

e. The office equipment, acquired on October 1, is expected to have a five-year life with no salvage value.

f. Three of the four months' prepaid rent have expired.

[continued on next page]

[continued from previous page]

Required

1. Prepare journal entries to record each of the December transactions and events for Business Solutions. Post those entries to the accounts in the ledger.
2. Prepare adjusting entries to reflect *a* through *f*. Post those entries to the accounts in the ledger.
3. Prepare an adjusted trial balance as of December 31, 2021.

Check (3) Adjusted trial balance totals, $109,034

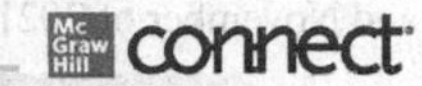

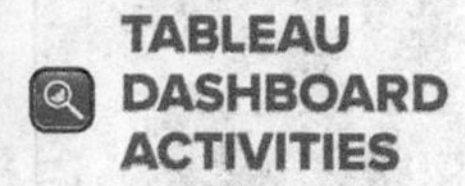

TABLEAU DASHBOARD ACTIVITIES

Tableau Dashboard Activities expose students to accounting analytics using visual displays. These assignments run in **Connect**. All are auto-gradable.

Tableau DA 3-1 Quick Study, Preparing adjusting entries, **P1, P2**—similar to QS 3-5 & 3-10

Tableau DA 3-2 Exercise, Preparing adjusting entries, **P1, P2, P3, P4**—similar to Exercises 3-9 & 3-11

Tableau DA 3-3 Mini-Case, Analyzing adjusting entries and preparing an adjusted trial balance, **P5**—similar to Exercises 3-10 & 3-12, QS 3-18

GENERAL LEDGER

General Ledger (GL) Assignments expose students to general ledger software similar to that in practice. **GL** is part of **Connect**, and **GL** assignments are auto-gradable and have algorithmic options. For the following **GL** assignments, prepare adjusting entries and determine their impact on net income. Financial statements are automatically generated based on entries recorded—this feature can be turned off.

GL 3-1 Based on the FastForward illustration in this chapter

For the following **GL** assignments, prepare the necessary adjustments, create the financial statements, and determine the impact each adjustment has on net income.

GL 3-2 Based on Problem 3-3A

GL 3-3 Extension of Problem 2-1A

GL 3-4 Extension of Problem 2-2A

GL 3-5 Based on Serial Problem SP 3

Accounting Analysis

connect

COMPANY ANALYSIS
A1

AA 3-1 Use **Apple**'s financial statements in Appendix A to answer the following.

1. Compute Apple's profit margin for fiscal years ended (*a*) September 28, 2019, and (*b*) September 29, 2018.
2. Is the change in Apple's profit margin favorable or unfavorable?
3. In 2019, did Apple's profit margin outperform or underperform the industry (assumed) average of 12%?

COMPARATIVE ANALYSIS
A1

AA 3-2 Key figures for the recent two years of both **Apple** and **Google** follow.

	Apple		Google	
$ millions	Current Year	Prior Year	Current Year	Prior Year
Net income	$ 55,256	$ 59,531	$ 34,343	$ 30,736
Net sales	260,174	265,595	161,857	136,819

Required

1. Compute profit margins for (*a*) Apple and (*b*) Google for the two years of data reported above.
2. In the *prior* year, which company is more successful on the basis of profit margin?

EXTENDED ANALYSIS
A1

AA 3-3 Key comparative figures for **Samsung, Apple,** and **Google** follow.

$ millions	Samsung	Apple	Google
Net income	$ 18,653	$ 55,256	$ 34,343
Net sales	197,691	260,174	161,857

Required

1. Compute profit margin for Samsung, Apple, and Google.
2. Which company is least successful on the basis of profit margin?

Discussion Questions

1. What is the difference between the cash basis and the accrual basis of accounting?
2. Why is the accrual basis of accounting generally preferred over the cash basis?
3. What type of business is most likely to select a fiscal year that corresponds to its natural business year instead of the calendar year?
4. What is a prepaid expense, and where is it reported in the financial statements?
5. What contra account is used when recording and reporting the effects of depreciation? Why is it used?
6. What is an accrued revenue? Give an example.
7. How is unearned revenue classified on the balance sheet?
8.[A] If a company initially records prepaid expenses with debits to expense accounts, what type of account is debited in the adjusting entries for those prepaid expenses?

Beyond the Numbers

ETHICS CHALLENGE
C1 P1

BTN 3-1 Jessica Boland works for Sea Biscuit Co. She and Farah Smith, her manager, are preparing adjusting entries for annual financial statements. Boland computes depreciation and records it as

Depreciation Expense—Equipment	123,000	
Accumulated Depreciation—Equipment		123,000

Smith agrees with her computation but says the credit entry should be directly to the Equipment account. Smith argues that while accumulated depreciation is technically correct, "it is less hassle not to use a contra account and just credit the Equipment account directly. And besides, the balance sheet shows the same amount for total assets under either method."

Required

1. How should depreciation be recorded? Do you support Boland or Smith?
2. Evaluate the strengths and weaknesses of Smith's reasons for preferring her method.
3. Indicate whether the situation Boland faces is an ethical problem. Explain.

COMMUNICATING IN PRACTICE
A1

BTN 3-2 The class should be divided into teams. Teams are to select an industry (such as automobile manufacturing, airlines, defense contractors), and each team member is to select a different company in that industry. Each team member is to acquire the annual report of the company selected. Annual reports can be downloaded from company websites or from the SEC's EDGAR database (SEC.gov).

Required

1. Use the annual report to compute the return on assets, debt ratio, and profit margin.
2. Communicate with team members via a meeting, e-mail, or telephone to discuss the meaning of the ratios, how different companies compare to each other, and the industry norm. The team must prepare a single memo reporting the ratios for each company and identifying the conclusions or consensus reached during the team's discussion. The memo is to be copied and distributed to the instructor and all classmates.

TEAMWORK IN ACTION
P1 P2 P3 P4

BTN 3-3 Four types of adjustments are described in the chapter: (1) prepaid expenses, (2) unearned revenues, (3) accrued expenses, and (4) accrued revenues.

Required

1. Form *learning teams* of four (or more) members. Each team member must select one of the four adjustments as an area of expertise (each team must have at least one expert in each area).
2. Form *expert teams* from the individuals who have selected the same area of expertise. Expert teams are to discuss and write a report that each expert will present to his or her learning team addressing the following:
   a. Description of the adjustment and why it's necessary.
   b. Example of a transaction or event, with dates and amounts, that requires adjustment.

[continued on next page]

[continued from previous page]

c. Adjusting entry(ies) for the example in requirement *b*.

d. Status of the affected account(s) before and after the adjustment in requirement *c*.

e. Effects on financial statements of not making the adjustment.

3. Each expert should return to his or her learning team. In rotation, each member should present his or her expert team's report to the learning team. Team discussion is encouraged.

ENTREPRENEURIAL DECISION

P2

BTN 3-4 Review this chapter's opening feature involving Emily and Betsy and Sword & Plough.

Required

1. Assume that Sword & Plough sells a $300 gift certificate to a customer, collecting the $300 cash in advance. Prepare the journal entry for (*a*) collection of the cash for delivery of the gift certificate to the customer and (*b*) revenue from the subsequent delivery of merchandise when the gift certificate is used.

2. How can keeping less inventory help to improve Sword & Plough's profit margin?

3. Emily and Betsy understand that many companies carry considerable inventory, and they are thinking of carrying additional inventory of merchandise for sale. Provide at least one reason for, and one reason against, carrying additional inventory.

4 Completing the Accounting Cycle

Chapter Preview

ACCOUNTING TOOL: WORK SHEET	CLOSING PROCESS	CLASSIFIED BALANCE SHEET
P1 Benefits of a work sheet	P2 Temporary accounts	C1 Classified balance sheet—Structure and categories
Preparing a work sheet	Closing entries	A1 Current ratio
Preparing financial statements	Post-closing trial balance	
	Accounting cycle	
NTK 4-1	NTK 4-2	NTK 4-3

Learning Objectives

CONCEPTUAL

C1 Explain and prepare a classified balance sheet.

ANALYTICAL

A1 Compute and analyze the current ratio.

PROCEDURAL

P1 Prepare a work sheet and explain its usefulness.

P2 Prepare closing entries and a post-closing trial balance.

P3 Appendix 4A—Prepare reversing entries and explain their purpose.

4 Completing the Accounting Cycle

Chapter Preview

ACCOUNTING TOOL: WORK SHEET	CLOSING PROCESS	CLASSIFIED BALANCE SHEET
P1 Benefits of a work sheet Preparing a work sheet Preparing financial statements	**P2** Temporary accounts Closing entries Post-closing trial balance Accounting cycle	**C1** Classified balance sheet—Structure and categories **A1** Current ratio
NTK 4-1	NTK 4-2	NTK 4-3

Learning Objectives

CONCEPTUAL

C1 Explain and prepare a classified balance sheet.

ANALYTICAL

A1 Compute and analyze the current ratio.

PROCEDURAL

P1 Prepare a work sheet and explain its usefulness.

P2 Prepare closing entries and a post-closing trial balance.

P3 *Appendix 4A*—Prepare reversing entries and explain their purpose.

It's a Snap!

"Creativity creates value"—**EVAN SPIEGEL**

J. Emilio Flores/Corbis/Getty Images

VENICE, CA—Evan Spiegel met his future co-founder Bobby Murphy in college. "We weren't cool," recalls Bobby, "so we tried to build things to be cool!" One of their cool projects was an app that could send messages that disappeared after a few seconds. This app would later be called **Snapchat** (**Snapchat.com**).

The first headquarters of Snapchat was the home of Evan's dad. However, within a matter of months, their app had over a million users.

As Snapchat grew, Evan and Bobby knew an effective accounting system was key to attracting investors. "One of the things I did underestimate," admits Evan, "was how much more important communication becomes [when seeking investors]."

Investors wanted to know revenues, costs, assets, and liabilities for Snapchat. "You really need to explain . . . how your business works," insists Evan.

To communicate "the Snap story," the entrepreneurs learned how to use work sheets and create classified financial statements. This included learning the accounting cycle. With accounting reports in hand, Evan and Bobby were able to secure additional financing. Exclaims Evan: "That was the greatest feeling of all time!"

Sources: *Snapchat website*, January 2021; *Vanity Fair*, October 2017; *LA Times*, March 2017; *Forbes*, January 2014

WORK SHEET AS A TOOL

Benefits of a Work Sheet (Spreadsheet)

P1 Prepare a work sheet and explain its usefulness.

A **work sheet** is a document that is used internally by companies to help with adjusting and closing accounts and with preparing financial statements. It is an internal accounting aid and is not a substitute for journals, ledgers, or financial statements. A work sheet:

- Helps in preparing financial statements.
- Reduces the risk of errors when working with many accounts and adjustments.
- Links accounts and adjustments to financial statements.
- Shows the effects of proposed or "what-if" transactions.

Decision Insight

Women in Accounting In a recent survey, it was reported that women make up roughly 50% of managers and senior managers at accounting firms. Women also make up about half of all supervisors and senior staff. If the current trend continues, women will soon hold the majority of manager and senior staff positions in accounting. Source: AICPA ■

Alexander Image/Shutterstock

Use of a Work Sheet

When a work sheet is used to prepare financial statements, it is constructed at the end of a period before the adjusting process. The complete work sheet includes a list of the accounts, their balances and adjustments, and their sorting into financial statement columns. To describe and interpret the work sheet, we use the information from FastForward. Preparing the work sheet has five steps.

① Step 1. Enter Unadjusted Trial Balance

Refer to Exhibit 4.1—green section. The first step in preparing a work sheet is to list the title of each account and its account number. This includes all accounts in the ledger plus any expected ones from adjusting entries. The unadjusted balance for each account is then entered in the correct Debit or Credit column of the unadjusted trial balance columns. The

EXHIBIT 4.1

Work Sheet

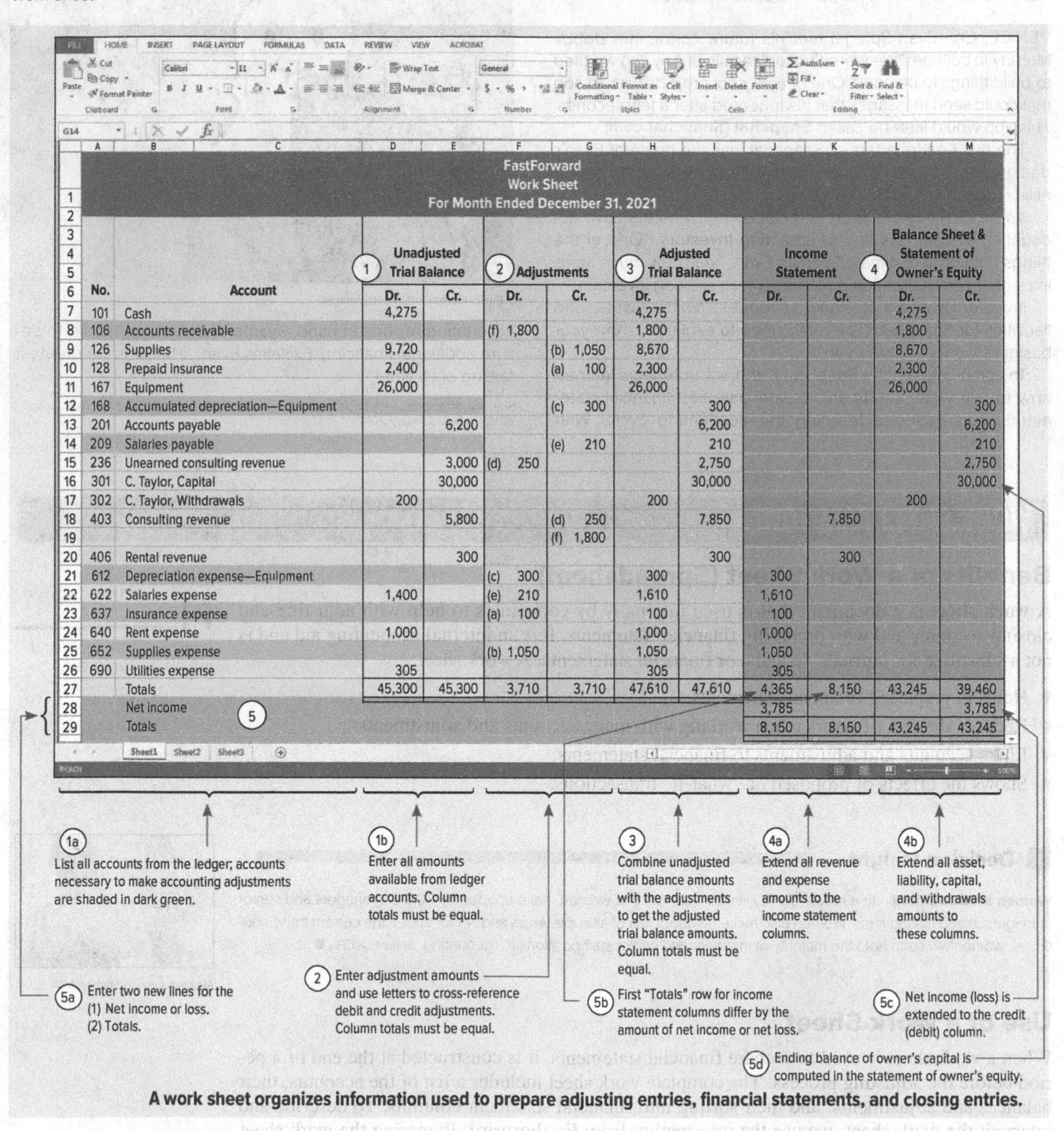

FastForward
Work Sheet
For Month Ended December 31, 2021

No.	Account	① Unadjusted Trial Balance Dr.	Cr.	② Adjustments Dr.	Cr.	③ Adjusted Trial Balance Dr.	Cr.	Income Statement Dr.	Cr.	④ Balance Sheet & Statement of Owner's Equity Dr.	Cr.
101	Cash	4,275				4,275				4,275	
106	Accounts receivable			(f) 1,800		1,800				1,800	
126	Supplies	9,720			(b) 1,050	8,670				8,670	
128	Prepaid insurance	2,400			(a) 100	2,300				2,300	
167	Equipment	26,000				26,000				26,000	
168	Accumulated depreciation—Equipment				(c) 300		300				300
201	Accounts payable		6,200				6,200				6,200
209	Salaries payable				(e) 210		210				210
236	Unearned consulting revenue		3,000	(d) 250			2,750				2,750
301	C. Taylor, Capital		30,000				30,000				30,000
302	C. Taylor, Withdrawals	200				200				200	
403	Consulting revenue		5,800		(d) 250		7,850		7,850		
					(f) 1,800						
406	Rental revenue		300				300		300		
612	Depreciation expense—Equipment			(c) 300		300		300			
622	Salaries expense	1,400		(e) 210		1,610		1,610			
637	Insurance expense			(a) 100		100		100			
640	Rent expense	1,000				1,000		1,000			
652	Supplies expense			(b) 1,050		1,050		1,050			
690	Utilities expense	305				305		305			
	Totals	45,300	45,300	3,710	3,710	47,610	47,610	4,365	8,150	43,245	39,460
	Net income ⑤							3,785			3,785
	Totals							8,150	8,150	43,245	43,245

A work sheet organizes information used to prepare adjusting entries, financial statements, and closing entries.

totals of these two columns must be equal. The light green section of Exhibit 4.1 shows FastForward's work sheet after completing this first step (dark green rows show accounts expected to arise from adjustments). Sometimes an account can require more than one adjustment, such as for Consulting Revenue. We add a blank line in this case.

2 Step 2. Enter Adjustments

Exhibit 4.1—yellow section. The second step is to enter adjustments in the Adjustments columns. The adjustments shown are the same ones shown in Exhibit 3.13. An identifying letter links the debit and credit of each adjustment. This is called *keying* the adjustments. After preparing a work sheet, **adjustments must still be entered in a journal and posted to the ledger.** The Adjustments columns provide the information for adjusting entries in the journal.

3 Step 3. Prepare Adjusted Trial Balance

Exhibit 4.1—blue section. The adjusted trial balance is prepared by combining the adjustments with the unadjusted balances for each account. As an example, the Prepaid Insurance account has a $2,400 debit balance in the Unadjusted Trial Balance columns. This $2,400 debit is combined with the $100 credit in the Adjustments columns to give Prepaid Insurance a $2,300 debit in the Adjusted Trial Balance columns. The totals of the Adjusted Trial Balance columns confirm debits and credits are equal.

4 Step 4. Sort Adjusted Trial Balance Amounts to Financial Statements

Exhibit 4.1—orange section. This step involves sorting account balances from the adjusted trial balance to their proper financial statement columns. Expenses go to the Income Statement Debit column, and revenues to the Income Statement Credit column. Assets and withdrawals go to the Balance Sheet & Statement of Owner's Equity Debit column. Liabilities and owner's capital go to the Balance Sheet & Statement of Owner's Equity Credit column.

5 Step 5. Total Statement Columns, Compute Income or Loss, and Balance Columns

Exhibit 4.1—purple section. Each financial statement column (from step 4) is totaled. The difference between the Debit and Credit column totals of the Income Statement columns is net income or net loss. This occurs because revenues are entered in the Credit column and expenses in the Debit column. If the Credit total exceeds the Debit total, there is net income. If the Debit total exceeds the Credit total, there is a net loss. For FastForward, the Credit total exceeds the Debit total, giving a $3,785 net income.

The net income from the Income Statement columns is then entered in the Balance Sheet & Statement of Owner's Equity Credit column. Adding net income to the last Credit column means that it is to be added to owner's capital. If a loss occurs, it is added to the Debit column. This means that it is to be subtracted from owner's capital. **The ending balance of owner's capital does not appear in the last two columns as a single amount, but it is computed in the statement of owner's equity** using these account balances. When net income or net loss is added to the Balance Sheet & Statement of Owner's Equity column, the totals of the last two columns must balance. If they do not, one or more errors have occurred.

Decision Maker

Entrepreneur You review the work sheet used to prepare financial statements. There is no depreciation adjustment, yet you own equipment. Does the absence of depreciation adjustment concern you? ■ *Answer:* Yes, you are concerned about the absence of a depreciation adjustment. Equipment does depreciate, and financial statements must recognize this occurrence. Its absence suggests an error (there is also the possibility that equipment is fully depreciated).

FrameStockFootages/Shutterstock

Preparing Financial Statements from a Work Sheet

A work sheet does not substitute for financial statements. It is a tool we use to help prepare financial statements. FastForward's financial statements are shown in Exhibit 4.2. Its income statement amounts are taken from the Income Statement columns of the work sheet. Amounts for its balance sheet and its statement of owner's equity are taken from the Balance Sheet & Statement of Owner's Equity columns of the work sheet.

EXHIBIT 4.2

Financial Statements Prepared from the Work Sheet

FASTFORWARD
Income Statement
For Month Ended December 31, 2021

Revenues		
Consulting revenue	$ 7,850	
Rental revenue	300	
Total revenues		$ 8,150
Expenses		
Depreciation expense—Equipment	300	
Salaries expense	1,610	
Insurance expense	100	
Rent expense	1,000	
Supplies expense	1,050	
Utilities expense	305	
Total expenses		4,365
Net income		$ 3,785

FASTFORWARD
Statement of Owner's Equity
For Month Ended December 31, 2021

C. Taylor, Capital, December 1		$ 0
Add: Investments by owner	$30,000	
Net income	3,785	33,785
		33,785
Less: Withdrawals by owner		200
C. Taylor, Capital, December 31		$33,585

FASTFORWARD
Balance Sheet
December 31, 2021

Assets		
Cash		$ 4,275
Accounts receivable		1,800
Supplies		8,670
Prepaid insurance		2,300
Equipment	$26,000	
Accumulated depreciation—Equipment	(300)	25,700
Total assets		$42,745
Liabilities		
Accounts payable		$ 6,200
Salaries payable		210
Unearned consulting revenue		2,750
Total liabilities		9,160
Equity		
C. Taylor, Capital		33,585
Total liabilities and equity		$42,745

NEED-TO-KNOW 4-1

Work Sheet

P1

The following 10-column work sheet contains the year-end unadjusted trial balance for Magic Company as of December 31. Complete the work sheet by entering the necessary adjustments, computing the adjusted account balances, extending the adjusted balances into the appropriate financial statement columns, and entering the amount of net income for the period. *Note:* The Magic, Capital account balance was $75,000 at December 31 of the *prior year*.

		Unadjusted Trial Balance		Adjustments		Adjusted Trial Balance		Income Statement		Balance Sheet and Statement of Owner's Equity	
No.	Account Title	Dr.	Cr.	Dr.	Cr.	Dr.	Cr.	Dr.	Cr.	Dr.	Cr.
101	Cash	13,000									
106	Accounts receivable	8,000									
183	Land	85,000									
201	Accounts payable		10,000								
251	Long-term notes payable		33,000								
301	Magic, Capital		75,000								
302	Magic, Withdrawals	20,000									
403	Services revenue		70,000								
622	Salaries expense	54,000									
650	Office supplies expense	8,000									
	Totals	188,000	188,000								
	Net income										
	Totals										

1. Prepare and complete the work sheet, starting with the unadjusted trial balance and including adjustments based on the following.
   a. The company has earned $9,000 in revenue that was not received or recorded at year-end.
   b. The company incurred $2,000 in salary expense that was not yet recorded or paid at year-end. Assume it records salary not yet paid as part of accounts payable.
   c. The long-term note payable was issued on December 31 this year. Thus, no interest has yet accrued on this loan.
2. Use information from the completed work sheet in part 1 to prepare adjusting journal entries.

3. Prepare the income statement and the statement of owner's equity for the year ended December 31 and the unclassified balance sheet at December 31.

Part 1 Solution

		Unadjusted Trial Balance		Adjustments		Adjusted Trial Balance		Income Statement		Balance Sheet and Statement of Owner's Equity	
No.	**Account Title**	**Dr.**	**Cr.**	**Dr.**	**Cr.**	**Dr.**	**Cr.**	**Dr.**	**Cr.**	**Dr.**	**Cr.**
101	Cash	13,000				13,000				13,000	
106	Accounts receivable	8,000		(a)9,000		17,000				17,000	
183	Land	85,000				85,000				85,000	
201	Accounts payable		10,000		(b)2,000		12,000				12,000
251	Long-term notes payable		33,000				33,000				33,000
301	Magic, Capital		75,000				75,000				75,000
302	Magic, Withdrawals	20,000				20,000				20,000	
403	Services revenue		70,000		(a)9,000		79,000		79,000		
622	Salaries expense	54,000		(b)2,000		56,000		56,000			
650	Office supplies expense	8,000				8,000		8,000			
	Totals	188,000	188,000	11,000	11,000	199,000	199,000	64,000	79,000	135,000	120,000
	Net income							15,000			15,000
	Totals							79,000	79,000	135,000	135,000

Part 2 Solution

(a) Dec. 31	Accounts Receivable	9,000	
	Services revenue		9,000
(b) Dec. 31	Salaries Expense	2,000	
	Accounts Payable		2,000
(c)	No entry required.		

Part 3 Solution

MAGIC COMPANY
Income Statement
For Year Ended December 31

Revenue		
Services revenue		$79,000
Expenses		
Salaries expense	$56,000	
Office supplies expense	8,000	
Total expenses		64,000
Net income		$15,000

MAGIC COMPANY
Statement of Owner's Equity
For Year Ended December 31

Magic, Capital, December 31, prior year	$75,000
Add: Investments by owner	0
Net income	15,000
	90,000
Less: Withdrawals by owner	20,000
Magic, Capital, December 31, current year	$70,000

MAGIC COMPANY
Balance Sheet
December 31

Assets	
Cash	$ 13,000
Accounts receivable..................	17,000
Land..................................	85,000
Total assets..........................	$115,000
Liabilities	
Accounts payable.....................	$ 12,000
Long-term notes payable.............	33,000
Total liabilities.......................	45,000
Equity	
Magic, Capital.........................	70,000
Total liabilities and equity............	$115,000

Do More: QS 4-1, QS 4-2, QS 4-3, QS 4-4, E 4-1, E 4-2, E 4-3, E 4-4

CLOSING PROCESS

P2 Prepare closing entires and a post-closing trial balance

The **closing process** occurs at the end of an accounting period *after* financial statements are completed. In the closing process we (1) identify accounts for closing, (2) record and post the closing entries, and (3) prepare a post-closing trial balance. The closing process has two purposes. First, it resets revenue, expense, and withdrawals account balances to zero at the end of each period. This is done so that these accounts can properly measure income and

TEMPORARY
PERMANENT

Temporary Accounts (closed at period-end)	Permanent Accounts (not closed at period-end)
Revenues	Assets
Expenses	Liabilities
Owner, Withdrawals	Owner, Capital
Income Summary	

withdrawals for the next period. Second, it updates the balance in the owner's capital account to match the amount reported on the statement of owner's equity and the balance sheet.

Temporary and Permanent Accounts

Temporary accounts relate to one accounting period. They include all income statement accounts, the owner withdrawals account, and the **Income Summary** account. They are temporary because such accounts are used for a period and then closed at period-end. **The closing process applies only to temporary accounts.**

Permanent accounts report on activities related to one or more future accounting periods. They include asset, liability, and owner capital accounts (all balance sheet accounts). **Permanent accounts are not closed each period and carry their ending balance into future periods.**

Recording Closing Entries

Closing entries transfer the end-of-period balances in revenue, expense, and withdrawals accounts to the permanent capital account. Closing entries are necessary at the end of each period after financial statements are prepared because

- Revenue, expense, and withdrawals accounts must begin each period with zero balances.
- Owner's capital must reflect prior periods' revenues, expenses, and withdrawals.

Point: If **Apple** did not make closing entries, prior year revenue from iPhone sales would be included with current year revenue.

An income statement reports revenues and expenses for an *accounting period*. Owner withdrawals are also reported for an accounting period. Because revenue, expense, and withdrawals accounts record information separately for each period, they must start each period with zero balances.

Exhibit 4.3 uses the adjusted account balances of FastForward (from the Adjusted Trial Balance columns of Exhibit 4.1 or from the left side of Exhibit 4.4) to show the four steps to close its temporary accounts.

① ② To close revenue and expense accounts, we transfer their balances to Income Summary. **Income Summary is a temporary account only used for the closing process** that contains a credit for total revenues (and gains) and a debit for total expenses (and losses).

EXHIBIT 4.3

Four-Step Closing

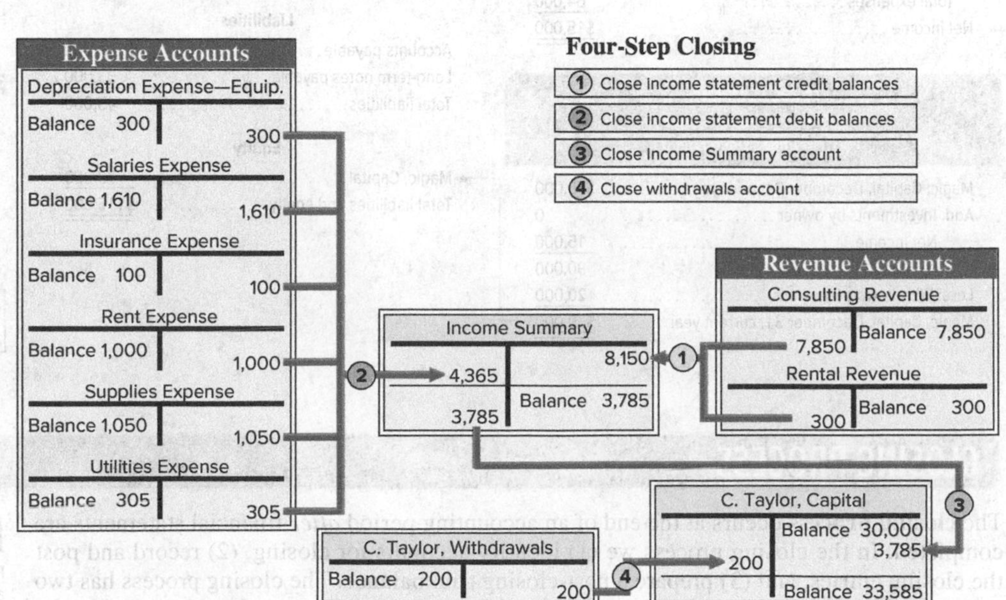

Point: C. Taylor, Capital is the only *permanent account* in Exhibit 4.3—meaning it is not closed, but it does have Income Summary closed to it.

③ The Income Summary balance, which equals net income or net loss, is transferred to the capital account.

④ The withdrawals account balance is transferred to the capital account. After closing entries are posted, the revenue, expense, withdrawals, and Income Summary accounts have zero balances and are said to be *closed* or *cleared*.

Exhibit 4.4 shows the four closing journal entries to apply the closing process of Exhibit 4.3.

EXHIBIT 4.4

Preparing Closing Entries

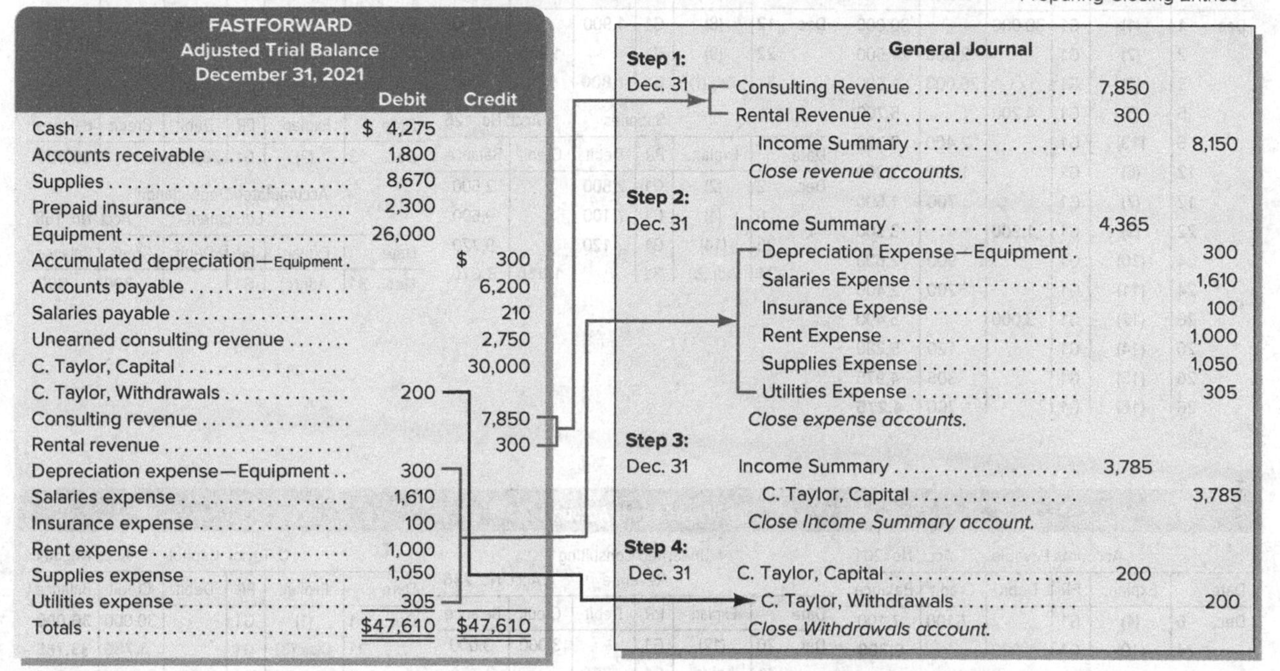

FASTFORWARD
Adjusted Trial Balance
December 31, 2021

	Debit	Credit
Cash	$ 4,275	
Accounts receivable	1,800	
Supplies	8,670	
Prepaid insurance	2,300	
Equipment	26,000	
Accumulated depreciation—Equipment		$ 300
Accounts payable		6,200
Salaries payable		210
Unearned consulting revenue		2,750
C. Taylor, Capital		30,000
C. Taylor, Withdrawals	200	
Consulting revenue		7,850
Rental revenue		300
Depreciation expense—Equipment	300	
Salaries expense	1,610	
Insurance expense	100	
Rent expense	1,000	
Supplies expense	1,050	
Utilities expense	305	
Totals	$47,610	$47,610

General Journal

Step 1: Dec. 31	Consulting Revenue	7,850	
	Rental Revenue	300	
	Income Summary		8,150
	Close revenue accounts.		
Step 2: Dec. 31	Income Summary	4,365	
	Depreciation Expense—Equipment		300
	Salaries Expense		1,610
	Insurance Expense		100
	Rent Expense		1,000
	Supplies Expense		1,050
	Utilities Expense		305
	Close expense accounts.		
Step 3: Dec. 31	Income Summary	3,785	
	C. Taylor, Capital		3,785
	Close Income Summary account.		
Step 4: Dec. 31	C. Taylor, Capital	200	
	C. Taylor, Withdrawals		200
	Close Withdrawals account.		

Step 1: Close Credit Balances in Revenue Accounts to Income Summary First, we close revenues to Income Summary. We bring accounts with credit balances to zero by debiting them. For FastForward, this is step 1 in Exhibit 4.4. The $8,150 credit entry to Income Summary equals total revenues for the period. This leaves revenue accounts with zero balances, and they are now ready to record revenues for next period.

Step 2: Close Debit Balances in Expense Accounts to Income Summary Second, we close expenses to Income Summary. We bring expense accounts' debit balances to zero by crediting them. With a balance of zero, these accounts are ready to record expenses for next period. This second closing entry for FastForward is step 2 in Exhibit 4.4.

Step 3: Close Income Summary to Owner's Capital After steps 1 and 2, the balance of Income Summary equals December net income of $3,785 ($8,150 credit less $4,365 debit). The third closing entry transfers the balance of the Income Summary account to the capital account. This entry closes the Income Summary account—see step 3 in Exhibit 4.4.

Step 4: Close Withdrawals Account to Owner's Capital The fourth closing entry transfers any debit balance in the withdrawals account to the owner's capital account—see step 4 in Exhibit 4.4. This entry gives the withdrawals account a zero balance, and the account is now ready to record next period's withdrawals.

Exhibit 4.5 shows the entire ledger of FastForward as of December 31 *after* adjusting and closing entries are posted. The temporary accounts (revenues, expenses, and withdrawals) have ending balances equal to zero.

EXHIBIT 4.5

General Ledger after the Closing Process for FastForward

Asset Accounts

Cash — Acct. No. 101

Date	Explan.	PR	Debit	Credit	Balance
Dec. 1	(1)	G1	30,000		30,000
2	(2)	G1		2,500	27,500
3	(3)	G1		26,000	1,500
5	(5)	G1	4,200		5,700
6	(13)	G1		2,400	3,300
12	(6)	G1		1,000	2,300
12	(7)	G1		700	1,600
22	(9)	G1	1,900		3,500
24	(10)	G1		900	2,600
24	(11)	G1		200	2,400
26	(12)	G1	3,000		5,400
26	(14)	G1		120	5,280
26	(15)	G1		305	4,975
26	(16)	G1		700	**4,275**

Accounts Receivable — Acct. No. 106

Date	Explan.	PR	Debit	Credit	Balance
Dec. 12	(8)	G1	1,900		1,900
22	(9)	G1		1,900	0
31	Adj.(f)	G1	1,800		**1,800**

Supplies — Acct. No. 126

Date	Explan.	PR	Debit	Credit	Balance
Dec. 2	(2)	G1	2,500		2,500
6	(4)	G1	7,100		9,600
26	(14)	G1	120		9,720
31	Adj.(b)	G1		1,050	**8,670**

Prepaid Insurance — Acct. No. 128

Date	Explan.	PR	Debit	Credit	Balance
Dec. 6	(13)	G1	2,400		2,400
31	Adj.(a)	G1		100	**2,300**

Equipment — Acct. No. 167

Date	Explan.	PR	Debit	Credit	Balance
Dec. 3	(3)	G1	26,000		**26,000**

Accumulated Depreciation—Equipment — Acct. No. 168

Date	Explan.	PR	Debit	Credit	Balance
Dec. 31	Adj.(c)	G1		300	**300**

Liability and Equity Accounts

Accounts Payable — Acct. No. 201

Date	Explan.	PR	Debit	Credit	Balance
Dec. 6	(4)	G1		7,100	7,100
24	(10)	G1	900		**6,200**

Salaries Payable — Acct. No. 209

Date	Explan.	PR	Debit	Credit	Balance
Dec. 31	Adj.(e)	G1		210	**210**

Unearned Consulting Revenue — Acct. No. 236

Date	Explan.	PR	Debit	Credit	Balance
Dec. 26	(12)	G1		3,000	3,000
31	Adj.(d)	G1	250		**2,750**

C. Taylor, Capital — Acct. No. 301

Date	Explan.	PR	Debit	Credit	Balance
Dec. 1	(1)	G1		30,000	30,000
31	Clos.(3)	G1		3,785	33,785
31	Clos.(4)	G1	200		**33,585**

C. Taylor, Withdrawals — Acct. No. 302

Date	Explan.	PR	Debit	Credit	Balance
Dec. 24	(11)	G1	200		200
31	Clos.(4)	G1		200	**0**

Revenue and Expense Accounts (Including Income Summary)

Consulting Revenue — Acct. No. 403

Date	Explan.	PR	Debit	Credit	Balance
Dec. 5	(5)	G1		4,200	4,200
12	(8)	G1		1,600	5,800
31	Adj.(d)	G1		250	6,050
31	Adj.(f)	G1		1,800	7,850
31	Clos.(1)	G1	7,850		**0**

Rental Revenue — Acct. No. 406

Date	Explan.	PR	Debit	Credit	Balance
Dec. 12	(8)	G1		300	300
31	Clos.(1)	G1	300		**0**

Depreciation Expense—Equipment — Acct. No. 612

Date	Explan.	PR	Debit	Credit	Balance
Dec. 31	Adj.(c)	G1	300		300
31	Clos.(2)	G1		300	**0**

Salaries Expense — Acct. No. 622

Date	Explan.	PR	Debit	Credit	Balance
Dec. 12	(7)	G1	700		700
26	(16)	G1	700		1,400
31	Adj.(e)	G1	210		1,610
31	Clos.(2)	G1		1,610	**0**

Insurance Expense — Acct. No. 637

Date	Explan.	PR	Debit	Credit	Balance
Dec. 31	Adj.(a)	G1	100		100
31	Clos.(2)	G1		100	**0**

Rent Expense — Acct. No. 640

Date	Explan.	PR	Debit	Credit	Balance
Dec. 12	(6)	G1	1,000		1,000
31	Clos.(2)	G1		1,000	**0**

Supplies Expense — Acct. No. 652

Date	Explan.	PR	Debit	Credit	Balance
Dec. 31	Adj.(b)	G1	1,050		1,050
31	Clos.(2)	G1		1,050	**0**

Utilities Expense — Acct. No. 690

Date	Explan.	PR	Debit	Credit	Balance
Dec. 26	(15)	G1	305		305
31	Clos.(2)	G1		305	**0**

Income Summary — Acct. No. 901

Date	Explan.	PR	Debit	Credit	Balance
Dec. 31	Clos.(1)	G1		8,150	8,150
31	Clos.(2)	G1	4,365		3,785
31	Clos.(3)	G1	3,785		**0**

Post-Closing Trial Balance

A **post-closing trial balance** is a list of permanent accounts and their balances after all closing entries. Only balance sheet (permanent) accounts are on a post-closing trial balance. A post-closing trial balance verifies that (1) total debits equal total credits for permanent accounts and (2) all temporary accounts have zero balances. FastForward's post-closing trial balance is in Exhibit 4.6 and often is the last step in the accounting process.

EXHIBIT 4.6

Post-Closing Trial Balance

FASTFORWARD
Post-Closing Trial Balance
December 31, 2021

	Debit	Credit
Cash	$ 4,275	
Accounts receivable	1,800	
Supplies	8,670	
Prepaid insurance	2,300	
Equipment	26,000	
Accumulated depreciation—Equipment		$ 300
Accounts payable		6,200
Salaries payable		210
Unearned consulting revenue		2,750
C. Taylor, Capital		33,585
Totals	$43,045	$43,045

Point: C. Taylor, Capital is computed as $30,000 + $3,785 − $200.

Decision Maker

Staff Accountant A friend shows you the post-closing trial balance she is working on. You review the statement and see a line item for rent expense. How do you know that an error exists? ■ *Answer:* This error is apparent in a post-closing trial balance because Rent Expense is a temporary account. Post-closing trial balances only contain permanent accounts.

nd3000/Shutterstock

NEED-TO-KNOW 4-2

Closing Entries

P2

Do More: QS 4-6, QS 4-7, QS 4-8, QS 4-9, E 4-6, E 4-7, E 4-8, E 4-9

Use the following adjusted account balances for Magic Company to prepare its closing entries.

Account Title	Debit	Credit
Cash	$ 13,000	
Accounts receivable	17,000	
Land	85,000	
Accounts payable		$ 12,000
Long-term notes payable		33,000
Magic, Capital		75,000
Magic, Withdrawals	20,000	
Services revenue		79,000
Salaries expense	56,000	
Supplies expense	8,000	
Totals	$199,000	$199,000

Solution

Date	Account	Debit	Credit
Dec. 31	Services revenue	79,000	
	Income Summary		79,000
	Close revenue account.		
Dec. 31	Income Summary	64,000	
	Salaries Expense		56,000
	Office Supplies Expense		8,000
	Close expense accounts.		

Date	Account	Debit	Credit
Dec. 31	Income Summary	15,000	
	Magic, Capital		15,000
	Close Income Summary.		
Dec. 31	Magic, Capital	20,000	
	Magic, Withdrawals		20,000
	Close Withdrawals account.		

ACCOUNTING CYCLE

The **accounting cycle** is the steps in preparing financial statements. It is called a *cycle* because the steps are repeated each reporting period. Exhibit 4.7 shows the 10 steps in the cycle. Steps 1 through 3 occur regularly as a company enters into transactions. Steps 4 through 9 are done at the end of a period. *Reversing entries* in step 10 are optional and are explained in Appendix 4A.

EXHIBIT 4.7

Steps in the Accounting Cycle*

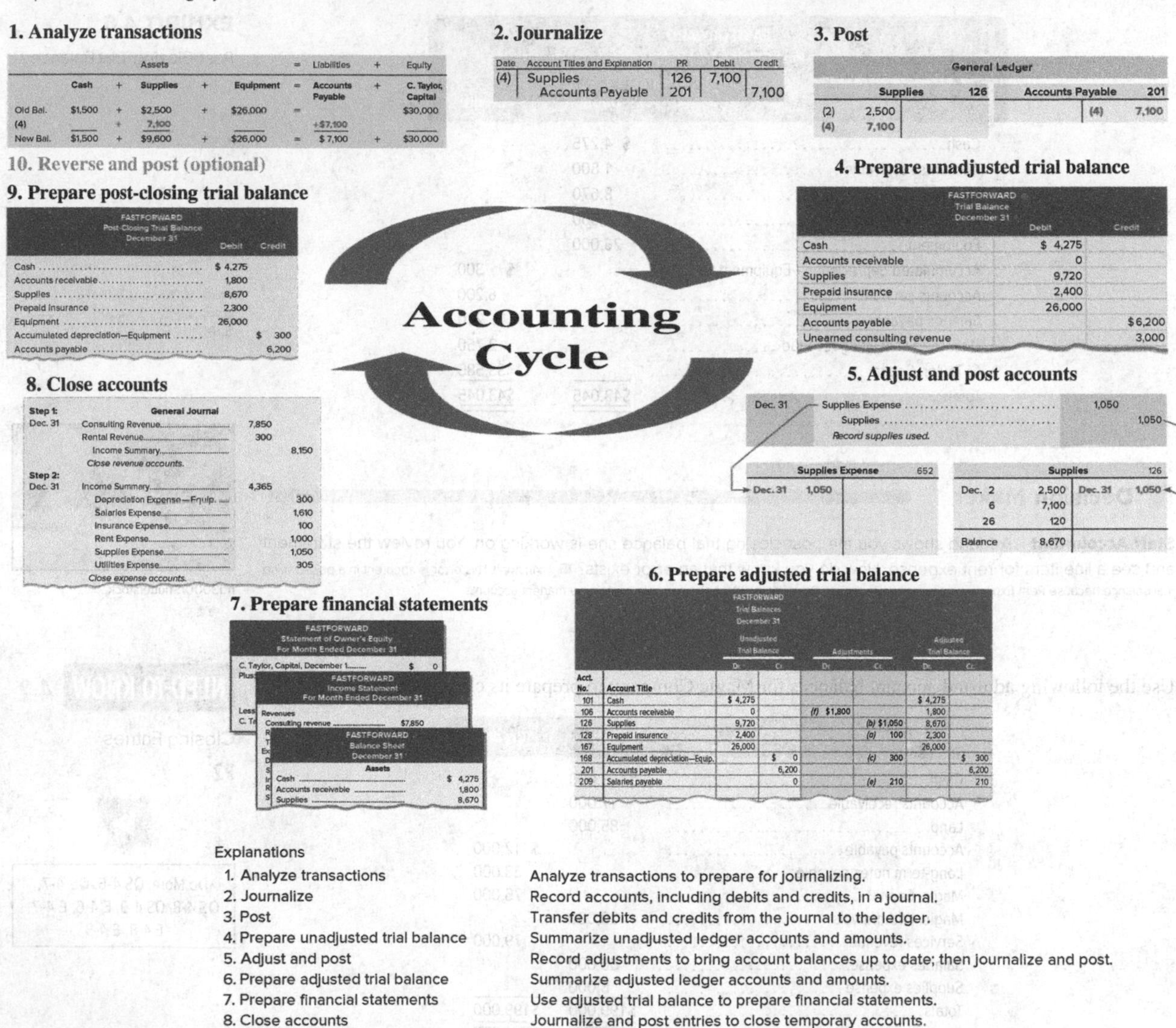

Explanations

1. Analyze transactions	Analyze transactions to prepare for journalizing.
2. Journalize	Record accounts, including debits and credits, in a journal.
3. Post	Transfer debits and credits from the journal to the ledger.
4. Prepare unadjusted trial balance	Summarize unadjusted ledger accounts and amounts.
5. Adjust and post	Record adjustments to bring account balances up to date; then journalize and post.
6. Prepare adjusted trial balance	Summarize adjusted ledger accounts and amounts.
7. Prepare financial statements	Use adjusted trial balance to prepare financial statements.
8. Close accounts	Journalize and post entries to close temporary accounts.
9. Prepare post-closing trial balance	Test clerical accuracy of the closing procedures.
10. Optional: Reverse and post	Reverse certain adjustments in the next period—optional step; see Appendix 4A.

* Steps 4, 6, and 9 can be done on a work sheet. A work sheet is useful in planning adjustments, but adjustments (step 5) must always be journalized and posted. Steps 3, 4, 6, and 9 are automatic with a computerized system.

CLASSIFIED BALANCE SHEET

C1

Explain and prepare a classified balance sheet.

This section describes a classified balance sheet. An **unclassified balance sheet** broadly groups accounts into assets, liabilities, and equity. One example is FastForward's balance sheet in Exhibit 4.2. A **classified balance sheet** organizes assets and liabilities into subgroups.

Classification Structure

A classified balance sheet typically contains the categories in Exhibit 4.8 (there is no required layout). An important classification is the separation between current (short-term) and noncurrent (long-term) for both assets and liabilities. Current items are expected to come due (either collected or owed) within one year or the company's operating cycle, whichever is longer. The **operating cycle** is the time span from when *cash is used* to acquire goods and services until *cash is received* from the sale of goods and services. Most operating cycles are less than one year, which means most companies use a one-year period to classify current and noncurrent items. To make it easy, assume an operating cycle of one year, unless we say otherwise.

A balance sheet lists current assets before noncurrent assets and current liabilities before noncurrent liabilities. Current assets and current liabilities are listed in order of how quickly they will be converted to, or paid in, cash.

EXHIBIT 4.8

Typical Categories in a Classified Balance Sheet

Assets	Liabilities and Equity
Current assets	**Current liabilities**
Noncurrent assets	**Noncurrent liabilities**
Long-term investments	**Equity**
Plant assets	
Intangible assets	

Classification Categories

The balance sheet for Snowboarding Components in Exhibit 4.9 shows the typical categories. Its assets are classified as either current or noncurrent. Its noncurrent assets include three main categories: long-term investments, plant assets, and intangible assets. Its liabilities are classified as either current or long-term. Not all companies use the same categories. **Jarden**, a producer of snowboards, reported a balance sheet with five asset classes: current assets; property, plant, and equipment; goodwill; intangibles; and other assets.

Current Assets **Current assets** are cash and other resources that are expected to be sold, collected, or used within one year or the company's operating cycle, whichever is longer. Examples are cash, short-term investments, accounts receivable, short-term notes receivable, merchandise inventory (goods for sale), and prepaid expenses.

Long-Term Investments **Long-term** (or *noncurrent*) **investments** include notes receivable and investments in stocks and bonds when they are expected to be held for more than the longer of one year or the operating cycle.

EXHIBIT 4.9

Example of a Classified Balance Sheet

SNOWBOARDING COMPONENTS
Balance Sheet
December 31, 2021

Assets			Liabilities		
Current assets			**Current liabilities**		
Cash	$ 6,500		Accounts payable	$ 15,300	
Accounts receivable	6,500		Wages payable	3,200	
Merchandise inventory	27,500		Unearned revenue	10,500	
Prepaid insurance	2,400		Total current liabilities		$ 29,000
Total current assets		$ 42,900	**Long-term liabilities**		
Long-term investments			Notes payable (due in ten years)	150,000	
Notes receivable (due in three years)	1,500		Total long-term liabilities		150,000
Investments in stocks and bonds	66,000		Total liabilities		179,000
Total long-term investments		67,500			
Plant assets					
Equipment	203,200		**Equity**		
Less accumulated depreciation	53,000	150,200	T. Hawk, Capital		164,800
Land		73,200			
Total plant assets		223,400			
Intangible assets		10,000			
Total assets		$343,800	Total liabilities and equity		$343,800

Plant Assets Plant assets are tangible assets that are both *long-lived* and *used to produce or sell products and services*. Examples are equipment, machinery, buildings, and land that are used to produce or sell products and services. Plant assets are also called *property, plant and equipment (PP&E)* or *fixed assets*.

Intangible Assets **Intangible assets** are long-term assets that benefit business operations but lack physical form. Examples are patents, trademarks, copyrights, franchises, and goodwill. Their value comes from the privileges or rights granted to or held by the owner.

Purestock/SuperStock

Current Liabilities **Current liabilities** are liabilities due to be paid or settled within one year or the operating cycle, whichever is longer. They usually are settled by paying out cash. Current liabilities include accounts payable, wages payable, taxes payable, interest payable, and unearned revenues. Also, any portion of a long-term liability due to be paid within one year or the operating cycle, whichever is longer, is a current liability.

Long-Term Liabilities **Long-term liabilities** are liabilities *not* due within one year or the operating cycle, whichever is longer. Notes payable, mortgages payable, bonds payable, and lease obligations are common long-term liabilities.

Equity Equity is the owner's claim on assets. For a proprietorship, this claim is reported in the equity section with an owner's capital account. Equity is not separated into current and noncurrent categories.

NEED-TO-KNOW 4-3

Classified Balance Sheet

C1

Use the following account balances from Magic Company's post-closing trial balance to prepare its classified balance sheet as of December 31.

Cash	$13,000	Accounts payable	$12,000
Accounts receivable	17,000	Long-term notes payable	33,000
Land	85,000	Magic, Capital	70,000

Solution

MAGIC COMPANY
Balance Sheet
December 31

Assets		Liabilities	
Current assets		Current liabilities	
Cash	$ 13,000	Accounts payable	$ 12,000
Accounts receivable	17,000	Total current liabilities	12,000
Total current assets	30,000	Long-term notes payable	33,000
Plant assets		Total liabilities	45,000
Land	85,000	**Equity**	
Total plant assets	85,000	Magic, Capital*	70,000
Total assets	$115,000	Total liabilities and equity	$115,000

*Computed as $75,000 beginning balance + $15,000 net income (from NTK 4-1) − $20,000 withdrawals.

Do More: QS 4-12, QS 4-15, QS 4-17, E 4-12, E 4-13, P 4-3

Current Ratio  **Decision Analysis**

A1 Compute and analyze the current ratio

An important use of financial statements is to help assess a company's ability to pay its debts in the near future. Such analysis affects decisions by suppliers when allowing a company to buy on credit. It also affects decisions by creditors when lending money to a company, including loan terms such as interest rate and due date. The **current ratio** is one measure of a company's ability to pay its short-term obligations. It is defined in Exhibit 4.10.

EXHIBIT 4.10 Current Ratio

$$\text{Current ratio} = \frac{\text{Current assets}}{\text{Current liabilities}}$$

Costco's current ratio for each of the last three years is in Exhibit 4.11. A current ratio of over 1.0 means that current obligations can be covered with current assets. For the most recent three years, Costco's current ratio has been slightly above or slightly below 1.0. This means Costco could face challenges in covering current liabilities. Although Costco has a better ratio than **Walmart** in each of the last three years, management must continue to monitor current assets and liabilities.

EXHIBIT 4.11 Computation and Analysis Using Current Ratio

Company	$ millions	Current Year	1 Year Ago	2 Years Ago
Costco	Current assets........	$23,485	$20,289	$17,317
	Current liabilities.....	$23,237	$19,926	$17,495
	Current ratio	**1.01**	**1.02**	**0.99**
Walmart	Current ratio	0.80	0.76	0.86

Decision Maker

Analyst You are analyzing a dirt bike company's ability to meet upcoming loan payments. You compute its current ratio as 1.2. You find that a major portion of accounts receivable is due from one client who has not made any payments in the past 12 months. Removing this receivable from current assets lowers the current ratio to 0.7. What do you conclude? ■ *Answer:* A current ratio of 1.2 suggests that current assets are sufficient to cover current liabilities. Removing the past-due receivable reduces the current ratio to 0.7. You conclude that the company will have difficulty meeting its loan payments.

Ingram Publishing

NEED-TO-KNOW 4-4

COMPREHENSIVE

Completing a Work Sheet, Recording Closing Entries, and Preparing Financial Statements

The partial work sheet of Midtown Repair Company at December 31 follows.

	Adjusted Trial Balance		Income Statement		Balance Sheet and Statement of Owner's Equity	
Account Title	**Debit**	**Credit**	**Debit**	**Credit**	**Debit**	**Credit**
Cash	95,600					
Prepaid insurance	16,000					
Prepaid rent	4,000					
Notes receivable (due in 5 years)	50,000					
Equipment	170,000					
Accumulated depreciation—Equipment		57,000				
Accounts payable		52,000				
Notes payable (due in 9 years)		63,000				
C. Trout, Capital		178,500				
C. Trout, Withdrawals	30,000					
Services revenue		180,800				
Interest revenue		7,500				
Depreciation expense—Equipment	28,500					
Wages expense	85,000					
Rent expense	48,000					
Insurance expense	6,000					
Interest expense	5,700					
Totals	538,800	538,800				

[continued on next page]

[continued from preceding page]

Required

1. Complete the work sheet by extending the adjusted trial balance totals to the appropriate financial statement columns.
2. Prepare closing entries for Midtown Repair Company.
3. Set up the Income Summary and the C. Trout, Capital accounts in the general ledger (in balance column format) and post the closing entries to these accounts.
4. Determine the balance of the C. Trout, Capital account to be reported on the December 31 current year balance sheet.
5. Prepare an income statement and a statement of owner's equity for the year-ended December 31. Prepare a classified balance sheet as of December 31. The balance in C. Trout, Capital on December 31 of the *prior year* was $178,500, and there are no owner investments during the year.

SOLUTION

1. Completing the work sheet.

	Adjusted Trial Balance		Income Statement		Balance Sheet and Statement of Owner's Equity	
Account Title	**Debit**	**Credit**	**Debit**	**Credit**	**Debit**	**Credit**
Cash	95,600				95,600	
Prepaid insurance	16,000				16,000	
Prepaid rent	4,000				4,000	
Notes receivable (due in 5 years)	50,000				50,000	
Equipment	170,000				170,000	
Accumulated depreciation—Equipment		57,000				57,000
Accounts payable		52,000				52,000
Notes payable (due in 9 years)		63,000				63,000
C. Trout, Capital		178,500				178,500
C. Trout, Withdrawals	30,000				30,000	
Services revenue		180,800		180,800		
Interest revenue		7,500		7,500		
Depreciation expense—Equipment	28,500		28,500			
Wages expense	85,000		85,000			
Rent expense	48,000		48,000			
Insurance expense	6,000		6,000			
Interest expense	5,700		5,700			
Totals	538,800	538,800	173,200	188,300	365,600	350,500
Net income			15,100			15,100
Totals			188,300	188,300	365,600	365,600

2. Closing entries.

Date	Account	Debit	Credit
Dec. 31	Services Revenue	180,800	
	Interest Revenue	7,500	
	Income Summary		188,300
	Close revenue accounts.		
Dec. 31	Income Summary	173,200	
	Depreciation Expense—Equipment		28,500
	Wages Expense		85,000
	Rent Expense		48,000
	Insurance Expense		6,000
	Interest Expense		5,700
	Close expense accounts.		

Date	Account	Debit	Credit
Dec. 31	Income Summary	15,100	
	C. Trout, Capital		15,100
	Close Income Summary account.		
Dec. 31	C. Trout, Capital	30,000	
	C. Trout, Withdrawals		30,000
	Close Withdrawals account.		

3. Set up the Income Summary and the Capital ledger accounts and post the closing entries.

Income Summary — Account No. 901

Date	Explanation	PR	Debit	Credit	Balance
Jan. 1	Beginning balance				0
Dec. 31	Close revenue accounts			188,300	188,300
31	Close expense accounts		173,200		15,100
31	Close Income Summary		15,100		0

C. Trout, Capital — Account No. 301

Date	Explanation	PR	Debit	Credit	Balance
Jan. 1	Beginning balance				178,500
Dec. 31	Close Income Summary			15,100	193,600
31	Close C. Trout, Withdrawals		30,000		163,600

4. The final capital balance of $163,600 (from part 3) will be reported on the December 31 current year balance sheet. The final capital balance reflects the increase from net income and the decrease from owner's withdrawals.

5.

MIDTOWN REPAIR COMPANY Income Statement For Year Ended December 31		
Revenues		
Services revenue	$180,800	
Interest revenue	7,500	
Total revenues		$188,300
Expenses		
Depreciation expense—Equipment	28,500	
Wages expense	85,000	
Rent expense	48,000	
Insurance expense	6,000	
Interest expense	5,700	
Total expenses		173,200
Net income		$ 15,100

MIDTOWN REPAIR COMPANY Statement of Owner's Equity For Year Ended December 31		
C. Trout, Capital, December 31, prior year		$178,500
Add: Investments by owner	$ 0	
Net income	15,100	15,100
		193,600
Less: Withdrawals by owner		30,000
C. Trout, Capital, December 31, current year		$163,600

MIDTOWN REPAIR COMPANY Balance Sheet December 31		
Assets		
Current assets		
Cash		$ 95,600
Prepaid insurance		16,000
Prepaid rent		4,000
Total current assets		115,600
Long-term investments		
Notes receivable		50,000
Plant assets		
Equipment	$170,000	
Less: Accumulated depreciation—Equipment	(57,000)	
Total plant assets		113,000
Total assets		$278,600
Liabilities		
Current liabilities		
Accounts payable		$ 52,000
Long-term liabilities		
Long-term notes payable		63,000
Total liabilities		115,000
Equity		
C. Trout, Capital		163,600
Total liabilities and equity		$278,600

APPENDIX

Reversing Entries 4A

P3 Prepare reversing entries and explain their purpose.

Reversing entries are optional. They are dated the first day of the next accounting period, and they reverse the debits and credits of adjusting entries using the same accounts and amounts. Reversing entries are used for adjusting entries involving accrued revenues and accrued expenses. The purpose of reversing entries is to simplify recordkeeping. Exhibit 4A.1 shows an example of FastForward's reversing entries. The top of the exhibit shows the adjusting entry FastForward recorded on December 31 for its employee's earned but unpaid salary. The entry recorded three days' salary of $210, which increased December's total salary expense to $1,610. The entry also recognized a liability of $210. The expense is reported on December's income statement. The expense account is then closed. The ledger on January 1, 2022, shows a $210 liability and a zero balance in the Salaries Expense account. At this point, the choice is made between using or not using reversing entries.

Accounting *without* Reversing Entries The path down the left side of Exhibit 4A.1 is described in the chapter. To summarize, when the next payday occurs on January 9, we record payment with a compound entry that debits both the expense and liability accounts and credits Cash. Posting that entry creates a $490 balance in the expense account and reduces the liability account balance to zero because the payable has been settled.

EXHIBIT 4A.1

Reversing Entries for an Accrued Expense

*Circled numbers in the *Balance* column indicate abnormal balances.

Accrue salaries expense on December 31, 2021

Salaries Expense	210	
Salaries Payable		210

Salaries Expense

Date	Expl.	Debit	Credit	Balance
2021				
Dec. 12	(7)	700		700
26	(16)	700		1,400
31	(e)	210		1,610

Salaries Payable

Date	Expl.	Debit	Credit	Balance
2021				
Dec. 31	(e)		210	210

WITHOUT Reversing Entries — OR — **WITH Reversing Entries**

WITHOUT Reversing Entries

No reversing entry recorded on Jan. 1, 2022

NO ENTRY

Salaries Expense

Date	Expl.	Debit	Credit	Balance
2022				

Salaries Payable

Date	Expl.	Debit	Credit	Balance
2021				
Dec. 31	(e)		210	210
2022				

Pay the accrued and current salaries on January 9, the first payday in 2022

Salaries Expense	490	
Salaries Payable	210	
Cash		700

Salaries Expense

Date	Expl.	Debit	Credit	Balance
2022				
Jan. 9		490		490

Salaries Payable

Date	Expl.	Debit	Credit	Balance
2021				
Dec. 31	(e)		210	210
2022				
Jan. 9		210		0

WITH Reversing Entries

Reversing entry recorded on Jan. 1, 2022

Salaries Payable	210	
Salaries Expense		210

Salaries Expense*

Date	Expl.	Debit	Credit	Balance
2022				
Jan. 1			210	(210)

Salaries Payable

Date	Expl.	Debit	Credit	Balance
2021				
Dec. 31	(e)		210	210
2022				
Jan. 1		210		0

Pay the accrued and current salaries on January 9, the first payday in 2022

Salaries Expense	700	
Cash		700

Salaries Expense*

Date	Expl.	Debit	Credit	Balance
2022				
Jan. 1			210	(210)
Jan. 9		700		490

Salaries Payable

Date	Expl.	Debit	Credit	Balance
2021				
Dec. 31	(e)		210	210
2022				
Jan. 1		210		0

Under both approaches, the expense and liability accounts have identical balances after the cash payment on January 9.

Salaries Expense ...... $490 Salaries Payable $0

Accounting *with* Reversing Entries The right side of Exhibit 4A.1 shows reversing entries. A reversing entry is the exact opposite of an adjusting entry. For FastForward, the Salaries Payable liability account is debited for $210, meaning that this account now has a zero balance after the entry is posted on January 1. The Salaries Payable account temporarily understates the liability, but this is not a problem because financial statements are not prepared before the liability is settled on January 9. The credit to the Salaries Expense account is unusual because it gives the account an *abnormal credit balance.* We highlight an abnormal balance by circling it. Because of the reversing entry, the January 9 entry to record payment debits the Salaries Expense account and credits Cash for the full $700 paid. It is the same as all other entries made to record 10 days' salary for the employee. We see that after the payment entry is posted, the Salaries Expense account has a $490 balance that reflects seven days' salary of $70 per day (see the lower right side of Exhibit 4A.1). The zero balance in the Salaries Payable account is now correct. The lower section of Exhibit 4A.1 shows that the expense and liability accounts have exactly the same balances whether reversing entries are used or not.

Point: If a company chooses to prepare reversing entries, all accruals are reversed. Deferrals are not reversed.

Summary: Cheat Sheet

WORK SHEET

Work sheet: Used to help with adjusting and closing accounts and with preparing financial statements.

Five Steps in Preparing Work sheet

1. Enter unadjusted trial balance—list every account that appears on financial statements and their balances.
2. Enter adjustments—enter the period-end adjustments.
3. Prepare adjusted trial balance—combine the unadjusted balances and adjustments for each account.
4. Sort adjusted trial balance amounts to financial statements—

Account Type	Financial Statement Column
Expenses	Income Statement *Debit*
Revenues	Income Statement *Credit*
Assets and withdrawals	Balance Sheet & Statement of Owner's Equity *Debit*
Liabilities and owner's capital	Balance Sheet & Statement of Owner's Equity *Credit*

5. Total statement columns, compute income or loss, and balance columns—if income statement Credit total exceeds Debit total, there is net income. If Debit total exceeds Credit total, there is a net loss. Net income (loss) is then entered in the Balance Sheet & Statement of Owner's Equity Credit (Debit) column.

No.	Account	① Unadjusted Trial Balance Dr.	Cr.	② Adjustments Dr.	Cr.	③ Adjusted Trial Balance Dr.	Cr.	④ Income Statement Dr.	Cr.	Balance Sheet & Statement of Owner's Equity Dr.	Cr.
101	Cash	4,275				4,275				4,275	
106	Accounts receivable	0		(f) 1,800		1,800				1,800	
126	Supplies	9,720			(b) 1,050	8,670				8,670	
128	Prepaid insurance	2,400			(a) 100	2,300				2,300	
167	Equipment	26,000				26,000				26,000	
168	Accumulated depreciation—Equipment				(c) 300		300				300
201	Accounts payable		6,200				6,200				6,200
209	Salaries payable				(e) 210		210				210
236	Unearned consulting revenue		3,000	(d) 250			2,750				2,750
301	C. Taylor, Capital		30,000				30,000				30,000
302	C. Taylor, Withdrawals	200				200				200	
403	Consulting revenue		5,800		(d) 250 (f) 1,800		7,850		7,850		
406	Rental revenue		300				300		300		
612	Depreciation expense—Equipment			(c) 300		300		300			
622	Salaries expense	1,400		(e) 210		1,610		1,610			
637	Insurance expense			(a) 100		100		100			
640	Rent expense	1,000				1,000		1,000			
652	Supplies expense			(b) 1,050		1,050		1,050			
690	Utilities expense	305				305		305			
	Totals	45,300	45,300	3,710	3,710	47,610	47,610	4,365	8,150	43,245	39,460
	Net income ⑤							3,785			3,785
	Totals							8,150	8,150	43,245	43,245

CLOSING PROCESS

Closing process: Occurs at period-end after financial statements have been prepared. Resets revenue, expense, and withdrawals balances to zero.

Temporary accounts: Closed at period-end. They consist of revenue, expense, withdrawals, and Income Summary.

Permanent accounts: *Not* closed at period-end. They consist of asset, liability, and owner capital (all balance sheet accounts).

Income Summary: A temporary account only used for the closing process that has a credit for total revenues and a debit for total expenses.

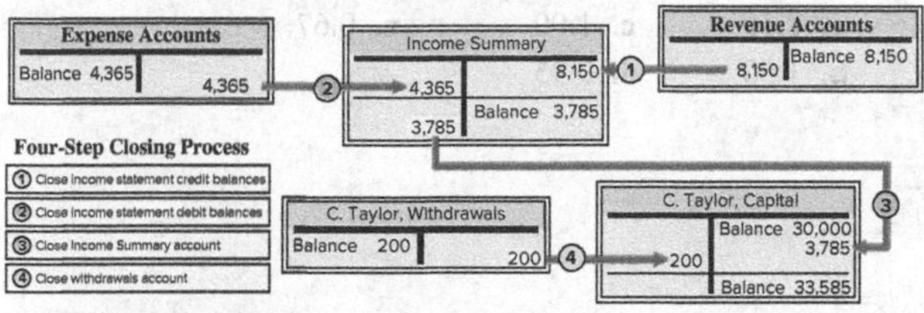

Closing Process Journal Entries by Step

		Dr.	Cr.
①	Consulting Revenue	7,850	
	Rental Revenue	300	
	Income Summary		8,150
②	Income Summary	4,365	
	Depreciation Expense—Equipment		300
	Salaries Expense		1,610
	Insurance Expense		100
	Rent Expense		1,000
	Supplies Expense		1,050
	Utilities Expense		305
③	Income Summary	3,785	
	C. Taylor, Capital		3,785
④	C. Taylor, Capital	200	
	C. Taylor, Withdrawals		200

Post-closing trial balance: A list of permanent accounts (assets, liabilities, equity) and their balances after all closing entries.

CLASSIFIED BALANCE SHEET

Classified balance sheet: Organizes assets and liabilities into meaningful subgroups.

Current vs. long-term classification: Current items are to be collected or owed within one year. Long-term items are expected after one year.

Current assets: Assets to be sold, collected, or used within one year. Examples are cash, short-term investments, accounts receivable, merchandise inventory, and prepaid expenses.

Long-term investments: Assets to be held for more than one year. Examples are notes receivable and long-term investments in stock and bonds.

Plant assets: Tangible assets used to produce or sell products and services. Examples are equipment, machinery, buildings, and land used in operations.

Intangible assets: Long-term assets that lack physical form. Examples are patents, trademarks, copyrights, franchises, and goodwill.

Current liabilities: Liabilities to be paid or settled within one year. Examples are accounts payable, wages payable, taxes payable, interest payable, unearned revenues, and current portions of notes or long-term debt.

Long-term liabilities: Liabilities not due within one year. Examples are notes payable, mortgages payable, bonds payable, and lease obligations.

Equity: The owner's claim on assets. For a proprietorship, this is the owner's capital account.

Common Layout of Classified Balance Sheet

Assets	Liabilities and Equity
Current assets	Current liabilities
Noncurrent assets	Noncurrent liabilities
Long-term investments	
Plant assets	Equity
Intangible assets	

Key Terms

Accounting cycle (136)
Classified balance sheet (136)
Closing entries (132)
Closing process (131)
Current assets (137)
Current liabilities (138)
Current ratio (139)
Income Summary (132)
Intangible assets (138)
Long-term investments (137)
Long-term liabilities (138)
Operating cycle (137)
Permanent accounts (132)
Post-closing trial balance (135)
Reversing entries (141)
Temporary accounts (132)
Unclassified balance sheet (136)
Work sheet (127)

Multiple Choice Quiz

1. G. Venda, owner of Venda Services, withdrew $25,000 from the business during the current year. The entry to close the withdrawals account at the end of the year is:

a. G. Venda, Withdrawals.........	25,000	
G. Venda, Capital.........		25,000
b. Income Summary.........	25,000	
G. Venda, Capital.........		25,000
c. G. Venda, Withdrawals.........	25,000	
Cash.........		25,000
d. G. Venda, Capital.........	25,000	
G. Venda, Withdrawals....		25,000

2. The following information is available for the R. Kandamil Company before closing the accounts. After all of the closing entries are made, what will be the balance in the R. Kandamil, Capital account?

Total revenues..	$300,000	R. Kandamil, Capital......	$100,000
Total expenses..	195,000	R. Kandamil, Withdrawals...	45,000

a. $360,000 **c.** $160,000 **e.** $60,000
b. $250,000 **d.** $150,000

3. Which of the following errors would cause the Balance Sheet & Statement of Owner's Equity columns of a work sheet to be out of balance?

a. Entering a revenue amount in the Balance Sheet & Statement of Owner's Equity Debit column.
b. Entering a liability amount in the Balance Sheet & Statement of Owner's Equity Credit column.
c. Entering an expense amount in the Balance Sheet & Statement of Owner's Equity Debit column.
d. Entering an asset amount in the Income Statement Debit column.
e. Entering a liability amount in the Income Statement Credit column.

4. The temporary account used only in the closing process to hold the amounts of revenues and expenses before the net difference is added or subtracted from the owner's capital account is called the

a. Closing account. **d.** Balance Column account.
b. Nominal account. **e.** Income Summary account.
c. Contra account.

5. Based on the following information from Repicor Company's balance sheet, what is its current ratio?

Current assets..........	$ 75,000	Current liabilities......	$ 50,000
Long-term investments ...	30,000	Long-term liabilities....	60,000
Plant assets	300,000	D. Repicor, Capital.....	295,000

a. 2.10 **c.** 1.00 **e.** 0.67
b. 1.50 **d.** 0.95

ANSWERS TO MULTIPLE CHOICE QUIZ

1. d **2.** c **3.** a **4.** e **5.** b

Superscript letter A denotes assignments based on Appendix 4A.

Select Quick Study and Exercise assignments feature Guided Example videos, called "Hints" in Connect. Hints use different numbers, and instructors can turn this feature on or off.

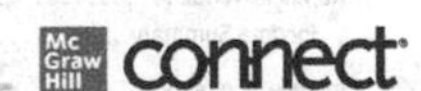

QUICK STUDY

QS 4-1
Ordering work sheet steps
P1

List the following steps in preparing a work sheet in the proper order.
a. Total the statement columns, compute net income (loss), and complete the work sheet.
b. Extend adjusted balances to appropriate financial statement columns.
c. Prepare an unadjusted trial balance on the work sheet.
d. Prepare an adjusted trial balance on the work sheet.
e. Enter adjustments data on the work sheet.

QS 4-2
Preparing a work sheet
P1

Determine the financial statement column (Income Statement column or the Balance Sheet & Statement of Owner's Equity column) where a normal account balance is extended.

a. Equipment **d.** Depreciation Expense **g.** Supplies
b. Owner, Withdrawals **e.** Accounts Receivable **h.** Rent Expense
c. Prepaid Rent **f.** Insurance Expense **i.** Cash

QS 4-3
Computing capital balance using work sheet **P1**

The following selected information is taken from the work sheet for Warton Company at its December 31 year-end. Determine the amount for B. Warton, Capital that should be reported on its current December 31 year-end balance sheet. *Note:* The B. Warton, Capital account balance was $72,000 on December 31 of the *prior year.*

	Income Statement		Balance Sheet & Statement of Owner's Equity	
	Dr.	Cr.	Dr.	Cr.
B. Warton, Capital				72,000
B. Warton, Withdrawals			39,000	
Totals	122,000	181,000		

QS 4-4
Preparing a partial work sheet
P1

The ledger of Claudell Company includes the following unadjusted normal balances: Prepaid Rent $1,000, Services Revenue $55,600, and Wages Expense $5,000. Adjustments are required for (*a*) prepaid rent expired $200; (*b*) accrued services revenue $900; and (*c*) accrued wages expense $700.

Prepare a 10-column work sheet with six rows for the following accounts: Prepaid Rent, Services Revenue, Wages Expense, Accounts Receivable, Wages Payable, and Rent Expense. Enter the unadjusted balances and the necessary adjustments on the work sheet and complete the work sheet for these accounts.

QS 4-5
Explaining temporary and permanent accounts
P2

Choose from the following list to best complete the statements below.

a. Temporary **c.** One or more **e.** Zero balances
b. Permanent **d.** One **f.** Income Summary

1. ______ accounts generally consist of all balance sheet accounts, and these accounts are not closed.
2. Permanent accounts report on activities related to ______ future accounting periods, and they carry their ending balances into the next period.
3. Temporary accounts accumulate data related to ______ accounting period.
4. ______ accounts include all income statement accounts, the withdrawals account, and the Income Summary account.

QS 4-6
Preparing closing entries
P2

The ledger of Mai Company includes the following accounts with normal balances as of December 31: D. Mai, Capital $9,000; D. Mai, Withdrawals $800; Services Revenue $13,000; Wages Expense $8,400; and Rent Expense $1,600. Prepare its December 31 closing entries.

QS 4-7
Preparing closing entries in T-accounts
P2

Set up T-accounts for the following accounts and amounts with normal balances as of December 31: K. Korver, Capital $18,000; K. Korver, Withdrawals $2,000; Services Revenue $33,000; Salaries Expense $25,000; Rent Expense $3,000; and Income Summary $0. (1) Post closing entries to each account's T-account. (2) Compute the ending balance of each T-account.

QS 4-8
Preparing closing entries
P2

Using Sierra Company's adjusted trial balance from QS 4-16, prepare its December 31 closing entries.

QS 4-9
Analyzing closing entries on owner's capital P2

Ace Company reports revenues of $40,000 and expenses of $31,000. The owner made no additional investments during the period but withdrew $5,000 cash from the business. After closing entries are recorded, determine the amount of the increase or decrease in the owner's capital account.

QS 4-10
Identifying post-closing accounts P2

For each account, identify whether it is included or excluded from a post-closing trial balance.

a. Accounts Receivable **c.** Cash **e.** Income Tax Expense
b. Salaries Expense **d.** Land **f.** Salaries Payable

QS 4-11
Identifying the accounting cycle P2

List the following steps of the accounting cycle in their proper order.

a. Posting the journal entries.
b. Journalizing and posting adjusting entries.
c. Preparing the adjusted trial balance.
d. Journalizing and posting closing entries.
e. Analyzing transactions and events.
f. Preparing the financial statements.
g. Preparing the unadjusted trial balance.
h. Journalizing transactions and events.
i. Preparing the post-closing trial balance.

QS 4-12
Classifying balance sheet items
C1

Common categories of a classified balance sheet include Current Assets, Long-Term Investments, Plant Assets, Intangible Assets, Current Liabilities, and Long-Term Liabilities. For each of the following items, identify the balance sheet category where the item would best appear.

1. Land
2. Notes payable (due in five years)
3. Accounts receivable
4. Trademarks
5. Accounts payable
6. Equipment
7. Wages payable
8. Cash

QS 4-13
Preparing an income statement
C1

Use the following selected accounts and amounts with normal balances from Buildex Co.'s adjusted trial balance to prepare its income statement for the year ended December 31. *Hint:* Not all accounts need to be used.

Cash	$ 9,000	Depreciation expense	$ 4,000
Building	98,000	Wages expense	45,000
Accounts payable	8,000	Insurance expense	3,000
Services revenue	60,000	Supplies expense	2,000
Interest revenue	5,000	Utilities expense	1,000

QS 4-14
Preparing a statement of owner's equity C1

J. Clancy owns Clancy Consulting. On December 31 of the *prior year,* the J. Clancy, Capital account balance was $20,000. During the current year, Clancy invests an additional $15,000 in assets but withdrew $11,000 cash. Clancy Consulting reports net income of $32,000 for the current year. Prepare a statement of owner's equity for Clancy Consulting for the *current year* ended December 31.

QS 4-15
Preparing a classified balance sheet
C1

Use the following selected accounts and amounts with normal balances from Juan Co. to prepare its classified balance sheet at December 31.

Wages payable	$ 1,000	Accounts receivable	$ 7,000
Building	100,000	Accumulated depreciation—Building	30,000
Cash	18,000	Notes payable (due in 5 years)	51,000
Interest payable	2,000	Notes receivable (due in 14 years)	20,000
L. Juan, Capital	50,000	Accounts payable	11,000

QS 4-16
Preparing an income statement & statement of owner's equity
C1

Use the following adjusted trial balance of Sierra Company to prepare its (1) income statement and (2) statement of owner's equity for the year ended December 31. The L. Sierra, Capital account balance was $10,500 on December 31 of the *prior year,* and there are no owner investments during the current year.

Adjusted Trial Balance	Debit	Credit
Cash	$ 5,000	
Prepaid insurance	500	
Notes receivable (due in 5 years)	4,000	
Buildings	20,000	
Accumulated depreciation—Buildings		$12,000
Accounts payable		2,500
Notes payable (due in 3 years)		3,000
L. Sierra, Capital		10,500
L. Sierra, Withdrawals	1,000	
Consulting revenue		9,500
Wages expense	3,500	
Depreciation expense—Buildings	2,000	
Insurance expense	1,500	
Totals	$37,500	$37,500

QS 4-17
Preparing a classified balance sheet C1

Use the information in the adjusted trial balance reported in QS 4-16 to prepare Sierra Company's *classified* balance sheet as of December 31.

QS 4-18
Computing the current ratio
A1

Compute Chavez Company's current ratio using the following information.

Accounts receivable	$18,000	Long-term notes payable	$21,000
Accounts payable	11,000	Office supplies	2,600
Buildings	45,000	Prepaid insurance	3,200
Cash	7,000	Unearned services revenue	3,000

QS 4-19A
Preparing reversing entries
P3

Geralt Company made an adjusting entry at its December 31 year-end for $800 of wages earned by employees but not yet paid. Geralt uses reversing entries. Prepare the reversing entry Geralt must record on January 1.

QS 4-20A
Preparing reversing entries
P3

On December 31, Yates Co. prepared an adjusting entry for $12,000 of earned but unrecorded consulting revenue. On January 16, Yates received $26,700 cash as payment in full for consulting work it provided that began on December 18 and ended on January 16. The company uses reversing entries.

a. Prepare the December 31 adjusting entry.
b. Prepare the January 1 reversing entry.
c. Prepare the January 16 cash receipt entry.

connect

EXERCISES

Exercise 4-1
Assigning account balances on a work sheet P1

These 16 accounts are from the Adjusted Trial Balance columns of a company's work sheet. Determine the letter of the financial statement column (A, B, C, or D) where a normal account balance is extended.

A. Debit column for the Income Statement columns.
B. Credit column for the Income Statement columns.
C. Debit column for the Balance Sheet & Statement of Owner's Equity columns.
D. Credit column for the Balance Sheet & Statement of Owner's Equity columns.

1. Interest Revenue
2. Machinery
3. Owner, Withdrawals
4. Depreciation Expense
5. Accounts Payable
6. Services Revenue
7. Owner, Capital
8. Interest Expense
9. Accounts Receivable
10. Accumulated Depreciation
11. Office Supplies
12. Insurance Expense
13. Interest Receivable
14. Cash
15. Rent Expense
16. Wages Payable

Exercise 4-2
Extending accounts to financial statement columns P1

The Adjusted Trial Balance columns of a work sheet for Planta Company follow. Complete the work sheet by extending the account balances into the appropriate financial statement columns and by entering the amount of net income for the reporting period.

		Adjusted Trial Balance		Income Statement		Balance Sheet and Statement of Owner's Equity	
No.	Account Title	Dr.	Cr.	Dr.	Cr.	Dr.	Cr.
101	Cash	$ 7,000					
106	Accounts receivable	27,200					
153	Trucks	42,000					
154	Accumulated depreciation—Trucks		$ 17,500				
183	Land	32,000					
201	Accounts payable		15,000				
209	Salaries payable		4,200				
236	Unearned revenue		3,600				
301	B. Planta, Capital		65,500				
302	B. Planta, Withdrawals	15,400					
403	Plumbing revenue		84,000				
611	Depreciation expense—Trucks	6,500					
622	Salaries expense	38,000					
640	Rent expense	13,000					
677	Miscellaneous expenses	8,700					
	Totals	$189,800	$189,800				
	Net income						
	Totals						

Check Net income, $17,800

Exercise 4-3
Preparing adjusting entries from a work sheet P1

Use the following information from the Adjustments columns of a work sheet to prepare the necessary adjusting journal entries (*a*) through (*e*).

[continued from preceding page]

		Unadjusted Trial Balance		Adjustments		Adjusted Trial Balance	
No.	Account Title	Dr.	Cr.	Dr.	Cr.	Dr.	Cr.
109	Interest receivable			(d) $ 880			
124	Office supplies				(b) $ 1,750		
128	Prepaid insurance				(a) 900		
164	Accumulated depreciation—Office equipment				(c) 2,200		
209	Salaries payable				(e) 560		
409	Interest revenue				(d) 880		
612	Depreciation expense—Office equipment			(c) 2,200			
620	Office salaries expense			(e) 560			
637	Insurance expense			(a) 900			
650	Office supplies expense			(b) 1,750			
	Totals			$6,290	$6,290		

Exercise 4-4
Completing work sheet adjustments
P1

The following data are taken from the unadjusted trial balance of the Westcott Company at December 31.

1. Use the following information to complete the Adjustments columns of the work sheet.

a. Depreciation on equipment, $3
b. Accrued salaries, $6
c. The $12 of unearned revenue has been earned
d. Supplies available at December 31, $15
e. Expired insurance, $15

2. Extend the balances in the Adjusted Trial Balance columns of the work sheet to the proper financial statement columns. Compute totals for those columns, including net income.

	Unadjusted Trial Balance		Adjustments		Adjusted Trial Balance		Income Statement		Balance Sheet & Statement of Owner's Equity	
Account	Dr.	Cr.	Dr.	Cr.	Dr.	Cr.	Dr.	Cr.	Dr.	Cr.
Cash	21									
Accounts receivable	12									
Supplies	24									
Prepaid insurance	18									
Equipment	39									
Accumulated depreciation—Equipment		15								
Accounts payable		6								
Salaries payable										
Unearned revenue		12								
W. Westcott, Capital		42								
W. Westcott, Withdrawals	6									
Services revenue		75								
Depreciation expense—Equipment										
Salaries expense	18									
Insurance expense										
Supplies expense										
Utilities expense	12									
Totals	150	150								
Net income										
Totals										

Exercise 4-5
Computing Income Summary and ending capital balance from closing entries
P2

Capri Company began the current period with a $20,000 credit balance in the K. Capri, Capital account. At the end of the period, the company's adjusted account balances include the following temporary accounts with normal balances.

Services revenue	$70,000	Interest revenue	$ 7,000
Salaries expense	38,000	K. Capri, Withdrawals	12,000
Depreciation expense	8,000	Utilities expense	4,600

1. After closing the revenue and expense accounts, what is the balance of the Income Summary account?
2. After all closing entries are journalized and posted, what is the balance of the K. Capri, Capital account?

Exercise 4-6
Completing the Income Statement columns and preparing closing entries
P1 P2

Following are Income Statement columns from a 10-column work sheet for Brown's Bike Rental Company.

1. Determine the amount that should be entered on the net income line of the work sheet.
2. Prepare the company's closing entries. The owner, H. Brown, did not make any withdrawals this period.

Account Title	Debit	Credit
Rental revenue		$120,000
Salaries expense	$ 46,300	
Insurance expense	7,400	
Supplies expense	16,000	
Bike repair expense	4,200	
Depreciation expense—Bikes	20,500	
Totals		
Net income		
Totals		

Exercise 4-7
Preparing a work sheet and recording closing entries
P1 P2

The following unadjusted trial balance contains the accounts and balances of Dylan Delivery Company as of December 31.

1. Use the following information about the company's adjustments to complete a 10-column work sheet.
   a. Unrecorded depreciation on the trucks at the end of the year is $40,000.
   b. Total amount of accrued interest expense at year-end is $6,000.
   c. Cost of unused supplies still available at year-end is $2,000.

2. (*a*) Prepare the year-end closing entries for this company. (*b*) Determine the capital amount to be reported on its year-end balance sheet. *Note:* The S. Dylan, Capital account balance was $307,000 on December 31 of the *prior year*.

Unadjusted Trial Balance		
Account Title	**Debit**	**Credit**
Cash	$ 16,000	
Accounts receivable	34,000	
Supplies	5,000	
Trucks	350,000	
Accumulated depreciation—Trucks		$ 80,000
Land	160,000	
Accounts payable		24,000
Interest payable		5,000
Long-term notes payable		100,000
S. Dylan, Capital		307,000
S. Dylan, Withdrawals	34,000	
Delivery revenue		263,000
Depreciation expense—Trucks	40,000	
Salaries expense	110,000	
Supplies expense	15,000	
Interest expense	5,000	
Repairs expense	10,000	
Totals	$779,000	$779,000

Check Adj. trial balance totals, $820,000; Net income, $39,000

Exercise 4-8
Preparing and posting closing entries
P2

Use the May 31 fiscal year-end information from the following ledger accounts (assume that all accounts have normal balances) to (*a*) prepare closing journal entries and (*b*) post those entries to ledger accounts.

General Ledger

M. Muncel, Capital — Acct. No. 301

Date	PR	Debit	Credit	Balance
May 31	G2			40,000

M. Muncel, Withdrawals — Acct. No. 302

Date	PR	Debit	Credit	Balance
May 31	G2			22,000

Services Revenue — Acct. No. 403

Date	PR	Debit	Credit	Balance
May 31	G2			76,000

Depreciation Expense — Acct. No. 603

Date	PR	Debit	Credit	Balance
May 31	G2			15,000

Salaries Expense — Acct. No. 622

Date	PR	Debit	Credit	Balance
May 31	G2			20,000

Insurance Expense — Acct. No. 637

Date	PR	Debit	Credit	Balance
May 31	G2			4,400

Rent Expense — Acct. No. 640

Date	PR	Debit	Credit	Balance
May 31	G2			8,400

Income Summary — Acct. No. 901

Date	PR	Debit	Credit	Balance

Check M. Muncel, Capital (ending balance), $46,200

Exercise 4-9
Preparing closing entries and a post-closing trial balance P2

Following are accounts and year-end adjusted balances of Cruz Company as of December 31.

1. Prepare the December 31 closing entries. The account number for Income Summary is 901.
2. Prepare the December 31 post-closing trial balance. *Note:* The A. Cruz, Capital account balance was $47,600 on December 31 of the *prior year*.

No.	Account Title	Debit	Credit
101	Cash	$19,000	
126	Supplies	13,000	
128	Prepaid insurance	3,000	
167	Equipment	24,000	
168	Accumulated depreciation—Equipment		$ 7,500
301	A. Cruz, Capital		47,600
302	A. Cruz, Withdrawals	7,000	
403	Services revenue		44,000
612	Depreciation expense—Equipment	3,000	
622	Salaries expense	22,000	
637	Insurance expense	2,500	
640	Rent expense	3,400	
652	Supplies expense	2,200	
	Totals	$99,100	$99,100

Exercise 4-10
Preparing an income statement & statement of owner's equity C1

Use the following adjusted trial balance at December 31 of Wilson Trucking Company to prepare the (1) income statement and (2) statement of owner's equity, for the year ended December 31. The K. Wilson, Capital account balance was $170,000 at December 31 of the *prior year*, and there were no owner investments during the current year.

Account Title	Debit	Credit
Cash	$ 8,000	
Accounts receivable	17,500	
Office supplies	3,000	
Trucks	172,000	
Accumulated depreciation—Trucks		$ 36,000
Land	85,000	
Accounts payable		12,000
Interest payable		4,000
Long-term notes payable		58,000
K. Wilson, Capital		170,000
K. Wilson, Withdrawals	20,000	
Trucking revenue		130,000
Depreciation expense—Trucks	23,500	
Salaries expense	61,000	
Office supplies expense	8,000	
Interest expense	12,000	
Totals	$410,000	$410,000

Exercise 4-11
Preparing a classified balance sheet C1

Use the information in the adjusted trial balance reported in Exercise 4-10 to prepare Wilson Trucking Company's *classified* balance sheet as of December 31.

Exercise 4-12
Preparing closing entries P2

Using Wilson Trucking Company's adjusted trial balance from E 4-10, prepare its December 31 closing entries.

Exercise 4-13
Preparing a classified balance sheet C1

Use the following selected accounts and amounts with normal balances from Andrea Co. to prepare its classified balance sheet at December 31.

Account	Amount	Account	Amount
Accounts payable	$ 8,000	Accounts receivable	$ 4,000
Land	30,000	Accumulated depreciation—Machinery	16,000
Cash	13,000	Notes payable (due in 7 years)	29,000
Salaries payable	1,000	Long-term investments in bonds	7,000
S. Andrea, Capital	42,000	Notes receivable (due in 4 years)	15,000
Machinery	20,000	Merchandise inventory	5,000
Prepaid insurance	2,000		

Exercise 4-14
Computing the current ratio
A1

(*a*) Use the information in the adjusted trial balance reported in Exercise 4-11 to compute the current ratio for Wilson Trucking. (*b*) Assuming Spalding (a competitor) has a current ratio of 1.5, which company is better able to pay its short-term obligations?

Exercise 4-15
Computing and analyzing the current ratio
A1

(*a*) Calculate the current ratio for each of the following competing companies. (*b*) Which competitor is in the best position to pay its short-term obligations?

	Edison	MAXT	Chatter	TRU	Gleeson
Current Assets	$79,040	104,880	45,080	85,680	61,000
Current Liabilities	$32,000	76,000	49,000	81,600	100,000

Exercise 4-16^A
Preparing reversing entries
P3

Hawk Company used the following information to prepare adjusting entries at its December 31 year-end. Prepare any necessary reversing entries for accounting adjustments *a* through *e* assuming that the company uses reversing entries.

a. The company earned $6,000 in service revenues that were not yet recorded at year-end.
b. The expired portion of prepaid insurance was $3,700.
c. The company earned $2,900 of its Unearned Revenue account balance.
d. Depreciation expense for office equipment was $3,300.
e. Employees earned, but have not been paid, salaries of $3,400.

Exercise 4-17^A
Preparing reversing entries
P3

Trey Co. entered into the following two transactions. Trey prepares financial statements annually at December 31.

a. Trey rents a building for $2,800 per month beginning December 1. By agreement, Trey paid cash for both December and January rent on January 2.
b. Trey rents space in a building it owns to a tenant for $850 per month. Trey agreed to allow the tenant to delay payment for December and January rent until January 3, when the tenant paid cash for both months.

Required

1. Prepare adjusting entries the company must record for these events as of December 31.
2. Assuming Trey does *not* use reversing entries, prepare journal entries to record Trey's payment of rent on January 2 and the collection of the tenant's rent on January 3.
3. Assuming Trey uses reversing entries, prepare reversing entries on January 1. Also prepare journal entries to record Trey's payment of rent on January 2 and the receipt of the tenant's rent on January 3.

connect

PROBLEM SET A

Problem 4-1A
Applying the accounting cycle
P2

On April 1, Jiro Nozomi created a new travel agency, Adventure Travel. The following transactions occurred during the company's first month.

Apr. 2 Nozomi invested $30,000 cash and computer equipment worth $20,000 in the company.
3 The company rented furnished office space by paying $1,800 cash for the first month's (April) rent.
4 The company purchased $1,000 of office supplies for cash.
10 The company paid $2,400 cash for a 12-month insurance policy. Coverage begins on April 11.
14 The company paid $1,600 cash for two weeks' salaries earned by employees.
24 The company collected $8,000 cash for commissions revenue.
28 The company paid $1,600 cash for two weeks' salaries earned by employees.
29 The company paid $350 cash for minor repairs to computer equipment.
30 The company paid $750 cash for this month's telephone bill.
30 Nozomi withdrew $1,500 cash from the company for personal use.

[continued on next page]

[continued from preceding page]
The company's chart of accounts follows.

101 Cash	209 Salaries Payable	637 Insurance Expense
106 Accounts Receivable	301 J. Nozomi, Capital	640 Rent Expense
124 Office Supplies	302 J. Nozomi, Withdrawals	650 Office Supplies Expense
128 Prepaid Insurance	403 Commissions Revenue	684 Repairs Expense
167 Computer Equipment	612 Depreciation Expense—Computer Equip.	688 Telephone Expense
168 Accumulated Depreciation—Computer Equip.	622 Salaries Expense	901 Income Summary

Required

1. Use the balance column format to set up each ledger account listed in its chart of accounts.
2. Prepare journal entries to record the transactions for April and post them to ledger accounts.
3. Prepare an unadjusted trial balance as of April 30.
4. Use the following information to journalize and post adjusting entries for the month.
   a. Prepaid insurance of $133 expired this month.
   b. At the end of the month, $600 of office supplies are still available.
   c. This month's depreciation on computer equipment is $500.
   d. Employees earned $420 of unpaid and unrecorded salaries as of month-end.
   e. The company earned $1,750 of commissions revenue that is not yet recorded at month-end.
5. Prepare the adjusted trial balance as of April 30. Prepare the income statement and the statement of owner's equity for the month of April and the balance sheet at April 30.
6. Prepare journal entries to close the temporary accounts and post these entries to the ledger.
7. Prepare a post-closing trial balance.

Check (3) Unadj. trial balance totals, $58,000

(4*a*) Dr. Insurance Expense, $133

(5) Net income, $2,197; Total assets, $51,117

(7) P-C trial balance totals, $51,617

Problem 4-2A
Preparing a work sheet, adjusting and closing entries, and financial statements
C1 P1 P2

The following unadjusted trial balance is for Ace Construction Co. at its June 30 current fiscal year-end. The credit balance of the V. Ace, Capital account was $53,660 on June 30 of the *prior year,* and the owner invested $35,000 cash during the current fiscal year.

Unadjusted Trial Balance
June 30

No.	Account Title	Debit	Credit
101	Cash	$ 18,500	
126	Supplies	9,900	
128	Prepaid insurance	7,200	
167	Equipment	132,000	
168	Accumulated depreciation—Equipment		$ 26,250
201	Accounts payable		6,800
203	Interest payable		0
208	Rent payable		0
210	Wages payable		0
213	Property taxes payable		0
251	Long-term notes payable		25,000
301	V. Ace, Capital		88,660
302	V. Ace, Withdrawals	33,000	
403	Construction revenue		132,100
612	Depreciation expense—Equipment	0	
623	Wages expense	46,860	
633	Interest expense	2,750	
637	Insurance expense	0	
640	Rent expense	12,000	
652	Supplies expense	0	
683	Property taxes expense	7,800	
684	Repairs expense	2,910	
690	Utilities expense	5,890	
	Totals	$278,810	$278,810

Required

1. Prepare and complete a 10-column work sheet for the current fiscal year, starting with the unadjusted trial balance and including adjustments using the following additional information.
   a. Supplies available at the end of the current fiscal year total $3,300.
   b. Cost of expired insurance for the current fiscal year is $3,800.
   c. Annual depreciation on equipment is $8,400.
   d. June utilities expense of $650 is not included in the unadjusted trial balance because the bill arrived after the trial balance was prepared. The $650 amount owed must be recorded.
   e. Employees have earned $1,800 of accrued and unpaid wages at fiscal year-end.
   f. Rent expense incurred and not yet paid or recorded at fiscal year-end is $500.
   g. Additional property taxes of $1,000 have been assessed for this fiscal year but have not been paid or recorded at fiscal year-end.
   h. $250 accrued interest for June has not yet been paid or recorded.
2. Using information from the completed 10-column work sheet in part 1, journalize the adjusting entries and the closing entries.
3. Prepare the income statement and the statement of owner's equity for the year ended June 30 and the classified balance sheet at June 30.

Check (3) Net income, $30,890; Total assets, $122,550; Current liabilities, $11,000

Problem 4-3A
Determining balance sheet classifications
C1

Common categories of a classified balance sheet include Current Assets, Long-Term Investments, Plant Assets, Intangible Assets, Current Liabilities, Long-Term Liabilities, and Equity. For each of the following items, identify the balance sheet category where the item typically would best appear. If an item does not appear on the balance sheet, indicate that instead.

1. Long-term investment in stock
2. Depreciation expense—Building
3. Prepaid rent (2 months of rent)
4. Interest receivable
5. Taxes payable (due in 5 weeks)
6. Automobiles
7. Notes payable (due in 3 years)
8. Accounts payable
9. Cash
10. Patents
11. Unearned services revenue
12. Trucks
13. Prepaid insurance (expires in 5 months)
14. Buildings
15. Store supplies
16. Office equipment
17. Land
18. Repairs expense
19. Office supplies
20. Wages payable

Problem 4-4A
Preparing financial statements and closing entries
C1 P2

The adjusted trial balance for Tybalt Construction on December 31 of the current year follows. Oro Tybalt invested $5,000 cash in the business during the year. The O. Tybalt, Capital account balance was $121,400 on December 31 of the *prior year*.

Adjusted Trial Balance
December 31

No.	Account Title	Debit	Credit
101	Cash	$ 5,000	
126	Supplies	31,100	
128	Prepaid insurance	7,000	
167	Equipment	40,000	
168	Accumulated depreciation—Equipment		$20,000
173	Building	150,000	
174	Accumulated depreciation—Building		50,000
183	Land	55,000	
201	Accounts payable		16,500
203	Interest payable		2,500

[continued on next page]

[continued from preceding page]

208	Rent payable		3,500
210	Wages payable		2,500
213	Property taxes payable		900
236	Unearned revenue		14,500
251	Long-term notes payable		60,000
301	O. Tybalt, Capital		126,400
302	O. Tybalt, Withdrawals	13,000	
403	Services revenue		97,000
406	Rent revenue		14,000
409	Interest revenue		4,100
606	Depreciation expense—Building	11,000	
612	Depreciation expense—Equipment	6,000	
623	Wages expense	52,900	
633	Interest expense	5,100	
637	Insurance expense	10,000	
640	Rent expense	13,400	
652	Supplies expense	7,400	
683	Property taxes expense	5,000	
	Totals	$411,900	$411,900

Required

Check (1) Total assets $218,100; Net income, $4,300

1. Prepare the income statement and the statement of owner's equity for the current year ended December 31, and the classified balance sheet at December 31.
2. Prepare the necessary closing entries at December 31 of the current year.

Problem 4-5A
Preparing financial statements and closing entries
C1 P2

The adjusted trial balance of Karise Repairs on December 31 follows.

Adjusted Trial Balance
December 31

No.	Account Title	Debit	Credit
101	Cash	$ 14,000	
124	Office supplies	1,300	
128	Prepaid insurance	2,050	
167	Equipment	50,000	
168	Accumulated depreciation—Equipment		$ 5,000
201	Accounts payable		14,000
210	Wages payable		600
301	C. Karise, Capital		33,000
302	C. Karise, Withdrawals	16,000	
403	Services revenue		90,950
612	Depreciation expense—Equipment	5,000	
623	Wages expense	37,500	
637	Insurance expense	800	
640	Rent expense	10,600	
650	Office supplies expense	3,600	
690	Utilities expense	2,700	
	Totals	$143,550	$143,550

Required

Check (1) Ending capital balance, $47,750; Net income, $30,750

1. Prepare an income statement and a statement of owner's equity for the year, and a classified balance sheet at December 31. *Note:* The C. Karise, Capital account balance was $33,000 on December 31 of the *prior year*, and there were no owner investments during the current year.
2. Prepare the December 31 closing entries.

Problem 4-6A^A
Preparing reversing entries
P3

The following six-column table for Hawkeye Ranges includes the unadjusted trial balance as of December 31.

	Unadjusted Trial Balance		Adjustments		Adjusted Trial Balance	
Account Title	**Dr.**	**Cr.**	**Dr.**	**Cr.**	**Dr.**	**Cr.**
Cash	$ 14,000					
Accounts receivable	0					
Supplies	6,500					
Equipment	135,000					
Accumulated depreciation—Equipment		$ 30,000				
Interest payable		0				
Salaries payable		0				
Unearned revenue		15,000				
Notes payable		75,000				
P. Hawkeye, Capital		50,250				
P. Hawkeye, Withdrawals	21,125					
Services revenue		42,000				
Depreciation expense—Equipment	0					
Salaries expense	30,000					
Interest expense	5,625					
Supplies expense	0					
Totals	$212,250	$212,250				

Required

1. Complete the six-column table by entering adjustments that reflect the following information.
   a. As of December 31, employees had earned $1,200 of unpaid and unrecorded salaries. The next payday is January 4, at which time $1,500 of salaries will be paid.
   b. Cost of supplies still available at December 31 total $3,000.
   c. An interest payment is made every three months. The amount of unrecorded accrued interest at December 31 is $1,875. The next interest payment, at an amount of $2,250, is due on January 15.
   d. Analysis of Unearned Revenue shows $5,800 remaining unearned at December 31.
   e. Revenue of $9,300 is accrued for services provided. Payment will be collected on January 31.
   f. Depreciation expense is $15,000.
2. Prepare journal entries for adjustments entered in the six-column table for part 1.
3. Prepare journal entries to reverse the effects of the adjusting entries that involve accruals.
4. Prepare journal entries to record cash payments and cash collections described in part 1 for January.

Check (1) Adjusted trial balance totals, $239,625

PROBLEM SET B

Problem 4-1B
Applying the accounting cycle
P2

On July 1, Lula Plume created a new self-storage business, Safe Storage Co. The following transactions occurred during the company's first month.

July 2	Plume invested $30,000 cash and buildings worth $150,000 in the company.
3	The company rented equipment by paying $2,000 cash for the first month's (July) rent.
5	The company purchased $2,400 of office supplies for cash.
10	The company paid $7,200 cash for a 12-month insurance policy. Coverage begins on July 11.
14	The company paid an employee $1,000 cash for two weeks' salary earned.
24	The company collected $9,800 cash for storage revenue from customers.
28	The company paid $1,000 cash for two weeks' salary earned by an employee.
29	The company paid $950 cash for minor repairs to buildings.
30	The company paid $400 cash for this month's telephone bill.
31	Plume withdrew $2,000 cash from the company for personal use.

The company's chart of accounts follows:

101	Cash	209	Salaries Payable	637	Insurance Expense
106	Accounts Receivable	301	L. Plume, Capital	640	Rent Expense
124	Office Supplies	302	L. Plume, Withdrawals	650	Office Supplies Expense
128	Prepaid Insurance	403	Storage Revenue	684	Repairs Expense
173	Buildings	606	Depreciation Expense—Buildings	688	Telephone Expense
174	Accumulated Depreciation—Buildings	622	Salaries Expense	901	Income Summary

[continued on next page]

[continued from preceding page]

Required

1. Use the balance column format to set up each ledger account listed in its chart of accounts.
2. Prepare journal entries to record the transactions for July and post them to ledger accounts.
3. Prepare an unadjusted trial balance as of July 31.
4. Use the following information to journalize and post adjusting entries for the month.
   a. Prepaid insurance of $400 expired this month.
   b. At the end of the month, $1,525 of office supplies are still available.
   c. This month's depreciation on buildings is $1,500.
   d. An employee earned $100 of unpaid and unrecorded salary as of month-end.
   e. The company earned $1,150 of storage revenue that is not yet recorded at month-end.
5. Prepare the adjusted trial balance as of July 31. Prepare the income statement and the statement of owner's equity for the month of July and the balance sheet at July 31.
6. Prepare journal entries to close the temporary accounts and post these entries to the ledger.
7. Prepare a post-closing trial balance.

Check (3) Unadj. trial balance totals, $189,800

(4*a*) Dr. Insurance Expense, $400

(5) Net income, $2,725; Total assets, $180,825

(7) P-C trial balance totals, $182,325

Problem 4-2B
Preparing a work sheet, adjusting and closing entries, and financial statements
C1 P1 P2

The following unadjusted trial balance is for Power Demolition Company at its April 30 current fiscal year-end. The credit balance of the J. Bonn, Capital account was $46,900 on April 30 of the *prior year*, and the owner invested $40,000 cash during the current fiscal year.

Unadjusted Trial Balance
April 30

No.	Account Title	Debit	Credit
101	Cash	$ 7,000	
126	Supplies	16,000	
128	Prepaid insurance	12,600	
167	Equipment	200,000	
168	Accumulated depreciation—Equipment		$ 14,000
201	Accounts payable		6,800
203	Interest payable		0
208	Rent payable		0
210	Wages payable		0
213	Property taxes payable		0
251	Long-term notes payable		30,000
301	J. Bonn, Capital		86,900
302	J. Bonn, Withdrawals	12,000	
403	Demolition revenue		187,000
612	Depreciation expense—Equipment	0	
623	Wages expense	41,400	
633	Interest expense	3,300	
637	Insurance expense	0	
640	Rent expense	13,200	
652	Supplies expense	0	
683	Property taxes expense	9,700	
684	Repairs expense	4,700	
690	Utilities expense	4,800	
	Totals	$ 324,700	$324,700

Required

1. Prepare and complete a 10-column work sheet for the current fiscal year, starting with the unadjusted trial balance and including adjustments using the following additional information.
   a. Supplies available at the end of the current fiscal year total $7,900.
   b. Cost of expired insurance for the current fiscal year is $10,600.
   c. Annual depreciation on equipment is $7,000.
   d. April utilities expense of $800 is not included in the unadjusted trial balance because the bill arrived after the trial balance was prepared. The $800 amount owed must be recorded.
   e. Employees have earned $2,000 of accrued and unpaid wages at fiscal year-end.
   f. Rent expense incurred and not yet paid or recorded at fiscal year-end is $3,000.

g. Additional property taxes of $550 have been assessed for this fiscal year but have not been paid or recorded at fiscal year-end.

h. $300 accrued interest for April has not yet been paid or recorded.

2. Using information from the completed 10-column work sheet in part 1, journalize the adjusting entries and the closing entries.

3. Prepare the income statement and the statement of owner's equity for the year ended April 30 and the classified balance sheet at April 30.

Check (3) Net income, $77,550; Total assets, $195,900; Current liabilities, $13,450

Problem 4-3B
Determining balance sheet classifications
C1

Common categories of a classified balance sheet include Current Assets, Long-Term Investments, Plant Assets, Intangible Assets, Current Liabilities, Long-Term Liabilities, and Equity. For each of the following items, identify the balance sheet category where the item typically would best appear. If an item does not appear on the balance sheet, indicate that instead.

1. Commissions revenue
2. Interest receivable
3. Long-term investment in stock
4. Prepaid insurance (4 months of rent)
5. Machinery
6. Notes payable (due in 15 years)
7. Copyrights
8. Rent payable
9. Trucks
10. Office equipment
11. Rent receivable
12. Salaries payable
13. Income taxes payable (due in 11 weeks)
14. Patents
15. Office supplies
16. Interest payable
17. Rent revenue
18. Notes receivable (due in 10 years)
19. Land
20. Depreciation expense—Trucks

Problem 4-4B
Preparing financial statements and closing entries
C1 P2

The adjusted trial balance for Anara Co. on December 31 of the current year follows. Petra Anara invested $40,000 cash in the business during the year. The P. Anara, Capital account balance was $52,800 on December 31 of the *prior year*.

Adjusted Trial Balance
December 31

No.	Account Title	Debit	Credit
101	Cash	$ 7,400	
126	Supplies	15,800	
128	Prepaid insurance	1,000	
167	Equipment	24,000	
168	Accumulated depreciation—Equipment		$ 4,000
173	Building	100,000	
174	Accumulated depreciation—Building		10,000
183	Land	30,500	
201	Accounts payable		3,500
203	Interest payable		1,750
208	Rent payable		400
210	Wages payable		1,280
213	Property taxes payable		3,330
236	Unearned revenue		9,150
251	Long-term notes payable		31,600
301	P. Anara, Capital		92,800
302	P. Anara, Withdrawals	8,000	
403	Services revenue		59,600
406	Rent revenue		4,500
409	Interest revenue		2,320
606	Depreciation expense—Building	2,000	
612	Depreciation expense—Equipment	1,000	
623	Wages expense	22,030	
633	Interest expense	1,550	
637	Insurance expense	1,525	
640	Rent expense	3,600	
652	Supplies expense	1,000	
683	Property taxes expense	4,825	
	Totals	$224,230	$224,230

[continued on next page]

[continued from preceding page]

Required

Check (1) Total assets, $164,700; Net income, $28,890

1. Prepare the income statement and the statement of owner's equity for the current year ended December 31, and the classified balance sheet at December 31.
2. Prepare the necessary closing entries at December 31 of the current year.

Problem 4-5B
Preparing financial statements and closing entries
C1 P2

Santo Company's adjusted trial balance on December 31 follows.

Adjusted Trial Balance December 31			
No.	**Account Title**	**Debit**	**Credit**
101	Cash	$ 14,450	
125	Store supplies	5,140	
128	Prepaid insurance	1,200	
167	Equipment	31,000	
168	Accumulated depreciation—Equipment		$ 8,000
201	Accounts payable		1,500
210	Wages payable		2,700
301	P. Santo, Capital		35,650
302	P. Santo, Withdrawals	15,000	
403	Services revenue		54,700
612	Depreciation expense—Equipment	2,000	
623	Wages expense	26,400	
637	Insurance expense	600	
640	Rent expense	3,600	
651	Store supplies expense	1,200	
690	Utilities expense	1,960	
	Totals	$102,550	$102,550

Required

Check (1) Ending capital balance, $39,590

1. Prepare an income statement and a statement of owner's equity for the year, and a classified balance sheet at December 31. *Note:* The P. Santo, Capital account balance was $35,650 on December 31 of the *prior year*, and there were no owner investments during the current year.
2. Prepare the December 31 closing entries.

Problem 4-6B[A]
Preparing reversing entries
P3

The following six-column table for Solutions Co. includes the unadjusted trial balance as of December 31.

	Unadjusted Trial Balance		Adjustments		Adjusted Trial Balance	
Account Title	**Dr.**	**Cr.**	**Dr.**	**Cr.**	**Dr.**	**Cr.**
Cash	$ 10,000					
Accounts receivable	0					
Supplies	7,600					
Machinery	50,000					
Accumulated depreciation—Machinery		$ 20,000				
Interest payable		0				
Salaries payable		0				
Unearned revenue		7,200				
Notes payable		30,000				
G. Clay, Capital		14,200				
G. Clay, Withdrawals	9,500					
Services revenue		32,450				
Depreciation expense—Machinery	0					
Salaries expense	24,500					
Interest expense	2,250					
Supplies expense	0					
Totals	$103,850	$103,850				

Required

1. Complete the six-column table by entering adjustments that reflect the following information.

a. As of December 31, employees had earned $400 of unpaid and unrecorded wages. The next payday is January 4, at which time $1,200 in wages will be paid.

b. Cost of supplies still available at December 31 is $3,450.

c. An interest payment is made every three months. The amount of unrecorded accrued interest at December 31 is $800. The next interest payment, at an amount of $900, is due on January 15.

d. Analysis of Unearned Revenue shows that $3,200 remains unearned at December 31.

e. Revenue of $2,450 is accrued for services provided. Payment will be collected on January 31.

f. Depreciation expense is $3,800.

2. Prepare journal entries for adjustments entered in the six-column table for part 1.

3. Prepare journal entries to reverse the effects of the adjusting entries that involve accruals.

4. Prepare journal entries to record cash payments and cash collections described in part 1 for January.

Check (1) Adjusted trial balance totals, $111,300

connect

SERIAL PROBLEM

Business Solutions

P2

*Serial problem began in Chapter 1. If previous chapter segments were not completed, the serial problem can begin at this point. It is available in **Connect** with an algorithmic option.*

SP 4 The December 31, 2021, adjusted trial balance of **Business Solutions** (reflecting its transactions from October through December of 2021) follows.

Alexander Image/Shutterstock

No.	Account Title	Debit	Credit
101	Cash	$ 48,372	
106	Accounts receivable	5,668	
126	Computer supplies	580	
128	Prepaid insurance	1,665	
131	Prepaid rent	825	
163	Office equipment	8,000	
164	Accumulated depreciation—Office equipment		$ 400
167	Computer equipment	20,000	
168	Accumulated depreciation—Computer equipment		1,250
201	Accounts payable		1,100
210	Wages payable		500
236	Unearned computer services revenue		1,500
301	S. Rey, Capital		73,000
302	S. Rey, Withdrawals	7,100	
403	Computer services revenue		31,284
612	Depreciation expense—Office equipment	400	
613	Depreciation expense—Computer equipment	1,250	
623	Wages expense	3,875	
637	Insurance expense	555	
640	Rent expense	2,475	
652	Computer supplies expense	3,065	
655	Advertising expense	2,753	
676	Mileage expense	896	
677	Miscellaneous expenses	250	
684	Repairs expense—Computer	1,305	
901	Income summary		0
	Totals	$109,034	$109,034

[continued on next page]

[continued from preceding page]

Required

1. Prepare an income statement for the three months ended December 31, 2021.
2. Prepare a statement of owner's equity for the three months ended December 31, 2021. *Hint:* The S. Rey, Capital account balance was $0 on October 1, and owner investments were $73,000 this period.
3. Prepare a classified balance sheet as of December 31, 2021.
4. Record and post the necessary closing entries as of December 31, 2021.
5. Prepare a post-closing trial balance as of December 31, 2021.

Check (5) Post-closing trial balance totals, $85,110

TABLEAU DASHBOARD ACTIVITIES

Tableau Dashboard Activities expose students to accounting analytics using visual displays. These assignments run in **Connect**. All are auto-gradable.

Tableau DA 4-1 Quick Study, Classifying balance sheet items, C3—similar to QS 4-12

Tableau DA 4-2 Exercise, Preparing a post-closing trial balance and current assets section of a balance sheet, P3, C3—similar to Exercise 4-9 and QS 4-15

Tableau DA 4-3 Mini-Case, Preparing a classified balance sheet, C3—similar to QS 4-17 and Exercise 4-13

GENERAL LEDGER

General Ledger (GL) Assignments expose students to general ledger software similar to that in practice. GL is part of **Connect**, and GL assignments are auto-gradable and have algorithmic options. For the following GL assignments, prepare adjusting entries and determine their impact on net income. Financial statements are automatically generated based on entries recorded—this feature can be turned off.

GL 4-1 Transactions from the FastForward illustration in this chapter

GL 4-2 Based on Problem 4-1A

GL 4-3 Based on Problem 4-2A

GL 4-4 Based on Problem 4-6A

GL 4-5 Based on Serial Problem SP 4

Accounting Analysis

COMPANY ANALYSIS

P2

AA 4-1 Refer to **Apple**'s financial statements in Appendix A to answer the following.

1. For the fiscal year ended September 28, 2019, what amount is credited to Income Summary to summarize its revenues earned? *Hint:* make sure to consider any "Other income" reported on Apple's income statement.
2. For the fiscal year ended September 28, 2019, what amount is debited to Income Summary to summarize its expenses incurred?
3. For the fiscal year ended September 28, 2019, what is the balance of its Income Summary account before it is closed?

COMPARATIVE ANALYSIS

A1

AA 4-2 Key figures for the recent two years of both **Apple** and **Google** follow.

	Apple		Google	
$ millions	Current Year	Prior Year	Current Year	Prior Year
Current assets	$162,819	$131,339	$152,578	$135,676
Current liabilities	105,718	115,929	45,221	34,620

Required

1. Compute current ratios for (*a*) Apple and (*b*) Google for the two years reported above.
2. In the current year, which company has the better ability to pay short-term obligations according to the current ratio?
3. Do (*a*) Apple's and (*b*) Google's current ratios underperform or outperform the industry (assumed) average ratio of 2.0?

EXTENDED ANALYSIS
A1

AA 4-3 The following selected information is available from **Samsung**'s financial statements.

$ millions	Current Year	Prior Year
Current assets.	$155,634	$149,896
Current liabilities.	54,728	$ 59,274

Required

1. Compute Samsung's current ratio for both the current year and the prior year.
2. In the current year, did Samsung's current ratio improve or worsen versus the prior year?

Discussion Questions

1. What are the steps in recording closing entries?
2. What accounts are affected by closing entries? What accounts are not affected?
3. What two purposes are accomplished by recording closing entries?
4. What is the purpose of the Income Summary account?
5. Explain whether an error has occurred if a post-closing trial balance includes a Depreciation Expense account.
6. What tasks are aided by a work sheet?
7. Why are the debit and credit entries in the Adjustments columns of the work sheet identified with letters?
8. What is a company's operating cycle?
9. What classes of assets and liabilities are shown on a typical classified balance sheet?
10. How is unearned revenue classified on the balance sheet?
11. What are the characteristics of plant assets?
12. [A] How do reversing entries simplify recordkeeping?
13. [A] If a company recorded accrued salaries expense of $500 at the end of its fiscal year, what reversing entry could be made? When would it be made?

Beyond the Numbers

ETHICS CHALLENGE
P2

BTN 4-1 On January 20, Tamira Nelson, the accountant for Picton Enterprises, is feeling pressure to complete the annual December 31 year-end financial statements. The company president has said he needs up-to-date financial statements to share with the bank on January 21 at a dinner meeting that has been called to discuss Picton's obtaining loan financing for a special building project. Tamira knows that she will not be able to gather all the needed information in the next 24 hours to prepare the entire set of adjusting entries. Those entries must be posted before the financial statements accurately portray the company's performance and financial position for the year ended December 31 (three weeks ago). Tamira ultimately decides to estimate several expense accruals at the last minute. When deciding on estimates for the expenses, she uses low estimates because she does not want to

[continued on next page]

[continued from preceding page]
make the financial statements look worse than they are. Tamira finishes the financial statements before the deadline and gives them to the president without mentioning that several account balances are estimates that she provided.

Required

1. Identify several courses of action that Tamira could have taken instead of the one she took.
2. If you were in Tamira's situation, what would you have done? Briefly justify your response.

COMMUNICATING IN PRACTICE
P2

BTN 4-2 One of your classmates states that a company's books should be ongoing and therefore not closed until that business is terminated. Write a half-page memo to this classmate explaining the concept of the closing process by drawing analogies between (1) a scoreboard for an athletic event and the revenue and expense accounts of a business or (2) a sports team's record book and the capital account. *Hint:* Think about what would happen if the scoreboard were not cleared before the start of a new game.

TEAMWORK IN ACTION
P1 P2

BTN 4-3 The unadjusted trial balance and information for the accounting adjustments of Noseworthy Investigators follow. Each team member involved in this project is to assume one of the four responsibilities listed. After completing each of these responsibilities, the team should work together to prove the accounting equation utilizing information from teammates (1 and 4). If your equation does not balance, you are to work as a team to resolve the error. The team's goal is to complete the task as quickly and accurately as possible.

Unadjusted Trial Balance

Account Title	Debit	Credit
Cash	$16,000	
Supplies	12,000	
Prepaid insurance	3,000	
Equipment	25,000	
Accumulated depreciation—Equipment		$ 7,000
Accounts payable		3,000
D. Noseworthy, Capital		34,000
D. Noseworthy, Withdrawals	6,000	
Investigation revenue		33,000
Rent expense	15,000	
Totals	$77,000	$77,000

Additional Year-End Information

a. Insurance that expired in the current period amounts to $2,200.
b. Equipment depreciation for the period is $4,000.
c. Unused supplies total $5,000 at period-end.
d. Services in the amount of $800 have been provided but have not been billed or collected.

Responsibilities for Individual Team Members

1. Determine the accounts and adjusted balances to be extended to the Balance Sheet columns of the work sheet for Noseworthy. Also determine total assets and total liabilities.
2. Determine the adjusted revenue account balance and prepare the entry to close this account.
3. Determine the adjusted account balances for expenses and prepare the entry to close these accounts.

4. Prepare T-accounts for both D. Noseworthy, Capital (reflecting the unadjusted trial balance amount) and Income Summary. Ask teammates assigned to parts 2 and 3 for the postings for Income Summary. Using that information, prepare and post both the third and fourth closing entries. Provide the team with the ending capital account balance.

5. The entire team should prove the accounting equation using post-closing balances.

ENTREPRENEURIAL DECISION

P2 C1

BTN 4-4 Review this chapter's opening feature involving Evan and Bobby and **Snapchat**.

1. Explain how a classified balance sheet can help Evan and Bobby know what bills are due when and whether they have the resources to pay those bills.

2. Why is it important for Evan and Bobby to match costs and revenues in a specific time period? How do closing entries help them in this regard?

3. What objectives are met when Evan and Bobby apply closing procedures each fiscal year-end?

5 Accounting for Merchandising Operations

Chapter Preview

MERCHANDISING ACTIVITIES	MERCHANDISING PURCHASES	MERCHANDISING SALES	MERCHANDISER REPORTING
C1 Income and inventory for merchandisers	**P1** Accounting for:	**P2** Accounting for:	**P3** Adjusting and closing
Operating cycle	Purchases discounts	Sales of merchandise	**P4** Multiple-step and single-step income statements
Inventory cost flows	Purchases returns and allowances	Sales discounts	**A1** Acid-test analysis
	Transportation costs	Sales returns and allowances	Gross margin analysis
NTK 5-1	**NTK 5-2**	**NTK 5-3**	**NTK 5-4, 5-5**

*All content is consistent with **new revenue recognition rules**. Details of new adjusting entries are in Appendix 5B.*

Learning Objectives

CONCEPTUAL

C1 Describe merchandising activities and cost flows.

ANALYTICAL

A1 Compute and analyze the acid-test ratio and gross margin ratio.

PROCEDURAL

P1 Analyze and record transactions for merchandise purchases using a perpetual system.

P2 Analyze and record transactions for merchandise sales using a perpetual system.

P3 Prepare adjustments and close accounts for a merchandising company.

P4 Define and prepare multiple-step and single-step income statements.

P5 *Appendix 5A*—Record and compare merchandising transactions using both periodic and perpetual inventory systems.

P6 *Appendix 5B*—Prepare adjustments for discounts, returns, and allowances per revenue recognition rules.

P7 *Appendix 5C*—Record and compare merchandising transactions using the gross method and net method.

State of the Art

"Go big or go home"—**KENDRA SCOTT**

AUSTIN, TX—Kendra Scott took $500 from savings and designed her first jewelry collection from her bedroom. "My mom's family was farmers and coal miners," says Kendra. "They were very hardworking folks." She applied that same work ethic to her passion for design and business. Today, **Kendra Scott** (KendraScott.com) jewelry and accessories are available from over 600 stores. Kendra has opened 75 of her own stores. "I'm a girl from Kenosha, Wisconsin," points out Kendra. "Who would've thought I'd be a fashion designer?"

Although Kendra has a knack for fashion, she attributes much of her company's success to an ability to analyze trends in customer tastes. Kendra regularly applies accounting analytics to sales, purchases, and inventory data. This allows her to see which products are selling well and which are piling up in inventory. According to Kendra, analyzing accounting data and engaging with customers enable the company to "hear what [the customer] wants, what she needs, and what's important to her."

Her company's accounting reports detail sales and gross profit information to help Kendra assess business and new opportunities. Those reports also help Kendra gauge how much she can devote to charity. "I decided that if someone would call me for a charitable donation . . . I would always have something to give," insists Kendra. "We don't turn anyone away."

Jarod Gibo

Kendra explains that accounting, merchandising, and fashion are a perfect blend. She admits, "I feel like the luckiest person alive."

Sources: *Kendra Scott website*, January 2021; *Success.com*, March 2016; *CBS*, March 2018

MERCHANDISING ACTIVITIES

C1 Describe merchandising activities and cost flows.

Previous chapters focused on accounting for service companies. A merchandising company's activities differ from those of a service company. **Merchandise** refers to products, also called *goods,* that a company buys to resell. A **merchandiser** earns net income by buying and selling merchandise. Merchandisers are wholesalers or retailers. A **wholesaler** buys products from manufacturers and sells them to retailers. A **retailer** buys products from manufacturers or wholesalers and sells them to consumers.

Reporting Income for a Merchandiser

Net income for a merchandiser equals revenues from selling merchandise minus both the cost of merchandise sold and other expenses—see Exhibit 5.1. Revenue from selling merchandise is called *sales,* and the expense of buying and preparing merchandise is called **cost of goods sold.** (Some service companies use the term *sales* instead of revenues; cost of goods sold is also called *cost of sales*.)

EXHIBIT 5.1 Computing Income for a Merchandising Company versus a Service Company

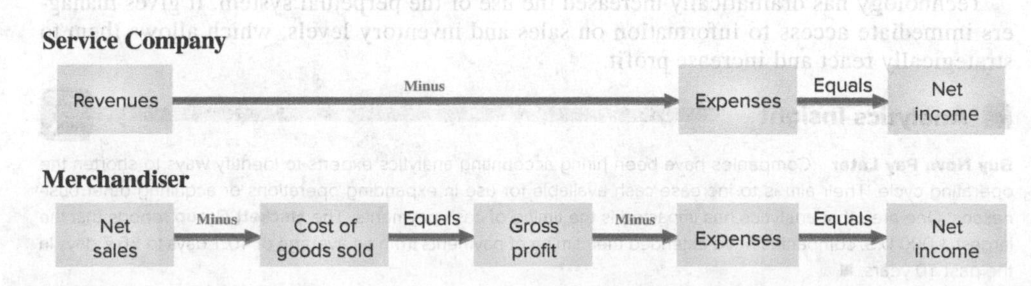

The income statements for a service company, **H&R Block**, and for a merchandiser, **Nordstrom**, are in Exhibit 5.2. We see that the merchandiser, Nordstrom, reports cost of goods sold, which is not reported by the service company. The merchandiser also reports **gross profit,** or **gross margin,** which is net sales minus cost of goods sold.

EXHIBIT 5.2

Income Statement for a Service Company and a Merchandising Company

Service Company

H&R Block Income Statement ($ millions)	
Revenues	$3,095
Expenses	2,672
Net income	$ 423

Merchandising Company

NORDSTROM INC. Income Statement ($ millions)	
Net sales	$15,524
Cost of goods sold	9,932
Gross profit	5,592
Expenses	5,096
Net income	$ 496

Reporting Inventory for a Merchandiser

A merchandiser's balance sheet has a current asset called *merchandise inventory,* an item not on a service company's balance sheet. **Merchandise inventory,** or simply **inventory,** refers to products that a company owns and intends to sell. Inventory cost includes the cost to buy the goods, ship them to the store, and make them ready for sale.

EXHIBIT 5.3

Merchandiser's Operating Cycle

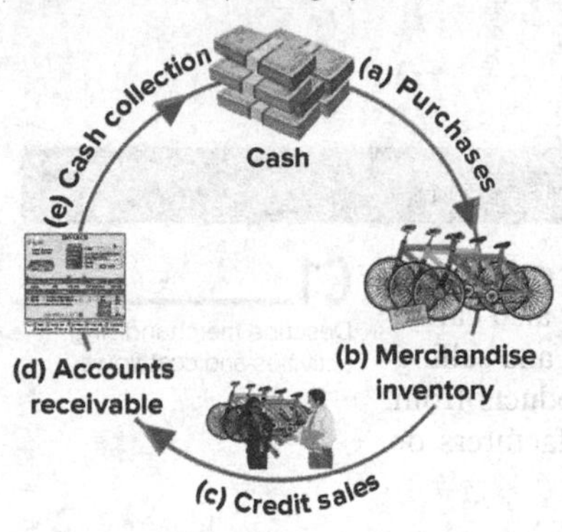

Operating Cycle for a Merchandiser

Exhibit 5.3 shows an operating cycle for a merchandiser with credit sales. The cycle moves from *(a)* cash purchases of merchandise to *(b)* inventory for sale to *(c)* credit sales to *(d)* accounts receivable to *(e)* receipt of cash. The length of an operating cycle differs across the types of businesses. Department stores often have operating cycles of two to five months. Operating cycles for grocery stores are usually from two to eight weeks. Companies try to keep their operating cycles short because assets tied up in inventory and receivables are not productive. Cash sales shorten operating cycles.

Inventory Systems

Exhibit 5.4 shows that a company's merchandise available for sale consists of what it begins with (beginning inventory) and what it purchases (net purchases). The merchandise available for sale is either sold (expensed on the income statement as cost of goods sold) or kept for future sales (as inventory, a current asset on the balance sheet).

EXHIBIT 5.4

Merchandiser's Cost Flow for a Single Time Period

Companies account for inventory in one of two ways: *perpetual system* or *periodic system.*

- **Perpetual inventory system** records cost of goods sold at the time of each sale.
- **Periodic inventory system** records cost of goods sold at the end of the period.

Technology has dramatically increased the use of the perpetual system. It gives managers immediate access to information on sales and inventory levels, which allows them to strategically react and increase profit.

Tobias Ackeborn/E+/Getty Images

Analytics Insight

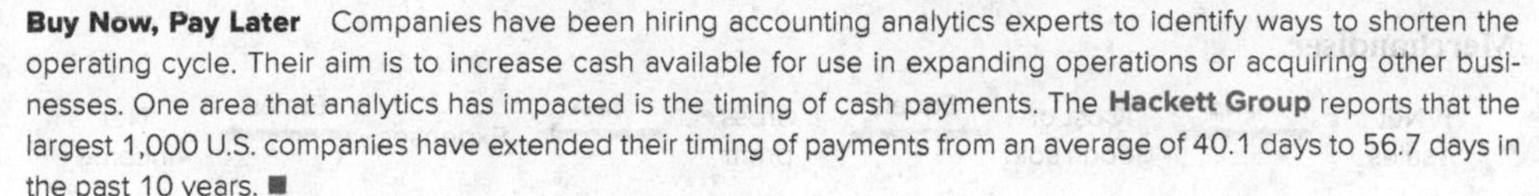

Buy Now, Pay Later Companies have been hiring accounting analytics experts to identify ways to shorten the operating cycle. Their aim is to increase cash available for use in expanding operations or acquiring other businesses. One area that analytics has impacted is the timing of cash payments. The **Hackett Group** reports that the largest 1,000 U.S. companies have extended their timing of payments from an average of 40.1 days to 56.7 days in the past 10 years. ■

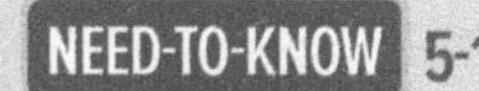

Merchandise Accounts and Computations

C1

Use the following information from a merchandising company and from a service company to complete the requirements.

SaveCo Merchandiser			
Supplies	$ 10	Expenses	$ 20
Beginning inventory	100	Net purchases	80
Ending inventory	50	Net sales	190

Hi-Tech Services			
Expenses	$170	Prepaid rent	$25
Revenues	200	Accounts payable	35
Cash	10	Supplies	65

1. For the merchandiser only, compute (a) goods available for sale, (b) cost of goods sold, and (c) gross profit.
2. Compute net income for each company.

Solution

1. a. Computation of goods available for sale (SaveCo).

Beginning inventory	$100
Plus: Net purchases	80
Goods available for sale	$180

b. Computation of cost of goods sold (SaveCo).

Beginning inventory	$100
Plus: Net purchases	80
Goods available for sale	180
Less: Ending inventory	50
Cost of goods sold	$130

c. Computation of gross profit (SaveCo).

Net sales	$190
Less: Cost of goods sold (from part b)	130
Gross profit	$ 60

2. Computation of net income for each company.

SaveCo Merchandiser	
Net sales	$190
Less: Cost of goods sold (from part 1b)	130
Gross profit	60
Less: Expenses	20
Net income	$ 40

Hi-Tech Services	
Revenues	$200
Less: Expenses	170
Net income	$ 30

Do More: QS 5-1, QS 5-2, QS 5-3, E 5-1, E 5-2

MERCHANDISE PURCHASES

P1 Analyze and record transactions for merchandise purchases using a perpetual system.

This section explains how we record purchases under different purchase terms.

Purchases without Cash Discounts

Z-Mart records a $500 cash purchase of merchandise on November 2 as follows.

Nov. 2	Merchandise Inventory	500	
	Cash		500
	Purchased goods for cash.		

Assets = Liabilities + Equity
+500
−500

If these goods are instead *purchased on credit,* Z-Mart makes the same entry except that Accounts Payable is credited instead of Cash.

Purchases with Cash Discounts

The purchase of goods on credit requires credit terms. **Credit terms** include the amounts and timing of payments from a buyer to a seller. To demonstrate, when sellers require payment within 60 days after the invoice date, credit terms are "n/60," meaning *net 60 days.*

Credit Terms Exhibit 5.5 explains credit terms. The amount of time allowed before full payment is due is the **credit period.** Sellers can grant a **cash discount** to encourage buyers to pay earlier. A buyer views a cash discount as a **purchases discount.** A seller views a cash discount as a **sales discount.** Any cash discounts are described on the invoice. The invoice date sets the discount and credit periods. For example, credit terms of "2/10, n/60" mean that full payment is due within a 60-day credit period, but the buyer can deduct 2% of the invoice amount if payment is made within 10 days of the invoice date. This reduced payment is only for the **discount period.**

EXHIBIT 5.5

Credit Terms

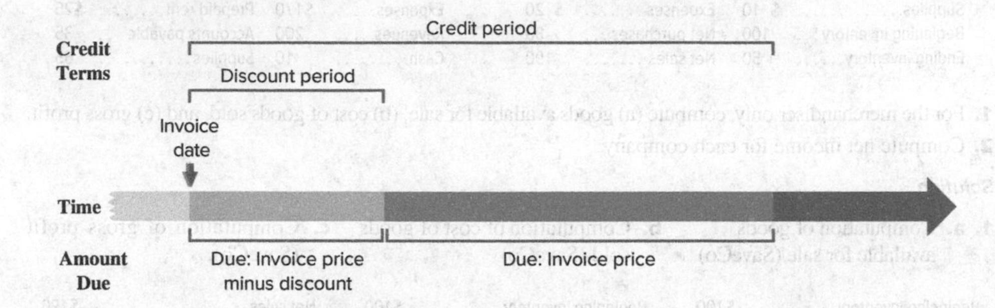

Invoice On November 2, Z-Mart purchases $500 of merchandise **on credit** with terms of 2/10, n/30. The invoice for this purchase is shown in Exhibit 5.6. This is a purchase invoice for Z-Mart (buyer) and a sales invoice for Trex (seller). The amount recorded for merchandise inventory includes its purchase cost, shipping fees, taxes, and any other costs necessary to make it ready for sale.

EXHIBIT 5.6

Invoice

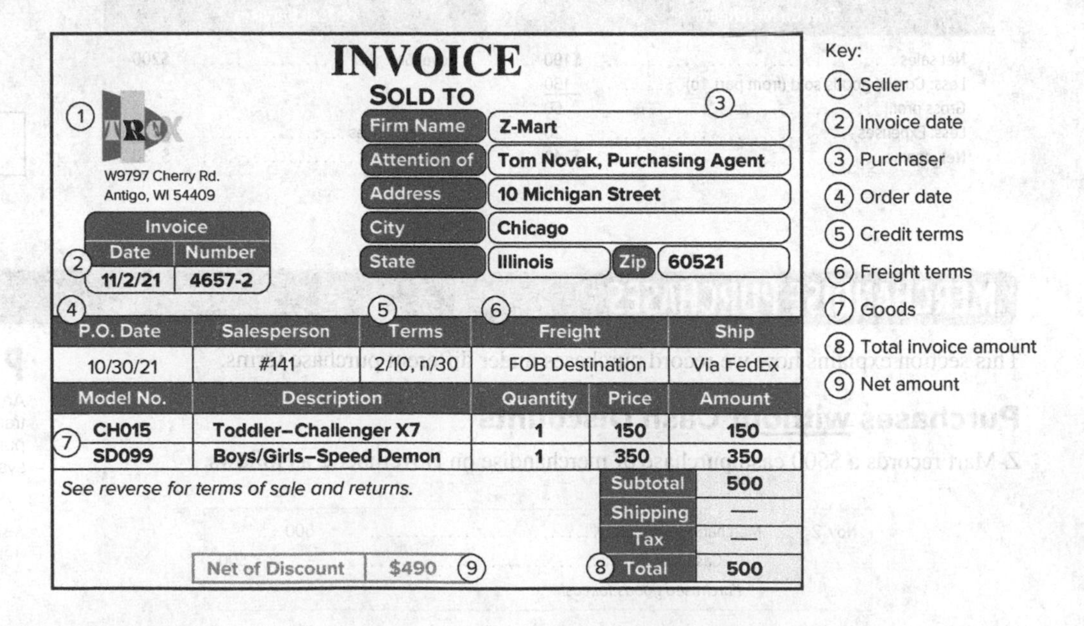

INVOICE

(1) TREX
W9797 Cherry Rd.
Antigo, WI 54409

(2) Invoice Date: 11/2/21 Number: 4657-2

SOLD TO (3)

Firm Name	Z-Mart
Attention of	Tom Novak, Purchasing Agent
Address	10 Michigan Street
City	Chicago
State	Illinois Zip 60521

(4) P.O. Date	Salesperson	(5) Terms	(6) Freight	Ship
10/30/21	#141	2/10, n/30	FOB Destination	Via FedEx

Model No.	Description	Quantity	Price	Amount
(7) CH015	Toddler–Challenger X7	1	150	150
SD099	Boys/Girls–Speed Demon	1	350	350
			Subtotal	500
			Shipping	—
			Tax	—
			(8) Total	500

See reverse for terms of sale and returns.

Net of Discount $490 (9)

Key:
(1) Seller
(2) Invoice date
(3) Purchaser
(4) Order date
(5) Credit terms
(6) Freight terms
(7) Goods
(8) Total invoice amount
(9) Net amount

Gross Method Z-Mart purchases $500 of merchandise on credit terms of 2/10, n/30. The November 2 invoice offers a 2% discount if paid within 10 days; if not, Z-Mart must pay the full amount within 30 days. The buyer has two options.

- Pay within discount period (Nov. 2 through Nov. 12): Due = $490.

or

- Pay after discount period (Nov. 13 through Dec. 2): Due = $500.

The $490 equals the $500 invoice minus $10 discount (computed as $500 × 2%).

On the purchase date, we do not know if payment will occur within the discount period. The **gross method** records the purchase at its *gross* (full) invoice amount. For Z-Mart, the purchase of $500 of merchandise with terms of 2/10, n/30 is recorded at $500. *The gross method is used* *here because it (1) complies with new revenue recognition rules, (2) is used more in practice, and (3) is easier and less costly to apply.*

Purchases on Credit Z-Mart's entry to record the November 2 purchase of $500 of merchandise on credit follows. (If Z-Mart has multiple suppliers, it helps to add the name to the payable, such as Accounts Payable—Trex.)

(a) Nov. 2	Merchandise Inventory	500	
	Accounts Payable		500
	Purchased goods, terms 2/10, n/30.		

Assets = Liabilities + Equity
+500 +500

Point: Appendix 5A repeats journal entries *a* through *g* using the periodic system.

Payment within Discount Period Good cash management means that invoices are not paid until the last day of the discount or credit period. This is because the buyer can use that money until payment is required. If Z-Mart pays the amount due on or before November 12, the entry is

(b1) Nov. 12	Accounts Payable	500	
	Merchandise Inventory		10
	Cash*		490
	*Paid for goods within discount period. *$500 × (100% − 2%)*		

Assets = Liabilities + Equity
−490 −500
− 10

The Merchandise Inventory account equals the $490 net cost of purchases after these entries, and the Accounts Payable account has a zero balance.

Accounts Payable			
		Nov. 2	500
Nov. 12	500		
		Bal.	0

Merchandise Inventory			
Nov. 2	500		
		Nov. 12	10
Bal.	490		

Cash			
		Nov. 12	490

Payment after Discount Period If the invoice is paid *after* November 12, the discount is lost. If Z-Mart pays the gross (full) amount due on December 2 (the n/30 due date), the entry is

(b2) Dec. 2	Accounts Payable	500	
	Cash		500
	Paid for goods outside discount period.		

Assets = Liabilities + Equity
−500 −500

Purchases with Returns and Allowances

Purchases returns are merchandise a buyer purchases but then returns. *Purchases allowances* refer to a seller granting a price reduction (allowance) to a buyer of defective or unacceptable merchandise.

Purchases Allowances On November 5, Z-Mart (buyer) agrees to a $30 allowance from Trex for defective merchandise (assume allowance is $30 whether paid within the discount period or not). Z-Mart's entry to update Merchandise Inventory and record the allowance follows. Z-Mart's allowance for defective merchandise reduces its account payable to the seller. If cash is refunded, Cash is debited instead of Accounts Payable.

(c1) Nov. 5	Accounts Payable	30	
	Merchandise Inventory		30
	Allowance for defective goods.		

Assets = Liabilities + Equity
−30 −30

Purchases Returns Returns of inventory are recorded at the amount charged for that inventory. On June 1, Z-Mart purchases $250 of merchandise with terms 2/10, n/60—see entries below. On June 3, Z-Mart returns $50 of those goods. When Z-Mart pays on June 11, it takes the 2% discount only on the $200 remaining balance ($250 − $50). When goods are returned, a buyer takes a discount on only the remaining balance. This means the discount is $4 (computed as $200 × 2%) and the cash payment is $196 (computed as $200 − $4).

Assets = Liabilities + Equity
+250 +250

Assets = Liabilities + Equity
−50 −50

Assets = Liabilities + Equity
−196 −200
− 4

		Debit	Credit
June 1	Merchandise Inventory	250	
	Accounts Payable		250
	Purchased goods, terms 2/10, n/60.		
(c2) June 3	Accounts Payable	50	
	Merchandise Inventory		50
	Returned goods to seller.		
June 11	Accounts Payable	200	
	Merchandise Inventory		4
	Cash		196
	Paid for $200 of goods less $4 discount.		

These T-accounts show the final $196 in inventory, the zero balance in Accounts Payable, and the $196 cash payment.

Example: If, on June 20, Z-Mart returns all goods paid for on June 11, the entry is
Cash 196
Merchandise Inventory ... 196

Accounts Payable			
		Jun. 1	250
Jun. 3	50		
Jun. 11	200		
		Bal.	0

Merchandise Inventory			
Jun. 1	250		
		Jun. 3	50
		Jun. 11	4
Bal.	196		

Cash			
		Jun. 11	196

Purchases and Transportation Costs

The buyer and seller must agree on who is responsible for paying freight (shipping) costs and who has the risk of loss during transit. This is the same as asking at what point ownership transfers from the seller to the buyer. The point of transfer is called the **FOB** (*free on board*) point.

Exhibit 5.7 covers two alternative points of transfer.

1. *FOB shipping point* means the buyer accepts ownership when the goods depart the seller's place of business. The buyer pays shipping costs and has the risk of loss in transit. The goods are part of the buyer's inventory when they are in transit because ownership has transferred to the buyer. **1-800-Flowers.com**, a floral merchandiser, uses FOB shipping point.
2. *FOB destination* means ownership of goods transfers to the buyer when the goods arrive at the buyer's place of business. The seller pays shipping charges and has the risk of loss in transit. The seller does not record revenue until the goods arrive at the destination.

When a buyer is responsible for paying transportation costs, the payment is made to a carrier or directly to the seller. The cost principle requires that transportation costs of a buyer (often

EXHIBIT 5.7

Ownership Transfer and Transportation Costs

Shipping Terms	Ownership Transfers at	Goods in Transit Owned by	Transportation Costs Paid by
FOB shipping point	Shipping point	Buyer	**Buyer** Merchandise Inventory ... # Cash .... #
FOB destination	Destination	Seller	**Seller** Delivery Expense ...... # Cash .... #

called *transportation-in* or *freight-in*) be part of the cost of merchandise inventory. Z-Mart's entry to record a $75 freight charge from **UPS** for merchandise purchased FOB shipping point is

(*d*) Nov. 24	Merchandise Inventory	75	
	Cash.		75
	Paid freight costs on goods.		

Assets = Liabilities + Equity
+75
−75

When a seller is responsible for paying shipping costs, it records these costs in a Delivery Expense account. Delivery expense, also called *transportation-out* or *freight-out,* is reported as a selling expense in the seller's income statement.

Itemized Costs of Purchases In summary, purchases are recorded as debits to Merchandise Inventory. Purchases discounts, returns, and allowances are credited to (subtracted from) Merchandise Inventory. Transportation-in is debited (added) to Merchandise Inventory. Z-Mart's itemized costs of merchandise purchases for the year are in Exhibit 5.8.

EXHIBIT 5.8
Itemized Costs of Merchandise Purchases

Itemized Costs of Merchandise Purchases	
Invoice cost of merchandise purchases	$ 235,800
Less: Purchases discounts received	(4,200)
Purchases returns and allowances.	(1,500)
Add: Costs of transportation-in	2,300
Total net cost of merchandise purchases	**$232,400**

The accounting system described here does not provide separate records (accounts) for total purchases, total purchases discounts, total purchases returns and allowances, and total transportation-in. Many companies collect this information in supplementary records to evaluate these costs. **Supplementary records,** or *supplemental records,* refer to information outside the usual ledger accounts.

Point: Purchase of inventory affects balance sheet accounts only.

Decision Ethics

PeopleImages/E+/Getty Images

Payables Manager As a new accounts payable manager, you are being trained by the outgoing manager. She explains that the system prepares checks for amounts net of favorable cash discounts, and the checks are dated the last day of the discount period. She tells you that checks are not mailed until five days later, adding that "the company gets free use of cash for an extra five days, and our department looks better." Do you continue this policy? ■ *Answer:* One point of view is that the late payment policy is unethical. A deliberate plan to make late payments means the company lies when it pretends to make payment within the discount period. Another view is that the late payment policy is acceptable. Some believe attempts to take discounts through late payments are accepted as "price negotiation."

NEED-TO-KNOW 5-2

Merchandise Purchases
P1

Prepare journal entries to record each of the following transactions. Assume a perpetual inventory system using the gross method for recording purchases.

Oct. 1 Purchased $1,000 of goods. Terms of the sale are 4/10, n/30, and FOB shipping point; the invoice is dated October 1.
3 Paid $30 cash for freight charges from UPS for the October 1 purchase.
7 Returned $50 of the $1,000 of goods from the October 1 purchase and received full credit.
11 Paid the amount due from the October 1 purchase (less the return on October 7).
31 *Assume the October 11 payment was never made.* Instead, payment of the amount due, less the return on October 7, occurred on October 31.

Do More: QS 5-4, QS 5-5, QS 5-6, QS 5-7, E 5-3, E 5-4, E 5-5, E 5-8

Solution

Oct. 1	Merchandise Inventory	1,000	
	Accounts Payable.		1,000
	Purchased goods, terms 4/10, n/30.		
Oct. 3	Merchandise Inventory	30	
	Cash.		30
	Paid freight on purchases FOB shipping point.		
Oct. 7	Accounts Payable	50	
	Merchandise Inventory.		50
	Returned goods.		

Oct. 11	Accounts Payable	950	
	Merchandise Inventory*		38
	Cash†		912
	Paid for goods within discount period. **$950 × 4% †$950 − ($950 × 4%)*		
Oct. 31	Accounts Payable‡.	950	
	Cash.		950
	Paid for goods outside discount period. ‡$1,000 − $50		

MERCHANDISE SALES

P2

Analyze and record transactions for merchandise sales using a perpetual system.

Merchandising companies must account for sales, sales discounts, sales returns and allowances, and cost of goods sold. Z-Mart has these items in its gross profit computation—see Exhibit 5.9. This shows that customers paid $314,700 for merchandise that cost Z-Mart $230,400, yielding a gross profit of $84,300.

EXHIBIT 5.9

Gross Profit Computation

Computation of Gross Profit	
Net sales (net of discounts, returns, and allowances)	$ 314,700
Cost of goods sold	230,400
Gross profit	**$ 84,300**

The perpetual accounting system requires that each sales transaction for a merchandiser, whether for cash or on credit, has *two entries:* one for revenue and one for cost.

1. **Revenue recorded (and asset increased) from the customer.**
2. **Cost of goods sold incurred (and asset decreased) to the customer.**

Sales without Cash Discounts

Revenue Side: Inflow of Assets Z-Mart sold $1,000 of merchandise on credit terms n/60 on November 12. The revenue part of this transaction is recorded as follows. This entry shows an increase in Z-Mart's assets in the form of accounts receivable. It also shows the increase in revenue (Sales). If the sale is for cash, debit Cash instead of Accounts Receivable.

Assets = Liabilities + Equity
+1,000 +1,000

Nov. 12	Accounts Receivable	1,000	
	Sales		1,000
	Sold goods on credit. [Revenue recognition.]		

Point: Gross profit on Nov. 12 sale:

Net sales	$1,000
Cost of goods sold	300
Gross profit	$ 700

Cost Side: Outflow of Assets The cost side of each sale requires that Merchandise Inventory decrease by that item's cost. The cost of the merchandise Z-Mart sold on November 12 is $300, and the entry to record the cost part of this transaction follows.

Assets = Liabilities + Equity
−300 −300

Nov. 12	Cost of Goods Sold	300	
	Merchandise Inventory		300
	Record cost of Nov. 12 sale. [Expense recognition.]		

Sales with Cash Discounts

Offering discounts on credit sales benefits a seller through earlier cash receipts and reduced collection efforts. The *gross method* records sales at the full amount and records sales discounts if, and when, they are taken. **The gross method is used here as it (1) complies with new revenue recognition rules, (2) is used more in practice, and (3) is easier and less costly to apply.** (The **net method** records sales at the net amount, which assumes all discounts are taken. See Appendix 5C.)

Sales on Credit Z-Mart makes a credit sale for $1,000 on November 12 with terms of 2/10, n/45 (cost of the merchandise sold is $300). The entries to record this sale follow.

Assets = Liabilities + Equity
+1,000 +1,000

Assets = Liabilities + Equity
−300 −300

Nov. 12	Accounts Receivable	1,000	
	Sales		1,000
	Sold goods, terms 2/10, n/45.		
Nov. 12	Cost of Goods Sold	300	
	Merchandise Inventory		300
	Record cost of Nov. 12 sale.		

Buyer Pays within Discount Period One option is for the buyer to pay $980 within the 10-day discount period ending November 22. The $20 sales discount is computed as $1,000 × 2%. If the customer pays on (or before) November 22, Z-Mart records the cash receipt as follows. **Sales Discounts** is a **contra revenue account,** meaning the Sales Discounts account is subtracted from the Sales account when computing net sales. The Sales Discounts account has a *normal debit balance* because it is subtracted from Sales, which has a normal credit balance.

Point: Net sales is the amount received from the customer.

Sales	$1,000
Sales discounts	(20)
Net sales	$ 980

Nov. 22	Cash*	980	
	Sales Discounts	20	
	Accounts Receivable		1,000
	Received payment on Nov. 12 sale less discount.		
	**$1,000 – ($1,000 × 2%)*		

Assets = Liabilities + Equity
+ 980 −20
−1,000

Buyer Pays after Discount Period The customer's second option is to wait 45 days until December 27 (or at least until after the discount period) and then pay $1,000. Z-Mart records that cash receipt as

Dec. 27	Cash	1,000	
	Accounts Receivable		1,000
	Received payment on Nov. 12 sale after discount period.		

Assets = Liabilities + Equity
+1,000
−1,000

Sales with Returns and Allowances

If a customer is unhappy with a purchase, many sellers allow the customer to either return the merchandise for a full refund (*sales return*) or keep the merchandise along with a partial refund (*sales allowance*).

Buyer Returns Goods—Revenue Side When a buyer returns goods, it impacts the seller's revenue *and* cost sides. When a return occurs, the seller debits **Sales Returns and Allowances**, a **contra revenue account** to Sales. Assume that a customer returns merchandise on December 29 that sold for $15 and cost $9; the revenue-side returns entry is

(e1) Dec. 29	Sales Returns and Allowances	15	
	Cash		15
	Goods returned from Nov. 12 sale.		

Assets = Liabilities + Equity
−15 −15

Buyer Returns Goods—Cost Side When a return occurs, the seller must reduce the cost of sales. If the merchandise returned is not defective and can be resold, the seller adds the cost of the returned goods back to inventory and reduces cost of goods sold as follows. (Advanced courses cover cases where goods are defective.)

(e2) Dec. 29	Merchandise Inventory	9	
	Cost of Goods Sold		9
	Returned goods are added back to inventory.		

Assets = Liabilities + Equity
+9 +9

Buyer Granted Allowances If a buyer is not satisfied with the goods, the seller might offer a price reduction for the buyer to keep the goods. There is no cost-side entry in this case as the inventory is not returned. On the revenue side, the seller debits Sales Returns and Allowances and credits Cash or Accounts Receivable depending on what's agreed. Assume that $40 of merchandise previously sold is defective. The seller gives a price reduction and credits the buyer's accounts receivable for $10. The seller records this allowance as follows.

Assets = Liabilities + Equity
−10 −10

(f) Nov. 24	Sales Returns and Allowances	10	
	Accounts Receivable		10
	Sales allowance granted.		

If the seller has already collected cash for the sale, the seller could give the price reduction in cash. For example, instead of crediting the buyer's Accounts Receivable in the entry above, the seller can credit Cash for $10.

Michael DeYoung/Blend Images

Decision Insight

What's Your Policy? Return policies are a competitive advantage for businesses. **REI** offers a 1-year return policy on nearly every product it sells. **Amazon** picks up returned items at your door. On the other hand, some stores like **Best Buy** allow only 14 days to return products. ■

NEED-TO-KNOW 5-3

Merchandise Sales

P2

Do More: QS 5-10, QS 5-11, QS 5-12, QS 5-13, E 5-6, E 5-7, E 5-9, E 5-10, E 5-12

Prepare journal entries to record each of the following transactions. Assume a perpetual inventory system and use of the gross method. Beginning inventory equals $9,000.

June 1 Sold 50 units of merchandise to a customer for $150 per unit under credit terms of 2/10, n/30, FOB shipping point, and the invoice is dated June 1. The 50 units of merchandise had cost $100 per unit.

7 The customer returns 2 units purchased on June 1 because those units did not fit its needs. The seller restores those units to its inventory (as they are not defective) and credits Accounts Receivable from the customer.

11 The seller receives the balance due from the June 1 sale to the customer less returns and allowances.

14 The customer discovers that 10 units have minor damage but keeps them because the seller sends a $50 cash payment allowance to compensate.

Solution

June 1	Accounts Receivable	7,500	
	Sales		7,500
	Sold goods. 50 units × $150		
June 1	Cost of Goods Sold	5,000	
	Merchandise Inventory		5,000
	Cost of sale. 50 units × $100		
June 7	Sales Returns and Allowances	300	
	Accounts Receivable		300
	Returns accepted. 2 units × $150		
June 7	Merchandise Inventory	200	
	Cost of Goods Sold		200
	Returns to inventory. 2 units × $100		

June 11	Cash	7,056	
	Sales Discounts*	144	
	Accounts Receivable		7,200
	Received payment.		
	**($7,500 − $300) × 2%*		
June 14	Sales Returns and Allowances	50	
	Cash		50
	Recorded allowance on goods.		

ADJUSTING AND CLOSING FOR MERCHANDISERS

P3

Prepare adjustments and close accounts for a merchandising company.

Exhibit 5.10 shows the flow of merchandising costs during a period and where these costs are reported at period-end. Specifically, beginning inventory plus the net cost of purchases is the merchandise available for sale. As inventory is sold, its cost is recorded in cost of goods sold on

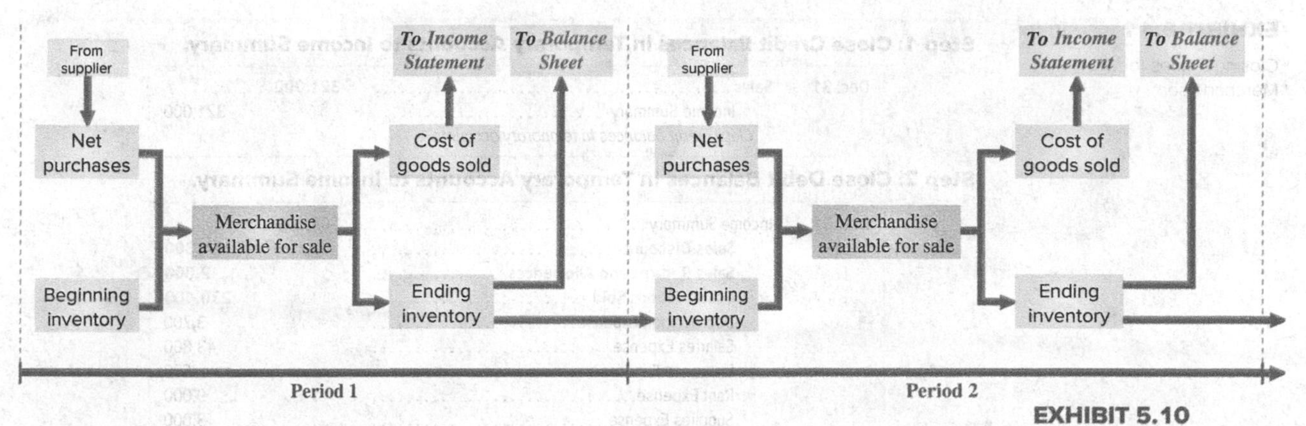

EXHIBIT 5.10

Merchandising Cost Flow in the Accounting Cycle

the income statement; what remains is ending inventory on the balance sheet. A period's ending inventory is the next period's beginning inventory.

Adjusting Entries for Merchandisers

Each of the steps in the accounting cycle described in the prior chapter applies to a merchandiser. We expand upon three steps of the accounting cycle for a merchandiser—adjustments, financial statement preparation, and closing.

Inventory Shrinkage—Adjusting Entry A merchandiser using a *perpetual* inventory system makes an adjustment to Merchandise Inventory for any loss of merchandise, including theft and deterioration. **Shrinkage** is the loss of inventory; it is computed by comparing a physical count of inventory with recorded amounts.

Z-Mart's Merchandise Inventory account at the end of the year has a balance of $21,250, but a physical count shows only $21,000 of inventory exists. The adjusting entry to record this $250 shrinkage is

Dec. 31	Cost of Goods Sold.	250	
	Merchandise Inventory.		250
	Adjust for $250 shrinkage.		

Assets = Liabilities + Equity
−250 −250

Sales Discounts, Returns, and Allowances—Adjusting Entries Revenue recognition rules require sales to be reported at the amount expected to be received. This means that period-end adjusting entries are commonly made for expected returns and allowances (both revenue and cost sides) and expected sales discounts. Appendix 5B covers these entries.

Closing Entries for Merchandisers

Closing entries are similar for service companies and merchandising companies. The difference is that we close some new temporary accounts that come from merchandising activities. Z-Mart has temporary accounts unique to merchandisers: Sales (of goods), Sales Discounts, Sales Returns and Allowances, and Cost of Goods Sold. The differences are in **red** in the closing entries of Exhibit 5.11. Sales, having a normal credit balance, is debited in step 1. Sales Discounts, Sales Returns and Allowances, and Cost of Goods Sold, having normal debit balances, are credited in step 2. The third and fourth closing entries are identical for a merchandiser and a service company.

EXHIBIT 5.11

Closing Entries for a Merchandiser

Step 1: Close Credit Balances in Temporary Accounts to Income Summary.

Dec. 31	Sales	321,000	
	Income Summary		321,000
	Close credit balances in temporary accounts.		

Step 2: Close Debit Balances in Temporary Accounts to Income Summary.

Dec. 31	Income Summary	308,100	
	Sales Discounts		4,300
	Sales Returns and Allowances		2,000
	Cost of Goods Sold		230,400
	Depreciation Expense		3,700
	Salaries Expense		43,800
	Insurance Expense		600
	Rent Expense		9,000
	Supplies Expense		3,000
	Advertising Expense		11,300
	Close debit balances in temporary accounts.		

Step 3: Close Income Summary.

Dec. 31	Income Summary	12,900	
	K. Marty, Capital		12,900

Step 4: Close Withdrawals.

Dec. 31	K. Marty, Capital	4,000	
	K. Marty, Withdrawals		4,000

Summary of Merchandising Entries

Exhibit 5.12 summarizes the adjusting and closing entries of a merchandiser (using a perpetual inventory system).

EXHIBIT 5.12

Summary of Key Merchandising Entries (using perpetual system and gross method)

	Merchandising Transactions	Merchandising Entries	Dr.	Cr.
Purchases	Purchasing merchandise for resale.	Merchandise Inventory	#	
		Cash or Accounts Payable		#
	Paying freight costs on purchases; FOB shipping point.	Merchandise Inventory	#	
		Cash		#
	Paying within discount period.	Accounts Payable	#	
		Merchandise Inventory		#
		Cash		#
	Paying outside discount period.	Accounts Payable	#	
		Cash		#
	Recording purchases returns or allowances.	Cash or Accounts Payable	#	
		Merchandise Inventory		#
Sales	Selling merchandise.	Cash or Accounts Receivable	#	
		Sales		#
		Cost of Goods Sold	#	
		Merchandise Inventory		#
	Receiving payment within discount period.	Cash	#	
		Sales Discounts	#	
		Accounts Receivable		#
	Receiving payment outside discount period.	Cash	#	
		Accounts Receivable		#
	Receiving sales returns of nondefective inventory.	Sales Returns and Allowances	#	
		Cash or Accounts Receivable		#
		Merchandise Inventory	#	
		Cost of Goods Sold		#
	Granting sales allowances.	Sales Returns and Allowances	#	
		Cash or Accounts Receivable		#
	Paying freight costs on sales; FOB destination.	Delivery Expense	#	
		Cash		#

Merchandising Events		Adjusting and Closing Entries	Dr.	Cr.
Adjusting	Adjustment for shrinkage (occurs when recorded amount larger than physical inventory).	Cost of Goods Sold	#	
		Merchandise Inventory		#
Closing	Closing temporary accounts with credit balances.	Sales	#	
		Income Summary		#
	Closing temporary accounts with debit balances.	Income Summary	#	
		Sales Returns and Allowances		#
		Sales Discounts		#
		Cost of Goods Sold		#
		Delivery Expense		#
		"Other Expenses"		#
	No change to closing Income Summary and Withdrawals.			

Merchandise Inventory	
Beginning inventory	
Purchases	Pur. returns
Freight-in (FOB shp pt)	Pur. allowances
	Pur. discounts
Customer returns	Shrinkage
Goods avail. for sale	COGS
Ending inventory	

NEED-TO-KNOW 5-4

Recording Shrinkage and Closing Entries

P3

A merchandising company's ledger on May 31, its fiscal year-end, includes the following accounts that have normal balances (it uses the perpetual inventory system). A physical count of its May 31 year-end inventory reveals that the cost of the merchandise inventory still available is $656. (a) Prepare the entry to record any inventory shrinkage. (b) Prepare the four closing entries as of May 31.

Merchandise inventory	$ 756	Sales	$4,300	Depreciation expense	$400
Z. Zee, Capital	2,300	Sales discounts	50	Salaries expense	600
Z. Zee, Withdrawals	150	Other operating expenses	300	Sales returns and allowances	250
		Cost of goods sold	2,100		

Do More: QS 5-14, QS 5-15, E 5-14, E 5-15, P 5-4

Solution

a.

		Dr.	Cr.
May 31	Cost of Goods Sold	100	
	Merchandise Inventory		100
	Adjust for shrinkage ($756 − $656).		

b.

		Dr.	Cr.
May 31	Sales	4,300	
	Income Summary		4,300
	Close temporary accounts with credit balances.		
May 31	Income Summary	3,800	
	Sales Discounts		50
	Sales Returns and Allowances		250
	Cost of Goods Sold*		2,200
	Depreciation Expense		400
	Salaries Expense		600
	Other Operating Expenses		300
	*Close temporary accounts with debit balances. *$2,100 (Unadj. bal.) + $100 (Shrinkage)*		

		Dr.	Cr.
May 31	Income Summary	500	
	Z. Zee, Capital		500
	Close Income Summary account.		
May 31	Z. Zee, Capital	150	
	Z. Zee, Withdrawals		150
	Close Withdrawals account.		

MORE ON FINANCIAL STATEMENT FORMATS

P4

Define and prepare multiple-step and single-step income statements.

This section covers two income statement formats: multiple-step and single-step. The classified balance sheet of a merchandiser also is covered.

Multiple-Step Income Statement

A **multiple-step income statement** details net sales and expenses and reports subtotals for various types of items. Exhibit 5.13 shows a multiple-step income statement. The statement has three main parts: (1) *gross profit,* which is net sales minus cost of goods sold; (2) *income from operations,* which is gross profit minus operating expenses; and (3) *net income,* which is income from operations plus or minus nonoperating items.

Operating expenses are separated into two sections. **Selling expenses** are costs to market and distribute products and services such as advertising of merchandise, store supplies and rent, and delivery of goods to customers. **General and administrative expenses** are costs to administer a company's overall operations such as office salaries, office equipment, and office supplies. Expenses are allocated between these two sections when they contribute to more than one. Z-Mart allocates rent expense of $9,000 from its store building between two sections: $8,100 to selling expense and $900 to general and administrative expenses.

EXHIBIT 5.13

Multiple-Step Income Statement

Z-MART
Income Statement
For Year Ended December 31, 2021

Sales		$321,000	
Less: Sales discounts	$ 4,300		
Sales returns and allowances	2,000	6,300	Gross profit computation
Net sales		314,700	
Cost of goods sold*		230,400	
Gross profit		84,300	
Operating expenses			
Selling expenses			
Depreciation expense—Store equipment	3,000		
Sales salaries expense	18,500		
Rent expense—Selling space	8,100		
Store supplies expense	1,200		
Advertising expense	11,300		
Total selling expenses		42,100	Income from operations computation
General and administrative expenses			
Depreciation expense—Office equipment	700		
Office salaries expense	25,300		
Insurance expense	600		
Rent expense—Office space	900		
Office supplies expense	1,800		
Total general and administrative expenses		29,300	
Total operating expenses		71,400	
Income from operations		12,900	
Other revenues and gains (expenses and losses)			
Interest revenue	1,000		Nonoperating activities computation
Gain on sale of building	2,500		
Interest expense	(1,500)		
Total other revenues and gains (expenses and losses)		2,000	
Net income		$ 14,900	

*Cost of goods sold:

Beginning inventory	$ 19,000
Net cost of purchases	232,400
Goods available for sale	251,400
Less ending inventory	21,000
Cost of goods sold	$230,400

Nonoperating activities consist of other expenses, revenues, losses, and gains that are unrelated to a company's operations. *Other revenues and gains* commonly include interest revenue, dividend revenue, rent revenue, and gains from asset disposals. *Other expenses and losses* commonly include interest expense, losses from asset disposals, and casualty losses. When there are no reportable nonoperating activities, its income from operations is simply labeled *net income*.

Single-Step Income Statement

A **single-step income statement** is shown in Exhibit 5.14. It lists cost of goods sold as another expense and shows only one subtotal for total expenses. Expenses are grouped into categories. Many companies use formats that combine features of both single- and multiple-step statements. Net income is the same under either format, so management chooses the format that best informs users.

EXHIBIT 5.14

Single-Step Income Statement

Z-MART Income Statement For Year Ended December 31, 2021		
Revenues		
Net sales		$314,700
Interest revenue		1,000
Gain on sale of building		2,500
Total revenues		318,200
Expenses		
Cost of goods sold	$230,400	
Selling expenses	42,100	
General and administrative expenses	29,300	
Interest expense	1,500	
Total expenses		303,300
Net income		$ 14,900

Classified Balance Sheet

The classified balance sheet reports merchandise inventory as a current asset, usually after accounts receivable, according to how quickly they can be converted to cash. Inventory is converted less quickly to cash than accounts receivable because inventory first must be sold before cash can be received. Exhibit 5.15 shows the current asset section of Z-Mart's classified balance sheet (other sections are similar to the previous chapter).

EXHIBIT 5.15

Classified Balance Sheet (partial) of a Merchandiser

Z-MART Balance Sheet (partial) December 31, 2021	
Current assets	
Cash	$ 8,200
Accounts receivable	11,200
Merchandise inventory	**21,000**
Office supplies	550
Store supplies	250
Prepaid insurance	300
Total current assets	$41,500

Point: Statement of owner's equity is the same for merchandisers and service companies.

NEED-TO-KNOW 5-5

Multiple- and Single-Step Income Statements

P4

Taret's adjusted account balances from its general ledger on April 30, its fiscal year-end, are shown here in random order. (a) Prepare a multiple-step income statement that begins with gross sales and includes separate categories for net sales, cost of goods sold, selling expenses, and general and administrative expenses. (b) Prepare a single-step income statement that begins with net sales and includes these expense categories: cost of goods sold, selling expenses, and general and administrative expenses.

Adjusted Account Balances	Debit	Credit
Merchandise inventory	$ 800	
Other (noninventory) assets	2,600	
Total liabilities		$ 500
Taret, Capital		2,100
Taret, Withdrawals	300	
Sales		9,500
Sales discounts	260	
Sales returns and allowances	240	
Cost of goods sold	6,500	
Sales salaries expense	450	
Rent expense—Selling space	400	
Store supplies expense	30	
Advertising expense	20	
Office salaries expense	420	
Rent expense—Office space	72	
Office supplies expense	8	
Totals	$12,100	$12,100

Solution

a. Multiple-step income statement.

TARET
Income Statement
For Year Ended April 30

Sales		$9,500
Less: Sales discounts	$260	
Sales returns and allowances	240	500
Net sales		9,000
Cost of goods sold		6,500
Gross profit		2,500
Operating expenses		
Selling expenses		
Sales salaries expense	450	
Rent expense—Selling space	400	
Store supplies expense	30	
Advertising expense	20	
Total selling expenses		900
General and administrative expenses		
Office salaries expense	420	
Rent expense—Office space	72	
Office supplies expense	8	
Total general and administrative expenses		500
Total operating expenses		1,400
Net income		$1,100

b. Single-step income statement.

TARET
Income Statement
For Year Ended April 30

Net sales		$9,000
Expenses		
Cost of goods sold	$6,500	
Selling expenses	900	
General and administrative expenses	500	
Total expenses		7,900
Net income		$1,100

Do More: QS 5-16 though QS 5-21, E 5-17, E 5-18, E 5-19

Decision Analysis

Acid-Test and Gross Margin Ratios

Acid-Test Ratio

A1 Compute and analyze the acid-test ratio and gross margin ratio.

One measure of a merchandiser's ability to pay its current liabilities (referred to as its *liquidity*) is the acid-test ratio. The **acid-test ratio,** also called *quick ratio,* is defined as *quick assets* (cash, short-term investments, and current receivables) divided by current liabilities—see Exhibit 5.16. It differs from the current ratio by excluding less liquid current assets such as inventory and prepaid expenses that take longer to be converted to cash.

EXHIBIT 5.16

Acid-Test (Quick) Ratio

$$\text{Acid-test ratio} = \frac{\text{Cash and cash equivalents} + \text{Short-term investments} + \text{Current receivables}}{\text{Current liabilities}}$$

Exhibit 5.17 shows both the acid-test and current ratios of **Nike** and **Under Armour** for three recent years. Nike's acid-test ratio implies that it has enough quick assets to cover current liabilities. It is also on par with its competitor, Under Armour. Nike's current ratio suggests it has more than enough current assets to cover current liabilities. Analysts might argue that Nike could invest some current assets in more productive assets. An acid-test ratio less than 1.0 means that current liabilities exceed quick assets. A rule of thumb is that the acid-test ratio should have a value near, or higher than, 1.0. Less than 1.0 raises liquidity concerns unless a company can get enough cash from sales or if liabilities are not due until late in the next period.

Izf/Shutterstock

EXHIBIT 5.17

Acid-Test and Current Ratios for Two Competitors

Company	$ millions	Current Year	1 Year Ago	2 Years Ago
Nike	Total quick assets	$ 8,935	$ 8,743	$ 9,856
	Total current assets	$16,525	$15,134	$16,061
	Total current liabilities	$ 7,866	$ 6,040	$ 5,474
	Acid-test ratio	**1.1**	**1.4**	**1.8**
	Current ratio	**2.1**	**2.5**	**2.9**
Under Armour	Acid-test ratio	1.1	0.9	0.9
	Current ratio	1.9	2.0	2.2

Decision Maker

Supplier A retailer requests to purchase supplies on credit from your company. You have no prior experience with this retailer. The retailer's current ratio is 2.1, its acid-test ratio is 0.5, and inventory makes up most of its current assets. Do you extend credit? ■ *Answer:* A current ratio of 2.1 suggests sufficient current assets to cover current liabilities. An acid-test ratio of 0.5 suggests, however, that quick assets can cover only about one-half of current liabilities. The retailer depends on money from sales of inventory to pay current liabilities. If sales decline, the likelihood that this retailer will default on its payments increases. You probably do not extend credit.

Gross Margin Ratio

Without enough gross profit, a merchandiser can fail. The gross margin ratio helps understand this link. It differs from the profit margin ratio in that it excludes all costs except cost of goods sold. The **gross margin ratio** (or *gross profit ratio*) is defined as *gross margin* (net sales minus cost of goods sold) divided by net sales—see Exhibit 5.18.

EXHIBIT 5.18

Gross Margin Ratio

$$\textbf{Gross margin ratio} = \frac{\textbf{Net sales} - \textbf{Cost of goods sold}}{\textbf{Net sales}}$$

Exhibit 5.19 shows the gross margin ratio of **Nike** for three recent years. For Nike, each $1 of sales in the current year yielded about 44.7¢ in gross margin to cover all expenses and still produce a net income. This 44.7¢ margin is up from 43.8¢ in the prior year. This increase is favorable.

EXHIBIT 5.19

Nike's Gross Margin Ratio

$ millions	Current Year	1 Year Ago	2 Years Ago
Gross margin..........	$17,474	$15,956	$15,312
Net sales..............	$39,117	$36,397	$34,350
Gross margin ratio	**44.7%**	**43.8%**	**44.6%**

Decision Maker

Financial Officer Your company has a 36% gross margin ratio and a 17% net profit margin ratio. Industry averages are 44% for gross margin and 16% for net profit margin. Do these comparative results concern you? ■ *Answer:* Your company's net profit margin is about equal to the industry average. However, gross margin shows that your company is paying far more in cost of goods sold or receiving far less in sales price than competitors. You should try to find the problem with cost of goods sold, sales, or both.

NEED-TO-KNOW 5-6

COMPREHENSIVE 1

Single- and Multiple-Step Income Statements, Closing Entries, and Analysis Using Acid-Test and Gross Margin Ratios

Use the following adjusted trial balance and additional information to complete the requirements.

KC ANTIQUES Adjusted Trial Balance December 31	Debit	Credit
Cash	$ 7,000	
Accounts receivable	13,000	
Merchandise inventory (ending)	60,000	
Store supplies	1,500	
Equipment	45,600	
Accumulated depreciation—Equipment		$ 16,600
Accounts payable		9,000
Salaries payable		2,000
K. Carter, Capital		79,000
K. Carter, Withdrawals	10,000	
Sales		343,250
Sales discounts	5,000	
Sales returns and allowances	6,000	
Cost of goods sold	159,900	
Depreciation expense—Store equipment	4,100	
Depreciation expense—Office equipment	1,600	
Sales salaries expense	30,000	
Office salaries expense	34,000	
Insurance expense	11,000	
Rent expense—Selling space	16,800	
Rent expense—Office space	7,200	
Store supplies expense	5,750	
Advertising expense	31,400	
Totals	$449,850	$449,850

Supplementary records for the year reveal the following itemized costs for merchandising activities.

Invoice cost of merchandise purchases	$150,000	Purchases returns and allowances	$2,700
Purchases discounts received	2,500	Cost of transportation-in	5,000

Required

1. Use the supplementary records to compute the total cost of merchandise purchases for the year.

2. Prepare a multiple-step income statement for the year. (Beginning inventory was $70,100.)

3. Prepare a single-step income statement for the year.

4. Prepare closing entries for KC Antiques at December 31.

5. Compute the acid-test ratio and the gross margin ratio. Explain the meaning of each ratio and interpret them for KC Antiques.

SOLUTION

1.

Invoice cost of merchandise purchases	$150,000
Less: Purchases discounts received	(2,500)
Purchases returns and allowances	(2,700)
Add: Cost of transportation-in	5,000
Total cost of merchandise purchases	$149,800

2. Multiple-step income statement.

KC ANTIQUES Income Statement For Year Ended December 31		
Sales		$343,250
Less: Sales discounts	$ 5,000	
Sales returns and allowances	6,000	11,000
Net sales		332,250
Cost of goods sold		159,900
Gross profit		172,350
Expenses		
Selling expenses		
Depreciation expense—Store equipment	4,100	
Sales salaries expense	30,000	
Rent expense—Selling space	16,800	
Store supplies expense	5,750	
Advertising expense	31,400	
Total selling expenses		88,050
General and administrative expenses		
Depreciation expense—Office equipment	1,600	
Office salaries expense	34,000	
Insurance expense	11,000	
Rent expense—Office space	7,200	
Total general and administrative expenses		53,800
Total operating expenses		141,850
Net income		$ 30,500

3. Single-step income statement.

KC ANTIQUES Income Statement For Year Ended December 31		
Net sales		$332,250
Expenses		
Cost of goods sold	$159,900	
Selling expenses	88,050	
General and administrative expenses	53,800	
Total expenses		301,750
Net income		$ 30,500

4.

Date	Account	Debit	Credit
Dec. 31	Sales	343,250	
	Income Summary		343,250
	Close credit balances in temporary accounts.		
Dec. 31	Income Summary	312,750	
	Sales Discounts		5,000
	Sales Returns and Allowances		6,000
	Cost of Goods Sold		159,900
	Depreciation Expense—Store Equipment		4,100
	Depreciation Expense—Office Equipment		1,600
	Sales Salaries Expense		30,000
	Office Salaries Expense		34,000
	Insurance Expense		11,000
	Rent Expense—Selling Space		16,800
	Rent Expense—Office Space		7,200
	Store Supplies Expense		5,750
	Advertising Expense		31,400
	Close debit balances in temporary accounts.		

Date	Account	Debit	Credit
Dec. 31	Income Summary	30,500	
	K. Carter, Capital		30,500
	Close Income Summary account.		
Dec. 31	K. Carter, Capital	10,000	
	K. Carter, Withdrawals		10,000
	Close Withdrawals account.		

5. Acid-test ratio = (Cash and equivalents + Short-term investments + Current receivables)/Current liabilities

= (Cash + Accounts receivable)/(Accounts payable + Salaries payable)

= ($7,000 + $13,000)/($9,000 + $2,000) = $20,000/$11,000 = 1.82

Gross margin ratio = Gross profit/Net sales = $172,350/$332,250 = 0.52 (or 52%)

KC Antiques has a healthy acid-test ratio of 1.82. This means it has $1.82 in liquid assets to satisfy each $1.00 in current liabilities. The gross margin of 0.52 shows that KC Antiques spends 48¢ ($1.00 – $0.52) of every dollar of net sales on the costs of acquiring the merchandise it sells. This leaves 52¢ of every dollar of net sales to cover other expenses incurred in the business and to provide a net profit.

NEED-TO-KNOW 5-7

COMPREHENSIVE 2

Recording Merchandising Transactions—Both Seller and Buyer

Prepare journal entries for the following transactions for both the seller (BMX) and buyer (Sanuk).

May 4 BMX sold $1,500 of merchandise on account to Sanuk, terms FOB shipping point, n/45, invoice dated May 4. The cost of the merchandise was $900.
6 Sanuk paid transportation charges of $30 on the May 4 purchase from BMX.
8 BMX sold $1,000 of merchandise on account to Sanuk, terms FOB destination, n/15, invoice dated May 8. The cost of the merchandise was $700. This sale permitted returns for 30 days.
10 BMX paid transportation costs of $50 for delivery of merchandise sold to Sanuk on May 8.
16 Sanuk returned $200 of merchandise purchased on May 8 for full credit. The merchandise, which had cost $140, is returned to inventory.
18 BMX received payment from Sanuk for the May 8 purchase.
21 BMX sold $2,400 of merchandise on account to Sanuk, terms FOB shipping point, 2/10, n/60. The cost of the merchandise was $1,440. This sale permitted returns for 90 days.
31 BMX received payment from Sanuk for the May 21 purchase, less discount.

Solution

	BMX (Seller)			Sanuk (Buyer)		
May 4	Accounts Receivable—Sanuk	1,500		Merchandise Inventory	1,500	
	Sales		1,500	Accounts Payable—BMX		1,500
	Cost of Goods Sold	900				
	Merchandise Inventory		900			
6	No entry.			Merchandise Inventory	30	
				Cash		30
8	Accounts Receivable—Sanuk	1,000		Merchandise Inventory	1,000	
	Sales		1,000	Accounts Payable—BMX		1,000
	Cost of Goods Sold	700				
	Merchandise Inventory		700			
10	Delivery Expense	50		No entry.		
	Cash		50			
16	Sales Returns & Allowances	200		Accounts Payable—BMX	200	
	Accounts Receivable—Sanuk		200	Merchandise Inventory		200
	Merchandise Inventory	140				
	Cost of Goods Sold		140			
18	Cash	800		Accounts Payable—BMX	800	
	Accounts Receivable—Sanuk		800	Cash		800
21	Accounts Receivable—Sanuk	2,400		Merchandise Inventory	2,400	
	Sales		2,400	Accounts Payable—BMX		2,400
	Cost of Goods Sold	1,440				
	Merchandise Inventory		1,440			
31	Cash	2,352		Accounts Payable—BMX	2,400	
	Sales Discounts	48		Merchandise Inventory		48
	Accounts Receivable—Sanuk		2,400	Cash		2,352

APPENDIX

5A Periodic Inventory System

P5 Record and compare merchandising transactions using both periodic and perpetual inventory systems.

A periodic inventory system requires updating the inventory account only at the *end of a period.* During the period, the Merchandise Inventory balance remains unchanged and cost of merchandise is recorded in a temporary *Purchases* account. When a company sells merchandise, it records revenue ***but not the cost of the goods sold.*** At the end of the period, it takes a *physical count of inventory* to get ending inventory. The cost of goods sold is then computed as cost of merchandise available for sale minus ending inventory.

Recording Merchandise Purchases Under a periodic system, the purchases, purchases returns and allowances, purchases discounts, and transportation-in transactions are recorded in separate temporary accounts. At period-end, each of these temporary accounts is closed, which updates the Merchandise Inventory account. To demonstrate, journal entries under the periodic inventory system are shown for the most common transactions (codes ***a*** through ***d*** link these transactions to those in the chapter). For comparison, perpetual system journal entries are shown to the right of each periodic entry. Differences are highlighted.

Credit Purchases with Cash Discounts The periodic system uses a temporary **Purchases** account that accumulates the cost of all purchase transactions during each period. The Purchases account has a normal debit balance, as it increases the cost of merchandise available for sale. Z-Mart's November 2 entry to record the purchase of merchandise for $500 on credit with terms of 2/10, n/30 is

(*a*)

Periodic			Perpetual		
Purchases	500		Merchandise Inventory	500	
Accounts Payable		500	Accounts Payable		500

Payment of Purchases The periodic system uses a temporary **Purchases Discounts** account that accumulates discounts taken during the period. If payment for transaction *a* is made *within the discount period,* the entry is

(*b1*)

Periodic			Perpetual		
Accounts Payable	500		Accounts Payable	500	
Purchases Discounts*		10	Merchandise Inventory*		10
Cash		490	Cash		490
*$500 × 2%			*$500 × 2%		

If payment for transaction *a* is made *after the discount period expires,* the entry is

(*b2*)

Periodic			Perpetual		
Accounts Payable	500		Accounts Payable	500	
Cash		500	Cash		500

Purchases Allowances The buyer and seller agree to a $30 purchases allowance for defective goods (whether paid within the discount period or not). In the periodic system, the temporary **Purchases Returns and Allowances** account accumulates the cost of all returns and allowances during a period. The buyer records the $30 allowance as

(*c1*)

Periodic			Perpetual		
Accounts Payable	30		Accounts Payable	30	
Purchases Returns and Allowances		30	Merchandise Inventory		30

Point: Purchases Discounts and Purchases Returns and Allowances are contra purchases accounts *and* have normal credit balances, as they both decrease the cost of merchandise available for sale.

Purchases Returns The buyer returns $50 of merchandise within the discount period. The entry is

(*c2*)

Periodic			Perpetual		
Accounts Payable	50		Accounts Payable	50	
Purchases Returns and Allowances		50	Merchandise Inventory		50

Transportation-In The buyer paid a $75 freight charge to transport goods with terms FOB shipping point. In the periodic system, this cost is recorded in a temporary **Transportation-In** account, which has a normal debit balance as it increases the cost of merchandise available for sale.

(*d*)

Periodic			Perpetual		
Transportation-In	75		Merchandise Inventory	75	
Cash		75	Cash		75

Recording Merchandise *Sales*

Journal entries under the periodic system are shown for the most common transactions (codes ***e*** through ***h*** link these transactions to those in the chapter). Perpetual system entries are shown to the right of each periodic entry. Differences are highlighted.

Credit Sales and Receipt of Payments Both the periodic and perpetual systems record sales entries similarly, using the gross method. The same holds for entries related to payment of receivables from sales both during and after the discount period. However, under the periodic system, the cost of goods sold is *not* recorded at the time of each sale (whereas it is under the perpetual system). The entry to record $1,000 in credit sales (costing $300) is

Periodic			Perpetual		
Accounts Receivable.........	1,000		Accounts Receivable.............	1,000	
Sales.................		1,000	Sales.....................		1,000
			Cost of Goods Sold..............	300	
No cost-side entry			Merchandise Inventory		300

Returns Received by Seller A customer returned merchandise for a cash refund. The goods sell for $15 and cost $9. (*Recall:* The periodic system records only the revenue effect, not the cost effect, for sales transactions.) The entry for the seller to take back the return is

	Periodic			Perpetual		
(*e1*)	Sales Returns and Allowances....	15		Sales Returns and Allowances	15	
	Cash		15	Cash.....................		15
(*e2*)				Merchandise Inventory	9	
	No entry			Cost of Goods Sold..........		9

Allowances Granted by Seller The seller gives a price reduction and credits the buyer's accounts receivable for $10. The entry is identical under the periodic and perpetual systems. The seller records this allowance as

	Periodic			Perpetual		
(*f*)	Sales Returns and Allowances....	10		Sales Returns and Allowances	10	
	Accounts Receivable		10	Accounts Receivable.........		10

Recording Adjusting Entries

Shrinkage—Adjusting Entry Adjusting entries for the two systems are in Exhibit 5A.1. The $250 shrinkage is only recorded under the perpetual system—see entry *z* in Exhibit 5A.1. Shrinkage in cost of goods is unknown using a periodic system because inventory is not continually updated and therefore cannot be compared to the physical count.

EXHIBIT 5A.1

Comparison of Adjusting Entries—Periodic and Perpetual

	Periodic—Adjusting Entries			Perpetual—Adjusting Entries		
(*z*)	None			Cost of Goods Sold	250	
				Merchandise Inventory		250
(*g*)	Sales Discounts..........	50		Sales Discounts	50	
	Allowance for Sales Discounts		50	Allowance for Sales Discounts ..		50
(*h1*)	Sales Returns and Allowances....	900		Sales Returns and Allowances	900	
	Sales Refund Payable		900	Sales Refund Payable........		900
(*h2*)	Inventory Returns Estimated	300		Inventory Returns Estimated.......	300	
	Purchases...............		300	Cost of Goods Sold.........		300
	Entries in gray are covered in Appendix 5B.			Entries in gray are covered in Appendix 5B.		

Expected Sales Discounts—Adjusting Entry Both the periodic and perpetual methods make a period-end adjusting entry under the gross method to estimate the $50 sales discounts arising from current-period sales that are likely to be taken in future periods. Z-Mart made the period-end adjusting entry *g* in Exhibit 5A.1 for expected sales discounts.

Expected Returns and Allowances—Adjusting Entry Both the periodic and perpetual inventory systems estimate returns and allowances arising from current-period sales that will occur in future periods. The adjusting entry for both systems is identical for the sales side, but slightly different for the cost side. The period-end entries *h1* and *h2* in Exhibit 5A.1 are used to record the updates to expected sales refunds of $900 and the cost side of $300. Under both systems, the seller sets up a **Sales Refund Payable** account, which is a current liability reflecting the amount expected to be refunded to customers, and an **Inventory Returns Estimated** account, which is a current asset reflecting the inventory estimated to be returned.

Recording Closing Entries

Periodic and perpetual inventory systems have slight differences in closing entries. The period-end Merchandise Inventory balance (unadjusted) is $19,000 under the periodic system. Because the periodic system does not update the Merchandise Inventory balance during the period, the $19,000 amount is the beginning inventory. A physical count of inventory taken at the end of the period reveals $21,000 of merchandise available. Closing entries for the two systems follow. Recording the periodic inventory balance is a two-step process. The ending inventory balance of $21,000 is entered by debiting the inventory account in the first closing entry. The beginning inventory balance of $19,000 is deleted by crediting the inventory account in the second closing entry.[1]

	Periodic—Closing Entries			Perpetual—Closing Entries		
(1)	Sales	321,000		Sales	321,000	
	Merchandise Inventory (ending)	**21,000**				
	Purchases Discounts	**4,200**				
	Purchases Returns and Allowances	**1,500**				
	Income Summary		347,700	Income Summary		321,000
(2)	Income Summary	334,800		Income Summary	308,100	
	Sales Discounts		4,300	Sales Discounts		4,300
	Sales Returns and Allowances		2,000	Sales Returns and Allowances		2,000
	Merch. Inven. (beginning)		**19,000**			
	Purchases		**235,800**	**Cost of Goods Sold**		**230,400**
	Transportation-In		**2,300**			
	Depreciation Expense		3,700	Depreciation Expense		3,700
	Salaries Expense		43,800	Salaries Expense		43,800
	Insurance Expense		600	Insurance Expense		600
	Rent Expense		9,000	Rent Expense		9,000
	Supplies Expense		3,000	Supplies Expense		3,000
	Advertising Expense		11,300	Advertising Expense		11,300
(3)	Income Summary	12,900		Income Summary	12,900	
	K. Marty, Capital		12,900	K. Marty, Capital		12,900
(4)	K. Marty, Capital	4,000		K. Marty, Capital	4,000	
	K. Marty, Withdrawals		4,000	K. Marty, Withdrawals		4,000

[1]This approach is called the *closing entry method*. An alternative approach, referred to as the *adjusting entry method,* would not make any entries to Merchandise Inventory in the closing entries, but instead would make two adjusting entries. Using Z-Mart data, the two adjusting entries would be (1) Dr. Income Summary and Cr. Merchandise Inventory for $19,000 each and (2) Dr. Merchandise Inventory and Cr. Income Summary for $21,000 each. The first entry removes the beginning balance of Merchandise Inventory, and the second entry records the actual ending balance.

By updating Merchandise Inventory and closing Purchases, Purchases Discounts, Purchases Returns and Allowances, and Transportation-In, the periodic system transfers the cost of sales amount to Income Summary. Review the periodic side of the closing entries and see that the red items affect Income Summary as follows.

Credit to Income Summary in the first closing entry includes amounts from	
Merchandise inventory (ending)	$ 21,000
Purchases discounts	4,200
Purchases returns and allowances	1,500
Debit to Income Summary in the second closing entry includes amounts from	
Merchandise inventory (beginning)	(19,000)
Purchases	(235,800)
Transportation-in	(2,300)
Net effect on Income Summary (net debit = cost of goods sold)	**$(230,400)**

This $230,400 effect on Income Summary is the cost of goods sold amount (which is equal to cost of goods sold reported in a perpetual inventory system). The periodic system transfers cost of goods sold to the Income Summary account but without using a Cost of Goods Sold account. Also, the periodic system does not separately measure shrinkage. Instead, it computes cost of goods available for sale, subtracts the cost of ending inventory, and defines the difference as cost of goods sold, which includes shrinkage.

Preparing Financial Statements The financial statements of a merchandiser using the periodic system are similar to those for a service company described in prior chapters. The income statement mainly differs by the inclusion of *cost of goods sold* and *gross profit*—of course, net sales is affected by discounts, returns, and allowances. The cost of goods sold section under the periodic system is shown here. The balance sheet mainly differs by the inclusion of *merchandise inventory,* inventory returns estimated, allowance for sales discounts, and sales refund payable. *Visit the Additional Student Resource section of the* **Connect** *eBook to view sample chart of accounts for periodic and perpetual systems.*

Calculation of Cost of Goods Sold	
Beginning inventory	$ 19,000
Net cost of purchases	232,400
Cost of goods available for sale	251,400
Less ending inventory	21,000
Cost of goods sold	$230,400

APPENDIX

5B Adjusting Entries under New Revenue Recognition Rules

P6 Prepare adjustments for discounts, returns, and allowances per revenue recognition rules.

Expected Sales Discounts—Adjusting Entry

New revenue recognition rules require sales to be reported at the amount expected to be received. This means that a period-end adjusting entry is made to estimate sales discounts for current-period sales that are expected to be taken in future periods. To demonstrate, assume Z-Mart has the following unadjusted balances.

Accounts Receivable	$11,250

Allowance for Sales Discounts	$0

Of the $11,250 of receivables, $2,500 of them are within the 2% discount period, for which we expect buyers to take $50 in future-period discounts (computed as $2,500 × 2%) arising from this period's sales. The adjusting entry for the $50 update to Allowance for Sales Discounts is

Assets = Liabilities + Equity
−50 −50

(g) Dec. 31	Sales Discounts	50	
	Allowance for Sales Discounts		50
	Adjustment for future discounts.		

Allowance for Sales Discounts is a **contra asset account** and is reported on the balance sheet as a reduction to the Accounts Receivable asset account. The Allowance for Sales Discounts account has a *normal credit balance* because it reduces Accounts Receivable, which has a normal debit balance. This adjusting entry results in both accounts receivable and sales being reported at expected amounts.*

Allowance for Sales Discounts		
	Beg. bal.	0
	Req. adj.	50
	Est. bal.	50

Balance Sheet—partial	
Accounts receivable	$11,250
Less allowance for sales discounts	50
Accounts receivable, net	$11,200

Income Statement—partial	
Sales	$321,000
Less sales discounts, returns & allowances	6,300
Net sales	$314,700

**Next Period Adjustment* The Allowance for Sales Discounts balance remains unchanged during a period except for the period-end adjusting entry. At next period-end, assume that Z-Mart computes an $80 balance for the Allowance for Sales Discounts. Using our three-step adjusting process we get:
Step 1: Current bal. is $50 credit in Allowance for Sales Discounts.
Step 2: Current bal. should be $80 credit in Allowance for Sales Discounts.
Step 3: Record entry to get from step 1 to step 2.

	Debit	Credit
Sales Discounts	30	
Allowance for Sales Discounts		30

Expected Returns and Allowances—Adjusting Entries

To avoid overstatement of sales and cost of sales, sellers estimate sales returns and allowances in the period of the sale. Estimating returns and allowances requires companies to maintain the following two balance sheet accounts that are set up with adjusting entries. Two adjusting entries are made: one for the revenue side *and* one for the cost side.

Current Asset→Inventory Returns Estimated

Current Liability→Sales Refund Payable

Revenue Side for Expected R&A When returns and allowances are expected, a seller sets up a **Sales Refund Payable** account, which is **a current liability showing the amount expected to be refunded to customers.** Assume that on December 31 the company estimates future sales refunds to be $1,200. Assume also that the *unadjusted balance* in Sales Refund Payable is a $300 credit. The adjusting entry for the $900 update to Sales Refund Payable follows. The Sales Refund Payable account is updated only during the adjusting entry process. Its balance remains unchanged during the period when actual returns and allowances are recorded.

		Debit	Credit
(h1) Dec. 31	Sales Returns and Allowances	900	
	Sales Refund Payable		900
	*Expected refund of sales.**		

Assets = Liabilities + Equity
+900 −900

*This entry uses our three-step adjusting process:
Step 1: Current bal. is $300 credit for Sales Refund Payable.
Step 2: Current bal. should be $1,200 credit for Sales Refund Payable.
Step 3: Record entry to get from step 1 to step 2.

Sales Refund Payable		
	Beg. bal.	300
	Req. adj.	900
	Est. bal.	1,200

Cost Side for Expected R&A On the cost side, some inventory is expected to be returned, which means that cost of goods sold recorded at the time of sale is overstated due to expected returns. A seller sets up an **Inventory Returns Estimated** account, which is **a current asset showing the inventory estimated to be returned.** Extending the example above, assume that the company estimates future inventory returns to be $500 (which is the cost side of the $1,200 expected returns and allowances above). Assume also that the (beginning) *unadjusted balance* in Inventory Returns Estimated is a $200 debit. The adjusting entry for the $300 update to expected returns follows. The Inventory Returns Estimated account is updated only during the adjusting entry process. Its balance remains unchanged during the period when actual returns and allowances are recorded. If estimates of returns and allowances prove too high or too low, we adjust future estimates accordingly.

		Debit	Credit
(h2) Dec. 31	**Inventory Returns Estimated**	300	
	Cost of Goods Sold		300
	*Expected return of inventory.**		

Assets = Liabilities + Equity
+300 +300

*This entry uses our three-step adjusting process:
Step 1: Current bal. is $200 debit for Inventory Returns Estimated.
Step 2: Current bal. should be $500 debit for Inventory Returns Estimated.
Step 3: Record entry to get from step 1 to step 2.

Inventory Returns Estimated		
Beg. bal.	200	
Req. adj.	300	
Est. bal.	500	

NEED-TO-KNOW 5-8

Estimating Discounts, Returns, and Allowances

P6

At the current year-end, a company shows the following unadjusted balances for selected accounts.

Allowance for Sales Discounts	$ 75 credit	Sales Discounts	$1,850 debit
Sales Refund Payable	800 credit	Sales Returns and Allowances	4,825 debit
Inventory Returns Estimated	450 debit	Cost of Goods Sold	9,875 debit

a. After an analysis of future sales discounts, the company estimates that the Allowance for Sales Discounts account should have a $275 credit balance. Prepare the current year-end adjusting journal entry for future sales discounts.

b. After an analysis of future sales returns and allowances, the company estimates that the Sales Refund Payable account should have an $870 credit balance (revenue side).

c. After an analysis of future inventory returns, the company estimates that the Inventory Returns Estimated account should have a $500 debit balance (cost side).

Solution

a. Dec. 31	Sales Discounts	200	
	Allowance for Sales Discounts		200
	Adjustment for future discounts. $275 Cr. − $75 Cr.		
b. Dec. 31	Sales Returns and Allowances	70	
	Sales Refund Payable		70
	Adjustment for future sales refund. $870 Cr. − $800 Cr.		
c. Dec. 31	Inventory Returns Estimated	50	
	Cost of Goods Sold		50
	Adjustment for future inventory returns. $500 Dr. − $450 Dr.		

Do More: QS 5-28, QS 5-29, E 5-25, E 5-26, E 5-27

APPENDIX

5C Net Method for Merchandising

P7

Record and compare merchandising transactions using the gross method and net method.

The **net method** records an invoice at its *net* amount (net of any cash discount). The **gross method,** covered earlier in the chapter, initially records an invoice at its gross (full) amount. This appendix records merchandising transactions using the net method. Differences with the gross method are highlighted.

When invoices are recorded at *net* amounts, any cash discounts are deducted from the balance of the Merchandise Inventory account when initially recorded. **This assumes that all cash discounts will be taken.** If any discounts are later lost, they are recorded in a **Discounts Lost** expense account reported on the income statement.

Perpetual Inventory System

PURCHASES—Perpetual A company purchases merchandise on November 2 at a $500 invoice price ($490 net) with terms of 2/10, n/30. Its November 2 entries under the gross and net methods are

Gross Method—Perpetual

Merchandise Inventory	500	
Accounts Payable		500

Net Method—Perpetual

Merchandise Inventory	490	
Accounts Payable		490

If the invoice is paid on (or before) November 12 within the discount period, it records

Gross Method—Perpetual

Accounts Payable	500	
Merchandise Inventory		10
Cash		490

Net Method—Perpetual

Accounts Payable	490	
Cash		490

If the invoice is paid *after the discount period,* it records

Gross Method—Perpetual			Net Method—Perpetual		
Accounts Payable	500		Accounts Payable	490	
			Discounts Lost*	10	
Cash		500	Cash		500

*For simplicity, we record Discounts Lost on the *payment date.*

SALES—Perpetual A company sells merchandise on November 2 at a $500 invoice price ($490 net) with terms of 2/10, n/30. The goods cost $200. Its November 2 entries are

Gross Method—Perpetual			Net Method—Perpetual		
Accounts Receivable..........	500		Accounts Receivable.............	490	
Sales.......................		500	Sales		490
Cost of Goods Sold...........	200		Cost of Goods Sold	200	
Merchandise Inventory ...		200	Merchandise Inventory		200

If cash is received on (or before) November 12 within the discount period, it records

Gross Method—Perpetual			Net Method—Perpetual		
Cash.........................	490		Cash..........................	490	
Sales Discounts..............	10				
Accounts Receivable		500	Accounts Receivable		490

If cash is received *after the discount period,* it records

Gross Method—Perpetual			Net Method—Perpetual		
Cash.........................	500		Cash..........................	500	
			Interest Revenue		10
Accounts Receivable		500	Accounts Receivable		490

Summary: Cheat Sheet

MERCHANDISING ACTIVITIES

Merchandise: Goods a company buys to resell.
Cost of goods sold: Costs of merchandise sold.
Gross profit (gross margin): Net sales minus cost of goods sold.
Computing net income (service company vs. merchandiser):

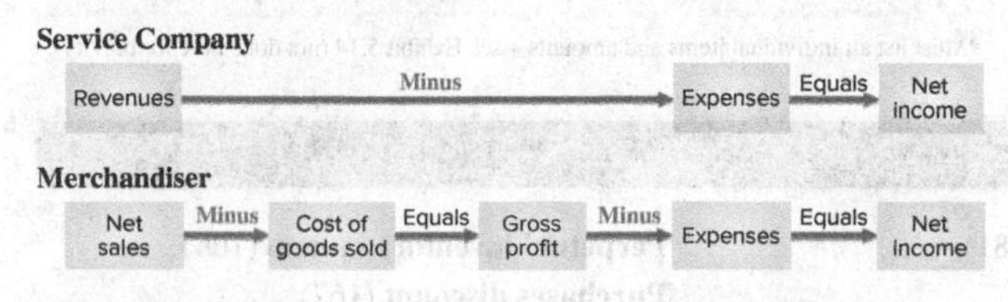

Inventory: Costs of merchandise owned but not yet sold. It is a current asset on the balance sheet.
Merchandise Cost Flows:

Perpetual inventory system: Updates accounting records for each purchase and each sale of inventory.
Periodic inventory system: Updates accounting records for purchases and sales of inventory only at the end of a period.

MERCHANDISING PURCHASES

Cash discount: A purchases discount on the price paid by the buyer, or a sales discount on the amount received for the seller.
Credit terms example: "2/10, n/60" means full payment is due within 60 days, but the buyer can deduct 2% of the invoice amount if payment is made within 10 days.
Gross method: Initially record purchases at gross (full) invoice amounts.

Purchasing Merchandise for Resale Entries:

Purchasing merchandise on credit	Merchandise Inventory........	500	
	Accounts Payable		500
Paying within discount period (Inventory reduced by discount taken)	Accounts Payable............	500	
	Merchandise Inventory ...		10
	Cash		490
Paying outside discount period	Accounts Payable............	500	
	Cash		500
Recording purchases returns or allowances	Cash or Accounts Payable	30	
	Merchandise Inventory ..		30

Transportation Costs and Ownership Transfer Rules:

Shipping Terms	Ownership Transfers at	Goods in Transit Owned by	Transportation Costs Paid by
FOB shipping point	Shipping point	Buyer	Buyer Merchandise Inventory .... # Cash .... #
FOB destination	Destination	Seller	Seller Delivery Expense .... # Cash .... #

MERCHANDISING SALES

Selling merchandise on credit	Accounts Receivable..........	1,000	
	Sales....................		1,000
	Cost of Goods Sold..........	300	
	Merchandise Inventory		300
Receiving payment within discount period	Cash..........................	980	
	Sales Discounts.............	20	
	Accounts Receivable		1,000

Receiving payment outside discount period	Cash..........................	1,000	
	Accounts Receivable		1,000

Sales Discounts: A contra revenue account, meaning Sales Discounts is subtracted from Sales when computing net sales.

Customer Merchandise Returns Entries:

Receiving sales returns of nondefective inventory	Sales Returns and Allowances..	15	
	Cash or Accounts Receivable		15
	Merchandise Inventory.......	9	
	Cost of Goods Sold.........		9

Sales allowance: A price reduction agreed to when a buyer is unsatisfied with the goods.

Recognizing sales allowances	Sales Returns and Allowances..	10	
	Cash or Accounts Receivable		10

MERCHANDISER REPORTING

Inventory shrinkage: An adjusting entry to account for the loss of inventory due to theft or deterioration. It is computed by comparing a physical count of inventory with recorded amounts.

Adjustment for shrinkage (occurs when recorded amount larger than physical inventory)	Cost of Goods Sold	250	
	Merchandise Inventory.......		250

Closing Entries: Differences between merchandisers and service companies in red.

Step 1: Close Credit Balances in Temporary Accounts to Income Summary	Sales......................	321,000	
	Income Summary		321,000

Step 2: Close Debit Balances in Temporary Accounts to Income Summary	Income Summary	308,100	
	Sales Discounts		4,300
	Sales Returns and Allowances..		2,000
	Cost of Goods Sold..........		230,400
	Other Expenses		71,400

Step 3: Close Income Summary (same entry as for service company)

Step 4: Close Withdrawals (same entry as for service company)

Multiple-step income statement: Three parts: (1) gross profit; (2) income from operations, which is gross profit minus operating expenses; and (3) net income, which is income from operations plus or minus nonoperating items.

Operating expenses: Separated into selling expenses and general & administrative expenses.

Selling expenses: Expenses of advertising merchandise, making sales, and delivering goods to customers.

General & administrative expenses: Expenses that support a company's overall operations, including accounting and human resources.

Nonoperating activities: Consist of expenses, revenues, losses, and gains that are unrelated to a company's main operations.

Multiple-Step Income Statement Example

Income Statement		
Sales......................................		$321,000
Less: Sales discounts..............................	$4,300	
Sales returns and allowances....................	2,000	6,300
Net sales..		314,700
Cost of goods sold		230,400
Gross profit		84,300
Operating expenses		
Selling expenses†		
General and administrative expenses†		
Total operating expenses		71,400
Income from operations		12,900
Total other revenues and gains (expenses and losses)		2,000
Net income		$ 14,900

†Must list all individual expenses and amounts—see Exhibit 5.13 (not done here for brevity).

Single-Step Income Statement Example

Income Statement	
Revenues	
Total revenues*	$318,200
Expenses	
Total expenses*	303,300
Net income	$ 14,900

*Must list all individual items and amounts—see Exhibit 5.14 (not done here for brevity).

Key Terms

Acid-test ratio (180)
Allowance for Sales Discounts (189)
Cash discount (167)
Cost of goods sold (165)
Credit period (167)
Credit terms (167)
Discount period (168)
Discounts Lost (190)
FOB (170)
General and administrative expenses (178)
Gross margin (166)
Gross margin ratio (181)
Gross method (190)
Gross profit (166)
Inventory (166)
Inventory Returns Estimated (189)
Merchandise (165)
Merchandise inventory (166)
Merchandiser (165)
Multiple-step income statement (178)
Net method (190)
Periodic inventory system (166)
Perpetual inventory system (166)
Purchases discount (167)
Retailer (165)
Sales discount (168)
Sales Refund Payable (189)
Sales Returns and Allowances (173)
Selling expenses (178)
Shrinkage (175)
Single-step income statement (179)
Supplementary records (171)
Wholesaler (165)

Multiple Choice Quiz

1. A company has $550,000 in net sales and $193,000 in gross profit. This means its cost of goods sold equals

a. $743,000. **c.** $357,000. **e.** $(193,000).
b. $550,000. **d.** $193,000.

2. A company purchased $4,500 of merchandise on May 1 with terms of 2/10, n/30. On May 6, it returned $250 of that merchandise. On May 8, it paid the balance owed for merchandise, taking any discount it is entitled to. The cash paid on May 8 is

a. $4,500. **c.** $4,160. **e.** $4,410.
b. $4,250. **d.** $4,165.

3. A company has cash sales of $75,000, credit sales of $320,000, sales returns and allowances of $13,700, and sales discounts of $6,000. Its net sales equal

a. $395,000. **c.** $300,300. **e.** $414,700.
b. $375,300. **d.** $339,700.

4. A company's quick assets are $37,500, its current assets are $80,000, and its current liabilities are $50,000. Its acid-test ratio equals

a. 1.600. **c.** 0.625. **e.** 0.469.
b. 0.750. **d.** 1.333.

5. A company's net sales are $675,000, its cost of goods sold is $459,000, and its net income is $74,250. Its gross margin ratio equals

a. 32%. **c.** 47%. **e.** 34%.
b. 68%. **d.** 11%.

ANSWERS TO MULTIPLE CHOICE QUIZ

1. c; Gross profit = $550,000 − $193,000 = $357,000
2. d; ($4,500 − $250) × (100% − 2%) = $4,165
3. b; Net sales = $75,000 + $320,000 − $13,700 − $6,000 = $375,300
4. b; Acid-test ratio = $37,500/$50,000 = 0.75
5. a; Gross margin ratio = ($675,000 − $459,000)/$675,000 = 32%

Superscript letter A, B, or C denotes assignments based on Appendix 5A, 5B, or 5C.

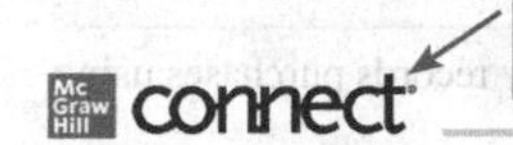

Select Quick Study and Exercise assignments feature Guided Example videos, called "Hints" in Connect. Hints use different numbers, and instructors can turn this feature on or off.

QUICK STUDY

QS 5-1
Applying merchandising terms
C1 P1

Match each phrase with its definition.

A. Sales discount
B. Credit period
C. Discount period
D. FOB destination
E. FOB shipping point
F. Gross profit
G. Merchandise inventory
H. Purchases discount

1. Goods a company owns and expects to sell to its customers.
2. Time period that can pass before a customer's full payment is due.
3. Seller's description of a cash discount granted to buyers in return for early payment.
4. Ownership of goods is transferred when the seller delivers goods to the carrier.
5. Purchaser's description of a cash discount received from a supplier of goods.
6. Difference between net sales and the cost of goods sold.
7. Time period in which a cash discount is available.
8. Ownership of goods is transferred when delivered to the buyer's place of business.

QS 5-2
Identifying inventory costs
C1

Costs of $5,000 were incurred to acquire goods and make them ready for sale. The goods were shipped to the buyer (FOB shipping point) for a cost of $200. Additional necessary costs of $400 were incurred to acquire the goods. No other incentives or discounts were available. Compute the buyer's total cost of merchandise inventory.

QS 5-3
Merchandise accounts and computations
C1

Use the following information (in random order) from a merchandising company and from a service company. *Hint:* Not all information may be necessary for the solutions.

a. For the merchandiser only, compute (1) goods available for sale, (2) cost of goods sold, and (3) gross profit.
b. Compute net income for each company.

McNeil Merchandising Company			
Accumulated depreciation	$ 700	Expenses	$1,450
Beginning inventory	5,000	Net purchases	3,900
Ending inventory	1,700	Net sales	9,500

Krug Service Company			
Expenses	$12,500	Prepaid rent	$ 800
Revenues	14,000	Accounts payable	200
Cash	700	Equipment	1,300

QS 5-4
Computing net invoice amounts
P1

Compute the amount to be paid for each of the four separate invoices assuming that all invoices are paid *within* the discount period.

	Merchandise (gross)	Terms		Merchandise (gross)	Terms
a.	$5,000	2/10, n/60	**c.**	$75,000	1/10, n/30
b.	$20,000	1/15, n/90	**d.**	$10,000	3/15, n/45

QS 5-5
Recording purchases, returns, and discounts taken
P1

Prepare journal entries to record each of the following transactions of a merchandising company. The company uses a perpetual inventory system and the gross method.

Nov. 5 Purchased 600 units of product at a cost of $10 per unit. Terms of the sale are 2/10, n/60; the invoice is dated November 5.
7 Returned 25 defective units from the November 5 purchase and received full credit.
15 Paid the amount due from the November 5 purchase, minus the return on November 7.

QS 5-6
Recording purchases and discounts taken
P1

Prepare journal entries to record each of the following transactions. The company records purchases using the gross method and a perpetual inventory system.

Aug. 1 Purchased merchandise with an invoice price of $60,000 and credit terms of 3/10, n/30.
11 Paid supplier the amount owed from the August 1 purchase.

QS 5-7
Recording purchases and discounts missed
P1

Prepare journal entries to record each of the following transactions. The company records purchases using the gross method and a perpetual inventory system.

Sep. 15 Purchased merchandise with an invoice price of $35,000 and credit terms of 2/5, n/15.
29 Paid supplier the amount owed on the September 15 purchase.

QS 5-8
Recording purchases and returns; **no** discounts
P1

Prepare journal entries to record each of the following transactions. The company records purchases using the gross method and a perpetual inventory system.

May 1 Purchased merchandise with a price of $800 and credit terms of n/30.
7 Returned merchandise that had a price of $100.
31 Paid the amount due from the May 1 purchase, minus the May 7 return.

QS 5-9
Recording purchases and allowances; **no** discounts
P1

Prepare journal entries to record each of the following transactions. The company records purchases using the gross method and a perpetual inventory system.

June 1 Purchased merchandise with a price of $450 and credit terms of n/45.
9 Received a $50 allowance (for scratched merchandise) toward the June 1 purchase.
July 16 Paid the amount due from the June 1 purchase, minus the June 9 allowance.

QS 5-10
Recording sales, returns, and discounts taken
P2

Prepare journal entries to record each of the following sales transactions of a merchandising company. The company uses a perpetual inventory system and the gross method.

Apr. 1 Sold merchandise for $3,000, with credit terms n/30; invoice dated April 1. The cost of the merchandise is $1,800.
4 The customer in the April 1 sale returned $300 of merchandise for full credit. The merchandise, which had cost $180, is returned to inventory.
8 Sold merchandise for $1,000, with credit terms of 1/10, n/30; invoice dated April 8. Cost of the merchandise is $700.
11 Received payment for the amount due from the April 1 sale less the return on April 4.

QS 5-11
Recording sales and returns; **no** discounts
P2

Prepare journal entries to record each of the following sales transactions of EcoMart Merchandising. EcoMart uses a *perpetual* inventory system and the *gross* method.

Oct. 1 Sold merchandise for $1,500, with credit terms n/30, invoice dated October 1. The cost of the merchandise is $900.
6 The customer in the October 1 sale returned $150 of merchandise for full credit. The merchandise, which had cost $90, is returned to inventory.
9 Sold merchandise for $700 cash. Cost of the merchandise is $450.
30 Received payment for the amount due from the October 1 sale less the return on October 6.

QS 5-12
Effects of sales transactions on income statement **P2**

Analyze each transaction in QS 5-11 by indicating its effects on the components of the income statement—specifically, identify the accounts and amounts (including + or −) for each transaction.

QS 5-13
Recording sales, returns, and allowances; **no** discounts
P2

Prepare journal entries to record each of the following sales transactions of TFC Merchandising. TFC uses a perpetual inventory system and the gross method.

May 1 Sold merchandise for $600, with credit terms n/60. The cost of the merchandise is $400.
9 The customer discovers slight defects in some units. TFC gives a price reduction (allowance) and credits the customer's accounts receivable for $40 to compensate for the defects.
June 4 The customer in the May 1 sale returned $75 of merchandise for full credit. The merchandise, which had cost $50, is returned to inventory.
30 Received payment for the amount due from the May 1 sale less the May 9 allowance and June 4 return.

QS 5-14
Accounting for shrinkage—perpetual system
P3

Telo Company's ledger on July 31, its fiscal year-end, shows merchandise inventory of $37,800 before accounting for any shrinkage. A physical count of its July 31 year-end inventory discloses that the cost of the merchandise inventory still available is $35,900. Prepare the entry to record any inventory shrinkage.

QS 5-15
Closing entries **P3**

Nix'It Company's ledger on July 31, its fiscal year-end, includes the following selected accounts that have normal balances. Nix'It uses the perpetual inventory system. Prepare the company's year-end closing entries.

T. Nix, Capital	$115,300	Sales returns and allowances	$ 6,500
T. Nix, Withdrawals	7,000	Cost of goods sold	106,900
Sales	170,000	Depreciation expense	10,300
Sales discounts	4,700	Salaries expense	32,500
		Miscellaneous expenses	5,000

QS 5-16
Identifying type of income statement
P4

Indicate whether each statement describes a multiple-step income statement or a single-step income statement.

1. Commonly reports detailed computations of net sales and other costs and expenses.
2. Statement limited to two main categories (revenues and expenses).
3. Reports gross profit on a separate line.
4. Separates income from operations from the other revenues and gains.

QS 5-17
Computing missing amounts using income statement relations
P4

Compute the missing amounts in the separate (partial) income statements A, B, and C.

	A	B	C
Sales	$?	$20,000	$90,000
Sales discounts	1,500	500	2,000
Sales returns and allowances	4,000	?	7,000
Net sales	35,000	16,500	?
Cost of goods sold	?	14,000	?
Gross profit	13,000	?	21,000

QS 5-18
Computing net sales and gross profit **P4**

Vitamix reports the following information for its year ended December 31: cash sales of $60,000; sales on credit of $90,000; general and administrative expenses of $17,000; sales returns of $11,000; cost of goods sold of $80,000; sales discounts of $2,000; and selling expenses of $24,000.
Compute (*a*) net sales and (*b*) gross profit.

QS 5-19
Preparing gross profit section of a multiple-step income statement **P4**

Using the year-end information from QS 5-18, prepare the gross profit section of a multiple-step income statement.

QS 5-20
Preparing a multiple-step income statement
P4

Save-the-Earth Co. reports the following income statement accounts for the year ended December 31. Prepare a multiple-step income statement that includes separate categories for net sales, cost of goods sold, selling expenses, and general and administrative expenses. Categorize the following accounts as selling expenses: Sales Staff Salaries Expense and Advertising Expense. Categorize the remaining expenses as general and administrative.

Sales discounts	$ 750	Office supplies expense	$ 500
Office salaries expense	2,000	Cost of goods sold	9,000
Rent expense—Office space	1,500	Sales	20,000
Advertising expense	500	Insurance expense	1,000
Sales returns and allowances	250	Sales staff salaries expense	2,500

QS 5-21
Preparing a classified balance sheet for a merchandiser
P4

Clear Water Co. reports the following balance sheet accounts as of December 31. Prepare a classified balance sheet.

Buildings	$25,000	Notes payable (due in 7 years)	$30,000
Accounts receivable	2,000	Office supplies	1,000
Land	15,000	O. Water, Capital	16,000
Merchandise inventory	7,000	Wages payable	3,000
Accounts payable	5,000	Accumulated Depreciation—Buildings	4,000
Cash	8,000		

QS 5-22
Computing and interpreting acid-test ratio
A1

The following information on current assets and current liabilities is for Belkin Company. (*a*) Compute Belkin's acid-test ratio. (*b*) If its competitor, Logit, has an acid-test ratio of 1.2, which company is better able to pay for current liabilities with its quick assets?

Cash	$1,490	Prepaid expenses	$ 700
Accounts receivable	2,800	Accounts payable	5,750
Inventory	6,000	Other current liabilities	850

QS 5-23
Computing and analyzing gross margin ratio
A1

(*a*) Compute net sales, gross profit, and the gross margin ratio for each of the four separate companies. (*b*) Which company has the best gross margin ratio?

	Carrier	Lennox	Trane	York
Sales	$150,000	$550,000	$38,700	$255,700
Sales discounts	5,000	17,500	600	4,800
Sales returns and allowances	20,000	6,000	5,100	900
Cost of goods sold	79,750	329,589	24,453	126,500

QS 5-24[A]
Contrasting periodic and perpetual systems
P5

Identify whether each description best applies to a periodic or a perpetual inventory system.

a. Updates the inventory account only at period-end.
b. Requires an adjusting entry to record inventory shrinkage.
c. Returns immediately affect the account balance of Merchandise Inventory.
d. Records cost of goods sold each time a sales transaction occurs.
e. Provides more timely information to managers.

QS 5-25[A]
Periodic: Computing cost of goods sold
P5

Chazen Company's inventory balance at the beginning of the year was $6,000. During the year, the company had Purchases of $30,000 and Purchases Returns and Allowances of $2,000. The company's inventory balance at the end of the year is $4,000.

Compute cost of goods sold for the year assuming Chazen uses the periodic inventory system.

QS 5-26[A]
Periodic: Recording purchases, returns, and discounts **P5**

Refer to QS 5-5 and prepare journal entries to record each of the merchandising transactions assuming that the company records purchases using the *gross* method and a *periodic* inventory system.

QS 5-27[A]
Periodic: Recording sales, returns, and discounts **P5**

Refer to QS 5-10 and prepare journal entries to record each of the merchandising transactions assuming that the company records purchases using the *gross* method and a *periodic* inventory system.

QS 5-28[B]
Recording estimates of future discounts
P6

ProBuilder has the following June 30 fiscal-year-end unadjusted balances: Allowance for Sales Discounts, $0; and Accounts Receivable, $10,000. Of the $10,000 of receivables, $2,000 are within a 3% discount period, meaning that it expects buyers to take $60 in future discounts arising from this period's sales.

a. Prepare the June 30 fiscal-year-end adjusting journal entry for future sales discounts.

b. Assume the same facts above *and* that there is a $10 fiscal-year-end unadjusted credit balance in the Allowance for Sales Discounts. Prepare the June 30 fiscal-year-end adjusting journal entry for future sales discounts.

QS 5-29[B]
Recording estimates of future returns
P6

ProBuilder reports merchandise sales of $50,000 and cost of merchandise sales of $20,000 in its first year of operations ending June 30. It makes fiscal-year-end adjusting entries for estimated future returns and allowances equal to 2% of sales, or $1,000, and 2% of cost of sales, or $400.

a. Prepare the June 30 fiscal-year-end adjusting journal entry for future returns and allowances related to sales.

b. Prepare the June 30 fiscal-year-end adjusting journal entry for future returns and allowances related to cost of sales.

QS 5-30[C]
Net method: Recording purchases, returns, and discounts **P7**

Refer to QS 5-5 and prepare journal entries to record each of the merchandising transactions assuming that the company records purchases using the *net* method and a *perpetual* inventory system.

QS 5-31[C]
Net method: Recording sales, returns, and discounts **P7**

Refer to QS 5-10 and prepare journal entries to record each of the merchandising transactions assuming that the company records purchases using the *net* method and a *perpetual* inventory system.

Mc Graw Hill connect

EXERCISES

Exercise 5-1
Computing revenues, expenses, and income
C1

Fill in the blanks in the following separate income statements *a* through *e*.

	a	b	c	d	e
Sales	$62,000	$43,500	$55,000	$?	$25,600
Cost of goods sold					
Merchandise inventory, beginning	8,000	17,050	7,500	8,000	4,560
Total cost of merchandise purchases	38,000	?	?	32,000	6,600
Merchandise inventory, ending	?	3,000	9,000	6,600	?
Cost of goods sold	34,050	16,000	?	?	7,000
Gross profit	?	?	12,750	45,600	?
Expenses	10,000	10,650	12,150	3,600	6,000
Net income (loss)	$?	$16,850	$ 600	$42,000	$?

Exercise 5-2
Operating cycle for merchandiser
C1

The operating cycle of a merchandiser with credit sales includes the following five activities. Starting with merchandise acquisition, identify the chronological order of these five activities.

a. Prepare merchandise for sale.
b. Collect cash from customers on account.
c. Make credit sales to customers.
d. Purchase merchandise.
e. Monitor and service accounts receivable.

Exercise 5-3
Recording purchases, purchases returns, and purchases allowances
P1

Prepare journal entries to record the following transactions for a retail store. The company uses a perpetual inventory system and the gross method.

Apr. 2 Purchased $4,600 of merchandise from Lyon Company with credit terms of 2/15, n/60, invoice dated April 2, and FOB shipping point.
3 Paid $300 cash for shipping charges on the April 2 purchase.
4 Returned to Lyon Company unacceptable merchandise that had an invoice price of $600.
17 Sent a check to Lyon Company for the April 2 purchase, net of the discount and the returned merchandise.
18 Purchased $8,500 of merchandise from Frist Corp. with credit terms of 1/10, n/30, invoice dated April 18, and FOB destination.
21 After negotiations over scuffed merchandise, received from Frist a $500 allowance toward the $8,500 owed on the April 18 purchase.
28 Sent check to Frist paying for the April 18 purchase, net of the allowance and the discount.

Check Apr. 28, Cr. Cash, $7,920

Exercise 5-4
Purchasing transactions
P1

Prepare journal entries to record the following transactions of Recycled Fashion retail store. Recycled Fashion uses a perpetual inventory system and the gross method.

Mar. 3 Purchased $1,150 of merchandise from GreenWorld Company with credit terms of 2/15, n/60, invoice dated March 3, and FOB shipping point.
4 Paid $75 cash for shipping charges on the March 3 purchase.
5 Returned to GreenWorld unacceptable merchandise that had an invoice price of $150.
18 Paid GreenWorld for the March 3 purchase, net of the discount and the returned merchandise.
19 Purchased $425 of merchandise from PeopleFirst Corp. with credit terms of 1/10, n/30, invoice dated March 19, and FOB destination.
21 After negotiations, received from PeopleFirst a $25 allowance (for scuffed merchandise) toward the $425 owed on the March 19 purchase.
29 Sent check to PeopleFirst paying for the March 19 purchase, net of the allowance and the discount.

Exercise 5-5
Determining inventory ownership and costs in transit
P1

For each transaction of Sealy Co., (*a*) determine whether or not Sealy owns the goods during transit. (*b*) If Sealy is responsible for transportation costs, record the entry for shipping costs assuming they are paid in cash and the perpetual inventory system is used.

1. Purchased goods FOB shipping point. Transportation costs are $600.
2. Sold goods FOB destination. Transportation costs are $200.
3. Sold goods FOB shipping point. Transportation costs are $350.
4. Purchased goods FOB destination. Transportation costs are $125.

Exercise 5-6
Recording sales, sales returns, and sales allowances
P2

Allied Merchandisers was organized on May 1. Macy Co. is a major customer (buyer) of Allied (seller) products. Prepare journal entries to record the following transactions for Allied assuming it uses a perpetual inventory system and the gross method.

May 3 Allied made its first and only purchase of inventory for the period on May 3 for 2,000 units at a price of $10 cash per unit (for a total cost of $20,000).
5 Allied sold 1,500 of the units in inventory for $14 per unit (invoice total: $21,000) to Macy Co. under credit terms 2/10, n/60. The goods cost Allied $15,000.
7 Macy returns 125 units because they did not fit the customer's needs (invoice amount: $1,750). Allied restores the units, which cost $1,250, to its inventory.
8 Macy discovers that 200 units are scuffed but are still of use and, therefore, keeps the units. Allied gives a price reduction (allowance) and credits Macy's accounts receivable for $300 to compensate for the damage.
15 Allied receives payment from Macy for the amount owed on the May 5 purchase; payment is net of returns, allowances, and any cash discount.

Exercise 5-7
Effects of sales transactions on income statement **P2**

Analyze each transaction in Exercise 5-6 by indicating its effects on the income statement—specifically, identify the accounts and amounts (including + or −) for each transaction.

Exercise 5-8
Recording purchases, purchases returns, and purchases allowances **P1**

Refer to Exercise 5-6 and prepare journal entries for Macy Co. to record each of the May transactions. Macy is a retailer that uses the gross method and a perpetual inventory system; it purchases these units for resale.

Exercise 5-9
Recording sales, purchases, and cash discounts—buyer *and* seller
P1 P2

Santa Fe Retailing purchased merchandise from Mesa Wholesalers with credit terms of 3/10, n/60 and an invoice price of $24,000. The merchandise had cost Mesa $16,000. Assume that both buyer and seller use a perpetual inventory system and the gross method.

1. Prepare entries that the *buyer* records for the (*a*) purchase, (*b*) cash payment *within* the discount period, and (*c*) cash payment *after* the discount period.
2. Prepare entries that the *seller* records for the (*a*) sale, (*b*) cash collection *within* the discount period, and (*c*) cash collection *after* the discount period.

Exercise 5-10
Recording sales, purchases, shipping, and returns—buyer *and* seller
P1 P2

Sydney Retailing (buyer) and Troy Wholesalers (seller) enter into the following transactions. Both Sydney and Troy use a perpetual inventory system and the gross method.

May 11 Sydney accepts delivery of $40,000 of merchandise it purchases for resale from Troy: invoice dated May 11, terms 3/10, n/90, FOB shipping point. The goods cost Troy $30,000. Sydney pays $345 cash to Express Shipping for delivery charges on the merchandise.
12 Sydney returns $1,400 of the $40,000 of goods to Troy, who receives them the same day and restores them to its inventory. The returned goods had cost Troy $1,050.
20 Sydney pays Troy for the amount owed. Troy receives the cash immediately.

1. Prepare journal entries that Sydney Retailing (buyer) records for these three transactions.
2. Prepare journal entries that Troy Wholesalers (seller) records for these three transactions.

Check (1) May 20, Cr. Cash, $37,442

Exercise 5-11
Inventory and cost of sales transactions in T-accounts
P1 P2

The following summarizes Tesla's merchandising activities for the year. Set up T-accounts for Merchandise Inventory and for Cost of Goods Sold. Enter each line item into one or both of the two T-accounts and compute the T-account balances.

Cost of merchandise sold to customers	$196,000
Merchandise inventory, beginning-of-year	25,000
Merchandise purchases, gross amount	192,500
Shrinkage on inventory as of year-end	800
Transportation-in for merchandise purchases	2,900
Cost of merchandise returned by customers (and restored to inventory)	2,100
Discounts received from suppliers on merchandise purchases	1,700
Returns to and allowances from suppliers on merchandise purchases	4,000

Check Ending Merch. Inventory, $20,000

Exercise 5-12
Recording purchases, sales, returns, and shipping
P1 P2

Prepare journal entries for the following merchandising transactions of Dollar Store assuming it uses a perpetual inventory system and the gross method.

Nov. 1 Dollar Store purchases merchandise for $1,500 on terms of 2/5, n/30, FOB shipping point, invoice dated November 1.
5 Dollar Store pays cash for the November 1 purchase.
7 Dollar Store discovers and returns $200 of defective merchandise purchased on November 1, and paid for on November 5, for a cash refund.
10 Dollar Store pays $90 cash for transportation costs for the November 1 purchase.
13 Dollar Store sells merchandise for $1,600 with terms n/30. The cost of the merchandise is $800.
16 Merchandise is returned to the Dollar Store from the November 13 transaction. The returned items are priced at $160 and cost $80; the items were not damaged and were returned to inventory.

Exercise 5-13
Recording purchases, sales, and returns; **no** discounts
P1 P2

Prepare journal entries for the following merchandising transactions of Powell Company assuming it uses a perpetual inventory system and the gross method.

May 1 Powell purchased merchandise with a price of $875 and credit terms of n/30.
12 Powell returned merchandise that had a price of $125.
31 Powell paid the amount due from the May 1 purchase, minus the May 12 return.
June 3 Powell sold merchandise for $450, with credit terms n/15. Cost of the merchandise is $300.
5 The customer discovers some of the units are scratched. Powell gives a price reduction (allowance) and credits the customer's accounts receivable for $20 to compensate for the scratches.
18 Powell received payment for the amount due from the June 3 sale less the June 5 allowance.

Exercise 5-14
Accounting for shrinkage
P3

At the beginning of the year, SnapIt had $10,000 of inventory. During the year, SnapIt purchased $35,000 of merchandise and sold $30,000 of merchandise. A physical count of inventory at year-end shows $14,000 of inventory exists. Prepare the entry to record inventory shrinkage.

Exercise 5-15
Preparing closing entries for a merchandiser
P3

The following listing of temporary accounts is from the December 31 adjusted trial balance of Emiko Co. Use these normal account balances to journalize closing entries.

	Debit	Credit		Debit	Credit
K. Emiko, Withdrawals	$ 33,000		Sales salaries expense	$ 49,700	
Sales		$529,000	Utilities expense	15,000	
Sales returns and allowances	17,500		Selling expenses	39,000	
Sales discounts	5,000		Administrative expenses	105,000	
Cost of goods sold	213,300				

Exercise 5-16
Impacts of inventory error on key accounts
P3

A retailer completed a physical count of ending merchandise inventory. When counting inventory, employees did not include $3,000 of incoming goods shipped by a supplier on December 31 under FOB shipping point. These goods had been recorded in Merchandise Inventory, but *they were not included in the physical count because they were in transit*. This means shrinkage was incorrectly overstated by $3,000.

Compute the amount of overstatement or understatement for each of the following amounts for this period.

a. Ending inventory **b.** Total assets **c.** Net income **d.** Total equity

Exercise 5-17
Computing net sales for multiple-step income statement
P4

A company reports the following sales-related information. Compute and prepare the net sales portion only of this company's multiple-step income statement.

Sales, gross	$200,000	Sales returns and allowances	$16,000
Sales discounts	4,000	Sales salaries expense	10,000

Exercise 5-18
Preparing a multiple-step income statement
P4

Fit-for-Life Foods reports the following income statement accounts for the year ended December 31. Prepare a multiple-step income statement that includes separate categories for net sales; cost of goods sold; selling expenses; general and administrative expenses; and other revenues, gains, expenses, and losses. Categorize the following accounts as selling expenses: Sales Salaries Expense, Rent Expense—Selling Space, TV Advertising Expense, and Sales Commission Expense. Categorize the remaining expenses as general and administrative.

Gain on sale of equipment	$ 6,250	Depreciation expense—Office copier	$ 500
Office supplies expense	700	Sales discounts	16,000
Insurance expense	1,300	Sales returns and allowances	4,000
Sales	220,000	TV advertising expense	2,000
Office salaries expense	32,500	Interest revenue	750
Rent expense—Selling space	10,000	Cost of goods sold	90,000
Sales salaries expense	23,000	Sales commission expense	13,000

Exercise 5-19
Preparing a classified balance sheet for a merchandiser
P4

Adams Co. reports the following balance sheet accounts as of December 31. Prepare a classified balance sheet.

Salaries payable	$ 6,000	D. Adams, Capital	$60,000
Buildings	55,000	Notes payable (due in 9 years)	30,000
Prepaid rent	7,000	Office supplies	2,000
Merchandise inventory	14,000	Land	22,000
Accounts payable	10,000	Accumulated depreciation—Building	5,000
Prepaid insurance	3,000	Mortgages payable (due in 5 years)	12,000
Accounts receivable	4,000	Cash	16,000

Exercise 5-20
Inventory error impact on ratios A1

Refer to the information in Exercise 5-16 and indicate whether the failure to include in-transit inventory as part of the physical count results in an overstatement, understatement, or no effect on the following ratios.

a. Gross margin ratio **b.** Profit margin ratio **c.** Acid-test ratio **d.** Current ratio

Exercise 5-21
Computing and analyzing the acid-test ratio
A1

a. Compute the acid-test ratio for each of the following separate cases.
b. Which company is in the best position to meet short-term obligations?

	Camaro	GTO	Torino
Cash	$2,000	$ 110	$1,000
Short-term investments	50	0	580
Current receivables	350	470	700
Inventory	2,600	2,420	4,230
Prepaid expenses	200	500	900
Total current assets	$5,200	$3,500	$7,410
Current liabilities	$2,000	$1,000	$3,800

Exercise 5-22[A]
Periodic: Recording purchases, returns, and allowances P5

Refer to Exercise 5-3 and prepare journal entries to record each of the merchandising transactions assuming that the buyer uses the *periodic inventory system* and the *gross method*.

Exercise 5-23[A]
Periodic: Recording sales, purchases, and discounts: buyer and seller P5

Refer to Exercise 5-9 and prepare journal entries to record each of the merchandising transactions assuming that the *periodic inventory system* and the *gross method* are used by both the buyer and the seller.

Exercise 5-24[A]
Periodic: Recording sales, purchases, shipping, and returns: buyer and seller P5

Refer to Exercise 5-10 and prepare journal entries to record each of the merchandising transactions assuming that the *periodic inventory system* and the *gross method* are used by both the buyer and the seller.

Exercise 5-25[B]
Recording estimates of future discounts
P6

Med Labs has the following December 31 year-end unadjusted balances: Allowance for Sales Discounts, $0; and Accounts Receivable, $5,000. Of the $5,000 of receivables, $1,000 are within a 2% discount period, meaning that it expects buyers to take $20 in future-period discounts arising from this period's sales.

a. Prepare the December 31 year-end adjusting journal entry for future sales discounts.
b. Assume the same facts above *and* that there is a $5 year-end unadjusted credit balance in Allowance for Sales Discounts. Prepare the December 31 year-end adjusting journal entry for future sales discounts.
c. Is Allowance for Sales Discounts a contra asset or a contra liability account?

Exercise 5-26[B]
Recording estimates of future returns
P6

Chico Company allows its customers to return merchandise within 30 days of purchase.

- At December 31, the end of its first year of operations, Chico estimates future-period merchandise returns of $60,000 (cost of $22,500) related to its current-year sales.
- A few days later, on January 3, a customer returns merchandise with a selling price of $2,000 for a cash refund; the returned merchandise cost $750 and is returned to inventory as it is not defective.

a. Prepare the December 31 year-end adjusting journal entry for estimated future sales returns and allowances (revenue side).
b. Prepare the December 31 year-end adjusting journal entry for estimated future inventory returns and allowances (cost side).
c. Prepare the January 3 journal entries to record the merchandise returned.

Exercise 5-27[B]
Recording estimates of future returns
P6

Lopez Company reports unadjusted first-year merchandise sales of $100,000 and cost of merchandise sales of $30,000.

a. Compute gross profit (using the unadjusted numbers above).
b. The company expects future returns and allowances equal to 5% of sales and 5% of cost of sales.
   1. Prepare the year-end adjusting entry to record the sales expected to be refunded.
   2. Prepare the year-end adjusting entry to record the cost side of sales returns and allowances.
   3. Recompute gross profit using the adjusted numbers from parts 1 and 2.
c. Is Sales Refund Payable an asset, liability, or equity account?
d. Is Inventory Returns Estimated an asset, liability, or equity account?

Exercise 5-28^C
Net method: Recording sales, purchases, shipping, and returns—buyer and seller **P7**

Refer to Exercise 5-10 and prepare journal entries to record each of the merchandising transactions assuming that the *perpetual inventory system* and the *net method* are used by both the buyer and the seller.

Exercise 5-29^C
Net & gross methods: Recording purchases, sales, returns, and discounts—buyer and seller **P7**

Piere Imports uses the perpetual system in accounting for merchandise inventory and had the following transactions during the month of October. Prepare entries to record these transactions assuming that Piere Imports records invoices (*a*) at gross amounts and (*b*) at net amounts.

Oct. 2 Purchased merchandise at a $3,000 price ($2,940 net), invoice dated October 2, terms 2/10, n/30.
10 Returned $500 ($490 net) of merchandise purchased on October 2 and debited its account payable for that amount.
17 Purchased merchandise at a $5,400 price ($5,292 net), invoice dated October 17, terms 2/10, n/30.
27 Paid for the merchandise purchased on October 17, less the discount.
31 Paid for the merchandise purchased on October 2.

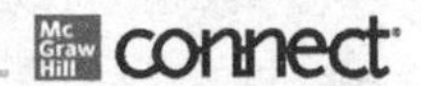

PROBLEM SET A

Problem 5-1A
Preparing journal entries for merchandising activities
P1 P2

Prepare journal entries to record the following merchandising transactions of Cabela's, which uses the perpetual inventory system and the gross method.

July 1 Purchased merchandise from Boden Company for $6,000 under credit terms of 1/15, n/30, FOB shipping point, invoice dated July 1.
2 Sold merchandise to Creek Co. for $900 under credit terms of 2/10, n/60, FOB shipping point, invoice dated July 2. The merchandise had cost $500.
3 Paid $125 cash for freight charges on the purchase of July 1.
8 Sold merchandise that had cost $1,300 for $1,700 cash.
9 Purchased merchandise from Leight Co. for $2,200 under credit terms of 2/15, n/60, FOB destination, invoice dated July 9.
11 Returned $200 of merchandise purchased on July 9 from Leight Co. and debited its account payable for that amount.
12 Received the balance due from Creek Co. for the invoice dated July 2, net of the discount.
16 Paid the balance due to Boden Company within the discount period.
19 Sold merchandise that cost $800 to Art Co. for $1,200 under credit terms of 2/15, n/60, FOB shipping point, invoice dated July 19.
21 Gave a price reduction (allowance) of $100 to Art Co. for merchandise sold on July 19 and credited Art's accounts receivable for that amount.
24 Paid Leight Co. the balance due, net of discount.
30 Received the balance due from Art Co. for the invoice dated July 19, net of discount.
31 Sold merchandise that cost $4,800 to Creek Co. for $7,000 under credit terms of 2/10, n/60, FOB shipping point, invoice dated July 31.

Check July 12, Dr. Cash, $882
July 16, Cr. Cash, $5,940
July 24, Cr. Cash, $1,960
July 30, Dr. Cash, $1,078

Problem 5-2A
Preparing journal entries for merchandising activities
P1 P2

Prepare journal entries to record the following merchandising transactions of Lowe's, which uses the perpetual inventory system and the gross method.

Aug. 1 Purchased merchandise from Aron Company for $7,500 under credit terms of 1/10, n/30, FOB destination, invoice dated August 1.
5 Sold merchandise to Baird Corp. for $5,200 under credit terms of 2/10, n/60, FOB destination, invoice dated August 5. The merchandise had cost $4,000.
8 Purchased merchandise from Waters Corporation for $5,400 under credit terms of 1/10, n/45, FOB shipping point, invoice dated August 8.
9 Paid $125 cash for shipping charges related to the August 5 sale to Baird Corp.
10 Baird returned merchandise from the August 5 sale that had cost Lowe's $400 and was sold for $600. The merchandise was restored to inventory.
12 After negotiations with Waters Corporation concerning problems with the purchases on August 8, Lowe's received a price reduction from Waters of $400 off the $5,400 of goods purchased. Lowe's debited accounts payable for $400.
14 At Aron's request, Lowe's paid $200 cash for freight charges on the August 1 purchase, reducing the amount owed (accounts payable) to Aron.

Check Aug. 9, Dr. Delivery Expense, $125

15 Received balance due from Baird Corp. for the August 5 sale less the return on August 10.
18 Paid the amount due Waters Corporation for the August 8 purchase less the price allowance from August 12.
19 Sold merchandise to Tux Co. for $4,800 under credit terms of n/10, FOB shipping point, invoice dated August 19. The merchandise had cost $2,400.
22 Tux requested a price reduction on the August 19 sale because the merchandise did not meet specifications. Lowe's gave a price reduction (allowance) of $500 to Tux and credited Tux's accounts receivable for that amount.
29 Received Tux's cash payment for the amount due from the August 19 sale less the price allowance from August 22.
30 Paid Aron Company the amount due from the August 1 purchase.

Aug. 18, Cr. Cash, $4,950

Aug. 29, Dr. Cash, $4,300

Problem 5-3A
Computing merchandising amounts and formatting income statements
C1 P4

Valley Company's adjusted account balances from its general ledger on August 31, its fiscal year-end, follows. It categorizes the following accounts as selling expenses: Sales Salaries Expense, Rent Expense—Selling Space, Store Supplies Expense, and Advertising Expense. It categorizes the remaining expenses as general and administrative.

Adjusted Account Balances	Debit	Credit
Merchandise inventory (ending)	$ 41,000	
Other (noninventory) assets	130,400	
Total liabilities		$ 25,000
K. Valley, Capital		104,550
K. Valley, Withdrawals	8,000	
Sales		225,600
Sales discounts	2,250	
Sales returns and allowances	12,000	
Cost of goods sold	74,500	
Sales salaries expense	32,000	
Rent expense—Selling space	8,000	
Store supplies expense	1,500	
Advertising expense	13,000	
Office salaries expense	28,500	
Rent expense—Office space	3,600	
Office supplies expense	400	
Totals	$355,150	$355,150

Beginning merchandise inventory was $25,400. Supplementary records of merchandising activities for the year ended August 31 reveal the following itemized costs.

Invoice cost of merchandise purchases	$92,000	Purchases returns and allowances	$4,500
Purchases discounts received	2,000	Costs of transportation-in	4,600

Required

1. Compute the company's net sales for the year.
2. Compute the company's total cost of merchandise purchased for the year.
3. Prepare a multiple-step income statement that includes separate categories for net sales, cost of goods sold, selling expenses, and general and administrative expenses.
4. Prepare a single-step income statement that includes these expense categories: cost of goods sold, selling expenses, and general and administrative expenses.

Check (2) $90,100

(3) Gross profit, $136,850; Net income, $49,850

(4) Total expenses, $161,500

Problem 5-4A
Preparing closing entries and interpreting information about discounts and returns C1 P3

Use the data for Valley Company in Problem 5-3A to complete the following requirement.

Required

Prepare closing entries as of August 31 (the perpetual inventory system is used).

Problem 5-5A
Preparing adjusting entries and income statements; computing gross margin, acid-test, and current ratios
A1 P3 P4

The following unadjusted trial balance is prepared at fiscal year-end for Nelson Company. Nelson Company uses a perpetual inventory system. It categorizes the following accounts as selling expenses: Depreciation Expense—Store Equipment, Sales Salaries Expense, Rent Expense—Selling Space, Store Supplies Expense, and Advertising Expense. It categorizes the remaining expenses as general and administrative.

NELSON COMPANY
Unadjusted Trial Balance

January 31	Debit	Credit
Cash	$ 1,000	
Merchandise inventory	12,500	
Store supplies	5,800	
Prepaid insurance	2,400	
Store equipment	42,900	
Accumulated depreciation—Store equipment		$ 15,250
Accounts payable		10,000
J. Nelson, Capital		32,000
J. Nelson, Withdrawals	2,200	
Sales		111,950
Sales discounts	2,000	
Sales returns and allowances	2,200	
Cost of goods sold	38,400	
Depreciation expense—Store equipment	0	
Sales salaries expense	17,500	
Office salaries expense	17,500	
Insurance expense	0	
Rent expense—Selling space	7,500	
Rent expense—Office space	7,500	
Store supplies expense	0	
Advertising expense	9,800	
Totals	$169,200	$169,200

Required

1. Prepare adjusting journal entries to reflect each of the following:
   a. Store supplies still available at fiscal year-end amount to $1,750.
   b. Expired insurance, an administrative expense, is $1,400 for the fiscal year.
   c. Depreciation expense on store equipment, a selling expense, is $1,525 for the fiscal year.
   d. To estimate shrinkage, a physical count of ending merchandise inventory is taken. It shows $10,900 of inventory is still available at fiscal year-end.
2. Prepare a multiple-step income statement for the year ended January 31 that begins with gross sales and includes separate categories for net sales, cost of goods sold, selling expenses, and general and administrative expenses.
3. Prepare a single-step income statement for the year ended January 31.
4. Compute the current ratio, acid-test ratio, and gross margin ratio as of January 31. (Round ratios to two decimals.)

Check (2) Gross profit, $67,750

(3) Total expenses, $106,775; Net income, $975

PROBLEM SET B

Problem 5-1B
Preparing journal entries for merchandising activities
P1 P2

Prepare journal entries to record the following merchandising transactions of IKEA, which uses the perpetual inventory system and gross method.

May 2 Purchased merchandise from Havel Co. for $10,000 under credit terms of 1/15, n/30, FOB shipping point, invoice dated May 2.
4 Sold merchandise to Rath Co. for $11,000 under credit terms of 2/10, n/60, FOB shipping point, invoice dated May 4. The merchandise had cost $5,600.
5 Paid $250 cash for freight charges on the purchase of May 2.
9 Sold merchandise that had cost $2,000 for $2,500 cash.
10 Purchased merchandise from Duke Co. for $3,650 under credit terms of 2/15, n/60, FOB destination, invoice dated May 10.
12 Returned $650 of merchandise purchased on May 10 from Duke Co. and debited its account payable for that amount.
14 Received the balance due from Rath Co. for the invoice dated May 4, net of the discount.
17 Paid the balance due to Havel Co. within the discount period.

Check May 14, Dr. Cash, $10,780

20 Sold merchandise that cost $1,450 to Tamer Co. for $2,800 under credit terms of 2/15, n/60, FOB shipping point, invoice dated May 20.
22 Gave a price reduction (allowance) of $300 to Tamer Co. for merchandise sold on May 20 and credited Tamer's accounts receivable for that amount.
25 Paid Duke Co. the balance due, net of the discount.
30 Received the balance due from Tamer Co. for the invoice dated May 20, net of discount and allowance.
31 Sold merchandise that cost $3,600 to Rath Co. for $7,200 under credit terms of 2/10, n/60, FOB shipping point, invoice dated May 31.

May 17, Cr. Cash, $9,900

May 30, Dr. Cash, $2,450

Problem 5-2B
Preparing journal entries for merchandising activities
P1 P2

Prepare journal entries to record the following merchandising transactions of Menards, which applies the perpetual inventory system and gross method.

July 3 Purchased merchandise from OLB Corp. for $15,000 under credit terms of 1/10, n/30, FOB destination, invoice dated July 3.
7 Sold merchandise to Brill Co. for $11,500 under credit terms of 2/10, n/60, FOB destination, invoice dated July 7. The merchandise had cost $7,750.
10 Purchased merchandise from Rupert Co. for $14,200 under credit terms of 1/10, n/45, FOB shipping point, invoice dated July 10.
11 Paid $300 cash for shipping charges related to the July 7 sale to Brill Co.
12 Brill returned merchandise from the July 7 sale that had cost Menards $1,450 and been sold for $2,000. The merchandise was restored to inventory.
14 After negotiations with Rupert Co. concerning problems with the merchandise purchased on July 10, Menards received a price reduction from Rupert of $1,200. Menards debited accounts payable for $1,200.
15 At OLB's request, Menards paid $200 cash for freight charges on the July 3 purchase, reducing the amount owed (accounts payable) to OLB.
17 Received balance due from Brill Co. for the July 7 sale less the return on July 12.
20 Paid the amount due Rupert Co. for the July 10 purchase less the price reduction granted on July 14.
21 Sold merchandise to Brown for $11,000 under credit terms of 1/10, n/30, FOB shipping point, invoice dated July 21. The merchandise had cost $7,000.
24 Brown requested a price reduction on the July 21 sale because the merchandise did not meet specifications. Menards gave a price reduction (allowance) of $1,000 to Brown and credited Brown's accounts receivable for that amount.
30 Received Brown's cash payment for the amount due from the July 21 sale less the price allowance from July 24.
31 Paid OLB Corp. the amount due from the July 3 purchase.

Check July 17, Dr. Cash, $9,310

July 30, Dr. Cash, $9,900

July 31, Cr. Cash, $14,800

Problem 5-3B
Computing merchandising amounts and formatting income statements
C1 P4

Barkley Company's adjusted account balances from its general ledger on March 31, its fiscal year-end, follows. It categorizes the following accounts as selling expenses: Sales Salaries Expense, Rent Expense—Selling Space, Store Supplies Expense, and Advertising Expense. It categorizes the remaining expenses as general and administrative.

Adjusted Account Balances	Debit	Credit
Merchandise inventory (ending)	$ 56,500	
Other (noninventory) assets	202,600	
Total liabilities		$ 42,500
C. Barkley, Capital		164,425
C. Barkley, Withdrawals	3,000	
Sales		332,650
Sales discounts	5,875	
Sales returns and allowances	20,000	
Cost of goods sold	115,600	
Sales salaries expense	44,500	
Rent expense—Selling space	16,000	
Store supplies expense	3,850	
Advertising expense	26,000	
Office salaries expense	40,750	
Rent expense—Office space	3,800	
Office supplies expense	1,100	
Totals	$539,575	$539,575

[continued on next page]

[continued from previous page]

Beginning merchandise inventory was $37,500. Supplementary records of merchandising activities for the year ended March 31 reveal the following itemized costs.

Invoice cost of merchandise purchases....	$138,500	Purchases returns and allowances......	$6,700
Purchases discounts received...........	2,950	Costs of transportation-in..............	5,750

Required

1. Compute the company's net sales for the year.
2. Compute the company's total cost of merchandise purchased for the year.
3. Prepare a multiple-step income statement that includes separate categories for net sales, cost of goods sold, selling expenses, and general and administrative expenses.
4. Prepare a single-step income statement that includes these expense categories: cost of goods sold, selling expenses, and general and administrative expenses.

Check (2) $134,600

(3) Gross profit, $191,175; Net income, $55,175

(4) Total expenses, $251,600

Problem 5-4B
Preparing closing entries and interpreting information about discounts and returns C1 P3

Use the data for Barkley Company in Problem 5-3B to complete the following requirement.

Required

Prepare closing entries as of March 31 (the perpetual inventory system is used).

Problem 5-5B
Preparing adjusting entries and income statements; computing gross margin, acid-test, and current ratios
P3 P4 A1

The following unadjusted trial balance is prepared at fiscal year-end for Foster Products Company. Foster Products Company uses a perpetual inventory system. It categorizes the following accounts as selling expenses: Depreciation Expense—Store Equipment, Sales Salaries Expense, Rent Expense—Selling Space, Store Supplies Expense, and Advertising Expense. It categorizes the remaining expenses as general and administrative.

FOSTER PRODUCTS COMPANY
Unadjusted Trial Balance

October 31	Debit	Credit
Cash	$ 7,400	
Merchandise inventory	24,000	
Store supplies	9,700	
Prepaid insurance	6,600	
Store equipment	81,800	
Accumulated depreciation—Store equipment		$ 32,000
Accounts payable		18,000
D. Foster, Capital		43,000
D. Foster, Withdrawals	2,000	
Sales		227,100
Sales discounts	1,000	
Sales returns and allowances	5,000	
Cost of goods sold	75,800	
Depreciation expense—Store equipment	0	
Sales salaries expense	31,500	
Office salaries expense	31,500	
Insurance expense	0	
Rent expense—Selling space	13,000	
Rent expense—Office space	13,000	
Store supplies expense	0	
Advertising expense	17,800	
Totals	$320,100	$320,100

Required

1. Prepare adjusting journal entries to reflect each of the following:
   a. Store supplies still available at fiscal year-end amount to $3,700.
   b. Expired insurance, an administrative expense, is $2,800 for the fiscal year.
   c. Depreciation expense on store equipment, a selling expense, is $3,000 for the fiscal year.

d. To estimate shrinkage, a physical count of ending merchandise inventory is taken. It shows $21,300 of inventory is still available at fiscal year-end.

2. Prepare a multiple-step income statement for the year ended October 31 that begins with gross sales and includes separate categories for net sales, cost of goods sold, selling expenses, and general and administrative expenses.

Check (2) Gross profit, $142,600

3. Prepare a single-step income statement for the year ended October 31.

4. Compute the current ratio, acid-test ratio, and gross margin ratio as of October 31. (Round ratios to two decimals.)

(3) Total expenses, $197,100; Net income, $24,000

Mc Graw Hill **connect**

SERIAL PROBLEM

Business Solutions

P1 P2 P3 P4

Serial problem began in Chapter 1. If previous chapter segments were not completed, the serial problem can begin at this point. It is available in ***Connect*** *with an algorithmic option.*

SP 5 Santana Rey created **Business Solutions** on October 1, 2021. The company has been successful, and its list of customers has grown. To accommodate the growth, the accounting system is modified to set up separate accounts for each customer. The following chart of accounts includes the account number used for each account and any balance as of December 31, 2021. Santana Rey decided to add a fourth digit with a decimal point to the 106 account number that had been used for the single Accounts Receivable account. This change allows the company to continue using the existing chart of accounts.

No.	Account Title	Dr.	Cr.	No.	Account Title	Dr.	Cr.
101	Cash	$48,372		210	Wages payable		$ 500
106.1	Alex's Engineering Co.	0		236	Unearned computer services revenue		1,500
106.2	Wildcat Services	0		301	S. Rey, Capital		80,360
106.3	Easy Leasing	0		302	S. Rey, Withdrawals	$0	
106.4	IFM Co.	3,000		403	Computer services revenue		0
106.5	Liu Corp.	0		413	Sales		0
106.6	Gomez Co.	2,668		414	Sales returns and allowances	0	
106.7	Delta Co.	0		415	Sales discounts	0	
106.8	KC, Inc.	0		502	Cost of goods sold	0	
106.9	Dream, Inc.	0		612	Depreciation expense—Office equipment	0	
119	Merchandise inventory	0		613	Depreciation expense—Computer equipment	0	
126	Computer supplies	580		623	Wages expense	0	
128	Prepaid insurance	1,665		637	Insurance expense	0	
131	Prepaid rent	825		640	Rent expense	0	
163	Office equipment	8,000		652	Computer supplies expense	0	
164	Accumulated depreciation—Office equipment		$ 400	655	Advertising expense	0	
				676	Mileage expense	0	
167	Computer equipment	20,000		677	Miscellaneous expenses	0	
168	Accumulated depreciation—Computer equipment		1,250	684	Repairs expense—Computer	0	
201	Accounts payable		1,100				

In response to requests from customers, S. Rey will begin selling computer software. The company will extend credit terms of 1/10, n/30, FOB shipping point, to all customers who purchase this merchandise. However, no cash discount is available on consulting fees. Additional accounts (Nos. 119, 413, 414, 415, and 502) are added to its general ledger to accommodate the company's new merchandising activities. Its transactions for January through March follow.

Jan. 4 The company paid cash to Lyn Addie for five days' work at the rate of $125 per day. Four of the five days relate to wages payable that were accrued in the prior year.

5 Santana Rey invested an additional $25,000 cash in the company.

7 The company purchased $5,800 of merchandise from Kansas Corp. with terms of 1/10, n/30, FOB shipping point, invoice dated January 7.

9 The company received $2,668 cash from Gomez Co. as full payment on its account.

11 The company completed a five-day project for Alex's Engineering Co. and billed it $5,500, which is the total price of $7,000 less the advance payment of $1,500. The company debited Unearned Computer Services Revenue for $1,500.

[continued on next page]

Alexander Image/Shutterstock

[continued from previous page]

13 The company sold merchandise with a retail value of $5,200 and a cost of $3,560 to Liu Corp., invoice dated January 13.
15 The company paid $600 cash for freight charges on the merchandise purchased on January 7.
16 The company received $4,000 cash from Delta Co. for computer services provided.
17 The company paid Kansas Corp. for the invoice dated January 7, net of the discount.
20 The company gave a price reduction (allowance) of $500 to Liu Corp. and credited Liu's accounts receivable for that amount.
22 The company received the balance due from Liu Corp., net of the discount and the allowance.
24 The company returned defective merchandise to Kansas Corp. and accepted a credit against future purchases (debited accounts payable). The defective merchandise invoice cost, net of the discount, was $496.
26 The company purchased $9,000 of merchandise from Kansas Corp. with terms of 1/10, n/30, FOB destination, invoice dated January 26.
26 The company sold merchandise with a $4,640 cost for $5,800 on credit to KC, Inc., invoice dated January 26.
31 The company paid cash to Lyn Addie for 10 days' work at $125 per day.
Feb. 1 The company paid $2,475 cash to Hillside Mall for another three months' rent in advance.
3 The company paid Kansas Corp. for the balance due, net of the cash discount, less the $496 credit from merchandise returned on January 24.
5 The company paid $600 cash to Facebook for an advertisement to appear on February 5 only.
11 The company received the balance due from Alex's Engineering Co. for fees billed on January 11.
15 S. Rey withdrew $4,800 cash from the company for personal use.
23 The company sold merchandise with a $2,660 cost for $3,220 on credit to Delta Co., invoice dated February 23.
26 The company paid cash to Lyn Addie for eight days' work at $125 per day.
27 The company reimbursed Santana Rey $192 cash for business automobile mileage. The company recorded the reimbursement as "Mileage Expense."
Mar. 8 The company purchased $2,730 of computer supplies from Harris Office Products on credit with terms of n/30, FOB destination, invoice dated March 8.
9 The company received the balance due from Delta Co. for merchandise sold on February 23.
11 The company paid $960 cash for minor repairs to the company's computer.
16 The company received $5,260 cash from Dream, Inc., for computing services provided.
19 The company paid the full amount due of $3,830 to Harris Office Products, consisting of amounts created on December 15 (of $1,100) and March 8.
24 The company billed Easy Leasing for $9,047 of computing services provided.
25 The company sold merchandise with a $2,002 cost for $2,800 on credit to Wildcat Services, invoice dated March 25.
30 The company sold merchandise with a $1,048 cost for $2,220 on credit to IFM Company, invoice dated March 30.
31 The company reimbursed Santana Rey $128 cash for business automobile mileage. The company recorded the reimbursement as "Mileage Expense."

The following additional facts are available for preparing adjustments on March 31 prior to financial statement preparation.

a. The March 31 amount of computer supplies still available totals $2,005.
b. Prepaid insurance coverage of $555 expired during this three-month period.
c. Lyn Addie has not been paid for seven days of work at the rate of $125 per day.
d. Prepaid rent of $2,475 expired during this three-month period.
e. Depreciation on the computer equipment for January 1 through March 31 is $1,250.
f. Depreciation on the office equipment for January 1 through March 31 is $400.
g. The March 31 amount of merchandise inventory still available totals $704.

Required

1. Prepare journal entries to record each of the January through March transactions.
2. Post the journal entries in part 1 to the accounts in the company's general ledger. *Note:* Begin with the ledger's post-closing adjusted balances as of December 31, 2021.
3. Prepare a 6-column work sheet (similar to the one shown in Exhibit 3.13) that includes the unadjusted trial balance, the March 31 adjustments (*a*) through (*g*), and the adjusted trial balance. Do not prepare closing entries and do not journalize the adjustments or post them to the ledger.

Check (2) Ending balances at March 31: Cash, $68,057; Sales, $19,240
(3) Unadj. TB totals, $151,557; Adj. TB totals, $154,082

4. Prepare an income statement (from the adjusted trial balance in part 3) for the three months ended March 31, 2022. (*a*) Use a single-step format. List all expenses without differentiating between selling expenses and general and administrative expenses. (*b*) Use a multiple-step format that begins with gross sales (service revenues plus gross product sales) and includes separate categories for net sales, cost of goods sold, selling expenses, and general and administrative expenses. Categorize the following accounts as selling expenses: Wages Expense, Mileage Expense, and Advertising Expense. Categorize the remaining expenses as general and administrative.

(4) Net income, $18,833

5. Prepare a statement of owner's equity (from the adjusted trial balance in part 3) for the three months ended March 31, 2022.
6. Prepare a classified balance sheet (from the adjusted trial balance) as of March 31, 2022.

(6) Total assets, $120,268

TABLEAU DASHBOARD ACTIVITIES

Tableau Dashboard Activities expose students to accounting analytics using visual displays. These assignments run in **Connect**. All are auto-gradable.

Tableau DA 5-1 Quick Study, Analyzing credit terms and computing gross profit, **C1, P1**—similar to QS 5-18

Tableau DA 5-2 Exercise, Analyzing credit terms and computing gross profit, **C1, P1**—similar to Exercise 5-17

Tableau DA 5-3 Mini-Case, Preparing a classified balance sheet, **P1, P4**—similar to Exercise 5-19

GENERAL LEDGER

connect

General Ledger (GL) Assignments For the following GL assignments, prepare journal entries highlighting the operating cycle of a merchandising company. A trial balance is automatically generated based on the journal entries recorded—this feature can be turned off.

GL 5-1 Based on Problem 5-1A

GL 5-2 Based on Problem 5-2A

GL 5-3 Based on Problem 5-5A

Accounting Analysis

connect

COMPANY ANALYSIS
A1

AA 5-1 Refer to **Apple**'s financial statements in Appendix A to answer the following.

Required

1. Assume that the amounts reported for inventories and cost of sales reflect items purchased in a form ready for resale. Compute the net cost of goods purchased for the year ended September 28, 2019.
2. Compute the current ratio and acid-test ratio as of September 28, 2019, and September 29, 2018. *Note:* Do not include vendor non-trade receivables with quick assets.
3. Does Apple's 2019 current ratio outperform or underperform the (assumed) industry average of 1.5?
4. Does Apple's 2019 acid-test ratio outperform or underperform the (assumed) industry average of 1.0?

COMPARATIVE ANALYSIS
A1

AA 5-2 Key comparative figures for **Apple** and **Google** follow.

	Apple		Google	
$ millions	Current Year	Prior Year	Current Year	Prior Year
Net sales	$260,174	$265,595	$161,857	$136,819
Cost of sales . . .	161,782	163,756	71,896	59,549

Required

1. Compute the amount of gross margin and the gross margin ratio for the two years shown for each of these companies.
2. Which company earns more in gross margin for each dollar of net sales for the current year?
3. Does the company's current-year gross margin underperform or outperform the 35% industry average in the case of (*a*) Apple and (*b*) Google?
4. Is the change in the company's current-year gross margin favorable or unfavorable for (*a*) Apple and (*b*) Google?

EXTENDED ANALYSIS
A1 P4

AA 5-3 Key comparative figures for **Samsung, Apple,** and **Google** follow.

$ millions	Samsung	Apple	Google
Net Sales	$197,691	$260,174	$161,857
Cost of Sales	126,336	161,782	71,896

Required

1. Compute the gross margin ratio for each of the three companies.
2. Is Samsung's gross margin ratio better or worse than that for (*a*) Apple? (*b*) Google?
3. Is the single-step or multiple-step income statement format used in the case of (*a*) Apple, (*b*) Google, and (*c*) Samsung?

Discussion Questions

1. What items appear in financial statements of merchandising companies but not in the statements of service companies?
2. In comparing the accounts of a merchandising company with those of a service company, what additional accounts would the merchandising company likely use, assuming it employs a perpetual inventory system?
3. Explain how a business can earn a positive gross profit on its sales and still have a net loss.
4. Why do companies offer a cash discount?
5. How does a company that uses a perpetual inventory system determine the amount of inventory shrinkage?
6. What is the difference between a sales discount and a purchases discount?
7. What is the difference between the single-step and multiple-step income statement formats?
8. Buyers negotiate purchase contracts with suppliers. What type of shipping terms should a buyer attempt to negotiate to minimize transportation costs?

Beyond the Numbers

ETHICS CHALLENGE
C1 P2

BTN 5-1 Amy Martin is a student who plans to attend approximately four professional events a year at her college. Each event necessitates payment of $100 to $200 for a new suit and accessories. After incurring a major hit to her savings for the first event, Amy develops a different approach. She buys the suit on credit the week before the event, wears it to the event, and returns it the next week to the store for a full refund on her charge card.

Required

1. Comment on the ethics exhibited by Amy and possible consequences of her actions.
2. How does the merchandising company account for the suits that Amy returns?

COMMUNICATING IN PRACTICE
C1 P3 P5

BTN 5-2 You are the financial officer for Music Plus, a retailer that sells goods for home entertainment needs. The business owner, Vic Velakturi, recently reviewed the annual financial statements you prepared and sent you an e-mail stating that he thinks you overstated net income. He explains that although he has invested a great deal in security, he is sure shoplifting and other forms of inventory shrinkage have occurred, but he does not see any deduction for shrinkage on the income statement. The store uses a perpetual inventory system.

Required

Prepare a brief memorandum that responds to the owner's concerns.

BTN 5-3 Official Brands's general ledger and supplementary records at the end of its current period reveal the following.

TEAMWORK IN ACTION

C1

Sales, gross	$600,000	Merchandise inventory (beginning of period)	$ 98,000
Sales returns & allowances	20,000	Invoice cost of merchandise purchases	360,000
Sales discounts	13,000	Purchases discounts received	9,000
Cost of transportation-in	22,000	Purchases returns and allowances	11,000
Operating expenses	50,000	Merchandise inventory (end of period)	84,000

Required

1. *Each* member of the team is to assume responsibility for computing *one* of the following items. You are not to duplicate your teammates' work. Get any necessary amounts to compute your item from the appropriate teammate. Each member is to explain his or her computation to the team in preparation for reporting to the class.
   a. Net sales
   b. Total cost of merchandise purchases
   c. Cost of goods sold
   d. Gross profit
   e. Net income
2. Check your net income with the instructor. If correct, proceed to step 3.
3. Assume that a physical inventory count finds that actual ending inventory is $76,000. Discuss how this affects previously computed amounts in step 1.

Point: In teams of four, assign the same student *a* and *e*. Rotate teams for reporting on a different computation and the analysis in step 3.

BTN 5-4 Refer to the opening feature about **Kendra Scott**. Assume the business reports current annual sales at approximately $1 million and prepares the following income statement.

ENTREPRENEURIAL DECISION

C1 P1

KENDRA SCOTT Income Statement For Current Year Ended December 31	
Net sales	$1,000,000
Cost of sales	610,000
Expenses (other than cost of sales)	200,000
Net income	$ 190,000

Assume the business sells to individuals and retailers, ranging from small shops to large chains. Assume that it currently offers credit terms of 1/15, n/60, and ships FOB destination. To improve its cash flow, it is considering changing credit terms to 3/10, n/30. In addition, it proposes to change shipping terms to FOB shipping point. It expects that the increase in discount rate will increase net sales by 9%, but the gross margin ratio (and ratio of cost of sales divided by net sales) is expected to remain unchanged. It also expects that delivery expenses will be zero under this proposal; thus, expenses other than cost of sales are expected to increase only 6%.

Required

1. Prepare a forecasted income statement for the *next* year ended December 31 based on the proposal.
2. Based on the forecasted income statement alone (from your part 1 solution), do you recommend that the business implement the new sales policies? Explain.
3. What else should the business consider before deciding whether to implement the new policies? Explain.

6 Inventories and Cost of Sales

Chapter Preview

INVENTORY BASICS	INVENTORY COSTING	INVENTORY VALUATION, ERRORS, AND ANALYSIS
C1 Determining inventory items	**P1** Inventory measurement:	**P2** Lower of cost or market
Determining inventory costs	Specific identification	**A2** Effects of inventory errors
Control of inventory	First-in, first-out	**A3** Inventory management
	Last-in, first-out	**P3** *Appendix:* Periodic system
	Weighted average	
	A1 Financial statements	
NTK 6-1	**NTK 6-2**	**NTK 6-3, 6-4**

Learning Objectives

CONCEPTUAL

C1 Identify the items and costs of merchandise inventory.

ANALYTICAL

A1 Analyze the effects of inventory methods for both financial and tax reporting.

A2 Analyze the effects of inventory errors on current and future financial statements.

A3 Assess inventory management using both inventory turnover and days' sales in inventory.

PROCEDURAL

P1 Compute inventory in a perpetual system using the methods of specific identification, FIFO, LIFO, and weighted average.

P2 Compute the lower of cost or market amount of inventory.

P3 *Appendix 6A*—Compute inventory in a periodic system using the methods of specific identification, FIFO, LIFO, and weighted average.

P4 *Appendix 6B*—Apply both the retail inventory and gross profit methods to estimate inventory.

Dream of Doing

"Humans are unbelievably data efficient"

—JEFF BEZOS

SEATTLE—Jeff Bezos, founder and CEO of **Amazon**, started the company in his garage. "The first initial start-up capital for Amazon.com came primarily from my parents, and they invested a large fraction of their life savings," recalls Jeff. "My dad's first question was, 'What's the Internet?' He wasn't making a bet on this company or this concept. He was making a bet on his son."

Jeff has grown Amazon from an online bookstore into one of the world's most valuable companies. Amazon's success is tied to several factors, including its accounting system and data analytics. Amazon is expanding its accounting system, using its sales and inventory accounting data to predict customer purchases and shipments before orders are placed.

While Jeff has been able to dominate the retail industry with accounting analytics, he has his sights set on groceries. With the acquisition of **Whole Foods**, Jeff has begun implementing the same accounting analytics to those stores.

To ensure fresh sourced produce at Whole Foods, Amazon set up an analytics-based inventory tracking system. Store managers receive inventory reports, often in the form of a **Tableau** Dashboard. The inventory system tracks all transactions and uses predictive analytics to identify which items to stock at which stores and when.

Sajjad Hussain/AFP/Getty Images

Jeff encourages young people to start businesses. He stresses the importance of accounting: "If you don't understand the details of your business, you are going to fail."

Sources: *Amazon website*, January 2021; *Biography.com*, January 2016; *Fundable*, June 2015; *GreenBiz*, August 2014; *Inc.com*, May 2014; *Bloomberg*, January 2013; *Wall Street Journal*, October 2011

INVENTORY BASICS

Determining Inventory Items

C1 Identify the items and costs of merchandise inventory.

Merchandise inventory includes all goods that a company owns and holds for sale. This is true regardless of where the goods are located when inventory is counted. Special attention is directed at goods in transit, goods on consignment, and goods that are damaged or obsolete.

Goods in Transit Does a buyer's inventory include goods in transit from a supplier? If ownership has passed to the buyer, the goods are included in the buyer's inventory. We determine this by reviewing shipping terms, which are illustrated in Exhibit 6.1.

- FOB shipping point—goods are included in buyer's inventory once they are shipped.
- FOB destination—goods are included in buyer's inventory after arrival at the destination.

EXHIBIT 6.1 Terms of Sale

Goods on Consignment Goods on consignment are goods sent by the owner, called the **consignor,** to another party, the **consignee.** A consignee sells goods for the owner. The consignor owns the consigned goods and reports them in its inventory. For example, **Upper Deck**

pays sports celebrities such as Russell Wilson of the Seattle Seahawks to sign memorabilia, which are offered to card shops on consignment. Upper Deck, the consignor, reports these items in its inventory until sold. The consignee *never* reports consigned goods in inventory.

Goods Damaged or Obsolete Damaged, obsolete (out-of-date), and deteriorated goods are not reported in inventory if they cannot be sold. If these goods can be sold at a lower price, they are included in inventory at **net realizable value.** Net realizable value is sales price minus the cost of making the sale. A loss is recorded when the damage or obsolescence occurs.

Determining Inventory Costs

Merchandise inventory includes costs to bring an item to a salable condition and location. Inventory costs include invoice cost minus any discount, plus any other costs. Other costs include shipping, storage, import duties, and insurance. The *expense recognition principle* says that inventory costs are expensed as cost of goods sold when inventory is sold.

Internal Controls and Taking a Physical Count

Fraud: Auditors observe employees as they count inventory. Auditors also take their own count to ensure accuracy.

Events can cause the Inventory account balance to be different than the actual inventory available. Such events include theft, loss, damage, and errors. Thus, nearly all companies take a *physical count of inventory* at least once each year. This physical count is used to adjust the Inventory account balance to the actual inventory available.

Decision Insight

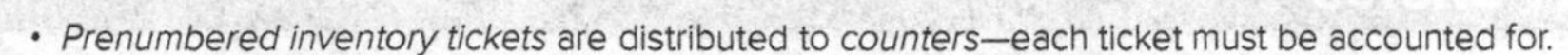

Peathegee Inc/Blend Images

Down for the Count A company applies internal controls when taking a physical count of inventory that usually include the following to minimize fraud and to increase reliability.

- *Prenumbered inventory tickets* are distributed to *counters*—each ticket must be accounted for.
- Counters of inventory are assigned and do not include those responsible for inventory.
- Counters confirm the existence, amount, and condition of inventory.
- A second count is taken by a different counter.
- A manager confirms all inventories are ticketed once, and only once. ■

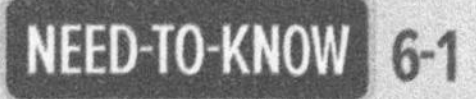

NEED-TO-KNOW 6-1

Inventory Items and Costs

C1

1. A master carver of wooden birds operates her business out of a garage. At the end of the current period, the carver has 17 units (carvings) in her garage, 3 of which were damaged by water and cannot be sold. She also has another 5 units in her truck, ready to deliver per a customer order, terms FOB destination, and another 11 units out on consignment at retail stores. How many units does she include in the business's period-end inventory?
2. A distributor of artistic iron-based fixtures acquires a piece for $1,000, terms FOB shipping point. Additional costs in obtaining it and offering it for sale include $150 for transportation-in, $300 for import duties, $100 for insurance during shipment, $200 for advertising, a $50 voluntary gratuity to the delivery person, $75 for enhanced store lighting, and $250 for sales staff salaries. For computing inventory, what cost is assigned to this artistic piece?

Solutions

1.

Units in ending inventory	
Units in storage	17 units
Less damaged (unsalable) units	(3)
Plus units in transit	5
Plus units on consignment	11
Total units in ending inventory	30 units

2.

Merchandise cost	$1,000
Plus:	
Transportation-in	150
Import duties	300
Insurance	100
Total inventory cost	$1,550

Do More: QS 6-1, QS 6-2, QS 6-3, E 6-1, E 6-2

INVENTORY COSTING UNDER A PERPETUAL SYSTEM

When identical items are purchased at different costs, we must decide which amounts to record in cost of goods sold (COGS) and which amounts remain in inventory. We describe four methods to assign costs to inventory and to cost of goods sold: (1) specific identification; (2) first-in, first-out (FIFO); (3) last-in, first-out (LIFO); and (4) weighted average.

Each method has a pattern for how costs flow through inventory. The cost flow assumption does not have to match the actual physical flow of goods. For example, **Kroger**'s grocery chain sells food first-in, first-out, meaning they sell the oldest food in inventory first. However, Kroger can use last-in, first-out to assign costs to food sold. With the exception of specific identification, the **physical flow and cost flow do not have to be the same.**

Inventory Cost Flow Methods

To show inventory cost flow methods, assume that three identical units are purchased separately at the following three dates and costs: May 1 at $45, May 3 at $65, and May 6 at $70. One unit is then sold on May 7 for $100. Exhibit 6.2 shows the flow of costs to either cost of goods sold on the income statement or inventory reported on the balance sheet for FIFO, LIFO, and weighted average.

EXHIBIT 6.2
Cost Flow Methods

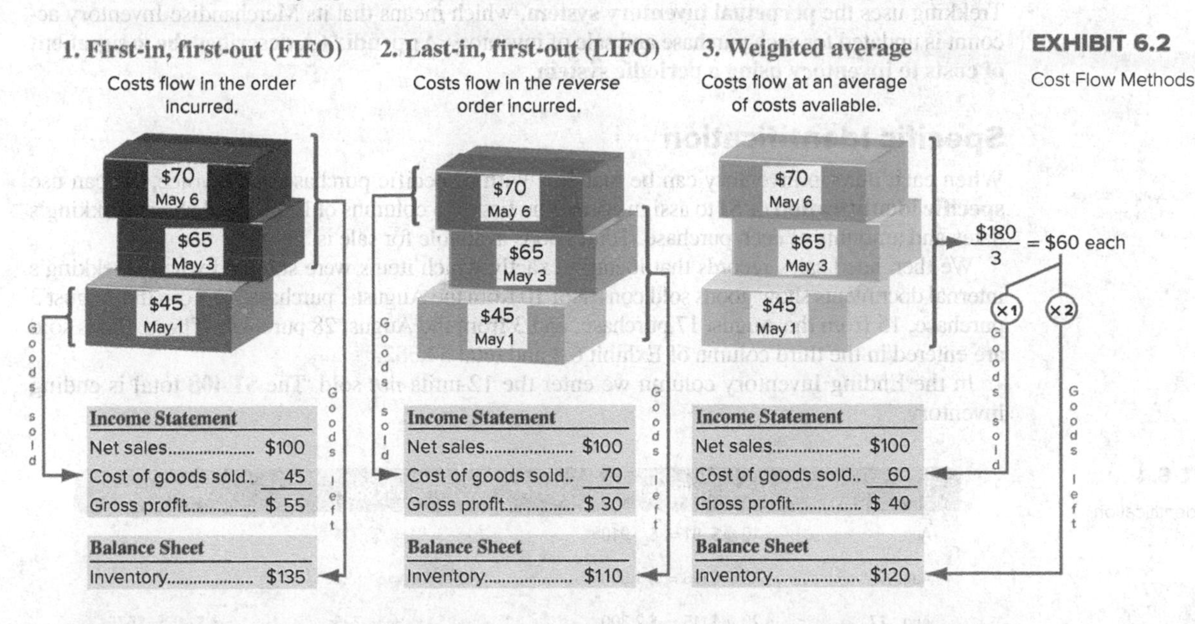

(1) *FIFO assumes costs flow in the order incurred.* The unit purchased on May 1 for $45 is the earliest cost incurred—it is sent to cost of goods sold on the income statement first. The remaining two units ($65 and $70) are reported in inventory on the balance sheet.

(2) *LIFO assumes costs flow in the reverse order incurred.* The unit purchased on May 6 for $70 is the most recent cost incurred—it is sent to cost of goods sold on the income statement. The remaining two units ($45 and $65) are reported in inventory on the balance sheet.

(3) *Weighted average assumes costs flow at an average of the costs available.* The units available at the May 7 sale average $60 in cost, computed as ($45 + $65 + $70)/3. One unit's $60 average cost is sent to cost of goods sold on the income statement. The remaining two units' average costs are reported in inventory at $120 on the balance sheet.

Cost flow methods impact gross profit and inventory numbers. Exhibit 6.2 shows that gross profit ranges from $30 to $55 due to the cost flow method.

Point: Recall inventory cost flow.

Beginning inventory + Net purchases
= Merchandise available for sale
Ending inventory + Cost of goods sold

The following sections on inventory costing use the *perpetual system*. Appendix 6A uses the periodic system. An instructor can choose to cover either one or both systems. If the perpetual system is skipped, then read Appendix 6A and return to the "Valuing Inventory at LCM and the Effects of Inventory Errors" section.

Inventory Costing Illustration

P1 Compute inventory in a perpetual system using the methods of specific identification, FIFO, LIFO, and weighted average.

This section demonstrates inventory costing methods. We use information from Trekking, a sporting goods store. Among its products, Trekking sells one type of mountain bike whose sales are directed at resorts that provide inexpensive bikes for guest use. We use Trekking's data from August. Its mountain bike (unit) inventory at the beginning of August and its purchases and sales during August are in Exhibit 6.3. It ends August with 12 bikes in inventory.

EXHIBIT 6.3 Purchases and Sales of Goods

Warut Chinsai/Shutterstock

Date	Activity	Units Acquired at Cost	Units Sold at Retail	Unit Inventory
Aug. 1	Beginning inventory........	10 units @ $ 91 = $ 910		10 units
Aug. 3	Purchases..............	15 units @ $106 = $ 1,590		25 units
Aug. 14	Sales..................		20 units @ $130	5 units
Aug. 17	Purchases..............	20 units @ $115 = $ 2,300		25 units
Aug. 28	Purchases..............	10 units @ $119 = $ 1,190		35 units
Aug. 30	Sales..................		23 units @ $150	**12 units**
	Totals................	**55 units** **$5,990**	**43 units**	
		Units available for sale; Goods available for sale	Units sold	Units left

Trekking uses the **perpetual inventory system**, which means that its Merchandise Inventory account is updated for each purchase and sale of inventory. **Appendix 6A describes the assignment of costs to inventory using a periodic system.**

Specific Identification

Point: Specific identification is common for custom-made inventory such as jewelry.

When each item in inventory can be matched with a specific purchase and invoice, we can use **specific identification** or **SI** to assign costs. The first two columns of Exhibit 6.4 show Trekking's dates and amounts of each purchase. Total goods available for sale is **$5,990.**

We then need sales records that identify exactly which items were sold and when. Trekking's internal documents show goods sold consist of 10 from the August 1 purchase, 15 from the August 3 purchase, 15 from the August 17 purchase, and 3 from the August 28 purchase. These goods sold are entered in the third column of Exhibit 6.4 and total **$4,582.**

In the Ending Inventory column we enter the 12 units *not* sold. The **$1,408** total is ending inventory.

EXHIBIT 6.4 Specific Identification

Date	Goods Available for Sale	Cost of Goods Sold	Ending Inventory
Aug. 1	10 @ $ 91 = $ 910	10 @ $ 91 = $ 910	
Aug. 3	15 @ $106 = $ 1,590	15 @ $106 = $1,590	
Aug. 17	20 @ $115 = $ 2,300	15 @ $115 = $1,725	5 @ $115 = $575
Aug. 28	10 @ $119 = $ 1,190	3 @ $119 = $ 357	7 @ $119 = $833
	$5,990	43 $4,582	12 = $1,408

Trekking's cost of goods sold reported on the income statement is **$4,582**, and ending inventory reported on the balance sheet is **$1,408**. The following graphic shows this flow of costs.

Trekking Bikes

SI Inventory $1,408

SI COGS $4,582

FIRST Bought

LAST Bought

Point: SI yields identical results under both periodic and perpetual.

First-In, First-Out

First-in, first-out (FIFO) assumes that inventory items are sold in the order acquired. When sales occur, the costs of the earliest units acquired are charged to cost of goods sold. This leaves the costs from the most recent purchases in ending inventory.

Exhibit 6.5 starts with beginning inventory of 10 bikes at $91 each.

Aug. 3 Purchased 15 bikes costing $106 each. We update the Inventory Balance column to consist of 10 bikes at $91 each *and* 15 bikes at $106 each.

Aug. 14 Sold 20 bikes. Using FIFO, we enter in the Cost of Goods Sold column the *first* 10 sold at the earliest cost of $91 each and the next 10 sold at a cost of $106 each. In the Inventory Balance column we enter the 5 *not* sold costing $106 each.

Aug. 17 Purchased 20 bikes costing $115 each. We add these to the Inventory Balance column.

Aug. 28 Purchased 10 bikes at $119 each. We add these to the Inventory Balance column.

Aug. 30 Sold 23 bikes. Using FIFO, in the Cost of Goods Sold column we enter the 23 bikes purchased *first*: 5 at $106 and then 18 at $115. This leaves 12 bikes costing $1,420 in ending inventory.

EXHIBIT 6.5

FIFO—Perpetual

Date	Goods Purchased	Cost of Goods Sold		Inventory Balance	
Aug. 1	Beginning balance			10 @ $ 91	= $ 910
Aug. 3	15 @ $106 = $1,590			10 @ $ 91 15 @ $106	= $ 2,500
Aug. 14		10 @ $ 91 = $ 910 10 @ $106 = $1,060	= $1,970	5 @ $106	= $ 530
Aug. 17	20 @ $115 = $2,300			5 @ $106 20 @ $115	= $ 2,830
Aug. 28	10 @ $119 = $1,190			5 @ $106 20 @ $115 10 @ $119	= $ 4,020
Aug. 30		5 @ $106 = $ 530 18 @ $115 = $2,070	= $2,600	2 @ $115 10 @ $119	= $1,420
			$4,570		

Merchandise Inventory (FIFO)

Debit		Credit	
Aug. 1	910		
Aug. 3	1,590		
		Aug. 14	1,970
Aug. 17	2,300		
Aug. 28	1,190		
		Aug. 30	2,600
Aug. 31	1,420		

The **$4,570** total in cost of good sold is reported on the income statement. The ending inventory of **$1,420** from the Inventory Balance column is reported on the balance sheet.

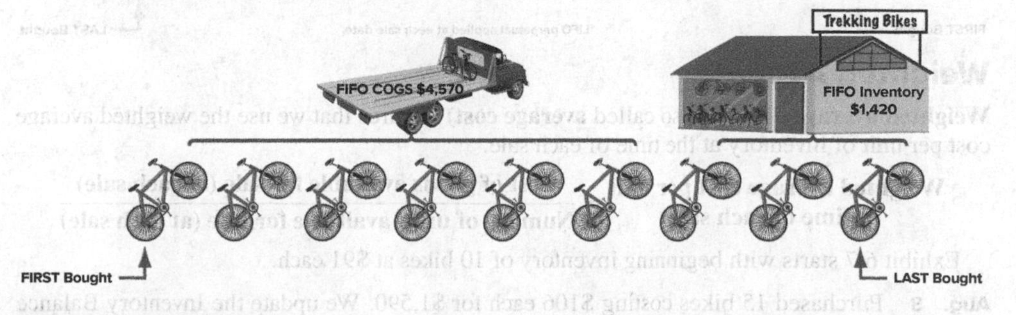

Point: For FIFO, the COGS and ending inventory are the same for periodic and perpetual.

Last-In, First-Out

Last-in, first-out (LIFO) assumes that the most recent purchases are sold first. These more recent costs are charged to the goods sold, and the costs of the earliest purchases are assigned to inventory.

Exhibit 6.6 starts with beginning inventory of 10 bikes at $91 each.

Aug. 3 Purchased 15 bikes costing $106 each. We update the Inventory Balance column to consist of 10 bikes at $91 each *and* 15 bikes at $106 each.

Aug. 14 Sold 20 bikes. Using LIFO, we enter in the Cost of Goods Sold column the 20 sold, *beginning with last units purchased:* 15 sold from the most recent purchase at $106 each, and the next 5 sold from the next most recent purchase at $91 each. In the Inventory Balance column we enter the 5 *not* sold at a cost of $91 each.

Aug. 17 Purchased 20 bikes costing $115 each. We add these to the Inventory Balance column.

Aug. 28 Purchased 10 bikes at $119 each. We add these to the Inventory Balance column.

Aug. 30 Sold 23 bikes. Using LIFO, in the Cost of Goods Sold column we enter the 23 bikes purchased *last*: 10 at $119 and then 13 at $115. This leaves 12 bikes costing $1,260 in ending inventory.

EXHIBIT 6.6

LIFO—Perpetual

Date	Goods Purchased	Cost of Goods Sold		Inventory Balance	
Aug. 1	Beginning balance			10 @ $ 91	= $ 910
Aug. 3	15 @ $106 = $1,590			10 @ $ 91 15 @ $106	= $ 2,500
Aug. 14		15 @ $106 = $1,590 5 @ $ 91 = $ 455	= $2,045	5 @ $ 91	= $ 455
Aug. 17	20 @ $115 = $2,300			5 @ $ 91 20 @ $115	= $ 2,755
Aug. 28	10 @ $119 = $1,190			5 @ $ 91 20 @ $115 10 @ $119	= $ 3,945
Aug. 30		10 @ $119 = $1,190 13 @ $115 = $1,495	= $2,685	5 @ $ 91 7 @ $115	= $1,260
			$4,730		

Merchandise Inventory (LIFO)

Debit		Credit	
Aug. 1	910		
Aug. 3	1,590		
		Aug. 14	2,045
Aug. 17	2,300		
Aug. 28	1,190		
		Aug. 30	2,685
Aug. 31	1,260		

The **$4,730** total in cost of good sold is reported on the income statement. The ending inventory of **$1,260** from the Inventory Balance column is reported on the balance sheet.

Trekking Bikes

LIFO Inventory $1,260

*LIFO COGS $4,730

FIRST Bought

*LIFO perpetual applied at each sale date.

LAST Bought

Weighted Average

Weighted average or **WA** (also called **average cost**) requires that we use the weighted average cost per unit of inventory at the time of each sale.

$$\textbf{Weighted average cost per unit at time of each sale} = \frac{\textbf{Cost of goods available for sale (at each sale)}}{\textbf{Number of units available for sale (at each sale)}}$$

Exhibit 6.7 starts with beginning inventory of 10 bikes at $91 each.

Aug. 3 Purchased 15 bikes costing $106 each for $1,590. We update the Inventory Balance column to consist of 10 bikes at $91 each and 15 bikes at $106 each. The *average cost* per bike for that inventory is $100, computed as $2,500/(10 bikes + 15 bikes).

Aug. 14 Sold 20 bikes. Applying WA, the 20 sold are assigned the $100 average cost. This leaves 5 bikes with an average cost of $100 each in inventory.

Aug. 17 Purchased 20 bikes at $115 each. We add these to the Inventory Balance column. The *average cost* per bike is now $112.

Aug. 28 Purchased 10 bikes at $119 each. We add these to the Inventory Balance column. The *average cost* per bike is now $114, computed as $3,990 / 35 bikes.

Aug. 30 Sold 23 bikes. Applying WA, the 23 sold are assigned the $114 average cost. This leaves 12 bikes costing $1,368 in ending inventory.

EXHIBIT 6.7

Weighted Average—Perpetual

Date	Goods Purchased	Cost of Goods Sold	Inventory Balance
Aug. 1	Beginning balance		10 @ $ 91 = $ 910 (10 @ $ 91 per unit)
Aug. 3	15 @ $106 = $1,590		10 @ $ 91 15 @ $106 } = $2,500 (25 @ $100 per unit)[a]
Aug. 14		20 @ $100 = $2,000	5 @ $100 = $ 500 (5 @ $100 per unit)[b]
Aug. 17	20 @ $115 = $2,300		5 @ $100 20 @ $115 } = $2,800 (25 @ $112 per unit)[c]
Aug. 28	10 @ $119 = $1,190		25 @ $112 10 @ $119 } = $3,990 (35 @ $114 per unit)[d]
Aug. 30		23 @ $114 = $2,622	12 @ $114 = $1,368 (12 @ $114 per unit)[e]
		$4,622	

[a]$100 per unit = ($2,500 inventory balance ÷ 25 units in inventory).
[b]$100 per unit = ($500 inventory balance ÷ 5 units in inventory).
[c]$112 per unit = ($2,800 inventory balance ÷ 25 units in inventory).
[d]$114 per unit = ($3,990 inventory balance ÷ 35 units in inventory).
[e]$114 per unit = ($1,368 inventory balance ÷ 12 units in inventory).

Merchandise Inventory (WA)

Aug. 1	910		
Aug. 3	1,590		
		Aug. 14	2,000
Aug. 17	2,300		
Aug. 28	1,190		
		Aug. 30	2,622
Aug. 31	1,368		

The **$4,622** total in cost of good sold is reported on the income statement. The ending inventory of **$1,368** from the Inventory Balance column is reported on the balance sheet.

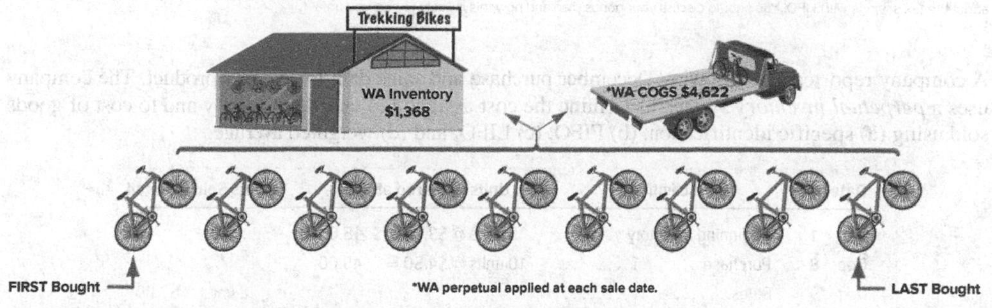

Financial Statement Effects of Costing Methods

A1 Analyze the effects of inventory methods for both financial and tax reporting.

When purchase prices do not change, each inventory costing method assigns the same cost amounts to inventory and to cost of goods sold. When purchase prices are different, the methods assign different cost amounts. We show these differences in Exhibit 6.8 using Trekking's data.

Rising Costs When purchase costs *regularly rise,* as in Trekking's case, the following occurs.

- FIFO reports the lowest cost of goods sold—yielding the highest gross profit and net income.
- LIFO reports the highest cost of goods sold—yielding the lowest gross profit and net income.
- Weighted average yields results between FIFO and LIFO.

EXHIBIT 6.8

Financial Statement Effects of Inventory Costing Methods

Trekking Company For Month Ended August 31	Specific Identification	FIFO	LIFO	Weighted Average
Income Statement				
Sales	$ 6,050	$ 6,050	$ 6,050	$ 6,050
Cost of goods sold	4,582	4,570	4,730	4,622
Gross profit	$ 1,468	$ 1,480	$ 1,320	$ 1,428
Balance Sheet				
Inventory	$1,408	$1,420	$1,260	$1,368

Falling Costs When costs *regularly decline,* the reverse occurs for FIFO and LIFO.

- FIFO gives the highest cost of goods sold—yielding the lowest gross profit and net income.
- LIFO gives the lowest cost of goods sold—yielding the highest gross profit and net income.

Method Advantages Each method offers advantages.

- FIFO—inventory on the balance sheet approximates its current cost; it also follows the actual flow of goods for most businesses.
- LIFO—cost of goods sold on the income statement approximates its current cost; it also better matches current costs with revenues.
- Weighted average—smooths out erratic changes in costs.
- Specific identification—matches the costs of items with the revenues they generate.

Point: LIFO inventory is often less than the inventory's replacement cost because LIFO inventory is valued using the oldest inventory purchase costs.

Tax Effects of Costing Methods

Inventory costs affect net income and have potential tax effects. Exhibit 6.8 shows that Trekking gains a temporary tax advantage by using LIFO because it has less income to be taxed. Many companies use LIFO for this reason. The IRS requires that when LIFO is used for tax reporting, it also must be used for financial reporting—called *LIFO conformity rule.*

Decision Ethics

Caia Image/Image Source

Inventory Manager Your compensation as inventory manager includes a bonus plan based on gross profit. Your superior asks your opinion on changing the inventory costing method from FIFO to LIFO. As costs are expected to continue to rise, your superior predicts that LIFO would match higher current costs against sales, thereby lowering taxable income (and gross profit). What do you recommend? ■ *Answer:* It seems your company can save (or at least postpone) taxes by switching to LIFO, but the switch is likely to reduce bonus money that you believe you have earned and deserve. Your best decision is to tell your superior about the tax savings with LIFO. You should discuss your bonus plan and how this is likely to hurt you unfairly.

Perpetual SI, FIFO, LIFO, and WA

P1

A company reported the following December purchase and sales data for its only product. The company uses a *perpetual inventory system.* Determine the cost assigned to ending inventory and to cost of goods sold using (a) specific identification, (b) FIFO, (c) LIFO, and (d) weighted average.

Date	Activities	Units Acquired at Cost		Units Sold at Retail
Dec. 1	Beginning inventory	5 units @ $3.00 =	$ 15.00	
Dec. 8	Purchase	10 units @ $4.50 =	45.00	
Dec. 9	Sales....................			8 units @ $7.00
Dec. 19	Purchase	13 units @ $5.00 =	65.00	
Dec. 24	Sales....................			18 units @ $8.00
Dec. 30	Purchase	8 units @ $5.30 =	42.40	
Totals	....	36 units	$167.40	26 units

For specific identification, ending inventory consists of 10 units, where 8 are from the December 30 purchase and 2 are from the December 8 purchase.

Solutions

a. Specific identification.

Date	Goods Available for Sale	Cost of Goods Sold		Ending Inventory	
Dec. 1	5 units @ $3.00 = $ 15.00	5 units @ $3.00 = $ 15.00			
Dec. 8	10 units @ $4.50 = $ 45.00	8 units @ $4.50 = $ 36.00		2 units @ $4.50 = $ 9.00	
Dec. 19	13 units @ $5.00 = $ 65.00	13 units @ $5.00 = $ 65.00			
Dec. 30	8 units @ $5.30 = $ 42.40			8 units @ $5.30 = $42.40	
	$167.40	26	$116.00	10	$51.40

b. FIFO—Perpetual.

Date	Goods Purchased	Cost of Goods Sold	Inventory Balance
Dec. 1			5 @ $3.00 = $ 15.00
Dec. 8	10 @ $4.50		5 @ $3.00 10 @ $4.50 } = $ 60.00
Dec. 9		5 @ $3.00 3 @ $4.50 } = $ 28.50	7 @ $4.50 = $ 31.50
Dec. 19	13 @ $5.00		7 @ $4.50 13 @ $5.00 } = $ 96.50
Dec. 24		7 @ $4.50 11 @ $5.00 } = $ 86.50	2 @ $5.00 = $ 10.00
Dec. 30	8 @ $5.30		2 @ $5.00 8 @ $5.30 } = **$52.40**
		$115.00	

Merchandise Inventory (FIFO)

	Debit		Credit
Beg. inventory	15.00		
Dec. 8	45.00		
		Dec. 9	28.50
Dec. 19	65.00		
		Dec. 24	86.50
Dec. 30	42.40		
End. inventory	52.40		

c. LIFO—Perpetual.

Date	Goods Purchased	Cost of Goods Sold	Inventory Balance
Dec. 1			5 @ $3.00 = $ 15.00
Dec. 8	10 @ $4.50		5 @ $3.00 10 @ $4.50 } = $ 60.00
Dec. 9		8 @ $4.50 = $ 36.00	5 @ $3.00 2 @ $4.50 } = $ 24.00
Dec. 19	13 @ $5.00		5 @ $3.00 2 @ $4.50 13 @ $5.00 } = $ 89.00
Dec. 24		13 @ $5.00 2 @ $4.50 3 @ $3.00 } = $ 83.00	2 @ $3.00 = $ 6.00
Dec. 30	8 @ $5.30		2 @ $3.00 8 @ $5.30 } = **$48.40**
		$119.00	

Merchandise Inventory (LIFO)

	Debit		Credit
Beg. inventory	15.00		
Dec. 8	45.00		
		Dec. 9	36.00
Dec. 19	65.00		
		Dec. 24	83.00
Dec. 30	42.40		
End. inventory	48.40		

d. Weighted Average—Perpetual.

Date	Goods Purchased	Cost of Goods Sold	Inventory Balance
Dec. 1			5 @ $3.00 = $15.00 (5 @ $3.00 per unit)
Dec. 8	10 @ $4.50		5 @ $3.00 10 @ $4.50 } = $60.00 ($60.00/15 units = $4.00 avg. cost)
Dec. 9		8 @ $4.00 = $ 32.00	7 @ $4.00 = $28.00 (7 @ $4.00 per unit)
Dec. 19	13 @ $5.00		7 @ $4.00 13 @ $5.00 } = $93.00 ($93.00/20 units = $4.65 avg. cost)
Dec. 24		18 @ $4.65 = $ 83.70	2 @ $4.65 = $ 9.30 (2 @ $4.65 per unit)
Dec. 30	8 @ $5.30		2 @ $4.65 8 @ $5.30 } = **$51.70** ($51.70/10 units = $5.17 avg. cost)
		$115.70	

Merchandise Inventory (WA)

	Debit		Credit
Beg. inventory	15.00		
Dec. 8	45.00		
		Dec. 9	32.00
Dec. 19	65.00		
		Dec. 24	83.70
Dec. 30	42.40		
End. inventory	51.70		

Do More: QS 6-5, QS 6-6, QS 6-7, QS 6-11, QS 6-12, QS 6-13, QS 6-14, E 6-3, E 6-5

VALUING INVENTORY AT LCM AND ANALYZING INVENTORY ERRORS

Lower of Cost or Market

P2 Compute the lower of cost or market amount of inventory.

After companies apply one of four costing methods (FIFO, LIFO, weighted average, or specific identification), inventory is reviewed to ensure it is reported at the **lower of cost or market (LCM).**

Computing the Lower of Cost or Market *Market* in the term *LCM* is *replacement cost* for LIFO, but *net realizable value* for the other three methods—advanced courses cover specifics. A decline in market value means a loss of value in inventory. When market value is lower than cost of inventory, a loss is recorded. When market value is higher than cost of inventory, no adjustment is made.

Point: LCM applied to each individual item always yields the lowest inventory.

LCM is applied in one of three ways: (1) to each individual item separately, (2) to major categories of items, or (3) to the whole of inventory. With the increasing use of technology and inventory tracking, companies increasingly apply LCM to each individual item separately. Accordingly, we show that method only; advanced courses cover other methods. To demonstrate LCM, we apply it to the ending inventory of a motorsports retailer in Exhibit 6.9.

EXHIBIT 6.9

Lower of Cost or Market Computations

Inventory Items	Units	Per Unit Cost	Per Unit Market	Total Cost	Total Market	LCM Applied to Items
Roadster......	20	$8,500	$7,000	$170,000	$140,000	$ 140,000
Sprint.........	10	5,000	6,000	50,000	60,000	50,000
Totals........				$220,000		$190,000

$140,000 is the lower of $170,000 or $140,000.

$190,000 is lower than $220,000 recorded cost.

For Roadster, $140,000 is the lower of the $170,000 cost and the $140,000 market. For Sprint, $50,000 is the lower of the $50,000 cost and the $60,000 market. This yields a $190,000 reported inventory, computed from $140,000 for Roadster plus $50,000 for Sprint.

Recording the Lower of Cost or Market Inventory is adjusted downward when total "LCM applied to items" is less than total cost of inventory. To demonstrate, if LCM is applied in Exhibit 6.9, the Merchandise Inventory account must be adjusted from the $220,000 recorded cost down to the $190,000 LCM amount as follows.

	Debit	Credit
Cost of Goods Sold..............................	30,000	
Merchandise Inventory........................		30,000
Adjust inventory cost to market.		

NEED-TO-KNOW 6-3

LCM Method

P2

A company has the following products in its ending inventory, along with cost and market values. (a) Compute the lower of cost or market for its inventory when applied *separately to each product.* (b) If the market amount is less than the recorded cost of the inventory, then record the December 31 LCM adjustment to the Merchandise Inventory account.

	Units	Cost per Unit	Market per Unit
Road bikes	5	$1,000	$800
Mountain bikes..........	4	500	600
Town bikes	10	400	450

Solution

a.

Inventory Items	Units	Cost per Unit	Market per Unit	Total Cost	Total Market	LCM Items
Road bikes	5	$1,000	$800	$ 5,000	$4,000	$ 4,000
Mountain bikes...............	4	500	600	2,000	2,400	2,000
Town bikes	10	400	450	4,000	4,500	4,000
Totals......................				$11,000		$ 10,000
LCM applied to each product....						$10,000

b.

Dec. 31	Cost of Goods Sold..............................	1,000	
	Merchandise Inventory.......................		1,000
	Adjust inventory cost to market ($11,000 – $10,000).		

Do More: QS 6-23, E 6-16, P 6-5

Financial Statement Effects of Inventory Errors

A2 Analyze the effects of inventory errors on current and future financial statements.

An inventory error causes misstatements in cost of goods sold, gross profit, net income, current assets, and equity. It also causes misstatements in the next period's statements because ending inventory of one period is the beginning inventory of the next. As we consider financial statement effects, we recall the following ***inventory relation.***

Income Statement Effects Exhibit 6.10 shows the effects of inventory errors in the current and next period's income statements.

- **Row 1, Year 1.** Understating ending inventory overstates cost of goods sold. This is because we subtract a smaller ending inventory in computing cost of goods sold. A higher cost of goods sold yields a lower income.
- **Row 1, Year 2.** Understated ending inventory for Year 1 becomes an understated beginning inventory for Year 2. If beginning inventory is understated, cost of goods sold is understated (because we are starting with a smaller amount). A lower cost of goods sold yields a higher income.
- **Row 2, Year 1.** Overstating ending inventory understates cost of goods sold. A lower cost of goods sold yields a higher income.
- **Row 2, Year 2.** Overstated ending inventory for Year 1 becomes an overstated beginning inventory for Year 2. If beginning inventory is overstated, cost of goods sold is overstated. A higher cost of goods sold yields a lower income.

EXHIBIT 6.10

Effects of Inventory Errors on the Income Statement

	Year 1		Year 2	
Ending Inventory	Cost of Goods Sold	Net Income	Cost of Goods Sold	Net Income
Understated ↓	Overstated ↑	Understated ↓	Understated ↓	Overstated ↑
Overstated ↑	Understated ↓	Overstated ↑	Overstated ↑	Understated ↓

Inventory Error Example Consider an inventory error for a company with $100,000 in sales for each of Year 1, Year 2, and Year 3. If this company has a steady $20,000 inventory level and makes $60,000 in purchases in each year, its cost of goods sold is $60,000 and its gross profit is $40,000.

Year 1 Impact Assume the company makes an error in computing its Year 1 ending inventory and reports $16,000 instead of the correct amount of $20,000. The effects of this error are in Exhibit 6.11. The $4,000 understatement of Year 1 ending inventory causes a $4,000 overstatement in Year 1 cost of goods sold and a $4,000 understatement in both gross profit and net income for Year 1.

EXHIBIT 6.11

Effects of Inventory Errors on Three Periods' Income Statements

Income Statements	Year 1		Year 2		Year 3	
Sales		$100,000		$100,000		$100,000
Cost of goods sold						
Beginning inventory	$20,000		$16,000*		$20,000	
Cost of goods purchased	60,000		60,000		60,000	
Goods available for sale	80,000		76,000		80,000	
Ending inventory	16,000*		20,000		20,000	
Cost of goods sold		64,000†		56,000†		60,000
Gross profit		36,000		44,000		40,000
Expenses		10,000		10,000		10,000
Net income		$ 26,000		$ 34,000		$ 30,000

*Correct amount is $20,000. †Correct amount is $60,000. Correct income is $30,000 for each year.

Example: If Year 1 ending inventory in Exhibit 6.11 is overstated by $3,000, cost of goods sold is understated by $3,000 in Year 1 and overstated by $3,000 in Year 2. Net income is overstated in Year 1 and understated in Year 2. Assets and equity are overstated in Year 1.

Year 2 Impact The Year 1 understated ending inventory becomes the Year 2 understated beginning inventory. This error causes an understatement in Year 2 cost of goods sold and a $4,000 overstatement in both gross profit and net income for Year 2.

Year 3 Impact The Year 1 understated ending inventory affects only that period and the next. It does not affect Year 3 results or any period thereafter.

Balance Sheet Effects Understating ending inventory understates both current and total assets. An understatement in ending inventory also yields an understatement in equity because of the understatement in net income. Exhibit 6.12 shows the effects of inventory errors on the current period's balance sheet amounts.

EXHIBIT 6.12

Effects of Inventory Errors on Current Period's Balance Sheet

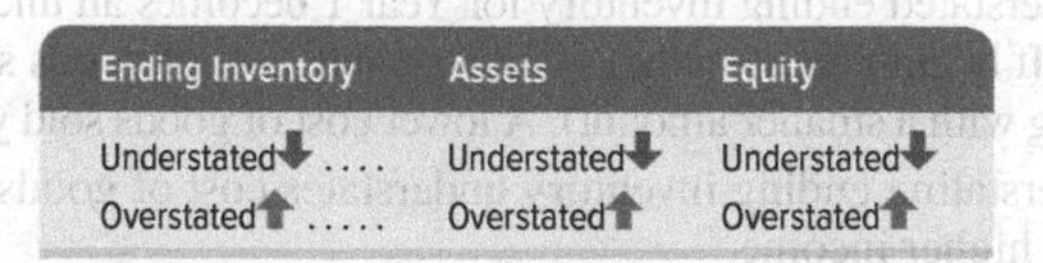

Ending Inventory	Assets	Equity
Understated ↓	Understated ↓	Understated ↓
Overstated ↑	Overstated ↑	Overstated ↑

Konstantin Inozemtsev/E+/Getty Images

Ethical Risk

Eyes in the Sky One of the largest builders, **Homex**, was accused of faking the construction and sale of 100,000 homes. How was it caught? When the SEC used satellite imagery to confirm the existence of homes, it found nothing but bare soil. SEC 2017-60 ■

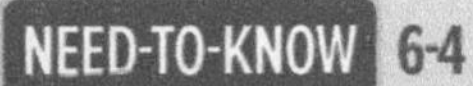

NEED-TO-KNOW 6-4

Effects of Inventory Errors

A2

A company had $10,000 of sales, and it purchased merchandise costing $7,000 in each of Year 1, Year 2, and Year 3. It also maintained a $2,000 physical inventory from the beginning to the end of that three-year period. In accounting for inventory, it made an error at the end of Year 1 that caused its Year 1 ending inventory to appear on its statements as $1,600 rather than the correct $2,000. (a) Determine the correct amount of the company's gross profit in each of Year 1, Year 2, and Year 3. (b) Prepare comparative income statements as in Exhibit 6.11 to show the effect of this error on the company's cost of goods sold and gross profit for each of Year 1, Year 2, and Year 3.

Solution

a. Correct gross profit = \$10,000 − \$7,000 = \$3,000 (for each year).

b. Cost of goods sold and gross profit figures follow.

	Year 1		Year 2		Year 3	
Sales		\$10,000		\$10,000		\$10,000
Cost of goods sold						
Beginning inventory	\$2,000		→\$1,600		→\$2,000	
Cost of purchases	7,000		7,000		7,000	
Goods available for sale	9,000		8,600		9,000	
Ending inventory	1,600		2,000		2,000	
Cost of goods sold		7,400		6,600		7,000
Gross profit		\$ 2,600		\$ 3,400		\$ 3,000

Do More: QS 6-24, E 6-17, P 6-6

Inventory Turnover and Days' Sales in Inventory  **Decision Analysis**

Inventory Turnover

Inventory turnover, also called *merchandise inventory turnover,* is defined in Exhibit 6.13. Inventory turnover tells how many *times* a company turns over (sells) its inventory in a period. It is used to assess whether management is doing a good job controlling the amount of inventory. A low ratio means the company may have more inventory than it needs or is struggling to sell inventory. A very high ratio means inventory might be too low. This can cause lost sales if customers must back-order merchandise. Inventory turnover has no simple rule except to say *a high ratio is preferable if inventory is adequate to meet demand.*

A3 Assess inventory management using both inventory turnover and days' sales in inventory

$$\textbf{Inventory turnover} = \frac{\textbf{Cost of goods sold}}{\textbf{Average inventory}}$$

EXHIBIT 6.13
Inventory Turnover

Days' Sales in Inventory

Days' sales in inventory is a ratio that shows how much inventory is available in terms of the number of days' sales. It can be interpreted as the number of days one can sell from existing inventory if no new items are purchased. This ratio reveals the buffer against out-of-stock inventory and is useful in evaluating how quickly inventory is being sold. It is defined in Exhibit 6.14. Days' sales in inventory uses *ending* inventory, whereas inventory turnover uses *average* inventory.

$$\textbf{Days' sales in inventory} = \frac{\textbf{Ending inventory}}{\textbf{Cost of goods sold}} \times 365$$

EXHIBIT 6.14
Days' Sales in Inventory

Analysis of Inventory Management

We apply the analysis tools in this section to **Costco** and **Walmart**, as shown in Exhibit 6.15. Costco's current year inventory turnover of 11.8 times means that it turns over its inventory 11.8 times per year. Costco's inventory turnover exceeded Walmart's turnover in each of the last three years. This is a positive for Costco, as we prefer inventory turnover to be high provided inventory is not out of stock and the company is not losing customers. Days' sales in inventory of 31.3 days means that Costco is carrying 31.3 days of sales in inventory. This inventory buffer seems sufficient. As long as Costco is not at risk of running out of stock, it prefers its assets not be tied up in inventory.

Point: Take care when comparing turnover ratios across companies that use different costing methods (such as FIFO and LIFO).

EXHIBIT 6.15

Inventory Turnover and Days' Sales in Inventory for Costco and Walmart

Company	Figure ($ millions)	Current Year	1 Year Ago	2 Years Ago
Costco	Cost of goods sold	$132,886	$123,152	$111,882
	Ending inventory	$ 11,395	$ 11,040	$ 9,834
	Inventory turnover........	**11.8 times**	**11.8 times**	**11.9 times**
	Days' sales in inventory	**31.3 days**	**32.7 days**	**32.1 days**
Walmart	Inventory turnover.........	8.8 times	8.6 times	8.3 times
	Days' sales in inventory	41.9 days	42.8 days	43.5 days

Decision Maker

Entrepreneur Your retail store has an inventory turnover of 5.0 and a days' sales in inventory of 73 days. The industry norm for inventory turnover is 4.4 and for days' sales in inventory is 74 days. What is your assessment of inventory management? ■ *Answer:* Your inventory turnover is higher than the norm, whereas days' sales in inventory approximates the norm. Because your turnover is already 14% better than average, you should probably direct attention to days' sales in inventory. You should see if you can reduce the level of inventory while maintaining service to customers. Given your higher turnover, you should be able to hold less inventory.

NEED-TO-KNOW 6-5

COMPREHENSIVE 1

Perpetual Method: Computing Inventory Using LIFO, FIFO, WA, and SI; Financial Statement Impacts; and Inventory Errors

Craig Company buys and sells one product. Its beginning inventory, purchases, and sales during the current year follow.

Date	Activity	Units Acquired at Cost	Units Sold at Retail	Unit Inventory
Jan. 1	Beg. inventory....	400 units @ $14 = $ 5,600		400 units
Jan. 15	Sale		200 units @ $30	200 units
Mar. 10	Purchase	200 units @ $15 = $ 3,000		400 units
Apr. 1	Sale		200 units @ $30	200 units
May 9	Purchase	300 units @ $16 = $ 4,800		500 units
Sep. 22	Purchase	250 units @ $20 = $ 5,000		750 units
Nov. 1	Sale		300 units @ $35	450 units
Nov. 28	Purchase	100 units @ $21 = $ 2,100		550 units
	Totals	1,250 units $20,500	700 units	

Additional tracking data for specific identification: Sold 400 units costing $14 each, 200 units costing $15 each, and 100 units costing $20 each.

Required

1. Compute the cost of goods available for sale.
2. Apply FIFO, LIFO, weighted average, and specific identification to compute ending inventory and cost of goods sold under each method using the *perpetual system*.
3. Compute gross profit under each method. Also, report the inventory amount reported on the balance sheet for each method.
4. In preparing financial statements for the current year, the financial officer was instructed to use FIFO but failed to do so and instead computed cost of goods sold according to LIFO, which led to a $1,400 overstatement in cost of goods sold from using LIFO. Determine the impact on current year income from the error. Also determine the effect of this error on next year's income.

SOLUTION

1. Cost of goods available for sale (this amount is the same for all methods).

Date		Units	Unit Cost	Cost
Jan. 1	Beg. inventory............	400	$14	$ 5,600
Mar. 10	Purchase...............	200	15	3,000
May 9	Purchase...............	300	16	4,800
Sep. 22	Purchase...............	250	20	5,000
Nov. 28	Purchase...............	100	21	2,100
	Total goods available for sale	1,250		$20,500

2a. FIFO **perpetual** method.

Date	Goods Purchased	Cost of Goods Sold	Inventory Balance	
Jan. 1	Beginning balance		400 @ $14	= $ 5,600
Jan. 15		200 @ $14 = $2,800	200 @ $14	= $ 2,800
Mar. 10	200 @ $15 = $3,000		200 @ $14 200 @ $15	= $ 5,800
Apr. 1		200 @ $14 = $2,800	200 @ $15	= $ 3,000
May 9	300 @ $16 = $4,800		200 @ $15 300 @ $16	= $ 7,800
Sep. 22	250 @ $20 = $5,000		200 @ $15 300 @ $16 250 @ $20	= $ 12,800
Nov. 1		200 @ $15 = $3,000 100 @ $16 = $1,600	200 @ $16 250 @ $20	= $ 8,200
Nov. 28	100 @ $21 = $2,100		200 @ $16 250 @ $20 100 @ $21	= $10,300
Total cost of goods sold		$10,200		

2b. LIFO **perpetual** method.

Date	Goods Purchased	Cost of Goods Sold	Inventory Balance	
Jan. 1	Beginning balance		400 @ $14	= $ 5,600
Jan. 15		200 @ $14 = $2,800	200 @ $14	= $ 2,800
Mar. 10	200 @ $15 = $3,000		200 @ $14 200 @ $15	= $ 5,800
Apr. 1		200 @ $15 = $3,000	200 @ $14	= $ 2,800
May 9	300 @ $16 = $4,800		200 @ $14 300 @ $16	= $ 7,600
Sep. 22	250 @ $20 = $5,000		200 @ $14 300 @ $16 250 @ $20	= $ 12,600
Nov. 1		250 @ $20 = $5,000 50 @ $16 = $ 800	200 @ $14 250 @ $16	= $ 6,800
Nov. 28	100 @ $21 = $2,100		200 @ $14 250 @ $16 100 @ $21	= $ 8,900
Total cost of goods sold		$11,600		

2c. Weighted average **perpetual** method.

Date	Goods Purchased	Cost of Goods Sold	Inventory Balance	
Jan. 1	Beginning balance		400 @ $14.00 ($5,600/400 units	= $ 5,600 = $14.00 avg. cost)
Jan. 15		200 @ $14.00 = $ 2,800	200 @ $14.00	= $ 2,800

[continued on next page]

[continued from previous page]

Date	Goods Purchased	Cost of Goods Sold	Inventory Balance
Mar. 10	200 @ $15.00 = $3,000		200 @ $14.00 200 @ $15.00 } = $ 5,800 ($5,800/400 units = $14.50 avg. cost)
Apr. 1		200 @ $14.50 = $ 2,900	200 @ $14.50 = $ 2,900
May 9	300 @ $16.00 = $4,800		200 @ $14.50 300 @ $16.00 } = $ 7,700 ($7,700/500 units = $15.40 avg. cost)
Sep. 22	250 @ $20.00 = $5,000		500 @ $15.40 250 @ $20.00 } = $ 12,700 ($12,700/750 units = $16.93† avg. cost)
Nov. 1		300 @ $16.93 = $ 5,079	450 @ $16.93 = $ 7,618.50
Nov. 28	100 @ $21.00 = $2,100		450 @ $16.93 100 @ $21.00 } = $9,718.50 ($9,718.50/550 units = $17.67 avg. cost)
Total cost of goods sold*		$10,779	

*Cost of goods sold ($10,779) plus ending inventory ($9,718.50) is $2.50 less than the cost of goods available for sale ($20,500) due to rounding.

†Rounded to 2 decimal places.

2d. Specific identification method.

Date	Goods Available for Sale	Cost of Goods Sold		Ending Inventory	
Jan. 1	400 @ $14 = $ 5,600	400 @ $14 = $ 5,600			
Mar. 10	200 @ $15 = $ 3,000	200 @ $15 = $ 3,000			
May 9	300 @ $16 = $ 4,800			300 @ $16 = $ 4,800	
Sep. 22	250 @ $20 = $ 5,000	100 @ $20 = $ 2,000		150 @ $20 = $ 3,000	
Nov. 28	100 @ $21 = $ 2,100			100 @ $21 = $ 2,100	
	$20,500	700	$10,600	550	$9,900

3.

	FIFO	LIFO	Weighted Average	Specific Identification
Income Statement				
Sales*	$ 22,500	$22,500	$ 22,500	$22,500
Cost of goods sold . . .	10,200	11,600	10,779	10,600
Gross profit	$ 12,300	$10,900	$ 11,721	$11,900
Balance Sheet				
Inventory	$10,300	$ 8,900	$9,718.50	$ 9,900

*Sales = (200 units × $30) + (200 units × $30) + (300 units × $35) = $22,500.

4. Mistakenly using LIFO when FIFO should have been used overstates cost of goods sold in the current year by $1,400, which is the difference between the FIFO and LIFO amounts of ending inventory. It understates income in the current year by $1,400. In the next year, income is overstated by $1,400 because of the understatement in beginning inventory.

NEED-TO-KNOW 6-6

COMPREHENSIVE 2

Periodic Method: Computing Inventory Using LIFO, FIFO, WA, and SI; Financial Statement Impacts; and Inventory Errors

Craig Company buys and sells one product. Its beginning inventory, purchases, and sales during the current year follow.

Date	Activity	Units Acquired at Cost	Units Sold at Retail	Unit Inventory
Jan. 1	Beg. inventory....	400 units @ $14 = $ 5,600		400 units
Jan. 15	Sale		200 units @ $30	200 units
Mar. 10	Purchase	200 units @ $15 = $ 3,000		400 units
Apr. 1	Sale		200 units @ $30	200 units
May 9	Purchase	300 units @ $16 = $ 4,800		500 units
Sep. 22	Purchase	250 units @ $20 = $ 5,000		750 units
Nov. 1	Sale		300 units @ $35	450 units
Nov. 28	Purchase	100 units @ $21 = $ 2,100		550 units
	Totals	1,250 units $20,500	700 units	

Additional tracking data for specific identification: Sold 400 units costing $14 each, 200 units costing $15 each, and 100 units costing $20 each.

Required

1. Compute the cost of goods available for sale.
2. Apply FIFO, LIFO, weighted average, and specific identification to compute ending inventory and cost of goods sold under each method using the *periodic system*.
3. Compute gross profit under each method. Also, report the inventory amount reported on the balance sheet for each method.
4. In preparing financial statements for the current year, the financial officer was instructed to use FIFO but failed to do so and instead computed cost of goods sold according to LIFO. Determine the impact of the error on current year income. Also determine the effect of this error on next year's income.

SOLUTION

1. Cost of goods available for sale (this amount is the same for all methods).

Date		Units	Unit Cost	Cost
Jan. 1	Beg. inventory............	400	$14	$ 5,600
Mar. 10	Purchase.................	200	15	3,000
May 9	Purchase.................	300	16	4,800
Sep. 22	Purchase.................	250	20	5,000
Nov. 28	Purchase.................	100	21	2,100
Total goods available for sale		1,250		$20,500

2a. FIFO **periodic** method.

Date	Goods Available for Sale	Cost of Goods Sold	Ending Inventory
Jan. 1	400 @ $14 = $ 5,600	400 @ $14 = $ 5,600	
Mar. 10	200 @ $15 = $ 3,000	200 @ $15 = $ 3,000	
May 9	300 @ $16 = $ 4,800	100 @ $16 = $ 1,600	200 @ $16 = $ 3,200
Sep. 22	250 @ $20 = $ 5,000		250 @ $20 = $ 5,000
Nov. 28	100 @ $21 = $ 2,100		100 @ $21 = $ 2,100
	$20,500	700 $10,200	550 $10,300

2b. LIFO **periodic** method.

Date	Goods Available for Sale	Cost of Goods Sold		Ending Inventory	
Jan. 1	400 @ $14 = $ 5,600			400 @ $14 = $5,600	
Mar. 10	200 @ $15 = $ 3,000	50 @ $15 = $ 750		150 @ $15 = $2,250	
May 9	300 @ $16 = $ 4,800	300 @ $16 = $ 4,800			
Sep. 22	250 @ $20 = $ 5,000	250 @ $20 = $ 5,000			
Nov. 28	100 @ $21 = $ 2,100	100 @ $21 = $ 2,100			
	$20,500	700	$12,650	550	$7,850

2c. Weighted average **periodic** method.

Date	Goods Available for Sale	Cost of Goods Sold	Ending Inventory
Jan. 1	400 @ $14 = $ 5,600		
Mar. 10	200 @ $15 = $ 3,000		
May 9	300 @ $16 = $ 4,800		
Sep. 22	250 @ $20 = $ 5,000		
Nov. 28	100 @ $21 = $ 2,100		
	1,250 units $20,500		
	= $16.40 ($20,500/1,250 units)	700 @ $16.40 = **$11,480**	550 @ $16.40 = **$9,020**

2d. Specific identification method.

Date	Goods Available for Sale	Cost of Goods Sold		Ending Inventory	
Jan. 1	400 @ $14 = $ 5,600	400 @ $14 = $ 5,600			
Mar. 10	200 @ $15 = $ 3,000	200 @ $15 = $ 3,000			
May 9	300 @ $16 = $ 4,800			300 @ $16 = $4,800	
Sep. 22	250 @ $20 = $ 5,000	100 @ $20 = $ 2,000		150 @ $20 = $3,000	
Nov. 28	100 @ $21 = $ 2,100			100 @ $21 = $2,100	
	$20,500	700	$10,600	550	$9,900

3.

	FIFO	LIFO	Weighted Average	Specific Identification
Income Statement				
Sales*	$ 22,500	$22,500	$ 22,500	$22,500
Cost of goods sold	10,200	12,650	11,480	10,600
Gross profit	$ 12,300	$ 9,850	$ 11,020	$11,900
Balance Sheet				
Inventory	**$10,300**	**$ 7,850**	**$ 9,020**	**$ 9,900**

*Sales = (200 units × $30) + (200 units × $30) + (300 units × $35) = $22,500.

4. Mistakenly using LIFO, when FIFO should have been used, overstates cost of goods sold in the current year by $2,450, which is the difference between the FIFO and LIFO amounts of ending inventory. It understates income in the current year by $2,450. In the next year, income is overstated by $2,450 because of the understatement in beginning inventory.

APPENDIX

Inventory Costing under a Periodic System

6A

P3

Compute inventory in a periodic system using the methods of specific identification, FIFO, LIFO, and weighted average.

This section demonstrates inventory costing methods. We use information from Trekking, a sporting goods store. Among its many products, Trekking sells one type of mountain bike whose sales are directed at resorts that provide inexpensive bikes for guest use. We use Trekking's data from August. Its mountain bike (unit) inventory at the beginning of August and its purchases and sales during August are shown in Exhibit 6A.1. It ends August with 12 bikes remaining in inventory.

EXHIBIT 6A.1

Purchases and Sales of Goods

Date	Activity	Units Acquired at Cost	Units Sold at Retail	Unit Inventory
Aug. 1	Beginning inventory.......	10 units @ $ 91 = $ 910		10 units
Aug. 3	Purchases..............	15 units @ $106 = $ 1,590		25 units
Aug. 14	Sales...................		20 units @ $130	5 units
Aug. 17	Purchases..............	20 units @ $115 = $ 2,300		25 units
Aug. 28	Purchases..............	10 units @ $119 = $ 1,190		35 units
Aug. 30	Sales...................		23 units @ $150	12 units
	Totals	55 units (Units available for sale) / $5,990 (Goods available for sale)	43 units (Units sold)	12 units (Units left)

Warut Chinsai/Shutterstock

Trekking uses the **periodic inventory system**, which means that its Merchandise Inventory account is updated at the end of each period (monthly for Trekking) to reflect purchases and sales. (Many companies use the periodic system for tracking costs [not so much for sales]. Reasons include the use of standard costs by some companies and dollar-value LIFO by others. Also, inventory values are identical under the periodic and perpetual methods when using Specific Identification and for FIFO.

Specific Identification

When each item in inventory can be matched with a specific purchase and invoice, we can use **specific identification** or **SI** to assign costs. The first two columns of Exhibit 6A.2 show Trekking's dates and amounts of each purchase. Total goods available for sale is **$5,990**.

We then need sales records that identify exactly which items were sold and when. Trekking's internal documents show goods sold consist of 10 from the August 1 purchase, 15 from the August 3 purchase, 15 from the August 17 purchase, and 3 from the August 28 purchase. These goods sold are entered in the third column of Exhibit 6.4 and total **$4,582**.

In the Ending Inventory column we enter the 12 units *not* sold. The **$1,408** total is ending inventory.

EXHIBIT 6A.2

Specific Identification

Date	Goods Available for Sale	Cost of Goods Sold	Ending Inventory
Aug. 1	10 @ $ 91 = $ 910	10 @ $ 91 = $ 910	
Aug. 3	15 @ $106 = $1,590	15 @ $106 = $1,590	
Aug. 17	20 @ $115 = $2,300	15 @ $115 = $1,725	5 @ $115 = $ 575
Aug. 28	10 @ $119 = $1,190	3 @ $119 = $ 357	7 @ $119 = $ 833
	$5,990	43 $4,582	12 $1,408

Point: Specific identification is common for custom-made inventory such as jewelry.

Trekking's cost of goods sold reported on the income statement is **$4,582**, and ending inventory reported on the balance sheet is **$1,408**. The following graphic shows these cost flows.

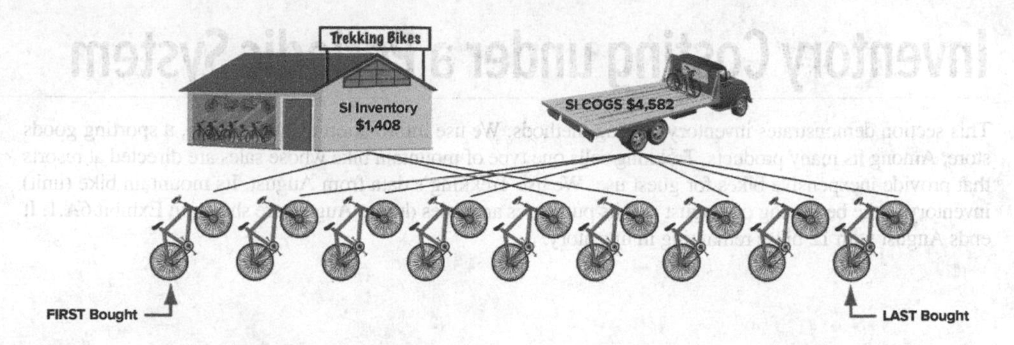

First-In, First-Out

First-in, first-out (FIFO) assumes that inventory items are sold in the order acquired. When sales occur, the costs of the earliest units acquired are charged to cost of goods sold. This leaves the costs from the most recent purchases in ending inventory.

The Goods Available for Sale column in Exhibit 6A.3 shows the units and costs making up the $5,990 goods available for sale (from Exhibit 6A.1). In the Cost of Goods Sold column we enter the 43 units sold, *beginning with the first units purchased:* 10 from August 1, then 15 from August 3, and 18 from August 17. The $4,570 total is cost of goods sold. In the Ending Inventory column we enter the 12 units *not* sold. The $1,420 total is ending inventory.

EXHIBIT 6A.3
FIFO—Periodic

Date	Goods Available for Sale	Cost of Goods Sold		Ending Inventory	
Aug. 1	10 @ $ 91 = $ 910	10 @ $ 91 = $ 910			
Aug. 3	15 @ $106 = $1,590	15 @ $106 = $1,590			
Aug. 17	20 @ $115 = $2,300	18 @ $115 = $2,070		2 @ $115 = $ 230	
Aug. 28	10 @ $119 = $1,190			10 @ $119 = $1,190	
	$5,990	43	$4,570	12	= $1,420

Trekking's ending inventory reported on the balance sheet is **$1,420**, and its cost of goods sold reported on the income statement is **$4,570**.

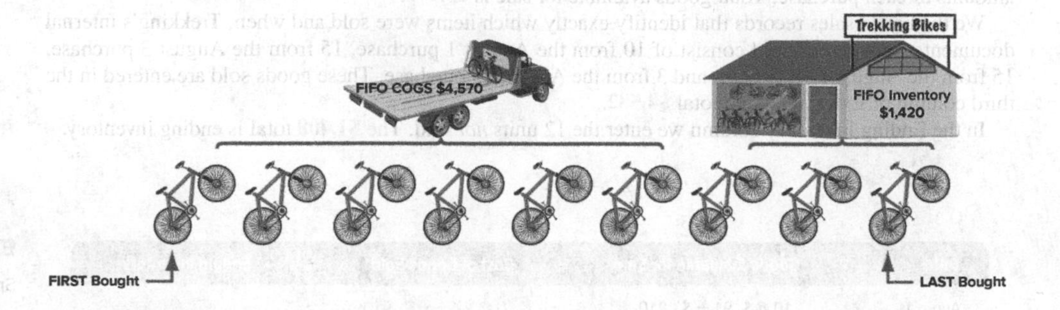

Last-In, First-Out

Last-in, first-out (LIFO) assumes that the most recent purchases are sold first. These more recent costs are charged to cost of goods sold, and the costs of the earliest purchases are assigned to inventory.

The Goods Available for Sale column in Exhibit 6A.4 shows the units and costs making up the $5,990 goods available for sale (from Exhibit 6A.1). In the Cost of Goods Sold column we enter the 43 units sold, ***beginning with the last units purchased:*** 10 from August 28, then 20 from August 17, and 13 from August 3. The $4,868 total is cost of goods sold. In the Ending Inventory column we enter the 12 units *not* sold. The $1,122 total is ending inventory.

EXHIBIT 6A.4

LIFO—Periodic

Date	Goods Available for Sale	Cost of Goods Sold	Ending Inventory
Aug. 1	10 @ $ 91 = $ 910		10 @ $ 91 = $ 910
Aug. 3	15 @ $106 = $1,590	13 @ $106 = $1,378	2 @ $106 = $ 212
Aug. 17	20 @ $115 = $2,300	20 @ $115 = $2,300	
Aug. 28	10 @ $119 = $1,190	10 @ $119 = $1,190	
	$5,990	43 $4,868	12 = $1,122

Trekking's ending inventory reported on the balance sheet is $1,122, and its cost of goods sold reported on the income statement is $4,868.

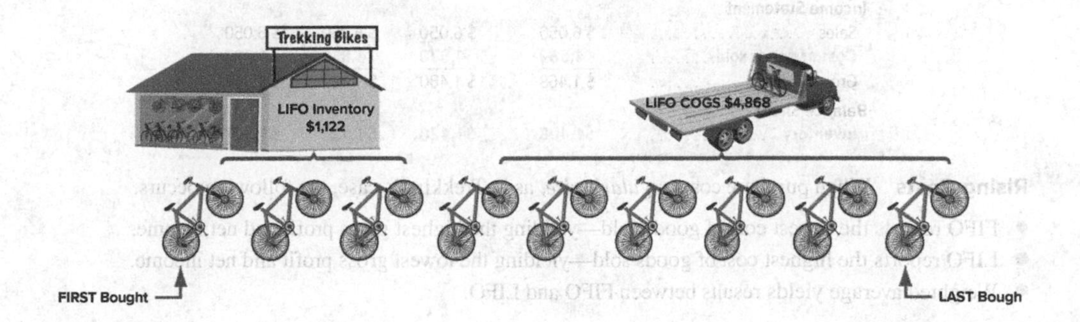

Weighted Average

Weighted average or **WA** (also called **average cost**) requires that we use the average cost per unit of inventory at the end of the period. Weighted average cost per unit equals the cost of goods available for sale divided by the units available. The Goods Available for Sale column in Exhibit 6A.5 shows the 55 units and costs making up the $5,990 goods available for sale (from Exhibit 6A.1). At the bottom of that column we compute average cost per unit as $5,990 / 55 units = $108.91. In the Cost of Goods Sold column we enter the 43 units sold times the $108.91 average cost. The $4,683 total is cost of goods sold. In the Ending Inventory column we enter the 12 units *not* sold times the $108.91 average cost. The $1,307 total is ending inventory.

EXHIBIT 6A.5

Weighted Average—Periodic

Date	Goods Available for Sale	Cost of Goods Sold	Ending Inventory
Aug. 1	10 @ $ 91 = $ 910		
Aug. 3	15 @ $106 = $1,590		
Aug. 17	20 @ $115 = $2,300		
Aug. 28	10 @ $119 = $1,190		
	55 units $5,990		
	= $108.91 ($5,990/55 units)	43 @ $108.91 = $4,683	12 @ $108.91 = $1,307

Trekking's ending inventory reported on the balance sheet is **$1,307**, and its cost of goods sold reported on the income statement is **$4,683**.

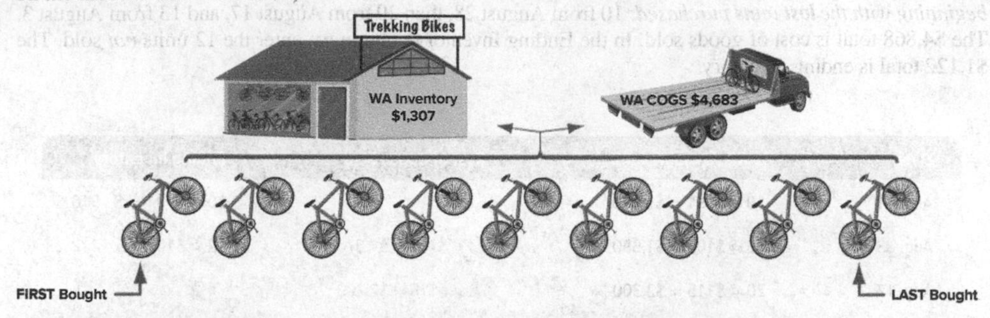

Financial Statement Effects of Costing Methods

When purchase prices do not change, each inventory costing method assigns the same cost amounts to inventory and to cost of goods sold. When purchase prices are different, the methods assign different cost amounts. We show these differences in Exhibit 6A.6 using Trekking's data.

EXHIBIT 6A.6

Financial Statement Effects of Inventory Costing Methods

Trekking Company For Month Ended August 31	Specific Identification	FIFO	LIFO	Weighted Average
Income Statement				
Sales	$ 6,050	$ 6,050	$ 6,050	$ 6,050
Cost of goods sold........	4,582	4,570	4,868	4,683
Gross profit	$ 1,468	$ 1,480	$ 1,182	$ 1,367
Balance Sheet				
Inventory	$1,408	$1,420	$1,122	$1,307

Rising Costs When purchase costs *regularly rise,* as in Trekking's case, the following occurs.

- FIFO reports the lowest cost of goods sold—yielding the highest gross profit and net income.
- LIFO reports the highest cost of goods sold—yielding the lowest gross profit and net income.
- Weighted average yields results between FIFO and LIFO.

Falling Costs When costs *regularly decline,* the reverse occurs for FIFO and LIFO. FIFO gives the highest cost of goods sold—yielding the lowest gross profit and net income. LIFO gives the lowest cost of goods sold—yielding the highest gross profit and net income.

Method Advantages Each method offers advantages.

- FIFO—inventory approximates its current cost; it also follows actual flow of goods for most businesses.
- LIFO—cost of goods sold approximates its current cost; it also better matches current costs with revenues.
- Weighted average—smooths out erratic changes in costs.
- Specific identification—matches the costs of items with the revenues they generate.

Point: LIFO inventory is often less than the inventory's replacement cost because LIFO inventory is valued using the oldest inventory purchase costs.

NEED-TO-KNOW 6-7

Periodic SI, FIFO, LIFO, and WA

P3

A company reported the following December purchases and sales data for its only product. The company uses a *periodic inventory system.* Determine the cost assigned to ending inventory and to cost of goods sold using (a) specific identification, (b) FIFO, (c) LIFO, and (d) weighted average. For specific identification, ending inventory consists of 10 units, where 8 are from the December 30 purchase and 2 are from the December 8 purchase.

Date	Activities	Units Acquired at Cost	Units Sold at Retail
Dec. 1	Beginning inventory	5 units @ $3.00 = $ 15.00	
Dec. 8	Purchase	10 units @ $4.50 = 45.00	
Dec. 9	Sales....................		8 units @ $7.00
Dec. 19	Purchase	13 units @ $5.00 = 65.00	
Dec. 24	Sales....................		18 units @ $8.00
Dec. 30	Purchase	8 units @ $5.30 = 42.40	
Totals	....	36 units $167.40	26 units

Solutions

a. Specific identification.

Date	Goods Available for Sale	Cost of Goods Sold		Ending Inventory	
Dec. 1	5 units @ $3.00 = $ 15.00	5 units @ $3.00 = $ 15.00			
Dec. 8	10 units @ $4.50 = $ 45.00	8 units @ $4.50 = $ 36.00		2 units @ $4.50 = $ 9.00	
Dec. 19	13 units @ $5.00 = $ 65.00	13 units @ $5.00 = $ 65.00			
Dec. 30	8 units @ $5.30 = $ 42.40			8 units @ $5.30 = $42.40	
	$167.40	26	$116.00	10	$51.40

b. FIFO—Periodic.

Date	Goods Available for Sale	Cost of Goods Sold		Ending Inventory	
Dec. 1	5 @ $3.00 = $ 15.00	5 @ $3.00 = $ 15.00			
Dec. 8	10 @ $4.50 = $ 45.00	10 @ $4.50 = $ 45.00			
Dec. 19	13 @ $5.00 = $ 65.00	11 @ $5.00 = $ 55.00		2 @ $5.00 = $10.00	
Dec. 30	8 @ $5.30 = $ 42.40			8 @ $5.30 = $42.40	
	$167.40	26	$115.00	10	$52.40

c. LIFO—Periodic.

Date	Goods Available for Sale	Cost of Goods Sold		Ending Inventory	
Dec. 1	5 @ $3.00 = $ 15.00			5 @ $3.00 = $15.00	
Dec. 8	10 @ $4.50 = $ 45.00	5 @ $4.50 = $ 22.50		5 @ $4.50 = $22.50	
Dec. 19	13 @ $5.00 = $ 65.00	13 @ $5.00 = $ 65.00			
Dec. 30	8 @ $5.30 = $ 42.40	8 @ $5.30 = $ 42.40			
	$167.40	26	$129.90	10	$37.50

d. WA—Periodic.

Date	Goods Available for Sale	Cost of Goods Sold	Ending Inventory
Dec. 1	5 @ $3.00 = $ 15.00		
Dec. 8	10 @ $4.50 = $ 45.00		
Dec. 19	13 @ $5.00 = $ 65.00		
Dec. 30	8 @ $5.30 = $ 42.40		
	36 units $167.40		
	= $4.65 ($167.40/36 units)	26 @ $4.65 = $120.90	10 @ $4.65 = $46.50

Do More: QS 6-8, QS 6-9, QS 6-10, QS 6-15, QS 6-16, QS 6-17, QS 6-18, E 6-6, E 6-7

APPENDIX

6B Inventory Estimation Methods

P4 Apply both the retail inventory and gross profit methods to estimate inventory.

Inventory sometimes is estimated for two reasons. First, companies often report **interim financial statements** (financial statements prepared for periods of less than one year), but they only annually take a physical count of inventory. Second, companies may require an inventory estimate if some casualty such as fire or flood makes taking a physical count impossible. Estimates are usually only required for companies that use the periodic system. Companies using a perpetual system would presumably have updated inventory data.

This appendix describes two methods to estimate inventory.

Retail Inventory Method To avoid the time-consuming process of taking a physical inventory, some companies use the **retail inventory method** to estimate cost of goods sold and ending inventory.

EXHIBIT 6B.1

Retail Inventory Method of Inventory Estimation

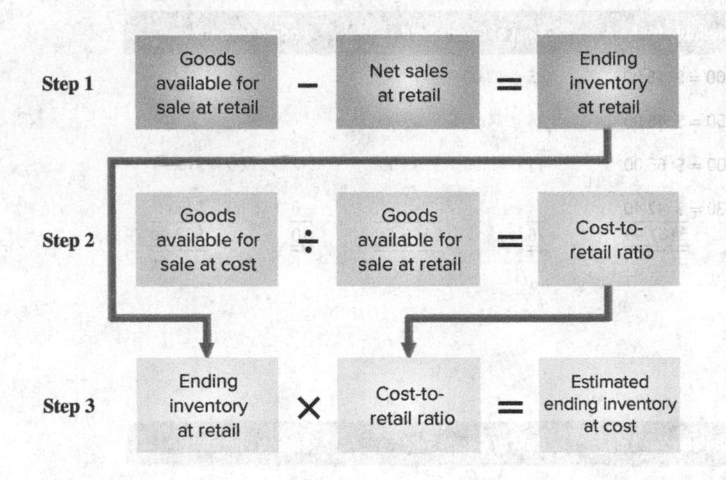

The retail inventory method uses a three-step process to estimate ending inventory. We need to know the amount of inventory a company had at the beginning of the period in both *cost* and *retail* amounts. We already explained how to compute the cost of inventory. The *retail amount of inventory* is measured using selling prices of inventory items. We also need to know the net amount of goods purchased (minus returns, allowances, and discounts) in the period, both at cost and at retail. The amount of net sales at retail also is needed. The process is shown in Exhibit 6B.1.

The reasoning behind the retail inventory method is that if we can get a good estimate of the cost-to-retail ratio, we can multiply ending inventory at retail by this ratio to estimate ending inventory at cost. Exhibit 6B.2 shows how these steps are applied to estimate ending inventory. First, we find that \$100,000 of goods (at retail selling prices) were available for sale. A total of \$70,000 of these goods were sold, leaving \$30,000 (retail value) of merchandise in ending inventory. Second, the cost of these goods is 60% of the \$100,000 retail value. Third, because cost for these goods is 60% of retail, the estimated cost of ending inventory is \$18,000.

EXHIBIT 6B.2

Estimated Inventory Using the Retail Inventory Method

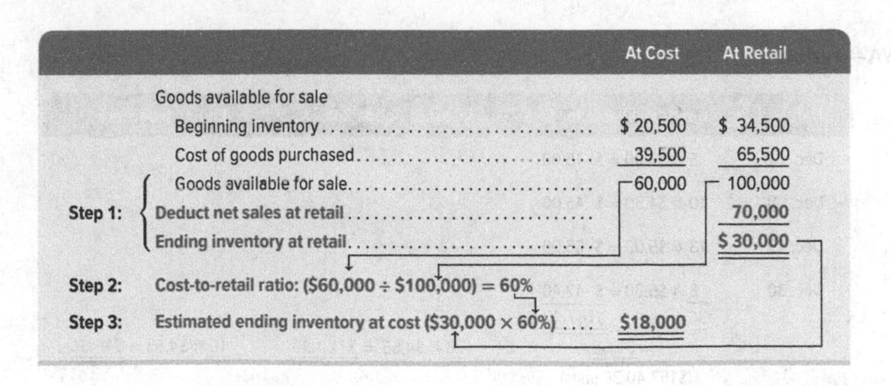

		At Cost	At Retail
	Goods available for sale		
	Beginning inventory	\$ 20,500	\$ 34,500
	Cost of goods purchased	39,500	65,500
Step 1:	Goods available for sale	60,000	100,000
	Deduct net sales at retail		**70,000**
	Ending inventory at retail		**\$ 30,000**
Step 2:	**Cost-to-retail ratio: (\$60,000 ÷ \$100,000) = 60%**		
Step 3:	**Estimated ending inventory at cost (\$30,000 × 60%)**	**\$18,000**	

Gross Profit Method

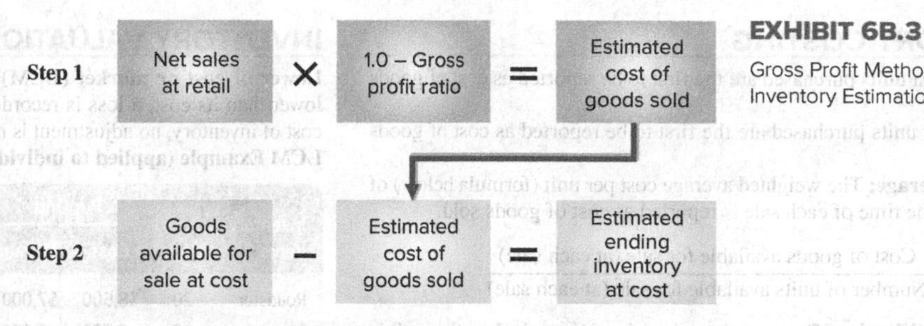

EXHIBIT 6B.3

Gross Profit Method of Inventory Estimation

The **gross profit method** estimates the cost of ending inventory by applying the gross profit ratio to net sales (at retail). This type of estimate often is used when inventory is destroyed, lost, or stolen. This method uses the historical relation between cost of goods sold and net sales to estimate the proportion of cost of goods sold making up current sales. This cost of goods sold estimate is then subtracted from cost of goods available for sale to estimate the ending inventory at cost. These two steps are shown in Exhibit 6B.3.

To demonstrate, assume that a company's inventory is destroyed by fire in March. When the fire occurs, the company's accounts show the following balances for January through March: Net Sales, $30,000; Beginning Inventory, $12,000 (at January 1); and Cost of Goods Purchased, $20,500. If this company's gross profit ratio is 30%, then 30% of each net sales dollar is gross profit and 70% is cost of goods sold. We show in Exhibit 6B.4 how this 70% is used to estimate lost inventory of $11,500.

EXHIBIT 6B.4

Estimated Inventory Using the Gross Profit Method

	Goods available for sale		
	Beginning inventory, January 1	$12,000	
	Cost of goods purchased	20,500	
	Goods available for sale (at cost)	32,500	
	Net sales at retail		$30,000
Step 1:	**Estimated cost of goods sold ($30,000 × 70%)**	(21,000)	← × 0.70
Step 2:	**Estimated March inventory at cost**	$11,500	

NEED-TO-KNOW 6-8

Retail Inventory Estimation

P4

Using the retail method and the following data, estimate the cost of ending inventory.

	Cost	Retail
Beginning inventory	$324,000	$530,000
Cost of goods purchased	195,000	335,000
Net sales		320,000

Solution

Estimated ending inventory (at cost) is $327,000. It is computed as follows.

Step 1: ($530,000 + $335,000) − $320,000 = $545,000

Step 2: $\frac{\$324,000 + \$195,000}{\$530,000 + \$335,000} = 60\%$

Step 3: $545,000 × 60% = $327,000

Do More: QS 6-26, E 6-20, E 6-21, P 6-9

Summary: Cheat Sheet

INVENTORY BASICS

FOB shipping point: Goods are included in buyer's inventory once they are shipped.

FOB destination: Goods are included in buyer's inventory after arrival at their destination.

Consignee: Never reports consigned goods in inventory; stays in consignor's inventory until sold.

Merchandise inventory: Includes any *necessary* costs to make an item ready for sale. Examples—shipping, storage, import fees, and insurance.

INVENTORY COSTING

FIFO: Earliest units purchased are the first to be reported as cost of goods sold.
LIFO: Latest units purchased are the first to be reported as cost of goods sold.
Weighted average: The weighted average cost per unit (formula below) of inventory at the time of each sale is reported as cost of goods sold.

$$\frac{\text{Cost of goods available for sale (at each sale)}}{\text{Number of units available for sale (at each sale)}}$$

Specific identification: Each unit is assigned a cost, and when that unit is sold, its cost is reported as cost of goods sold.

Cost Flow Assumptions Example

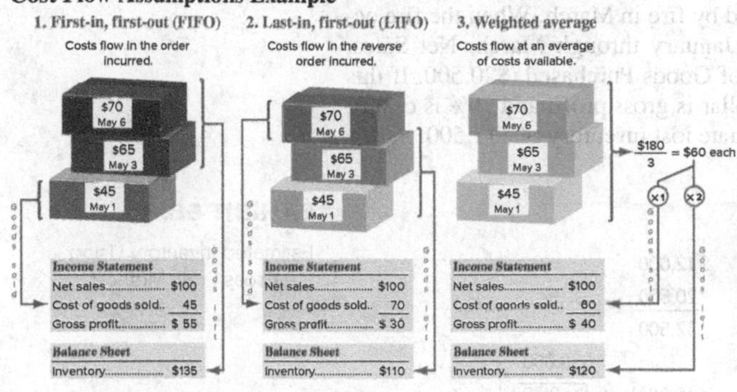

Financial Statement Effects
Rising Costs—FIFO reports lowest cost of goods sold and highest net income. LIFO reports highest cost of goods sold and lowest income. Weighted average reports results in between LIFO and FIFO.
Falling Costs—FIFO reports highest cost of goods sold and lowest net income. LIFO reports lowest cost of goods sold and highest income.

INVENTORY VALUATION, ERRORS & ANALYSIS

Lower of cost or market (LCM): When market value of inventory is lower than its cost, a loss is recorded. When market value is higher than cost of inventory, no adjustment is made.
LCM Example (applied to individual items separately)

Inventory Items	Units	Per Unit Cost	Per Unit Market	Total Cost	Total Market	LCM Applied to Items
Roadster	20	$8,500	$7,000	$170,000	$140,000	$ 140,000
Sprint	10	5,000	6,000	50,000	60,000	50,000
Totals				$220,000		$190,000

Roadster: $140,000 is the lower of the $170,000 cost and $140,000 market.
Sprint: $50,000 is the lower of the $50,000 cost and $60,000 market.
LCM: Results in a $190,000 reported inventory.

LCM Journal Entry: To get from $220,000 reported inventory to the $190,000 LCM inventory, make the following entry.

Cost of Goods Sold	30,000	
Merchandise Inventory		30,000

Effects of Overstated or Understated Inventory for Income Statement

Ending Inventory	Year 1 Cost of Goods Sold	Year 1 Net Income	Year 2 Cost of Goods Sold	Year 2 Net Income
Understated ↓	Overstated ↑	Understated ↓	Understated ↓	Overstated ↑
Overstated ↑	Understated ↓	Overstated ↑	Overstated ↑	Understated ↓

Effects of Overstated or Understated Inventory for Balance Sheet

Ending Inventory	Assets	Equity
Understated ↓	Understated ↓	Understated ↓
Overstated ↑	Overstated ↑	Overstated ↑

Key Terms

Average cost (218, 233)
Consignee (213)
Consignor (213)
Days' sales in inventory (225)
First-in, first-out (FIFO) (217, 232)
Gross profit method (237)
Interim financial statements (236)
Inventory turnover (225)
Last-in, first-out (LIFO) (217, 232)
Lower of cost or market (LCM) (222)
Net realizable value (214)
Retail inventory method (236)
Specific identification (SI) (216, 226)
Weighted average (WA) (218, 233)

Multiple Choice Quiz

Use the following information from Marvel Company for the month of July to answer questions 1 through 4.

July 1	Beginning inventory	75 units @ $25 each
July 3	Purchase	348 units @ $27 each
July 8	Sale	300 units
July 15	Purchase	257 units @ $28 each
July 23	Sale	275 units

1. **Perpetual:** Assume that Marvel uses a *perpetual* FIFO inventory system. What is the dollar value of its ending inventory?
   a. $2,940 b. $2,685 c. $2,625 d. $2,852 e. $2,705

2. **Perpetual:** Assume that Marvel uses a *perpetual* LIFO inventory system. What is the dollar value of its ending inventory?
   a. $2,940 b. $2,685 c. $2,625 d. $2,852 e. $2,705

3. **Perpetual and Periodic:** Assume that Marvel uses a specific identification inventory system. Its ending inventory consists of 20 units from beginning inventory, 40 units from the July 3 purchase, and 45 units from the July 15 purchase. What is the dollar value of its ending inventory?
   a. $2,940 b. $2,685 c. $2,625 d. $2,852 e. $2,840

4. Periodic: Assume that Marvel uses a *periodic* FIFO inventory system. What is the dollar value of its ending inventory?

a. $2,940 **c.** $2,625 **e.** $2,705
b. $2,685 **d.** $2,852

5. Periodic: A company reports the following beginning inventory and purchases, and it ends the period with 30 units in inventory.

Beginning inventory . . .	100 units at $10 cost per unit
Purchase 1	40 units at $12 cost per unit
Purchase 2	20 units at $14 cost per unit

i) Compute ending inventory using the FIFO *periodic* system.
a. $400 **b.** $1,460 **c.** $1,360 **d.** $300

ii) Compute cost of goods sold using the LIFO *periodic* system.
a. $400 **b.** $1,460 **c.** $1,360 **d.** $300

6. A company has cost of goods sold of $85,000 and ending inventory of $18,000. Its days' sales in inventory equals

a. 49.32 days. **c.** 4.72 days. **e.** 1,723.61 days.
b. 0.21 day. **d.** 77.29 days.

ANSWERS TO MULTIPLE CHOICE QUIZ

1. a; FIFO perpetual

Date	Goods Purchased	Cost of Goods Sold	Inventory Balance
July 1			75 units @ $25 = $ 1,875
July 3	348 units @ $27 = $9,396		75 units @ $25 348 units @ $27 } = $11,271
July 8		75 units @ $25 225 units @ $27 } = $ 7,950	123 units @ $27 = $ 3,321
July 15	257 units @ $28 = $7,196		123 units @ $27 257 units @ $28 } = $10,517
July 23		123 units @ $27 152 units @ $28 } = $ 7,577	105 units @ $28 = $2,940
		575 $15,527	

2. b; LIFO perpetual

Date	Goods Purchased	Cost of Goods Sold	Inventory Balance
July 1			75 units @ $25 = $ 1,875
July 3	348 units @ $27 = $9,396		75 units @ $25 348 units @ $27 } = $11,271
July 8		300 units @ $27 = $ 8,100	75 units @ $25 48 units @ $27 } = $ 3,171
July 15	257 units @ $28 = $7,196		75 units @ $25 48 units @ $27 257 units @ $28 } = $10,367
July 23		257 units @ $28 18 units @ $27 } = $ 7,682	75 units @ $25 30 units @ $27 } = $ 2,685
		575 $15,782	

3. e; Specific identification (perpetual and periodic are identical for specific identification)—Ending inventory computation follows.

Date	Goods Available for Sale	Cost of Goods Sold	Ending Inventory
July 1	75 @ $25 = $ 1,875	55 @ $25 = $ 1,375	20 @ $25 = $ 500
July 3	348 @ $27 = $ 9,396	308 @ $27 = $ 8,316	40 @ $27 = $1,080
July 15	257 @ $28 = $ 7,196	212 @ $28 = $ 5,936	45 @ $28 = $1,260
	$18,467	575 $15,627	105 $2,840

4. a;

Date	Goods Available for Sale	Cost of Goods Sold	Ending Inventory
July 1	75 @ $25 = $ 1,875	75 @ $25 = $ 1,875	
July 3	348 @ $27 = $ 9,396	348 @ $27 = $ 9,396	
July 15	257 @ $28 = $ 7,196	152 @ $28 = $ 4,256	105 @ $28 = $2,940
	$18,467	575 $15,527	105 $2,940

5. **i)** a;

Date	Goods Available for Sale		Cost of Goods Sold		Ending Inventory	
Beg. Inv.	100 @ $10 = $1,000		100 @ $10 = $1,000			
Pur. 1	40 @ $12 = $ 480		30 @ $12 = $ 360		10 @ $12 = $120	
Pur. 2	20 @ $14 = $ 280				20 @ $14 = $280	
		$1,760	130	$1,360	30	$400

5. **ii)** b;

Date	Goods Available for Sale		Cost of Goods Sold		Ending Inventory	
Beg. Inv.	100 @ $10 = $1,000		70 @ $10 = $ 700		30 @ $10 = $300	
Pur. 1	40 @ $12 = $ 480		40 @ $12 = $ 480			
Pur. 2	20 @ $14 = $ 280		20 @ $14 = $ 280			
		$1,760	130	$1,460	30	$300

6. d; Days' sales in inventory = (Ending inventory/Cost of goods sold) × 365
= ($18,000/$85,000) × 365
= 77.29 days

Superscript letter A or B denotes assignments based on Appendix 6A or 6B.

Select Quick Study and Exercise assignments feature Guided Example videos, called "Hints" in Connect. Hints use different numbers, and instructors can turn this feature on or off.

QUICK STUDY

QS 6-1
Inventory ownership
C1

Homestead Crafts, a distributor of handmade gifts, operates out of owner Emma Finn's house. At the end of the current period, Emma looks over her inventory and finds that she has the following.

- 1,300 units (products) in her basement, 20 of which were damaged by water and cannot be sold.
- 350 units in her van, ready to deliver per a customer order, terms FOB destination.
- 80 units out on consignment to a friend who owns a retail store.

How many total units should Emma include in her company's period-end inventory?

QS 6-2
Inventory costs
C1

A car dealer acquires a used car for $14,000, with terms FOB shipping point. Compute total inventory costs assigned to the used car if additional costs include the following.

- $250 for transportation-in.
- $300 for shipping insurance.
- $900 for car import duties.
- $150 for advertising.
- $1,250 for sales staff salaries.
- $180 for trimming shrubs.

QS 6-3
Inventory costs
C1

A solar panel dealer acquires a used panel for $9,000, with terms FOB shipping point. Compute total inventory costs assigned to the used panel if additional costs include the following.

- $1,500 for sales staff salaries.
- $280 for transportation-in by train.
- $110 for online advertising.
- $135 for shipping insurance.
- $550 for used panel restoration.
- $300 for lawn care.

QS 6-4
Computing goods available for sale P1

Wattan Company reports beginning inventory of 10 units at $60 each. Every week for four weeks it purchases an additional 10 units at respective costs of $61, $62, $65, and $70 per unit for weeks 1 through 4. Compute the cost of goods available for sale and the units available for sale for this four-week period. Assume that no sales occur during those four weeks.

QS 6-5
Perpetual: Inventory costing with FIFO
P1

A company reports the following beginning inventory and two purchases for the month of January. On January 26, the company sells 350 units. Ending inventory at January 31 totals 150 units.

	Units	Unit Cost
Beginning inventory on January 1.	320	$3.00
Purchase on January 9	80	3.20
Purchase on January 25	100	3.34

Required

Assume the perpetual inventory system is used. Determine the costs assigned to ending inventory when costs are assigned based on the FIFO method. (Round per unit costs and inventory amounts to cents.)

QS 6-6
Perpetual: Inventory costing with LIFO P1

Refer to the information in QS 6-5 and assume the perpetual inventory system is used. Determine the costs assigned to ending inventory when costs are assigned based on LIFO. (Round per unit costs and inventory amounts to cents.)

QS 6-7
Perpetual: Inventory costing with weighted average P1

Refer to the information in QS 6-5 and assume the perpetual inventory system is used. Determine the costs assigned to ending inventory when costs are assigned based on the weighted average method. (Round per unit costs and inventory amounts to cents.)

QS 6-8A
Periodic: Inventory costing with FIFO P3

Refer to the information in QS 6-5 and assume the periodic inventory system is used. Determine the costs assigned to ending inventory when costs are assigned based on the FIFO method. (Round per unit costs and inventory amounts to cents.)

QS 6-9A
Periodic: Inventory costing with LIFO P3

Refer to the information in QS 6-5 and assume the periodic inventory system is used. Determine the costs assigned to ending inventory when costs are assigned based on the LIFO method. (Round per unit costs and inventory amounts to cents.)

QS 6-10A
Periodic: Inventory costing with weighted average P3

Refer to the information in QS 6-5 and assume the periodic inventory system is used. Determine the costs assigned to ending inventory when costs are assigned based on the weighted average method. (Round per unit costs and inventory amounts to cents.)

QS 6-11
Perpetual: Assigning costs with FIFO

P1

Trey Monson starts a merchandising business on December 1 and enters into the following three inventory purchases. Also, on December 15, Monson sells 15 units for $20 each.

Purchases on December 7.	10 units @ $ 6 cost
Purchases on December 14.	20 units @ $12 cost
Purchases on December 21.	15 units @ $14 cost

Required

Monson uses a perpetual inventory system. Determine the costs assigned to the December 31 ending inventory based on the FIFO method.

QS 6-12
Perpetual: Inventory costing with LIFO P1

Refer to the information in QS 6-11 and assume the perpetual inventory system is used. Determine the costs assigned to ending inventory when costs are assigned based on the LIFO method.

QS 6-13
Perpetual: Inventory costing with weighted average P1

Refer to the information in QS 6-11 and assume the perpetual inventory system is used. Determine the costs assigned to ending inventory when costs are assigned based on the weighted average method. (Round per unit costs and inventory amounts to cents.)

QS 6-14
Perpetual: Inventory costing with specific identification P1

Refer to the information in QS 6-11 and assume the perpetual inventory system is used. Determine the costs assigned to ending inventory when costs are assigned based on specific identification. Of the units sold, eight are from the December 7 purchase and seven are from the December 14 purchase.

QS 6-15A
Periodic: Inventory costing with FIFO P3

Refer to the information in QS 6-11 and assume the periodic inventory system is used. Determine the costs assigned to ending inventory when costs are assigned based on the FIFO method.

QS 6-16A
Periodic: Inventory costing with LIFO P3

Refer to the information in QS 6-11 and assume the periodic inventory system is used. Determine the costs assigned to ending inventory when costs are assigned based on the LIFO method.

QS 6-17[A]
Periodic: Inventory costing with weighted average P3

Refer to the information in QS 6-11 and assume the periodic inventory system is used. Determine the costs assigned to ending inventory when costs are assigned based on the weighted average method. (Round per unit costs and inventory amounts to cents.)

QS 6-18[A]
Periodic: Inventory costing with specific identification P3

Refer to the information in QS 6-11 and assume the periodic inventory system is used. Determine the costs assigned to ending inventory when costs are assigned based on specific identification. Of the units sold, eight are from the December 7 purchase and seven are from the December 14 purchase.

QS 6-19
Contrasting inventory costing methods
A1

Identify the inventory costing method (SI, FIFO, LIFO, or WA) best described by each of the following separate statements. Assume a period of increasing costs.

1. Results in the highest cost of goods sold.
2. Yields the highest net income.
3. Has the lowest tax expense because of reporting the lowest net income.
4. Better matches current costs with revenues.
5. Precisely matches the costs of items with the revenues they generate.

QS 6-20
Using income statement relations to compute missing amounts A1

Compute the missing amounts in the separate income statements A, B, and C.

	A	B	C
Sales	$?	$20,000	$90,000
Cost of goods sold	40,000	?	30,000
Gross profit	35,000	11,500	?
Expenses	?	6,000	?
Net income	13,000	?	21,000

QS 6-21
Determining financial statement impact of FIFO vs. LIFO A1

Complete the following table by indicating whether FIFO or LIFO results in the *lower* reported amount for each of the three accounting measures.

	Lowest Ending Inventory	Lowest Cost of Goods Sold	Lowest Net Income
Rising costs			
Falling costs			

QS 6-22
Identifying income tax effect of FIFO vs. LIFO A1

Spade Co. is considering either FIFO or LIFO. Determine which method results in the lowest income tax expense in the current year when (*a*) inventory costs are rising and (*b*) inventory costs are falling. The income tax rate is 20% and is calculated as a percentage of net income.

QS 6-23
Applying LCM to inventories
P2

Ames Trading Co. has the following products in its ending inventory. Compute lower of cost or market for inventory applied separately to each product.

Product	Quantity	Cost per Unit	Market per Unit
Mountain bikes....	11	$600	$550
Skateboards......	13	350	425
Gliders..........	26	800	700

QS 6-24
Inventory errors
A2

In taking a physical inventory at the end of Year 1, Grant Company forgot to count certain units and understated ending inventory by $10,000. Determine how this error affects each of the following.

a. Year 1 cost of goods sold
b. Year 1 net income
c. Year 2 cost of goods sold
d. Year 2 net income

QS 6-25
Analyzing inventory A3

Endor Company begins the year with $140,000 of goods in inventory. At year-end, the amount in inventory has increased to $180,000. Cost of goods sold for the year is $1,200,000. Compute Endor's inventory turnover and days' sales in inventory. Assume there are 365 days in the year.

QS 6-26[B]
Estimating inventories—gross profit method P4

Confucius Bookstore's inventory is destroyed by a fire on September 5. The following data for the current year are available from the accounting records. Estimate the cost of the inventory destroyed.

Beginning inventory, Jan. 1	$190,000
Jan. 1 through Sept. 5 purchases (net)	$352,000
Jan. 1 through Sept. 5 sales (net)	$685,000
Current year's estimated gross profit rate	44%

connect

EXERCISES

Exercise 6-1
Inventory ownership C1

1. At year-end, Barr Co. had shipped $12,500 of merchandise FOB destination to Lee Co. Which company should include the $12,500 of merchandise in transit as part of its year-end inventory?
2. Parris Company has shipped $20,000 of goods to Harlow Co., and Harlow Co. has arranged to sell the goods for Parris. Identify the consignor and the consignee. Which company should include any unsold goods as part of its inventory?

Exercise 6-2
Inventory costs C1

Walberg Associates, antique dealers, purchased goods for $75,000. Terms of the purchase were FOB shipping point, and the cost of transporting the goods to Walberg Associates's warehouse was $2,400. Walberg Associates insured the shipment at a cost of $300. Prior to putting the goods up for sale, they cleaned and refurbished them at a cost of $980. Determine the cost of inventory.

Exercise 6-3
Perpetual: Inventory costing methods P1

Laker Company reported the following January purchases and sales data for its only product.

Date	Activities	Units Acquired at Cost	Units Sold at Retail
Jan. 1	Beginning inventory	140 units @ $6.00 = $ 840	
Jan. 10	Sales		100 units @ $15
Jan. 20	Purchase	60 units @ $5.00 = 300	
Jan. 25	Sales		80 units @ $15
Jan. 30	Purchase	180 units @ $4.50 = 810	
	Totals	380 units $1,950	180 units

Required

The company uses a perpetual inventory system. Determine the cost assigned to ending inventory and to cost of goods sold using (*a*) specific identification, (*b*) weighted average, (*c*) FIFO, and (*d*) LIFO. (Round per unit costs and inventory amounts to cents.) For specific identification, ending inventory consists of 180 units from the January 30 purchase, 5 units from the January 20 purchase, and 15 units from beginning inventory.

Exercise 6-4
Perpetual: Journalizing transactions P1

Refer to sales and purchases data from Exercise 6-3 and record journal entries for Laker Company's sales and purchases transactions. Assume for this assignment that the company uses a perpetual inventory system and FIFO. All sales and purchases are made on account, and no discounts are offered.

Exercise 6-5
Perpetual: Gross profit effects of inventory methods A1

Use the data in Exercise 6-3 to compute gross profit for the month of January for Laker Company similar to that in Exhibit 6.8 for the four inventory methods.

1. Which method yields the highest gross profit?
2. Does gross profit using weighted average fall above, between, or below that using FIFO and LIFO?
3. If costs were rising instead of falling, which method would yield the highest gross profit?

Exercise 6-6[A]
Periodic: Inventory costing P3

Refer to the information in Exercise 6-3 and assume the periodic inventory system is used. Determine the costs assigned to ending inventory and to cost of goods sold using (*a*) specific identification, (*b*) weighted average, (*c*) FIFO, and (*d*) LIFO. (Round per unit costs and inventory amounts to cents.) For specific identification, ending inventory consists of 180 units from the January 30 purchase, 5 units from the January 20 purchase, and 15 units from beginning inventory.

Exercise 6-7^A
Periodic: Gross profit effects of inventory methods
P3 A1

Use the data and results from Exercise 6-6^A to compute gross profit for the month of January for the company similar to that in Exhibit 6.8 for the four inventory methods.

Required

1. Which method yields the highest gross profit?
2. Does gross profit using weighted average fall above, between, or below that using FIFO and LIFO?
3. If costs were rising instead of falling, which method would yield the highest gross profit?

Exercise 6-8
Perpetual: Inventory costing methods—FIFO and LIFO
P1

Hemming Co. reported the following current year purchases and sales for its only product.

Date	Activities	Units Acquired at Cost		Units Sold at Retail
Jan. 1	Beginning inventory	200 units @ $10 =	$ 2,000	
Jan. 10	Sales....................			150 units @ $40
Mar. 14	Purchase	350 units @ $15 =	5,250	
Mar. 15	Sales....................			300 units @ $40
July 30	Purchase	450 units @ $20 =	9,000	
Oct. 5	Sales....................			430 units @ $40
Oct. 26	Purchase	100 units @ $25 =	2,500	
	Totals	1,100 units	$18,750	880 units

Required

Hemming uses a perpetual inventory system. Determine the costs assigned to ending inventory and to cost of goods sold using (*a*) FIFO and (*b*) LIFO. (*c*) Compute the gross profit for each method.

Exercise 6-9
Specific identification
P1

Refer to the information in Exercise 6-8. Ending inventory consists of 45 units from the March 14 purchase, 75 units from the July 30 purchase, and all 100 units from the October 26 purchase. Using the specific identification method, compute (*a*) the cost of goods sold and (*b*) the gross profit.

Exercise 6-10^A
Periodic: Inventory costing
P3

Refer to the information in Exercise 6-8 and assume the periodic inventory system is used. Determine the costs assigned to ending inventory and to cost of goods sold using (*a*) FIFO and (*b*) LIFO. (*c*) Compute the gross profit for each method.

Exercise 6-11
Perpetual: Inventory costing methods—FIFO and LIFO
P1

Tree Seedlings has the following current year purchases and sales for its only product.

Date	Activities	Units Acquired at Cost	Units Sold at Retail
Jan. 1	Beginning inventory	40 units @ $2 = $ 80	
Jan. 3	Sales....................		30 units @ $8
Feb. 14	Purchase	70 units @ $3 = $210	
Feb. 15	Sales....................		60 units @ $8
June 30	Purchase	90 units @ $4 = $360	
Nov. 6	Sales....................		86 units @ $8
Nov. 19	Purchase	20 units @ $5 = $100	
	Totals	220 units $750	176 units

Required

The company uses a perpetual inventory system. Determine the costs assigned to ending inventory and to cost of goods sold using (*a*) FIFO and (*b*) LIFO. (*c*) Compute the gross profit for each method.

Exercise 6-12
Perpetual: Journalizing transactions P1

Refer to sales and purchases data from Exercise 6-11 and record journal entries for Tree Seedlings's sales and purchases transactions. Assume for this assignment that the company uses a perpetual inventory system and LIFO. All sales and purchases are made on account, and no discounts are offered.

Exercise 6-13^A
Periodic: Inventory costing methods—FIFO and LIFO P3

Refer to the information in Exercise 6-11 and assume the periodic inventory system is used. Determine the costs assigned to ending inventory and to cost of goods sold using (*a*) FIFO and (*b*) LIFO. (*c*) Compute the gross profit for each method.

Exercise 6-14[A]
Periodic: Cost flow assumptions
P3

Lopez Company reported the following current year data for its only product. The company uses a periodic inventory system, and its ending inventory consists of 150 units—50 from each of the last three purchases. Determine the cost assigned to ending inventory and to cost of goods sold using (*a*) specific identification, (*b*) weighted average, (*c*) FIFO, and (*d*) LIFO. (Round per unit costs and inventory amounts to cents.) (*e*) Which method yields the highest net income?

Jan. 1	Beginning inventory	96 units @ $2.00 =	$ 192
Mar. 7	Purchase	220 units @ $2.25 =	495
July 28	Purchase	544 units @ $2.50 =	1,360
Oct. 3	Purchase	480 units @ $2.80 =	1,344
Dec. 19	Purchase	160 units @ $2.90 =	464
	Totals	1,500 units	$3,855

Check Inventory: LIFO, $313.50; FIFO, $435.00

Exercise 6-15[A]
Periodic: Cost flow assumptions
P3

Flora's Gifts reported the following current-month data for its only product. The company uses a periodic inventory system, and its ending inventory consists of 60 units—50 units from the January 6 purchase and 10 units from the January 25 purchase. Determine the cost assigned to ending inventory and to cost of goods sold using (*a*) specific identification, (*b*) weighted average, (*c*) FIFO, and (*d*) LIFO. (Round per unit costs and inventory amounts to cents.) (*e*) Which method yields the lowest net income?

Jan. 1	Beginning inventory	138 units @ $3.00 =	$ 414
Jan. 6	Purchase	300 units @ $2.80 =	840
Jan. 17	Purchase	540 units @ $2.30 =	1,242
Jan. 25	Purchase	22 units @ $2.00 =	44
	Totals	1,000 units	$2,540

Check Inventory: LIFO, $180.00; FIFO, $131.40

Exercise 6-16
Lower of cost or market
P2

Martinez Company's ending inventory includes the following items. Compute the lower of cost or market for ending inventory applied separately to each product.

Product	Units	Cost per Unit	Market per Unit
Helmets.........	24	$50	$54
Bats............	17	78	72
Shoes...........	38	95	91
Uniforms........	42	36	36

Check LCM = $7,394

Exercise 6-17
Analyzing inventory errors
A2

Vibrant Company had $850,000 of sales in each of Year 1, Year 2, and Year 3, and it purchased merchandise costing $500,000 in each of those years. It also maintained a $250,000 physical inventory from the beginning to the end of that three-year period. In accounting for inventory, it made an error at the end of Year 1 that caused its Year 1 ending inventory to appear on its statements as $230,000 rather than the correct $250,000.

1. Determine the correct amount of the company's gross profit in each of Year 1, Year 2, and Year 3.
2. Prepare comparative income statements as in Exhibit 6.11 to show the effect of this error on the company's cost of goods sold and gross profit for each of Year 1, Year 2, and Year 3.

Exercise 6-18
Comparing LIFO numbers to FIFO numbers; ratio analysis
A3

Cruz Company uses LIFO for inventory costing and reports the following financial data. It also recomputed inventory and cost of goods sold using FIFO for comparison purposes.

	Year 2	Year 1
LIFO inventory..........................	$160	$110
LIFO cost of goods sold	740	680
FIFO inventory	240	110
FIFO cost of goods sold	660	645
Current assets (using LIFO)	220	180
Current assets (using FIFO).............	300	180
Current liabilities.....................	200	170

1. Compute its current ratio, inventory turnover, and days' sales in inventory for Year 2 using (*a*) LIFO numbers and (*b*) FIFO numbers.
2. Comment on and interpret the results of part 1.

Check (1) FIFO: Current ratio, 1.5; Inventory turnover, 3.8 times

Exercise 6-19
Inventory turnover and days' sales in inventory
A3

Use the following information for Palmer Co. to compute inventory turnover for Year 3 and Year 2, and its days' sales in inventory at December 31, Year 3 and Year 2. From Year 2 to Year 3, did Palmer improve its (*a*) inventory turnover and (*b*) days' sales in inventory?

	Year 3	Year 2	Year 1
Cost of goods sold	$643,825	$426,650	$391,300
Ending inventory.	97,400	87,750	92,500

Exercise 6-20^B
Estimating ending inventory—retail method
P4

Dakota Company had net sales (at retail) of $260,000. The following additional information is available from its records. Use the retail inventory method to estimate Dakota's year-end inventory at cost.

	At Cost	At Retail
Beginning inventory.	$ 63,800	$128,400
Cost of goods purchased.	115,060	196,800

Check End. inventory at cost, $35,860

Exercise 6-21^B
Estimating ending inventory—gross profit method P4

On January 1, JKR Shop had $225,000 of beginning inventory at cost. In the first quarter of the year, it purchased $795,000 of merchandise, returned $11,550, and paid freight charges of $18,800 on purchased merchandise, terms FOB shipping point. The company's gross profit averages 30%, and the store had $1,000,000 of net sales (at retail) in the first quarter of the year.

Use the gross profit method to estimate its cost of inventory at the end of the first quarter.

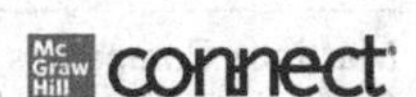

PROBLEM SET A

Problem 6-1A
Perpetual: Alternative cost flows
P1

Warnerwoods Company uses a perpetual inventory system. It entered into the following purchases and sales transactions for March. (For specific identification, units sold consist of 80 units from beginning inventory, 340 units from the March 5 purchase, 40 units from the March 18 purchase, and 120 units from the March 25 purchase.

Date	Activities	Units Acquired at Cost	Units Sold at Retail
Mar. 1	Beginning inventory	100 units @ $50 per unit	
Mar. 5	Purchase	400 units @ $55 per unit	
Mar. 9	Sales.		420 units @ $85 per unit
Mar. 18	Purchase	120 units @ $60 per unit	
Mar. 25	Purchase	200 units @ $62 per unit	
Mar. 29	Sales.		160 units @ $95 per unit
	Totals	820 units	580 units

Required

1. Compute cost of goods available for sale and the number of units available for sale.
2. Compute the number of units in ending inventory.
3. Compute the cost assigned to ending inventory using (*a*) FIFO, (*b*) LIFO, (*c*) weighted average, and (*d*) specific identification. (Round all amounts to cents.)
4. Compute gross profit earned by the company for each of the four costing methods in part 3.

Problem 6-2A^A
Periodic: Alternative cost flows
P3

Refer to the information in Problem 6-1A and assume the periodic inventory system is used.

Required

1. Compute cost of goods available for sale and the number of units available for sale.
2. Compute the number of units in ending inventory.
3. Compute the cost assigned to ending inventory using (*a*) FIFO, (*b*) LIFO, (*c*) weighted average, and (*d*) specific identification. (Round all amounts to cents.)
4. Compute gross profit earned by the company for each of the four costing methods in part 3.

Problem 6-3A
Perpetual: Alternative cost flows
P1

Montoure Company uses a perpetual inventory system. It entered into the following calendar-year purchases and sales transactions. (For specific identification, units sold consist of 600 units from beginning inventory, 300 from the February 10 purchase, 200 from the March 13 purchase, 50 from the August 21 purchase, and 250 from the September 5 purchase.)

Date	Activities	Units Acquired at Cost	Units Sold at Retail
Jan. 1	Beginning inventory	600 units @ $45 per unit	
Feb. 10	Purchase	400 units @ $42 per unit	
Mar. 13	Purchase	200 units @ $27 per unit	
Mar. 15	Sales................		800 units @ $75 per unit
Aug. 21	Purchase	100 units @ $50 per unit	
Sep. 5	Purchase	500 units @ $46 per unit	
Sep. 10	Sales................		600 units @ $75 per unit
	Totals	1,800 units	1,400 units

Required

1. Compute cost of goods available for sale and the number of units available for sale.
2. Compute the number of units in ending inventory.
3. Compute the cost assigned to ending inventory using (*a*) FIFO, (*b*) LIFO, (*c*) weighted average, and (*d*) specific identification. (Round all amounts to cents.)
4. Compute gross profit earned by the company for each of the four costing methods in part 3.

Analysis Component

5. The company's manager earns a bonus based on a percent of gross profit. Which method of inventory costing produces the highest bonus for the manager?

Problem 6-4A^A^
Periodic: Alternative cost flows
P3

Refer to the information in Problem 6-3A and assume the periodic inventory system is used.

Required

1. Compute cost of goods available for sale and the number of units available for sale.
2. Compute the number of units in ending inventory.
3. Compute the cost assigned to ending inventory using (*a*) FIFO, (*b*) LIFO, (*c*) weighted average, and (*d*) specific identification. (Round all amounts to cents.)
4. Compute gross profit earned by the company for each of the four costing methods in part 3.

Analysis Component

5. The company's manager earns a bonus based on a percentage of gross profit. Which method of inventory costing produces the highest bonus for the manager?

Problem 6-5A
Lower of cost or market
P2

A physical inventory of Liverpool Company taken at December 31 reveals the following.

Item	Units	Cost per Unit	Market per Unit
Car audio equipment			
Speakers	345	$ 90	$ 98
Stereos	260	111	100
Amplifiers	326	86	95
Subwoofers	204	52	41
Security equipment			
Alarms	480	150	125
Locks	291	93	84
Cameras	212	310	322
Binocular equipment			
Tripods	185	70	84
Stabilizers	170	97	105

Required

1. Compute the lower of cost or market for the inventory applied separately to each item.
2. If the market amount is less than the recorded cost of the inventory, then record the LCM adjustment to the Merchandise Inventory account.

Check (1) $273,054

Problem 6-6A
Analysis of inventory errors
A2

Navajo Company's year-end financial statements show the following. The company recently discovered that in making physical counts of inventory, it had made the following errors: Year 1 ending inventory is understated by $56,000 and Year 2 ending inventory is overstated by $20,000.

For Year Ended December 31	Year 1	Year 2	Year 3
(*a*) Cost of goods sold....	$ 615,000	$ 957,000	$ 780,000
(*b*) Net income.........	230,000	285,000	241,000
(*c*) Total current assets ...	1,255,000	1,365,000	1,200,000
(*d*) Total equity.........	1,387,000	1,530,000	1,242,000

Required

1. For each key financial statement figure—(*a*), (*b*), (*c*), and (*d*) above—prepare a table similar to the following to show the adjustments necessary to correct the reported amounts.

Figure: ______	Year 1	Year 2	Year 3
Reported amount			
Adjustments for: Year 1 error.....			
Year 2 error.....			
Corrected amount			

Check (1) Corrected net income: Year 1, $286,000; Year 2, $209,000; Year 3, $261,000

2. What is the total error in combined net income for the three-year period resulting from the inventory errors? Explain.

Problem 6-7A^A
Periodic: Alternative cost flows P3

Seminole Co. began the year with 23,000 units of product in its January 1 inventory costing $15 each. It made four purchases of its product during the year as follows. The company uses a periodic inventory system. On December 31, a physical count reveals that 40,000 units of its product remain in inventory.

Mar. 7.....	30,000 units @ $18 each	Aug. 1......	23,000 units @ $25 each
May 25.....	39,000 units @ $20 each	Nov. 10......	35,000 units @ $26 each

Required

1. Compute the number and total cost of the units available for sale during the year.
2. Compute the amounts assigned to ending inventory and the cost of goods sold using (*a*) FIFO, (*b*) LIFO, and (*c*) weighted average. (Round all amounts to cents.)

Check (2) Cost of goods sold: FIFO, $2,115,000; LIFO, $2,499,000; WA, $2,310,000

Problem 6-8A^A
Periodic: Income comparisons and cost flows
A1 P3

QP Corp. sold 4,000 units of its product at $50 per unit during the year and incurred operating expenses of $5 per unit in selling the units. It began the year with 700 units in inventory and made successive purchases of its product as follows.

Jan. 1	Beginning inventory	700 units @ $18 per unit
Feb. 20	Purchase	1,700 units @ $19 per unit
May 16	Purchase	800 units @ $20 per unit
Oct. 3	Purchase	500 units @ $21 per unit
Dec. 11	Purchase	2,300 units @ $22 per unit
	Total	6,000 units

Required

1. Prepare comparative year-end income statements for the three inventory costing methods of FIFO, LIFO, and weighted average. (Round all amounts to cents.) Include a detailed cost of goods sold section as part of each statement. The company uses a periodic inventory system.
2. How would the financial results from using the three alternative inventory costing methods change if the company had been experiencing *declining* costs in its purchases of inventory?
3. What advantages and disadvantages are offered by using (*a*) LIFO and (*b*) FIFO? Assume the continuing trend of *increasing* costs.

Problem 6-9A[B]
Retail inventory method
P4

The records of Alaska Company provide the following information for the year ended December 31.

	At Cost	At Retail
Beginning inventory, January 1	$ 469,010	$ 928,950
Cost of goods purchased	3,376,050	6,381,050
Sales		5,595,800
Sales returns		42,800

Required

1. Use the retail inventory method to estimate the company's year-end inventory at cost.
2. A year-end physical inventory at retail prices yields a total inventory of $1,686,900. Prepare a calculation showing the company's loss from shrinkage at cost and at retail.

Check (1) Inventory, $924,182 cost
(2) Inventory shortage at cost, $36,873

Problem 6-10A[B]
Gross profit method **P4**

Wayward Company wants to prepare interim financial statements for the first quarter. The company wishes to avoid making a physical count of inventory. Wayward's gross profit rate averages 34%. The following information for the first quarter is available from its records.

Beginning inventory, January 1	$ 302,580
Cost of goods purchased	941,040
Sales	1,211,160
Sales returns	8,410

Required

Use the gross profit method to estimate the company's first-quarter ending inventory.

Check Estimated ending inventory, $449,805

PROBLEM SET B

Problem 6-1B
Perpetual: Alternative cost flows
P1

Ming Company uses a perpetual inventory system. It entered into the following purchases and sales transactions for April. (For specific identification, units sold consist of 20 units from beginning inventory, 30 units from the April 6 purchase, and 10 units from the April 25 purchase.)

Date	Activities	Units Acquired at Cost	Units Sold at Retail
Apr. 1	Beginning inventory	20 units @ $3,000 per unit	
Apr. 6	Purchase	30 units @ $3,500 per unit	
Apr. 9	Sales		35 units @ $12,000 per unit
Apr. 17	Purchase	5 units @ $4,500 per unit	
Apr. 25	Purchase	10 units @ $4,800 per unit	
Apr. 30	Sales		25 units @ $14,000 per unit
	Total	65 units	60 units

Required

1. Compute cost of goods available for sale and the number of units available for sale.
2. Compute the number of units in ending inventory.
3. Compute the cost assigned to ending inventory using (*a*) FIFO, (*b*) LIFO, (*c*) weighted average, and (*d*) specific identification. (Round all amounts to cents.)
4. Compute gross profit earned by the company for each of the four costing methods in part 3.

Problem 6-2B[A]
Periodic: Alternative cost flows
P3

Refer to the information in Problem 6-1B and assume the periodic inventory system is used.

Required

1. Compute cost of goods available for sale and the number of units available for sale.
2. Compute the number of units in ending inventory.
3. Compute the cost assigned to ending inventory using (*a*) FIFO, (*b*) LIFO, (*c*) weighted average, and (*d*) specific identification. (Round all amounts to cents.)
4. Compute gross profit earned by the company for each of the four costing methods in part 3.

Problem 6-3B
Perpetual: Alternative cost flows
P1

Aloha Company uses a perpetual inventory system. It entered into the following calendar-year purchases and sales transactions. (For specific identification, units sold consist of 80 units from beginning inventory, 300 units from the May 6 purchase, and 100 units from the May 25 purchase.)

Date	Activities	Units Acquired at Cost	Units Sold at Retail
May 1	Beginning inventory	150 units @ $300 per unit	
May 6	Purchase	350 units @ $350 per unit	
May 9	Sales................		180 units @ $1,200 per unit
May 17	Purchase	80 units @ $450 per unit	
May 25	Purchase	100 units @ $458 per unit	
May 30	Sales................		300 units @ $1,400 per unit
	Total	680 units	480 units

Required

1. Compute cost of goods available for sale and the number of units available for sale.
2. Compute the number of units in ending inventory.
3. Compute the cost assigned to ending inventory using (*a*) FIFO, (*b*) LIFO, (*c*) weighted average, and (*d*) specific identification. (Round all amounts to cents.)
4. Compute gross profit earned by the company for each of the four costing methods in part 3.

Analysis Component

5. If the company's manager earns a bonus based on a percent of gross profit, which method of inventory costing will the manager likely prefer?

Problem 6-4B[A]
Periodic: Alternative cost flows
P3

Refer to the information in Problem 6-3B and assume the periodic inventory system is used.

Required

1. Compute cost of goods available for sale and the number of units available for sale.
2. Compute the number of units in ending inventory.
3. Compute the cost assigned to ending inventory using (*a*) FIFO, (*b*) LIFO, (*c*) weighted average, and (*d*) specific identification. (Round all amounts to cents.)
4. Compute gross profit earned by the company for each of the four costing methods in part 3.

Analysis Component

5. If the company's manager earns a bonus based on a percentage of gross profit, which method of inventory costing will the manager likely prefer?

Problem 6-5B
Lower of cost or market
P2

A physical inventory of Office Necessities Company taken at December 31 reveals the following.

Item	Units	Cost per Unit	Market per Unit
Office furniture			
Desks	536	$261	$305
Chairs	395	227	256
Mats	687	49	43
Bookshelves	421	93	82
Filing cabinets			
Two-drawer	114	81	70
Four-drawer	298	135	122
Lateral	75	104	118
Office equipment			
Projectors	370	168	200
Copiers	475	317	288
Phones	302	125	117

Required

Check (1) $580,054

1. Compute the lower of cost or market for the inventory applied separately to each item.
2. If the market amount is less than the recorded cost of the inventory, then record the LCM adjustment to the Merchandise Inventory account.

Problem 6-6B
Analysis of inventory errors
A2

Hallam Company's year-end financial statements show the following. The company recently discovered that in making physical counts of inventory, it had made the following errors: Year 1 ending inventory is overstated by $18,000 and Year 2 ending inventory is understated by $26,000.

For Year Ended December 31	Year 1	Year 2	Year 3
(a) Cost of goods sold	$207,200	$213,800	$197,030
(b) Net income	175,800	212,270	184,910
(c) Total current assets	276,000	277,500	272,950
(d) Total equity...........	314,000	315,000	346,000

Required

1. For each key financial statement figure—(*a*), (*b*), (*c*), and (*d*) above—prepare a table similar to the following to show the adjustments necessary to correct the reported amounts.

Figure: ________	Year 1	Year 2	Year 3
Reported amount			
Adjustments for: Year 1 error....			
Year 2 error....			
Corrected amount			

2. What is the total error in combined net income for the three-year period resulting from the inventory errors? Explain.

Check (1) Corrected net income: Year 1, $157,800; Year 2, $256,270; Year 3, $158,910

Problem 6-7B^A
Periodic: Alternative cost flows
P3

Seneca Co. began the year with 6,500 units of product in its January 1 inventory costing $35 each. It made four purchases of its product during the year as follows. The company uses a periodic inventory system. On December 31, a physical count reveals that 8,500 units of its product remain in inventory.

Jan. 4	11,500 units @ $33 each	July 9	11,000 units @ $29 each
May 18	13,400 units @ $32 each	Nov. 21	7,600 units @ $27 each

Required

1. Compute the number and total cost of the units available for sale during the year.
2. Compute the amounts assigned to ending inventory and the cost of goods sold using (*a*) FIFO, (*b*) LIFO, and (*c*) weighted average. (Round all amounts to cents.)

Check (2) Cost of goods sold: FIFO, $1,328,700; LIFO, $1,266,500; WA, $1,294,800

Problem 6-8B^A
Periodic: Income comparisons and cost flows
A1 P3

Shepard Company sold 4,000 units of its product at $100 per unit during the year and incurred operating expenses of $15 per unit in selling the units. It began the year with 840 units in inventory and made successive purchases of its product as follows.

Jan. 1	Beginning inventory	840 units @ $58 per unit
Apr. 2	Purchase	600 units @ $59 per unit
June 14	Purchase	1,205 units @ $61 per unit
Aug. 29	Purchase	700 units @ $64 per unit
Nov. 18	Purchase	1,655 units @ $65 per unit
	Total	5,000 units

Required

1. Prepare comparative year-end income statements for the three inventory costing methods of FIFO, LIFO, and weighted average. (Round all amounts to cents.) Include a detailed cost of goods sold section as part of each statement. The company uses a periodic inventory system.
2. How would the financial results from using the three alternative inventory costing methods change if the company had been experiencing decreasing prices in its purchases of inventory?
3. What advantages and disadvantages are offered by using (*a*) LIFO and (*b*) FIFO? Assume the continuing trend of increasing costs.

Problem 6-9B[B]
Retail inventory method
P4

The records of Macklin Co. provide the following information for the year ended December 31.

	At Cost	At Retail
Beginning inventory, January 1	$ 90,022	$115,610
Cost of goods purchased	502,250	761,830
Sales		782,300
Sales returns		3,460

Required

1. Use the retail inventory method to estimate the company's year-end inventory.
2. A year-end physical inventory at retail prices yields a total inventory of $80,450. Prepare a calculation showing the company's loss from shrinkage at cost and at retail.

Check (1) Inventory, $66,555 cost
(2) Inventory shortage at cost, $12,251.25

Problem 6-10B[B]
Gross profit method
P4

Otingo Equipment Co. wants to prepare interim financial statements for the first quarter. The company wishes to avoid making a physical count of inventory. Otingo's gross profit rate averages 35%. The following information for the first quarter is available from its records.

Beginning inventory, January 1	$ 802,880
Cost of goods purchased	2,209,636
Sales	3,760,260
Sales returns	79,300

Required

Use the gross profit method to estimate the company's first-quarter ending inventory.

Check Est. ending inventory, $619,892

SERIAL PROBLEM
Business Solutions
A3 P2

Alexander Image/Shutterstock

Serial problem began in Chapter 1. If previous chapter segments were not completed, the serial problem can begin at this point. It is available in ***Connect*** *with an algorithmic option.*

SP 6

Part A

Santana Rey of **Business Solutions** is evaluating her inventory to determine whether it must be adjusted based on lower of cost or market rules. Business Solutions has three different types of software in its inventory, and the following information is available for each.

Inventory Items	Units	Cost per Unit	Market per Unit
Office productivity	3	$ 76	$ 74
Desktop publishing	2	103	100
Accounting	3	90	96

Required

Compute the lower of cost or market for ending inventory assuming Rey applies the lower of cost or market rule to each product in inventory. Must Rey adjust the reported inventory value? Explain.

Part B

Selected accounts and balances for the three months ended March 31, 2022, for Business Solutions follow.

Beginning inventory, January 1	$ 0
Cost of goods sold	14,052
Ending inventory, March 31	704

Required

1. Compute inventory turnover and days' sales in inventory for the three months ended March 31, 2022.
2. Assess the company's performance if competitors average 15 times for inventory turnover and 25 days for days' sales in inventory.

Mc Graw Hill connect

Tableau Dashboard Activities expose students to accounting analytics using visual displays. These assignments run in **Connect**. All are auto-gradable.

Tableau DA 6-1 Quick Study, Computing goods available for sale and assigning costs using specific identification, **P1**—similar to QS 6-14

Tableau DA 6-2 Exercise, Perpetual inventory costing methods, **P1, A1**—similar to Exercise 6-3

Tableau DA 6-3 Mini-Case, Perpetual inventory costing methods, **P1, A1**—similar to Exercise 6-5

Tableau DA 6-4A Exercise, Periodic income effects of LIFO and FIFO, **P3**—similar to Exercise 6-6

Tableau DA 6-5A Mini-Case, Periodic income effects of LIFO and FIFO, **P3**—similar to Exercise 6-7

Accounting Analysis

Mc Graw Hill connect

COMPANY ANALYSIS
C1 A3

AA 6-1 Use **Apple**'s financial statements in Appendix A to answer the following.

Required

1. What amount of inventories did Apple report as a current asset (*a*) on September 28, 2019? (*b*) On September 29, 2018?
2. Inventories make up what percent of total assets (*a*) on September 28, 2019? (*b*) On September 29, 2018?
3. Assuming Apple has enough inventory to meet demand, does Apple prefer inventory to be a lower or higher percentage of total assets?
4. Compute (*a*) inventory turnover for fiscal year ended September 28, 2019, and (*b*) days' sales in inventory as of September 28, 2019.

COMPARATIVE ANALYSIS
A3

AA 6-2 Comparative figures for **Apple** and **Google** follow.

	Apple			Google		
$ millions	Current Year	One Year Prior	Two Years Prior	Current Year	One Year Prior	Two Years Prior
Inventory	$ 4,106	$ 3,956	$ 4,855	$ 999	$ 1,107	$ 749
Cost of sales	161,782	163,756	141,048	71,896	59,549	45,583

Required

1. Compute inventory turnover for each company for the most recent two years shown.
2. Compute days' sales in inventory for each company for the three years shown.
3. Did the current year inventory turnover underperform or outperform the industry's average turnover of 15 in the case of (*a*) Apple and (*b*) Google?

EXTENDED ANALYSIS
A3

AA 6-3 Key figures for **Samsung** follow.

$ millions	Current Year	One Year Prior	Two Years Prior
Inventory..............	$ 22,966	$ 24,870	$ 22,708
Cost of sales...........	126,336	113,598	117,515

Required

1. For the most recent two years, compute Samsung's (*a*) inventory turnover and (*b*) days' sales in inventory.
2. Is the change in Samsung's inventory turnover favorable or unfavorable?
3. Did the current year inventory turnover for Samsung underperform or outperform the industry's average turnover of 15?

Discussion Questions

1. Describe how costs flow from inventory to cost of goods sold for the following methods: (*a*) FIFO and (*b*) LIFO.
2. Where is the amount of merchandise inventory disclosed in the financial statements?
3. If costs are declining, will the LIFO or FIFO method of inventory valuation yield the lower cost of goods sold? Why?
4. If inventory errors are said to correct themselves, why are accounting users concerned when such errors are made?
5. Explain the following statement: "Inventory errors correct themselves."
6. What is the meaning of *market* as it is used in determining the lower of cost or market for inventory?
7. What factors contribute to (or cause) inventory shrinkage?
8.[B] When preparing interim financial statements, what two methods can companies utilize to estimate cost of goods sold and ending inventory?

Beyond the Numbers

ETHICS CHALLENGE
A1

BTN 6-1 Golf Challenge Corp. is a retail sports store carrying golf apparel and equipment. The store is at the end of its second year of operation and is struggling. A major problem is that its cost of inventory has continually increased in the past two years. In the first year of operations, the store assigned inventory costs using LIFO. A loan agreement the store has with its bank, its prime source of financing, requires the store to maintain a certain profit margin and current ratio. The store's owner is currently looking over Golf Challenge's preliminary financial statements for its second year. The numbers are not favorable. The only way the store can meet the financial ratios agreed on with the bank is to change from LIFO to FIFO. The store originally decided on LIFO because of its tax advantages. The owner recalculates ending inventory using FIFO and submits those numbers and statements to the loan officer for the required bank review. The owner thankfully reflects on the available latitude in choosing the inventory costing method.

Required

1. How does Golf Challenge's use of FIFO improve its net profit margin and current ratio?
2. Is the action by Golf Challenge's owner ethical? Explain.

COMMUNICATING IN PRACTICE
A1

BTN 6-2 You are a financial adviser with a client in the wholesale produce business that just completed its first year of operations. Due to weather conditions, the cost of acquiring produce to resell has escalated during the latter part of this period. Your client, Javonte Gish, mentions that because her business sells perishable goods, she has striven to maintain a FIFO flow of goods. Although sales are good, the increasing cost of inventory has put the business in a tight cash position. Gish has expressed concern regarding the ability of the business to meet income tax obligations.

Required

Prepare a memorandum that identifies, explains, and justifies the inventory method you recommend that Ms. Gish adopt.

TAKING IT TO THE NET
A3

APPLE

BTN 6-3 Access the September 29, 2018, 10-K report for **Apple, Inc.** (ticker: AAPL), filed on November 5, 2018, from the EDGAR filings at SEC.gov.

Required

1. What products are manufactured by Apple?
2. What inventory method does Apple use? *Hint:* See Note 1 to its financial statements.
3. Compute its gross profit and gross profit ratio for the 2018 fiscal year. Comment on your computations—assume an industry average of 40% for the gross profit ratio.
4. Compute its inventory turnover and days' sales in inventory for the year ended September 29, 2018. Comment on your computations—assume an industry average of 15 for inventory turnover and 9 for days' sales in inventory.

TEAMWORK IN ACTION

A1 P1

BTN 6-4 Each team member has the responsibility to become an expert on an inventory method. This expertise will be used to facilitate teammates' understanding of the concepts relevant to that method.

1. Each learning team member should select an area for expertise by choosing one of the following inventory methods: specific identification, LIFO, FIFO, or weighted average.
2. Form expert teams made up of students who have selected the same area of expertise. The instructor will identify where each expert team will meet.
3. Using the following data, each expert team must collaborate to develop a presentation that illustrates the relevant concepts and procedures for its inventory method. Each team member must write the presentation in a format that can be shown to the learning team.

Point: Step 1 allows four choices or areas for expertise. Larger teams will have some duplication of choice, but the specific identification method should not be duplicated.

Data: The company uses a **perpetual** inventory system. It had the following beginning inventory and current year purchases of its product.

Jan. 1	Beginning inventory	50 units @ $100 = $ 5,000
Jan. 14	Purchase	150 units @ $120 = 18,000
Apr. 30	Purchase	200 units @ $150 = 30,000
Sep. 26	Purchase	300 units @ $200 = 60,000

The company transacted sales on the following dates at a $350 per unit sales price.

Jan. 10	30 units..........	specific cost: 30 @ $100
Feb. 15	100 units..........	specific cost: 100 @ $120
Oct. 5	350 units..........	specific cost: 100 @ $150 and 250 @ $200

Concepts and Procedures to Illustrate in Expert Presentation

a. Identify and compute the costs to assign to the units sold. (Round per unit costs to three decimals.)
b. Identify and compute the costs to assign to the units in ending inventory. (Round inventory balances to the dollar.)
c. How likely is it that this inventory costing method will reflect the actual physical flow of goods? How relevant is that factor in determining whether this is an acceptable method to use?
d. What is the impact of this method versus others in determining net income and income taxes?
e. How closely does the ending inventory amount reflect replacement cost?

4. Re-form learning teams. In rotation, each expert is to present to the team the presentation developed in part 3. Experts are to encourage and respond to questions.

ENTREPRENEURIAL DECISION

A3

BTN 6-5 Review the chapter's opening feature highlighting Jeff Bezos and **Whole Foods**. Assume that the business consistently maintains an inventory level of $30,000, meaning that its average and ending inventory levels are the same. Also assume its annual cost of sales is $120,000. To cut costs, the business proposes to slash inventory to a constant level of $15,000 with no impact on cost of sales. The business plans to work with suppliers to get quicker deliveries and to order smaller quantities more often.

Required

1. Compute the company's inventory turnover and its days' sales in inventory under (*a*) current conditions and (*b*) proposed conditions.
2. Evaluate and comment on the merits of the proposal given your analysis for part 1. Identify any concerns you might have about the proposal.

7 Accounting Information Systems

Chapter Preview

ACCOUNTING SYSTEM AND JOURNAL BASICS	SALES JOURNAL	CASH RECEIPTS JOURNAL	PURCHASES JOURNAL	CASH PAYMENTS JOURNAL
C1 Principles Components **C2** Journals Controlling accounts Subsidiary ledgers	**P1** Journalizing Posting Proving Returns and allowances	**P2** Journalizing Posting Footing and cross footing	**P3** Journalizing Posting Proving	**P4** Journalizing Posting General journal transactions
NTK 7-1, 7-2	**NTK 7-3**	**NTK 7-4**	**NTK 7-5**	**NTK 7-6**

Learning Objectives

CONCEPTUAL

C1 Identify the principles and components of accounting information systems.

C2 Explain special journals, controlling accounts, and subsidiary ledgers.

ANALYTICAL

A1 Compute days' payable outstanding and explain its use in assessing payments to suppliers.

PROCEDURAL

P1 Journalize and post transactions using a sales journal.

P2 Journalize and post transactions using a cash receipts journal.

P3 Journalize and post transactions using a purchases journal.

P4 Journalize and post transactions using a cash payments journal.

Out of the Box

"Execute like there's no tomorrow, strategize like there will be"—**AARON LEVIE**

LOS ALTOS, CA—Aaron Levie, Dylan Smith, Jeff Queisser, and Sam Ghods met in high school. "[Aaron] was a magician, and I was very much a hard core nerd," recalls Jeff. Beyond magic and nerdiness, the four friends were interested in information systems. The four friends launched **Box (Box.com)**, a cloud storage solution.

An immediate concern was how to obtain money to get started. "A couple of 19- and 20-year-olds starting a business isn't that old school," admits Dylan. Then a surprise occurred. As a result of a cold e-mail to Mark Cuban, the *Shark Tank* TV star, the founders received an investment of $350,000.

As the number of businesses and individuals using their service skyrocketed, the owners realized they needed to get their accounting system in order. This included setting up internal controls to guard against errors and fraud and creating special journals and accounting ledgers. Aaron insists that reliable accounting "platforms not only offer agility and productivity, but also an opportunity for better security."

Box maintains special journals for sales, cash receipts, purchases, and cash payments. Because Box has many customers paying to use its services, Box has subsidiary accounts receivable ledgers for each customer. It also has subsidiary accounts payable ledgers.

Kelly Redinger/Design Pics

The larger message of Box according to Aaron is, "Take the stodgiest, oldest, slowest moving industry you can find . . . and build amazing software for it."

Sources: *Box website*, January 2021; *Yahoo Finance*, January 2016; *Inc.*, October 2012; *BBC*, May 2013; *TechRepublic*, March 2014; *CrunchBase.com*, 2016

SYSTEM PRINCIPLES

C1 Identify the principles and components of accounting information systems.

Accounting information systems collect and process data from transactions and events, organize them in reports, and communicate results to decision makers. Accounting systems help users make more informed decisions and better understand the risks and returns of different strategies. Five principles of accounting information systems are shown in Exhibit 7.1.

Control Principle The **control principle** prescribes that an accounting information system have internal controls. **Internal controls** are procedures that help managers control and monitor business activities. They include policies to protect company assets and ensure compliance with laws and regulations.

EXHIBIT 7.1

System Principles

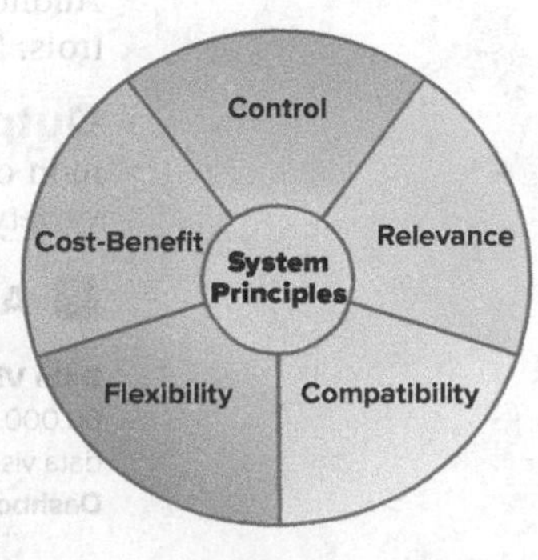

Relevance Principle The **relevance principle** prescribes that an accounting information system report useful, understandable, and timely information for decision making.

Compatibility Principle The **compatibility principle** prescribes that an accounting information system conform with a company's activities, personnel, and structure.

Flexibility Principle The **flexibility principle** prescribes that an accounting information system be able to adapt to changes in the company, business environment, and needs of decision makers. Technological advances, competitive pressures, consumer tastes, regulations, and company activities constantly evolve. A system must be designed to adapt to these changes.

Cost-Benefit Principle The **cost-benefit principle** prescribes that the benefits from an activity in an accounting information system outweigh the costs of that activity. For example, the benefits of producing a specific report must outweigh the costs of time and effort to produce that report. Decisions regarding other system principles (control, relevance, compatibility, and flexibility) are also affected by the cost-benefit principle.

Hero/Fancy/Corbis/Glow Images

Decision Insight

Who Owns the System? **Nintendo**'s stock increased greatly after the huge success of *Pokémon Go*. However, few investors read Nintendo's disclosures that said it owned less than one-third of the company that developed the app. When investors realized this, the stock dropped 17%, representing over $6 billion in value. ■

SYSTEM COMPONENTS

Point: Computerized systems provide more accuracy and speed than manual.

The five **components of accounting systems** are source documents, input devices, information processors, information storage, and output devices. These components apply whether a system is computerized or manual. Exhibit 7.2 shows these components.

EXHIBIT 7.2
Accounting System Components

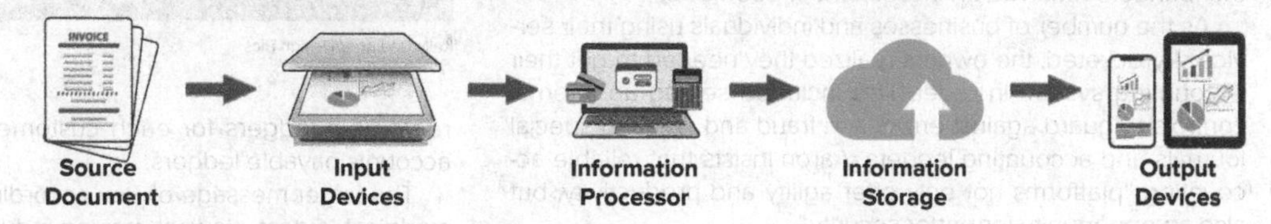

Source Documents

Source documents provide the information processed by an accounting system. Examples include bank statements and checks, invoices from suppliers, customer bills, sales receipts, and employee earnings records. Accurate source documents are crucial to accounting information systems. Input of wrong information damages the reliability of the information system.

Point: Control procedures limit the possibility of entering wrong data.

Input Devices

Input devices take information from source documents and transfer it to information processing. These devices convert data on source documents to a form usable by the system. Journal entries are a type of input device. Keyboards and scanners are the most common input devices in business.

Point: Controls ensure that only authorized individuals input data into the system.

Information Processors

Information processors summarize information for use in analysis and reporting. An information processor includes journals, ledgers, working papers, and posting procedures. Each assists in transforming raw data to useful information.

Information Storage

Information storage keeps data accessible to information processors. After being input and processed, data are stored for use in future analyses and reports. Auditors rely on this database when they audit both financial statements and a company's controls. Modern systems depend increasingly on cloud storage.

Output Devices

Output devices make accounting information available to users. Common output devices are printers, monitors, and smartphones. Output devices provide users a variety of items including customer bills, financial statements, and internal reports.

Analytics Insight

Data Visualization Research suggests that data is best conveyed visually. In fact, the human brain processes visuals 60,000 times faster than text. Also, infographics are 30 times more likely to be read than text. **Tableau**, the most popular data visualization tool, helps those with accounting knowledge convey key information to decision makers. See **Tableau Dashboard Activities** in Connect to start developing these skills. Sources: U of Minnesota; Kissmetrics ■

NEED-TO-KNOW 7-1

System Principles and Components

C1

Match each numbered description with the principle, component, or descriptor that it best reflects.

A. Control principle
B. Relevance principle
C. Compatibility principle
D. Flexibility principle
E. Cost-benefit principle
F. Source documents
G. Input devices
H. Information processors
I. Information storage
J. Output devices

1. Capture information from source documents and transfer to information processing.
2. Keeps data accessible to information processors.
3. Systems that summarize information for use.
4. Means to take information out of an accounting system and make it available to users.
5. Provide the information processed by the accounting system.
6. Prescribes that benefits from an activity in a system outweigh the costs.
7. Prescribes that a system be adaptable to changes in the company, environment, and user needs.
8. Prescribes that a system conform with a company's activities, personnel, and structure.
9. Prescribes that a system report useful, understandable, and timely information.
10. Prescribes that a system have internal controls.

Solution

1. G **2.** I **3.** H **4.** J **5.** F **6.** E **7.** D **8.** C **9.** B **10.** A

Do More: QS 7-1, QS 7-2

SPECIAL JOURNALS AND SUBSIDIARY LEDGERS

This chapter covers special journals using a *perpetual* inventory system.

C2 Explain special journals, controlling accounts, and subsidiary ledgers.

Basics of Special Journals

A **general journal** is an all-purpose journal in which we can record any transaction. To enhance internal control and reduce costs, transactions are organized into common groups. A **special journal** is used to record and post transactions of similar type. Special journals accumulate debits and credits of similar transactions and post amounts as column *totals* instead of individual amounts. The general journal is used for transactions not covered by special journals and for adjusting, closing, and correcting entries. Most transactions of a merchandiser are categorized into the journals shown in Exhibit 7.3. Special journals allow an *efficient division of labor,* which is also an effective control procedure.

Point: Companies use as many special journals as necessary.

Point: A specific transaction is recorded in only *one* journal.

EXHIBIT 7.3

Using Special Journals with a General Journal

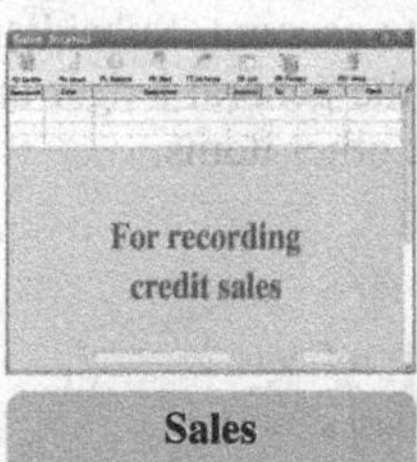

Sales Journal

Cash Receipts Journal

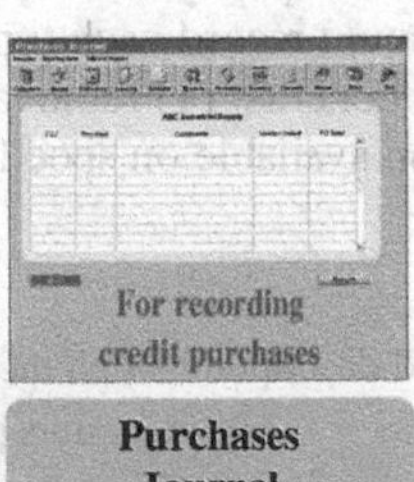

Purchases Journal

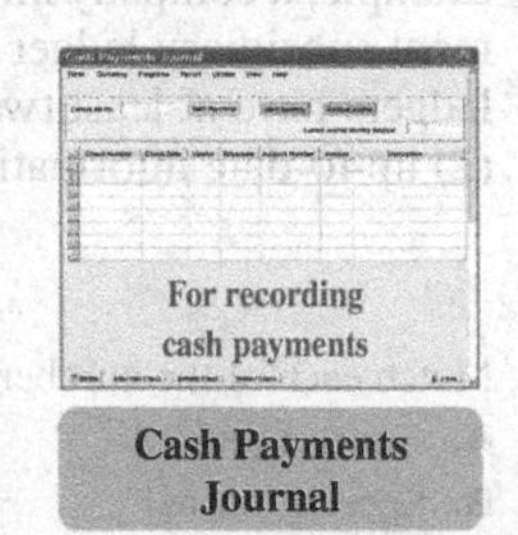

Cash Payments Journal

General Journal

Special journals are different for different types of businesses. A business creates special journals for its most common transactions, such as sales, cash receipts, purchases, and cash payments (or disbursements). The following sections give one example of a common systems design, but other designs are possible.

Subsidiary Ledgers

A **subsidiary ledger** is a list of individual accounts with a common characteristic. A subsidiary ledger has detailed information on specific accounts in the general ledger. Two of the most important are:

- **Accounts receivable ledger**—stores transaction data of individual customers.
- **Accounts payable ledger**—stores transaction data of individual suppliers.

Accounts Receivable Ledger When a company has more than one credit customer, the accounts receivable records must show how much *each* customer purchased, paid, and has yet to pay. A *subsidiary ledger*, called the **accounts receivable ledger,** is set up to keep a separate account for each customer. The general ledger usually has a single Accounts Receivable account that equals the total of its subsidiary ledgers.

Point: When a general ledger account has a subsidiary ledger, any transaction that impacts one of them also impacts the other.

The left side of Exhibit 7.4 shows the relation between the Accounts Receivable account in the general ledger and its individual accounts in the subsidiary ledger. After all items are posted, the balance in the Accounts Receivable account must equal the total of all balances of its customers' accounts. The Accounts Receivable account is said to control the accounts receivable ledger and is called a **controlling account.**

Point: A *control account* is any general ledger account that summarizes subsidiary ledger data.

Accounts Payable Ledger Companies buy on credit from several suppliers and keep a separate account for each supplier by having an Accounts Payable controlling account in the general ledger and a separate account for each supplier (creditor) in an **accounts payable ledger**—see the right side of Exhibit 7.4.

EXHIBIT 7.4

Controlling Accounts and Subsidiary Ledgers

General Ledger

General Ledger — Accounts Receivable

General Ledger — Accounts Payable

Accounts Receivable Subsidiary Ledger

Accounts Payable Subsidiary Ledger

Subsidiary Ledgers

Albert Co. | Frank Booth | Jason Henry | Ace Mfg. | ITT Company | Smite Company

Other Subsidiary Ledgers Subsidiary ledgers are used for several other accounts. For example, a company might keep only one Equipment account in its general ledger, but its equipment subsidiary ledger could record each type of equipment in a separate account. Subsidiary ledgers have at least two benefits: (1) removal of excessive details from the general ledger and (2) up-to-date information available on specific customers, suppliers, and other items.

NEED-TO-KNOW 7-2

Journals and Ledgers

C2

Match each of the numbered descriptions with the term, title, or phrase that it best reflects.

A. General journal
B. Special journal
C. Subsidiary ledger
D. Accounts receivable ledger
E. Accounts payable ledger
F. Controlling account
G. Sales journal
H. Cash receipts journal
I. Purchases journal
J. Cash payments journal

1. Used to record all cash payments.
2. Used to record all credit purchases.
3. Used to record all receipts of cash.
4. Used to record sales of inventory on credit.
5. Stores transaction data of individual customers.
6. Stores transaction data of individual suppliers.
7. Account that is said to control a specific subsidiary ledger.
8. Contains detailed information on a specific account from the general ledger.
9. Used to record and post transactions of similar type.
10. All-purpose journal in which any transaction can be recorded.

Solution

1. J **2.** I **3.** H **4.** G **5.** D **6.** E **7.** F **8.** C **9.** B **10.** A

Do More: QS 7-3, QS 7-4, E 7-5

SALES JOURNAL

P1 Journalize and post transactions using a sales journal.

A **sales journal** is used to record sales of inventory *on credit.* Sales of inventory *for cash* are recorded in a cash receipts journal. Sales of *noninventory* assets on credit are recorded in the general journal.

Journalizing Each sale on credit is recorded separately in a sales journal. Information about each sale is taken from the sales receipt or invoice. The top part of Exhibit 7.5 shows a sales journal from a merchandiser. It has columns for recording the date, customer's name, invoice number, posting reference, and the sales and cost amounts of each credit sale.

Point: The sales journal in Exhibit 7.5 is called a **columnar journal,** which is any journal with more than one column.

Each transaction recorded in the sales journal yields an entry in the Accounts Receivable Dr., Sales Cr. column. We use one column for these two accounts. Each transaction in the sales journal yields an entry in the Cost of Goods Sold Dr., Inventory Cr. column. To demonstrate, on February 2, the company sold merchandise on credit to Jason Henry for $450. The invoice number is 307, and the cost of this merchandise is $315. This information is shown on one line in the sales journal. The Posting Reference (PR) column is not used when entering transactions but instead is used when posting.

Posting Posting from a sales journal is shown in the arrow lines of Exhibit 7.5. There are two types of posting: (1) posting to the subsidiary ledger(s) and (2) posting to the general ledger.

Posting to Subsidiary Ledger Transactions in the sales journal are posted to customer accounts in the accounts receivable ledger to keep customer accounts up to date. When sales recorded in the sales journal are individually posted to customer accounts in the accounts

EXHIBIT 7.5

Sales Journal with Posting

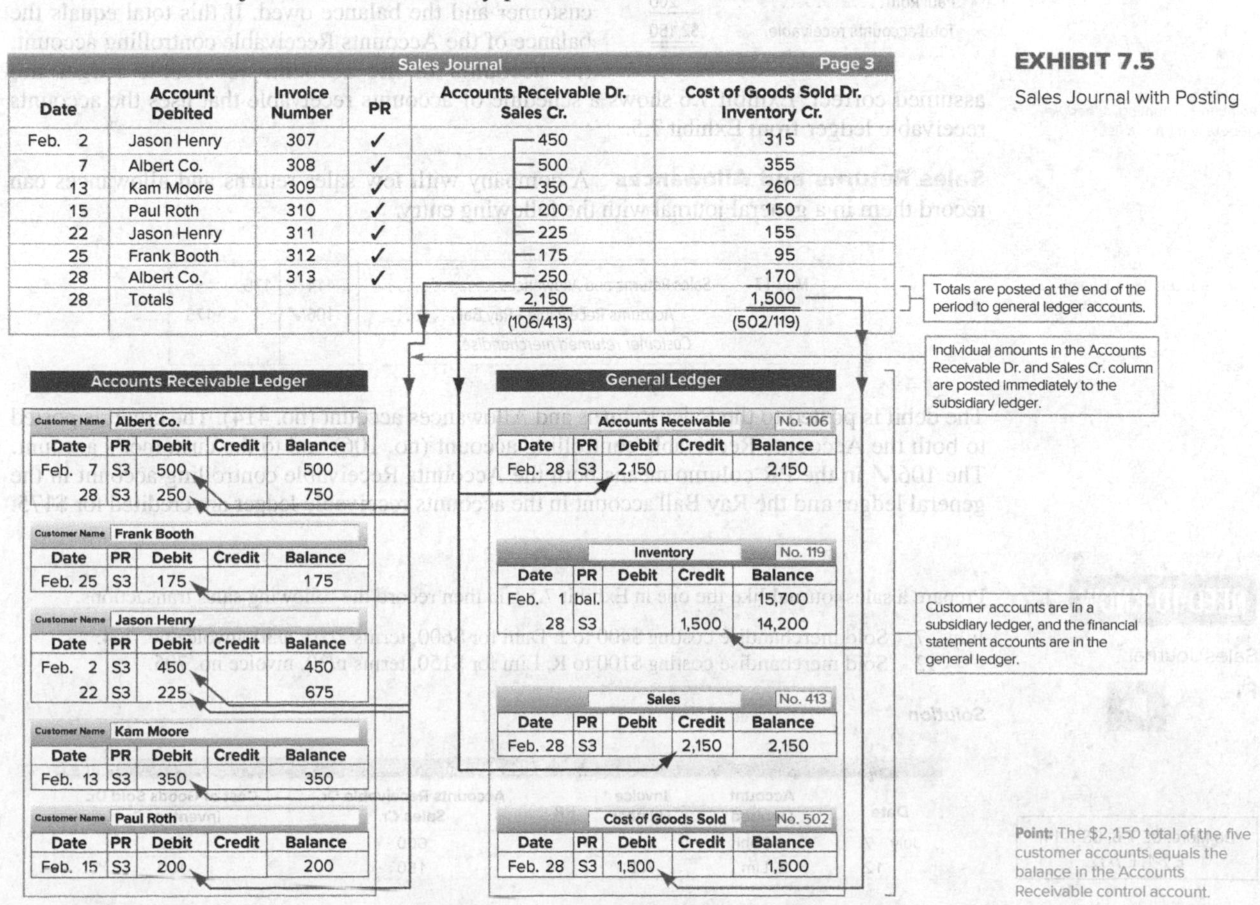
Totals are posted at the end of the period to general ledger accounts.
Individual amounts in the Accounts Receivable Dr. and Sales Cr. column are posted immediately to the subsidiary ledger.
Customer accounts are in a subsidiary ledger, and the financial statement accounts are in the general ledger.

Sales Journal — Page 3

Date	Account Debited	Invoice Number	PR	Accounts Receivable Dr. Sales Cr.	Cost of Goods Sold Dr. Inventory Cr.
Feb. 2	Jason Henry	307	✓	450	315
7	Albert Co.	308	✓	500	355
13	Kam Moore	309	✓	350	260
15	Paul Roth	310	✓	200	150
22	Jason Henry	311	✓	225	155
25	Frank Booth	312	✓	175	95
28	Albert Co.	313	✓	250	170
28	Totals			2,150	1,500
				(106/413)	(502/119)

Accounts Receivable Ledger

Customer Name: Albert Co.

Date	PR	Debit	Credit	Balance
Feb. 7	S3	500		500
28	S3	250		750

Customer Name: Frank Booth

Date	PR	Debit	Credit	Balance
Feb. 25	S3	175		175

Customer Name: Jason Henry

Date	PR	Debit	Credit	Balance
Feb. 2	S3	450		450
22	S3	225		675

Customer Name: Kam Moore

Date	PR	Debit	Credit	Balance
Feb. 13	S3	350		350

Customer Name: Paul Roth

Date	PR	Debit	Credit	Balance
Feb. 15	S3	200		200

General Ledger

Accounts Receivable — No. 106

Date	PR	Debit	Credit	Balance
Feb. 28	S3	2,150		2,150

Inventory — No. 119

Date	PR	Debit	Credit	Balance
Feb. 1	bal.			15,700
28	S3		1,500	14,200

Sales — No. 413

Date	PR	Debit	Credit	Balance
Feb. 28	S3		2,150	2,150

Cost of Goods Sold — No. 502

Date	PR	Debit	Credit	Balance
Feb. 28	S3	1,500		1,500

Point: The $2,150 total of the five customer accounts equals the balance in the Accounts Receivable control account.

receivable ledger, check marks are entered in the sales journal's PR column. Check marks are used rather than account numbers because customer accounts are arranged alphabetically in the accounts receivable ledger. The equality of debits and credits is always maintained in the general ledger.

Posting to General Ledger The sales journal's account columns are totaled at the end of each period (the month of February in this case). For the "sales" column, the $2,150 total is debited to Accounts Receivable and credited to Sales in the general ledger (see Exhibit 7.5). For the "cost" column, the $1,500 total is debited to Cost of Goods Sold and credited to Inventory in the general ledger. When totals are posted to accounts in the general ledger, the account numbers are entered below the column total in the sales journal for tracking. For example, we enter (106/413) below the total in the sales column after this amount is posted to account number 106 (Accounts Receivable) and account number 413 (Sales).

Point: Postings are automatic in a computerized system.

The PR column of subsidiary ledgers shows the journal and page number from which an amount is taken. Items posted from the sales journal have the initial ***S*** before their journal page numbers in a PR column. The cash receipts journal uses ***R***; the cash payments or disbursements journal uses ***D***; the purchases journal uses ***P***; and the general journal uses ***G***.

EXHIBIT 7.6

Schedule of Accounts Receivable

Schedule of Accounts Receivable February 28	
Albert Co.	$ 750
Frank Booth	175
Jason Henry	675
Kam Moore	350
Paul Roth	200
Total accounts receivable	$2,150

Proving the Ledgers Account balances in the general ledger and subsidiary ledgers are proved (reviewed) for accuracy after posting. To do this, we first prepare a trial balance of the general ledger to confirm that debits equal credits. Second, we use a subsidiary ledger to prepare a *schedule* of individual accounts and amounts. A **schedule of accounts receivable** lists each customer and the balance owed. If this total equals the balance of the Accounts Receivable controlling account, the accounts in the accounts receivable ledger are assumed correct. Exhibit 7.6 shows a schedule of accounts receivable that uses the accounts receivable ledger from Exhibit 7.5.

Point: In accounting, *schedule* generally means a list.

Sales Returns and Allowances A company with few sales returns and allowances can record them in a general journal with the following entry.

Assets = Liabilities + Equity
−175 −175

May 17	Sales Returns and Allowances	414	175	
	Accounts Receivable—Ray Ball	106/✓		175
	Customer returned merchandise.			

The debit is posted to the Sales Returns and Allowances account (no. 414). The credit is posted to both the Accounts Receivable controlling account (no. 106) and to the customer's account. The 106/✓ in the PR column means both the Accounts Receivable controlling account in the general ledger and the Ray Ball account in the accounts receivable ledger are credited for $175.

NEED-TO-KNOW 7-3

Sales Journal

P1

Prepare a sales journal like the one in Exhibit 7.5 and then record the following sales transactions.

July 7 Sold merchandise costing $400 to J. Dahl for $600, terms 2/10, n/30, invoice no. 704.
12 Sold merchandise costing $100 to R. Lim for $150, terms n/30, invoice no. 705.

Solution

Sales Journal — Page 3

Date	Account Debited	Invoice Number	PR	Accounts Receivable Dr. Sales Cr.	Cost of Goods Sold Dr. Inventory Cr.
July 7	J. Dahl	704		600	400
12	R. Lim	705		150	100

Do More: QS 7-6, QS 7-14, E 7-1, E 7-12

CASH RECEIPTS JOURNAL

P2 Journalize and post transactions using a cash receipts journal.

A **cash receipts journal** is used to record all receipts of cash (all transactions that include a debit to Cash). Cash receipts are separated into three types: (1) cash from credit customers in payment of their accounts, (2) cash from cash sales, and (3) cash from other sources. The cash receipts journal in Exhibit 7.7 has a separate credit column for each of these three types.

EXHIBIT 7.7

Cash Receipts Journal with Posting

Cash Receipts Journal — Page 2

Date	Account Credited	Explanation	PR	Cash Dr.	Sales Discount Dr.	Accounts Receivable Cr.	Sales Cr.	Other Accounts Cr.	Cost of Goods Sold Dr. Inventory Cr.
Feb. 7	Sales	Cash sales	✗	4,450			4,450		3,150
12	Jason Henry	Invoice, 2/2	✓	441	9	450			
14	Sales	Cash sales	✗	3,925			3,925		2,950
17	Albert Co.	Invoice, 2/7	✓	490	10	500			
20	Notes Payable	Note to bank	245	750				750	
21	Sales	Cash sales	✗	4,700			4,700		3,400
22	Interest revenue	Bank account	409	250				250	
23	Kam Moore	Invoice, 2/13	✓	343	7	350			
25	Paul Roth	Invoice, 2/15	✓	196	4	200			
28	Sales	Cash sales	✗	4,225			4,225		3,050
28	Totals			19,770	30	1,500	17,300	1,000	12,550
				(101)	(415)	(106)	(413)	(✗)	(502/119)

Individual amounts in the Other Accounts Cr. column and the Accounts Receivable Cr. column are posted immediately.

Column totals, except for Other Accounts Cr. column, are posted at the end of the period.

Accounts Receivable Ledger

Customer Name: Albert Co.

Date	PR	Debit	Credit	Balance
Feb. 7	S3	500		500
17	R2		500	0
28	S3	250		250

Customer Name: Frank Booth

Date	PR	Debit	Credit	Balance
Feb. 25	S3	175		175

Customer Name: Jason Henry

Date	PR	Debit	Credit	Balance
Feb. 2	S3	450		450
12	R2		450	0
22	S3	225		225

Customer Name: Kam Moore

Date	PR	Debit	Credit	Balance
Feb. 13	S3	350		350
23	R2		350	0

Customer Name: Paul Roth

Date	PR	Debit	Credit	Balance
Feb. 15	S3	200		200
25	R2		200	0

General Ledger

Cash — No. 101

Date	PR	Debit	Credit	Balance
Feb. 28	R2	19,770		19,770

Accounts Receivable — No. 106

Date	PR	Debit	Credit	Balance
Feb. 28	S3	2,150		2,150
28	R2		1,500	650

Inventory — No. 119

Date	PR	Debit	Credit	Balance
Feb. 1	bal.			15,700
28	S3		1,500	14,200
28	R2		12,550	1,650

Notes Payable — No. 245

Date	PR	Debit	Credit	Balance
Feb. 20	R2		750	750

General Ledger (continued)

Interest Revenue — No. 409

Date	PR	Debit	Credit	Balance
Feb. 22	R2		250	250

Sales — No. 413

Date	PR	Debit	Credit	Balance
Feb. 28	S3		2,150	2,150
28	R2		17,300	19,450

Sales Discounts — No. 415

Date	PR	Debit	Credit	Balance
Feb. 28	R2	30		30

Cost of Goods Sold — No. 502

Date	PR	Debit	Credit	Balance
Feb. 28	S3	1,500		1,500
28	R2	12,550		14,050

Point: The $650 total of the five customer accounts equals the balance in Accounts Receivable control account.

Cash from Credit Customers

Journalizing To record cash received in payment of a customer's account, the customer's name is first entered in the Account Credited column—see transactions dated February 12, 17, 23, and 25. Then the amounts debited to both Cash and Sales Discount (if any) are entered in their columns, and the amount credited to the customer's account is entered in the Accounts Receivable Cr. column.

Posting Individual amounts in the Accounts Receivable Cr. column are posted immediately to customer accounts in the subsidiary accounts receivable ledger. The $1,500 column total is posted at the end of the period (month in this case) as a credit to the Accounts Receivable controlling account in the general ledger.

Example: Record in the cash receipts journal a $700 cash sale of land when the land carries a $700 original cost. *Answer:* Debit the Cash column for $700, and credit the Other Accounts column for $700 (the account credited is Land).

Cash Sales

Journalizing Each cash sale is entered in the Cash Dr. column and the Sales Cr. column. The February 7, 14, 21, and 28 transactions are examples. Each cash sale also yields an entry to Cost of Goods Sold Dr. and Inventory Cr. for the cost of merchandise—see the far right column.

Posting For cash sales, an *x* in the PR column means that its amount is not individually posted. We do post the $17,300 Sales Cr. total and the $12,550 total from the "cost" column.

Cash from Other Sources

Journalizing Examples of cash from other sources are money borrowed from a bank, cash interest received, and cash sale of noninventory assets. The February 20 and 22 transactions are examples. The Other Accounts Cr. column is used for these transactions.

Posting These transactions are immediately posted to their general ledger accounts.

Footing, Crossfooting, and Posting

Point: Subsidiary ledgers and their controlling accounts are *in balance* only after all posting is complete.

To be sure that total debits and credits in a journal are equal, we crossfoot column totals before posting them. To *foot* a column of numbers is to add it. To *crossfoot* in this case is to add the Debit column totals, then add the Credit column totals, and verify that the Debit and Credit column totals are equal. Footing and crossfooting of the numbers in Exhibit 7.7 result in the report in Exhibit 7.8.

EXHIBIT 7.8

Footing and Crossfooting Journal Totals

Debit Columns		Credit Columns	
Cash	$19,770	Accounts Receivable	$ 1,500
Sales Discounts	30	Sales	17,300
Cost of Goods Sold	12,550	Other Accounts	1,000
		Inventory	12,550
Total	$32,350	Total	$32,350

At the end of the period, the total amounts from the columns of the cash receipts journal are posted to their general ledger accounts. The Other Accounts Cr. column total is not posted because the individual amounts are directly posted to their general ledger accounts. An *x* below the Other Accounts Cr. column indicates this column total is not posted. The account numbers for the column totals that are posted are entered in parentheses below each column.

Inti St. Clair/Digital Vision/Getty Images

Decision Maker

Entrepreneur You want to know how quickly customers are paying their bills. Where do you find this information? ■ *Answer:* The accounts receivable ledger lists detailed information for each customer's account, including the amounts, dates of transactions, and dates of payments. It shows how long customers wait before paying their bills.

NEED-TO-KNOW 7-4

Cash Receipts Journal

P2

Prepare a cash receipts journal like the one in Exhibit 7.7 and then record the following cash receipts transactions.

July 1 The company borrowed $5,000 cash by signing a note payable to the bank.
2 C. Ming, the owner, contributed $1,000 cash to the company.
11 The company sold merchandise costing $100 to Mulan for $400 cash.
29 The company received $950 cash from Chan in payment of a July 7 purchase (where the company sold merchandise costing $700 on credit to Chan for $1,000, subject to a $50 sales discount if paid within 30 days).

Solution

Cash Receipts Journal									Page 2
Date	Account Credited	Explanation	PR	Cash Dr.	Sales Discount Dr.	Accounts Receivable Cr.	Sales Cr.	Other Accounts Cr.	Cost of Goods Sold Dr. Inventory Cr.
July 1	Notes Payable	Note to bank		5,000				5,000	
2	C. Ming, Capital	Contribution		1,000				1,000	
11	Sales	Cash sale		400			400		100
29	Chan	Invoice, 7/7		950	50	1,000			

Do More: QS 7-7, E 7-3, E 7-13, P 7-2

PURCHASES JOURNAL

P3 Journalize and post transactions using a purchases journal.

A **purchases journal** is used to record all credit purchases, including those for inventory. Purchases using cash are recorded in the cash payments journal.

Journalizing The Accounts Payable Cr. column in Exhibit 7.9 is used to record the amounts owed to each creditor. Inventory purchases are recorded using the Inventory Dr. column.

EXHIBIT 7.9

Purchases Journal with Posting

Purchases Journal								Page 1
Date	Account	Date of Invoice	Terms	PR	Accounts Payable Cr.	Inventory Dr.	Office Supplies Dr.	Other Accounts Dr.
Feb. 3	Horning Supply Co.	2/3	n/30	✓	350	275	75	
5	Ace Mfg. Co.	2/5	2/10, n/30	✓	200	200		
13	Wynet & Co.	2/13	2/10, n/30	✓	150	150		
20	Smite Co.	2/20	2/10, n/30	✓	300	300		
25	Ace Mfg. Co.	2/25	2/10, n/30	✓	100	100		
28	Store Supplies/ITT Co.	2/28	n/30	125/✓	225	125	25	75
28	Totals				1,325 (201)	1,150 (119)	100 (124)	75 (X)

Individual amounts in the Other Accounts Dr. column and the Accounts Payable Cr. column are posted immediately.

Column totals, except for the Other Accounts Dr. column, are posted at the end of the period.

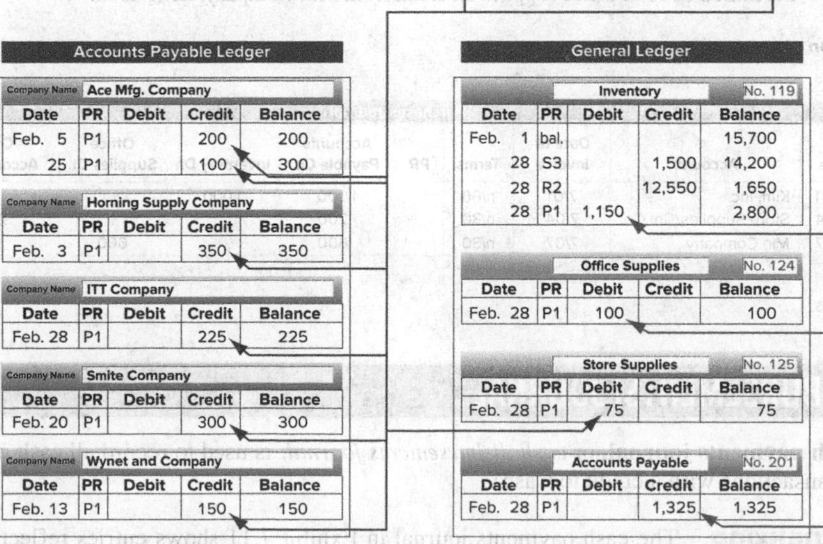

Accounts Payable Ledger

Company Name: Ace Mfg. Company				
Date	PR	Debit	Credit	Balance
Feb. 5	P1		200	200
25	P1		100	300

Company Name: Horning Supply Company				
Date	PR	Debit	Credit	Balance
Feb. 3	P1		350	350

Company Name: ITT Company				
Date	PR	Debit	Credit	Balance
Feb. 28	P1		225	225

Company Name: Smite Company				
Date	PR	Debit	Credit	Balance
Feb. 20	P1		300	300

Company Name: Wynet and Company				
Date	PR	Debit	Credit	Balance
Feb. 13	P1		150	150

General Ledger

Inventory				No. 119
Date	PR	Debit	Credit	Balance
Feb. 1	bal.			15,700
28	S3		1,500	14,200
28	R2		12,550	1,650
28	P1	1,150		2,800

Office Supplies				No. 124
Date	PR	Debit	Credit	Balance
Feb. 28	P1	100		100

Store Supplies				No. 125
Date	PR	Debit	Credit	Balance
Feb. 28	P1	75		75

Accounts Payable				No. 201
Date	PR	Debit	Credit	Balance
Feb. 28	P1		1,325	1,325

Point: The $1,325 total of the five vendor accounts equals the balance in the Accounts Payable control account.

To demonstrate, inventory costing $200 is purchased from Ace Manufacturing on February 5. The creditor's name (Ace) is entered in the Account column, the invoice date is entered in the Date of Invoice column, the purchase terms are entered in the Terms column, and the $200 amount is entered in the Accounts Payable Cr. and the Inventory Dr. columns. When a purchase has an amount recorded in the Other Accounts Dr. column, the Account column shows

Point: Each transaction in the purchases journal has a credit to Accounts Payable. Debit accounts will vary.

the general ledger account debited. For example, the February 28 transaction has purchases of inventory, office supplies, and store supplies from ITT. The journal has no column for store supplies, so the Other Accounts Dr. column is used. In this case, Store Supplies is entered in the Account column along with the creditor's name (ITT). This purchases journal also includes a separate column for credit purchases of office supplies. Each company decides what separate columns are necessary.

Point: The Other Accounts Dr. column allows the purchases journal to be used for any purchase on credit.

Posting The amounts in the Accounts Payable Cr. column are immediately posted to individual creditor accounts in the accounts payable subsidiary ledger. Individual amounts in the Other Accounts Dr. column are immediately posted to their general ledger accounts. At the end of the period, all column totals except the Other Accounts Dr. column are posted to their general ledger accounts.

EXHIBIT 7.10

Schedule of Accounts Payable

Schedule of Accounts Payable February 28	
Ace Mfg. Company	$ 300
Horning Supply Company	350
ITT Company	225
Smite Company	300
Wynet & Company	150
Total accounts payable	$1,325

Point: The balance in the Accounts Payable controlling account must equal the total of the individual account balances in the accounts payable subsidiary ledger after posting.

Proving the Ledger Accounts payable balances in the subsidiary ledger are proved after posting. We prove the subsidiary ledger by preparing a **schedule of accounts payable,** which is a list of accounts from the accounts payable ledger with their balances and the total. If the total of the individual balances equals the balance of the Accounts Payable controlling account, the accounts in the accounts payable ledger are assumed correct. Exhibit 7.10 shows a schedule of accounts payable drawn from the accounts payable ledger of Exhibit 7.9.

NEED-TO-KNOW 7-5

Purchases Journal

P3

Prepare a purchases journal like the one in Exhibit 7.9 and then record the following purchases transactions.

July 1 Purchased $1,000 of merchandise on credit from Kim, Inc., terms n/60.
4 Purchased $200 of store supplies from Chi Company on credit, terms n/30.
7 Purchased $600 of office supplies on credit from Min Company, terms n/30.

Solution

Purchases Journal								Page 1
Date	Account	Date of Invoice	Terms	PR	Accounts Payable Cr.	Inventory Dr.	Office Supplies Dr.	Other Accounts Dr.
July 1	Kim, Inc.	7/01	n/60		1,000	1,000		
4	Store Supplies/Chi Co.	7/04	n/30		200			200
7	Min Company	7/07	n/30		600		600	

Do More: QS 7-8, E 7-6, E 7-10

CASH PAYMENTS (DISBURSEMENTS) JOURNAL

P4

Journalize and post transactions using a cash payments journal.

A **cash payments journal,** or *cash disbursements journal,* is used to record all cash payments (all transactions with a credit to Cash).

Journalizing The cash payments journal in Exhibit 7.11 shows entries reflecting cash payments. Credits to Inventory reflect purchase discounts. For example, on February 15, the company pays Ace on account (credit terms of 2/10, n/30—see February 5 transaction in Exhibit 7.9). Because payment occurs in the discount period, the company pays $196 ($200 invoice less $4 discount). The $4 discount is credited to Inventory.

When a company purchases inventory for cash, it is recorded using the Other Accounts Dr. column and the Cash Cr. column as shown in the February 3 and 12 transactions. Generally, the Other Accounts column is used to record cash payments on items for which no column exists.

EXHIBIT 7.11

Cash Payments Journal with Posting

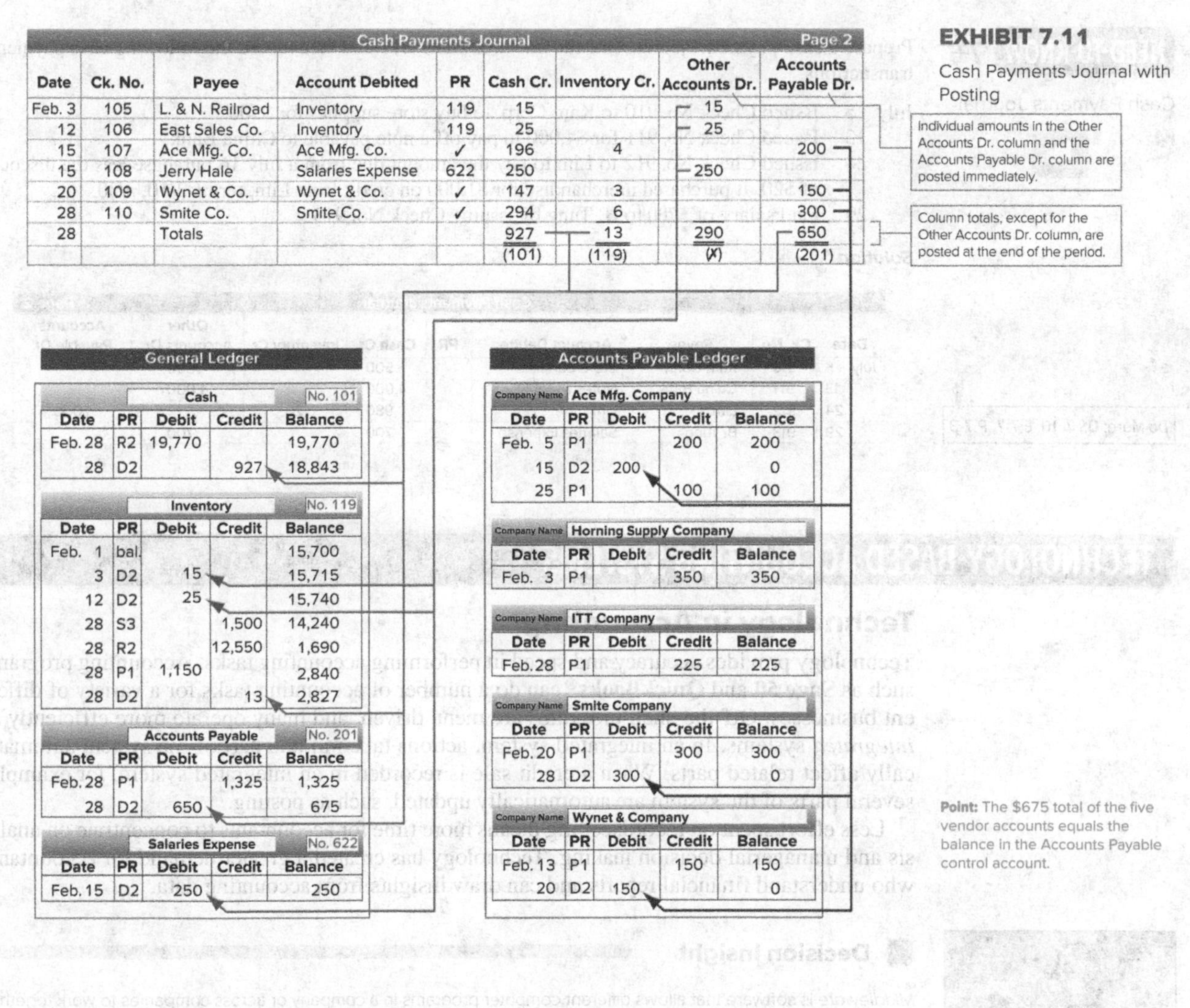

Cash Payments Journal — Page 2

Date	Ck. No.	Payee	Account Debited	PR	Cash Cr.	Inventory Cr.	Other Accounts Dr.	Accounts Payable Dr.
Feb. 3	105	L. & N. Railroad	Inventory	119	15		15	
12	106	East Sales Co.	Inventory	119	25		25	
15	107	Ace Mfg. Co.	Ace Mfg. Co.	✓	196	4		200
15	108	Jerry Hale	Salaries Expense	622	250		250	
20	109	Wynet & Co.	Wynet & Co.	✓	147	3		150
28	110	Smite Co.	Smite Co.	✓	294	6		300
28		Totals			927	13	290	650
					(101)	(119)	(✗)	(201)

Individual amounts in the Other Accounts Dr. column and the Accounts Payable Dr. column are posted immediately.
Column totals, except for the Other Accounts Dr. column, are posted at the end of the period.

General Ledger

Cash — No. 101

Date	PR	Debit	Credit	Balance
Feb. 28	R2	19,770		19,770
28	D2		927	18,843

Inventory — No. 119

Date	PR	Debit	Credit	Balance
Feb. 1	bal.			15,700
3	D2	15		15,715
12	D2	25		15,740
28	S3		1,500	14,240
28	R2		12,550	1,690
28	P1	1,150		2,840
28	D2		13	2,827

Accounts Payable — No. 201

Date	PR	Debit	Credit	Balance
Feb. 28	P1		1,325	1,325
28	D2	650		675

Salaries Expense — No. 622

Date	PR	Debit	Credit	Balance
Feb. 15	D2	250		250

Accounts Payable Ledger

Company Name: Ace Mfg. Company

Date	PR	Debit	Credit	Balance
Feb. 5	P1		200	200
15	D2	200		0
25	P1		100	100

Company Name: Horning Supply Company

Date	PR	Debit	Credit	Balance
Feb. 3	P1		350	350

Company Name: ITT Company

Date	PR	Debit	Credit	Balance
Feb. 28	P1		225	225

Company Name: Smite Company

Date	PR	Debit	Credit	Balance
Feb. 20	P1		300	300
28	D2	300		0

Company Name: Wynet & Company

Date	PR	Debit	Credit	Balance
Feb. 13	P1		150	150
20	D2	150		0

Point: The $675 total of the five vendor accounts equals the balance in the Accounts Payable control account.

For example, on February 15, the company pays salaries expense of $250. The amount is recorded using the Other Accounts Dr. column, and the title of the account debited (Salaries Expense) is entered in the Account Debited column.

The cash payments journal has a column titled Ck. No. (check number). The identifying number of the paper or electronic check (or ACH) is entered in this column.

Point: When a cash payments journal has a column for check numbers, it is sometimes called a **check register**.

Posting Individual amounts in the Other Accounts Dr. column of a cash payments journal are immediately posted to their general ledger accounts. Individual amounts in the Accounts Payable Dr. column are also immediately posted to creditors' accounts in the subsidiary accounts payable ledger. At the end of the period, we post the Accounts Payable Dr. column total to the Accounts Payable controlling account. Also, the Inventory Cr. column total is posted to the Inventory account, and the Cash Cr. column total is posted to the Cash account.

General Journal Transactions

When special journals are used, we still need a general journal for adjusting, closing, and any other transactions for which no special journal has been set up. Examples of these other transactions might include purchases returns and allowances, purchases of plant assets by issuing a note payable, sales returns if a sales returns and allowances journal is not used, and receipt of a note receivable from a customer.

NEED-TO-KNOW 7-6

Cash Payments Journal

P4

Prepare a cash payments journal like the one in Exhibit 7.11 and then record the following cash payments transactions.

July 5 Issued Check No. 910 to Kam Corp. to buy store supplies for $500.
13 Issued Check No. 911 for $4,000 to pay off a note payable to China Bank.
24 Issued Check No. 912 to Lim to pay the amount due from a July 16 purchase less the discount of $20. It purchased merchandise for $1,000 on credit from Lim, terms 2/10, n/30.
29 Paid salary of $700 to B. Tung by issuing Check No. 913.

Solution

Cash Payments Journal — Page 2

Date	Ck. No.	Payee	Account Debited	PR	Cash Cr.	Inventory Cr.	Other Accounts Dr.	Accounts Payable Dr.
July 5	910	Kam Corp.	Store Supplies		500		500	
13	911	China Bank	Notes Payable		4,000		4,000	
24	912	Lim	Lim		980	20		1,000
29	913	B. Tung	Salaries Expense		700		700	

Do More: QS 7-10, E 7-7, P 7-3

TECHNOLOGY-BASED ACCOUNTING SYSTEMS

Technology in Accounting

Technology provides accuracy and speed in performing accounting tasks. Accounting programs such as **Sage 50** and **QuickBooks®** can do a number of accounting tasks for a variety of different businesses. Off-the-shelf programs are menu driven, and many operate more efficiently as *integrated* systems. In an integrated system, actions taken in one part of the system automatically affect related parts. When a credit sale is recorded in an integrated system, for example, several parts of the system are automatically updated, such as posting.

Less effort spent on recordkeeping means more time for accountants to concentrate on analysis and managerial decision making. Technology has created a greater demand for accountants who understand financial reports and can draw insights from accounting data.

Hiraman/E+/Getty Images

Decision Insight

Middleware is software that allows different computer programs in a company or across companies to work together. It allows transfer of purchase orders, invoices, and other electronic documents between accounting systems. For example, suppliers can monitor their buyers' inventory levels for production and shipping purposes. ■

Data Processing in Accounting

Accounting systems are different in how input is entered and processed.

- **Online processing** enters and processes data as soon as source documents are available. This means that databases are immediately updated.
- **Batch processing** accumulates source documents for a period of time and then processes them all at once such as daily, weekly, or monthly.

The advantage of online processing is timeliness. The advantage of batch processing is that it requires only periodic updating of databases. The disadvantage of batch processing is the lack of up-to-date information for managers.

Computer Networks in Accounting

Networking, or linking computers with each other, can create information advantages (and cost efficiencies). **Computer networks** are links among computers giving users access to common databases, programs, and hardware. The network setups by **UPS** and **FedEx** allow multiple users to connect to a common database to track packages and bill customers.

Enterprise Resource Planning Software

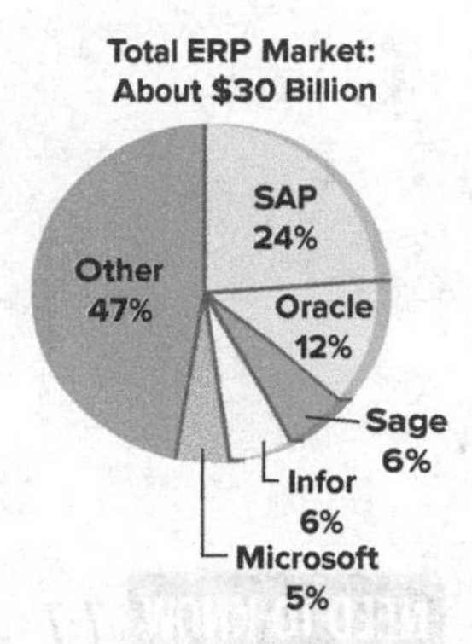

Enterprise resource planning (ERP) software includes the programs that manage a company's operations. They extend from order taking to manufacturing to accounting. ERP can help speed decision making, identify costs for reduction, and give managers control over operations. For many managers, ERP allows them to scrutinize the business, identify where inventories are piling up, and see what plants are most efficient.

Several companies offer ERP software. **SAP** leads the market, with **Oracle** a distant second (*AMR Research*). SAP is used by more than half of the world's 500 largest companies.

ERP is increasingly used by small business. One-third of Oracle's sales in North America are to companies with less than $500 million in annual revenue.

Data Analytics and Data Visualization

Data analytics is a process of analyzing data to identify meaningful relations and trends. In accounting, data analytics helps individuals make informed business decisions. **Dr Pepper Snapple Group** uses data analytics to send accounting information to its sales route staff via an app in real time. Staff can then make data-driven decisions on what sales and promotions to offer retailers. Data analytics also tracks their progress relative to projections.

Data visualization is a graphical presentation of data to help people understand its significance. Software is used to create meaningful visuals that inform key decision makers. **Tableau** is the most popular data visualization software. **NASA** uses data visualization to depict its plans and five-year budget in a graphic titled *Funding the Final Frontier.* This graphic shows the budget breakdown for space exploration, science, space operations, and other activities.

Cloud Computing

Cloud computing is the delivery of computing as a service rather than a product. Cloud computing uses applications via the web instead of installing them on individual computers. This means that companies lease, rather than purchase, those applications.

When a company uses cloud computing, users and their clients can access the same applications and share data. Accountants and analysts can similarly access data for quicker and easier processing and analysis. For example, all invoices could be offloaded to a web-based bill management system, where documentation, payments, and recordkeeping could all be handled in the cloud.

Days' Payable Outstanding — Decision Analysis

A1 Compute days' payable outstanding and explain its use in assessing payments to suppliers.

Days' payable outstanding is the average length of time that payables are deferred until payment is made. Delaying payment allows the buyer to increase available cash. However, excessive delays can hurt the buyer's relationship with the seller. Days' payable outstanding (DPO) is defined in Exhibit 7.12. Cost of goods sold is in the denominator because payables relate to the purchase of goods, which are recorded at cost.

EXHIBIT 7.12 Days' Payable Outstanding (DPO)

$$\textbf{Days' payable outstanding (DPO)} = \frac{\textbf{Accounts payable}}{\textbf{Cost of goods sold}} \times 365$$

We compute DPO in Exhibit 7.13 for **Costco** and **Walmart**. Costco's DPO is less than Walmart's in each of the last three years. This means that, on average, Walmart takes longer to pay its suppliers. Many investors view this as positive because it suggests that Walmart is negotiating better terms with its suppliers that allow Walmart to defer payment. However, if DPO is excessively large relative to its peers, investors worry that a company will hurt its relationship with suppliers by paying later than its peers. In managing DPO, companies wish to maximize available cash (using a higher DPO) while not hurting supplier relations.

EXHIBIT 7.13 Days' Payable Outstanding for Two Competitors

Company	Figure ($ millions)	Current Year	One Year Prior	Two Years Prior
Costco	Accounts payable	$ 11,679	$ 11,237	$ 9,608
	Cost of goods sold	$132,886	$123,152	$111,882
	Days' payable outstanding	**32.1 days**	**33.3 days**	**31.3 days**
Walmart	**Days' payable outstanding**	**44.6 days**	**45.1 days**	**41.9 days**

Decision Maker

Analyst A company under analysis has a days' payable outstanding (DPO) of 15 days. The industry norm is 32 days and this company's usual credit terms are n/30. What is your assessment of DPO? ■ Answer: DPO is less than the norm and lower than the usual credit period. This suggests that the company can further delay payments to suppliers (and increase its level of available cash) and not hurt its relationship with suppliers.

NEED-TO-KNOW 7-7

COMPREHENSIVE

Using Special Journals for Recording Transactions; preparing a trial balance and subsidiary ledgers for receivables and payables

Pepper Company completed the following selected transactions and events during March of this year. (Terms of all credit sales for the company are 2/10, n/30.)

Mar. 4 Sold merchandise on credit to Jennifer Nelson, Invoice No. 954, for $16,800 (cost is $12,200).
6 Purchased $1,220 of office supplies on credit from Mack Company, terms n/30.
6 Sold merchandise on credit to Dennie Hoskins, Invoice No. 955, for $10,200 (cost is $8,100).
11 Purchased $52,600 of merchandise, terms 2/10, n/30, from Defore Industries.
12 Borrowed $26,000 cash by giving Commerce Bank a long-term note payable.
14 Received cash payment from Jennifer Nelson for the March 4 sale less the discount of $336 (Invoice No. 954).
16 Returned $200 of merchandise to Defore Industries from the March 11 purchase. Pepper debited Accounts Payable for the returned amount.
16 Received cash payment from Dennie Hoskins for the March 6 sale less the discount of $204 (Invoice No. 955).
18 Purchased $22,850 of store equipment on credit from Schmidt Supply, terms n/30.
20 Sold merchandise on credit to Marjorie Allen, Invoice No. 956, for $5,600 (cost is $3,800).
21 Sent Defore Industries Check No. 516 in payment of its March 11 purchase less the return and the discount of $1,048.
22 Purchased $41,625 of merchandise, terms 2/10, n/30, from Welch Company.
26 Issued a $600 allowance to Marjorie Allen for defective merchandise Pepper sold on March 20. Pepper credited Accounts Receivable.
31 Issued Check No. 517 in payment of $15,900 sales salaries for the month.
31 Cash sales for the month are $134,680 (cost is $67,340). Pepper enters cash sales in the cash receipts journal at the end of each month.

Required

1. Open the following selected general ledger accounts: Cash (101), Accounts Receivable (106), Inventory (119), Office Supplies (124), Store Equipment (165), Accounts Payable (201), Long-Term Notes Payable (251), Sales (413), Sales Returns and Allowances (414), Sales Discounts (415), Cost of Goods Sold (502), and Sales Salaries Expense (621). Open the following accounts receivable ledger accounts: Marjorie Allen, Dennie Hoskins, and Jennifer Nelson. Open the following accounts payable ledger accounts: Defore Industries, Mack Company, Schmidt Supply, and Welch Company.
2. Enter the transactions using a sales journal, a purchases journal, a cash receipts journal, a cash payments journal, and a general journal. Regularly post to the individual customer and creditor accounts. Also, post any amounts that should be posted as individual amounts to general ledger accounts. Foot and crossfoot the journals and make the month-end postings. *Pepper Co. uses the perpetual inventory system.*
3. Prepare a trial balance for the selected general ledger accounts in part 1 and prove the accuracy of subsidiary ledgers by preparing schedules of accounts receivable and accounts payable.

SOLUTION

Sales Journal — Page 2

Date	Account Debited	Invoice Number	PR	Accounts Receivable Dr. Sales Cr.	Cost of Goods Sold Dr. Inventory Cr.
Mar. 4	Jennifer Nelson	954	✓	16,800	12,200
6	Dennie Hoskins	955	✓	10,200	8,100
20	Marjorie Allen	956	✓	5,600	3,800
31	Totals			32,600	24,100
				(106/413)	(502/119)

Cash Receipts Journal — Page 3

Date	Account Credited	Explanation	PR	Cash Dr.	Sales Discount Dr.	Accounts Receivable Cr.	Sales Cr.	Other Accounts Cr.	Cost of Goods Sold Dr. Inventory Cr.
Mar. 12	L.T. Notes Payable	Note to bank	251	26,000				26,000	
14	Jennifer Nelson	Invoice 954, 3/4	✓	16,464	336	16,800			
16	Dennie Hoskins	Invoice 955, 3/6	✓	9,996	204	10,200			
31	Sales	Cash sales	x	134,680			134,680		67,340
31	Totals			187,140	540	27,000	134,680	26,000	67,340
				(101)	(415)	(106)	(413)	(x)	(502/119)

Purchases Journal — Page 3

Date	Account	Date of Invoice	Terms	PR	Accounts Payable Cr.	Inventory Dr.	Office Supplies Dr.	Other Accounts Dr.
Mar. 6	Office Supplies/Mack Co	3/6	n/30	✓	1,220		1,220	
11	Defore Industries	3/11	2/10, n/30	✓	52,600	52,600		
18	Store Equipment/Schmidt Supp	3/18	n/30	165/✓	22,850			22,850
22	Welch Company	3/22	2/10, n/30	✓	41,625	41,625		
31	Totals				118,295	94,225	1,220	22,850
					(201)	(119)	(124)	(x)

Cash Payments Journal — Page 3

Date	Ck. No.	Payee	Account Debited	PR	Cash Cr.	Inventory Cr.	Other Accounts Dr.	Accounts Payable Dr.
Mar. 21	516	Defore Industries	Defore Industries	✓	51,352	1,048		52,400
31	517	Payroll	Sales Salaries Expense	621	15,900		15,900	
31		Totals			67,252	1,048	15,900	52,400
					(101)	(119)	(x)	(201)

General Journal — Page 2

Date	Account	PR	Debit	Credit
Mar. 16	Accounts Payable—Defore Industries	201/✓	200	
	Inventory	119		200
	Record merchandise returned.			
26	Sales Returns and Allowances	414	600	
	Accounts Receivable—Marjorie Allen	106/✓		600
	Record allowance issued.			

Accounts Receivable Ledger

Marjorie Allen

Date	PR	Debit	Credit	Balance
Mar. 20	S2	5,600		5,600
26	G2		600	5,000

Dennie Hoskins

Date	PR	Debit	Credit	Balance
Mar. 6	S2	10,200		10,200
16	R3		10,200	0

Jennifer Nelson

Date	PR	Debit	Credit	Balance
Mar. 4	S2	16,800		16,800
14	R3		16,800	0

Accounts Payable Ledger

Defore Industries

Date	PR	Debit	Credit	Balance
Mar. 11	P3		52,600	52,600
16	G2	200		52,400
21	D3	52,400		0

Mack Company

Date	PR	Debit	Credit	Balance
Mar. 6	P3		1,220	1,220

Schmidt Supply

Date	PR	Debit	Credit	Balance
Mar. 18	P3		22,850	22,850

Welch Company

Date	PR	Debit	Credit	Balance
Mar. 22	P3		41,625	41,625

General Ledger (covering transactions provided)

Cash — Acct. No. 101

Date	PR	Debit	Credit	Balance
Mar. 31	R3	187,140		187,140
31	D3		67,252	119,888

Accounts Receivable — Acct. No. 106

Date	PR	Debit	Credit	Balance
Mar. 26	G2		600	(600)
31	S2	32,600		32,000
31	R3		27,000	5,000

Inventory — Acct. No. 119

Date	PR	Debit	Credit	Balance
Mar. 16	G2		200	(200)
21	D3		1,048	(1,248)
31	P3	94,225		92,977
31	S2		24,100	68,877
31	R3		67,340	1,537

Office Supplies — Acct. No. 124

Date	PR	Debit	Credit	Balance
Mar. 31	P3	1,220		1,220

Store Equipment — Acct. No. 165

Date	PR	Debit	Credit	Balance
Mar. 18	P3	22,850		22,850

Accounts Payable — Acct. No. 201

Date	PR	Debit	Credit	Balance
Mar. 16	G2	200		(200)
31	P3		118,295	118,095
31	D3	52,400		65,695

Long-Term Notes Payable — Acct. No. 251

Date	PR	Debit	Credit	Balance
Mar. 12	R3		26,000	26,000

Sales — Acct. No. 413

Date	PR	Debit	Credit	Balance
Mar. 31	S2		32,600	32,600
31	R3		134,680	167,280

Sales Returns and Allowances — Acct. No. 414

Date	PR	Debit	Credit	Balance
Mar. 26	G2	600		600

Sales Discounts — Acct. No. 415

Date	PR	Debit	Credit	Balance
Mar. 31	R3	540		540

Cost of Goods Sold — Acct. No. 502

Date	PR	Debit	Credit	Balance
Mar. 31	R3	67,340		67,340
31	S2	24,100		91,440

Sales Salaries Expense — Acct. No. 621

Date	PR	Debit	Credit	Balance
Mar. 31	D3	15,900		15,900

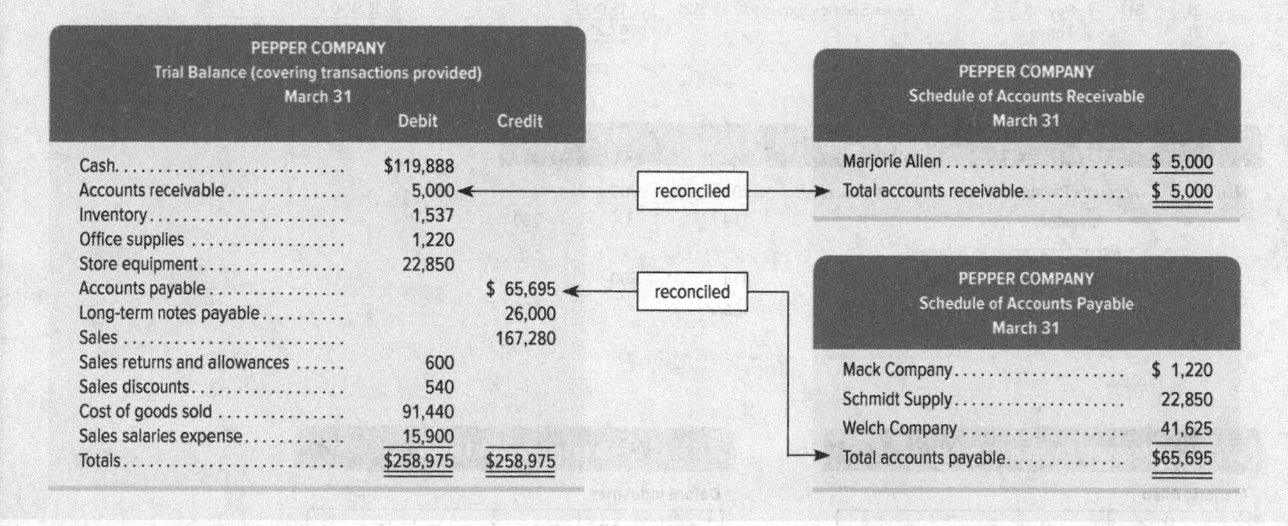

PEPPER COMPANY
Trial Balance (covering transactions provided)
March 31

	Debit	Credit
Cash	$119,888	
Accounts receivable	5,000	
Inventory	1,537	
Office supplies	1,220	
Store equipment	22,850	
Accounts payable		$ 65,695
Long-term notes payable		26,000
Sales		167,280
Sales returns and allowances	600	
Sales discounts	540	
Cost of goods sold	91,440	
Sales salaries expense	15,900	
Totals	$258,975	$258,975

PEPPER COMPANY
Schedule of Accounts Receivable
March 31

Marjorie Allen	$ 5,000
Total accounts receivable	$ 5,000

PEPPER COMPANY
Schedule of Accounts Payable
March 31

Mack Company	$ 1,220
Schmidt Supply	22,850
Welch Company	41,625
Total accounts payable	$65,695

Summary: Cheat Sheet

ACCOUNTING SYSTEM & JOURNAL BASICS

Control principle: A system has internal controls, which are procedures that help managers control a business.

Relevance principle: Accounting info is useful and timely.

Compatibility principle: System conforms to company structure.

Flexibility principle: System adapts to internal/external changes.

Cost-benefit principle: Benefits from an activity outweigh the costs.

Source documents: Information processed by the system.

Input devices: Transfer info from source documents to processing.

Information processors: Summarize info for use in reporting.

Information storage: Keeps data accessible.

Output devices: Make info available to users.

General journal: All-purpose journal for adjusting, closing, and any other transactions for which there is no special journal. Transactions include sales of *noninventory* assets on credit, purchases returns and allowances, purchases of plant assets by issuing a note payable, sales returns and allowances, and receipt of a note receivable.

Special journal: Used to record and post transactions of similar type.

Subsidiary ledger: A list of individual accounts detailing a specific account in the general ledger.

SALES JOURNAL

Sales journal: Used to record sales of inventory on credit.

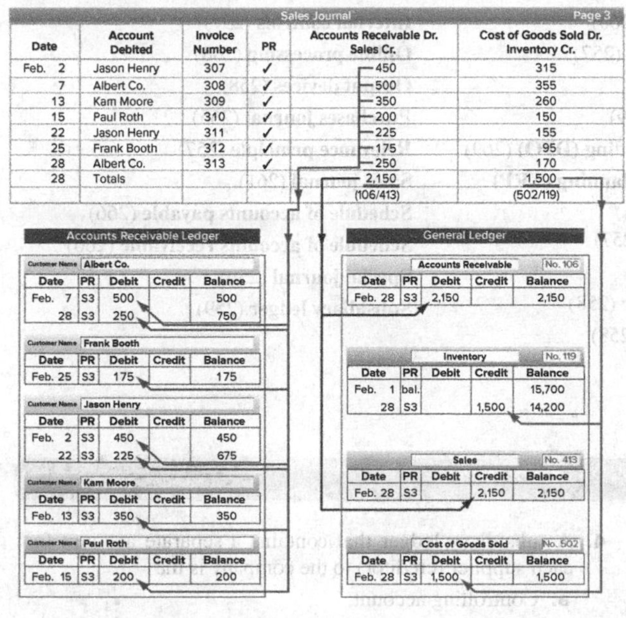

Sales Journal — Page 3

Date	Account Debited	Invoice Number	PR	Accounts Receivable Dr. Sales Cr.	Cost of Goods Sold Dr. Inventory Cr.
Feb. 2	Jason Henry	307	✓	450	315
7	Albert Co.	308	✓	500	355
13	Kam Moore	309	✓	350	260
15	Paul Roth	310	✓	200	150
22	Jason Henry	311	✓	225	155
25	Frank Booth	312	✓	175	95
28	Albert Co.	313	✓	250	170
28	Totals			2,150	1,500
				(106/413)	(502/119)

Accounts Receivable Ledger

Customer Name: Albert Co.

Date	PR	Debit	Credit	Balance
Feb. 7	S3	500		500
28	S3	250		750

Customer Name: Frank Booth

Date	PR	Debit	Credit	Balance
Feb. 25	S3	175		175

Customer Name: Jason Henry

Date	PR	Debit	Credit	Balance
Feb. 2	S3	450		450
22	S3	225		675

Customer Name: Kam Moore

Date	PR	Debit	Credit	Balance
Feb. 13	S3	350		350

Customer Name: Paul Roth

Date	PR	Debit	Credit	Balance
Feb. 15	S3	200		200

General Ledger

Accounts Receivable — No. 106

Date	PR	Debit	Credit	Balance
Feb. 28	S3	2,150		2,150

Inventory — No. 119

Date	PR	Debit	Credit	Balance
Feb. 1	bal.			15,700
28	S3		1,500	14,200

Sales — No. 413

Date	PR	Debit	Credit	Balance
Feb. 28	S3		2,150	2,150

Cost of Goods Sold — No. 502

Date	PR	Debit	Credit	Balance
Feb. 28	S3	1,500		1,500

Schedule of accounts receivable: Lists each customer and the balance owed. Used to prove that the Accounts Receivable controlling account and the total of individual accounts in its subsidiary ledger are equal.

Sales returns and allowances: Record them in a general journal with the following entry.

May 17	Sales Returns and Allowances.	414	175	
	Accounts Receivable—Ray Ball.	106/✓		175
	Customer returned merchandise.			

CASH RECEIPTS JOURNAL

Cash receipts journal: Used to record all receipts of cash, including (1) cash from credit customers in payment of their accounts—as well as discounts, (2) cash from cash sales, and (3) cash from all other sources.

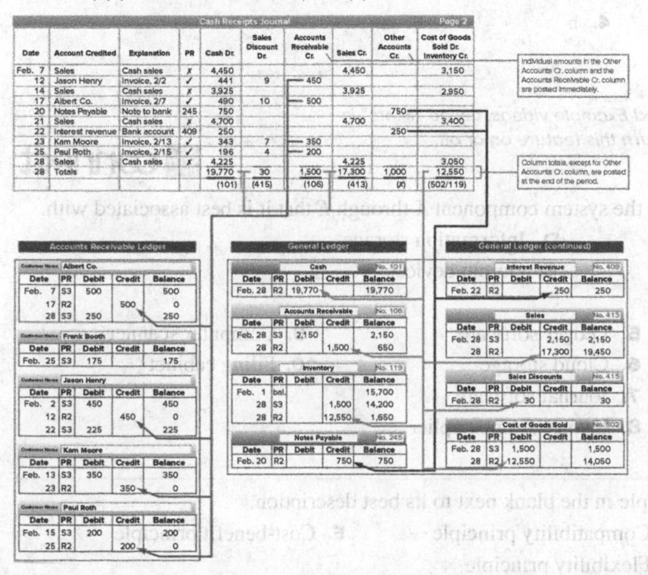

Cash Receipts Journal — Page 2

Date	Account Credited	Explanation	PR	Cash Dr.	Sales Discount Dr.	Accounts Receivable Cr.	Sales Cr.	Other Accounts Cr.	Cost of Goods Sold Dr. Inventory Cr.
Feb. 7	Sales	Cash sales	✗	4,450			4,450		3,150
12	Jason Henry	Invoice, 2/2	✓	441	9	450			
14	Sales	Cash sales	✗	3,925			3,925		2,950
17	Albert Co.	Invoice, 2/7	✓	490	10	500			
20	Notes Payable	Note to bank	245	750				750	
21	Sales	Cash sales	✗	4,700			4,700		3,400
22	Interest revenue	Bank account	409	250				250	
23	Kam Moore	Invoice, 2/13	✓	343	7	350			
25	Paul Roth	Invoice, 2/15	✓	196	4	200			
28	Sales	Cash sales	✗	4,225			4,225		3,050
28	Totals			19,770	30	1,500	17,300	1,000	12,550
				(101)	(415)	(106)	(413)	(✗)	(502/119)

Individual amounts in the Other Accounts Cr. column and the Accounts Receivable Cr. column are posted immediately.

Column totals, except for Other Accounts Cr. column, are posted at the end of the period.

Accounts Receivable Ledger

Customer Name: Albert Co.

Date	PR	Debit	Credit	Balance
Feb. 7	S3	500		500
17	R2		500	0
28	S3	250		250

Customer Name: Frank Booth

Date	PR	Debit	Credit	Balance
Feb. 25	S3	175		175

Customer Name: Jason Henry

Date	PR	Debit	Credit	Balance
Feb. 2	S3	450		450
12	R2		450	0
22	S3	225		225

Customer Name: Kam Moore

Date	PR	Debit	Credit	Balance
Feb. 13	S3	350		350
23	R2		350	0

Customer Name: Paul Roth

Date	PR	Debit	Credit	Balance
Feb. 15	S3	200		200
25	R2		200	0

General Ledger

Cash — No. 101

Date	PR	Debit	Credit	Balance
Feb. 28	R2	19,770		19,770

Accounts Receivable — No. 106

Date	PR	Debit	Credit	Balance
Feb. 28	S3	2,150		2,150
28	R2		1,500	650

Inventory — No. 119

Date	PR	Debit	Credit	Balance
Feb. 1	bal.			15,700
28	S3		1,500	14,200
28	R2		12,550	1,650

Notes Payable — No. 245

Date	PR	Debit	Credit	Balance
Feb. 20	R2		750	750

General Ledger (continued)

Interest Revenue — No. 409

Date	PR	Debit	Credit	Balance
Feb. 22	R2		250	250

Sales — No. 413

Date	PR	Debit	Credit	Balance
Feb. 28	S3		2,150	2,150
28	R2		17,300	19,450

Sales Discounts — No. 415

Date	PR	Debit	Credit	Balance
Feb. 28	R2	30		30

Cost of Goods Sold — No. 502

Date	PR	Debit	Credit	Balance
Feb. 28	S3	1,500		1,500
28	R2	12,550		14,050

Footing and crossfooting: To be sure that total debits and credits in a journal are equal, we crossfoot column totals. To foot a column of numbers is to add it. To crossfoot is to check if debit and credit column totals are equal.

PURCHASES JOURNAL

Purchases journal: Used to record all credit purchases, including those for inventory and supplies.

Purchases Journal — Page 1

Date	Account	Date of Invoice	Terms	PR	Accounts Payable Cr.	Inventory Dr.	Office Supplies Dr.	Other Accounts Dr.
Feb. 3	Horning Supply Co.	2/3	n/30	✓	350	275	75	
5	Ace Mfg. Co.	2/5	2/10, n/30	✓	200	200		
13	Wynet & Co.	2/13	2/10, n/30	✓	150	150		
20	Smite Co.	2/20	2/10, n/30	✓	300	300		
25	Ace Mfg. Co.	2/25	2/10, n/30	✓	100	100		
28	Store Supplies/ITT Co.	2/28	n/30	125/✓	225	125	25	75
28	Totals				1,325	1,150	100	75
					(201)	(119)	(124)	(✗)

Accounts Payable Ledger

Company Name: Ace Mfg. Company

Date	PR	Debit	Credit	Balance
Feb. 5	P1		200	200
25	P1		100	300

Company Name: Horning Supply Company

Date	PR	Debit	Credit	Balance
Feb. 3	P1		350	350

Company Name: ITT Company

Date	PR	Debit	Credit	Balance
Feb. 28	P1		225	225

Company Name: Smite Company

Date	PR	Debit	Credit	Balance
Feb. 20	P1		300	300

Company Name: Wynet and Company

Date	PR	Debit	Credit	Balance
Feb. 13	P1		150	150

General Ledger

Inventory — No. 119

Date	PR	Debit	Credit	Balance
Feb. 1	bal.			15,700
28	S3		1,500	14,200
28	R2		12,550	1,650
28	P1	1,150		2,800

Office Supplies — No. 124

Date	PR	Debit	Credit	Balance
Feb. 28	P1	100		100

Store Supplies — No. 125

Date	PR	Debit	Credit	Balance
Feb. 28	P1	75		75

Accounts Payable — No. 201

Date	PR	Debit	Credit	Balance
Feb. 28	P1		1,325	1,325

Schedule of accounts payable: Lists each creditor's accounts payable and the balance owed. Used to prove that the Accounts Payable controlling account and the total of individual accounts in its subsidiary ledger are equal.

CASH PAYMENTS JOURNAL

Cash payments journal: Used to record all cash payments, including cash payments for inventory, salaries, and accounts payable—minus discounts.

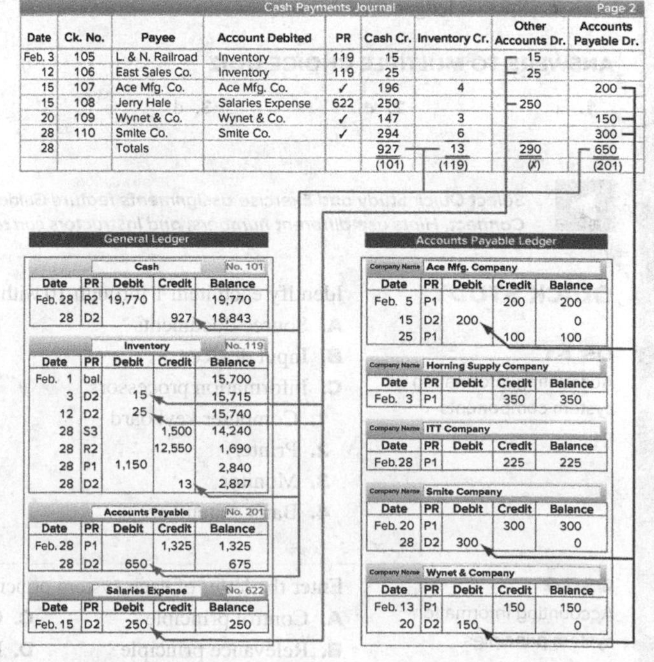

Cash Payments Journal — Page 2

Date	Ck. No.	Payee	Account Debited	PR	Cash Cr.	Inventory Cr.	Other Accounts Dr.	Accounts Payable Dr.
Feb. 3	105	L. & N. Railroad	Inventory	119	15		15	
12	106	East Sales Co.	Inventory	119	25		25	
15	107	Ace Mfg. Co.	Ace Mfg. Co.	✓	196	4		200
15	108	Jerry Hale	Salaries Expense	622	250		250	
20	109	Wynet & Co.	Wynet & Co.	✓	147	3		150
28	110	Smite Co.	Smite Co.	✓	294	6		300
28		Totals			927	13	290	650
					(101)	(119)	(✗)	(201)

General Ledger

Cash — No. 101

Date	PR	Debit	Credit	Balance
Feb. 28	R2	19,770		19,770
28	D2		927	18,843

Inventory — No. 119

Date	PR	Debit	Credit	Balance
Feb. 1	bal.			15,700
3	D2	15		15,715
12	D2	25		15,740
28	S3		1,500	14,240
28	R2		12,550	1,690
28	P1	1,150		2,840
28	D2		13	2,827

Accounts Payable — No. 201

Date	PR	Debit	Credit	Balance
Feb. 28	P1		1,325	1,325
28	D2	650		675

Salaries Expense — No. 622

Date	PR	Debit	Credit	Balance
Feb. 15	D2	250		250

Accounts Payable Ledger

Company Name: Ace Mfg. Company

Date	PR	Debit	Credit	Balance
Feb. 5	P1		200	200
15	D2	200		0
25	P1		100	100

Company Name: Horning Supply Company

Date	PR	Debit	Credit	Balance
Feb. 3	P1		350	350

Company Name: ITT Company

Date	PR	Debit	Credit	Balance
Feb. 28	P1		225	225

Company Name: Smite Company

Date	PR	Debit	Credit	Balance
Feb. 20	P1		300	300
28	D2	300		0

Company Name: Wynet & Company

Date	PR	Debit	Credit	Balance
Feb. 13	P1		150	150
20	D2	150		0

Key Terms

Accounting information system (257)
Accounts payable ledger (259)
Accounts receivable ledger (259)
Batch processing (268)
Cash payments journal (266)
Cash receipts journal (263)
Check register (267)
Columnar journal (261)
Compatibility principle (257)
Components of accounting systems (258)
Computer network (268)
Control principle (257)
Controlling account (260)
Cost-benefit principle (257)
Data analytics (269)
Data visualization (269)
Days' payable outstanding (DPO) (269)
Enterprise resource planning (ERP) software (269)
Flexibility principle (257)
General journal (259)
Information processor (258)
Information storage (258)
Input device (258)
Internal controls (257)
Online processing (268)
Output devices (258)
Purchases journal (265)
Relevance principle (257)
Sales journal (261)
Schedule of accounts payable (266)
Schedule of accounts receivable (266)
Special journal (259)
Subsidiary ledger (259)

Multiple Choice Quiz

1. The sales journal is used to record
- **a.** Credit sales.
- **b.** Cash sales.
- **c.** Cash receipts.
- **d.** Cash purchases.
- **e.** Credit purchases.

2. The purchases journal is used to record
- **a.** Credit sales.
- **b.** Cash sales.
- **c.** Cash receipts.
- **d.** Cash purchases.
- **e.** Credit purchases.

3. The ledger that contains the financial statement accounts of a company is the
- **a.** General journal.
- **b.** Column balance journal.
- **c.** Special ledger.
- **d.** General ledger.
- **e.** Special journal.

4. A subsidiary ledger that contains a separate account for each supplier (creditor) to the company is the
- **a.** Controlling account.
- **b.** Accounts payable ledger.
- **c.** Accounts receivable ledger.
- **d.** General ledger.
- **e.** Special journal.

5. Enterprise resource planning software
- **a.** Refers to programs that help manage company operations.
- **b.** Is another name for spreadsheet programs.
- **c.** Uses batch processing of business information.
- **d.** Is substantially declining in use.
- **e.** Is another name for database programs.

ANSWERS TO MULTIPLE CHOICE QUIZ

1. a **2.** e **3.** d **4.** b **5.** a

Select Quick Study and Exercise assignments feature Guided Example videos, called "Hints" in Connect. Hints use different numbers, and instructors can turn this feature on or off.

QUICK STUDY

QS 7-1
Accounting information system components
C1

Identify each item 1 through 10 with the system component *A* through *E* that it is best associated with.

A. Source documents
B. Input devices
C. Information processors
D. Information storage
E. Output devices

1. Computer keyboard
2. Printer
3. Monitor
4. Bank statement
5. Ledger software
6. Cloud storage
7. Journal software
8. Invoice from supplier
9. Computer scanner
10. Filing cabinet

QS 7-2
Accounting information system principles
C1

Enter the letter of each system principle in the blank next to its best description.

A. Control principle
B. Relevance principle
C. Compatibility principle
D. Flexibility principle
E. Cost-benefit principle

1. The accounting information system helps monitor activities.
2. The accounting information system conforms to the company's business activities.
3. The accounting information system changes in response to technological advances and competitive pressures.
4. Affects all other accounting information system principles.
5. The accounting information system provides timely information for effective decision making.

QS 7-3 Identifying general and subsidiary ledgers **C2**

For each account, indicate whether it appears in the general ledger or the subsidiary ledger.

a. Accounts Receivable—Martin
b. Interest Expense
c. Prepaid Rent
d. Accounts Payable—Julie
e. Notes Payable
f. Store Supplies

QS 7-4 Controlling accounts and subsidiary ledgers **C2**

Following is information from Fredrickson Company for its first month of business.

1. Identify the balances listed in the accounts receivable subsidiary ledger.
2. Identify the Accounts Receivable balance listed in the general ledger at month's end.

Credit Sales			Cash Collections		
Jan. 10	Stern Company........	$4,000	Jan. 20	Stern Company........	$2,000
19	Diaz Brothers	1,600	28	Diaz Brothers	1,600
23	Rex Company.........	2,500	31	Rex Company.........	1,300

QS 7-5 Identifying the special journal of entry **P1 P2 P3 P4**

Wilcox Electronics uses a sales journal, purchases journal, cash receipts journal, cash payments journal, and general journal. Identify the journal in which each transaction should be recorded.

a. Sold merchandise on credit.
b. Purchased shop supplies on credit.
c. Paid an employee's salary in cash.
d. Borrowed cash from the bank.
e. Sold merchandise for cash.
f. Purchased merchandise on credit.
g. Purchased inventory for cash.
h. Paid cash to a creditor.

QS 7-6 Sales journal **P1**

Caesar Company uses a sales journal, purchases journal, cash receipts journal, cash payments journal, and general journal. Prepare a sales journal like the one in Exhibit 7.5. Journalize the following transactions that should be recorded in the sales journal.

June 5 Purchased $1,000 of merchandise on credit from Roman Corp.
9 Sold merchandise costing $200 to R. Allen for $325, terms n/10, Invoice No. 2080.
12 Sold merchandise costing $300 to J. Meyer for $450 cash, Invoice No. 2081.
19 Received $325 cash from R. Allen to pay for the June 9 purchase.
27 Sold merchandise costing $400 to B. Kraft for $550, terms n/10, Invoice No. 2082.

QS 7-7 Cash receipts journal **P2**

Li Company uses a sales journal, purchases journal, cash receipts journal, cash payments journal, and general journal. Prepare a cash receipts journal like the one in Exhibit 7.7. Journalize the following transactions that should be recorded in the cash receipts journal.

May 1 C. Li, the owner, contributed $9,000 cash to the company.
7 The company purchased $5,000 of merchandise on credit from Gomez, terms n/30.
9 The company sold merchandise costing $400 to E. James for $500 on credit, terms n/10.
15 The company borrowed $1,000 cash by signing a note payable to the bank.
18 The company received $500 cash from E. James in payment of the May 9 purchase.
24 The company sold merchandise costing $150 to B. Cox for $200 cash.

QS 7-8 Purchases journal **P3**

Peachtree Company uses a sales journal, purchases journal, cash receipts journal, cash payments journal, and general journal. Prepare a purchases journal like the one in Exhibit 7.9. Journalize the following transactions that should be recorded in the purchases journal.

May 1 Purchased $10,100 of merchandise on credit from Krause, Inc., terms n/30.
8 Sold merchandise costing $900 to G. Seles for $1,500 on credit subject to a $30 sales discount if paid within 30 days.
14 Purchased $240 of store supplies from Chang Company on credit, terms n/30.
17 Purchased $260 of office supplies on credit from Monder Company, terms n/30.
24 Sold merchandise costing $400 to D. Air for $650 cash.
28 Purchased store supplies from Porter's for $90 cash.
29 Paid Krause, Inc., $10,100 cash for the merchandise purchased on May 1.

QS 7-9
Identifying journal of entry
P1 P2 P3 P4

Refer to QS 7-8 and for each of the transactions identify the journal in which it would be recorded. Assume the company uses a sales journal, purchases journal, cash receipts journal, cash payments journal, and general journal.

QS 7-10
Cash payments journal
P4

Greenleaf Company uses a sales journal, purchases journal, cash receipts journal, cash payments journal, and general journal. Prepare a cash payments journal like the one in Exhibit 7.11. Journalize the following transactions that should be recorded in the cash payments journal.

June 3 Issued Check No. 380 to Skipp Corp. to buy office supplies for $235.
5 Purchased merchandise for $3,200 on credit from Buck Co., terms n/15.
20 Issued Check No. 381 for $3,200 to Buck Co. to pay for the June 5 purchase.
23 Paid salary of $4,800 to T. Bourne by issuing Check No. 382.
26 Issued Check No. 383 for $2,250 to pay off a note payable to UT Bank.

QS 7-11
Entries in the general journal
P1 P2 P3 P4

Biloxi Gifts uses a sales journal, purchases journal, cash receipts journal, cash payments journal, and general journal. Journalize its transactions that should be recorded in the general journal. For those not recorded in the general journal, identify the special journal where each should be recorded.

Nov. 2 The company purchased $2,600 of merchandise on credit from the Midland Co., terms 2/10, n/30.
12 The owner, T. Biloxi, contributed an automobile worth $17,000 to the company.
16 The company sold $1,200 of merchandise (cost is $800) on credit to K. Myer, terms n/30.
19 Biloxi granted K. Myer an allowance (price reduction) of $175 for merchandise sold on November 16. Biloxi credited Accounts Receivable for that amount.

QS 7-12
Identifying transactions from subsidiary ledgers
P1 P2 P3 P4

Following are (1) two transactions involving a customer as reported in the accounts receivable subsidiary ledger *and* (2) two transactions involving a supplier as reported in the accounts payable subsidiary ledger. Identify the journal in which each of the four transactions is recorded.

Accounts Receivable Ledger
Customer Name J. Adamo

Date	PR	Debit	Credit	Balance
Feb. 3	S3	350		350
13	R2		350	0

Accounts Payable Ledger
Company Name Waze Company

Date	PR	Debit	Credit	Balance
Feb. 21	P1		600	600
27	D2	600		0

QS 7-13
Indicating journals used for posting
P1 P2 P3 P4

The following T-accounts show postings of selected transactions. Indicate the journal used in recording each of these postings *a* through *e*.

Cash

(d)	500	(e)	300

Accounts Receivable

(b)	1,600	(d)	500

Inventory

(a)	1,400	(c)	1,000

Accounts Payable

(e)	300	(a)	1,400

Sales

		(b)	1,600

Cost of Goods Sold

(c)	1,000		

QS 7-14
Accounts receivable ledger; posting to accounts
P1

Warton Company posts individual sales to the accounts receivable subsidiary ledger immediately. At the end of each month, Warton posts the end-of-month totals to the general ledger.

July 2	Mary Mack	$ 8,600
8	Eric Horner	11,100
10	Troy Wilson	13,400
14	Hong Jiang	20,500
20	Troy Wilson	11,200
29	Mary Mack	7,300
	Total credit sales	$72,100

1. Open an accounts receivable subsidiary ledger with a T-account for each customer. Post the amounts to the subsidiary ledger.
2. Open an Accounts Receivable controlling T-account and a Sales T-account to reflect general ledger accounts. Post the end-of-month total to these accounts.
3. Prepare a schedule of accounts receivable and prove (confirm) that its total equals the Accounts Receivable controlling account balance.

QS 7-15
Days' payable outstanding
A1

Wentz Co. made it a priority to negotiate better credit terms with its suppliers so it could defer payments longer. (*a*) Use the following information for Wentz Co. to compute days' payable outstanding for Year 1 and Year 2. (*b*) Does Wentz Co. appear to have negotiated better credit terms in Year 2 than in Year 1?

	Year 2	Year 1
Accounts payable	$ 4,110	$ 2,740
Cost of goods sold	50,000	40,000

connect

EXERCISES

Exercise 7-1
Sales journal
P1

Finer Company uses a sales journal, purchases journal, cash receipts journal, cash payments journal, and general journal. Prepare a sales journal like the one in Exhibit 7.5. Journalize the following transactions that should be recorded in the sales journal.

May 2 Sold merchandise costing $300 to B. Facer for $450 cash, Invoice No. 5703.
5 Purchased $2,400 of merchandise on credit from Marchant Corp.
7 Sold merchandise costing $800 to J. Dryer for $1,250, terms 2/10, n/30, Invoice No. 5704.
8 Borrowed $9,000 cash by signing a note payable to the bank.
12 Sold merchandise costing $200 to R. Lamb for $340, terms n/30, Invoice No. 5705.
16 Received $1,225 cash from J. Dryer to pay for the purchase of May 7.
19 Sold used store equipment (noninventory) for $900 cash to Golf, Inc.
25 Sold merchandise costing $500 to T. Taylor for $750, terms n/30, Invoice No. 5706.

Exercise 7-2
Identifying journal of entry
P1 P2 P3 P4

Refer to Exercise 7-1 and for each of the transactions identify the journal in which it would be recorded. Assume the company uses a sales journal, purchases journal, cash receipts journal, cash payments journal, and general journal.

Exercise 7-3
Cash receipts journal
P2

Ali Co. uses a sales journal, purchases journal, cash receipts journal, cash payments journal, and general journal. Prepare a cash receipts journal like the one in Exhibit 7.7. Journalize the following transactions that should be recorded in the cash receipts journal.

Nov. 3 The company purchased $3,200 of merchandise on credit from Hart Co., terms n/20.
7 The company sold merchandise costing $840 to J. Than for $1,000 on credit, subject to a $20 sales discount if paid by the end of the month.
9 The company borrowed $3,750 cash by signing a note payable to the bank.
13 J. Ali, the owner, contributed $5,000 cash to the company.
18 The company sold merchandise costing $250 to B. Cox for $330 cash.
22 The company paid Hart Co. $3,200 cash for the merchandise purchased on November 3.
27 The company received $980 cash from J. Than in payment of the November 7 purchase.
30 The company paid salaries of $1,650 in cash.

Exercise 7-4
Identifying journal of entry
P1 P2 P3 P4

Refer to Exercise 7-3 and for each of the transactions identify the journal in which it would be recorded. Assume the company uses a sales journal, purchases journal, cash receipts journal, cash payments journal, and general journal.

Exercise 7-5
Controlling accounts and subsidiary ledgers
C2

Following is information from Jesper Company for its first month of business.

1. Identify the balances listed in the accounts payable subsidiary ledger.
2. Identify the Accounts Payable balance listed in the general ledger at month's end.

Credit Purchases				Cash Paid			
Jan.	9	Bailey Company	$14,000	Jan.	19	Bailey Company	$10,100
	18	Johnson Brothers	6,600		27	Johnson Brothers	6,600
	22	Preston Company	6,200		31	Preston Company	5,400

Exercise 7-6
Purchases journal
P3

Gomez Company uses a sales journal, purchases journal, cash receipts journal, cash payments journal, and general journal. Prepare a purchases journal like the one in Exhibit 7.9. Journalize the following transactions that should be recorded in the purchases journal.

[continued on next page]

[continued from previous page]

July 1 Purchased $14,500 of merchandise on credit from Hector Co., terms n/15.
4 Sold merchandise costing $320 to C. Paul for $430 cash.
8 Purchased $420 of office supplies from Zhang Co. on credit, terms n/30.
15 Paid Hector $14,500 cash for the merchandise purchased on July 1.
21 Purchased $885 of store supplies on credit from Staples, terms n/30.
22 Sold merchandise costing $2,000 to MicroTran for $2,500 on credit, terms n/30.
23 Purchased office supplies from Depot for $305 cash.
25 Purchased $3,000 of merchandise on credit from Alfredo Co., terms n/30.
27 Paid employee salaries of $1,650 in cash.

Exercise 7-7
Cash payments journal
P4

Marx Supply uses a sales journal, purchases journal, cash receipts journal, cash payments journal, and general journal. Prepare a cash payments journal like the one in Exhibit 7.11. Journalize the following transactions that should be recorded in the cash payments journal.

Apr. 3 Purchased merchandise for $2,950 on credit from Seth, Inc., terms 2/10, n/30.
9 Issued Check No. 210 to Kitt Corp. to buy store supplies for $650.
12 Sold merchandise costing $500 to C. Myrs for $770 on credit, terms n/30.
17 Issued Check No. 211 for $1,400 to pay off a note payable to City Bank.
20 Purchased merchandise for $4,500 on credit from Lite, terms 2/10, n/30.
28 Issued Check No. 212 to Lite to pay the amount due for the April 20 purchase less the $90 discount.
29 Paid salary of $1,800 to B. Dock by issuing Check No. 213.
30 Issued Check No. 214 to Seth, Inc., for $2,950 to pay for the April 3 purchase.

Exercise 7-8
Identifying journal of entry
P1 P2 P3 P4

Refer to Exercise 7-7 and for each of the transactions identify the journal in which it would be recorded. Assume the company uses a sales journal, purchases journal, cash receipts journal, cash payments journal, and general journal.

Exercise 7-9
Entries in general journal
P1 P2 P3 P4

Smith Auto uses a sales journal, purchases journal, cash receipts journal, cash payments journal, and general journal. Journalize its transactions that should be recorded in the general journal. For those not recorded in the general journal, identify the special journal where each should be recorded.

July 3 The company purchased $3,100 of merchandise on credit from Advanced Parts, terms n/60.
6 The company sold $600 of merchandise for cash (cost is $450) to O'Reily.
7 The owner, A. Smith, contributed equipment worth $5,000 to the company.
9 The company sold $750 of used equipment (noninventory) on credit to Junk Yard, terms n/30.
13 The company sold $3,200 of merchandise (cost is $2,800) on credit to J. Bell, terms n/30.
15 The company granted J. Bell an allowance (price reduction) of $500 for merchandise purchased on July 13. Smith Auto credited Accounts Receivable for that amount.
22 The company purchased a building for $20,000 by issuing a note payable.
26 The company paid salaries of $4,400 with cash.

Exercise 7-10
Purchases journal and error identification
P3

A company that records credit purchases in a purchases journal and records purchases returns in a general journal made the following errors. Enter *A*, *B*, or *C* indicating when each error should be discovered.

A. When preparing the schedule of accounts payable.
B. When crossfooting the purchases journal.
C. When preparing the trial balance.

1. Made an addition error in totaling the Office Supplies column of the purchases journal.
2. Made an addition error in determining the balance of a creditor's subsidiary account.
3. Posted a purchases return to the Accounts Payable account and to the creditor's subsidiary account but did not post the purchases return to the Inventory account.
4. Correctly recorded an $8,000 purchase in the purchases journal but posted it to the creditor's subsidiary account as an $800 purchase.
5. Posted a purchases return to the Inventory account and to the Accounts Payable account but did not post to the creditor's subsidiary account.

Exercise 7-11
Special journal transactions and error discovery
P4

Post Pharmacy uses the following journals: sales journal, purchases journal, cash receipts journal, cash payments journal, and general journal. The following two transactions were processed.

June 5 Post Pharmacy purchased merchandise priced at $14,000, subject to credit terms of 2/10, n/30.
14 Post Pharmacy paid the net amount due for the merchandise purchased on June 5.

In journalizing the June 14 payment, the pharmacy debited Accounts Payable for $14,000 but failed to record the cash discount on the purchase. Cash was properly credited for the actual $13,720 paid.

a. In what journals would the June 5 and the June 14 transactions be recorded?

b. What procedure is likely to discover the error in journalizing the June 14 transaction?

Exercise 7-12
Posting to subsidiary ledger accounts; preparing a schedule of accounts receivable
P1

At the end of May, the sales journal of Mountain View appears as follows.

Sales Journal					Page 2
Date	Account Debited	Invoice Number	PR	Accounts Receivable Dr. Sales Cr.	Cost of Goods Sold Dr. Inventory Cr.
May 6	Aaron Reckers	190		3,880	3,120
10	Sara Reed	191		2,940	2,325
17	Anna Page	192		1,850	1,480
25	Sara Reed	193		1,340	1,075
31	Totals			10,010	8,000

Mountain View also recorded an allowance (price reduction) given to Anna Page with the following entry.

May 20	Sales Returns and Allowances	350	
	Accounts Receivable—Anna Page		350
	Record allowance to customer.		

Required

1. Open an accounts receivable subsidiary ledger that has a T-account for each customer listed in the sales journal. Post to the customer accounts the entries in the sales journal and any portion of the general journal entry that affects a customer's account.

2. Open a general ledger that has T-accounts for Accounts Receivable, Inventory, Sales, Sales Returns and Allowances, and Cost of Goods Sold. May's beginning balance of inventory was $20,000. Post the sales journal and any portion of the general journal entry that affects these accounts.

3. Prepare a schedule of accounts receivable and prove (confirm) that its total equals the balance in the Accounts Receivable controlling account.

Check (3) Ending Accounts Receivable, $9,660

Exercise 7-13
Identifying posting reference **P2**

Following is a cash receipts journal and a partial chart of accounts for a company. For each posting reference *a* through *k*, enter (1) an *x* for an amount not individually posted, (2) a ✓ for individual posting to the customer's account in the accounts receivable subsidiary ledger, or (3) an *account number* for a posting to the general ledger.

Cash Receipts Journal									
Date	Account Credited	Explanation	PR	Cash Dr.	Sales Discount Dr.	Accounts Receivable Cr.	Sales Cr.	Other Accounts Cr.	Cost of Goods Sold Dr. Inventory Cr.
May 1	Interest revenue	Bank account	*(a)*	100				100	
10	Notes Payable	Note to bank	*(b)*	3,000				3,000	
17	K. Korver	Invoice, 5/2	*(c)*	693	7	700			
18	E. Bled	Invoice, 5/9	*(d)*	1,200		1,200			
31	Sales	Cash sales	*(e)*	2,000			2,000		1,150
31	Totals			6,993	7	1,900	2,000	3,100	1,150
				(f)	*(g)*	*(h)*	*(i)*	*(j)*	*(k)*

Account	No.	Account	No.
Cash.	101	Interest revenue.	409
Accounts Receivable	106	Sales	413
Inventory.	119	Sales discount	415
Notes payable.	245	Cost of goods sold	502

Exercise 7-14
Days' payable outstanding
A1

The following companies are competitors in the same industry and have many of the same suppliers. (*a*) Calculate days' payable outstanding for each of the following companies (round to one decimal). (*b*) Assuming each company has positive relations with its suppliers, which company has likely negotiated the best credit terms?

	Accounts Payable	Cost of Goods Sold
Vizio.	$1,200	$20,000
Panasonic	1,920	28,000
TCL.	970	12,000

PROBLEM SET A

Problem 7-1A
Special journals, subsidiary ledgers, trial balance
P1 P2 P3 P4

Church Company completes these transactions and events during March of the current year (terms for all its credit sales are 2/10, n/30).

Mar. 1 Purchased $43,600 of merchandise from Van Industries, terms 2/15, n/30.
2 Sold merchandise on credit to Min Cho, Invoice No. 854, for $16,800 (cost is $8,400).
3 Purchased $1,230 of office supplies on credit from Gabel Company, terms n/30.
3 Sold merchandise on credit to Linda Witt, Invoice No. 855, for $10,200 (cost is $5,800).
6 Borrowed $82,000 cash from Federal Bank by signing a long-term note payable.
9 Purchased $21,850 of office equipment on credit from Spell Supply, terms n/30.
10 Sold merchandise on credit to Jovita Albany, Invoice No. 856, for $5,600 (cost is $2,900).
12 Received payment from Min Cho for the March 2 sale less the discount of $336.
13 Sent Van Industries Check No. 416 in payment of the March 1 invoice less the discount of $872.
13 Received payment from Linda Witt for the March 3 sale less the discount of $204.
14 Purchased $32,625 of merchandise from the CD Company, terms 2/10, n/30.
15 Issued Check No. 417 for $18,300; payee is Payroll, in payment of sales salaries expense for the first half of the month.
15 Cash sales for the first half of the month are $34,680 (cost is $20,210). These cash sales are recorded in the cash receipts journal on March 15.
16 Purchased $1,770 of store supplies on credit from Gabel Company, terms n/30.
17 Returned $2,425 of unsatisfactory merchandise purchased on March 14 to CD Company. Church reduces Accounts Payable by that amount.
19 Returned $630 of office equipment purchased on March 9 to Spell Supply. Church reduces Accounts Payable by that amount.
20 Received payment from Jovita Albany for the sale of March 10 less the discount of $112.
23 Issued Check No. 418 to CD Company in payment of the March 14 purchase less the March 17 return and the $604 discount.
27 Sold merchandise on credit to Jovita Albany, Invoice No. 857, for $14,910 (cost is $7,220).
28 Sold merchandise on credit to Linda Witt, Invoice No. 858, for $4,315 (cost is $3,280).
31 Issued Check No. 419 for $18,300; payee is Payroll, in payment of sales salaries expense for the last half of the month.
31 Cash sales for the last half of the month are $30,180 (cost is $16,820). These cash sales are recorded in the cash receipts journal on March 31.
31 Verify that amounts impacting customer and creditor accounts were posted and that any amounts that should have been posted as individual amounts to the general ledger accounts were posted. Foot and crossfoot the journals and make the month-end postings.

Required

1. Open the following general ledger accounts: Cash; Accounts Receivable; Inventory (March 1 beg. bal. is $10,000); Office Supplies; Store Supplies; Office Equipment; Accounts Payable; Long-Term Notes Payable; Z. Church, Capital (March 1 beg. bal. is $10,000); Sales; Sales Discounts; Cost of Goods Sold; and Sales Salaries Expense. Open the following accounts receivable subsidiary ledger accounts: Jovita Albany, Min Cho, and Linda Witt. Open the following accounts payable subsidiary ledger accounts: Gabel Company, Van Industries, Spell Supply, and CD Company.

2. Enter these transactions in a sales journal, purchases journal, cash receipts journal, cash payments journal, or general journal. Number all journal pages as page 2.

3. (*a*) Prepare a trial balance of the general ledger. (*b*) Prove the accuracy of the subsidiary ledgers by preparing schedules of both accounts receivable and accounts payable.

Check Trial balance totals, $232,905

Problem 7-2A
Special journals, subsidiary ledgers, and schedule of accounts receivable
P1 P2

Wiset Company completes these transactions during April of the current year (the terms of all its credit sales are 2/10, n/30).

Apr. 2 Purchased $14,300 of merchandise on credit from Noth Company, terms 2/10, n/60.
3 Sold merchandise on credit to Page Alistair, Invoice No. 760, for $4,000 (cost is $3,000).
3 Purchased $1,480 of office supplies on credit from Custer, Inc., terms n/30.
4 Issued Check No. 587 to *World View* for advertising expense of $899.
5 Sold merchandise on credit to Paula Kohr, Invoice No. 761, for $8,000 (cost is $6,500).
6 Returned $80 of office supplies purchased on April 3 to Custer, Inc. Wiset reduces Accounts Payable by that amount.
9 Purchased $12,125 of store equipment on credit from Hal's Supply, terms n/30.

11 Sold merchandise on credit to Nic Nelson, Invoice No. 762, for $10,500 (cost is $7,000).
12 Issued Check No. 588 to Noth Company in payment of its April 2 purchase less the discount of $286.
13 Received payment from Page Alistair for the April 3 sale less the discount of $80.
13 Sold $5,100 of merchandise on credit to Page Alistair (cost is $3,600), Invoice No. 763.
14 Received payment from Paula Kohr for the April 5 sale less the discount of $160.
16 Issued Check No. 589 for $10,750; payee is Payroll, in payment of sales salaries expense for the first half of the month.
16 Cash sales for the first half of the month are $52,840 (cost is $35,880). These cash sales are recorded in the cash receipts journal on April 16.
17 Purchased $13,750 of merchandise on credit from Grant Company, terms 2/10, n/30.
18 Borrowed $60,000 cash from First State Bank by signing a long-term note payable.
20 Received payment from Nic Nelson for the April 11 sale less the discount of $210.
20 Purchased $830 of store supplies on credit from Hal's Supply, terms n/30.
23 Returned $750 of defective merchandise purchased on April 17 to Grant Company. Wiset reduces Accounts Payable by that amount.
23 Received payment from Page Alistair for the April 13 sale less the discount of $102.
25 Purchased $11,375 of merchandise on credit from Noth Company, terms 2/10, n/60.
26 Issued Check No. 590 to Grant Company in payment of its April 17 invoice less the return and the $260 discount.
27 Sold $3,170 of merchandise on credit to Paula Kohr, Invoice No. 764 (cost is $2,520).
27 Sold $6,700 of merchandise on credit to Nic Nelson, Invoice No. 765 (cost is $4,305).
30 Issued Check No. 591 for $10,750; payee is Payroll, in payment of the sales salaries expense for the last half of the month.
30 Cash sales for the last half of the month are $73,975 (cost is $58,900). These cash sales are recorded in the cash receipts journal on April 30.

Required

1. Prepare a sales journal and cash receipts journal. Number both journal pages as page 3. Enter the transactions of Wiset Company that should be journalized in the sales journal and those that should be journalized in the cash receipts journal. Ignore transactions that should be journalized in a purchases journal, cash payments journal, or general journal.
2. Open the following general ledger accounts: Cash; Accounts Receivable; Inventory; Long-Term Notes Payable; B. Wiset, Capital; Sales; Sales Discounts; and Cost of Goods Sold. Enter the March 31 balances for Cash ($85,000), Inventory ($125,000), Long-Term Notes Payable ($110,000), and B. Wiset, Capital ($100,000). Also open accounts receivable subsidiary ledger accounts for Paula Kohr, Page Alistair, and Nic Nelson.
3. Verify that amounts that should be posted as individual amounts from the journals have been posted. (Such items are immediately posted.) Foot and crossfoot the journals and make the month-end postings.
4. (*a*) Prepare a trial balance of the general ledger accounts opened as required for part 2. (*b*) Prove the accuracy of the subsidiary ledger by preparing a schedule of accounts receivable.

Check Trial balance totals, $434,285

Problem 7-3A
Special journals, subsidiary ledgers, and schedule of accounts payable
P3 P4

The April transactions of Wiset Company are described in Problem 7-2A.

Required

1. Prepare a general journal, purchases journal, and cash payments journal. Number all journal pages as page 3. Enter the transactions of Wiset Company that should be journalized in the general journal, purchases journal, or cash payments journal. Ignore transactions that should be journalized in a sales journal or cash receipts journal.
2. Open the following general ledger accounts: Cash; Inventory; Office Supplies; Store Supplies; Store Equipment; Accounts Payable; Long-Term Notes Payable; B. Wiset, Capital; Sales Salaries Expense; and Advertising Expense. Enter the March 31 balances of Cash ($85,000), Inventory ($125,000), Long-Term Notes Payable ($110,000), and B. Wiset, Capital ($100,000). Also open accounts payable subsidiary ledger accounts for Hal's Supply, Noth Company, Grant Company, and Custer, Inc.
3. Verify that amounts that should be posted as individual amounts from the journals have been posted. (Such items are immediately posted.) Foot and crossfoot the journals and make the month-end postings.
4. (*a*) Prepare a trial balance of the general ledger accounts opened as required for part 2. (*b*) Prepare a schedule of accounts payable.

Check Trial balance totals, $235,730

PROBLEM SET B

Problem 7-1B
Special journals, subsidiary ledgers, trial balance
P1 P2 P3 P4

Grassley Company completes these transactions during November of the current year (terms for all its credit sales are 2/10, n/30).

Nov. 1 Purchased $5,058 of office equipment on credit from Brun Supply, terms n/30.
2 Borrowed $88,500 cash from Wisconsin Bank by signing a long-term note payable.
4 Purchased $33,500 of merchandise from BLR Industries, terms 2/10, n/30.
5 Purchased $1,040 of store supplies on credit from Grebe Company, terms n/30.
8 Sold merchandise on credit to Cyd Rounder, Invoice No. 439, for $6,550 (cost is $3,910).
10 Sold merchandise on credit to Carlos Mantel, Invoice No. 440, for $13,500 (cost is $8,500).
11 Purchased $2,557 of merchandise from Lo Company, terms 2/10, n/30.
12 Sent BLR Industries Check No. 633 in payment of its November 4 purchase less the discount of $670.
15 Issued Check No. 634 for $6,585; payee is Payroll, in payment of sales salaries expense for the first half of the month.
15 Cash sales for the first half of the month are $18,170 (cost is $9,000). These cash sales are recorded in the cash receipts journal on November 15.
15 Sold merchandise on credit to Tori Tripp, Invoice No. 441, for $5,250 (cost is $2,450).
16 Purchased $459 of office supplies on credit from Grebe Company, terms n/30.
17 Returned $557 of unsatisfactory merchandise purchased on November 11 to Lo Company. Grassley reduces Accounts Payable by that amount.
18 Received payment from Cyd Rounder for the November 8 sale less the discount of $131.
19 Received payment from Carlos Mantel for the November 10 sale less the discount of $270.
19 Issued Check No. 635 to Lo Company in payment of its November 11 purchase less the return and the $40 discount.
22 Sold merchandise on credit to Carlos Mantel, Invoice No. 442, for $3,695 (cost is $2,060).
24 Sold merchandise on credit to Tori Tripp, Invoice No. 443, for $4,280 (cost is $2,130).
25 Received payment from Tori Tripp for the sale of November 15 less the discount of $105.
26 Returned $922 of office equipment purchased on November 1 to Brun Supply. Grassley reduces Accounts Payable by that amount.
30 Issued Check No. 636 for $6,585; payee is Payroll, in payment of sales salaries expense for the last half of the month.
30 Cash sales for the last half of the month are $16,703 (cost is $10,200). These cash sales are recorded in the cash receipts journal on November 30.
30 Verify that amounts impacting customer and creditor accounts were posted and that any amounts that should have been posted as individual amounts to the general ledger accounts were posted. Foot and crossfoot the journals and make the month-end postings.

Required

1. Open the following general ledger accounts: Cash; Accounts Receivable; Inventory (Nov. 1 beg. bal. is $40,000); Office Supplies; Store Supplies; Office Equipment; Accounts Payable; Long-Term Notes Payable; C. Grassley, Capital (Nov. 1 beg. bal. is $40,000); Sales; Sales Discounts; Cost of Goods Sold; and Sales Salaries Expense. Open the following accounts receivable subsidiary ledger accounts: Carlos Mantel, Tori Tripp, and Cyd Rounder. Open the following accounts payable subsidiary ledger accounts: Grebe Company, BLR Industries, Brun Supply, and Lo Company.

2. Enter these transactions in a sales journal, purchases journal, cash receipts journal, cash payments journal, or general journal. Number all journal pages as page 2.

3. (*a*) Prepare a trial balance of the general ledger. (*b*) Prove the accuracy of the subsidiary ledgers by preparing schedules of both accounts receivable and accounts payable.

Check Trial balance totals, $202,283

Problem 7-2B
Special journals, subsidiary ledgers, schedule of accounts receivable
P1 P2

Acorn Industries completes these transactions during July of the current year (the terms of all its credit sales are 2/10, n/30).

July 1 Purchased $6,500 of merchandise on credit from Teton Company, terms 2/10, n/30.
3 Issued Check No. 300 to *The Weekly* for advertising expense of $625.
5 Sold merchandise on credit to Kim Nettle, Invoice No. 918, for $19,200 (cost is $10,500).
6 Sold merchandise on credit to Ruth Blake, Invoice No. 919, for $7,500 (cost is $4,300).
7 Purchased $1,250 of store supplies on credit from Plaine, Inc., terms n/30.
8 Returned $250 of store supplies purchased on July 7 to Plaine, Inc. Acorn reduces Accounts Payable by that amount.
9 Purchased $38,220 of store equipment on credit from Charm's Supply, terms n/30.

10 Issued Check No. 301 to Teton Company in payment of its July 1 purchase less the discount of $130.
13 Sold merchandise on credit to Ashton Moore, Invoice No. 920, for $8,550 (cost is $5,230).
14 Sold merchandise on credit to Kim Nettle, Invoice No. 921, for $5,100 (cost is $3,800).
15 Received payment from Kim Nettle for the July 5 sale less the discount of $384.
15 Issued Check No. 302 for $31,850; payee is Payroll, in payment of sales salaries expense for the first half of the month.
15 Cash sales for the first half of the month are $118,350 (cost is $76,330). These cash sales are recorded in the cash receipts journal on July 15.
16 Received payment from Ruth Blake for the July 6 sale less the discount of $150.
17 Purchased $7,200 of merchandise on credit from Drake Company, terms 2/10, n/30.
20 Purchased $650 of office supplies on credit from Charm's Supply, terms n/30.
21 Borrowed $15,000 cash from College Bank by signing a long-term note payable.
23 Received payment from Ashton Moore for the July 13 sale less the discount of $171.
24 Received payment from Kim Nettle for the July 14 sale less the discount of $102.
24 Returned $2,400 of defective merchandise purchased on July 17 to Drake Company. Acorn reduces Accounts Payable by that amount.
26 Purchased $9,770 of merchandise on credit from Teton Company, terms 2/10, n/30.
27 Issued Check No. 303 to Drake Company in payment of its July 17 purchase less the return and the $96 discount.
29 Sold merchandise on credit to Ruth Blake, Invoice No. 922, for $17,500 (cost is $10,850).
30 Sold merchandise on credit to Ashton Moore, Invoice No. 923, for $16,820 (cost is $9,840).
31 Issued Check No. 304 for $31,850; payee is Payroll, in payment of the sales salaries expense for the last half of the month.
31 Cash sales for the last half of the month are $80,244 (cost is $53,855). These cash sales are recorded in the cash receipts journal on July 31.

Required

1. Prepare a sales journal and cash receipts journal. Number both journals as page 3. Enter the transactions of Acorn Industries that should be journalized in the sales journal and those that should be journalized in the cash receipts journal. Ignore transactions that should be journalized in a purchases journal, cash payments journal, or general journal.
2. Open the following general ledger accounts: Cash; Accounts Receivable; Inventory; Long-Term Notes Payable; R. Acorn, Capital; Sales; Sales Discounts; and Cost of Goods Sold. Enter the June 30 balances for Cash ($100,000), Inventory ($200,000), Long-Term Notes Payable ($200,000), and R. Acorn, Capital ($100,000). Also open accounts receivable subsidiary ledger accounts for Kim Nettle, Ashton Moore, and Ruth Blake.
3. Verify that amounts that should be posted as individual amounts from the journals have been posted. (Such items are immediately posted.) Foot and crossfoot the journals and make the month-end postings.
4. (*a*) Prepare a trial balance of the general ledger accounts opened as required for part 2. (*b*) Prove the accuracy of the subsidiary ledger by preparing a schedule of accounts receivable.

Check Trial balance totals, $588,264

Problem 7-3B
Special journals, subsidiary ledgers, and schedule of accounts payable
P3 P4

The July transactions of Acorn Industries are described in Problem 7-2B.

Required

1. Prepare a general journal, purchases journal, and cash payments journal. Number all journal pages as page 3. Enter the transactions of Acorn Industries that should be journalized in the general journal, purchases journal, or cash payments journal. Ignore transactions that should be journalized in a sales journal or cash receipts journal.
2. Open the following general ledger accounts: Cash; Inventory; Office Supplies; Store Supplies; Store Equipment; Accounts Payable; Long-Term Notes Payable; R. Acorn, Capital; Sales Salaries Expense; and Advertising Expense. Enter the June 30 balances of Cash ($100,000), Inventory ($200,000), Long-Term Notes Payable ($200,000), and R. Acorn, Capital ($100,000). Also open accounts payable subsidiary ledger accounts for Charm's Supply, Teton Company, Drake Company, and Plaine, Inc.
3. Verify that amounts that should be posted as individual amounts from the journals have been posted. (Such items are immediately posted.) Foot and crossfoot the journals and make the month-end postings.
4. (*a*) Prepare a trial balance of the general ledger accounts opened as required for part 2. (*b*) Prepare a schedule of accounts payable.

Check Trial balance totals, $349,640

SERIAL PROBLEM

Business Solutions

P1 P2 P3 P4

Alexander Image/Shutterstock

Serial problem began in Chapter 1. If previous chapter segments were not completed, the serial problem can begin at this point. It is available in ***Connect*** *with an algorithmic option.*

SP 7 Assume that Santana Rey expands **Business Solutions**'s system to include special journals.

Required

1. Locate the transactions related to January through March 2022 for Business Solutions in Chapter 5.
2. Enter the Business Solutions transactions for January through March in a sales journal (insert "n/a" in the Invoice column), cash receipts journal, purchases journal (use Computer Supplies heading instead of Office Supplies), cash payments journal (insert "n/a" in the Check Number column), or general journal. Number journal pages as page 2. If the transaction does not specify the name of the payee, state "not specified" in the Payee column of the cash payments journal.
3. The transactions on the following dates should be journalized in the general journal: January 5, 11, 20, and 24 and March 24. Do not record and post the adjusting entries for the end of March.

COMPREHENSIVE PROBLEM

Using special journals to record and post transactions; preparing adjusting and closing entries; preparing a trial balance and financial statements; completing subsidiary ledgers for receivables and payables

This Comprehensive Problem requires account balances from the April month-end, which are available in Connect or in the Working Papers. Assume it is Monday, May 1, the first business day of the month, and you have just been hired as the accountant for Colo Company, which operates with monthly accounting periods. All of the company's accounting work is completed through the end of April, and its ledgers show April 30 balances. During your first month on the job, the company experiences the following transactions and events (terms for all its credit sales are 2/10, n/30 unless stated differently).

May 1 Issued Check No. 3410 to S&P Management Co. in payment of the May rent for $3,710. Charge $2,968 to Rent Expense—Selling Space, and charge $742 to Rent Expense—Office Space. (Use two lines to record the transaction.)

2 Sold merchandise on credit to Hensel Company, Invoice No. 8785, for $6,100 (cost is $4,100).

2 Issued an allowance (price reduction) of $175 to Knox Co. for merchandise sold on April 28. The total selling price (gross) was $4,725.

3 Issued a refund of $798 to Peyton Products for the return of merchandise purchased on April 29. Colo's Accounts Payable was reduced by that amount.

4 Purchased the following on credit from Gear Supply Co.: merchandise, $37,072; store supplies, $574; and office supplies, $83. Invoice dated May 4, terms n/30.

5 Received payment from Knox Co. for the balance from the April 28 ($4,550) sale less the May 2 return and the $91 discount.

8 Issued Check No. 3411 to Peyton Products to pay for the $7,098 of merchandise purchased on April 29 less the May 3 return and the $126 discount.

9 Sold store supplies (noninventory) to the business next door at their cost of $350 cash. *Hint:* Enter "Store Supplies" only in the Account Credited column.

10 Purchased $4,074 of office equipment on credit from Gear Supply Co., terms n/30.

11 Received payment from Hensel Company for the May 2 sale less the discount of $122.

11 Purchased $8,800 of merchandise from Garcia, Inc., terms 2/10, n/30.

12 Received an $854 price reduction from Gear Supply Co. for the return of office equipment received on May 10. Colo debited Accounts Payable by that amount.

15 Issued Check No. 3412, payable to Payroll, in payment of sales salaries, $5,320, and office salaries, $3,150.

15 Cash sales for the first half of the month are $59,220 (cost is $38,200). These cash sales are recorded in the cash receipts journal on May 15.

15 Post to the customer and creditor accounts. Also post individual items that are not included in column totals at the end of the month to the general ledger accounts.

16 Sold merchandise on credit to Hensel Company, Invoice No. 8786, for $3,990 (cost is $1,890).

17 Purchased $13,650 of merchandise from Fink Corp., terms 2/10, n/60.

19 Issued Check No. 3413 to Garcia, Inc., in payment of its May 11 purchase less the discount of $176.

22 Sold merchandise to Lee Services, Invoice No. 8787, for $6,850 (cost is $4,990), terms 2/10, n/60.

23 Issued Check No. 3414 to Fink Corp. in payment of its May 17 purchase less the discount of $273.

24 Purchased the following on credit from Gear Supply Co.: merchandise, $8,120; store supplies, $630; and office supplies, $280. Terms n/30.

25 Purchased $3,080 of merchandise from Peyton Products, terms 2/10, n/30.

26 Sold merchandise on credit to Crane Corp., Invoice No. 8788, for $14,210 (cost is $8,230).

26 Issued Check No. 3415 to Perennial Power in payment of the May electric bill, $1,283.
29 The owner of Colo Company, Jenny Colo, used Check No. 3416 to withdraw $7,000 cash from the business for personal use.
30 Received payment from Lee Services for the May 22 sale less the discount of $137.
30 Issued Check No. 3417, payable to Payroll, in payment of sales salaries, $5,320, and office salaries, $3,150.
31 Cash sales for the last half of the month are $66,052 (cost is $42,500). These cash sales are recorded in the cash receipts journal on May 31.
31 Post to the customer and creditor accounts. Also post individual items that are not included in column totals at the end of the month to the general ledger accounts. Foot and crossfoot the journals and make the month-end postings.

Required

1. Enter these transactions in a sales journal, purchases journal, cash receipts journal, cash payments journal, or general journal (number all journal pages as page 2). Post when instructed to do so. Assume a perpetual inventory system.
2. Prepare a trial balance in the Trial Balance columns of the work sheet provided. Complete the work sheet using the following information for accounting adjustments.
   a. Expired insurance, $553.
   b. Ending store supplies inventory, $2,632.
   c. Ending office supplies inventory, $504.
   d. Depreciation of store equipment, $567.
   e. Depreciation of office equipment, $329.

   Prepare and post adjusting and closing entries.
3. Prepare a May multiple-step income statement, a May statement of owner's equity, and a May 31 classified balance sheet.
4. (*a*) Prepare a post-closing trial balance. (*b*) Prove the accuracy of subsidiary ledgers by preparing schedules of both accounts receivable and accounts payable.

Check (2) Unadjusted trial balance totals, $545,020; Adjustments column totals, $2,407

(3) Net income, $31,647; Total assets, $385,791

connect

TABLEAU DASHBOARD ACTIVITIES

Tableau Dashboard Activities expose students to accounting analytics using visual displays. These assignments run in **Connect.** All are auto-gradable.

Tableau DA 7-1 Quick Study, Identifying journal of entry, **P1, P2, P3, P4**—similar to Exercise 7-2

Tableau DA 7-2 Exercise, Sales journal and cash receipts journal, **P1, P2**—similar to Exercises 7-1 and 7-3.

Tableau DA 7-3 Mini-Case, Purchases journal, cash payments journal, and accounts payable subsidiary ledger, **P3, P4**—similar to Exercises 7-5, 7-6, and 7-7.

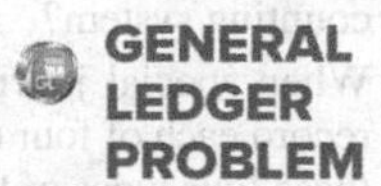

The **General Ledger** tool in *Connect* automates several of the procedural steps in the accounting cycle so that the accounting professional can focus on the impacts of each transaction on the various financial reports.

GL 7-1 General Ledger assignment **GL 7-1,** based on Problem 7-1A, highlights the relation between the subidiary ledgers and the control accounts. Prepare journal entries for a merchandiser, both purchase and sale transactions.

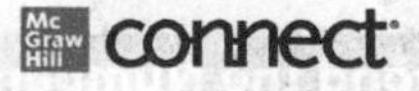

Accounting Analysis

connect

COMPANY ANALYSIS
A1

AA 7-1 Refer to **Apple**'s financial statements in Appendix A.

1. What amount of accounts payable did Apple report on (*a*) September 28, 2019? (*b*) On September 29, 2018?
2. Compute days' payable outstanding for fiscal year ended (*a*) September 28, 2019, and (*b*) September 29, 2018.
3. Does Apple appear to be taking more or less time to pay its suppliers in fiscal year 2019 versus 2018?

COMPARATIVE ANALYSIS

A1

AA 7-2 Key figures for **Apple** and **Google** follow.

$ millions	Apple		Google	
	Current Year	Prior Year	Current Year	Prior Year
Accounts payable	$ 46,236	$ 55,888	$ 5,561	$ 4,378
Cost of goods sold	161,782	163,756	71,896	59,549

Required

1. Compute days' payable outstanding for each company for the most recent two years.
2. For the current year, which company took more time to pay its suppliers?

EXTENDED ANALYSIS

A1

AA 7-3 Key figures for **Samsung** and **Google** follow.

$ millions	Samsung		Google
	Current Year	One Prior Year	Current Year
Accounts payable	$ 7,480	$ 7,276	$ 5,561
Cost of goods sold	126,336	113,598	71,896

Required

1. Compute Samsung's days' payable outstanding for the most recent two years.
2. Assuming Samsung is not at risk of damaging its relationships with suppliers, does it prefer days' payable outstanding to increase or decrease?
3. For the current year, did Samsung or Google take more time to pay its suppliers (based on days' payable outstanding)?

Discussion Questions

1. What are five basic components of an accounting system?
2. What are source documents? Give two examples.
3. What are the five fundamental principles of accounting information systems?
4. What is the purpose of an input device? Give examples of input devices for computer systems.
5. What purpose is served by the output devices of an accounting system?
6. When special journals are used, they are usually used to record each of four different types of transactions. What are these four types of transactions?
7. What notations are entered into the Posting Reference column of a ledger account?
8. When a general journal entry is used to record sales returns, the credit of the entry must be posted twice. Does this cause the trial balance to be out of balance? Explain.
9. Credits to customer accounts and credits to Other Accounts are individually posted from a cash receipts journal such as the one in Exhibit 7.7. Why not put both types of credits in the same column and save journal space?
10. Why should sales to and receipts of cash from credit customers be recorded and posted immediately?

Beyond the Numbers

ETHICS CHALLENGE

C1

BTN 7-1 Erica Gray, CPA, is a sole practitioner. She has been practicing as an auditor for 10 years. Recently a long-standing audit client asked Gray to design and implement an integrated computer-based accounting information system. The fees associated with this additional engagement with the client are very attractive. However, Gray wonders if she can remain objective on subsequent audits in her evaluation of the client's accounting system and its records if she was responsible for its design and implementation. Gray knows that professional auditing standards require her to remain independent in fact and appearance from her auditing clients.

Required

1. What do you believe auditing standards are mainly concerned with when they require independence in fact? In appearance?
2. Why is it important that auditors remain independent of their clients?
3. Do you think Gray can accept this engagement and remain independent? Justify your response.

COMMUNICATING IN PRACTICE
C2

BTN 7-2 Your friend, Wendy Geiger, owns a small retail store that sells candies and nuts. Geiger acquires her goods from a few select vendors. She generally makes purchase orders by phone and on credit. Sales are primarily for cash. Geiger keeps her own manual accounting system using a general journal and a general ledger. At the end of each business day, she records one summary entry for cash sales. Geiger recently began offering items in creative gift packages. This has increased sales substantially, and she is now receiving orders from corporate and other clients who order large quantities and prefer to buy on credit. As a result of increased credit transactions in both purchases and sales, keeping the accounting records has become extremely time-consuming. Geiger wants to continue to maintain her own manual system and calls you for advice. Write a memo to her advising how she might modify her current manual accounting system to accommodate the expanded business activities. Geiger is accustomed to checking her ledger by using a trial balance. Your memo should explain the advantages of what you propose and of any other verification techniques you recommend.

TEAMWORK IN ACTION
P1 P2 P3 P4

BTN 7-3 Each member of the team is to assume responsibility for one of the following tasks.

a. Journalizing in the purchases journal.
b. Journalizing in the cash payments journal.
c. Maintaining and verifying the accounts payable ledger.
d. Journalizing in the sales journal and the general journal.
e. Journalizing in the cash receipts journal.
f. Maintaining and verifying the accounts receivable ledger.

The team should abide by the following procedures in carrying out responsibilities.

Required

1. After tasks *a* through *f* are assigned, each team member is to quickly read the list of transactions in Problem 7-1A, identifying with initials the journal in which each transaction is to be recorded. Upon completion, the team leader is to read transaction dates, and the appropriate team member is to vocalize responsibility. Any disagreement between teammates must be resolved.
2. Journalize and continually update subsidiary ledgers. Journal recorders should alert teammates assigned to subsidiary ledgers when an entry must be posted to their subsidiary ledger.
3. Team members responsible for tasks *a*, *b*, *d*, and *e* are to summarize and prove journals; members responsible for tasks *c* and *f* are to prepare both payables and receivables schedules.
4. The team leader is to take charge of the general ledger, rotating team members to obtain amounts to be posted. The person responsible for a journal must complete posting references in that journal. Other team members should verify the accuracy of account balance computations. To avoid any abnormal account balances, post in the following order: P, S, G, R, D. (*Note:* Posting any necessary individual general ledger amounts is also done at this time.)
5. The team leader is to read out general ledger account balances while another team member fills in the trial balance form. Concurrently, one member should keep a running balance of debit account balance totals and another credit account balance totals. Verify the final total of the trial balance and the schedules. If necessary, the team must resolve any errors. Turn in the trial balance and schedules to the instructor.

ENTREPRENEURIAL DECISION
P1

BTN 7-4 Refer to the chapter's opening feature about Aaron, Dylan, Jeff, and Sam and their company, **Box**. Their company deals with the cloud storage needs of numerous suppliers and customers.

Required

1. Identify the special journals that Box would be likely to use in its operations. Also identify any subsidiary ledgers that it would likely use.
2. Box hopes to double yearly sales within five years from its current $10 million annual assumed amount. Also assume that its sales growth projections are as follows.

Year	One Year Hence	Two Years Hence	Three Years Hence	Four Years Hence	Five Years Hence
Projected growth in sales (from the preceding year)	0%	20%	15%	25%	20%

Estimate Box's projected sales for each year (round to the nearest dollar). If this pattern of sales growth holds, will Box achieve its goal of doubling sales in five years?

8 Cash, Fraud, and Internal Control

Chapter Preview

FRAUD AND INTERNAL CONTROL	CONTROL OF CASH	TOOLS OF CONTROL AND ANALYSIS
C1 Purpose and principles of controls	**C2** Definition and reporting of cash	**P2** Control of petty cash
Technology and controls	**P1** Control of cash receipts	**P3** Bank reconciliation as a control tool
Limitations of controls	Control of cash payments	**A1** Assessing liquidity
NTK 8-1	**NTK 8-2**	**NTK 8-3, 8-4**

Learning Objectives

CONCEPTUAL

C1 Define internal control and identify its purpose and principles.

C2 Define cash and cash equivalents and explain how to report them.

ANALYTICAL

A1 Compute the days' sales uncollected ratio and use it to assess liquidity.

PROCEDURAL

P1 Apply internal control to cash receipts and payments.

P2 Explain and record petty cash fund transactions.

P3 Prepare a bank reconciliation.

P4 *Appendix 8A*—Describe use of documentation and verification to control cash payments.

Driving Force

Brendan Smialowski/AFP/Getty Images

"Believe in yourself"—**JEAN LIU**

BEIJING—Most of us are familiar with **Uber** and **Lyft**. However, Jean Liu and **Didi Chuxing**, or **DiDi** for short, are quietly building the world's largest ride-sharing service.

Often referred to as the "Uber of China," DiDi already facilitates twice as many rides as Uber, Lyft, and all other ride-sharing services combined. Jean, DiDi's president, is viewed as a keen businesswoman and is listed among *Forbes*'s most influential women.

Jean's (and DiDi's) success has not been achieved without setbacks. The company had to strengthen its internal controls to ensure rider safety, including adding a feature to alert law enforcement in case of an emergency. Jean also deals with complaints about the enormous amounts of cash DiDi uses. Jean insists cash is necessary to expand operations and says, "we wouldn't be where we are today without burning cash."

DiDi already facilitates over 20 million rides per day, yet Jean is thinking of the future. That future includes using accounting data for use in predictive analytics: "If 100 people go downstairs and try to get a car, that wouldn't work," explains Jean. "But what if the network knows [using accounting data] that at this moment, there will always be 100 people coming out of this building? . . . Then we can match perfectly."

"The key to a successful business is understanding the customers' expectations," insists Jean, "and half the customers are women!"

Sources: *DiDi Chuxing website*, January 2021; *FT.com*, December 2016

FRAUD AND INTERNAL CONTROL

Purpose of Internal Control

C1 Define internal control and identify its purpose and principles.

Managers or owners of small businesses often control the entire operation. They know if the business is actually receiving the assets and services it paid for. Most companies, however, cannot maintain personal supervision and must rely on internal controls.

Internal Control System Managers use an internal control system to monitor and control business activities. An **internal control system** is policies and procedures used to

- Protect assets.
- Ensure reliable accounting.
- Promote efficient operations.
- Uphold company policies.

Deepadesigns/Shutterstock

Managers use internal control systems to prevent avoidable losses, plan operations, and monitor company and employee performance. For example, internal controls for **UnitedHealth Group** protect patient records and privacy.

Sarbanes-Oxley Act (SOX) **Sarbanes-Oxley Act (SOX)** requires managers and auditors of companies whose stock is traded on an exchange (called *public companies*) to document and verify internal controls. Following are some of the requirements.

- The company must have effective internal controls.
- Auditors must evaluate internal controls.
- Violators receive harsh penalties—up to 25 years in prison with fines.
- Auditors' work is overseen by the *Public Company Accounting Oversight Board* (PCAOB).

Committee of Sponsoring Organizations (COSO) **Committee of Sponsoring Organizations (COSO)** lists five ingredients of internal control that add to the quality of accounting information.

- **Control environment**—company structure, ethics, and integrity for internal control.
- **Risk assessment**—identify, analyze, and manage risk factors.
- **Control activities**—policies and procedures to reduce risk of loss.
- **Information & communication**—reports to internal and external parties.
- **Monitoring**—regular review of internal control effectiveness.

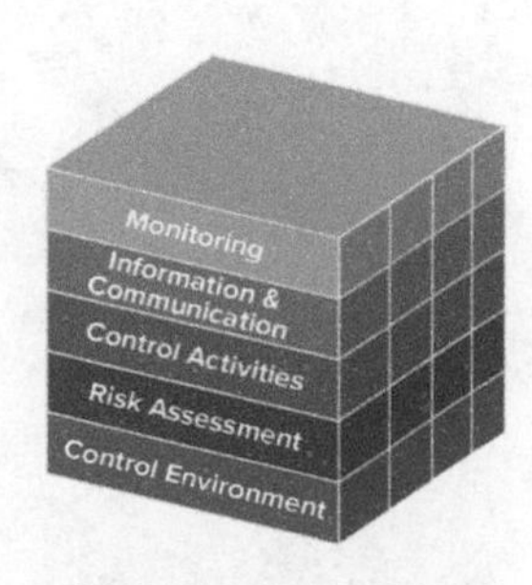

Principles of Internal Control

Internal control varies from company to company, but internal control principles apply to all companies. The **principles of internal control** are to

A control system is only as strong as its weakest link

1. Establish responsibilities.
2. Maintain adequate records.
3. Insure assets and bond key employees.
4. Separate recordkeeping from custody of assets.
5. Divide responsibility for related transactions.
6. Apply technological controls.
7. Perform regular and independent reviews.

Establish Responsibilities Responsibility for a task should be clearly established and assigned to one person. When a problem occurs in a company where responsibility is not established, determining who is at fault is difficult. For example, if two salesclerks share the same cash register and cash is missing, neither clerk can be held accountable. To prevent this problem, a company can use separate cash drawers for each clerk.

Point: Many companies have a mandatory vacation policy for employees who handle cash. When another employee must cover for the one on vacation, it is more difficult to hide cash frauds.

Maintain Adequate Records Good recordkeeping helps protect assets and helps managers monitor company activities. When there are detailed records of equipment, for example, items are unlikely to be lost or stolen without detection. Similarly, transactions are less likely to be entered in wrong accounts if a chart of accounts is used. Preprinted forms are also part of good internal control. When sales slips are properly designed, employees can record information efficiently with fewer errors. When sales slips are prenumbered, each slip is the responsibility of one salesperson, preventing the salesperson from stealing cash by making a sale and destroying the sales slip. Computerized point-of-sale systems achieve the same control results.

Insure Assets and Bond Key Employees Assets should be insured against losses, and employees handling lots of cash and easily transferable assets should be bonded. An employee is *bonded* when a company purchases an insurance policy, or a bond, against theft by that employee. Bonding discourages theft because bonded employees know the bonding company will pursue reported theft.

Separate Recordkeeping from Custody of Assets A person who controls or has access to an asset must not have access to that asset's accounting records. This principle reduces the risk of theft or waste of an asset because the person with control over it knows that another person keeps its records. Also, a recordkeeper who does not have access to the asset has no reason to falsify records. This means that to steal an asset and hide the theft from the records, two or more people must *collude*—or agree in secret to commit the fraud.

Point: ACFE estimates that employee fraud costs more than $150,000 per incident.

Divide Responsibility for Related Transactions Responsibility for a transaction should be divided between two or more individuals or departments. This ensures the work of one person acts as a check on the other to prevent fraud and errors. This principle, called *separation of duties,* does not mean duplication of work. For example, when a company orders inventory, the task should be split among several employees. One employee submits a request to purchase inventory, a second employee approves the request, a third employee makes the payment, and a fourth employee records the transaction.

Apply Technological Controls Cash registers, time clocks, and ID scanners are examples of devices that can improve internal control. A cash register with a locked-in tape or electronic file makes a record of each cash sale. A time clock records the exact hours worked by an employee. ID scanners limit access to authorized individuals.

Perform Regular and Independent Reviews Regular reviews of internal controls help ensure that procedures are followed. These reviews are preferably done by auditors not directly involved in the activities. Auditors evaluate the efficiency and effectiveness of internal controls. Many companies pay for audits by independent auditors. These auditors test the company's financial records and evaluate the effectiveness of internal controls.

Technology, Fraud, and Internal Control

Principles of internal control are relevant no matter what the technological state of the accounting system, from manual to fully automated. Technology allows us quicker access to information and improves managers' abilities to monitor and control business activities. This section describes technological impacts we must be alert to.

Reduced Processing Errors Technology reduces, but does not eliminate, errors in processing information. Less human involvement can cause data entry errors to go undiscovered. Also, errors in software can produce consistent but inaccurate processing of transactions.

More Extensive Testing of Records When accounting records are kept manually, only small samples of data are usually checked for accuracy. When data are accessible using technology, large samples or even the entire database can be tested quickly.

New Evidence of Processing Technology makes it possible to record additional transaction details not possible with manual systems. For example, a system can record who made the entry, the date and time, the source of the entry, and so on. This means that internal control depends more on the design and operation of the information system and less on the analysis of its resulting documents.

Separation of Duties A company with few employees risks losing separation of duties. For example, the person who designs the information system should not operate it. The company also must separate control over programs and files from the activities related to cash receipts and payments. For example, a computer operator should not control check-writing activities.

Increased E-Commerce Amazon and eBay are examples of successful e-commerce companies. All e-commerce transactions involve at least three risks: (1) credit card number theft, (2) computer viruses, and (3) impersonation or identity theft. Companies use technological internal controls to combat these risks.

Blockchain as a Control

Blockchain is viewed as a new, more secure type of accounting ledger. A blockchain ledger is continuously and simultaneously updated and verified. Blockchain technology makes it difficult for the ledger to be modified without a detailed record of changes. Records cannot be destroyed or hidden as the record is shared and stored by multiple users.

Valery Bandarchyk/Valery Bondjangobeat/jangobeat/123RF

While blockchain is commonly known as the technology that verifies and facilitates **Bitcoin** transactions, accounting and consulting firms are investing heavily in this technology. **Deloitte** built a blockchain software platform to assist businesses in implementing the technology. **PWC** offers auditing services that verify the effectiveness of a company's blockchain technologies.

Blockchain technology has implications for auditors who test internal controls. Auditors focus more on testing the effectiveness of a company's blockchain processes and technology than on verifying the accuracy of its output. Advanced courses cover the details.

Limitations of Internal Control

Internal controls have limitations from (1) human error or fraud and (2) the cost-benefit constraint. *Human error* occurs from carelessness, misjudgment, or confusion. *Human fraud* is intentionally defeating internal controls, such as management override, for personal gain. The **fraud triangle** shows three factors that push a person to commit fraud.

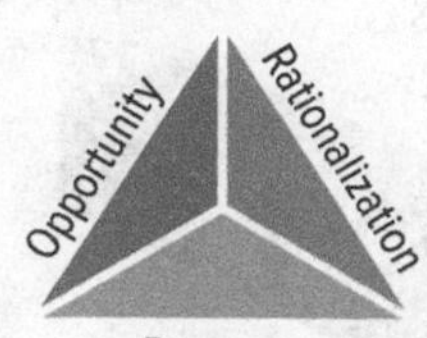

- **Opportunity.** A person must be able to commit fraud with a low risk of getting caught.
- **Pressure,** or incentive. A person must feel pressure or have incentive to commit fraud.
- **Rationalization,** or attitude. A person justifies fraud or does not see its criminal nature.

The *cost-benefit constraint* says that the costs of internal controls must not exceed their benefits. Analysis of costs and benefits considers all factors, including morale. For example, most companies have a legal right to read employees' e-mails but rarely do unless there is evidence of potential harm.

Hacker's Guide to Cyberspace

Pharming Viruses attached to e-mails and websites monitor keystrokes; when you sign on to financial websites, it steals your passwords.

Phishing Hackers send e-mails to you posing as banks; you are asked for information using fake websites where they steal your passwords and personal data.

Wi-Phishing Cybercrooks set up wireless networks hoping you will use them to connect to the web; passwords and data are stolen when you connect.

Bot-Networking Hackers send out spam and viruses from your PC.

Typo-Squatting Hackers set up websites with addresses similar to legit businesses; when you make a typo and hit their sites, they infect your PC.

nd3000/Shutterstock

Decision Insight

All Thumbs Internal control failures can cost a company and its customers millions. **Amazon** learned the hard way when its web services failed. This failure led hundreds of websites to slow down. Reports say this failure cost companies in the S&P 500 index $150 million. The culprit? A typo in Amazon's code. ■

NEED-TO-KNOW 8-1

Internal Controls

C1

Identify each procedure below as an internal control strength or weakness.

1. The cash drawer is accessible to any worker with an employee ID card.
2. The same employee requests, approves, and pays for inventory to streamline processes.
3. The recordkeeper for inventory does not have access to that inventory.
4. Employees who handle cash are bonded through an insurance policy.
5. To save on auditing costs, company employees now audit their own records.
6. Detailed records are kept of suppliers and accounts payable.

Do More: QS 8-1, QS 8-2, QS 8-3, E 8-1, E 8-2, E 8-3, P 8-1

Solution

1. Weakness **2.** Weakness **3.** Strength **4.** Strength **5.** Weakness **6.** Strength

CONTROL OF CASH

C2

Define cash and cash equivalents and explain how to report them.

Cash is easily hidden and moved. Internal controls protect cash and meet three guidelines.

1. Handling cash is separate from recordkeeping of cash.
2. Cash receipts are promptly deposited in a bank.
3. Cash payments are made by check or electronic funds transfer (EFT).

The first guideline applies separation of duties to minimize errors and fraud. When duties are separated, two or more people must collude to steal cash and hide this action. The second guideline uses immediate deposits of all cash receipts to produce an independent record of the cash received. It also reduces the chance of cash theft (or loss). The third guideline uses payments by check to develop an independent record of cash payments. It also reduces the risk of cash theft (or loss).

Cash, Cash Equivalents, and Liquidity

Liquidity refers to a company's ability to pay for its current liabilities. Cash and similar assets are called **liquid assets** because they can be readily used to pay for liabilities. The most liquid assets are usually reported first on a balance sheet; the least liquid assets are reported last.

Cash includes currency, coins, and deposits in bank accounts. Cash also includes items that can be deposited in these accounts such as customer checks, cashier's checks, certified checks, and money orders. **Cash equivalents** are short-term, highly liquid investment assets meeting two criteria: (1) readily convertible to a known cash amount and (2) close enough to their due date so that their market value will not greatly change. Only investments within three months of their due date usually meet these criteria. Cash equivalents are short-term investments such as U.S. Treasury bills. Most companies combine cash equivalents with cash on the balance sheet.

Point: Companies invest idle cash in cash equivalents to increase income.

Cash Management

A common reason companies fail is inability to manage cash. Companies must plan both cash receipts and cash payments. Goals of cash management are to

1. Plan cash receipts to meet cash payments when due.
2. Keep a minimum level of cash necessary to operate.

The *treasurer* is responsible for cash management. Effective cash management involves applying the following cash management strategies.

- **Encourage collection of receivables.** The quicker customers and others pay the company, the quicker it can use the money. Some companies offer discounts for quicker payments.
- **Delay payment of liabilities.** The more delayed a company is in paying others, the more time it has to use the money. Companies regularly wait to pay bills until the last day allowed.
- **Keep only necessary assets.** Acquiring expensive and rarely used assets can cause cash shortages. Some companies lease warehouses or rent equipment to avoid large up-front payments.
- **Plan expenditures.** Companies must look at seasonal and business cycles to plan expenditures when money is available.
- **Invest excess cash.** Excess cash earns no return and should be invested in productive assets like factories. Excess cash from seasonal cycles can be placed in a short-term investment for interest.

Control of Cash Receipts

Internal control of cash receipts ensures that cash received is properly recorded and deposited. Cash receipts commonly arise from transactions such as cash sales and collections of customer accounts. This section explains internal control over two types of cash receipts: over-the-counter and by mail.

P1 Apply internal control to cash receipts and payments.

Over-the-Counter Cash Receipts

Over-the-counter cash sales should be recorded on a cash register after each sale, and customers should get a receipt. Cash registers should hold a permanent, locked-in record of each transaction. The register is often linked with the accounting system. Less advanced registers record each transaction on a paper tape or electronic file locked inside the register.

Point: Many businesses have signs that read: If you receive no receipt, your purchase is free! This helps ensure that clerks ring up all transactions on registers.

Custody over cash should be separate from recordkeeping. The clerk who has access to cash in the register should not have access to its record. At the end of the clerk's work period, the clerk should count the cash in the register, record the amount, and turn over the cash and record to the company cashier. The cashier, like the clerk, has access to the cash but should not have access to accounting records (or the register tape or file). A third employee, often a supervisor, compares the record of total register transactions with the cash receipts reported by the cashier. This record is used for a journal entry recording over-the-counter cash receipts. The third employee has access to the records for cash but not to the actual cash. The clerk and the cashier have access to cash but not to the accounting records.

None of them can make a mistake or steal cash without the difference being noticed (see the following diagram).

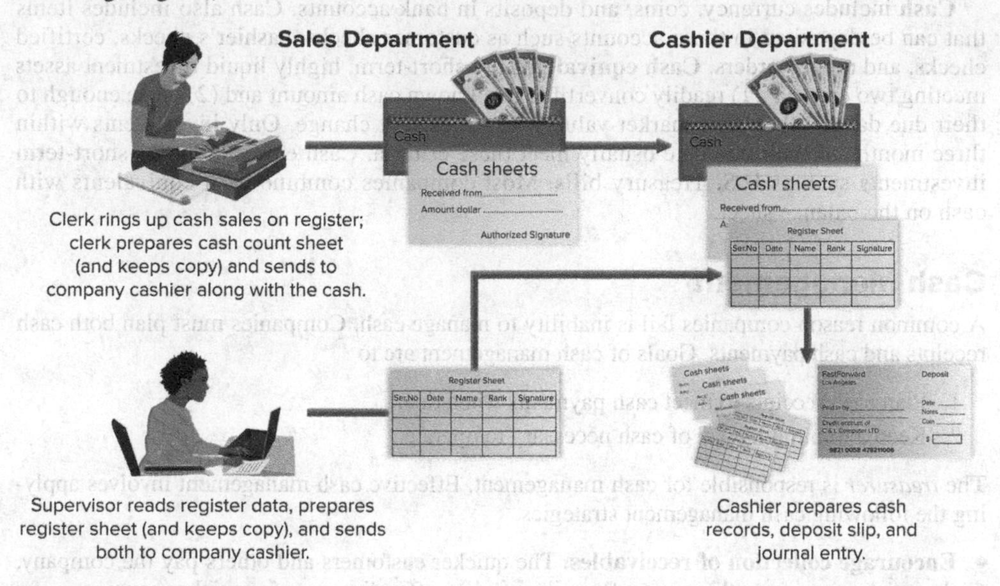
Sales Department
Cashier Department
Cash
Cash sheets
Received from
Amount dollar
Authorized Signature
Clerk rings up cash sales on register; clerk prepares cash count sheet (and keeps copy) and sends to company cashier along with the cash.
Register Sheet
Supervisor reads register data, prepares register sheet (and keeps copy), and sends both to company cashier.
Cashier prepares cash records, deposit slip, and journal entry.

Cash Over and Short One or more customers can be given too much or too little change. This means that at the end of a work period, the cash in a cash register might not equal the record of cash receipts. This difference is reported in the **Cash Over and Short** account, also called *Cash Short and Over,* which is an income statement account recording the income effects of cash overages and cash shortages. If a cash register's record shows $550 but the count of cash in the register is $555, the entry to record cash sales and its overage is

Assets = Liabilities + Equity
+555 + 5
+550

Cash	555	
Cash Over and Short		5
Sales		550
Record cash sales and a cash overage.		

Alternatively, if a cash register's record shows $625 but the count of cash in the register is $621, the entry to record cash sales and its shortage is

Assets = Liabilities + Equity
+621 − 4
+625

Cash	621	
Cash Over and Short	4	
Sales		625
Record cash sales and a cash shortage.		

Because customers are more likely to dispute being shortchanged than being given too much change, the Cash Over and Short account usually has a debit balance. A debit balance reflects an expense. It is reported on the income statement as part of selling, general, and administrative expenses. (Because the amount is usually small, it is often reported as part of *miscellaneous expenses*—or as part of *miscellaneous revenues* if it has a credit balance.)

Cash Receipts by Mail Two people are assigned the task of opening the mail. In this case, theft of cash receipts by mail requires collusion between these two employees. The person(s) opening the mail enters a list (in triplicate) of money received. This list has each sender's name, the amount, and an explanation of why the money was sent. The first copy is sent with the money to the cashier. A second copy is sent to the recordkeeper. A third copy is kept by the person(s) who opened the mail. The cashier deposits the money in a bank, and the recordkeeper records the amounts received.

This process is good internal control because the bank's record of cash deposited must agree with the records from each of the three. If the mail person(s) does not report all receipts correctly, customers will question their account balances. If the cashier does not deposit all the cash, the bank balance does not agree with the recordkeeper's cash balance. The recordkeeper does not have access to cash and has no opportunity to steal cash. This system makes errors and fraud highly unlikely. The exception is employee collusion.

Control of Cash Payments

Control of cash payments is important as most large thefts occur from payment of fake invoices. One key to controlling cash payments is to require all payments to be made by check. The only exception is small payments made from petty cash. Another key is to deny access to accounting records to anyone other than the owner who has the authority to sign checks. A small-business owner often signs checks and knows that the items being paid for are actually received. Large businesses cannot maintain personal supervision and must rely on internal controls described here, including the voucher system and petty cash system.

Cash Budget Projected cash receipts and cash payments are summarized in a *cash budget.* If there is enough cash for operations, companies wish to minimize the cash they hold because of its risk of theft and its low return versus other assets.

Voucher System of Control A **voucher system** is a set of procedures and approvals designed to control cash payments and the acceptance of liabilities that consist of

- Verifying, approving, and recording liabilities for cash payment.
- Issuing checks for payment of verified, approved, and recorded liabilities.

A voucher system's control over cash payments begins when a company incurs a liability that will result in cash payment. The system only allows authorized departments and individuals to incur liabilities and limits the type of liabilities. In a large retail store, for example, only a purchasing department is authorized to incur liabilities for inventory. Purchasing, receiving, and paying for merchandise are divided among several departments (or individuals). These departments include the one requesting the purchase, the purchasing department, the receiving department, and the accounting department.

To coordinate and control responsibilities of these departments, a company uses several different business documents. Exhibit 8.1 shows how documents are accumulated in a **voucher,** which is an internal document (or file) used to collect information to control cash payments and to ensure that a transaction is properly recorded. This specific example begins with a *purchase requisition* (a request to purchase merchandise) and ends with issuing a *check.*

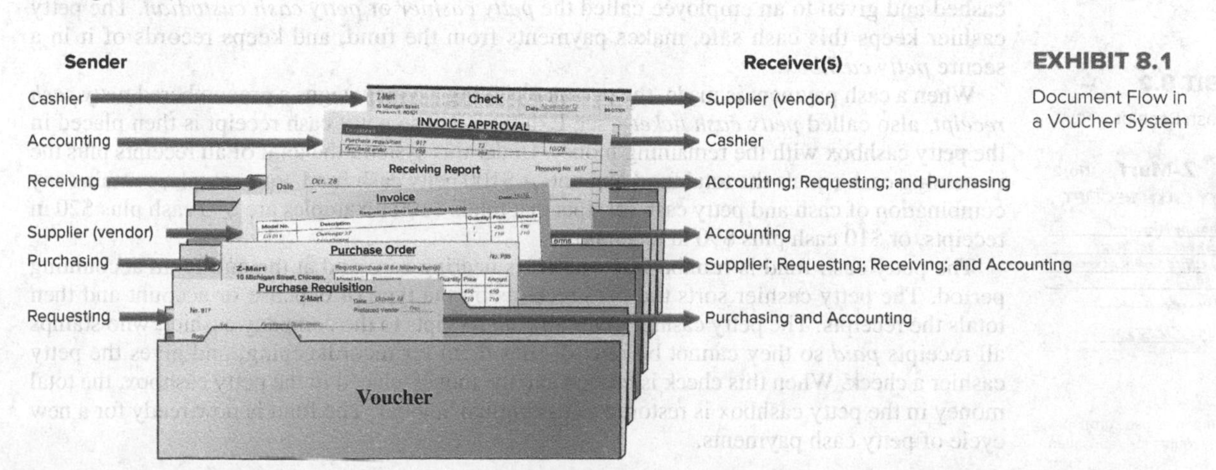

EXHIBIT 8.1
Document Flow in a Voucher System

A voucher system should be applied to all payments (except those using petty cash). When a company receives a monthly telephone bill, it should review the charges, prepare a voucher (file), and insert the bill. This transaction is then recorded. If the amount is due, a check is issued. If not, the voucher is filed for payment on its due date. Without records, an employee could collude with a supplier to get more than one payment, payment for excessive amounts, or payment for goods and services not received. A voucher system helps prevent such frauds.

J.R. Bale/Alamy Stock Photo

Ethical Risk

Steal Away The Association of Certified Fraud Examiners (ACFE) reports that 87% of fraud is from asset theft. Of those asset thefts, a few stand out—in both frequency and median loss. Namely, cash is most frequently stolen through billing (22%) and theft (20%), followed by expense reimbursements (14%), skimming (12%), check tampering (11%), and payroll (9%). Interestingly, the average loss per incident is greatest for check tampering ($158,000) and billing ($100,000). *Source:* "Report to the Nations," ACFE. ■

NEED-TO-KNOW 8-2

Control of Cash Receipts and Payments

P1 C2

Which of the following statements are true regarding the control of cash receipts and cash payments?

1. Over-the-counter cash sales should be recorded on a cash register after each sale.
2. Custody over cash should be separate from the recordkeeping of cash.
3. For control of cash receipts that arrive through the mail, two people should be present for opening that mail.
4. One key to controlling cash payments is to require that no expenditures be made by check; instead, all expenditures should be made from petty cash.
5. A voucher system of control should be applied only to purchases of inventory and never to other expenditures.

Solution

1. True 2. True 3. True 4. False 5. False

Do More: QS 8-4, QS 8-7, QS 8-8, E 8-4, E 8-5, E 8-6, E 8-7

P2

Explain and record petty cash fund transactions.

Petty Cash System of Control

To avoid writing checks for small amounts, a company sets up a **petty cash** system. *Petty cash payments* are small payments for items such as shipping fees, minor repairs, and low-cost supplies.

Operating a Petty Cash Fund

A petty cash fund requires estimating the amount of small payments to be made during a short period such as a week or month. A check is then drawn by the company cashier for an amount slightly in excess of this estimate. The check is cashed and given to an employee called the *petty cashier* or *petty cash custodian*. The petty cashier keeps this cash safe, makes payments from the fund, and keeps records of it in a secure *petty cashbox*.

When a cash payment is made, the person receiving payment signs a prenumbered *petty cash receipt,* also called *petty cash ticket*—see Exhibit 8.2. The petty cash receipt is then placed in the petty cashbox with the remaining money. Under this system, the total of all receipts plus the remaining cash equals the total fund amount. A $100 petty cash fund, for example, contains any combination of cash and petty cash receipts that totals $100 (examples are $80 cash plus $20 in receipts, or $10 cash plus $90 in receipts).

EXHIBIT 8.2

Petty Cash Receipt

Z-Mart No. 2
PETTY CASH RECEIPT
For Office supplies used
Date November 15, 2021
Charge to Office Supplies Expense
Amount $4.75
Approved by [signature]
Received by [signature]

The petty cash fund is reimbursed when it is nearing zero and at the end of an accounting period. The petty cashier sorts the paid receipts by the type of expense or account and then totals the receipts. The petty cashier gives all paid receipts to the company cashier, who stamps all receipts *paid* so they cannot be reused, files them for recordkeeping, and gives the petty cashier a check. When this check is cashed and the money placed in the petty cashbox, the total money in the petty cashbox is restored to its original amount. The fund is now ready for a new cycle of petty cash payments.

Point: Companies use surprise petty cash counts for verification.

Illustrating a Petty Cash Fund Assume Z-Mart sets up a petty cash fund on November 1. A $75 check is drawn and cashed, and the proceeds given to the petty cashier. The entry to record the setup of this petty cash fund is

Nov. 1	Petty Cash	75	
	Cash		75
	Establish a petty cash fund.		

Assets = Liabilities + Equity
+75
−75

After the petty cash fund is established, the Petty Cash account is not debited or credited again unless the amount of the fund is changed.

Next, assume that Z-Mart's petty cashier makes several November payments from petty cash. On November 27, after making a $46.50 cash payment for tile cleaning, only $3.70 cash remains in the fund. The petty cashier then summarizes and totals the petty cash receipts as shown in Exhibit 8.3.

EXHIBIT 8.3

Petty Cash Payments Report

Petty Cash Payments Report		
Merchandise Inventory (transportation-in)		
Nov. 5	Transport of merchandise purchased	$ 15.05
Office Supplies Expense		
Nov. 15	Purchase of office supplies immediately used	4.75
Delivery Expense		
Nov. 18	Customer's package delivered	5.00
Miscellaneous Expense		
Nov. 27	Tile cleaning	46.50
Total		$71.30

Point: This report also can include receipt number and names of those who approved and received cash payment (see Need-to-Know 8-3).

The petty cash payments report and all receipts are given to the company cashier in exchange for a $71.30 check to reimburse the fund. The petty cashier cashes the check and puts the $71.30 cash in the petty cashbox. The company records this reimbursement as follows. A petty cash fund is usually reimbursed at the end of an accounting period so that expenses are recorded in the proper period, even if the fund is not low on money.

Nov. 27	Merchandise Inventory	15.05	
	Office Supplies Expense	4.75	
	Delivery Expense	5.00	
	Miscellaneous Expenses	46.50	
	Cash*		71.30
	Reimburse petty cash.		
	**$75 fund bal. − $3.70 cash remaining.*		

Assets = Liabilities + Equity
−71.30 −46.50
+15.05 − 5.00
− 4.75

Increasing or Decreasing a Petty Cash Fund A decision to increase or decrease a petty cash fund is often made when reimbursing it. Assume Z-Mart decides to *increase* its petty cash fund from $75 to $100 on November 27 when it reimburses the fund. The entries required are to (1) reimburse the fund as usual (see the preceding November 27 entry) and (2) increase the fund amount as follows.

Nov. 27	Petty Cash	25	
	Cash		25
	Increase petty cash fund from $75 to $100.		

Instead, if it *decreases* the petty cash fund from $75 to $55 on November 27, the entry is

Nov. 27	Cash	20	
	Petty Cash		20
	Decrease petty cash fund from $75 to $55.		

Summary of Petty Cash Accounting

Event	Petty Cash	Cash	Expenses
Set up fund	Debit	Credit	—
Reimburse fund.....	—	Credit	Debit
Increase fund	Debit	Credit	—
Decrease fund......	Credit	Debit	—

Cash Over and Short Sometimes a petty cashier fails to get a receipt for payment or overpays for the amount due. When this occurs and the fund is later reimbursed, the petty cash payments report plus the cash remaining will not equal the fund balance. This mistake causes the fund to be *short*. This shortage is recorded as an expense in the reimbursing entry with a debit to the Cash Over and Short account. (An *overage* in the petty cash fund is recorded with a credit to Cash Over and Short in the reimbursing entry.)

Following is the June 1 entry to reimburse a $200 petty cash fund when its payments report shows $178 in miscellaneous expenses and only $15 cash remains.

$200 Petty Cash Fund

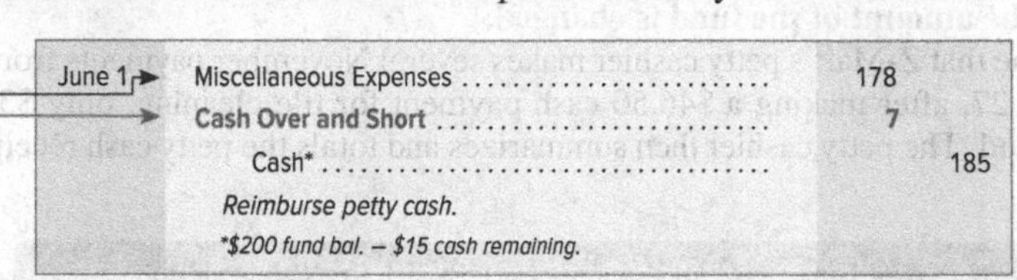

June 1	Miscellaneous Expenses	178	
	Cash Over and Short	7	
	Cash*		185
	Reimburse petty cash.		

**$200 fund bal. − $15 cash remaining.*

Ethical Risk

Take a Hint There are clues to fraudulent activities. Clues from accounting include (1) an increase in customer refunds—could be fake, (2) missing documents—could be used for fraud, (3) differences between bank deposits and cash receipts—could be cash embezzled, and (4) delayed recording—could reflect fraudulent records. Clues from employees include (1) lifestyle change—could be embezzlement, (2) too close with suppliers—could signal fraudulent transactions, and (3) refusal to leave job, even for vacations—could conceal fraudulent activities. ■

NEED-TO-KNOW 8-3

Petty Cash System

P2

Bacardi Company established a $150 petty cash fund with Eminem as the petty cashier. When the fund balance reached $19 cash, Eminem prepared a petty cash payments report, which follows.

Petty Cash Payments Report

Receipt No.	Account Charged		Approved by	Received by
12	Delivery Expense................	$ 29	Eminem	A. Smirnoff
13	Merchandise Inventory..........	18	Eminem	J. Daniels
15	(Omitted)......................	32	Eminem	C. Carlsberg
16	Miscellaneous Expense..........	41	(Omitted)	J. Walker
	Total	$120		

Required

1. Identify four internal control weaknesses from the petty cash payments report.
2. Prepare general journal entries to record
   a. Establishment of the petty cash fund.
   b. Reimbursement of the fund. (Assume for this part only that petty cash Receipt No. 15 was issued for miscellaneous expenses.)
3. What is the Petty Cash account balance immediately before reimbursement? After reimbursement?

Solution

1. Four internal control weaknesses that are apparent from the payments report include
   a. Petty cash Receipt No. 14 is missing. This raises questions about the petty cashier's management of the fund.
   b. The $19 cash balance means that $131 has been withdrawn ($150 − $19 = $131). However, the total amount of the petty cash receipts is only $120 ($29 + $18 + $32 + $41). The fund is $11 short of cash ($131 − $120 = $11). Management should investigate.
   c. The petty cashier (Eminem) did not sign petty cash Receipt No. 16. This could have been a mistake on his part or he might not have authorized the payment.
   d. Petty cash Receipt No. 15 does not say which account to charge. Management should check with C. Carlsberg and the petty cashier (Eminem) about the transaction. Without further information, debit Miscellaneous Expense.

2. Petty cash general journal entries.

a. Entry to establish the petty cash fund.

Petty Cash	150	
Cash		150

b. Entry to reimburse the fund.

Delivery Expense	29	
Merchandise Inventory	18	
Miscellaneous Expense ($41 + $32)	73	
Cash Over and Short	11	
Cash ($150 fund bal. − $19 cash rem.)		131

3. The Petty Cash account balance *always* equals its fund balance, in this case $150. This account balance does not change unless the fund is increased or decreased.

Do More: QS 8-9, E 8-8, E 8-9, E 8-10, P 8-2, P 8-3

BANKING ACTIVITIES AS CONTROLS

Basic Bank Services

Banks safeguard cash and provide detailed records of cash transactions. They provide services and documents that help control cash, which is the focus of this section.

Bank Account, Deposit, and Check A *bank account* is used to deposit money for safekeeping and helps control withdrawals. Persons authorized to write checks on the account must sign a **signature card,** which the bank uses to verify signatures.

Each bank deposit has a **deposit ticket,** which lists items such as currency, coins, and checks deposited along with amounts. The bank gives the customer a receipt as proof of the deposit. Exhibit 8.4 shows a deposit ticket.

Point: Firms often have multiple bank accounts for different needs and for specific transactions such as payroll.

EXHIBIT 8.4

Deposit Ticket

Front

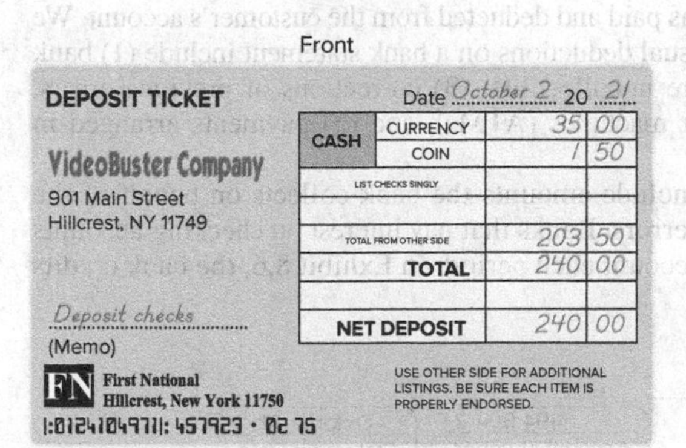
DEPOSIT TICKET

Date October 2, 20 21

VideoBuster Company
901 Main Street
Hillcrest, NY 11749

CASH	CURRENCY	35 00
	COIN	1 50
LIST CHECKS SINGLY		
TOTAL FROM OTHER SIDE		203 50
TOTAL		240 00
NET DEPOSIT		240 00

Deposit checks
(Memo)

USE OTHER SIDE FOR ADDITIONAL LISTINGS. BE SURE EACH ITEM IS PROPERLY ENDORSED.

FN First National
Hillcrest, New York 11750

I:012410497II: 457923 • 02 75

Back

	CHECKS LIST SINGLY	DOLLARS	CENTS
1	14-287/939	90	50
2	82-759/339	82	80
3	76-907/919	30	20
4			
5			
6			
7			
8			
9			
10			
11			
TOTAL		203	50

ENTER TOTAL ON THE FRONT OF THIS TICKET

To withdraw money, the depositor can use a **check,** which is a document telling the bank to pay a specified amount to a designated recipient. A check involves three parties: a *maker* who signs the check, a *payee* who is the recipient, and a *bank* (or *payer*) on which the check is drawn. The bank provides the depositor the checks. Exhibit 8.5 shows one type of check. It has an optional *remittance advice* explaining the payment. The *memo* line is used for an explanation.

Electronic Funds Transfer **Electronic funds transfer (EFT)** is the electronic transfer of cash from one party to another. Companies are increasingly using EFT because of its convenience and low cost. Payroll, rent, utilities, insurance, and interest payments are usually done by EFT. The bank statement lists cash withdrawals by EFT with the checks and other deductions. Cash receipts by EFT are listed with deposits and other additions.

EXHIBIT 8.5

Check with Remittance Advice

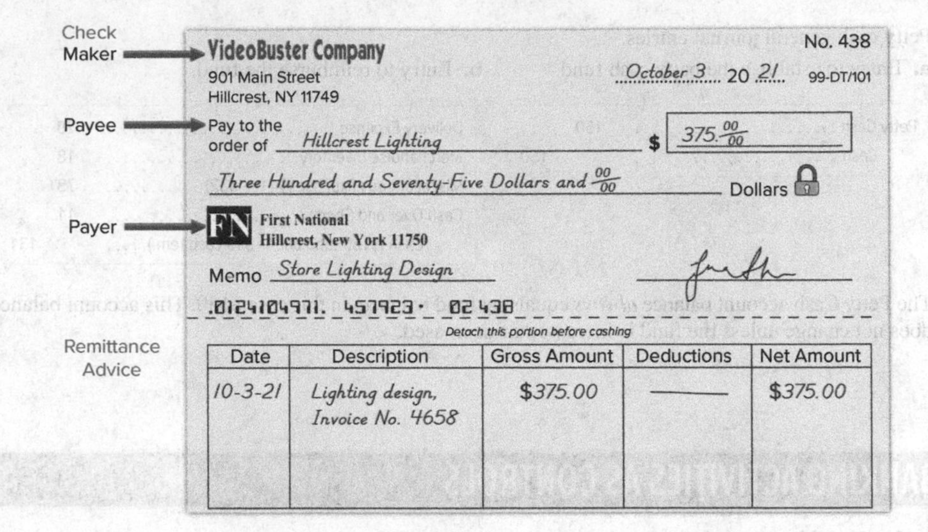

Date	Description	Gross Amount	Deductions	Net Amount
10-3-21	Lighting design, Invoice No. 4658	$375.00	——	$375.00

Types of Check Fraud (CkFraud.org)

- Forged signatures—legitimate checks with fake payer signature
- Forged endorsements—stolen check that is endorsed and cashed by someone other than the payee
- Counterfeit checks—fraudulent checks with fake payer signature
- Altered checks—legitimate check altered (such as changed payee or amount) to benefit perpetrator
- Check kiting—deposit check from one bank account (without sufficient funds) into a second bank account

Bank Statement

Point: Good control is to send a copy of the bank statement directly to a party without access to cash or recordkeeping.

Usually once a month, the bank sends a **bank statement** showing the account activity. Different banks use different formats for their bank statements, but all of them include the following.

1. Beginning-of-period account balance.
2. Withdrawals and other decreases to the account during the period.
3. Deposits and other increases to the account during the period.
4. End-of-period account balance.

Exhibit 8.6 shows one type of bank statement.

Canceled checks are checks the bank has paid and deducted from the customer's account. We say such checks *cleared the bank.* Other usual deductions on a bank statement include (1) bank service fees, (2) checks deposited that are uncollectible, (3) corrections of previous errors, (4) withdrawals through automated teller machines (ATMs), and (5) payments arranged in advance by a depositor.

Increases to the depositor's account include amounts the bank collects on behalf of the depositor and the corrections of previous errors. Banks that pay interest on checking accounts credit interest earned to the depositor's account each period. In Exhibit 8.6, the bank credits $8 of interest to the account.

EXHIBIT 8.6

Bank Statement

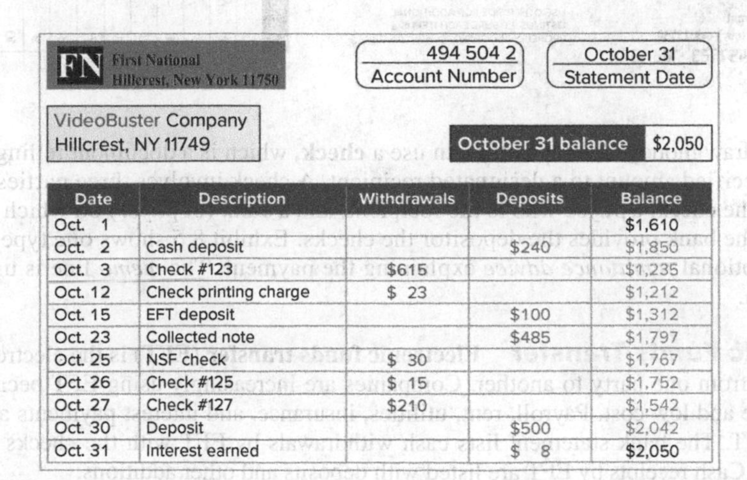
FN First National
Hillcrest, New York 11750

494 504 2 — Account Number

October 31 — Statement Date

VideoBuster Company
Hillcrest, NY 11749

October 31 balance $2,050

Date	Description	Withdrawals	Deposits	Balance
Oct. 1				$1,610
Oct. 2	Cash deposit		$240	$1,850
Oct. 3	Check #123	$615		$1,235
Oct. 12	Check printing charge	$ 23		$1,212
Oct. 15	EFT deposit		$100	$1,312
Oct. 23	Collected note		$485	$1,797
Oct. 25	NSF check	$ 30		$1,767
Oct. 26	Check #125	$ 15		$1,752
Oct. 27	Check #127	$210		$1,542
Oct. 30	Deposit		$500	$2,042
Oct. 31	Interest earned		$ 8	$2,050

Bank Reconciliation

P3 Prepare a bank reconciliation.

The balance of a checking account on the bank statement rarely equals the depositor's book balance (from its records). This is due to information that one party has that the other does not. We must therefore verify the accuracy of both the depositor's records and the bank's records. To do this, we prepare a **bank reconciliation** to explain differences between the checking account balance in the depositor's records and the balance on the bank statement. The person preparing the bank reconciliation should not be responsible for processing cash receipts, managing checks, or maintaining cash records. The following explains bank and book adjustments.

Point: *Books* refer to accounting records.

Bank Balance Adjustments

\+ **Deposits in transit. Deposits in transit** are deposits made and recorded in the depositor's books but not yet listed on the bank statement. For example, companies can make deposits (in the night depository) after the bank is closed. If such a deposit occurred on a bank statement date, it would not appear on this period's statement. The bank would record such a deposit on the next business day, and it would appear on the next period's bank statement. Deposits mailed to the bank near the end of a period also can be in transit and not listed on the bank statement.

− **Outstanding checks. Outstanding checks** are checks written by the depositor, subtracted on the depositor's books, and sent to the payees but not yet turned in for payment at the bank statement date.

± **Bank errors.** Any errors made by the bank are accounted for in the reconciliation. To find errors, we (a) compare deposits on the bank statement with deposits in the accounting records and (b) compare canceled checks on the bank statement with checks recorded in the accounting records.

Book Balance Adjustments

\+ **Interest earned and unrecorded cash receipts.** Banks sometimes collect notes for depositors. Banks also receive electronic funds transfers to the depositor's account. When a bank collects an item, it is added to the depositor's account, less any service fee. The bank statement also includes any interest earned.

− **Bank fees and NSF checks.** A company sometimes deposits another party's check that is uncollectible. This check is called a *nonsufficient funds (NSF)* check. The bank initially increases the depositor's account for the check. When the check is uncollectible, the bank reduces the depositor's account for that check. The bank may charge the depositor a fee for processing an uncollectible check. Other bank charges include printing new checks and service fees.

± **Book errors.** Any errors made by the depositor in the company books are accounted for in the reconciliation. To find errors, we use the same procedures described in the "Bank errors" section above.

Adjustments Summary Following is a summary of bank and book adjustments. Each of these items has already been recorded by either the bank or the company, but not both.

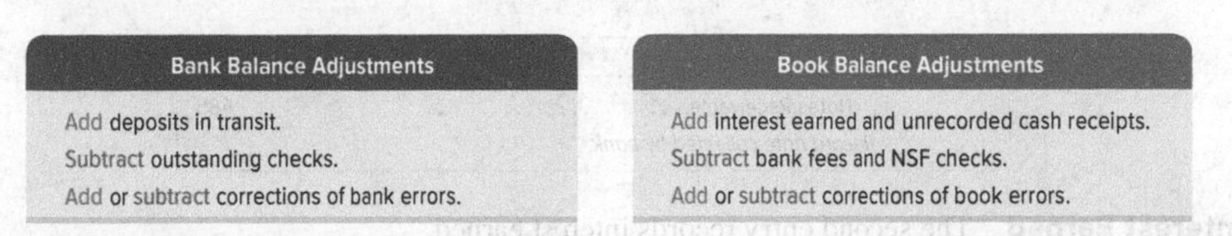

Bank Balance Adjustments	Book Balance Adjustments
Add deposits in transit.	Add interest earned and unrecorded cash receipts.
Subtract outstanding checks.	Subtract bank fees and NSF checks.
Add or subtract corrections of bank errors.	Add or subtract corrections of book errors.

Bank Reconciliation Demonstration In preparing the bank reconciliation, refer to Exhibit 8.7 and steps ❶ through ❽.

❶ Enter VideoBuster's bank balance of $2,050 taken from the October 31 bank statement.

Point: Outstanding checks are identified by comparing canceled checks on the bank statement with checks recorded. This includes identifying any outstanding checks listed on the *previous* period's bank reconciliation.

❷ Add any unrecorded deposits and bank errors that understate the bank balance to the bank balance. VideoBuster's $145 deposit in the bank's night depository on October 31 is not listed on its bank statement.

❸ Subtract any outstanding checks and bank errors that overstate the bank balance from the bank balance. VideoBuster's comparison of canceled checks with its books shows two checks outstanding: No. 124 for $150 and No. 126 for $200.

❹ Compute the *adjusted bank balance*.

❺ Enter VideoBuster's cash account book balance of $1,405 from its Oct. 31 accounting records.

❻ Add any unrecorded cash receipts, interest earned, and errors understating the book balance to the book balance. VideoBuster's bank statement shows the bank collected a note receivable and increased VideoBuster's account for $485. The bank statement also shows $8 for interest earned that was not yet recorded on the books.

❼ Subtract any unrecorded bank fees, NSF checks, and errors overstating the book balance from the book balance. Deductions on VideoBuster's bank statement that are not yet recorded include (a) a $23 charge for check printing and (b) an NSF check for $30. (The NSF check is dated October 16 and was in the book balance.)

❽ Compute the *adjusted book balance*.

Verify that the two adjusted balances from steps 4 and 8 are equal (reconciled).

EXHIBIT 8.7

Bank Reconciliation

VIDEOBUSTER
Bank Reconciliation
October 31

①	Bank statement balance		$ 2,050	⑤	Book balance		$ 1,405
②	Add			⑥	Add		
	Deposit of Oct. 31 in transit		145		Collected note	$485	
			2,195		Interest earned	8	493
③	Deduct						1,898
	Outstanding checks			⑦	Deduct		
	No. 124	$150			Check printing charge	23	
	No. 126	200	350		NSF check	30	53
④	**Adjusted bank balance**		**$1,845**	⑧	**Adjusted book balance**		**$1,845**

Balances are equal (reconciled)

Entries from a Bank Reconciliation

A bank reconciliation often finds unrecorded items that need recording by the company. In VideoBuster's reconciliation, the adjusted balance of $1,845 is the correct balance as of October 31. But the company's accounting records show a $1,405 balance. We make journal entries so that the book balance equals the adjusted balance. **Only items impacting the *book balance* need entries.** Exhibit 8.7 shows that four entries are required.

Collection of Note The first entry is to record collection of a note receivable by the bank.

Assets = Liabilities + Equity
+485
−485

Oct. 31	Cash	485	
	Notes Receivable		485
	Record note collected by bank.		

Interest Earned The second entry records interest earned.

Assets = Liabilities + Equity
+8 +8

Oct. 31	Cash	8	
	Interest Revenue		8
	Record interest earned in checking account.		

Check Printing The third entry records expenses for the check printing charge.

Oct. 31	Miscellaneous Expenses	23	
	Cash		23
	Check printing charge.		

Assets = Liabilities + Equity
−23 −23

NSF Check The fourth entry records the NSF check that is returned as uncollectible. The check was from T. Woods in payment of his account. The bank deducted $30 total from Video-Buster's account. This means the entry must reverse the effects of the original entry when the check was received.

Oct. 31	Accounts Receivable—T. Woods	30	
	Cash		30
	Charge Woods's account for $30 NSF check.		

Assets = Liabilities + Equity
+30
−30

After these four entries are recorded, the book balance of cash is adjusted to the correct amount of $1,845 (the adjusted book balance). The Cash T-account to the side shows the computation, where entries match the steps in Exhibit 8.7.

Cash			
Unadj. bal.	1,405		
⑥	485	⑦	23
⑥	8	⑦	30
Adj. bal.	1,845		

Point: Need-to-Know 8-4 shows an entry for an error correction.

Ethical Risk

Root Cause The Association of Certified Fraud Examiners (ACFE) reports that the primary factor contributing to fraud is the lack of internal controls (30%), followed by the override of existing controls (19%), lack of management review (18%), poor tone at the top (10%), and lack of competent oversight (8%). These findings highlight the importance of internal controls over cash. *Source:* "Report to the Nations," ACFE. ■

3D_creation/Shutterstock

NEED-TO-KNOW 8-4

Bank Reconciliation

P3

The following information is available to reconcile Gucci's book balance of cash with its bank statement cash balance as of December 31.

a. The December 31 cash balance according to the accounting records is $1,610, and the bank statement cash balance for that date is $1,900.

b. Gucci's December 31 daily cash receipts of $800 were placed in the bank's night depository on December 31 but do not appear on the December 31 bank statement.

c. Gucci's comparison of canceled checks with its books shows three checks outstanding: No. 6242 for $200, No. 6273 for $400, and No. 6282 for $100.

d. When the December checks are compared with entries in the accounting records, it is found that Check No. 6267 had been correctly drawn (subtracted from the bank balance) for $340 to pay for office supplies but was erroneously entered in the accounting records as $430.

e. The bank statement shows the bank collected a note receivable and increased Gucci's account for $470. Gucci had not recorded this transaction before receiving the statement.

f. The bank statement included an NSF check for $150 received from Prada Inc. in payment of its account. It also included a $20 charge for check printing. Gucci had not recorded these transactions before receiving the statement.

Required

1. Prepare the bank reconciliation for this company as of December 31.
2. Prepare the journal entries to make Gucci's book balance of cash equal to the reconciled cash balance as of December 31.

[continued on next page]

[continued from previous page]

Solutions

Part 1

GUCCI Bank Reconciliation December 31					
Bank statement balance		$1,900	Book balance		$1,610
Add			Add		
Deposit of Dec. 31		800	Error (Ck. 6267)	$ 90	
		2,700	Collected note	470	560
					2,170
Deduct			Deduct		
Outstanding Checks No. 6242	$200		NSF check	150	
6273	400		Printing fee	20	
6282	100	700			170
Adjusted bank balance		$2,000	Adjusted book balance		$2,000

Do More: QS 8-10, QS 8-11, QS 8-12, E 8-11, E 8-12, E 8-13, E 8-14

Part 2

Dec. 31	Cash	90	
	Office Supplies		90
	Correct an entry error.		
Dec. 31	Cash	470	
	Notes Receivable		470
	Record note collection.		

Dec. 31	Accounts Receivable—Prada Inc.	150	
	Cash		150
	Charge account for NSF check.		
Dec. 31	Miscellaneous Expenses	20	
	Cash		20
	Record check printing charge.		

Decision Analysis  Days' Sales Uncollected

A1 Compute the days' sales uncollected ratio and use it to assess liquidity.

One measure of how quickly a company can convert its accounts receivable into cash is the **days' sales uncollected,** also called *days' sales in receivables,* which is defined in Exhibit 8.8. We use days' sales uncollected to estimate how much time is likely to pass before the current amount of accounts receivable is received in cash. It is used to determine if cash is being collected quickly enough to pay upcoming obligations.

EXHIBIT 8.8

Days' Sales Uncollected

$$\textbf{Days' sales uncollected} = \frac{\textbf{Accounts receivable}}{\textbf{Net sales}} \times 365$$

Days' sales uncollected are shown for **Starbucks** and **Jack in the Box** in Exhibit 8.9. Days' sales uncollected for Starbucks is 12.1 days for the current year, computed as ($879/$26,509) × 365 days. This means it takes 12.1 days to collect cash from ending accounts receivable. This number reflects one or more of the following factors: a company's ability to collect receivables, customer financial health, customer payment strategies, and discount terms. To further assess Starbucks, we compare it to Jack in the Box. We see that Starbucks's 12.1 days' sales uncollected is better than Jack in the Box's 17.3 days' sales uncollected for the current year. Starbucks took less time to collect its receivables. The less time money is tied up in receivables, the better.

EXHIBIT 8.9

Analysis Using Days' Sales Uncollected

Company	Figure ($ millions)	Current Year	1 Year Ago	2 Years Ago
Starbucks	Accounts receivable	$ 879	$ 693	$ 870
	Net sales	$26,509	$24,720	$22,387
	Days' sales uncollected	**12.1 days**	**10.2 days**	**14.2 days**
Jack in the Box	Accounts receivable	$ 45	$ 57	$ 60
	Net sales	$ 950	$ 870	$ 1,097
	Days' sales uncollected	**17.3 days**	**23.9 days**	**20.0 days**

Decision Maker

Sales Representative The sales staff are told to help reduce days' sales uncollected for cash management purposes. What can you, a salesperson, do to reduce days' sales uncollected? ■ *Answer:* A salesperson can (1) push cash sales over credit, (2) identify customers most delayed in their payments and require earlier payments or cash sales, and (3) eliminate credit sales to customers that never pay.

NEED-TO-KNOW 8-5

COMPREHENSIVE

Preparing Bank Reconciliation and Entries

Prepare a bank reconciliation for Jamboree Enterprises for the month ended November 30 and make any necessary entries to the book balance of cash. The following information is available as of November 30.

a. On November 30, the company's book balance of cash is $16,380, but its bank statement shows a $38,520 cash balance.

b. Checks No. 2024 for $4,810 and No. 2026 for $5,000 are outstanding.

c. In comparing the canceled checks on the bank statement with the entries in the accounting records, it is found that Check No. 2025 in payment of rent is correctly drawn (subtracted from the bank balance) for $1,000 but is erroneously entered in the accounting records as $880.

d. The November 30 deposit of $17,150 was placed in the night depository after banking hours on that date, and this deposit amount does not appear on the bank statement.

e. In reviewing the bank statement, a check written by Jumbo Enterprises in the amount of $160 was erroneously drawn against Jamboree's account.

f. The bank statement says that the bank collected a $30,000 note and $900 of interest was earned. These transactions were not recorded by Jamboree prior to receiving the statement.

g. The bank statement lists a $1,100 NSF check received from a customer, Marilyn Welch. Jamboree had not recorded the return of this check before receiving the statement.

h. Bank service charges for November total $40. These charges were not recorded by Jamboree before receiving the statement.

SOLUTION

JAMBOREE ENTERPRISES
Bank Reconciliation
November 30

Bank statement balance		$ 38,520	Book balance		$ 16,380
Add			Add		
Deposit of Nov. 30	$17,150		Collection of note	$30,000	
Bank error (Jumbo)	160	17,310	Interest earned	900	30,900
		55,830			47,280
Deduct			Deduct		
Outstanding checks			NSF check (M. Welch)	1,100	
No. 2024	4,810		Recording error (No. 2025)	120	
No. 2026	5,000	9,810	Service charge	40	1,260
Adjusted bank balance		**$46,020**	**Adjusted book balance**		**$46,020**

Required Entries for Jamboree

Date	Account	Debit	Credit
Nov. 30	Cash	30,000	
	Notes Receivable		30,000
	Record collection of note.		
Nov. 30	Cash	900	
	Interest Revenue		900
	Record collection of revenue.		
Nov. 30	Accounts Receivable—M. Welch	1,100	
	Cash		1,100
	Reinstate account due from an NSF check.		

Date	Account	Debit	Credit
Nov. 30	Rent Expense	120	
	Cash		120
	Correct recording error on Check No. 2025.		
Nov. 30	Miscellaneous Expenses	40	
	Cash		40
	Record bank service charges.		

APPENDIX

8A Documentation and Verification

P4

Describe use of documentation and verification to control cash payments.

This appendix covers the documents of a typical voucher system of control.

Purchase Requisition Department managers are usually not allowed to place orders directly with suppliers for control purposes. Instead, a department manager must inform the purchasing department of its needs by preparing and signing a **purchase requisition,** which lists the merchandise requested to be purchased—see Exhibit 8A.1. Two copies of the purchase requisition are sent to the purchasing department, which then sends one copy to the accounting department. When the accounting department receives a purchase requisition, it creates and maintains a voucher for this transaction. The requesting department keeps a third copy.

EXHIBIT 8A.1

Purchase Requisition

Z-Mart

PURCHASE REQUISITION No. 917

From *Sporting Goods Department*
To *Purchasing Department*

Date *October 28*
Preferred Vendor *Trex*

Request purchase of the following item(s):

MODEL NO.	DESCRIPTION	QUANTITY
CH 015	Toddler–Challenger X7	1
SD 099	Boys/Girls–Speed Demon	1

Reason for Request *Replenish inventory*
Approval for Request *T.Z.*
For Purchasing Department use only: Order Date *Oct. 30* P.O. No. *P98*

Purchase Order A **purchase order** is a document the purchasing department uses to place an order with a **vendor** (seller or supplier). A purchase order authorizes a vendor to ship merchandise at the stated price and terms—see Exhibit 8A.2. When the purchasing department receives a purchase requisition, it prepares at least five copies of a purchase order. The copies are distributed as follows: *copy 1* to the vendor as a purchase request to ship merchandise; *copy 2,* along with a copy of the purchase requisition, to the accounting department, where it is entered in the voucher and used in approving payment of the invoice; *copy 3* to the requesting department to inform its manager of the purchase; *copy 4* to the receiving department without order quantity so it can compare with goods received and provide an independent count of goods received; and *copy 5* kept on file by the purchasing department.

EXHIBIT 8A.2

Purchase Order

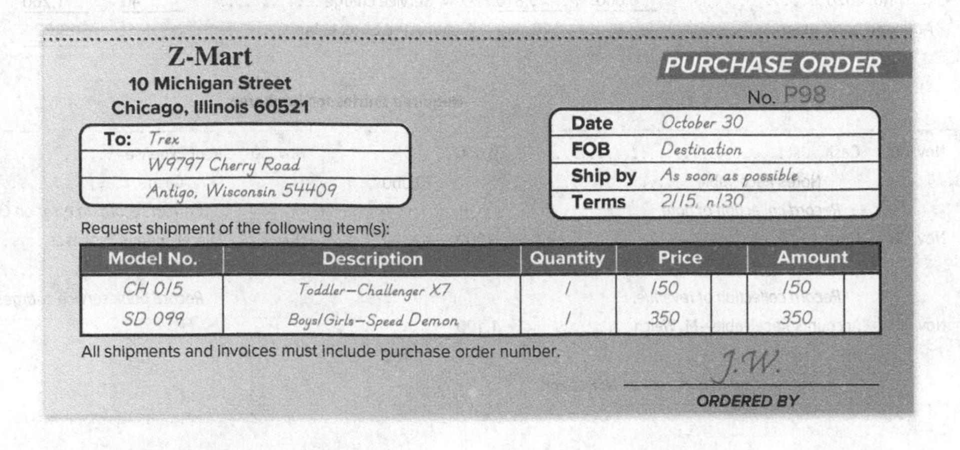

Z-Mart
10 Michigan Street
Chicago, Illinois 60521

PURCHASE ORDER
No. P98

To: *Trex*
W9797 Cherry Road
Antigo, Wisconsin 54409

Date	*October 30*
FOB	*Destination*
Ship by	*As soon as possible*
Terms	*2/15, n/30*

Request shipment of the following item(s):

Model No.	Description	Quantity	Price	Amount
CH 015	Toddler–Challenger X7	1	150	150
SD 099	Boys/Girls–Speed Demon	1	350	350

All shipments and invoices must include purchase order number.

J.W.
ORDERED BY

Invoice An **invoice** is an itemized statement of goods prepared by the vendor listing the customer's name, items sold, sales prices, and terms of sale. An invoice is also a bill sent to the buyer from the supplier. From the vendor's point of view, it is a *sales invoice*. The buyer, or **vendee,** treats it as a *purchase invoice*. The invoice is sent to the buyer's accounting department, where it is placed in the voucher. (Refer back to Exhibit 5.6, which shows Z-Mart's purchase invoice.)

Receiving Report Many companies have a receiving department to receive all merchandise and purchased assets. When each shipment arrives, this receiving department counts the goods and checks them for damage and agreement with the purchase order. It then prepares four or more copies of a **receiving report,** which is used within the company to notify that ordered goods have been received and to describe the quantities and condition of the goods. One copy is sent to accounting and placed in the voucher. Copies also are sent to the requesting department and the purchasing department to notify them that the goods have arrived. The receiving department keeps a copy in its files.

Invoice Approval When a receiving report arrives, the accounting department should have copies of the following documents in the voucher: purchase requisition, purchase order, and invoice. With the information in these documents, the accounting department can record the purchase and approve its payment. In approving an invoice for payment, it checks and compares information across all documents. To verify this information and to ensure that no step is missing, it often uses an **invoice approval,** also called *check authorization*—see Exhibit 8A.3. An invoice approval is a checklist of steps necessary for approving an invoice for recording and payment. It is a separate document either filed in the voucher or preprinted (or stamped) on the voucher.

EXHIBIT 8A.3
Invoice Approval

INVOICE APPROVAL

DOCUMENT		BY	DATE
Purchase requisition	917	TZ	Oct. 28
Purchase order	P98	JW	Oct. 30
Receiving report	R85	SK	Nov. 3
Invoice:	4657		Nov. 12
Price		JK	Nov. 12
Calculations		JK	Nov. 12
Terms		JK	Nov. 12
Approved for payment		BC	

As each step in the checklist is approved, the person initials the invoice approval and records the current date. Final approval means the following steps have occurred.

1. **Requisition check:** Items on invoice are requested per purchase requisition.
2. **Purchase order check:** Items on invoice are ordered per purchase order.
3. **Receiving report check:** Items on invoice are received per receiving report.
4. **Invoice check: Price:** Invoice prices are as agreed with the vendor.
   Calculations: Invoice has no mathematical errors.
   Terms: Terms are as agreed with the vendor.

Point: Recording a purchase is initiated by an invoice approval, not an invoice. An invoice approval verifies that the amount is consistent with that requested, ordered, and received. This controls and verifies purchases and related liabilities.

Point: Auditors, when auditing inventory, check a sampling of purchases by reviewing the purchase order, receiving report, and invoice.

Voucher Once an invoice has been checked and approved, the voucher is complete. A complete voucher is a record summarizing a transaction. Once the voucher certifies a transaction, it authorizes recording an obligation. A voucher also contains approval for paying the obligation on an appropriate date.

Completion of a voucher usually requires a person to enter certain information on both the inside and outside of the voucher. Typical information required on the inside of a voucher is on the left-hand side of Exhibit 8A.4, and that for the outside is on the right-hand side. This information is taken from the invoice and the supporting documents filed in the voucher. A complete voucher is sent to an authorized individual (often called an *auditor*). This person performs a final review, approves the accounts and amounts for debiting (called the *accounting distribution*), and authorizes recording of the voucher.

After a voucher is approved and recorded (in a journal called a **voucher register**), it is filed by its due date. A check is then sent on the payment date from the cashier, the voucher is marked "paid," and the voucher is sent to the accounting department and recorded (in a journal called the **check register**). The person issuing checks relies on the approved voucher and its signed supporting documents as

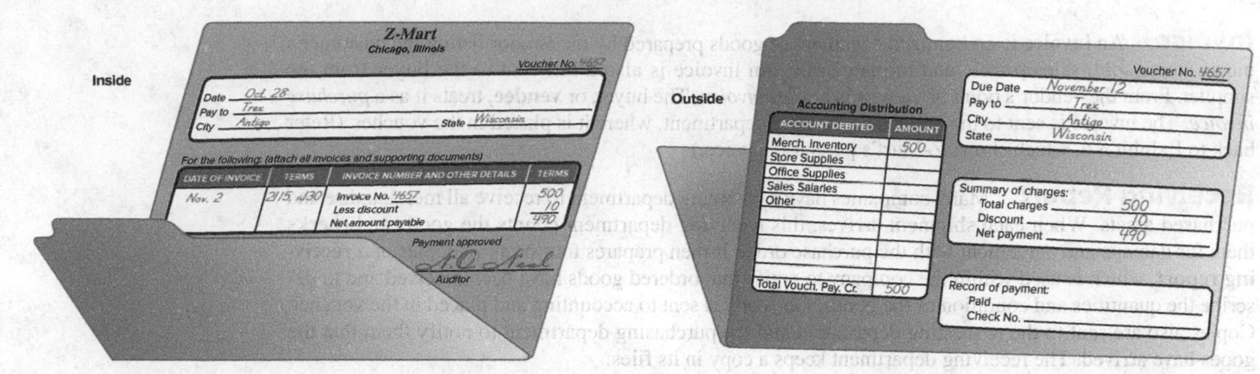

EXHIBIT 8A.4

A Voucher

proof that an obligation has been incurred and must be paid. The purchase requisition and purchase order confirm the purchase was authorized. The receiving report shows that items have been received, and the invoice approval form verifies that the invoice has been checked for errors. There is little chance for error and even less chance for fraud without collusion unless all the documents and signatures are forged.

Summary: Cheat Sheet

FRAUD AND INTERNAL CONTROL

Principles of Internal Control

Establish responsibilities: Responsibility for a task should be assigned to one person. If responsibility is not established, determining who is at fault is difficult.

Maintain adequate records: Good recordkeeping helps protect assets and helps managers monitor company activities.

Insure assets and bond key employees: Assets should be insured, and employees handling cash and easily transferable assets should be bonded.

Separate recordkeeping from custody of assets: An employee who has access to an asset must not have access to that asset's accounting records.

Divide responsibility for related transactions: Responsibility for a transaction should be divided between two or more individuals or departments. One person's work is a check on the others to prevent errors. This is *not* duplication of work.

Apply technological controls: Use technology such as ID scanners to protect assets and improve control.

Perform regular and independent reviews: Regular reviews of internal controls should be performed by outside reviewers, preferably auditors.

CONTROL OF CASH

Cash account: Includes currency, coins, checks, and deposits in bank accounts.

Cash equivalents: Short-term, liquid investment assets meeting two criteria: (1) convertible to a known cash amount and (2) close to their due date, usually within 3 months. An example is a U.S. Treasury bill.

Cash management strategies: (a) Encourage early collection of receivables, (b) delay payment of liabilities, (c) keep only necessary assets, (d) plan expenditures, and (e) invest excess cash.

Over-the-Counter Cash Receipt Control Procedures

- Sales are recorded on a cash register after each sale, and customers are given a receipt.
- Cash registers hold a locked-in record of each transaction and often are linked with the accounting system.
- Custody over cash is separate from recordkeeping. The clerk who has access to cash in the register cannot access accounting records. The recordkeeper cannot access the cash.

Cash Over and Short Journal Entries

If cash received is *more* than recorded cash sales:

Account	Debit	Credit
Cash	555	
Cash Over and Short		5
Sales		550

If cash received is *less* than recorded cash sales:

Account	Debit	Credit
Cash	621	
Cash Over and Short	4	
Sales		625

Cash Receipts by Mail Control Procedures

- Two people are tasked with opening mail. Theft of cash would require collusion between these two employees.
- A list (in triplicate) is kept of each sender's name, the amount, and an explanation of why money was sent. The first copy is sent with the money to the cashier. A second copy is sent to the recordkeeper. The employees who opened the mail keep the third copy. The cashier deposits the money in a bank, and the recordkeeper records amounts received.
- No employee has access to both accounting records and cash.

Cash Payment Control Procedures

- Require all payments to be made by check or EFT. The only exception is small payments made from petty cash.
- Deny access to records to employees who can sign checks (other than the owner).

Voucher system: Set of procedures to control cash payments. Applied to all payments.

TOOLS OF CONTROL AND ANALYSIS

Petty cash: System of control used for small payments.

Entry to set up a petty cash fund:

Account	Debit	Credit
Petty Cash	75	
Cash		75

Reimburse and record expenses for petty cash:

Merchandise Inventory	15.05	
Office Supplies Expense	4.75	
Delivery Expense	5.00	
Miscellaneous Expenses	46.50	
Cash		71.30

Increasing a petty cash fund (after reimbursement):

Petty Cash	25	
Cash		25

Decreasing a petty cash fund (after reimbursement):

Cash	20	
Petty Cash		20

Petty cash fund has unexplained shortage:

Miscellaneous Expenses	178	
Cash Over and Short	7	
Cash		185

Canceled checks: Checks the bank has paid and deducted from the customer's account.

Bank reconciliation adjustments:

Bank Balance Adjustments	Book Balance Adjustments
Add deposits in transit.	Add interest earned and unrecorded cash receipts.
Subtract outstanding checks.	Subtract bank fees and NSF checks.
Add or subtract corrections of bank errors.	Add or subtract corrections of book errors.

Entries from Bank Reconciliation—Examples

Collection of note:

Cash	485	
Notes Receivable		485

Interest earned:

Cash	8	
Interest Revenue		8

Bank fees:

Miscellaneous Expenses	23	
Cash		23

NSF checks:

Accounts Receivable—Name	30	
Cash		30

Key Terms

Bank reconciliation (301)
Bank statement (300)
Blockchain (291)
Canceled checks (300)
Cash (293)
Cash equivalents (293)
Cash Over and Short (294)
Check (299)
Check register (307)
Committee of Sponsoring Organizations (COSO) (289)
Days' sales uncollected (304)
Deposit ticket (299)
Deposits in transit (301)
Electronic funds transfer (EFT) (299)
Fraud triangle (291)
Internal control system (289)
Invoice (307)
Invoice approval (307)
Liquid assets (292)
Liquidity (292)
Outstanding checks (301)
Petty cash (296)
Principles of internal control (290)
Purchase order (306)
Purchase requisition (306)
Receiving report (307)
Sarbanes-Oxley Act (SOX) (289)
Signature card (299)
Vendee (307)
Vendor (306)
Voucher (295)
Voucher register (307)
Voucher system (295)

Multiple Choice Quiz

1. The following information is available for Hapley Co.
   - November 30 bank statement shows a $1,895 balance.
   - General ledger shows a $1,742 balance at November 30.
   - A $795 deposit in the bank's night depository on November 30 does not appear on the November 30 bank statement.
   - Outstanding checks amount to $638 at November 30.
   - A customer's $320 note was collected by the bank and deposited in Hapley's account in November.
   - A bank service charge of $10 is deducted by the bank and appears on the November 30 bank statement.

   How will the customer's note appear on Hapley's November 30 bank reconciliation?
   a. $320 is an addition to the book balance of cash.
   b. $320 is a deduction from the book balance of cash.
   c. $320 is an addition to the bank balance of cash.
   d. $320 is a deduction from the bank balance of cash.
   e. $335 is an addition to the bank balance of cash.

2. Using the information from question 1, what is the reconciled balance on Hapley's November 30 bank reconciliation?
   a. $2,052
   b. $1,895
   c. $1,742
   d. $2,201
   e. $1,184

3. A company replenishes its $500 petty cash fund. Its petty cashbox has $75 cash and petty cash receipts of $420 in repairs expense. The entry to replenish the fund includes

a. A debit to Cash for $75.
b. A credit to Cash for $75.
c. A credit to Petty Cash for $420.
d. A credit to Cash Over and Short for $5.
e. A debit to Cash Over and Short for $5.

4. A company had net sales of $84,000 and accounts receivable of $6,720. Its days' sales uncollected is

a. 3.2 days **b.** 18.4 days **c.** 230.0 days **d.** 29.2 days **e.** 12.5 days

ANSWERS TO MULTIPLE CHOICE QUIZ

1. a; recognizes cash collection of note by bank.
2. a; the bank reconciliation follows.

Bank Reconciliation November 30			
Balance per bank statement .	$1,895	Balance per books.......	$1,742
Add: Deposit in transit	795	Add: Note collected......	320
Deduct: Outstanding checks .	(638)	Deduct: Service charge...	(10)
Reconciled balance.........	$2,052	Reconciled balance......	$2,052

3. e; The entry follows.

Repairs expense	420	
Cash Over and Short.........	5	
Cash		425

4. d; ($6,720/$84,000) × 365 = 29.2 days

Superscript letter A denotes assignments based on Appendix 8A.

Select Quick Study and Exercise assignments feature Guided Example videos, called "Hints" in Connect. Hints use different numbers, and instructors can turn this feature on or off.

QUICK STUDY

QS 8-1
Internal control objectives
C1

Indicate which statements are true and which are false.

1. Separation of recordkeeping for assets from the custody over assets helps reduce fraud.
2. The primary objective of internal control procedures is to safeguard the business against theft from government agencies.
3. Internal control procedures should be designed to protect assets from waste and theft.
4. Separating the responsibility for a transaction between two or more individuals or departments will not help prevent someone from creating a fictitious invoice and paying the money to himself.

QS 8-2
COSO internal control components
C1

COSO lists five components of internal control: control environment, risk assessment, control activities, information and communication, and monitoring. Indicate the COSO component that matches with each of the following internal control activities.

a. Independent review of controls
b. Executives' strong ethics
c. Reporting of control effectiveness
d. Analyses of fraud risk factors

QS 8-3
Applying fraud triangle
C1

Identify the fraud triangle risk factor (opportunity, pressure, or rationalization) in each situation.

1. Employees are told to report increased income or be fired.
2. Several salesclerks share the same cash drawer.
3. A worker did not receive a bonus this year and now feels it's okay to use the company credit card for personal expenses.
4. Doors safeguarding valuable merchandise are not locked with a passcode.
5. An employee feels underpaid and believes stealing inventory is justified.

QS 8-4
Cash and equivalents
C2

Choose from the following list of terms and phrases to best complete the following statements.

a. Cash **c.** Outstanding check **e.** Cash over and short
b. Cash equivalents **d.** Liquidity **f.** Voucher system

1. The ______ category includes currency, coins, and deposits in bank accounts.
2. The term ______ refers to a company's ability to pay for its current liabilities.
3. The ______ category includes short-term, highly liquid investment assets that are readily convertible to a known cash amount and sufficiently close to their due dates so that their market value will not greatly change.

QS 8-5
Reporting cash and cash equivalents
C2

Anna's Cookies combines cash and cash equivalents on the balance sheet. Using the following information, determine the amount reported for cash and cash equivalents.

- $100 in coins held in store registers
- $600 in accounts payable to suppliers
- $1,000 cash in a safe at the store
- $4,000 cash in checking accounts
- $1,700 worth of equipment
- $5,000 note receivable due in 10 years

QS 8-6
Control of cash
C2

Determine whether each procedure described below is an internal control strength or weakness.

1. The same employee is in charge of recordkeeping and depositing cash receipts.
2. All large payments are made by electronic funds transfer (EFT).
3. Cash receipts of large amounts are kept in an office drawer and deposited every six months.

QS 8-7
Internal control for cash
P1

Identify each of the following statements as either true or false.

a. A guideline for safeguarding cash is that all cash receipts be deposited monthly or yearly.
b. A voucher system of control is a control system exclusively for cash receipts.
c. A guideline for safeguarding cash is to separate the duties of those who have custody of cash from those who keep cash records.
d. Separation of duties eliminates the possibility of collusion to steal an asset and hide the theft from the records.

QS 8-8
Cash Over and Short
P1

Record the journal entry for Sales and for Cash Over and Short for each of the following separate situations.

a. The cash register's record shows $420 of cash sales, but the count of cash in the register is $430.
b. The cash register's record shows $980 of cash sales, but the count of cash in the register is $972.

QS 8-9
Petty cash accounting
P2

1. Brooks Agency set up a petty cash fund for $150. At the end of the current period, the fund contained $28 and had the following receipts: entertainment, $70; postage, $30; and printing, $22. Prepare journal entries to record (*a*) establishment of the fund and (*b*) reimbursement of the fund at the end of the current period.
2. Identify the two events from the following that cause a Petty Cash account to be credited in a journal entry.
   a. Fund amount is being reduced. **c.** Fund is being eliminated.
   b. Fund amount is being increased. **d.** Fund is being established.

QS 8-10
Bank reconciliation
P3

For *a* through *g*, indicate whether its amount (1) affects the bank or book side of a bank reconciliation, (2) is an addition or a subtraction in a bank reconciliation, and (3) requires a journal entry.

	Bank or Book Side	Add or Subtract	Entry or Not
a. Interest on cash balance	______	______	______
b. Bank service charges	______	______	______
c. Minimum balance bank fee	______	______	______
d. Outstanding checks	______	______	______
e. Collection of note by bank	______	______	______
f. NSF checks	______	______	______
g. Deposits in transit.	______	______	______

QS 8-11
Bank reconciliation
P3

Nolan Company's Cash account shows a $22,352 debit balance and its bank statement shows $21,332 on deposit at the close of business on June 30. Prepare a bank reconciliation using the following information.

a. Outstanding checks as of June 30 total $3,713.
b. The June 30 bank statement lists $41 in bank service charges; the company has not yet recorded the cost of these services.
c. In reviewing the bank statement, a $90 check written by the company was mistakenly recorded in the company's books as $99.
d. June 30 cash receipts of $4,724 were placed in the bank's night depository after banking hours and were not recorded on the June 30 bank statement.
e. The bank statement included a $23 credit for interest earned on the company's cash in the bank. The company has not yet recorded interest earned.

QS 8-12
Bank reconciliation
P3

Organic Food Co.'s Cash account shows a $5,500 debit balance and its bank statement shows $5,160 on deposit at the close of business on August 31. Prepare a bank reconciliation using the following information.

a. August 31 cash receipts of $1,240 were placed in the bank's night depository after banking hours and were not recorded on the August 31 bank statement.
b. The bank statement shows a $120 NSF check from a customer; the company has not yet recorded this NSF check.
c. Outstanding checks as of August 31 total $1,120.
d. In reviewing the bank statement, an $80 check written by Organic Fruits was mistakenly drawn against Organic Food's account.
e. The August 31 bank statement lists $20 in bank service charges; the company has not yet recorded the cost of these services.

QS 8-13
Entries from bank reconciliation **P3**

Using the information in QS 8-12, prepare any necessary journal entries that Organic Food Co. must record as a result of preparing the bank reconciliation.

QS 8-14
Preparing current assets section of balance sheet
C2

Use the following information to prepare the current assets section of Lima Company's classified balance sheet as of December 31.

Adjusted Trial Balance	Debit	Credit
Cash and equivalents	$ 4,000	
Accounts receivable	2,000	
Merchandise inventory	5,000	
Prepaid insurance	1,000	
Land	20,000	
Accounts payable		$ 3,000
M. Lima, Capital		26,000
Sales		17,000
Cost of goods sold	8,000	
Wages expense	6,000	
Totals	46,000	46,000

QS 8-15
Days' sales uncollected
A1

The following annual account balances are from Armour Sports at December 31.

	Year 2	Year 1
Accounts receivable	$ 100,000	$ 85,000
Net sales	2,500,000	2,000,000

a. What is the change in the number of days' sales uncollected between Year 1 and Year 2?
b. From the analysis in part *a*, is the company's collection of receivables improving?

QS 8-16[A]
Documents in a voucher system **P4**

Management uses a voucher system to help control and monitor cash payments. Which one or more of the four documents listed below are prepared as part of a voucher system of control?

a. Purchase order **b.** Outstanding check **c.** Invoice **d.** Voucher

connect

EXERCISES

Exercise 8-1
Identifying internal control failures
C1

Identify the internal control principle that was violated in each of the following separate situations.

a. The recordkeeper left town after the owner discovered a large sum of money had disappeared. An audit found that the recordkeeper had written and signed several checks made payable to his fiancée and recorded the checks as salaries expense.

b. An employee was put in charge of handling cash. That employee later stole cash from the business. The company incurred an *uninsured* loss of $184,000.

c. There is $500 in cash missing from a cash register drawer. Three salesclerks shared the cash register drawer, so the owner cannot determine who is at fault.

Exercise 8-2
Identifying internal control principles
C1

Whole Fruits Market took the following actions to improve internal controls. For each of the following actions, identify the internal control principle the company followed.

a. The recordkeeper is prohibited from having control over cash.

b. An insurance (bonding) policy is purchased against losses from theft by a cashier.

c. Each cashier is designated a specific cash drawer and is solely responsible for cash in that drawer.

d. Detailed records of inventory are kept to ensure items lost or stolen do not go unnoticed.

e. Digital time clocks are used to register which employees are at work at what times.

f. External auditors are regularly hired to evaluate internal controls.

Exercise 8-3
Internal control strengths and weaknesses
C1

Determine whether each procedure described below is an internal control strength or weakness; then identify the internal control principle violated or followed for each procedure.

1. The same employee requests, records, and makes payment for purchases of inventory.

2. The company saves money by having employees involved in operations perform the only review of internal controls.

3. Time is saved by not updating records for use of supplies.

4. The recordkeeper is not allowed to write checks or initiate EFTs.

5. Each salesclerk is in charge of her own cash drawer.

Exercise 8-4
Cash management strategies
C2

Determine whether each policy below is good or bad cash management; then identify the cash management strategy violated or followed for each policy.

1. Bills are paid as soon as they are received.

2. Cash receipts and cash payments are regularly planned and reviewed.

3. Excess cash is put in checking accounts, earning no interest income.

4. Customers are regularly allowed to pay after due dates without concern.

5. Rarely used equipment is rented rather than purchased.

Exercise 8-5
Cash and cash equivalents
C2

Specter Co. combines cash and cash equivalents on the balance sheet. Using the following information, determine the amount reported on the year-end balance sheet for cash and cash equivalents.

- $3,000 cash deposit in checking account.
- $20,000 bond investment due in 20 years.
- $5,000 U.S. Treasury bill due in 1 month.
- $200, 3-year loan to an employee.
- $1,000 of currency and coins.
- $500 of accounts receivable.

Exercise 8-6
Control of cash receipts
P1

Determine whether each cash receipts procedure is an internal control strength or weakness.

1. If a salesclerk makes an error in recording a cash sale, she can access the register's electronic record to correct the transaction.

2. All sales transactions, even those for less than $1, are recorded on a cash register.

3. Two employees are tasked with opening mail that contains cash receipts.

4. One of the two employees tasked with opening mail is also the recordkeeper for the business.

5. The supervisor has access to both cash and the accounting records.

6. Receipts are given to customers only for sales that are above $20.

Exercise 8-7
Voucher system and control of cash payments
P1

Determine whether each cash payment procedure is an internal control strength or weakness.

1. A voucher system is used for all payments of liabilities.
2. The owner of a small business has authority to write and sign checks.
3. When the owner is out of town, the recordkeeper is in charge of signing checks.
4. To save time, all departments are allowed to incur liabilities.
5. Payments over $100 are made by check.
6. Requesting and receiving merchandise are handled by the same department.

Exercise 8-8
Petty cash fund with a shortage P2

Check (2) Cr. Cash, $246 and (3) Cr. Cash, $50

Waupaca Company establishes a $350 petty cash fund on September 9. On September 30, the fund shows $104 in cash along with receipts for the following expenditures: transportation-in, $40; postage expenses, $123; and miscellaneous expenses, $80. The petty cashier could not account for a $3 shortage in the fund.

The company uses the perpetual system in accounting for merchandise inventory. Prepare (1) the September 9 entry to establish the fund, (2) the September 30 entry to reimburse the fund, and (3) an October 1 entry to increase the fund to $400.

Exercise 8-9
Petty cash fund with an overage
P2

EcoMart establishes a $1,050 petty cash fund on May 2. On May 30, the fund shows $326 in cash along with receipts for the following expenditures: transportation-in, $120; postage expenses, $369; and miscellaneous expenses, $240. The petty cashier could not account for a $5 overage in the fund. The company uses the perpetual system in accounting for merchandise inventory.

Prepare the (1) May 2 entry to establish the fund, (2) May 30 entry to reimburse the fund [*Hint:* Credit Cash Over and Short for $5 and credit Cash for $724], and (3) June 1 entry to increase the fund to $1,200.

Exercise 8-10
Petty cash fund accounting
P2

Palmona Co. establishes a $200 petty cash fund on January 1. On January 8, the fund shows $38 in cash along with receipts for the following expenditures: postage, $74; transportation-in, $29; delivery expenses, $16; and miscellaneous expenses, $43. Palmona uses the perpetual system in accounting for merchandise inventory.

1. Prepare the entry to establish the fund on January 1.
2. Prepare the entry to reimburse the fund on January 8 under two *separate* situations.
   a. To reimburse the fund.
   b. To reimburse the fund and increase it to $450. *Hint:* Make two entries.

Exercise 8-11
Bank reconciliation and journal entries
P3

Prepare a table with the following headings for a monthly bank reconciliation dated September 30. Indicate whether each item should be added to or subtracted from the book or bank balance and whether it should or should not appear on the September 30 reconciliation. For items that add or subtract from the book balance column, place a *Dr.* or *Cr.* after the "Add" or "Subtract" to show the accounting impact on Cash.

Item	Bank Balance	Book Balance		Shown or Not Shown on Reconciliation
	Add or Subtract	Add or Subtract	Dr. or Cr.	Shown or Not Shown

1. NSF check from a customer is shown on the bank statement but not yet recorded by the company.
2. Interest earned on the September cash balance in the bank is not yet recorded by the company.
3. Deposit made on September 5 and processed by the bank on September 6.
4. Checks written by another depositor but mistakenly charged against this company's account.
5. Bank service charge for September is not yet recorded by the company.
6. Checks outstanding on August 31 that cleared the bank in September.
7. Check written against the company's account and cleared by the bank; erroneously not recorded by the company's recordkeeper.
8. A note receivable is collected by the bank for the company, but it is not yet recorded by the company.
9. Checks written and mailed to payees on October 2.
10. Checks written by the company and mailed to payees on September 30.
11. Night deposit made on September 30 after the bank closed.
12. Bank fees for check printing are not yet recorded by the company.

Exercise 8-12
Bank reconciliation
P3

Del Gato Clinic's Cash account shows an $11,589 debit balance and its bank statement shows $10,555 on deposit at the close of business on June 30. Prepare its bank reconciliation using the following information.

a. Outstanding checks as of June 30 total $1,829.

b. The June 30 bank statement lists a $16 bank service charge.

c. Check No. 919, listed with the canceled checks, was correctly drawn for $467 in payment of a utility bill on June 15. Del Gato Clinic mistakenly recorded it with a debit to Utilities Expense and a credit to Cash in the amount of $476.

d. The June 30 cash receipts of $2,856 were placed in the bank's night depository after banking hours and were not recorded on the June 30 bank statement.

Check Reconciled bal., $11,582

Exercise 8-13
Entries from bank reconciliation P3

Using the information in Exercise 8-12, prepare any necessary journal entries that Del Gato Clinic must record as a result of preparing the bank reconciliation.

Exercise 8-14
Bank reconciliation
P3

Wright Company's Cash account shows a $27,500 debit balance and its bank statement shows $25,800 on deposit at the close of business on May 31. Prepare its bank reconciliation using the following information.

a. The May 31 bank statement lists $100 in bank service charges; the company has not yet recorded the cost of these services.

b. Outstanding checks as of May 31 total $5,600.

c. May 31 cash receipts of $6,200 were placed in the bank's night depository after banking hours and were not recorded on the May 31 bank statement.

d. In reviewing the bank statement, a $400 check written by Smith Company was mistakenly drawn against Wright's account.

e. The bank statement shows a $600 NSF check from a customer; the company has not yet recorded this NSF check.

Check Reconciled bal., $26,800

Exercise 8-15
Preparing a balance sheet
C2

Use the following accounts with normal balances to prepare Bosco Company's classified balance sheet as of December 31.

Merchandise inventory	$ 3,000	Land	$24,000
Accounts receivable	5,000	Buildings	40,000
Cash and equivalents	7,000	Accounts payable	10,000
Notes payable (due in 8 years)	15,000	Wages payable	2,000
Accumulated depreciation—Buildings	22,000	A. Bosco, Capital	30,000

Exercise 8-16
Computing and analyzing days' sales uncollected A1

Barga Co.'s net sales for Year 1 and Year 2 are $730,000 and $1,095,000, respectively. Its year-end balances of accounts receivable follow: Year 1, $65,000; and Year 2, $123,000.

a. Compute its days' sales uncollected at the end of each year.

b. Did days' sales uncollected improve or worsen in Year 2 versus Year 1?

Exercise 8-17[A]
Documents in a voucher system
P4

Match each document in a voucher system with its description.

Document

1. Purchase requisition
2. Purchase order
3. Invoice
4. Receiving report
5. Invoice approval
6. Voucher

Description

A. An itemized statement of goods prepared by the vendor listing the customer's name, items sold, sales prices, and terms of sale.

B. An internal file used to store documents and information to control cash payments and to ensure that a transaction is properly authorized and recorded.

C. A document used to place an order with a vendor that authorizes the vendor to ship ordered merchandise at the stated price and terms.

D. A checklist of steps necessary for the approval of an invoice for recording and payment; also known as a check authorization.

E. A document used by department managers to inform the purchasing department to place an order with a vendor.

F. A document used to notify the appropriate persons that ordered goods have arrived, including a description of the quantities and condition of goods.

PROBLEM SET A

Problem 8-1A
Analyzing internal control
C1

Following are five separate cases involving internal control issues.

a. Chi Han receives all incoming customer cash receipts for her employer and posts the customer payments to their respective accounts.

b. At Tico Company, Julia and Trevor alternate lunch hours. Julia is the petty cash custodian, but if someone needs petty cash when she is at lunch, Trevor fills in as custodian.

c. Nori Nozumi posts all patient charges and payments at the Hopeville Medical Clinic. Each night Nori backs up the computerized accounting system but does not password lock her computer.

d. Ben Shales prides himself on hiring quality workers who require little supervision. As office manager, Ben gives his employees full discretion over their tasks and for years has seen no reason to perform independent reviews of their work.

e. Carla Farah's manager has told her to reduce costs. Carla decides to raise the deductible on the plant's property insurance from $5,000 to $10,000. This cuts the property insurance premium in half. In a related move, she decides that bonding the plant's employees is a waste of money because the company has not experienced any losses due to employee theft. Carla saves the entire amount of the bonding insurance premium by dropping the bonding insurance.

Required

1. For each case, identify the principle(s) of internal control that is violated.

2. Recommend what should be done to adhere to principles of internal control in each case.

Problem 8-2A
Establishing, reimbursing, and adjusting petty cash
P2

Kiona Co. set up a petty cash fund for payments of small amounts. The following transactions involving the petty cash fund occurred in May (the last month of the company's fiscal year).

May 1 Prepared a company check for $300 to establish the petty cash fund.

15 Prepared a company check to replenish the fund for the following expenditures made since May 1.

- *a.* Paid $88 for janitorial expenses.
- *b.* Paid $53.68 for miscellaneous expenses.
- *c.* Paid postage expenses of $53.50.
- *d.* Paid $47.15 to Facebook for advertising expense.
- *e.* Counted $62.15 remaining in the petty cashbox.

16 Prepared a company check for $200 to increase the fund to $500.

31 The petty cashier reports that $288.20 cash remains in the fund. A company check is drawn to replenish the fund for the following expenditures made since May 15.

- *f.* Paid postage expenses of $147.36.
- *g.* Reimbursed the office manager for mileage expense, $23.50.
- *h.* Paid $34.75 in delivery expense for products to a customer, terms FOB destination.

31 The company decides that the May 16 increase in the fund was too large. It reduces the fund by $100, leaving a total of $400.

Required

Prepare journal entries to establish the fund on May 1, to replenish it on May 15 and on May 31, and to reflect any increase or decrease in the fund balance on May 16 and May 31.

Check Cr. to Cash: May 15, $237.85; May 16, $200.00

Problem 8-3A
Establishing, reimbursing, and increasing petty cash
P2

Nakashima Gallery had the following petty cash transactions in February of the current year. Nakashima uses the perpetual system to account for merchandise inventory.

Feb. 2 Wrote a $400 check to establish a petty cash fund.

5 Purchased paper for the copier for $14.15 that is immediately used.

9 Paid $32.50 shipping charges (transportation-in) on merchandise purchased for resale, terms FOB shipping point. These costs are added to merchandise inventory.

12 Paid $7.95 postage to deliver a contract to a client.

14 Reimbursed Adina Sharon, the manager, $68 for mileage on her car.

20 Purchased office paper for $67.77 that is immediately used.

23 Paid a courier $20 to deliver merchandise sold to a customer, terms FOB destination.

25 Paid $13.10 shipping charges (transportation-in) on merchandise purchased for resale, terms FOB shipping point. These costs are added to merchandise inventory.

27 Paid $54 for postage expenses.

28 The fund had $120.42 remaining in the petty cashbox. Sorted the petty cash receipts by accounts affected and exchanged them for a check to reimburse the fund for expenditures.
28 The petty cash fund amount is increased by $100 to a total of $500.

Required

1. Prepare the journal entry to establish the petty cash fund.
2. Prepare a petty cash payments report for February with these categories: delivery expense, mileage expense, postage expense, merchandise inventory (for transportation-in), and office supplies expense.
3. Prepare the journal entries for part 2 to both (*a*) reimburse and (*b*) increase the fund amount.

Check Cash credit: (3*a*) $279.58; (3*b*) $100.00

Problem 8-4A
Preparing a bank reconciliation and recording entries
P3

The following information is available to reconcile Branch Company's book balance of cash with its bank statement cash balance as of July 31.

a. On July 31, the company's Cash account has a $27,497 debit balance, but its July bank statement shows a $27,233 cash balance.
b. Check No. 3031 for $1,482, Check No. 3065 for $382, and Check No. 3069 for $2,281 are outstanding checks as of July 31.
c. Check No. 3056 for July rent expense was correctly written and drawn for $1,270 but was erroneously entered in the accounting records as $1,250.
d. The July bank statement shows the bank collected $7,955 cash on a note for Branch. Branch had not recorded this event before receiving the statement.
e. The bank statement shows an $805 NSF check. The check had been received from a customer, Evan Shaw. Branch has not yet recorded this check as NSF.
f. The July statement shows a $25 bank service charge. It has not yet been recorded in miscellaneous expenses because no previous notification had been received.
g. Branch's July 31 daily cash receipts of $11,514 were placed in the bank's night depository on that date but do not appear on the July 31 bank statement.

Required

1. Prepare the bank reconciliation for this company as of July 31.
2. Prepare the journal entries necessary to make the company's book balance of cash equal to the reconciled cash balance as of July 31.

Check (1) Reconciled balance, $34,602; (2) Cr. Notes Receivable, $8,000

Problem 8-5A
Preparing a bank reconciliation and recording entries
P3

Chavez Company most recently reconciled its bank statement and book balances of cash on August 31 and it reported two checks outstanding, No. 5888 for $1,028 and No. 5893 for $494. Check No. 5893 was still outstanding as of September 30. The following information is available for its September 30 reconciliation.

Date	Description	Withdrawals	Deposits	Balance
Sep. 1				$16,800
Sep. 3	Check #5888	$1,028		$15,772
Sep. 4	Check #5902	$ 719		$15,053
Sep. 5	Cash deposit		$1,103	$16,156
Sep. 7	Check #5901	$1,824		$14,332
Sep. 12	Cash deposit		$2,226	$16,558
Sep. 17	NSF check	$ 600		$15,958
Sep. 20	Check #5905	$ 937		$15,021
Sep. 21	Cash deposit		$4,093	$19,114
Sep. 22	Check #5903	$ 399		$18,715
Sep. 22	Check #5904	$2,090		$16,625
Sep. 25	Cash deposit		$2,351	$18,976
Sep. 28	Check #5907	$ 213		$18,763
Sep. 29	Check #5909	$1,807		$16,956
Sep. 30	Collected note		$1,485	$18,441
Sep. 30	Interest earned		$ 12	$18,453

[continued on next page]

[continued from previous page]

From Chavez Company's Accounting Records

Cash Receipts Deposited	
Date	**Cash Debit**
Sep. 5	1,103
12	2,226
21	4,093
25	2,351
30	1,682
	11,455

Cash Payments	
Check No.	**Cash Credit**
5901	1,824
5902	719
5903	399
5904	2,060
5905	937
5906	982
5907	213
5908	388
5909	1,807
	9,329

Cash					Acct. No. 101
Date	**Explanation**	**PR**	**Debit**	**Credit**	**Balance**
Aug. 31	Balance				15,278
Sep. 30	Total receipts	R12	11,455		26,733
30	Total payments	D23		9,329	17,404

Additional Information (*a*) Check No. 5904 is correctly drawn for $2,090 to pay for computer equipment; however, the recordkeeper misread the amount and entered it in the accounting records with a debit to Computer Equipment and a credit to Cash of $2,060. (*b*) The NSF check shown in the statement was originally received from a customer, S. Nilson, in payment of her account. Its return has not yet been recorded by the company. (*c*) The collection of the note on September 30 is not yet recorded by the company.

Required

1. Prepare the September 30 bank reconciliation for this company.

2. Prepare journal entries to adjust the book balance of cash to the reconciled balance.

Check (1) Reconciled balance, $18,271; (2) Cr. Notes Receivable, $1,485

PROBLEM SET B

Problem 8-1B
Analyzing internal control
C1

Following are five separate cases involving internal control issues.

a. Tywin Company keeps very poor records of its equipment. Instead, the company asserts its employees are honest and would never steal from the company.

b. Marker Theater has a computerized order-taking system for its tickets. The system is backed up once a year.

c. Sutton Company has two employees handling acquisitions of inventory. One employee places purchase orders and pays vendors. The second employee receives the merchandise.

d. The owner of Super Pharmacy uses a check software/printer to prepare checks, making it difficult for anyone to alter the amount of a check. The check software/printer, which is not password protected, is on the owner's desk in an office that contains company checks and is normally unlocked.

e. To ensure the company retreat would not be cut, the manager of Lavina Company decided to save money by canceling the external audit of internal controls.

Required

1. For each case, identify the principle(s) of internal control that is violated.

2. Recommend what should be done to adhere to principles of internal control in each case.

Problem 8-2B
Establishing, reimbursing, and adjusting petty cash
P2

Moya Co. establishes a petty cash fund for payments of small amounts. The following transactions involving the petty cash fund occurred in January (the last month of the company's fiscal year).

Jan. 3 A company check for $150 is written and made payable to the petty cashier to establish the petty cash fund.

14 A company check is written to replenish the fund for the following expenditures made since January 3.

a. Purchased office supplies for $14.29 that are immediately used.

b. Paid $19.60 COD shipping charges on merchandise purchased for resale, terms FOB shipping point. Moya uses the perpetual system to account for inventory.

c. Paid $38.57 to All-Tech for repairs expense to a computer.

d. Paid $12.82 for items classified as miscellaneous expenses.

e. Counted $62.28 remaining in the petty cashbox.

15 Prepared a company check for $50 to increase the fund to $200.

31 The petty cashier reports that $17.35 remains in the fund. A company check is written to replenish the fund for the following expenditures made since January 14.

f. Paid $50 to *The Smart Shopper* in advertising expense for January's newsletter.

g. Paid $48.19 for postage expenses.

h. Paid $78 to Smooth Delivery for delivery expense of merchandise, terms FOB destination.

31 The company decides that the January 15 increase in the fund was too little. It increases the fund by another $50.

Required

Prepare journal entries (in dollars and cents) to establish the fund on January 3, to replenish it on January 14 and January 31, and to reflect any increase or decrease in the fund balance on January 15 and 31.

Check Cr. to Cash: Jan. 14, $87.72; Jan. 31 (total), $232.65

Problem 8-3B
Establishing, reimbursing, and increasing petty cash
P2

Blues Music Center had the following petty cash transactions in March of the current year. Blues uses the perpetual system to account for merchandise inventory.

Mar. 5 Wrote a $250 check to establish a petty cash fund.
6 Paid $12.50 shipping charges (transportation-in) on merchandise purchased for resale, terms FOB shipping point. These costs are added to merchandise inventory.
11 Paid $10.75 in delivery expense on merchandise sold to a customer, terms FOB destination.
12 Purchased office file folders for $14.13 that are immediately used.
14 Reimbursed Bob Geldof, the manager, $11.65 for office supplies purchased and used.
18 Purchased office printer paper for $20.54 that is immediately used.
27 Paid $45.10 shipping charges (transportation-in) on merchandise purchased for resale, terms FOB shipping point. These costs are added to merchandise inventory.
28 Paid postage expense of $18.
30 Reimbursed Geldof $56.80 for mileage expense.
31 Cash of $61.53 remained in the fund. Sorted the petty cash receipts by accounts affected and exchanged them for a check to reimburse the fund for expenditures.
31 The petty cash fund amount is increased by $50 to a total of $300.

Required

1. Prepare the journal entry to establish the petty cash fund.
2. Prepare a petty cash payments report for March with these categories: delivery expense, mileage expense, postage expense, merchandise inventory (for transportation-in), and office supplies expense.
3. Prepare the journal entries for part 2 to both (*a*) reimburse and (*b*) increase the fund amount.

Check (2) Total expenses, $189.47
(3*a* & 3*b*) Total Cr. to Cash, $238.47

Problem 8-4B
Preparing a bank reconciliation and recording entries
P3

The following information is available to reconcile Severino Co.'s book balance of cash with its bank statement cash balance as of December 31.

a. The December 31 cash balance according to the accounting records is $32,878.30, and the bank statement cash balance for that date is $46,822.40.

b. Check No. 1242 for $410.40, Check No. 1273 for $4,589.30, and Check No. 1282 for $400 are outstanding checks as of December 31.

c. Check No. 1267 had been correctly drawn for $3,456 to pay for office supplies but was erroneously entered in the accounting records as $3,465.

d. The bank statement shows a $762.50 NSF check received from a customer, Titus Industries, in payment of its account. The statement also shows a $99 bank fee in miscellaneous expenses for check printing. Severino had not yet recorded these transactions.

e. The bank statement shows that the bank collected $18,980 cash on a note receivable for the company. Severino did not record this transaction before receiving the statement.

f. Severino's December 31 daily cash receipts of $9,583.10 were placed in the bank's night depository on that date but do not appear on the December 31 bank statement.

Required

1. Prepare the bank reconciliation for this company as of December 31.
2. Prepare the journal entries necessary to make the company's book balance of cash equal to the reconciled cash balance as of December 31.

Check (1) Reconciled balance, $51,005.80; (2) Cr. Notes Receivable, $18,980.00

Problem 8-5B
Preparing a bank reconciliation and recording entries
P3

Shamara Systems most recently reconciled its bank balance on April 30 and reported two checks outstanding at that time, No. 1771 for $781 and No. 1780 for $1,425.90. Check No. 1780 was still outstanding as of May 31. The following information is available for its May 31 reconciliation.

Date	Description	Withdrawals	Deposits	Balance
May 1				$18,290.70
May 1	Check #1771	$ 781.00		$17,509.70
May 2	Check #1783	$ 382.50		$17,127.20
May 4	Check #1782	$1,285.50		$15,841.70
May 4	Cash deposit		$2,438.00	$18,279.70
May 11	Check #1784	$1,449.60		$16,830.10
May 14	Cash deposit		$2,898.00	$19,728.10
May 18	NSF check	$ 431.80		$19,296.30
May 22	Cash deposit		$1,801.80	$21,098.10
May 25	Collected note		$7,350.00	$28,448.10
May 25	Check #1787	$8,032.50		$20,415.60
May 26	Check #1785	$ 63.90		$20,351.70
May 26	Cash deposit		$2,079.00	$22,430.70
May 29	Check #1788	$ 654.00		$21,776.70
May 31	Bank service charge	$ 14.00		$21,762.70

From Shamara Systems's Accounting Records

Cash Receipts Deposited

Date	Cash Debit
May 4	2,438.00
14	2,898.00
22	1,801.80
26	2,079.00
31	2,727.30
	11,944.10

Cash Payments

Check No.	Cash Credit
1782	1,285.50
1783	382.50
1784	1,449.60
1785	63.90
1786	353.10
1787	8,032.50
1788	644.00
1789	639.50
	12,850.60

Cash Acct. No. 101

Date		Explanation	PR	Debit	Credit	Balance
Apr.	30	Balance				16,083.80
May	31	Total receipts	R7	11,944.10		28,027.90
	31	Total payments	D8		12,850.60	15,177.30

Additional Information (*a*) Check No. 1788 is correctly drawn for $654 to pay for May utilities; however, the recordkeeper misread the amount and entered it in the accounting records with a debit to Utilities Expense and a credit to Cash for $644. The bank paid and deducted the correct amount. (*b*) The NSF check shown in the statement was originally received from a customer, W. Sox, in payment of her account. The company has not yet recorded its return. (*c*) The collection of the note on May 25 has not yet been recorded by the company.

Required

1. Prepare the May 31 bank reconciliation for Shamara Systems.
2. Prepare journal entries to adjust the book balance of cash to the reconciled balance.

Check (1) Reconciled balance, $22,071.50; (2) Cr. Notes Receivable, $7,350.00

connect

SERIAL PROBLEM

Business Solutions
P3

Serial problem began in Chapter 1. If previous chapter segments were not completed, the serial problem can begin at this point. It is available in ***Connect*** *with an algorithmic option.*

SP 8 Santana Rey receives the March bank statement for **Business Solutions** on April 11, 2022. The March 31 bank statement shows an ending cash balance of $67,566. The general ledger Cash account, No. 101, shows an ending cash balance per books of $68,057 as of March 31 (prior to any reconciliation). A comparison of the bank statement with the general ledger Cash account, No. 101, reveals the following.

a. The bank erroneously cleared a $500 check against the company account in March that S. Rey did not issue. The check was actually issued by Business Systems.

b. On March 25, the bank statement lists a $50 charge for a safety deposit box. Santana has not yet recorded this expense.

c. On March 26, the bank statement lists a $102 charge for printed checks that Business Solutions ordered from the bank. Santana has not yet recorded this expense.

d. On March 31, the bank statement lists $33 interest earned on Business Solutions's checking account for the month of March. Santana has not yet recorded this revenue.

e. S. Rey notices that the check she issued for $128 on March 31, 2022, has not yet cleared the bank.

f. S. Rey verifies that all deposits made in March do appear on the March bank statement.

Alexander Image/Shutterstock

Required

1. Prepare a bank reconciliation for Business Solutions for the month ended March 31, 2022.
2. Prepare any necessary entries. Use Miscellaneous Expenses, No. 677, for any bank charges. Use Interest Revenue, No. 404, for any interest earned on the checking account for March.

Check (1) Adj. bank bal., $67,938

TABLEAU DASHBOARD ACTIVITIES

Tableau Dashboard Activities expose students to accounting analytics using visual displays. These assignments run in **Connect**. All are auto-gradable.

Tableau DA 8-1 Quick Study, Identifying components of a bank reconciliation, **P3**—similar to QS 8-10

Tableau DA 8-2 Exercise, Preparing a bank reconciliation, **P3**—similar to Exercise 8-12

Tableau DA 8-3 Mini-Case, Entries from a bank reconciliation, **P3**—similar to Exercises 8-11 and 8-13

GENERAL LEDGER

General Ledger (GL) Assignments expose students to general ledger software similar to that in practice. GL is part of **Connect.**

GL 8-1 prepare journal entries related to petty cash and assess the impact of each transaction on net income.

Accounting Analysis

COMPANY ANALYSIS C2 A1

AA 8-1 Use **Apple**'s financial statements in Appendix A to answer the following.

1. Identify the total amount of cash and cash equivalents for fiscal years ended (*a*) September 28, 2019, and (*b*) September 29, 2018.
2. Compute cash and cash equivalents as a percent (rounded to one decimal) of total current assets, total current liabilities, total shareholders' equity, and total assets at fiscal year-end for both 2019 and 2018.
3. Compute the percent change (rounded to one decimal) between the beginning and ending year amounts of cash and cash equivalents for fiscal years ended (*a*) September 28, 2019, and (*b*) September 29, 2018. The beginning balance of cash and cash equivalents is $20,289 (millions) for fiscal year 2018.
4. Compute the days' sales uncollected (rounded to one decimal) as of (*a*) September 28, 2019, and (*b*) September 29, 2018.
5. Does Apple's collection of receivables in part 4 show a favorable or unfavorable change?

COMPARATIVE ANALYSIS A1

AA 8-2 Key comparative figures for **Apple** and **Google** follow.

	Apple		Google	
$ millions	Current Year	Prior Year	Current Year	Prior Year
Accounts receivable	$ 22,926	$ 23,186	$ 25,326	$ 20,838
Net sales	260,174	265,595	161,857	136,819

Required

1. Compute days' sales uncollected (rounded to one decimal) for the current year and the prior year for (*a*) Apple and (*b*) Google.
2. Which company had more success collecting receivables?

EXTENDED ANALYSIS C2 A1

AA 8-3 Key figures for **Samsung** follow.

$ millions	Current Year	Prior Year
Cash..........................	$ 23,069	$ 26,033
Accounts receivable............	33,730	31,703
Current assets.................	155,634	149,896
Total assets...................	302,511	291,179
Current liabilities............	54,728	59,274
Shareholders' equity	225,559	212,580
Net sales......................	197,691	209,163

[continued on next page]

[continued from previous page]

Required

1. Compute cash and cash equivalents as a percent (rounded to one decimal) of total current assets, total assets, total current liabilities, and total shareholders' equity for both years.
2. Compute the percentage change (rounded to one decimal) between the current-year and prior-year cash balances.
3. Compute the days' sales uncollected (rounded to one decimal) at the end of both the (*a*) current year and (*b*) prior year.
4. Does Samsung's collection of receivables show a favorable or unfavorable change?

Discussion Questions

1. List the seven broad principles of internal control.
2. Internal control procedures are important in every business, but at what stage in the development of a business do they become especially critical?
3. Why should responsibility for related transactions be divided among different departments or individuals?
4. Why should the person who keeps the records of an asset not be the person responsible for its custody?
5. When a store purchases merchandise, why are individual departments not allowed to directly deal with suppliers?
6. What are the limitations of internal controls?
7. Which of the following assets—inventory, building, accounts receivable, or cash—is most liquid? Which is least liquid?
8. What is a petty cash receipt? Who should sign it?
9. Why should cash receipts be deposited on the day of receipt?
10. Franco Co.'s recordkeeper left town after the manager discovered that a large sum of money had been stolen. The recordkeeper had written and signed several checks made payable to her fiancé and then recorded the checks as salaries expense. The fiancé, who cashed the checks but never worked for the company, left town with the recordkeeper. The company had an uninsured loss of $184,000. Evaluate Franco's internal control system and indicate which principles of internal control were ignored.
11. Recommend an internal control procedure for each situation: (*a*) A concession company has one employee who sells towels, coolers, and sunglasses at the beach. Each day, the employee is given enough towels, coolers, and sunglasses to last through the day and enough cash to make change. The money is kept in a box at the stand. (*b*) An antique store has one employee who is given cash and sent to garage sales each weekend. The employee pays cash for any merchandise acquired that the antique store resells.
12. Cash receipts from customers are received by the company with regular mail. The recordkeeper opens these letters and deposits the cash received each day. (*a*) Identify any internal control problem(s) in this arrangement. (*b*) What changes to its internal control system do you recommend?
13. Why would companies invest their idle cash in cash equivalents?
14. (*a*) The voucher system of control establishes procedures for what two processes? (*b*) When is the voucher initially prepared?

Beyond the Numbers

ETHICS CHALLENGE

C1

BTN 8-1 Harriet Knox, Ralph Patton, and Marcia Diamond work for a family physician, Dr. Gwen Conrad, who is in private practice. Dr. Conrad is knowledgeable about office management practices and has segregated the cash receipt duties as follows. Knox opens the mail and prepares a triplicate list of money received. She sends one copy of the list to Patton, the cashier, who deposits the receipts daily in the bank. Diamond, the recordkeeper, receives a copy of the list and posts payments to patients' accounts. About once a month the office clerks have an expensive lunch they pay for as follows. First, Patton endorses a patient's check in Dr. Conrad's name and cashes it at the bank. Knox then destroys the remittance advice accompanying the check. Finally, Diamond posts payment to the customer's account as a miscellaneous credit. The three justify their actions by their relatively low pay and knowledge that Dr. Conrad will likely never miss the money.

Required

1. Who is the best person in Dr. Conrad's office to reconcile the bank statement?
2. Would a bank reconciliation uncover this office fraud?
3. What are some procedures to detect this type of fraud?
4. Suggest additional internal controls that Dr. Conrad could implement.

COMMUNICATING IN PRACTICE
P4

BTN 8-2 Assume you are a business consultant. The owner of a company sends you an e-mail expressing concern that the company is not taking advantage of its discounts offered by vendors. The company currently uses the gross method of recording purchases. The owner is considering a review of all invoices and payments from the previous period. Due to the volume of purchases, however, the owner recognizes that this is time-consuming and costly. The owner *seeks your advice about monitoring purchase discounts* in the future. Provide a response in memorandum form. *Hint:* It will help to review the recording of purchase discounts in Appendix 5C.

TEAMWORK IN ACTION
C1

BTN 8-3 Organize the class into teams. Each team must prepare a list of 10 internal controls a consumer could observe in a typical retail department store. When called upon, the team's spokesperson must be prepared to share controls identified by the team that have not been shared by another team's spokesperson.

ENTREPRENEURIAL DECISION
C1 P1

BTN 8-4 Review the opening feature of this chapter that highlights Jean Liu and **Didi Chuxing** (or **DiDi**). The company plans to open a kiosk in the Ferry Building in San Francisco to sell shirts, hats, and other merchandise. Other retail outlets and expansion plans may be in the works.

Required

1. List the seven principles of internal control and explain how a retail outlet might implement each of the principles in its store.
2. Do you believe that a retail outlet will need to add controls to the business as it expands? Explain.

9 Accounting for Receivables

Chapter Preview

VALUING RECEIVABLES	DIRECT WRITE-OFF METHOD	ALLOWANCE METHOD	NOTES RECEIVABLE
C1 Sales on credit	P1 Recording bad debts	P2 Recording and writing off bad debts	C2 Maturity and interest
Sales on bank card	Recovery of bad debts	Recovery of bad debts	P4 Accounting for notes
Sales on installment	When to use direct write-off	P3 Estimating bad debts	C3 Selling and pledging
			A1 Receivable turnover
NTK 9-1	NTK 9-2	NTK 9-3, 9-4	NTK 9-5

Learning Objectives

CONCEPTUAL

C1 Describe accounts receivable and how they occur and are recorded.

C2 Describe a note receivable, the computation of its maturity date, and the recording of its existence.

C3 Explain how receivables can be converted to cash before maturity.

ANALYTICAL

A1 Compute accounts receivable turnover and use it to help assess financial condition.

PROCEDURAL

P1 Apply the direct write-off method to accounts receivable.

P2 Apply the allowance method to accounts receivable.

P3 Estimate uncollectibles based on sales and accounts receivable.

P4 Record the honoring and dishonoring of a note and adjustments for interest.

Deserving Credit

"We've got something"—**NICHOLE MUSTARD**

SAN FRANCISCO—Nichole Mustard studied zoology in college. She planned to work in a lab after graduating until she found out that meant working with mice. "A bunch of mice was not a great future," laughs Nichole. Instead, Nichole completed some accounting courses, which gave her the skills to help co-found **Credit Karma (CreditKarma.com)**, a free credit report and financial management site.

Credit Karma provides users their current credit score along with a tracking feature that shows how their credit score has changed over time. One's credit score is driven by many factors, including on-time payment history, usage of credit, number of derogatory marks, and number of accounts. Credit card companies and financial institutions use credit scores to determine whether or not to extend credit.

Credit Karma, Inc.

Nichole initially struggled with how to make money from this free service. "It was like hitting a brick wall," recalls Nichole. Things changed when Nichole began to apply predictive analytics to give recommendations on which credit cards and loans are likely to be approved. "It was like lights going on," says Nichole.

Today, financial institutions pay Credit Karma for referrals. When approving customers for use of credit cards and loans, the financial institution has a receivable from its customer. Interest is charged for loans and past-due credit card balances.

Nichole focuses on helping others. "To do this in a way that's really actually helping consumers and not just making money," insists Nichole, "that feels great!"

Sources: *Credit Karma website*, January 2021; *Business Insider*, August 2018

VALUING ACCOUNTS RECEIVABLE

A *receivable* is an amount due from another party. The two most common receivables are accounts receivable and notes receivable. Other receivables include interest receivable, rent receivable, tax refund receivable, and receivables from employees.

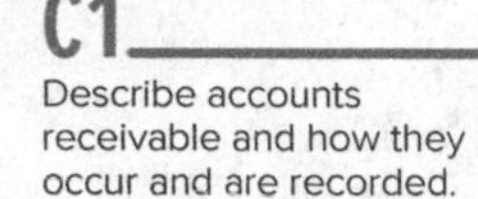
C1

Describe accounts receivable and how they occur and are recorded.

Accounts receivable are amounts due from customers for credit sales. Exhibit 9.1 shows amounts of receivables and their percent of total assets for some well-known companies.

EXHIBIT 9.1
Accounts Receivable

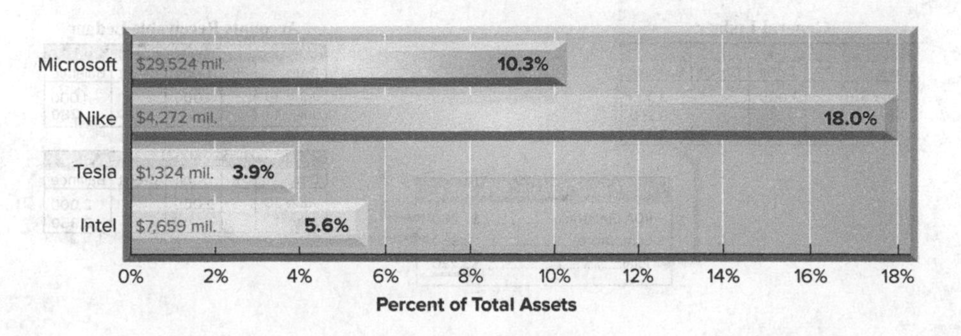

Sales on Credit Credit sales are recorded by increasing (debiting) Accounts Receivable. The general ledger has a single Accounts Receivable account called a *control* account. A company uses a separate account for each customer to track how much that customer purchases, has already paid, and still owes. A supplementary record has a separate account for each customer and is called the *accounts receivable ledger* or *accounts receivable subsidiary ledger*.

Exhibit 9.2 shows the relation between the Accounts Receivable account in the general ledger and its customer accounts in the accounts receivable ledger for TechCom, a small wholesaler. TechCom's accounts receivable reports a $3,000 ending balance for June 30. TechCom has two credit customers: CompStore and RDA Electronics. Its *schedule of accounts receivable* shows that the $3,000 balance of the Accounts Receivable account in the general ledger equals the total of its two customers' balances in the accounts receivable ledger.

EXHIBIT 9.2

General Ledger and the Accounts Receivable Ledger (before July 1)

General Ledger

Accounts Receivable

Date	PR	Debit	Credit	Balance
June 30		3,000		3,000

Accounts Receivable Ledger

RDA Electronics

Date	PR	Debit	Credit	Balance
June 30		1,000		1,000

CompStore

Date	PR	Debit	Credit	Balance
June 30		2,000		2,000

Schedule of Accounts Receivable

RDA Electronics	$1,000
CompStore	2,000
Total	$3,000

To see how to record accounts receivable from credit sales, we look at two transactions between TechCom and its credit customers—see Exhibit 9.3. The first is a credit sale of $950 to CompStore. The second is a collection of $720 from RDA Electronics from a prior credit sale.

EXHIBIT 9.3

Accounts Receivable Transactions

Assets = Liabilities + Equity
+950 +950

Assets = Liabilities + Equity
+720
−720

July 1	Accounts Receivable—CompStore	950	
	Sales		950
	*Record credit sales.**		
July 1	Cash	720	
	Accounts Receivable—RDA Electronics		720
	Record collection of credit sales.		

*We omit the entry to Dr. Cost of Sales and Cr. Inventory to focus on sales and receivables.

Exhibit 9.4 shows the general ledger and the accounts receivable ledger after recording the two July 1 transactions. The general ledger shows the effects of the sale, the collection, and the resulting balance of $3,230. These transactions are also shown in the individual customer accounts: RDA Electronics's ending balance is $280 and CompStore's ending balance is $2,950. The $3,230 total of customer accounts equals the balance of the Accounts Receivable account in the general ledger.

EXHIBIT 9.4

General Ledger and the Accounts Receivable Ledger (after July 1)

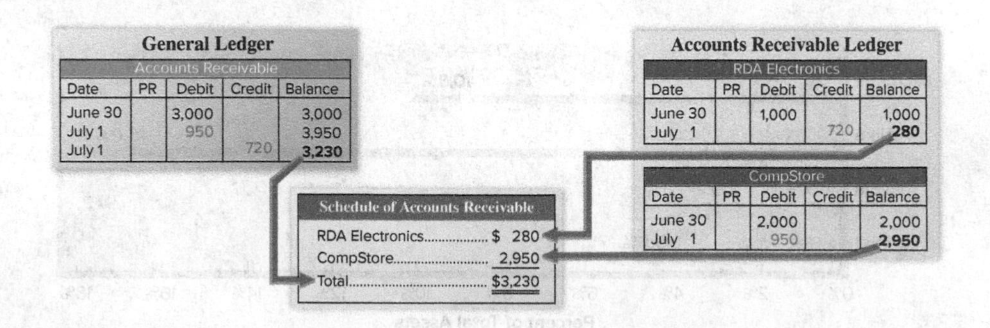

General Ledger

Accounts Receivable

Date	PR	Debit	Credit	Balance
June 30		3,000		3,000
July 1		950		3,950
July 1			720	3,230

Accounts Receivable Ledger

RDA Electronics

Date	PR	Debit	Credit	Balance
June 30		1,000		1,000
July 1			720	280

CompStore

Date	PR	Debit	Credit	Balance
June 30		2,000		2,000
July 1		950		2,950

Schedule of Accounts Receivable

RDA Electronics	$ 280
CompStore	2,950
Total	$3,230

Sales on Bank Credit Cards Most companies allow customers to pay using bank (or third-party) credit cards, such as **Visa**, **Mastercard**, or **American Express**, and debit cards. Sellers allow customers to use credit cards and debit cards for several reasons. First, the seller does not have to decide who gets credit and how much. Second, the seller avoids the risk of customers not paying (this risk is transferred to the card company). Third, the seller typically receives cash from the card company sooner than had it granted credit directly to customers. Fourth, more credit options for customers can lead to more sales.

The seller pays a fee when a card is used by the customer, often ranging from 1% to 5% of card sales. This fee reduces the cash received by the seller. If TechCom has $100 of credit card sales with a 4% fee, the entry follows. Some sellers report Credit Card Expense in the income statement as a discount subtracted from sales to get net sales. Other sellers report

Point: JCPenney reported third-party credit card costs exceed $10 million.

it as a selling expense or an administrative expense. In this text, we report credit card expense as a selling expense.

July 15	Cash	96	
	Credit Card Expense	4	
	Sales		100
	*Record credit card sales less 4% credit card expense.**		

*We omit the entry to Dr. Cost of Sales and Cr. Inventory to focus on credit card expense.

Assets = Liabilities + Equity
+96 +100
−4

Decision Maker

Dragon Images/Shutterstock

Entrepreneur As a small retailer, you are considering allowing customers to use credit cards. Until now, your store accepted only cash. What analysis do you use to decide? ■ *Answer:* This analysis must weigh benefits versus costs. The main benefit is the potential to increase sales by attracting customers who prefer credit cards. The main cost is the fee charged by the credit card company. We must estimate the expected increase in sales from allowing credit cards and then subtract (1) normal costs and expenses and (2) card fees from the expected sales increase. If analysis shows an increase in profit, the store should probably accept credit cards.

NEED-TO-KNOW 9-1

Credit Card Sales

C1

Prepare journal entries to record the following transactions for a retailer that uses the perpetual inventory system.

Jan. 2 Sold merchandise for $1,000 (that had cost $600) and accepted the customer's AA Bank Card. AA charges a 5% fee.

6 Sold merchandise for $400 (that had cost $300) and accepted the customer's VIZA Card. VIZA charges a 3% fee.

Solution

Jan. 2	Cash	950	
	Credit Card Expense*	50	
	Sales		1,000
	Record credit card sales less 5% fee.		
	**($1,000 × 0.05)*		
Jan. 2	Cost of Goods Sold	600	
	Merchandise Inventory		600
	Record cost of sales.		

Jan. 6	Cash	388	
	Credit Card Expense†	12	
	Sales		400
	Record credit card sales less 3% fee.		
	†($400 × 0.03)		
Jan. 6	Cost of Goods Sold	300	
	Merchandise Inventory		300
	Record cost of sales.		

Do More: QS 9-1, E 9-1, E 9-2

DIRECT WRITE-OFF METHOD

P1 Apply the direct write-off method to accounts receivable.

When a company directly grants credit to customers, it expects some customers will not pay what they promised. The accounts of these customers are *uncollectible accounts,* or **bad debts.** Uncollectible accounts are an expense of selling on credit. Why do companies sell on credit if they expect uncollectible accounts? The answer is that companies believe that granting credit will increase total sales enough to offset bad debts. Companies use two methods for uncollectible accounts: (1) direct write-off method and (2) allowance method.

Recording and Writing Off Bad Debts The **direct write-off method** records the loss from an uncollectible account receivable when it is determined to be uncollectible. No attempt is made to predict bad debts expense. If TechCom determines on January 23 that it cannot collect $520 owed by its customer J. Kent, it records the loss as follows. The debit in this entry charges the uncollectible amount directly to the current period's Bad Debts Expense account. The credit removes its balance from the Accounts Receivable account.

Assets = Liabilities + Equity
−520 −520

Jan. 23	Bad Debts Expense	520	
	Accounts Receivable—J. Kent		520
	Write off an uncollectible account.		

Recovering a Bad Debt Sometimes an account written off is later collected. If the account of J. Kent that was written off directly to Bad Debts Expense is later collected in full, then we record two entries.

Assets = Liabilities + Equity
+520 +520

Assets = Liabilities + Equity
+520
−520

Mar. 11	Accounts Receivable—J. Kent	520	
	Bad Debts Expense		520
	Reinstate account previously written off.		
Mar. 11	Cash	520	
	Accounts Receivable—J. Kent		520
	Record full payment of account.		

Direct write-off method
Advantages:
- Simple
- No estimates needed

Disadvantages:
- Receivables and income temporarily overstated
- Bad debts expense often not matched with sales

Using Direct Write-Off Method Many publicly traded companies and thousands of privately held companies use the direct write-off method; they include **Rand Medical Billing, Gateway Distributors, First Industrial Realty, New Frontier Energy, Globalink, and Sub Surface Waste Management**. The following disclosure by **Pharma-Bio Serv** is the usual justification: Bad debts are mainly accounted for using the direct write-off method . . . this method approximates that of the allowance method.

Companies weigh at least two concepts when considering use of the direct write-off method: (1) *Expense recognition*—requires expenses be reported in the same period as the sales they helped produce. (2) *Materiality* constraint—GAAP permits use of the simple, low-cost direct write-off method when its results approximate those using the allowance method.

NEED-TO-KNOW 9-2

Entries under Direct Write-Off Method

P1

A retailer uses the direct write-off method. Record the following transactions.

Feb. 14 The retailer determines that it cannot collect $400 of its accounts receivable from a customer named ZZZ Company.

Apr. 1 ZZZ Company unexpectedly pays its account in full to the retailer, which then records its recovery of this bad debt.

Solution

Feb. 14	Bad Debts Expense	400	
	Accounts Receivable—ZZZ Co.		400
	Write off an account.		
Apr. 1	Accounts Receivable—ZZZ Co.	400	
	Bad Debts Expense		400
	Reinstate an account previously written off.		
Apr. 1	Cash	400	
	Accounts Receivable—ZZZ Co.		400
	Record cash received on credit.		

Do More: QS 9-2, QS 9-3, E 9-4

ALLOWANCE METHOD

The **allowance method** for bad debts matches the *estimated* loss from uncollectible accounts receivable against the sales they helped produce. We use estimated losses because when sales occur, sellers do not know which customers will not pay. This means that at the end of each period, the allowance method requires an estimate of the total bad debts expected from that period's sales. This method has two advantages over the direct write-off method: (1) It records estimated bad debts expense in the period when the related sales are recorded and (2) it reports accounts receivable on the balance sheet at the estimated amount to be collected.

P2

Apply the allowance method to accounts receivable.

Recording Bad Debts Expense The allowance method estimates bad debts expense at the end of each accounting period and records it with an adjusting entry. TechCom had credit sales of $300,000 in its first year of operations. At the end of the first year, $20,000 of credit sales were uncollected. TechCom estimates that $1,500 of its accounts receivable is uncollectible and makes the following adjusting entry. (*How to estimate bad debts is explained in the next section.*)

Method	Bad Debts Expense Recorded . . .
Direct write-off. . .	*In future,* when accounts are uncollectible.
Allowance.	*Currently,* using estimated uncollectibles.

Dec. 31	Bad Debts Expense	1,500	
	Allowance for Doubtful Accounts.		1,500
	Record estimated bad debts.		

Assets = Liabilities + Equity
−1,500 −1,500

The estimated Bad Debts Expense of $1,500 is reported on the income statement (as either a selling expense or an administrative expense). The **Allowance for Doubtful Accounts** is a contra asset account. TechCom's account balances for Accounts Receivable and the Allowance for Doubtful Accounts follow.

Allowance method

Advantages:
- Receivables fairly stated
- Bad debts expense matched with sales
- Writing off bad debt does not affect net receivables or income

Disadvantages:
- Estimates needed

Accounts Receivable			
Dec. 31	20,000		

Allowance for Doubtful Accounts			
		Dec. 31	1,500

The Allowance for Doubtful Accounts credit balance of $1,500 reduces accounts receivable to its **realizable value,** which is the amount expected to be received. Although credit customers owe $20,000 to TechCom, only $18,500 is expected from customers. (TechCom still bills its customers for $20,000.) In the balance sheet, the Allowance for Doubtful Accounts is subtracted from Accounts Receivable and is reported in either of the following ways.

Current assets		
Accounts receivable	$20,000	
Less allowance for doubtful accounts	1,500	$18,500

or

Current assets	
Accounts receivable (net of $1,500 doubtful accounts).	$18,500

Writing Off a Bad Debt When specific accounts become uncollectible, they are written off against the Allowance for Doubtful Accounts. TechCom decides that J. Kent's $520 account is uncollectible and makes the following entry to write it off.

Jan. 23	Allowance for Doubtful Accounts	520	
	Accounts Receivable—J. Kent.		520
	Write off an uncollectible account.		

Assets = Liabilities + Equity
+520
−520

Point: Bad Debts Expense is not debited in the write-off because it was recorded in the period when sales occurred.

This entry removes $520 from the Accounts Receivable account (and the subsidiary ledger). The general ledger accounts appear as follows.

Accounts Receivable			
Dec. 31	20,000	Jan. 23	520

Allowance for Doubtful Accounts			
Jan. 23	520	Dec. 31	1,500

The write-off does *not* affect the realizable value of accounts receivable; see Exhibit 9.5. Neither total assets nor net income is affected by the write-off of a specific account. Instead, both assets and net income are affected in the period when bad debts expense is predicted and recorded with an adjusting entry.

EXHIBIT 9.5

Before and After Write-Off of a Bad Debt

	Before Write-Off	After Write-Off
Accounts receivable	$ 20,000	$ 19,480
Less allowance for doubtful accounts	1,500	980
Realizable value of accounts receivable	$18,500	$18,500

Exhibit 9.6 portrays the allowance method. It shows the creation of the allowance for future write-offs—adding to a cookie jar. It also shows the decrease of the allowance through write-offs—taking cookies from the jar.

EXHIBIT 9.6

Allowance for Doubtful Accounts

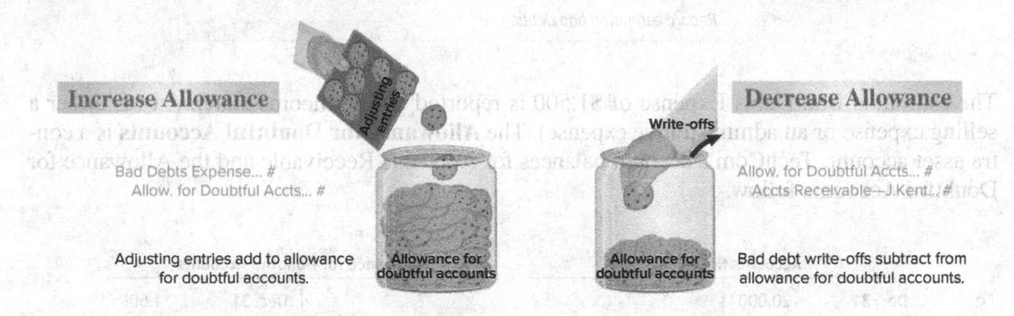

Recovering a Bad Debt

If an account that was written off is later collected, two entries are made. The first is to reverse the write-off and reinstate the customer's account. The second is to record the collection of the reinstated account. If on March 11 Kent pays in full his account previously written off, the entries are

Mar. 11	Accounts Receivable—J. Kent	520	
	Allowance for Doubtful Accounts		520
	Reinstate account previously written off.		
Mar. 11	Cash	520	
	Accounts Receivable—J. Kent		520
	Record full payment of account.		

Assets = Liabilities + Equity
+520
−520

Assets = Liabilities + Equity
+520
−520

Kent paid the entire amount previously written off, but sometimes a customer pays only a portion. If we believe this customer will later pay in full, we return the entire amount owed to accounts receivable (in the first entry only). If we expect no further collection, we return only the amount paid.

Elnur/Shutterstock

Analytics Insight

Customer Analytics Financial institutions and credit card companies use data analytics to predict the risk of extending credit to customers. When evaluating a customer, they use analytics that include credit scores, income, employment, and payment history. ■

NEED-TO-KNOW 9-3

Entries under Allowance Method

P2

Do More: QS 9-4, QS 9-5, QS 9-6, E 9-5, E 9-6, E 9-7, E 9-8

A retailer uses the allowance method. Record the following transactions.

Dec. 31 The retailer estimates $3,000 of its accounts receivable are uncollectible at its year-end.
Feb. 14 The retailer determines that it cannot collect $400 of its accounts receivable from a customer named ZZZ Company.
Apr. 1 ZZZ Company unexpectedly pays its account in full to the retailer, which then records its recovery of this bad debt.

Solution

Date	Account	Debit	Credit
Dec. 31	Bad Debts Expense.	3,000	
	Allowance for Doubtful Accounts		3,000
	Record estimated bad debts.		
Feb. 14	Allowance for Doubtful Accounts.	400	
	Accounts Receivable—ZZZ Co.		400
	Write off an account.		

Date	Account	Debit	Credit
Apr. 1	Accounts Receivable—ZZZ Co.	400	
	Allowance for Doubtful Accounts		400
	Reinstate an account previously written off.		
Apr. 1	Cash.	400	
	Accounts Receivable—ZZZ Co.		400
	Record cash received on credit.		

ESTIMATING BAD DEBTS FOR ALLOWANCE METHOD

P3

Estimate uncollectibles based on sales and accounts receivable.

Bad debts expense is estimated under the allowance method. This section covers methods for estimating bad debts expense.

Percent of Sales Method

The *percent of sales method,* or *income statement method,* assumes that a percent of credit sales for the period is uncollectible. For example, Musicland has credit sales of $400,000 in 2021. Musicland estimates 0.6% of credit sales to be uncollectible. This means Musicland expects $2,400 of bad debts expense from its sales ($400,000 × 0.006) and makes the following adjusting entry.

Date	Account	Debit	Credit
Dec. 31	Bad Debts Expense	2,400	
	Allowance for Doubtful Accounts		2,400
	Record estimated bad debts.		

Assets	=	Liabilities	+	Equity
−2,400				−2,400

Allowance for Doubtful Accounts, a balance sheet account, is not closed at period-end. Unless a company is in its first period of operations, its Allowance for Doubtful Accounts balance rarely equals the Bad Debts Expense balance. (When computing bad debts expense as a percent of sales, managers monitor and adjust the percent so it is not too high or too low.)

Point: When using the *percent of sales method* for estimating uncollectibles, and because the "Unadj. bal." in Bad Debts Expense is always $0, the adjusting entry amount always equals the % of sales.

Percent of Receivables Method

The *percent of accounts receivable method,* a *balance sheet method,* assumes that a percent of a company's receivables is uncollectible. This percent is based on experience and economic trends. Total receivables is multiplied by this percent to get the estimated uncollectible amount as reported in the balance sheet as Allowance for Doubtful Accounts.

Assume Musicland has $50,000 of accounts receivable on December 31, 2021. It estimates 5% of its receivables is uncollectible. This means that *after* the adjusting entry is posted, we want the Allowance for Doubtful Accounts to show a $2,500 credit balance (5% of $50,000). Musicland's beginning balance is $2,200 on December 31, 2020—see Exhibit 9.7.

EXHIBIT 9.7

Allowance for Doubtful Accounts after Bad Debts Adjusting Entry

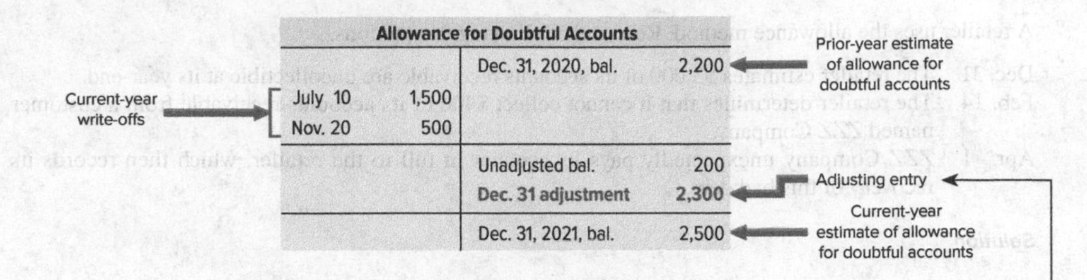

Allowance for Doubtful Accounts			
		Dec. 31, 2020, bal.	2,200
July 10	1,500		
Nov. 20	500		
		Unadjusted bal.	200
		Dec. 31 adjustment	2,300
		Dec. 31, 2021, bal.	2,500

Prior-year estimate of allowance for doubtful accounts
Current-year write-offs
Adjusting entry
Current-year estimate of allowance for doubtful accounts

During 2021, accounts of customers are written off on July 10 and November 20. The account has a $200 credit balance *before* the December 31, 2021, adjustment. The adjusting entry to give the allowance account the estimated $2,500 balance is

Assets = Liabilities + Equity
−2,300 −2,300

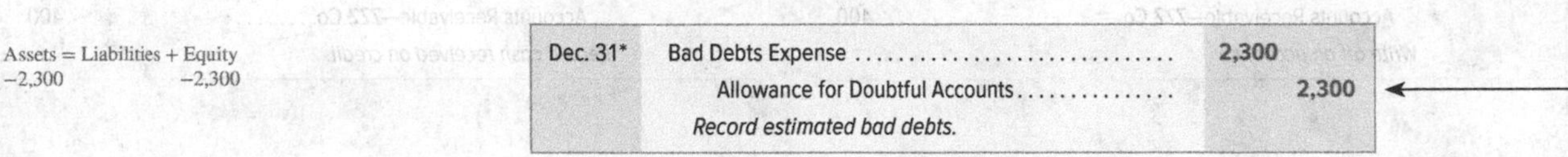

Dec. 31*	Bad Debts Expense	2,300	
	Allowance for Doubtful Accounts		2,300
	Record estimated bad debts.		

*The adjusting entry applies our three-step adjusting entry process:
Step 1: Current balance for Allowance account is $200 credit.
Step 2: Current balance for Allowance account should be $2,500 credit.
Step 3: Record entry to get from step 1 to step 2.

Aging of Receivables Method

The **aging of accounts receivable** method, another *balance sheet method,* is applied like the percent of receivables method except that several percentages are used (versus one) to estimate the allowance. Each receivable is classified by how long it is past its due date. Then estimates of uncollectible amounts are made assuming that the longer an amount is past due, the more likely it is uncollectible. After the amounts are classified (or aged), experience is used to estimate the percent of each uncollectible class. These percents are multiplied by the amounts in each class to get the estimated balance of the Allowance for Doubtful Accounts. An example schedule is shown in Exhibit 9.8.

Exhibit 9.8 lists each customer's balance assigned to one of five classes based on its days past due. The amounts in each class are totaled and multiplied by the estimated percent of uncollectible accounts for each class. To explain, Musicland has $3,700 in accounts receivable that are 31 to 60 days past due. Management estimates 10% of the amounts in this class are uncollectible, or a total of $370 ($3,700 × 10%). Similar analysis is done for each class. The final total of

EXHIBIT 9.8

Aging of Accounts Receivable

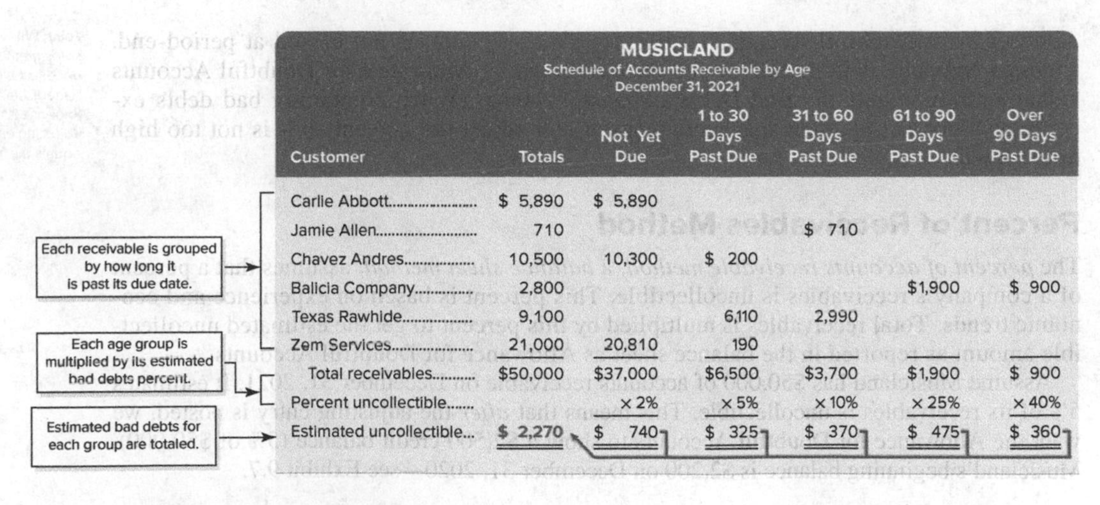

MUSICLAND
Schedule of Accounts Receivable by Age
December 31, 2021

Customer	Totals	Not Yet Due	1 to 30 Days Past Due	31 to 60 Days Past Due	61 to 90 Days Past Due	Over 90 Days Past Due
Carlie Abbott	$ 5,890	$ 5,890				
Jamie Allen	710			$ 710		
Chavez Andres	10,500	10,300	$ 200			
Balicia Company	2,800				$1,900	$ 900
Texas Rawhide	9,100		6,110	2,990		
Zem Services	21,000	20,810	190			
Total receivables	$50,000	$37,000	$6,500	$3,700	$1,900	$ 900
Percent uncollectible		× 2%	× 5%	× 10%	× 25%	× 40%
Estimated uncollectible	$ 2,270	$ 740	$ 325	$ 370	$ 475	$ 360

Each receivable is grouped by how long it is past its due date.
Each age group is multiplied by its estimated bad debts percent.
Estimated bad debts for each group are totaled.

$2,270 ($740 + $325 + $370 + $475 + $360) shown in the first column is the estimated balance for the Allowance for Doubtful Accounts.

Unadjusted Credit Balance in the Allowance Account Exhibit 9.9 shows that because the allowance account has an unadjusted credit balance of $200, the required adjustment to the

EXHIBIT 9.9

Adjustment for the Accounts Receivable Method

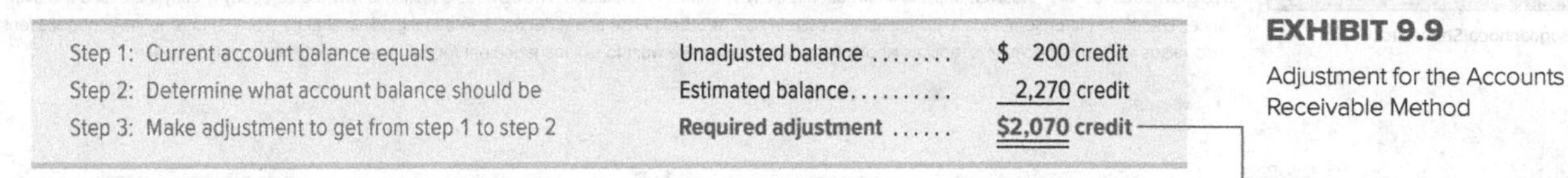

Step 1: Current account balance equals	Unadjusted balance	$ 200 credit
Step 2: Determine what account balance should be	Estimated balance..........	2,270 credit
Step 3: Make adjustment to get from step 1 to step 2	**Required adjustment**	**$2,070 credit**

Allowance for Doubtful Accounts is $2,070. (We can use a T-account for this analysis as shown to the side.) This analysis yields the following end-of-period adjusting entry.

Allowance for Doubtful Accounts		
	Unadj. bal.	200
	Req. adj.	**2,070**
	Est. bal.	2,270

Dec. 31	Bad Debts Expense	2,070	
	Allowance for Doubtful Accounts..............		2,070
	Record estimated bad debts.		

Assets = Liabilities + Equity
−2,070 −2,070

Unadjusted Debit Balance in the Allowance Account If the allowance account had an unadjusted *debit* balance of $500 instead of the $200 credit balance, its required adjustment would be computed as follows.

Point: A debit balance implies that write-offs for that period exceed the total allowance.

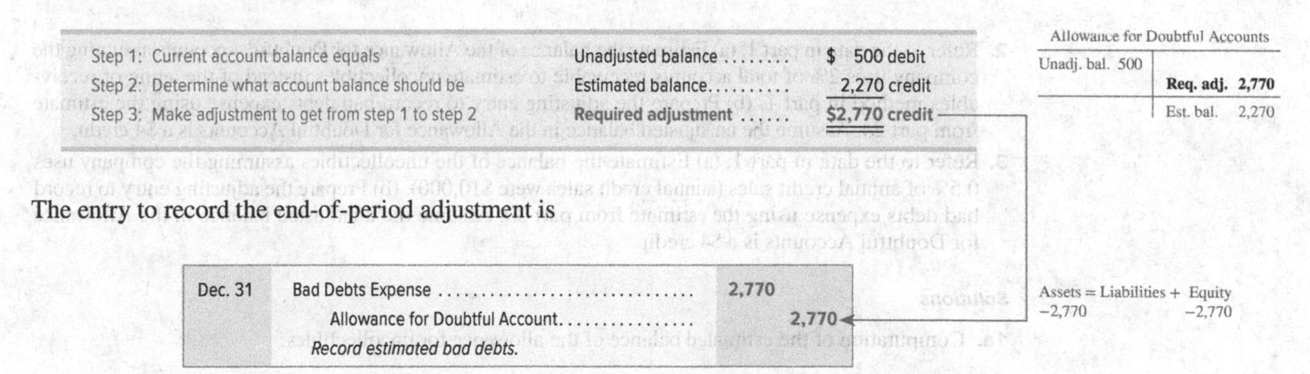

Step 1: Current account balance equals	Unadjusted balance	$ 500 debit
Step 2: Determine what account balance should be	Estimated balance..........	2,270 credit
Step 3: Make adjustment to get from step 1 to step 2	**Required adjustment**	**$2,770 credit**

Allowance for Doubtful Accounts		
Unadj. bal. 500		
	Req. adj.	**2,770**
	Est. bal.	2,270

The entry to record the end-of-period adjustment is

Dec. 31	Bad Debts Expense	2,770	
	Allowance for Doubtful Account...............		2,770
	Record estimated bad debts.		

Assets = Liabilities + Equity
−2,770 −2,770

Estimating Bad Debts—Summary of Methods Exhibit 9.10 summarizes the three estimation methods. The aging of accounts receivable method focuses on specific accounts and is usually the most reliable of the estimation methods.

EXHIBIT 9.10

Methods to Estimate Bad Debts under the Allowance Method

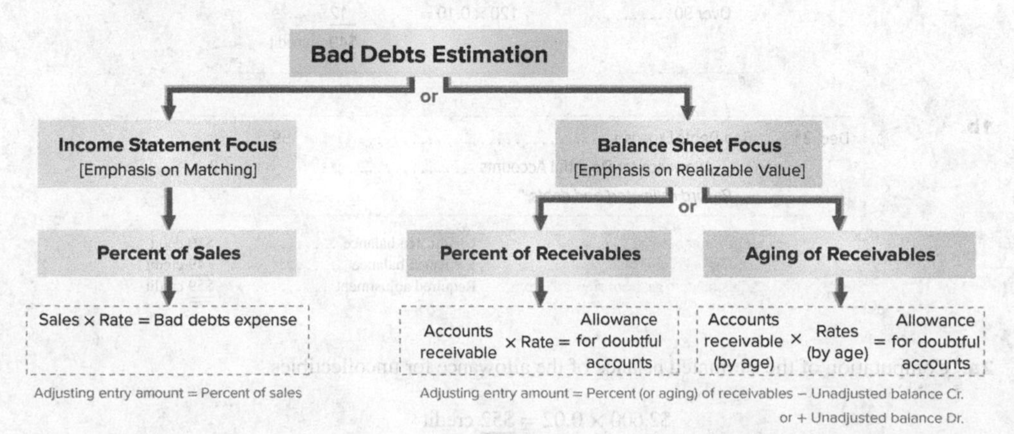

Bogdanhoda/Shutterstock

Decision Maker

Labor Union One week prior to labor contract negotiations, financial statements are released showing no income growth. A 10% growth was predicted. Your analysis finds that the company increased its allowance for uncollectibles from 1.5% to 4.5% of receivables. Without this change, income would show a 9% growth. Does this analysis impact negotiations? ■ *Answer:* Yes, this information is likely to impact negotiations. The obvious question is why the company greatly increased this allowance. The large increase means a substantial increase in bad debts expense and a decrease in earnings. This change (coming prior to labor negotiations) also raises concerns because it reduces labor's bargaining power. We want to ask management for documentation justifying this increase.

NEED-TO-KNOW 9-4

Estimating Bad Debts

P3

At its December 31 year-end, a company estimates uncollectible accounts using the allowance method.

1. It prepared the following aging of receivables analysis. (a) Estimate the balance of the Allowance for Doubtful Accounts using the aging of accounts receivable method. (b) Prepare the adjusting entry to record bad debts expense using the estimate from part *a*. Assume the unadjusted balance in the Allowance for Doubtful Accounts is a $10 debit.

		Days Past Due				
	Total	0	1 to 30	31 to 60	61 to 90	Over 90
Accounts receivable	$2,600	$2,000	$300	$80	$100	$120
Percent uncollectible		1%	2%	5%	7%	10%

2. Refer to the data in part 1. (a) Estimate the balance of the Allowance for Doubtful Accounts assuming the company uses 2% of total accounts receivable to estimate uncollectibles instead of the aging of receivables method in part 1. (b) Prepare the adjusting entry to record bad debts expense using the estimate from part 2*a*. Assume the unadjusted balance in the Allowance for Doubtful Accounts is a $4 credit.

3. Refer to the data in part 1. (a) Estimate the balance of the uncollectibles assuming the company uses 0.5% of annual credit sales (annual credit sales were $10,000). (b) Prepare the adjusting entry to record bad debts expense using the estimate from part 3*a*. Assume the unadjusted balance in the Allowance for Doubtful Accounts is a $4 credit.

Solutions

1a. Computation of the estimated balance of the allowance for uncollectibles.

Not due	$2,000 × 0.01 =	$20	
1 to 30	300 × 0.02 =	6	
31 to 60	80 × 0.05 =	4	
61 to 90	100 × 0.07 =	7	
Over 90	120 × 0.10 =	12	
		$49	credit

1b.

Dec. 31	Bad Debts Expense	59	
	Allowance for Doubtful Accounts		59
	*Record estimated bad debts.**		

Allowance for Doubtful Accounts			
Unadj. Dec. 31	10		
		Adj. Dec. 31	59
		Est. bal. Dec. 31	49

Step 1:	Current account balance equals	*Unadjusted balance	$10 debit
Step 2:	Determine what account balance should be	Estimated balance	49 credit
Step 3:	Make adjustment to get from step 1 to step 2	Required adjustment	$59 credit

2a. Computation of the estimated balance of the allowance for uncollectibles.

$2,600 × 0.02 = $52 credit

2b.

Dec. 31	Bad Debts Expense	48	
	Allowance for Doubtful Accounts		48
	*Record estimated bad debts.**		

Step 1: Current account balance equals	*Unadjusted balance	$ 4 credit
Step 2: Determine what account balance should be	Estimated balance	52 credit
Step 3: Make adjustment to get from step 1 to step 2	Required adjustment	$48 credit

Allowance for Doubtful Accounts		
	Unadj. Dec. 31	4
	Adj. Dec. 31	**48**
	Est. bal. Dec. 31	52

3a. Computation of the estimated balance of the bad debts expense.

$$\$10{,}000 \times 0.005 = \underline{\underline{\$50}} \text{ credit}$$

3b.

Dec. 31	Bad Debts Expense	50	
	Allowance for Doubtful Accounts		50
	Record estimated bad debts.		

Do More: QS 9-7, QS 9-8, QS 9-9, E 9-9, E 9-10, E 9-11, E 9-12, E 9-13, E 9-14

NOTES RECEIVABLE

C2 Describe a note receivable, the computation of its maturity date, and the recording of its existence.

A **promissory note** is a written promise to pay a specified amount, usually with interest, either on demand or at a stated future date. Promissory notes are used in many transactions, including paying for products and services and lending and borrowing money. Sellers sometimes ask for a note to replace an account receivable when a customer requests more time to pay a past-due account. Sellers prefer notes when the credit period is long and when the receivable is for a large amount. If a lawsuit is needed to collect from a customer, a note is the customer's written promise to pay the debt, its amount, and its terms.

Exhibit 9.11 shows a promissory note dated July 10, 2021. For this note, Julia Browne promises to pay TechCom or to its order a specified amount ($1,000), called the **principal of a note,** at a stated future date (October 8, 2021). As the one who signed the note and promised to pay it, Browne is the **maker of the note.** As the person to whom the note is payable, TechCom is the **payee of the note.** To Browne, the note is a liability called a *note payable*. To TechCom, the same note is an asset called a *note receivable*. This note's interest rate is 12%, as written on the note. **Interest** is the charge for using the money until its due date. To a borrower, interest is an expense. To a lender, it is revenue.

EXHIBIT 9.11

Promissory Note

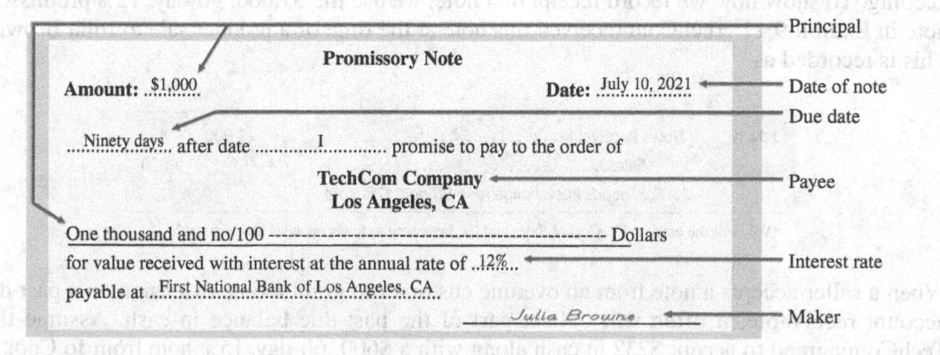

Computing Maturity and Interest

This section covers a note's maturity date, period covered, and interest computation.

Maturity Date and Period The **maturity date of a note** is the day the note (principal and interest) must be repaid. The *period* of a note is the time from the note's (contract) date to its maturity date. Many notes mature in less than a full year, and the period they cover is often expressed in days. As an example, a 90-day note dated July 10 matures on October 8. This count is shown in Exhibit 9.12. The period of a note is sometimes expressed in months or years. When months are used, the note is payable in the month of its maturity on the *same day of the month* as its original date. A nine-month note dated July 10, for example, is payable on April 10. The same rule applies when years are used.

Point: When counting days, omit the day a note is issued, but count the due date.

EXHIBIT 9.12

Maturity Date Computation

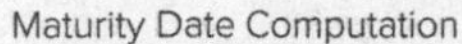

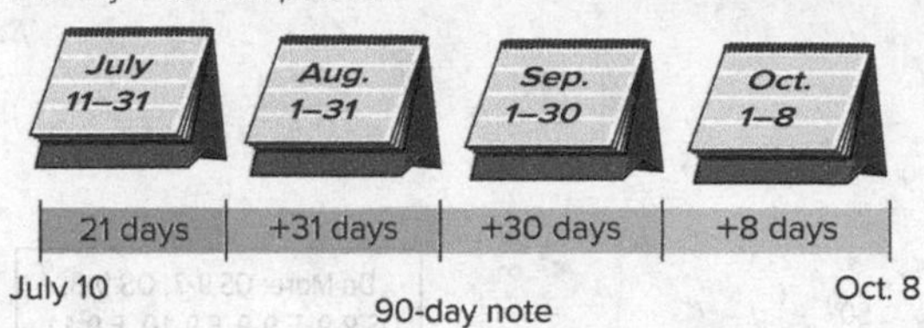

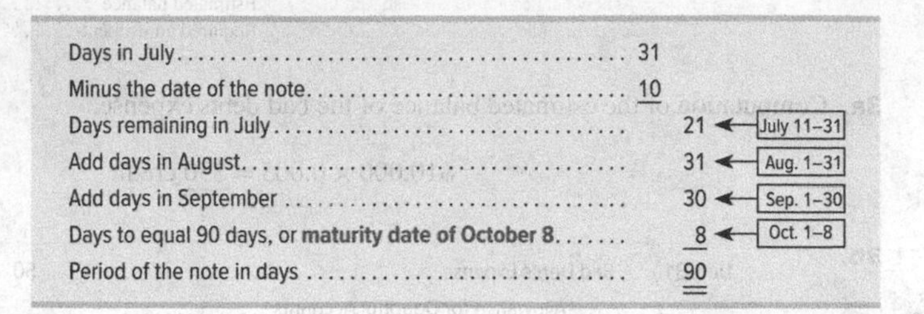

Days in July	31	
Minus the date of the note	10	
Days remaining in July	21	July 11–31
Add days in August	31	Aug. 1–31
Add days in September	30	Sep. 1–30
Days to equal 90 days, or **maturity date of October 8**	8	Oct. 1–8
Period of the note in days	90	

Point: Excel for maturity date.

	A	B
1	Note date	10-Jul
2	# of days	90
3	Maturity	

=B1+B2 = 8-Oct

Interest Computation

Interest is the cost of borrowing money for the borrower and the profit from lending money for the lender. Unless otherwise stated, the rate of interest on a note is the rate charged for the use of principal for one year (*annual rate*). The formula for computing interest on a note is in Exhibit 9.13.

EXHIBIT 9.13

Computation of Interest

$$\text{Principal of the note} \times \text{Annual interest rate} \times \text{Time expressed in fraction of year} = \text{Interest}$$

To simplify interest computations, a year is commonly treated as having 360 days (called the *banker's rule* and widely used in business transactions). **We treat a year as having 360 days for interest computations in examples and assignments.** Using the promissory note in Exhibit 9.11, where we have a 90-day, 12%, $1,000 note, the total interest follows.

Point: If the *banker's rule* is not used, interest is **$29.589041**. The *banker's rule* yields $30, which is easier to account for than $29.589041.

$$\$1{,}000 \times 12\% \times \frac{90}{360} = \$1{,}000 \times 0.12 \times 0.25 = \$30$$

Recording Notes Receivable

Notes receivable are usually recorded in a single Notes Receivable account to simplify record-keeping. To show how we record receipt of a note, we use the $1,000, 90-day, 12% promissory note in Exhibit 9.11. TechCom received this note at the time of a product sale to Julia Browne. This is recorded as

Assets = Liabilities + Equity
+1,000 +1,000

July 10*	Notes Receivable	1,000	
	Sales		1,000
	Sold goods in exchange for a 90-day, 12% note.		

*We omit the entry to Dr. Cost of Sales and Cr. Inventory to focus on sales and receivables.

When a seller accepts a note from an overdue customer to grant a time extension on a past-due account receivable, it often will collect part of the past-due balance in cash. Assume that TechCom agreed to accept $232 in cash along with a $600, 60-day, 15% note from Jo Cook to settle her $832 past-due account. TechCom makes the following entry.

Assets = Liabilities + Equity
+232
+600
−832

Oct. 5	Cash	232	
	Notes Receivable	600	
	Accounts Receivable—J. Cook		832
	Received cash and note to settle account.		

Valuing and Settling Notes

P4 Record the honoring and dishonoring of a note and adjustments for interest.

Recording an Honored Note The principal and interest of a note are due on its maturity date. The maker of the note usually *honors* the note and pays it in full. When J. Cook pays the note above on its due date, TechCom records it as follows. Interest revenue is reported on the income statement.

Date	Account	Debit	Credit
Dec. 4	Cash	615	
	Notes Receivable		600
	Interest Revenue		15
	Collect note with interest of $600 × 15% × 60/360.		

Assets = Liabilities + Equity
+615 +15
−600

Recording a Dishonored Note When a note's maker does not pay at maturity, the note is *dishonored.* Dishonoring a note does not mean the maker no longer has to pay. The payee still tries to collect. How do companies report this? The balance of the Notes Receivable account should only include notes that have not matured. When a note is dishonored, we remove the amount of this note from Notes Receivable and charge it to an account receivable from its maker. Assume that J. Cook dishonors the note at maturity. The following records the dishonoring of the note.

Point: *Maturity value* of a note equals principal plus interest earned.

Date	Account	Debit	Credit
Dec. 4	Accounts Receivable—J. Cook	615	
	Interest Revenue		15
	Notes Receivable		600
	Charge account of J. Cook for a dishonored note and interest of $600 × 15% × 60/360.		

Assets = Liabilities + Equity
+615 +15
−600

Charging a dishonored note to accounts receivable does two things. First, it removes the note from the Notes Receivable account and records the dishonored note in the maker's account. Second, if the maker of the dishonored note asks for credit in the future, his or her account will show the dishonored note.

Recording End-of-Period Interest Adjustment When notes receivable are outstanding at period-end, any accrued interest is recorded. Assume on December 16 TechCom accepts a $3,000, 60-day, 12% note from a customer. When TechCom's accounting period ends on December 31, $15 of interest has accrued on this note ($3,000 × 12% × 15/360). The following adjusting entry records this revenue.

Date	Account	Debit	Credit
Dec. 31	Interest Receivable	15	
	Interest Revenue		15
	Record accrued interest earned.		

Assets = Liabilities + Equity
+15 +15

Interest revenue is on the income statement, and interest receivable is on the balance sheet as a current asset. When the December 16 note is collected on February 14, TechCom's entry to record the cash receipt is

Date	Account	Debit	Credit
Feb. 14	Cash	3,060	
	Interest Revenue		45
	Interest Receivable		15
	Notes Receivable		3,000
	Received payment of note and its interest.		

Assets = Liabilities + Equity
+3,060 +45
−15
−3,000

Total interest on the 60-day note is $60 ($3,000 × 12% × 60/360). The $15 credit to Interest Receivable is the collection of interest accrued from the December 31 entry. The $45 interest revenue is from holding the note from January 1 to February 14.

NEED-TO-KNOW 9-5

Honoring and Dishonoring Notes

C2 P4

Do More: QS 9-11 through 9-17, E 9-18 through E 9-21

Ace Company purchases $1,400 of merchandise from Zitco on December 16. Zitco accepts Ace's $1,400, 90-day, 12% note as payment. Zitco's accounting period ends on December 31.

a. Prepare entries for Zitco on December 16 and December 31.

b. Prepare Zitco's March 16 entry if Ace dishonors the note.

c. Instead of the facts in part *b*, prepare Zitco's March 16 entry if Ace honors the note.

d. Assume the facts in part *b* (Ace dishonors the note). Then, on March 31, Zitco writes off the receivable from Ace Company. Prepare that write-off entry assuming that Zitco uses the allowance method.

Solution

a.

Dec. 16	Note Receivable—Ace	1,400	
	Sales†		1,400
Dec. 31	Interest Receivable	7	
	Interest Revenue (*$1,400 × 12% × 15/360*)		7

b.

Mar. 16	Accounts Receivable—Ace	1,442	
	Interest Revenue (*$1,400 × 12% × 75/360*)		35
	Interest Receivable		7
	Notes Receivable—Ace		1,400

c.

Mar. 16	Cash	1,442	
	Interest Revenue		35
	Interest Receivable		7
	Notes Receivable—Ace		1,400

d.

Mar. 31	Allowance for Doubtful Accounts	1,442	
	Accounts Receivable—Ace		1,442

†The entry for Cost of Goods Sold is not shown as cost of merchandise is not provided.

Disposal of Receivables

C3 Explain how receivables can be converted to cash before maturity.

Companies convert receivables to cash before they are due if they need cash or do not want to deal with collecting receivables. This is usually done by (1) selling them or (2) using them as security for a loan.

Selling Receivables A company can sell its receivables to a finance company or bank. The buyer, called a *factor,* acquires ownership of the receivables and receives cash when they come due. The seller is charged a *factoring fee*. By incurring a factoring fee, the seller gets cash earlier and can pass the risk of bad debts to the factor. The seller also avoids costs of billing and accounting for receivables. If TechCom sells $20,000 of its accounts receivable and is charged a 4% factoring fee, it records this sale as follows.

Assets = Liabilities + Equity
+19,200 −800
−20,000

Aug. 15	Cash	19,200	
	Factoring Fee Expense	800	
	Accounts Receivable		20,000
	Sold accounts receivable for cash less 4% fee.		

Pledging Receivables A company can borrow money by *pledging* its receivables as security for the loan. If the borrower defaults on (does not pay) the loan, the lender is paid from the cash receipts of the receivables. The borrower discloses pledging receivables in financial statement footnotes. If TechCom borrows $35,000 and pledges its receivables as security, it records

Assets = Liabilities + Equity
+35,000 + 35,000

Aug. 20	Cash	35,000	
	Notes Payable		35,000
	Borrow with a note secured by pledging receivables.		

Decision Maker

Saravutpics/Shutterstock

Analyst/Auditor You are reviewing accounts receivable of a coffee grower. Over the past five years, the allowance account as a percentage of gross accounts receivable shows a steady downward trend. What does this finding suggest? ■ *Answer:* The downward trend means the company is reducing the relative amount charged to bad debts expense each year. This action could be to increase net income. Alternatively, collections may have improved and fewer bad debts are justified.

Accounts Receivable Turnover  Decision Analysis

Accounts receivable turnover helps assess the quality and liquidity of receivables. *Quality* of receivables is the likelihood of collection without loss. *Liquidity* of receivables is the speed of collection. **Accounts receivable turnover** measures how often, on average, receivables are collected during the period and is defined in Exhibit 9.14.

EXHIBIT 9.14

Accounts Receivable Turnover

$$\textbf{Accounts receivable turnover} = \frac{\textbf{Net sales}}{\textbf{Average accounts receivable, net}}$$

A1 Compute accounts receivable turnover and use it to help assess financial condition.

The denominator is the *average* accounts receivable, net balance, computed as (Beginning balance + Ending balance) ÷ 2. TechCom has an accounts receivable turnover of 5.1. This means its average accounts receivable balance is converted into cash 5.1 times during the period, which is pictured here.

5.1 times per year

1 2 3 4 5

Jan. Feb. Mar. Apr. May June July Aug. Sep. Oct. Nov. Dec.

Accounts receivable turnover shows how well management is doing in granting credit to customers. A high turnover suggests that management should consider using less strict credit terms to increase sales. A low turnover suggests management should consider more strict credit terms and more aggressive collection efforts to avoid having assets tied up in accounts receivable.

Exhibit 9.15 shows accounts receivable turnover for **Visa** and **Mastercard**. Visa's current-year turnover is 16.7, computed as $22,977/$1,375 ($ millions). This means that Visa's average accounts receivable balance was converted into cash 16.7 times in the current year. Its turnover slightly decreased in the current year (16.7) compared with one year ago (17.6). Visa's turnover also exceeds that for Mastercard in each of these three years. Both Visa and Mastercard seem to be doing an adequate job of managing receivables.

EXHIBIT 9.15

Analysis Using Accounts Receivable Turnover

Company	Figure ($ millions)	Current Year	1 Year Ago	2 Years Ago
Visa	Net sales	$22,977	$20,609	$18,358
	Average accounts receivable, net	$ 1,375	$ 1,170	$ 1,087
	Accounts receivable turnover	**16.7**	**17.6**	**16.9**
Mastercard	Net sales	$16,883	$14,950	$12,497
	Average accounts receivable, net	$ 2,395	$ 2,123	$ 1,693
	Accounts receivable turnover	**7.0**	**7.0**	**7.4**

Decision Maker

Dietitian Your private practice is barely profitable, so you hire an analyst. The analyst says, *"Accounts receivable turnover is too low. Tighter credit policies are recommended along with discontinuing service to those most delayed in payments."* What actions do you take? ■ *Answer:* Both suggestions are probably financially wise recommendations, but we may be troubled by eliminating services to those less able to pay. One alternative is to follow the recommendations but start a care program directed at clients less able to pay for services. This allows you to continue services to clients less able to pay and to discontinue services to clients able but unwilling to pay.

NEED-TO-KNOW 9-6

COMPREHENSIVE

Recording Accounts and Notes Receivable Transactions; Estimating Bad Debts

Clayco Company completes the following transactions during the year.

July 14 Writes off a $750 account receivable arising from a sale to Briggs Company that dates to 10 months ago. (Clayco Company uses the allowance method.)

30 Clayco Company receives a $1,000, 90-day, 10% note in exchange for merchandise sold to Sumrell Company (the merchandise cost $600).

Aug. 15 Receives $2,000 cash plus a $10,000 note from JT Co. in exchange for merchandise that sells for $12,000 (its cost is $8,000). The note is dated August 15, bears 12% interest, and matures in 120 days.

Nov. 1 Completes a $200 credit card sale with a 4% fee (the cost of sales is $150). The cash is transferred immediately from the credit card company.

3 Sumrell Company refuses to pay the note that was due to Clayco Company on October 28. Prepare the journal entry to charge the dishonored note plus accrued interest to Sumrell Company's accounts receivable.

5 Completes a $500 credit card sale with a 5% fee (the cost of sales is $300). The cash is transferred immediately from the credit card company.

15 Receives the full amount of $750 from Briggs Company that was previously written off on July 14. Record the bad debts recovery.

Dec. 13 Receives payment of principal plus interest from JT for the August 15 note.

Required

1. Prepare Clayco Company's journal entries to record these transactions.

2. Prepare a year-end adjusting journal entry as of December 31 for each separate situation.

a. Bad debts are estimated to be $20,400 by aging accounts receivable. The unadjusted balance of the Allowance for Doubtful Accounts is a $1,000 debit.

b. Alternatively, assume that bad debts are estimated using the percent of sales method. The Allowance for Doubtful Accounts had a $1,000 debit balance before adjustment, and the company estimates bad debts to be 1% of its credit sales of $2,000,000.

SOLUTION

1.

Date	Account	Debit	Credit
July 14	Allowance for Doubtful Accounts	750	
	Accounts Receivable—Briggs Co.		750
	Wrote off an uncollectible account.		
July 30	Notes Receivable—Sumrell Co.	1,000	
	Sales		1,000
	Sold merchandise for a 90-day, 10% note.		
July 30	Cost of Goods Sold	600	
	Merchandise Inventory		600
	Record the cost of July 30 sale.		
Aug. 15	Cash	2,000	
	Notes Receivable—JT Co.	10,000	
	Sales		12,000
	Sold merchandise for $2,000 cash and $10,000 note.		
Aug. 15	Cost of Goods Sold	8,000	
	Merchandise Inventory		8,000
	Record the cost of Aug. 15 sale.		
Nov. 1	Cash	192	
	Credit Card Expense	8	
	Sales		200
	Record credit card sale less a 4% credit card expense.		
Nov. 1	Cost of Goods Sold	150	
	Merchandise Inventory		150
	Record the cost of Nov. 1 sale.		

Date	Account	Debit	Credit
Nov. 3	Accounts Receivable—Sumrell Co.	1,025	
	Interest Revenue		25
	Notes Receivable—Sumrell Co.		1,000
	Charge account of Sumrell Co. for a $1,000 dishonored note and interest of $1,000 × 10% × 90/360.		
Nov. 5	Cash	475	
	Credit Card Expense	25	
	Sales		500
	Record credit card sale less a 5% credit card expense.		
Nov. 5	Cost of Goods Sold	300	
	Merchandise Inventory		300
	Record the cost of Nov. 5 sale.		
Nov. 15	Accounts Receivable—Briggs Co.	750	
	Allowance for Doubtful Accounts		750
	Reinstate account of Briggs Co. previously written off.		
Nov. 15	Cash	750	
	Accounts Receivable—Briggs Co.		750
	Cash received in full payment of account.		
Dec. 13	Cash	10,400	
	Interest Revenue		400
	Note Receivable—JT Co.		10,000
	Collect note with interest of $10,000 × 12% × 120/360.		

2a. Aging of accounts receivable method.

Dec. 31	Bad Debts Expense	21,400	
	Allowance for Doubtful Accounts		21,400
	Adjust allowance account from a $1,000 debit balance to a $20,400 credit balance.		

2b. Percent of sales method. (For the income statement approach, which requires estimating bad debts as a percent of sales or credit sales, the Allowance for Doubtful Accounts balance is *not* considered when making the adjusting entry.)

Dec. 31	Bad Debts Expense	20,000	
	Allowance for Doubtful Accounts		20,000
	Record bad debts expense as 1% × $2,000,000 of credit sales.		

Summary: Cheat Sheet

VALUING RECEIVABLES

Accounts Receivable: Amounts due from customers for credit sales.

Credit sales and later collection:

Accounts Receivable—CompStore	950	
Sales		950
Cash	720	
Accounts Receivable—RDA Electronics		720

Sales using bank credit card:

Cash	96	
Credit Card Expense	4	
Sales		100

DIRECT WRITE-OFF METHOD

Direct write-off method: Record bad debt expense when an account is determined to be uncollectible.

Writing off a bad debt under *direct method:*

Bad Debts Expense	520	
Accounts Receivable—J. Kent		520

Bad debt later recovered under *direct method:*

Accounts Receivable—J. Kent	520	
Bad Debts Expense		520
Cash	520	
Accounts Receivable—J. Kent		520

ALLOWANCE METHOD

Allowance method: Matches estimated loss from uncollectible accounts receivable against the sales they helped produce.

Estimating bad debts:

Bad Debts Expense	1,500	
Allowance for Doubtful Accounts		1,500

Allowance for Doubtful Accounts: A contra asset account that reduces accounts receivable. It has a normal credit balance.

Writing off a bad debt under *allowance method:*

Allowance for Doubtful Accounts	520	
Accounts Receivable—J. Kent		520

Bad debt later recovered under *allowance method:*

Accounts Receivable—J. Kent	520	
Allowance for Doubtful Accounts		520
Cash	520	
Accounts Receivable—J. Kent		520

ESTIMATING BAD DEBTS USING ALLOWANCE METHOD

When using the allowance method, we often use one of the following methods to estimate bad debts.

- **Percent of sales:** Uses a percent of credit sales for the period to estimate bad debts.
- **Percent of accounts receivable:** Uses a percent of total accounts receivable to estimate bad debts.
- **Aging of accounts receivable:** Applies increasing percentages to accounts receivable (classified by days past due) to estimate bad debts.

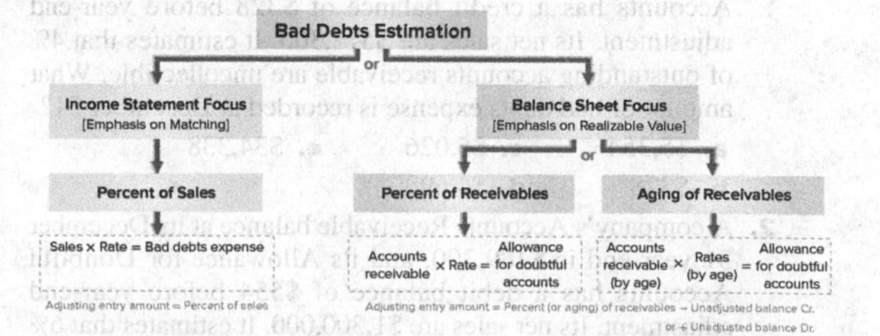

NOTES RECEIVABLE

Note receivable: A promise to pay a specified amount of money at a future date.

Principal of a note: Amount promised to be repaid.

Maturity date: Day the note must be repaid.

Interest formula (year assumed to have 360 days):

Principal of the note	×	Annual interest rate	×	Time expressed in fraction of year	=	Interest

Note receivable from sales:

Notes Receivable	1,000	
Sales		1,000

Note receivable and cash in exchange for accounts receivable:

Cash	232	
Notes Receivable	600	
Accounts Receivable—J. Cook		832

Note is *honored;* cash received in full (with interest):

Cash	615	
Notes Receivable		600
Interest Revenue		15

Note is *dishonored;* accounts receivable and interest recorded:

Accounts Receivable—J. Cook	615	
Interest Revenue		15
Notes Receivable		600

Accrue interest on note receivable:

Interest Receivable	15	
Interest Revenue		15

Note is *honored;* when note term runs over two periods:

Cash	3,060	
Interest Revenue		45
Interest Receivable		15
Notes Receivable		3,000

Factoring (selling) receivables: Accounts receivable are sold to a bank and the seller is charged a *factoring fee*.

Sale of receivables for cash with a charged factoring fee:

Cash	19,200	
Factoring Fee Expense	800	
Accounts Receivable		20,000

Pledging of receivables: Borrowing money by ***pledging*** receivables as security for a loan. Borrower discloses pledging in notes to financial statement.

Key Terms

Accounts receivable (325)
Accounts receivable turnover (339)
Aging of accounts receivable (332)
Allowance for Doubtful Accounts (329)
Allowance method (329)
Bad debts (327)
Direct write-off method (327)
Interest (335)
Maker of the note (335)
Maturity date of a note (335)
Payee of the note (335)
Principal of a note (335)
Promissory note (or note) (335)
Realizable value (329)

Multiple Choice Quiz

1. A company's Accounts Receivable balance at its December 31 year-end is $125,650, and its Allowance for Doubtful Accounts has a credit balance of $328 before year-end adjustment. Its net sales are $572,300. It estimates that 4% of outstanding accounts receivable are uncollectible. What amount of bad debts expense is recorded at December 31?

a. $5,354 **c.** $5,026 **e.** $34,338
b. $328 **d.** $4,698

2. A company's Accounts Receivable balance at its December 31 year-end is $489,300, and its Allowance for Doubtful Accounts has a debit balance of $554 before year-end adjustment. Its net sales are $1,300,000. It estimates that 6% of outstanding accounts receivable are uncollectible. What amount of bad debts expense is recorded at December 31?

a. $29,912 **c.** $78,000 **e.** $554
b. $28,804 **d.** $29,358

3. Total interest to be earned on a $7,500, 5%, 90-day note is

a. $93.75. **c.** $1,125.00. **e.** $125.00.
b. $375.00. **d.** $31.25.

4. A company receives a $9,000, 8%, 60-day note. The maturity value of the note is

a. $120. **c.** $9,120. **e.** $9,720.
b. $9,000. **d.** $720.

5. A company has net sales of $489,600 and average accounts receivable of $40,800. What is its accounts receivable turnover?

a. 0.08 **c.** 1,341.00 **e.** 111.78
b. 30.41 **d.** 12.00

ANSWERS TO MULTIPLE CHOICE QUIZ

1. d; Desired balance in Allowance for Doubtful Accounts ($125,650 × 0.04) = $ 5,026 cr.
   Current balance in Allowance for Doubtful Accounts = (328) cr.
   Bad debts expense to be recorded = $ 4,698
2. a; Desired balance in Allowance for Doubtful Accounts ($489,300 × 0.06) = $29,358 cr.
   Current balance in Allowance for Doubtful Accounts = 554 dr.
   Bad debts expense to be recorded = $29,912
3. a; $7,500 × 0.05 × 90/360 = $93.75
4. c; Principal amount $9,000
   Interest accrued .... 120 ($9,000 × 0.08 × 60/360)
   Maturity value $9,120
5. d; $489,600/$40,800 = 12

Select Quick Study and Exercise assignments feature Guided Example videos, called "Hints" in Connect. Hints use different numbers, and instructors can turn this feature on or off.

QUICK STUDY

QS 9-1 Credit card sales **C1**

Prepare journal entries for the following credit card sales transactions. The company uses the perpetual inventory system.

1. Sold $20,000 of merchandise, which cost $15,000, on Mastercard credit cards. Mastercard charges a 5% fee.
2. Sold $5,000 of merchandise, which cost $3,000, on an assortment of bank credit cards. These cards charge a 4% fee.

QS 9-2 Direct write-off method **P1**

Solstice Company determines on October 1 that it cannot collect $50,000 of its accounts receivable from its customer P. Moore. Apply the direct write-off method to record this loss as of October 1.

QS 9-3 Recovering a bad debt **P1**

Solstice Company determines on October 1 that it cannot collect $50,000 of its accounts receivable from its customer P. Moore. It uses the direct write-off method to record this loss as of October 1. On October 30, P. Moore unexpectedly pays his account in full to Solstice Company. Record Solstice's entries for recovery of this bad debt.

QS 9-4 Distinguishing between allowance method and direct write-off method **P1 P2**

Indicate whether each statement best describes the allowance method or the direct write-off method.

1. Does not predict bad debts expense.
2. Accounts receivable on the balance sheet is reported at net realizable value.
3. The write-off of a specific account does not affect net income.
4. When an account is written off, the debit is to Bad Debts Expense.
5. Usually does *not* best match sales and expenses because bad debts expense is not recorded until an account becomes uncollectible, which usually occurs in a period after the credit sale.
6. Estimates bad debts expense related to the sales recorded in that period.

QS 9-5 Comparing direct write-off and allowance method entries **P1 P2**

Flynn Co. determines that it cannot collect $7,000 of its accounts receivable from its customer, MDC. Record the journal entry required of Flynn under (*a*) the direct write-off method and (*b*) the allowance method.

QS 9-6 Allowance method for bad debts **P2**

Gomez Corp. uses the allowance method to account for uncollectibles. On January 31, it wrote off an $800 account of a customer C. Green. On March 9, it receives a $300 payment from Green.

1. Prepare the journal entry for January 31.
2. Prepare the journal entries for March 9; assume no additional money is expected from Green.

QS 9-7 Reporting allowance for doubtful accounts **P2**

On December 31 of Swift Co.'s first year, $50,000 of accounts receivable was not yet collected. Swift estimated that $2,000 of its accounts receivable was uncollectible and recorded the year-end adjusting entry.

1. Compute the realizable value of accounts receivable reported on Swift's year-end balance sheet.
2. On January 1 of Swift's second year, it writes off a customer's account for $300. Compute the realizable value of accounts receivable on January 1 after the write-off.

QS 9-8
Percent of accounts receivable method
P3

Warner Company's year-end unadjusted trial balance shows accounts receivable of $99,000, allowance for doubtful accounts of $600 (credit), and sales of $280,000. Uncollectibles are estimated to be 1.5% of accounts receivable.

1. Prepare the December 31 year-end adjusting entry for uncollectibles.

2. What amount would have been used in the year-end adjusting entry if the allowance account had a year-end unadjusted debit balance of $300?

QS 9-9
Percent of sales method
P3

BioWare's year-end unadjusted trial balance shows accounts receivable of $17,000 and sales of $150,000. Uncollectibles are estimated to be 2% of sales. Prepare the December 31 year-end adjusting entry for uncollectibles using the percent of sales method.

QS 9-10
Aging of receivables method
P3

Net Zero Products, a wholesaler of sustainable raw materials, prepares the following aging of receivables analysis. (1) Estimate the balance of the Allowance for Doubtful Accounts using the aging of accounts receivable method. (2) Prepare the adjusting entry to record bad debts expense assuming the unadjusted balance in the Allowance for Doubtful Accounts is a $1,000 credit.

		Days Past Due				
	Total	0	1 to 30	31 to 60	61 to 90	Over 90
Accounts receivable.....	$115,200	$80,000	$18,000	$7,200	$4,000	$6,000
Percent uncollectible		1%	3%	5%	8%	11%

QS 9-11
Computing interest
C2

Complete the following table by filling in missing amounts.

Principal of Note	Annual Interest Rate	Time Period	Interest
$10,000	8%	90 days	$?
40,000	?	180 days	2,000
?	4	270 days	900

QS 9-12
Computing note interest and maturity date
C2

Determine the maturity date and compute interest for each note.

Note	Contract Date	Principal	Interest Rate	Period of Note (Term)
1............	March 1	$10,000	6%	60 days
2............	May 15	15,000	8	90 days
3............	October 20	8,000	4	45 days

QS 9-13
Note receivable **C2**

On August 2, Jun Co. receives a $6,000, 90-day, 12% note from customer Ryan Albany as payment on his $6,000 account receivable. (1) Compute the maturity date for this note. (2) Prepare Jun's journal entry for August 2.

QS 9-14
Note receivable honored
P4

On August 2, Jun Co. receives a $6,000, 90-day, 12% note from customer Ryan Albany as payment on his $6,000 account receivable. Prepare Jun's journal entry assuming the note is honored by the customer on October 31 of that same year.

QS 9-15
Note receivable interest and maturity **P4**

On December 1, Daw Co. accepts a $10,000, 45-day, 6% note from a customer.

1. Prepare the year-end adjusting entry to record accrued interest revenue on December 31.

2. Prepare the entry required on the note's maturity date assuming it is honored.

QS 9-16
Computing interest revenue for two periods **P4**

On April 1 of Year 1, Respawn accepted a $10,000, 12-month, 8% note from a customer in granting a time extension on his past-due account receivable. Respawn's year-end is December 31. Compute interest revenue recorded by Respawn in Year 1 and Year 2.

Prepare journal entries to record the following transactions of Namco.

April 1 Accepted a $5,000, 90-day, 4% note from Travis in granting a time extension on his past-due account receivable.
June 30 Travis dishonored his note.

QS 9-17
Dishonoring a note
P4

Record the sale by Balus Company of $125,000 in accounts receivable on May 1. Balus is charged a 2.5% factoring fee.

QS 9-18
Factoring receivables C3

Selected accounts from Fair Trader Co.'s adjusted trial balance for the year ended December 31 follow. Prepare its income statement.

QS 9-19
Preparing an income statement
C3 P2 P4

Factoring fees	$ 300	Interest revenue	$ 3,000
Insurance expense	4,000	Salaries expense	22,000
Sales	50,000	Supplies expense	200
Rent expense	15,000	Bad debt expense	1,000

Selected accounts from Bennett Co.'s adjusted trial balance for the year ended December 31 follow. Prepare a classified balance sheet. *Note:* Allowance for doubtful accounts is reported and subtracted from accounts receivable on the company's balance sheet.

QS 9-20
Preparing a balance sheet
C3 P2 P4

Prepaid rent	$ 1,000	Accounts payable	$2,500
Accounts receivable	10,000	Allowance for doubtful accounts	500
Cash	12,000	Notes payable (due in 10 years)	6,000
A. Bennett, Capital	18,000	Notes receivable (due in 4 years)	4,000

The following data are for Rocky Company. *(a)* Compute Rocky's accounts receivable turnover. *(b)* If its competitor, Dixon, has an accounts receivable turnover of 7.5, which company appears to be doing a better job of managing its receivables?

QS 9-21
Accounts receivable turnover
A1

	Current Year	1 Year Ago
Accounts receivable, net	$153,400	$138,500
Net sales	861,105	910,600

Mc Graw Hill connect

EXERCISES

Exercise 9-1
Accounts receivable subsidiary ledger; schedule of accounts receivable
C1

Vail Company recorded the following transactions during November.

Date	Account	Debit	Credit
Nov. 5	Accounts Receivable—Ski Shop	4,615	
	Sales		4,615
10	Accounts Receivable—Welcome Inc.	1,350	
	Sales		1,350
13	Accounts Receivable—Zia Co.	832	
	Sales		832
21	Sales Returns and Allowances	209	
	Accounts Receivable—Zia Co.		209
30	Accounts Receivable—Ski Shop	2,713	
	Sales		2,713

1. Open a general ledger having T-accounts for Accounts Receivable, Sales, and Sales Returns and Allowances. Also open an accounts receivable subsidiary ledger having a T-account for each of its three customers. Post these entries to both the general ledger and the accounts receivable ledger.
2. Prepare a schedule of accounts receivable (see Exhibit 9.4) and compare its total with the balance of the Accounts Receivable controlling account as of November 30.

Check Accounts Receivable ending balance, $9,301

Exercise 9-2
Accounting for credit card sales
C1

Levine Company uses the perpetual inventory system. Prepare journal entries to record the following credit card transactions of Levine Company.

Apr. 8 Sold merchandise for $8,400 (that had cost $6,000) and accepted the customer's Suntrust Bank Card. Suntrust charges a 4% fee.

12 Sold merchandise for $5,600 (that had cost $3,500) and accepted the customer's Continental Card. Continental charges a 2.5% fee.

Exercise 9-3
Computing cash collections C1

Grande Co. had credit sales of $20,000 in the current period. Accounts Receivable had a beginning balance of $4,000 and an ending balance of $5,000. Compute its cash collections from its credit sales for the current period.

Exercise 9-4
Direct write-off method
P1

Dexter Company uses the direct write-off method. Prepare journal entries to record the following transactions.

Mar. 11 Dexter determines that it cannot collect $45,000 of its accounts receivable from Leer Co.

29 Leer Co. unexpectedly pays its account in full to Dexter Company. Dexter records its recovery of this bad debt.

Exercise 9-5
Writing off receivables
P2

On January 1, Wei Company begins the accounting period with a $30,000 credit balance in Allowance for Doubtful Accounts.

a. On February 1, the company determined that $6,800 in customer accounts was uncollectible; specifically, $900 for Oakley Co. and $5,900 for Brookes Co. Prepare the journal entry to write off those two accounts.

b. On June 5, the company unexpectedly received a $900 payment on a customer account, Oakley Company, that had previously been written off in part *a*. Prepare the entries to reinstate the account and record the cash received.

Exercise 9-6
Recording and reporting allowance for doubtful accounts
P2

In its first year of operations, Cloudbox has credit sales of $200,000. Its year-end balance in Accounts Receivable is $10,000, and the company estimates that $1,500 of its accounts receivable is uncollectible.

a. Prepare the year-end adjusting entry to estimate bad debts expense.

b. Prepare the current assets section of Cloudbox's classified balance sheet assuming Inventory is $22,000, Cash is $14,000, and Prepaid Rent is $3,000. *Note:* The company reports Accounts receivable, net on the balance sheet.

Exercise 9-7
Determining bad debts expense using financial disclosures
P2

Helix reported the following information in its financial statements. Write-offs of accounts receivable were $200 in the current year. Helix did not recover any write-offs. Determine bad debts expense for the current year.

At December 31	Current Year	Prior Year
Accounts receivable	$5,000	$4,000
Allowance for doubtful accounts	400	350
Accounts receivable, net	$4,600	$3,650

Exercise 9-8
Financial statement impact of receivables transactions
P2

Analyze each of the following transactions by showing the effects on the accounting equation—specifically, identify the accounts and amounts (including + or −) for each transaction.

a. The company provides $20,000 of services on credit.

b. The company estimates that $800 of its accounts receivable is uncollectible.

c. The company writes off a customer's entire $300 account as uncollectible.

Exercise 9-9
Comparing direct write-off and allowance method entries
P1 P2

Prepare journal entries for Sal Co. to record the following under (*a*) the direct write-off method and (*b*) the allowance method.

May 3 Sal Co. determines that it cannot collect its accounts receivable of $2,000 from Joey Co.

21 Sal Co. unexpectedly receives payment of $2,000 cash from Joey Co. toward its previously written-off account. Sal records recovery of this bad debt.

Exercise 9-10
Percent of sales method; write-off
P3

At year-end December 31, Chan Company estimates its bad debts as 1% of its annual credit sales of $487,500. Chan records its bad debts expense for that estimate. On the following February 1, Chan decides that the $580 account of P. Park is uncollectible and writes it off as a bad debt. On June 5, Park unexpectedly pays the amount previously written off.

Prepare Chan's journal entries to record the transactions of December 31, February 1, and June 5.

Exercise 9-11
Financial statement impact of bad debts expense and write-offs P3

Using information from Exercise 9-10, determine the impact of the December 31, February 1, and June 5 transactions on the accounting equation. For each transaction, indicate whether there would be an increase, decrease, or no effect, for Assets, Liabilities, and Equity.

Exercise 9-12
Percent of sales method P3

Warner Company's year-end unadjusted trial balance shows accounts receivable of $99,000, allowance for doubtful accounts of $600 (credit), and sales of $140,000. Uncollectibles are estimated to be 1% of sales. Prepare the December 31 year-end adjusting entry for uncollectibles.

Exercise 9-13
Percent of accounts receivable method P3

Mazie Supply Co. uses the percent of accounts receivable method. On December 31, it has outstanding accounts receivable of $55,000, and it estimates that 2% will be uncollectible.

Prepare the year-end adjusting entry to record bad debts expense under the assumption that the Allowance for Doubtful Accounts has (*a*) a $415 credit balance before the adjustment and (*b*) a $291 debit balance before the adjustment.

Exercise 9-14
Aging of receivables method P3

Daley Company prepared the following aging of receivables analysis at December 31.

		Days Past Due				
	Total	0	1 to 30	31 to 60	61 to 90	Over 90
Accounts receivable......	$570,000	$396,000	$90,000	$36,000	$18,000	$30,000
Percent uncollectible.....		1%	2%	5%	7%	10%

a. Estimate the balance of the Allowance for Doubtful Accounts using aging of accounts receivable.

b. Prepare the adjusting entry to record bad debts expense using the estimate from part *a*. Assume the unadjusted balance in the Allowance for Doubtful Accounts is a $3,600 credit.

c. Prepare the adjusting entry to record bad debts expense using the estimate from part *a*. Assume the unadjusted balance in the Allowance for Doubtful Accounts is a $100 debit.

Exercise 9-15
Percent of receivables method P3

Refer to the information in Exercise 9-14 to complete the following requirements.

a. Estimate the balance of the Allowance for Doubtful Accounts assuming the company uses 4.5% of total accounts receivable to estimate uncollectibles, instead of the aging of receivables method.

b. Prepare the adjusting entry to record bad debts expense using the estimate from part *a*. Assume the unadjusted balance in the Allowance for Doubtful Accounts is a $12,000 credit.

c. Prepare the adjusting entry to record bad debts expense using the estimate from part *a*. Assume the unadjusted balance in the Allowance for Doubtful Accounts is a $1,000 debit.

Exercise 9-16
Aging of receivables schedule P3

Following is a list of credit customers along with their amounts owed and the days past due at December 31. Also shown are five classifications of accounts receivable and estimated bad debts percent for each class.

1. Create an aging of accounts receivable schedule similar to Exhibit 9.8 and calculate the estimated balance for the Allowance for Doubtful Accounts.

2. Assuming an unadjusted credit balance of $100, record the required adjustment to the Allowance for Doubtful Accounts.

Customer	Accounts Receivable	Days Past Due
BCC Company	$4,000	12
Lannister Co.	1,000	0
Mike Properties	5,000	107
Ted Reeves	500	72
Jen Steffens	2,000	35

Days Past Due	0	1 to 30	31 to 60	61 to 90	Over 90
Percent uncollectible..........	1%	3%	5%	8%	12%

Exercise 9-17
Estimating bad debts
P3

At December 31, Folgeys Coffee Company reports the following results for its calendar year.

Cash sales...........	$900,000	Credit sales..........	$300,000

Its year-end unadjusted trial balance includes the following items.

Accounts receivable......	$125,000 debit	Allowance for doubtful accounts......	$5,000 debit

Check Dr. Bad Debts Expense: (1) $9,000

(3) $12,500

1. Prepare the adjusting entry to record bad debts expense assuming uncollectibles are estimated to be 3% of credit sales.

2. Prepare the adjusting entry to record bad debts expense assuming uncollectibles are estimated to be 1% of total sales.

3. Prepare the adjusting entry to record bad debts expense assuming uncollectibles are estimated to be 6% of year-end accounts receivable.

Exercise 9-18
Notes receivable transactions
C2

Check Dec. 31, Cr. Interest Revenue, $38

Prepare journal entries for the following transactions of Danica Company.

Dec. 13 Accepted a $9,500, 45-day, 8% note in granting Miranda Lee a time extension on her past-due account receivable.
31 Prepared an adjusting entry to record the accrued interest on the Lee note.

Exercise 9-19
Notes receivable transactions
P4

Check Jan. 27, Dr. Cash, $9,595

June 1, Dr. Cash, $5,125

Refer to the information in Exercise 9-18 and prepare the journal entries for the *following year* for Danica Company.

Jan. 27 Received Lee's payment for principal and interest on the note dated December 13.
Mar. 3 Accepted a $5,000, 10%, 90-day note in granting a time extension on the past-due account receivable of Tomas Company.
17 Accepted a $2,000, 30-day, 9% note in granting H. Cheng a time extension on his past-due account receivable.
Apr. 16 Cheng dishonored his note.
May 1 Wrote off the Cheng account against the Allowance for Doubtful Accounts.
June 1 Received the Tomas payment for principal and interest on the note dated March 3.

Exercise 9-20
Honoring a note
P4

Prepare journal entries to record transactions for Vitalo Company.

Nov. 1 Accepted a $6,000, 180-day, 8% note from Kelly White in granting a time extension on her past-due account receivable.
Dec. 31 Adjusted the year-end accounts for the accrued interest earned on the White note.
Apr. 30 White honored her note when presented for payment.

Exercise 9-21
Dishonoring a note
P4

Prepare journal entries to record the following transactions of Ridge Company.

Mar. 21 Accepted a $9,500, 180-day, 8% note from Tamara Jackson in granting a time extension on her past-due account receivable.
Sep. 17 Jackson dishonored her note.
Dec. 31 After trying several times to collect, Ridge Company wrote off Jackson's account against the Allowance for Doubtful Accounts.

Exercise 9-22
Selling and pledging accounts receivable
C3

On November 30, Petrov Co. has $128,700 of accounts receivable and uses the perpetual inventory system. (1) Prepare journal entries to record the following transactions. (2) Which transaction would most likely require a note to the financial statements?

Dec. 4 Sold $7,245 of merchandise (that had cost $5,000) to customers on credit, terms n/30.
9 Sold $20,000 of accounts receivable to Main Bank. Main charges a 4% factoring fee.
17 Received $5,859 cash from customers in payment on their accounts.
27 Borrowed $10,000 cash from Main Bank, pledging $12,500 of accounts receivable as security for the loan.

Exercise 9-23
Accounts receivable turnover
A1

The following information is from the annual financial statements of Raheem Company. (1) Compute its accounts receivable turnover for Year 2 and Year 3. (2) Assuming its competitor has a turnover of 11, is Raheem performing better or worse at collecting receivables than its competitor?

	Year 3	Year 2	Year 1
Net sales	$405,140	$335,280	$388,000
Accounts receivable, net (year-end)	44,800	41,400	34,800

connect

PROBLEM SET A

Problem 9-1A
Sales on credit and sales on credit cards
C1

Mayfair Co. completed the following transactions and uses a perpetual inventory system.

June 4 Sold $650 of merchandise on credit (that had cost $400) to Natara Morris, terms n/15.
5 Sold $6,900 of merchandise (that had cost $4,200) to customers who used their Zisa cards. Zisa charges a 3% fee.
6 Sold $5,850 of merchandise (that had cost $3,800) to customers who used their Access cards. Access charges a 2% fee.
8 Sold $4,350 of merchandise (that had cost $2,900) to customers who used their Access cards. Access charges a 2% fee.
13 Wrote off the account of Abigail McKee against the Allowance for Doubtful Accounts. The $429 balance in McKee's account was from a credit sale last year.
18 Received Morris's check in full payment for the June 4 purchase.

Check June 18, Dr. Cash, $650

Required

Prepare journal entries to record these transactions and events.

Problem 9-2A
Estimating and reporting bad debts
P2 P3

At December 31, Hawke Company reports the following results for its calendar year.

Cash sales	$1,905,000	Credit sales	$5,682,000

In addition, its unadjusted trial balance includes the following items.

Accounts receivable	$1,270,100 debit	Allowance for doubtful accounts	$16,580 debit

Required

1. Prepare the adjusting entry to record bad debts under each separate assumption.
a. Bad debts are estimated to be 1.5% of credit sales.
b. Bad debts are estimated to be 1% of total sales.
c. An aging analysis estimates that 5% of year-end accounts receivable are uncollectible.
2. Show how Accounts Receivable and the Allowance for Doubtful Accounts appear on its December 31 balance sheet given the facts in part 1*a*.
3. Show how Accounts Receivable and the Allowance for Doubtful Accounts appear on its December 31 balance sheet given the facts in part 1*c*.

Check Bad Debts Expense: (1*a*) $85,230, (1*c*) $80,085

Problem 9-3A
Aging accounts receivable and accounting for bad debts
P2 P3

On December 31, Jarden Co.'s Allowance for Doubtful Accounts has an unadjusted credit balance of $14,500. Jarden prepares a schedule of its December 31 accounts receivable by age.

	A	B	C
1	Accounts Receivable	Age of Accounts Receivable	Expected Percent Uncollectible
2	$830,000	Not yet due	1.25%
3	254,000	1 to 30 days past due	2.00
4	86,000	31 to 60 days past due	6.50
5	38,000	61 to 90 days past due	32.75
6	12,000	Over 90 days past due	68.00

[continued on next page]

[continued from previous page]

Required

1. Compute the required balance of the Allowance for Doubtful Accounts at December 31 using an aging of accounts receivable.
2. Prepare the adjusting entry to record bad debts expense at December 31.

Check (2) Dr. Bad Debts Expense, $27,150

Analysis Component

3. On June 30 of the next year, Jarden concludes that a customer's $4,750 receivable is uncollectible and the account is written off. Does this write-off directly affect Jarden's net income?

Problem 9-4A
Accounts receivable transactions and bad debts adjustments
C1 P2 P3

Liang Company began operations in Year 1. During its first two years, the company completed a number of transactions involving sales on credit, accounts receivable collections, and bad debts. These transactions are summarized as follows.

Year 1

a. Sold $1,345,434 of merchandise (that had cost $975,000) on credit, terms n/30.
b. Wrote off $18,300 of uncollectible accounts receivable.
c. Received $669,200 cash in payment of accounts receivable.
d. In adjusting the accounts on December 31, the company estimated that 1.5% of accounts receivable would be uncollectible.

Check (d) Dr. Bad Debts Expense, $28,169

Year 2

e. Sold $1,525,634 of merchandise on credit (that had cost $1,250,000), terms n/30.
f. Wrote off $27,800 of uncollectible accounts receivable.
g. Received $1,204,600 cash in payment of accounts receivable.
h. In adjusting the accounts on December 31, the company estimated that 1.5% of accounts receivable would be uncollectible.

(h) Dr. Bad Debts Expense, $32,199

Required

Prepare journal entries to record Liang's summarized transactions and its year-end adjustments to record bad debts expense. (The company uses the perpetual inventory system, and it applies the allowance method for its accounts receivable. Round to the nearest dollar.)

Problem 9-5A
Analyzing and journalizing notes receivable transactions
C2 C3 P4

The following transactions are from Ohlm Company.

Year 1

Dec. 16 Accepted a $10,800, 60-day, 8% note in granting Danny Todd a time extension on his past-due account receivable.
31 Made an adjusting entry to record the accrued interest on the Todd note.

Year 2

Feb. 14 Received Todd's payment of principal and interest on the note dated December 16.
Mar. 2 Accepted a $6,100, 8%, 90-day note in granting a time extension on the past-due account receivable from Midnight Co.
17 Accepted a $2,400, 30-day, 7% note in granting Ava Privet a time extension on her past-due account receivable.
Apr. 16 Privet dishonored her note.
May 31 Midnight Co. dishonored its note.
Aug. 7 Accepted a $7,440, 90-day, 10% note in granting a time extension on the past-due account receivable of Mulan Co.
Sep. 3 Accepted a $2,100, 60-day, 10% note in granting Noah Carson a time extension on his past-due account receivable.
Nov. 2 Received payment of principal plus interest from Carson for the September 3 note.
Nov. 5 Received payment of principal plus interest from Mulan for the August 7 note.
Dec. 1 Wrote off the Privet account against the Allowance for Doubtful Accounts.

Check Feb. 14, Cr. Interest Revenue, $108

May 31, Cr. Interest Revenue, $122

Nov. 2, Cr. Interest Revenue, $35

Required

1. Prepare journal entries to record these transactions and events.

Analysis Component

2. If Ohlm pledged its receivables as security for a loan from the bank, where on the financial statements does it disclose this pledge of receivables?

PROBLEM SET B

Problem 9-1B
Sales on credit and sales on credit cards **C1**

Archer Co. completed the following transactions and uses a perpetual inventory system.

Aug. 4 Sold $3,700 of merchandise on credit (that had cost $2,000) to McKenzie Carpenter, terms n/10.
10 Sold $5,200 of merchandise (that had cost $2,800) to customers who used their Commerce Bank credit cards. Commerce charges a 3% fee.
11 Sold $1,250 of merchandise (that had cost $900) to customers who used their Goldman cards. Goldman charges a 2% fee.
14 Received Carpenter's check in full payment for the August 4 purchase.
15 Sold $3,250 of merchandise (that had cost $1,758) to customers who used their Goldman cards. Goldman charges a 2% fee.
22 Wrote off the account of Craw Co. against the Allowance for Doubtful Accounts. The $498 balance in Craw Co.'s account was from a credit sale last year.

Check Aug. 14, Dr. Cash, $3,700

Required

Prepare journal entries to record these transactions and events.

Problem 9-2B
Estimating and reporting bad debts
P2 P3

At December 31, Ingleton Company reports the following results for the year.

Cash sales..................	$1,025,000	Credit sales	$1,342,000

In addition, its unadjusted trial balance includes the following items.

Accounts receivable.......	$575,000 debit	Allowance for doubtful accounts	$7,500 credit

Required

1. Prepare the adjusting entry to record bad debts under each separate assumption.
   a. Bad debts are estimated to be 2.5% of credit sales.
   b. Bad debts are estimated to be 1.5% of total sales.
   c. An aging analysis estimates that 6% of year-end accounts receivable are uncollectible.
2. Show how Accounts Receivable and the Allowance for Doubtful Accounts appear on its December 31 balance sheet given the facts in part *1a.*
3. Show how Accounts Receivable and the Allowance for Doubtful Accounts appear on its December 31 balance sheet given the facts in part *1c.*

Check Dr. Bad Debts Expense: (1*b*) $35,505, (1*c*) $27,000

Problem 9-3B
Aging accounts receivable and accounting for bad debts
P2 P3

At December 31, Hovak Co.'s Allowance for Doubtful Accounts has an unadjusted debit balance of $3,400. Hovak prepares a schedule of its December 31 accounts receivable by age.

	A	B	C
1	Accounts Receivable	Age of Accounts Receivable	Expected Percent Uncollectible
2	$396,400	Not yet due	2.0%
3	277,800	1 to 30 days past due	4.0
4	48,000	31 to 60 days past due	8.5
5	6,600	61 to 90 days past due	39.0
6	2,800	Over 90 days past due	82.0

[continued on next page]

[continued from previous page]

Required

1. Compute the required balance of the Allowance for Doubtful Accounts at December 31 using an aging of accounts receivable.
2. Prepare the adjusting entry to record bad debts expense at December 31.

Check (2) Dr. Bad Debts Expense, $31,390

Analysis Component

3. On July 31 of the following year, Hovak concludes that a customer's $3,455 receivable is uncollectible and the account is written off. Does this write-off directly affect Hovak's net income?

Problem 9-4B
Accounts receivable transactions and bad debts adjustments
C1 P2 P3

Sherman Co. began operations in Year 1. During its first two years, the company completed several transactions involving sales on credit, accounts receivable collections, and bad debts. These transactions are summarized as follows.

Year 1

a. Sold $685,350 of merchandise on credit (that had cost $500,000), terms n/30.
b. Received $482,300 cash in payment of accounts receivable.
c. Wrote off $9,350 of uncollectible accounts receivable.
d. In adjusting the accounts on December 31, the company estimated that 1% of accounts receivable would be uncollectible.

Check (d) Dr. Bad Debts Expense, $11,287

Year 2

e. Sold $870,220 of merchandise on credit (that had cost $650,000), terms n/30.
f. Received $990,800 cash in payment of accounts receivable.
g. Wrote off $11,090 of uncollectible accounts receivable.
h. In adjusting the accounts on December 31, the company estimated that 1% of accounts receivable would be uncollectible.

(h) Dr. Bad Debts Expense, $9,773

Required

Prepare journal entries to record Sherman's summarized transactions and its year-end adjusting entries to record bad debts expense. (The company uses the perpetual inventory system, and it applies the allowance method for its accounts receivable.)

Problem 9-5B
Analyzing and journalizing notes receivable transactions
C2 C3 P4

The following transactions are from Springer Company.

Year 1

Nov. 1 Accepted a $4,800, 90-day, 8% note in granting Steve Julian a time extension on his past-due account receivable.
Dec. 31 Made an adjusting entry to record the accrued interest on the Julian note.

Year 2

Jan. 30 Received Julian's payment for principal and interest on the note dated November 1.
Feb. 28 Accepted a $12,600, 30-day, 8% note in granting a time extension on the past-due account receivable from King Co.
Mar. 1 Accepted a $6,200, 60-day, 12% note in granting Myron Shelley a time extension on his past-due account receivable.
30 The King Co. dishonored its note.
Apr. 30 Received payment of principal plus interest from M. Shelley for the March 1 note.
June 15 Accepted a $2,000, 72-day, 8% note in granting a time extension on the past-due account receivable of Ryder Solon.
21 Accepted a $9,500, 90-day, 8% note in granting J. Felton a time extension on his past-due account receivable.
Aug. 26 Received payment of principal plus interest from R. Solon for the June 15 note.
Sep. 19 Received payment of principal plus interest from J. Felton for the June 21 note.
Nov. 30 Wrote off King's account against the Allowance for Doubtful Accounts.

Check Jan. 30, Cr. Interest Revenue, $32

Apr. 30, Cr. Interest Revenue, $124

Sep. 19, Cr. Interest Revenue, $190

[continued on next page]

Required

1. Prepare journal entries to record these transactions and events.

Analysis Component

2. If Springer pledged its receivables as security for a loan from the bank, where on the financial statements does it disclose this pledge of receivables?

Mc Graw Hill connect

Serial problem began in Chapter 1. If previous chapter segments were not completed, the serial problem can begin at this point. It is available in ***Connect*** *with an algorithmic option.*

SERIAL PROBLEM

Business Solutions

P1 P2

Alexander Image/Shutterstock

SP 9 Santana Rey, owner of **Business Solutions**, realizes that she needs to begin accounting for bad debts expense. Assume that Business Solutions has total revenues of $44,000 during the first three months of 2022 and that the Accounts Receivable balance on March 31, 2022, is $22,867.

Required

1. Prepare the adjusting entry to record bad debts expense on March 31, 2022, under each separate assumption. There is a zero unadjusted balance in the Allowance for Doubtful Accounts at March 31.
   a. Bad debts are estimated to be 1% of total revenues.
   b. Bad debts are estimated to be 2% of accounts receivable. (Round to the dollar.)
2. Assume that Business Solutions's Accounts Receivable balance at June 30, 2022, is $20,250 and that one account of $100 has been written off against the Allowance for Doubtful Accounts since March 31, 2022. If Rey uses the method in part 1*b*, what adjusting journal entry is made to recognize bad debts expense on June 30, 2022?
3. Should Rey consider adopting the direct write-off method of accounting for bad debts expense rather than one of the allowance methods considered in part 1? Explain.

Check (2) Dr. Bad Debts Expense, $48

Mc Graw Hill connect

TABLEAU DASHBOARD ACTIVITIES

Tableau Dashboard Activities expose students to accounting analytics using visual displays. These assignments run in **Connect**. All are auto-gradable.

Tableau DA 9-1 Quick Study, Percent of accounts receivable method, **P3**—similar to QS 9-8

Tableau DA 9-2 Exercise, Percent of sales method, percent of receivables method, and aging of receivables method, **P3**—similar to QS 9-8,9,10

Tableau DA 9-3 Mini-Case, Aging of receivables method and adjusting entries, **P3**—similar to Exercise 9-14

GENERAL LEDGER

General Ledger (GL) Assignments expose students to general ledger software similar to that in practice. GL is part of **Connect**, and GL assignments are auto-gradable and have algorithmic options.

GL 9-1 analyzes transactions relating to accounts and notes receivable and their impact on interest revenue.

Accounting Analysis

Mc Graw Hill connect

COMPANY ANALYSIS

A1

AA 9-1 Use **Apple**'s financial statements in Appendix A to answer the following.

1. What is the amount of Apple's accounts receivable as of September 28, 2019?
2. Compute Apple's accounts receivable turnover as of September 28, 2019.
3. Apple's most liquid assets include (*a*) cash and cash equivalents, (*b*) marketable securities (current), (*c*) accounts receivable, and (*d*) inventory. Compute the percentage that these liquid assets (in total) make up of current liabilities as of September 28, 2019, and as of September 29, 2018.
4. Did Apple's liquid assets as a percentage of current liabilities improve or worsen as of its fiscal 2019 year-end compared to its fiscal 2018 year-end?

COMPARATIVE ANALYSIS
A1 P2

AA 9-2 Comparative figures for **Apple** and **Google** follow.

$ millions	Apple			Google		
	Current Year	One Year Prior	Two Years Prior	Current Year	One Year Prior	Two Years Prior
Accounts receivable, net . .	$ 22,926	$ 23,186	$ 17,874	$ 25,326	$ 20,838	$ 18,336
Net sales	260,174	265,595	229,234	161,857	136,819	110,855

Required

1. Compute the accounts receivable turnover for the two most recent years for (*a*) Apple and (*b*) Google.
2. Which company more quickly collects its accounts receivable in the current year?

EXTENDED ANALYSIS
C1 A1

AA 9-3 Key figures for **Samsung** follow.

$ millions	Current Year	One Year Prior
Accounts receivable, net	$ 30,144	$ 29,060
Sales	197,691	209,163

1. Compute Samsung's accounts receivable turnover for the current year.
2. In the current year, does Samsung's accounts receivable turnover underperform or outperform the industry (assumed) average of 7?

Discussion Questions

1. How do sellers benefit from allowing their customers to use credit cards?
2. Why does the direct write-off method of accounting for bad debts usually fail to match revenues and expenses?
3. Explain the accounting constraint of materiality.
4. Why might a business prefer a note receivable to an account receivable?
5. Explain why writing off a bad debt against the Allowance for Doubtful Accounts does not reduce the estimated realizable value of a company's accounts receivable.
6. Why does the Bad Debts Expense account usually not have the same adjusted balance as the Allowance for Doubtful Accounts?

Beyond the Numbers

ETHICS CHALLENGE
P2 P3

BTN 9-1 Anton Blair is the manager of a medium-size company. A few years ago, Blair persuaded the owner to base a part of his compensation on the net income the company earns each year. Each December he estimates year-end financial figures in anticipation of the bonus he will receive. If the bonus is not as high as he would like, he offers several recommendations to the accountant for year-end adjustments. One of his favorite recommendations is for the controller to reduce the estimate of doubtful accounts.

Required

1. What effect does lowering the estimate for doubtful accounts have on the income statement and balance sheet?
2. Do you believe Blair's recommendation to adjust the allowance for doubtful accounts is within his rights as manager, or do you believe this action is an ethics violation? Justify your response.
3. What type of internal control(s) might be useful for this company in overseeing the manager's recommendations for accounting changes?

BTN 9-2 As the accountant for Pure-Air Distributing, you attend a sales managers' meeting devoted to a discussion of credit policies. At the meeting, you report that bad debts expense is estimated to be $59,000 and accounts receivable at year-end amount to $1,750,000 less a $43,000 allowance for doubtful accounts. Sid Omar, a sales manager, expresses confusion over why bad debts expense and the allowance for doubtful accounts are different amounts. Write a one-page memorandum to him explaining why a difference in bad debts expense and the allowance for doubtful accounts is not unusual. The company estimates bad debts expense as 2% of sales.

COMMUNICATING IN PRACTICE
P2 P3

BTN 9-3 Access **eBay**'s January 30, 2019, filing of its 10-K report for the year ended December 31, 2018, at SEC.gov.

TAKING IT TO THE NET
C1 P3

Required

1. What is the amount of eBay's net accounts receivable at December 31, 2018, and at December 31, 2017?
2. "Financial Statement Schedule II" of its 10-K report lists eBay's allowance for doubtful accounts (including authorized credits). For the two years ended December 31, 2018 and 2017, identify its allowance for doubtful accounts (including authorized credits), and then compute it as a percent of gross accounts receivable.
3. Do you believe that these percentages are reasonable based on what you know about eBay? Explain.

BTN 9-4 Each member of a team is to participate in estimating uncollectibles using the aging schedule and percents shown in Problem 9-3A. The division of labor is up to the team. Your goal is to accurately complete this task as soon as possible. After estimating uncollectibles, check your estimate with the instructor. If the estimate is correct, the team then should prepare the adjusting entry and the presentation of accounts receivable (net) for the December 31 year-end balance sheet.

TEAMWORK IN ACTION
P2 P3

BTN 9-5 Nichole Mustard and **Credit Karma** are introduced in the chapter's opening feature. Assume that they are considering two options.

ENTREPRENEURIAL DECISION
C1

Plan A. The company would begin selling access to a premium version of its website. The new online customers would use their credit cards. The company has the capability of selling the premium service with no additional investment in hardware or software. Annual credit sales are expected to increase by $250,000.

Costs associated with Plan A: Additional wages related to these new sales are $135,500; credit card fees will be 4.75% of sales; and additional recordkeeping costs will be 6% of sales. Premium service sales will reduce advertising revenues by $8,750 annually because some customers will now only use the premium service.

Plan B. The company would begin selling merchandise. It would make additional annual credit sales of $500,000.

Costs associated with Plan B: Cost of these new sales is $375,000; additional recordkeeping and shipping costs will be 4% of sales; and uncollectible accounts will be 6.2% of sales.

Required

1. Compute the additional annual net income or loss expected under (*a*) Plan A and (*b*) Plan B.
2. Should the company pursue either plan? Discuss both the financial and nonfinancial factors relevant to this decision.

Check (1*b*) Additional net income, $74,000

10 Plant Assets, Natural Resources, and Intangibles

Chapter Preview

PLANT ASSETS	NATURAL RESOURCES	INTANGIBLES
C1 Cost determination	**P3** Cost determination	**P4** Cost determination
P1 Depreciation	Depletion	Amortization
C2 Partial years and changes in estimates	Presentation	Types of intangibles
C3 Additional expenditures	Plant assets tied into extracting resources	**A1** Analyze asset usage
P2 Disposal		
NTK 10-1, 10-2, 10-3	**NTK 10-4**	**NTK 10-5**

Learning Objectives

CONCEPTUAL

C1 Compute the cost of plant assets.

C2 Explain depreciation for partial years and changes in estimates.

C3 Distinguish between revenue and capital expenditures, and account for them.

ANALYTICAL

A1 Compute total asset turnover and apply it to analyze a company's use of assets.

PROCEDURAL

P1 Compute and record depreciation using the straight-line, units-of-production, and declining-balance methods.

P2 Account for asset disposal through discarding or selling an asset.

P3 Account for natural resource assets and their depletion.

P4 Account for intangible assets.

P5 *Appendix 10A*—Account for asset exchanges.

To Boldly Go

"We're at the dawn of a new era"—**Elon Musk**

LOS ANGELES—Elon Musk's main goal in life is to help ensure the survival of mankind by populating Mars! "You back up your hard drive," explains Elon, "maybe we should back up life, too." To achieve his goal, Elon started **SpaceX**, an aerospace manufacturer and space transportation company.

SpaceX is working to build a spaceship capable of going to Mars. Elon vows, "We're going to make it happen." To fund his dream, Elon uses business innovations, with help from accounting analytics.

One breakthrough occurred when Elon was analyzing financial reports issued by NASA and concluded that NASA was spending too much building rockets to go to the International Space Station. He believed that if NASA outsourced its rocket production to SpaceX, NASA's costs would decline. SpaceX now builds rockets for NASA for one-tenth of their prior cost.

A key factor in Elon's cost-savings analysis is that SpaceX launches reusable rockets. Instead of building new rockets for each launch, SpaceX makes substantial repairs, called *betterments* or *extraordinary repairs,* to previously launched rockets. SpaceX was the first to apply this concept, which continues to save NASA billions.

Joe Marino-Bill Cantrell/UPI/Alamy Stock Photo

Elon pushes to solve big problems. "When something is important enough," insists Elon, "you do it even if the odds are not in your favor."

Sources: *SpaceX website*, January 2021; *GQ*, December 2015; *CBS*, May 2012

Section 1—Plant Assets

Plant assets are tangible assets used in a company's operations that have a useful life of more than one accounting period. Plant assets are also called *plant and equipment; property, plant and equipment (PP&E);* or *fixed assets.* Exhibit 10.1 shows plant assets as a percentage of total assets for several companies.

EXHIBIT 10.1

Plant Assets

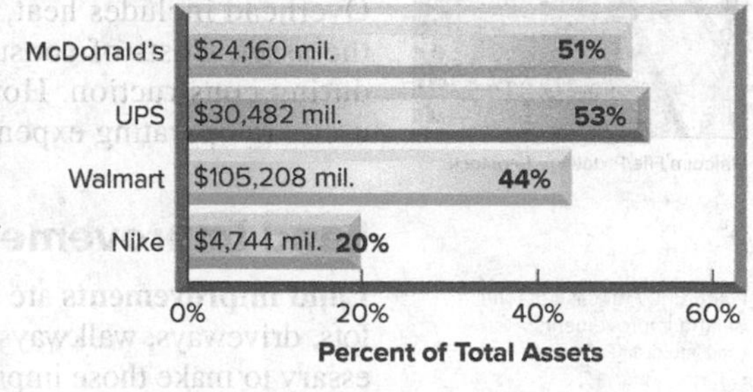

Plant assets are set apart from other assets by two important features. First, *plant assets are used in operations.* A computer purchased to resell is reported on the balance sheet as inventory. If the same computer is used in operations, it is a plant asset. Another example is land held for expansion, which is reported as a long-term investment. Instead, if this land holds a factory used in operations, the land is a plant asset.

The second important feature is that *plant assets have useful lives extending over more than one accounting period.* This makes plant assets different from current assets such as supplies that are normally used up within one period.

Exhibit 10.2 shows four issues in accounting for plant assets: (1) computing the costs of plant assets, (2) allocating the costs of plant assets, (3) accounting for subsequent expenditures to plant assets, and (4) recording the disposal of plant assets. The following sections discuss these issues.

EXHIBIT 10.2

Accounting for Plant Assets

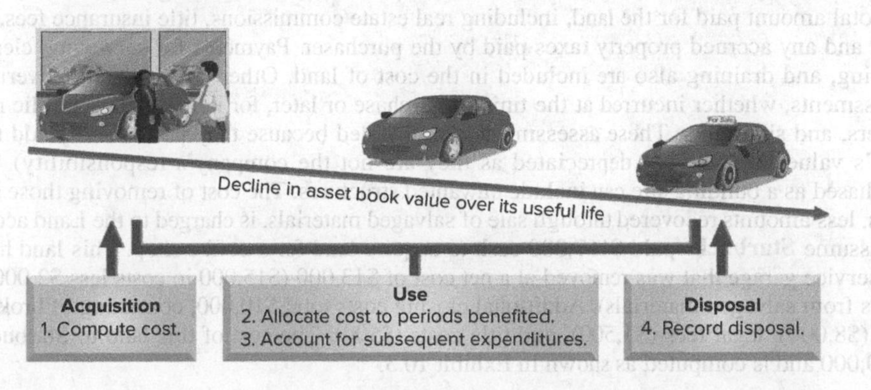

COST DETERMINATION

C1 Compute the cost of plant assets.

Plant assets are recorded at cost when acquired. **Cost** includes all expenditures necessary to get an asset in place and ready for use. The cost of a machine, for example, includes its invoice cost minus any discount, plus necessary shipping, assembling, installing, and testing costs. Examples are the costs of building a base for a machine, installing electrical hookups, and testing the asset before using it in operations.

To be recorded as part of the cost of a plant asset, an expenditure must be normal, reasonable, and necessary in preparing it for its intended use. If an asset is damaged during unpacking, the repairs are not added to its cost. Instead, they are charged to an expense account. Costs to modify or customize a new plant asset are added to the asset's cost. This section explains how to determine the cost of plant assets for its four major classes.

Machinery and Equipment

The costs of machinery and equipment consist of all costs normal and necessary to purchase them and prepare them for their intended use. These include the purchase price, taxes, transportation charges, insurance while in transit, and the installing, assembling, and testing of the machinery and equipment.

Buildings

Malcolm Fife/Pixtal/age fotostock

A Building account consists of the costs of purchasing or constructing a building that is used in operations. A purchased building's costs include its purchase price, taxes, title fees, and lawyer fees. Its costs also include all expenditures to ready it for its intended use, including necessary repairs or renovations. When a company constructs a building or any plant asset for its own use, its costs include materials and labor plus indirect overhead cost. Overhead includes heat, lighting, power, and depreciation on machinery used to construct the asset. Costs of construction also include design fees, building permits, and insurance during construction. However, costs such as insurance to cover the asset *after* it is being used are operating expenses.

Land Improvements

Point: Entry for cash purchase of land improvements:
Land Improvements .... #
Cash .... #

Land improvements are additions to land and have limited useful lives. Examples are parking lots, driveways, walkways, fences, and lighting systems. Land improvements include costs necessary to make those improvements ready for their intended use.

Land

Land is the earth's surface and has an indefinite (unlimited) life. Land includes costs necessary to make it ready for its intended use. When land is purchased for a building site, its cost includes the total amount paid for the land, including real estate commissions, title insurance fees, legal fees, and any accrued property taxes paid by the purchaser. Payments for surveying, clearing, grading, and draining also are included in the cost of land. Other costs include government assessments, whether incurred at the time of purchase or later, for items such as public roads, sewers, and sidewalks. These assessments are included because they permanently add to the land's value (and are not depreciated as they are not the company's responsibility). Land purchased as a building site can include unwanted structures. The cost of removing those structures, less amounts recovered through sale of salvaged materials, is charged to the Land account.

Assume **Starbucks** paid $167,000 cash to acquire land for a coffee shop. This land had an old service garage that was removed at a net cost of $13,000 ($15,000 in costs less $2,000 proceeds from salvaged materials). Additional closing costs total $10,000, consisting of brokerage fees ($8,000), legal fees ($1,500), and title costs ($500). The cost of this land to Starbucks is $190,000 and is computed as shown in Exhibit 10.3.

Cash price of land	$ 167,000
Net cost of garage removal	13,000
Closing costs	10,000
Cost of land	$190,000

Entry for cash purchase of land:

Land	190,000	
Cash		190,000
Record purchase of land.		

EXHIBIT 10.3
Recording Cost of Land

Lump-Sum Purchase

Plant assets sometimes are purchased as a group in a single transaction for a lump-sum price. This transaction is called a *lump-sum purchase,* or *group, bulk,* or *basket purchase.* When this occurs, we allocate the cost to the assets acquired based on their *relative market* (or *appraised*) *values.* Assume **CarMax** paid $90,000 cash to acquire a group of items consisting of a building appraised at $60,000 and land appraised at $40,000. The $90,000 cost is allocated based on appraised values, as shown in Exhibit 10.4. The entry to record the lump-sum purchase also is shown in Exhibit 10.4.

	Appraised Value	Percent of Total	Apportioned Cost
Building	$ 60,000	60% ($60,000/$100,000)	$54,000 ($90,000 × 60%)
Land	40,000	40 ($40,000/$100,000)	36,000 ($90,000 × 40%)
Totals	$100,000	100%	$ 90,000

Entry for lump-sum cash purchase:

Building	54,000	
Land	36,000	
Cash		90,000
Record costs of assets.		

EXHIBIT 10.4
Lump-Sum Purchase

NEED-TO-KNOW 10-1
Cost Determination
C1

Compute the recorded cost of a new machine given the following payments related to its purchase: gross purchase price, $700,000; sales tax, $49,000; purchase discount taken, $21,000; freight cost—terms FOB shipping point, $3,500; normal assembly costs, $3,000; cost of necessary machine platform, $2,500; and cost of parts used in maintaining machine, $4,200.

Solution

$737,000 = $700,000 + $49,000 − $21,000 + $3,500 + $3,000 + $2,500

Do More: QS 10-1, QS 10-2, E 10-1, E 10-2, E 10-3

DEPRECIATION

P1
Compute and record depreciation using the straight-line, units-of-production, and declining-balance methods.

Depreciation is the process of allocating the cost of a plant asset to expense while it is in use. Depreciation does not measure the decline in the asset's market value or its physical deterioration. This section covers computing depreciation.

Factors in Computing Depreciation

Factors that determine depreciation are (1) cost, (2) salvage value, and (3) useful life.

Cost The cost of a plant asset consists of all necessary and reasonable expenditures to acquire it and to prepare it for its intended use.

Salvage Value **Salvage value,** also called *residual value* or *scrap value,* is an estimate of the asset's value at the end of its useful life. This is the amount the owner expects to receive from disposing of the asset at the end of its useful life. If the asset is expected to be traded in on a new asset, its salvage value is the expected trade-in value. If we expect disposal costs, the salvage value equals the expected amount received from disposal less any disposal costs.

Useful Life **Useful life** of a plant asset is the length of time it is used in a company's operations. Useful life, or *service life,* might not be as long as the asset's total productive life. For example, the productive life of a computer can be eight years or more. Some companies, however, trade in old computers for new ones every two years. In this case, these computers

Point: Useful life and salvage value are estimates.

have a two-year useful life. The useful life of a plant asset is impacted by inadequacy and obsolescence. **Inadequacy** is the inability of a plant asset to meet its demands. **Obsolescence** is the process of becoming outdated and no longer used.

Depreciation Methods

Depreciation methods are used to allocate a plant asset's cost over its useful life. The most frequently used method is the straight-line method. The units-of-production and double-declining methods are also commonly used. We explain all three methods. Computations in this section use information about a machine used by **Reebok** and **Adidas** to inspect athletic shoes before packaging. Data for this machine are in Exhibit 10.5.

EXHIBIT 10.5

Data for Machine

Cost	$10,000	Useful life:	
Salvage value	1,000	Accounting periods	5 years
Depreciable cost	$ 9,000	Units inspected	36,000 shoes

Straight-Line Method **Straight-line depreciation** charges the same amount to each period of the asset's useful life. A two-step process is used. We first compute the **depreciable cost** of the asset, also called *cost to be depreciated.* It is computed as asset total cost minus salvage value. Second, depreciable cost is divided by the number of accounting periods in the asset's useful life. The computation for the inspection machine is in Exhibit 10.6.

EXHIBIT 10.6

Straight-Line Depreciation Formula

$$\frac{\textbf{Cost} - \textbf{Salvage value}}{\textbf{Useful life in periods}} = \frac{\$10,000 - \$1,000}{5 \text{ years}} = \$1,800 \text{ per year}$$

Point: Excel for SLN.

	A	B
1	Cost	$10,000
2	Salvage	$1,000
3	Life	5
4	SLN depr.	

=SLN(B1,B2,B3) = $1,800

If this machine is purchased on December 31, 2020, and used during its predicted useful life of five years, the straight-line method allocates equal depreciation to each of the years 2021 through 2025. We make the following adjusting entry at the end of each of the five years to record straight-line depreciation.

Dec. 31	Depreciation Expense	1,800	
	Accumulated Depreciation—Machinery		1,800
	Record annual depreciation.		

Assets = Liabilities + Equity
−1,800 −1,800

The $1,800 Depreciation Expense is reported on the income statement. The $1,800 **Accumulated Depreciation is a contra asset account to the Machinery account on the balance sheet.** Accumulated Depreciation has a normal credit balance. The left graph in Exhibit 10.7 shows the $1,800 per year expense reported in each of the five years. The right graph shows the Machinery account balance (net) on each of the six December 31 balance sheets.

EXHIBIT 10.7

Financial Statement Effects of Straight-Line Depreciation

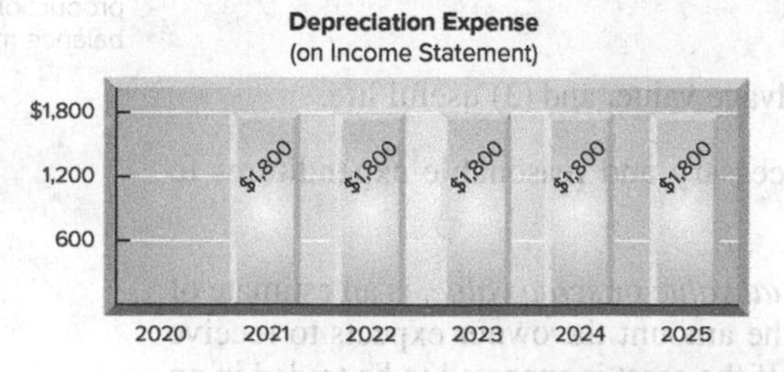

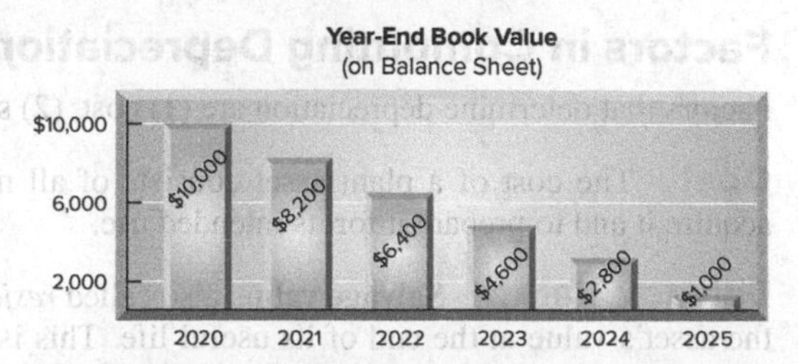

The net balance sheet amount is the **asset book value,** or *book value,* and is the asset's total cost minus accumulated depreciation. For example, at the end of the first year, its book value is $8,200, which is $10,000 minus $1,800, and is reported in the balance sheet as follows.

Book value = Cost − Accumulated depreciation

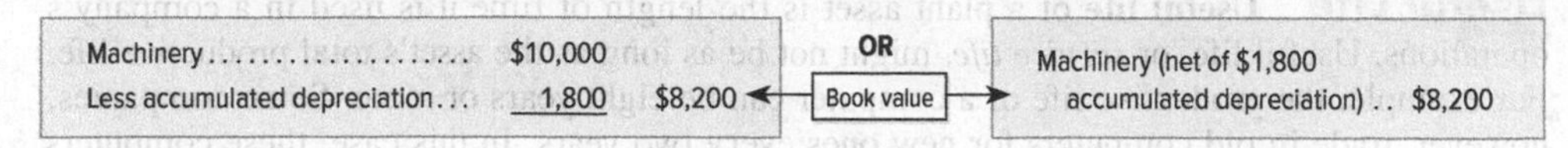

Machinery $10,000
Less accumulated depreciation... 1,800 $8,200
Book value
OR
Machinery (net of $1,800 accumulated depreciation) .. $8,200

We also can compute the *straight-line depreciation rate,* which is 100% divided by the number of periods in the asset's useful life. For the inspection machine, this rate is 20% (100% ÷ 5 years, or 20% per period). We use this rate, along with other information, to compute the machine's *straight-line depreciation schedule* shown in Exhibit 10.8. This exhibit shows (1) straight-line depreciation is the same each period, (2) accumulated depreciation is the total of current and prior periods' depreciation expense, and (3) book value declines each period until it equals salvage value.

EXHIBIT 10.8

Straight-Line Depreciation Schedule

	Depreciation for the Period			End of Period	
Annual Period	Depreciable Cost*	Depreciation Rate	Depreciation Expense	Accumulated Depreciation	Book Value†
2020	—	—	—	—	$10,000
2021	$9,000	20%	$1,800	$1,800	8,200
2022	9,000	20	1,800	3,600	6,400
2023	9,000	20	1,800	5,400	4,600
2024	9,000	20	1,800	7,200	2,800
2025	9,000	20	1,800	9,000	**1,000**
			$9,000 ←	$10,000 cost − $1,000 salvage	

*$10,000 − $1,000. †Book value is total cost minus accumulated depreciation.

Units-of-Production Method The use of some plant assets varies greatly from one period to the next. For example, a builder might use a piece of equipment for a month and then not use it again for several months. When equipment use varies from period to period, the units-of-production depreciation method can better match expenses with revenues. **Units-of-production depreciation** charges a varying amount for each period depending on an asset's *usage*. A two-step process is used.

1. Compute *depreciation per unit* as the asset's total cost minus salvage value and then divide by the total units expected to be produced during its useful life. Units of production can be expressed in product or other units such as hours used or miles driven.
2. Compute *depreciation expense* for the period by multiplying the depreciation per unit by the units produced in the period.

The computation for the machine described in Exhibit 10.5 is in Exhibit 10.9. The company reports that 7,000 shoes are inspected and sold in its first year.

EXHIBIT 10.9

Units-of-Production Depreciation Formula

Step 1 $\textbf{Depreciation per unit} = \dfrac{\textbf{Cost − Salvage value}}{\textbf{Total units of production}} = \dfrac{\$10{,}000 - \$1{,}000}{36{,}000 \text{ shoes}} = \$0.25 \text{ per shoe}$

Step 2 **Depreciation expense = Depreciation per unit × Units produced in period**

$0.25 per shoe × 7,000 shoes = $1,750

Using data on the number of units inspected (shoes produced) by the machine, we compute the *units-of-production depreciation schedule* in Exhibit 10.10. For example, depreciation for the first year is $1,750 (7,000 shoes at $0.25 per shoe). Depreciation for the second year is $2,000 (8,000 shoes at $0.25 per shoe). Exhibit 10.10 shows (1) depreciation expense depends on unit output, (2) accumulated depreciation is the total of current and prior periods' depreciation expense, and (3) book value declines each period until it equals salvage value. **Once an asset's book value equals its salvage value, depreciation stops.**

Example: Refer to Exhibit 10.10. If the number of shoes inspected in 2025 is 5,500, what is depreciation for 2025? *Answer:* $1,250 (never depreciate below salvage value)

EXHIBIT 10.10

Units-of-Production Depreciation Schedule

Annual Period	Depreciation for the Period: Number of Units	Depreciation per Unit	Depreciation Expense	End of Period: Accumulated Depreciation	Book Value
2020	—	—	—	—	$10,000
2021	7,000	$0.25	**$1,750**	$1,750	8,250
2022	8,000	0.25	**2,000**	3,750	6,250
2023	9,000	0.25	**2,250**	6,000	4,000
2024	7,000	0.25	**1,750**	7,750	2,250
2025	5,000	0.25	**1,250**	9,000	1,000
	36,000 units	$10,000 cost − $1,000 salvage →	**$9,000**	Salvage value is not depreciated.	

SL rate = $\frac{100\%}{\text{Useful life}}$

DDB rate = $\frac{200\%}{\text{Useful life}}$

Point: Excel for DDB.

	A	B
1	Cost	$10,000
2	Salvage	$1,000
3	Life	5
4	DDB depr.	
5	1	
6	2	
7	etc.	

=DDB(B1,B2,B3,A5) = $4,000

=DDB(B1,B2,B3,A6) = $2,400

Declining-Balance Method An **accelerated depreciation method** has more depreciation in the early years and less depreciation in later years. The most common accelerated method is the **declining-balance method,** which uses a depreciation rate that is a multiple of the straight-line rate. A common depreciation rate is double the straight-line rate. This is called *double-declining-balance (DDB)*. This is done in three steps.

1. Compute the asset's straight-line depreciation rate.
2. Double the straight-line rate.
3. Compute depreciation by multiplying this rate by the asset's beginning-period book value.

The first-year depreciation computation for the machine described in Exhibit 10.5 is in Exhibit 10.11. The three steps are

1. Divide 100% by five years to get the straight-line rate of 20%, or 1/5, per year.
2. Double this 20% rate to get the declining-balance rate of 40%, or 2/5, per year.
3. Compute depreciation as 40%, or 2/5, multiplied by the beginning-period book value.

EXHIBIT 10.11

Double-Declining-Balance Depreciation Formula*

Step 1 Straight-line rate = 100% ÷ Useful life = 100% ÷ 5 years = 20%

Step 2 Double-declining-balance rate = 2 × Straight-line rate = 2 × 20% = 40%

Step 3 Depreciation expense = Double-declining-balance rate × Beginning-period book value

40% × $10,000 = $4,000 (for 2021)

*In simple form: DDB depreciation = (2 × Beginning-period book value)/Useful life.

The *double-declining-balance depreciation schedule* is in Exhibit 10.12. The schedule follows the formula except for year 2025, when depreciation is $296. This $296 is not equal to 40% × $1,296, or $518.40. If we had used the $518.40 for depreciation in 2025, the ending book value would equal $777.60, which is less than the $1,000 salvage value. Instead, the $296 is computed as $1,296 book value minus $1,000 salvage value (for the year when DDB depreciation cuts into salvage value).

EXHIBIT 10.12

Double-Declining-Balance Depreciation Schedule

Annual Period	Depreciation for the Period: Beginning-of-Period Book Value	Depreciation Rate	Depreciation Expense	End of Period: Accumulated Depreciation	Book Value
2020	—	—	—	—	$10,000
2021	$10,000	40%	**$4,000**	$4,000	6,000
2022	6,000	40	**2,400**	6,400	3,600
2023	3,600	40	**1,440**	7,840	2,160
2024	2,160	40	**864**	8,704	1,296
2025	1,296	40	**296**	9,000	1,000
		$10,000 cost − $1,000 salvage →	**$9,000**	Salvage value is not depreciated.	

Comparing Depreciation Methods Exhibit 10.13 shows depreciation for each year under the three methods. While depreciation per period differs, total depreciation of $9,000 is the same over the useful life.

EXHIBIT 10.13

Depreciation Expense for the Different Methods

Period	Straight-Line	Units-of-Production	Double-Declining-Balance
2021	$1,800	$1,750	$4,000
2022	1,800	2,000	2,400
2023	1,800	2,250	1,440
2024	1,800	1,750	864
2025	1,800	1,250	296
Totals	$9,000	$9,000	$9,000

Popular Methods

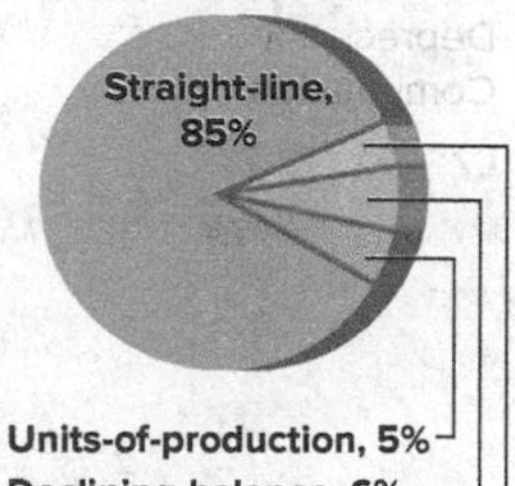

Units-of-production, 5%
Declining-balance, 6%
Accelerated & other, 4%

Depreciation for Tax Reporting Many companies use accelerated depreciation in computing taxable income. Reporting higher depreciation expense in the early years of an asset's life reduces the company's taxable income in those years and increases it in later years. The goal is to *postpone* its tax payments. The U.S. tax law has rules for depreciating assets. These rules include the **Modified Accelerated Cost Recovery System (MACRS),** which allows straight-line depreciation for some assets but requires accelerated depreciation for most kinds of assets. MACRS is *not* acceptable for financial reporting because it does not consider an asset's useful life or salvage value.

Partial-Year Depreciation

C2 Explain depreciation for partial years and changes in estimates.

When an asset is purchased or sold at a time other than the beginning or end of an accounting period, depreciation is recorded for part of that period.

Mid-Period Asset Purchase Assume that the machine in Exhibit 10.5 is purchased and placed in service on October 1, 2020, and the annual accounting period ends on December 31. Because this machine is used for three months in 2020, the calendar-year income statement reports depreciation for those three months. Using straight-line depreciation, we compute three months' depreciation of $450 as follows.

$$\frac{\$10{,}000 - \$1{,}000}{5 \text{ years}} \times \frac{3}{12} = \$450$$

Point: Assets purchased on days 1 through 15 of a month are usually recorded as purchased on the 1st of that month. Assets purchased on days 16 to month-end are recorded as if purchased on the 1st of the next month. The same applies to asset sales.

Mid-Period Asset Sale Assume that the machine above is sold on June 1, 2025. Depreciation is recorded in 2025 for the period January 1 through June 1 as follows.

$$\frac{\$10{,}000 - \$1{,}000}{5 \text{ years}} \times \frac{5}{12} = \$750$$

Change in Estimates

Depreciation is based on estimates of salvage value and useful life. If our estimate of an asset's useful life and/or salvage value changes, what should we do? The answer is to use the new estimate to compute depreciation for current and future periods. Revising an estimate of the useful life or salvage value of a plant asset is called a **change in an accounting estimate** and only affects current and future financial statements. We do not go back and restate (change) prior years' statements. This applies to all depreciation methods.

Let's return to the machine in Exhibit 10.8 using straight-line depreciation. At the beginning of this asset's third year, its book value is $6,400. Assume that at the beginning of its third year, the estimated number of years remaining in its useful life changes from three to four years *and* its estimate of salvage value changes from $1,000 to $400. Depreciation for each of the four remaining years is computed as in Exhibit 10.14.

	Original Depreciation	Revised Depreciation
2020	–	–
2021	$1,800	$1,800
2022	1,800	1,800
2023	1,800	1,500
2024	1,800	1,500
2025	1,800	1,500
2026	–	1,500
	$9,000	$9,600

EXHIBIT 10.14

Revised Straight-Line Depreciation

$$\frac{\textbf{Book value} - \textbf{Revised salvage value}}{\textbf{Revised remaining useful life}} = \frac{\$6{,}400 - \$400}{4 \text{ years}} = \$1{,}500 \text{ per year}$$

Standret/Shutterstock

Decision Ethics

Controller You are the controller for a struggling tulip grower. Depreciation of equipment is its largest expense. Competitors depreciate equipment over three years. The company president tells you to revise useful lives of equipment from three to six years. What should you do? ■ *Answer:* The president's instructions may be an honest and reasonable prediction of the future. However, you might confront the president if you believe the aim is only to increase income.

NEED-TO-KNOW 10-2

Depreciation Computations

C2 P1

Part 1. A machine costing $22,000 with a five-year life and an estimated $2,000 salvage value is installed on January 1. The manager estimates the machine will produce 1,000 units of product during its life. It actually produces the following units: 200 in Year 1, 400 in Year 2, 300 in Year 3, 80 in Year 4, and 30 in Year 5. The total units produced by the end of Year 5 exceed the original estimate—this difference was not predicted. (The machine must not be depreciated below its estimated salvage value.) Compute depreciation for each year under straight-line, units-of-production, and double-declining-balance.

Part 2. In early January, a company acquires equipment for $3,800. The company estimates this equipment has a useful life of three years and a salvage value of $200. On January 1 of the third year, the company changes its estimates to a total four-year useful life and zero salvage value. Using the straight-line method, what is depreciation expense for the third year?

Solution—Part 1

Year	Depreciation Expense		
	Straight-Line[a]	Units-of-Production[b]	Double-Declining-Balance[c]
1	$ 4,000	$ 4,000	$ 8,800
2	4,000	8,000	5,280
3	4,000	6,000	3,168
4	4,000	1,600	1,901
5	4,000	400	851
Totals...........	$20,000	$20,000	$20,000

[a]Straight-line: Expense per year = ($22,000 − $2,000)/5 years = $4,000 per year

[b]Units-of-production: Expense per unit = ($22,000 − $2,000)/1,000 units = $20 per unit

Year	Units	Depreciation per Unit	Depreciation Expense	Accum. Deprec.	Book Value
1..........	200	$20	$ 4,000	$ 4,000	$18,000
2..........	400	20	8,000	12,000	10,000
3..........	300	20	6,000	18,000	4,000
4..........	80	20	1,600	19,600	2,400
5..........	30	20	400*	20,000*	2,000
Total			$20,000		

*30 × $20 = $600; however, $600 would make accumulated depreciation exceed the $20,000 total depreciable cost. This means we take only enough depreciation in Year 5, a total of $400, to decrease book value to the asset's $2,000 salvage value (never lower).

[c]Double-declining-balance: (100%/5) × 2 = 40% depreciation rate

Year	Beginning Book Value	Depreciation Expense (40% of Beg. book value)	Accumulated Depreciation at Year-End	Ending Book Value (Cost less Accumulated Depreciation)
1.........	$22,000	$ 8,800	$ 8,800	$13,200
2.........	13,200	5,280	14,080	7,920
3.........	7,920	3,168	17,248	4,752
4.........	4,752	1,901*	19,149	2,851
5.........	2,851	851†	20,000	2,000
Total......		$20,000		

*Rounded to the nearest dollar.
†Set depreciation in Year 5 to reduce book value to the $2,000 salvage value; namely, instead of $1,140 ($2,851 × 40%), we use the maximum of $851 ($2,851 − $2,000).

Solution—Part 2

($3,800 − $200)/3 years = $1,200 (original depreciation per year)

$1,200 × 2 years = $2,400 (accumulated depreciation at date of change in estimate)

($3,800 − $2,400)/2 years = **$700** (revised depreciation)

Do More: QS 10-4 through QS 10-10, E 10-4 through E 10-13

ADDITIONAL EXPENDITURES

C3 Distinguish between revenue and capital expenditures, and account for them.

Plant assets require maintenance, repairs, and improvements. We must decide whether to expense or capitalize these expenditures (to capitalize is to increase the asset account).

Revenue expenditures, also called *income statement expenditures,* are costs that do not materially increase the plant asset's life or capabilities. They are recorded as expenses on the current-period income statement.

Capital expenditures, also called *balance sheet expenditures,* are costs of plant assets that provide benefits for longer than the current period. They increase the asset on the balance sheet.

Ordinary Repairs

Ordinary repairs are expenditures to keep an asset in good operating condition. Ordinary repairs do not extend an asset's useful life or increase its productivity beyond original expectations. Examples are normal costs of cleaning, lubricating, changing oil, and replacing small parts of a machine. Ordinary repairs are *revenue expenditures.* This means their costs are reported as expenses on the current-period income statement. Following this rule, **Brunswick** reports that "maintenance and repair costs are expensed as incurred." If Brunswick's current-year repair costs are $9,500, it makes the following entry.

Dec. 31	Repairs Expense	9,500	
	Cash		9,500
	Record ordinary repairs of equipment.		

Assets = Liabilities + Equity
−9,500 −9,500

Betterments and Extraordinary Repairs

Betterments and extraordinary repairs are *capital expenditures.*

Betterments (Improvements) **Betterments,** or *improvements,* are expenditures that make a plant asset more efficient or productive. A betterment often involves adding a component to an asset or replacing an old component with a better one and does not always increase useful life. An example is replacing manual controls on a machine with automatic controls. One special type of betterment is an *addition,* such as adding a new dock to a warehouse. Because a betterment benefits future periods, it is debited to the asset account as a capital expenditure. The new book value (less salvage value) is then depreciated over the asset's remaining useful life. Assume a company pays $8,000 for a machine with an eight-year useful life and no salvage value. After three years and $3,000 of depreciation, it adds an automated control system to the machine at a cost of $1,800. The cost of the betterment is added to the Machinery account with the following entry.

Jan. 2	Machinery	1,800	
	Cash		1,800
	Record installation of automated system.		

Assets = Liabilities + Equity
+1,800
−1,800

After this entry, the remaining cost to be depreciated is $6,800, computed as $8,000 − $3,000 + $1,800. Depreciation for the remaining five years is $1,360 per year, computed as $6,800/5 years.

Additional Expenditures	Examples	Expense Timing	Entry
Ordinary repairs	• Cleaning • Lubricating • Adjusting • Repainting	Expensed currently	Repairs Expense..... # Cash............ #
Betterments and extraordinary repairs	• Replacing main parts • Major asset expansions	Expensed in future	Asset (such as Equip.) # Cash............ #

Extraordinary Repairs (Replacements)

Extraordinary repairs are expenditures that extend the asset's useful life beyond its original estimate. Their costs are debited to the asset account. Both extraordinary repairs and betterments require revising future depreciation.

DISPOSALS OF PLANT ASSETS

P2 Account for asset disposal through discarding or selling an asset.

Disposal of plant assets occurs in one of three ways: discarding, sale, or exchange. Discarding and selling are covered here; Appendix 10A covers exchanges. The steps for disposing of plant assets are in Exhibit 10.15.

EXHIBIT 10.15

Accounting for Disposals

1. Record depreciation up to the date of disposal—this also updates Accumulated Depreciation.
2. Record the removal of the disposed asset's account balances—including its accumulated depreciation.
3. Record any cash (and/or other assets) received or paid in the disposal.
4. Record any gain or loss—equal to the value of any assets received minus the disposed asset's book value.

Discarding Plant Assets

A plant asset is *discarded* when it is no longer useful to the company and it has no market value. Assume that a machine costing $9,000 with accumulated depreciation of $9,000 is discarded. When accumulated depreciation equals the asset's cost, it is said to be *fully depreciated* (zero book value). The entry to record the discarding of this asset is

Assets = Liabilities + Equity
+9,000
−9,000

June 5	Accumulated Depreciation—Machinery	9,000	
	Machinery		9,000
	Discarding of fully depreciated machinery.		

This entry reflects all four steps of Exhibit 10.15. Step 1 is unnecessary because the machine is fully depreciated. Step 2 is reflected in the debit to Accumulated Depreciation and credit to Machinery. Because no other asset is involved, step 3 is irrelevant. Finally, because book value is zero and no other asset is involved, no gain or loss is recorded in step 4.

How do we account for discarding an asset that is not fully depreciated or one whose depreciation is not up-to-date? To answer this, consider equipment costing $8,000 with accumulated depreciation of $6,000 on December 31 of the prior fiscal year-end. This equipment is being depreciated by $1,000 per year using the straight-line method over eight years with zero salvage. On July 1 of the current year it is discarded. Step 1 is to bring depreciation up-to-date.

Point: Recording depreciation expense up-to-date gives an up-to-date book value for determining gain or loss.

Assets = Liabilities + Equity
−500 −500

July 1	Depreciation Expense	500	
	Accumulated Depreciation—Equipment		500
	Record 6 months' depreciation ($1,000 × 6/12).		

Steps 2 through 4 of Exhibit 10.15 are reflected in the second (and final) entry.

Assets = Liabilities + Equity
+6,500 −1,500
−8,000

July 1	Accumulated Depreciation—Equipment............	6,500	
	Loss on Disposal of Equipment	1,500	
	Equipment		8,000
	Discard equipment with a $1,500 book value.		

This loss is computed by comparing the equipment's $1,500 book value ($8,000 − $6,000 − $500) with the zero net cash proceeds. The loss is reported in the Other Expenses and Losses section of the income statement. Discarding an asset can sometimes require a cash payment that would increase the loss.

Selling Plant Assets

To demonstrate selling plant assets, consider BTO's March 31 sale of equipment that cost $16,000 and has accumulated depreciation of $12,000 at December 31 of the prior year-end. Annual depreciation on this equipment is $4,000 using straight-line. Step 1 of this sale is to record depreciation expense and update accumulated depreciation to March 31 of the current year.

Mar. 31	Depreciation Expense	1,000	
	Accumulated Depreciation—Equipment		1,000
	Record 3 months' depreciation ($4,000 × 3/12).		

Assets = Liabilities + Equity
−1,000 −1,000

Steps 2 through 4 need one final entry that depends on the amount received from the sale. We cover three different possibilities.

Sale at Book Value If BTO receives $3,000 cash, an amount equal to the equipment's book value as of March 31 (book value = $16,000 − $12,000 − $1,000), no gain or loss is recorded. The entry is

Sale price = Book value → No gain or loss

Mar. 31	Cash	3,000	
	Accumulated Depreciation—Equipment............	13,000	
	Equipment		16,000
	Record sale of equipment for no gain or loss.		

Assets = Liabilities + Equity
+3,000
+13,000
−16,000

Sale above Book Value If BTO receives $7,000, an amount that is $4,000 above the equipment's $3,000 book value as of March 31, a gain is recorded. The entry is

Sale price > Book value → Gain

Mar. 31	Cash	7,000	
	Accumulated Depreciation—Equipment............	13,000	
	Gain on Disposal of Equipment................		4,000
	Equipment		16,000
	Record sale of equipment for a $4,000 gain.		

Assets = Liabilities + Equity
+7,000 +4,000
+13,000
−16,000

Sale below Book Value If BTO receives $2,500, an amount that is $500 below the equipment's $3,000 book value as of March 31, a loss is recorded. The entry is

Sale price < Book value → Loss

Mar. 31	Cash	2,500	
	Loss on Disposal of Equipment..................	500	
	Accumulated Depreciation—Equipment............	13,000	
	Equipment		16,000
	Record sale of equipment for a $500 loss.		

Assets = Liabilities + Equity
+2,500 −500
+13,000
−16,000

NEED-TO-KNOW 10-3

Additional Expenditures and Asset Disposals

C3 P2

Part 1. A company pays $1,000 for equipment expected to last four years and have a $200 salvage value. Prepare journal entries to record the following costs related to the equipment.

a. During the second year of the equipment's life, $400 cash is paid for a new component expected to materially increase the equipment's productivity.

b. During the third year, $250 cash is paid for normal repairs necessary to keep the equipment in good working order.

c. During the fourth year, $500 is paid for repairs expected to increase the useful life of the equipment from four to five years.

Part 2. A company owns a machine that cost $500 and has accumulated depreciation of $400. Prepare the entry to record the disposal of the machine on January 2 in each separate situation.

a. The company disposed of the machine, receiving nothing in return.
b. The company sold the machine for $80 cash.
c. The company sold the machine for $100 cash.
d. The company sold the machine for $110 cash.

Solution—Part 1

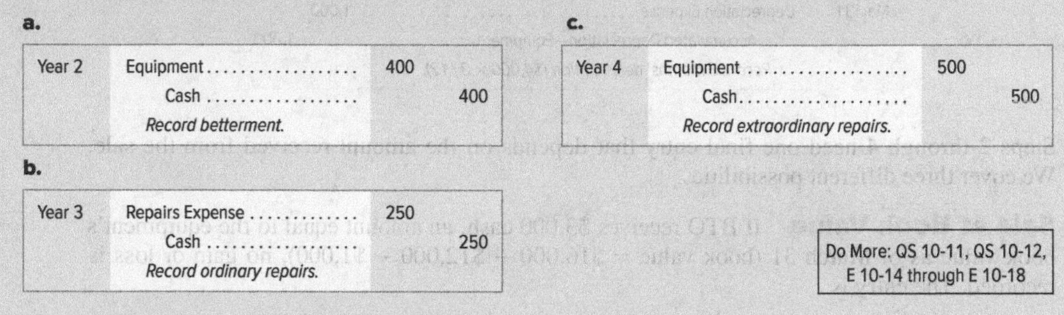

a.

Year 2	Equipment	400	
	Cash		400
	Record betterment.		

b.

Year 3	Repairs Expense	250	
	Cash		250
	Record ordinary repairs.		

c.

Year 4	Equipment	500	
	Cash		500
	Record extraordinary repairs.		

Do More: QS 10-11, QS 10-12, E 10-14 through E 10-18

Solution—Part 2 (*Note:* Book value of machine = $500 − $400 = $100)

a. Disposed of at no value.

Jan. 2	Loss on Disposal of Machine	100	
	Accumulated Depreciation—Machine	400	
	Machine		500
	Record disposal of machine.		

b. Sold for $80 cash.

Jan. 2	Cash	80	
	Loss on Sale of Machine	20	
	Accumulated Depreciation—Machine	400	
	Machine		500
	Record sale of machine below book value.		

c. Sold for $100 cash.

Jan. 2	Cash	100	
	Accumulated Depreciation—Machine	400	
	Machine		500
	Record sale of machine at book value.		

d. Sold for $110 cash.

Jan. 2	Cash	110	
	Accumulated Depreciation—Machine	400	
	Gain on Sale of Machine		10
	Machine		500
	Record sale of machine above book value.		

Section 2—Natural Resources

P3 Account for natural resource assets and their depletion.

Natural resources are assets that are physically consumed when used. Examples are standing timber, mineral deposits, and oil and gas fields. These assets are soon-to-be inventories of raw materials after cutting, mining, or pumping. Until that conversion happens, they are reported as noncurrent assets under either plant assets or their own category using titles such as *Timberlands, Mineral deposits,* or *Oil reserves.*

Cost Determination and Depletion

Natural resources are recorded at cost, which includes all expenditures necessary to acquire the resource and prepare it for use. **Depletion** is the process of allocating the cost of a natural resource to the period when it is consumed. Natural resources are reported on the balance sheet at cost minus *accumulated depletion.* The depletion expense per period is usually based on units extracted from cutting, mining, or pumping. This is similar to units-of-production depreciation.

To demonstrate, consider a mineral deposit with an estimated 250,000 tons of available ore. It is purchased for $500,000, and we expect zero salvage value. The depletion charge per ton of ore mined is $2, computed as $500,000 ÷ 250,000 tons. If 85,000 tons are mined and sold in the first year, the depletion charge for that year is $170,000. These computations are in Exhibit 10.16.

EXHIBIT 10.16

Depletion Formula

$$\text{Step 1 Depletion per unit} = \frac{\text{Cost} - \text{Salvage value}}{\text{Total units of capacity}} = \frac{\$500{,}000 - \$0}{250{,}000 \text{ tons}} = \$2 \text{ per ton}$$

$$\text{Step 2 Depletion expense} = \text{Depletion per unit} \times \text{Units extracted and sold in period}$$
$$= \$2 \times 85{,}000 = \$170{,}000$$

Depletion expense for the first year is recorded as follows.

Dec. 31	Depletion Expense—Mineral Deposit	170,000	
	Accumulated Depletion—Mineral Deposit		170,000
	Record depletion of the mineral deposit.		

Assets = Liabilities + Equity
−170,000 −170,000

The period-end balance sheet reports the mineral deposit as shown in Exhibit 10.17.

EXHIBIT 10.17

Balance Sheet Presentation of Natural Resources

Mineral deposit	$500,000	
Less accumulated depletion . .	170,000	$330,000

OR

Mineral deposit (net of $170,000 accumulated depletion)	$330,000

Because all 85,000 tons of the mined ore are sold during the year, the entire $170,000 of depletion is reported on the income statement. If some of the ore remains unsold at year-end, the depletion related to the unsold ore is carried forward on the balance sheet and reported as Ore Inventory, a current asset. Altering our example, assume that of the 85,000 tons mined the first year, only 70,000 tons are sold. We record depletion of $140,000 (70,000 tons × $2 depletion per unit) and the remaining ore inventory of $30,000 (15,000 tons × $2 depletion per unit) as follows.

Dec. 31	Depletion Expense—Mineral Deposit	140,000	
	Ore Inventory	30,000	
	Accumulated Depletion—Mineral Deposit		170,000
	Record depletion and inventory of mineral deposit.		

Assets = Liabilities + Equity
−170,000 −140,000
+30,000

Plant Assets Tied into Extracting

Mining, cutting, or pumping natural resources requires machinery, equipment, and buildings. When the usefulness of these plant assets is directly related to the depletion of a natural resource, their costs are depreciated using the units-of-production method in proportion to the depletion of the natural resource. For example, if a machine is permanently installed in a mine and 10% of the ore is mined and sold in the period, then 10% of the machine's cost (minus any salvage value) is depreciated. The same procedure is used when a machine is abandoned once resources are extracted. If the machine will be used at another site when extraction is complete, it is depreciated over its own useful life.

BeyondImages/iStock/Getty Images

Ethical Risk

Play It Safe Long-term assets must be safeguarded against theft, misuse, and damage. Controls include use of security tags, monitoring of rights infringements, and approvals of asset disposals. A study reports that 43% of employees in operations and services witnessed the wasting, mismanaging, or abusing of assets in the past year (KPMG). ■

NEED-TO-KNOW 10-4

Depletion Accounting

P3

A company acquires a zinc mine at a cost of $750,000 on January 1. At that same time, it incurs additional costs of $100,000 to access the mine, which is estimated to hold 200,000 tons of zinc. The estimated value of the land after the zinc is removed is $50,000.

1. Prepare the January 1 entry(ies) to record the cost of the zinc mine.
2. Prepare the December 31 year-end adjusting entry if 50,000 tons of zinc are mined, but only 40,000 tons are sold the first year.

Solution

1.

Date	Account	Debit	Credit
Jan. 1	Zinc Mine	850,000	
	Cash		850,000
	Record cost of zinc mine.		

2. Depletion per unit = ($750,000 + $100,000 − $50,000)/200,000 tons = $4.00 per ton

Date	Account	Debit	Credit
Dec. 31	Depletion Expense—Zinc Mine	160,000	
	Zinc Inventory	40,000	
	Accumulated Depletion—Zinc Mine		200,000
	Record depletion of zinc mine (50,000 × $4.00).		

Do More: QS 10-13, E 10-19, E 10-20, P 10-7

Section 3—Intangibles

P4 Account for intangible assets.

Intangible assets are nonphysical assets used in operations that give companies long-term rights or competitive advantages. Examples are patents, copyrights, licenses, leaseholds, franchises, and trademarks. Lack of physical substance does not always mean an intangible asset. For example, notes and accounts receivable lack physical substance but are not intangibles. This section covers common types of intangible assets.

Cost Determination and Amortization

An intangible asset is recorded at cost when purchased. Intangibles can have limited lives or indefinite lives. If an intangible has a **limited life,** its cost is expensed over its estimated useful life using **amortization.** If an intangible asset has an **indefinite life**—meaning that no legal, competitive, economic, or other factors limit its useful life—it is not amortized. If an intangible with an indefinite life is later judged to have a limited life, it is amortized over that limited life.

Amortization of intangible assets is similar to depreciation. However, only the straight-line method is used for amortizing intangibles *unless* the company can show that another method is preferred. Amortization is recorded in a contra account, Accumulated Amortization, which has a normal credit balance. The acquisition cost of intangible assets is disclosed along with the accumulated amortization. The disposal of an intangible asset involves removing its book value, recording any other asset(s) received or given up, and recognizing any gain or loss for the difference.

Many intangibles have limited lives due to laws, contracts, or other reasons. Examples are patents, copyrights, and leaseholds. The cost of intangible assets is amortized over the periods expected to benefit from their use, but this period cannot be longer than the assets' legal existence. Other intangibles such as trademarks and trade names have indefinite lives and are not amortized. An intangible asset that is not amortized is tested annually for **impairment**—if necessary, an impairment loss is recorded. (Details are in advanced courses.)

Intangible assets are often in a separate section of the balance sheet immediately after plant assets. For example, **Nike** follows this approach in reporting nearly $300 million of intangible assets in its balance sheet, plus $140 million in goodwill. Companies usually disclose their amortization periods for intangibles. The remainder of our discussion focuses on accounting for specific types of intangible assets.

Jiangsihui/Shutterstock

Types of Intangibles

Patents The federal government grants patents to encourage the invention of new technology and processes. A **patent** is an exclusive right granted to its owner to manufacture and sell a patented item or to use a process for 20 years. When patent rights are purchased, the cost to acquire the rights is debited to an account called Patents. If the owner engages in lawsuits to successfully defend a patent, the cost of lawsuits is debited to the Patents account; if the defense is unsuccessful, the book value of the patent is expensed. However, the costs of research and development leading to a new patent are expensed when incurred.

A patent's cost is amortized over its estimated useful life (not to exceed 20 years). If we purchase a patent costing $25,000 with a useful life of 10 years, we make the following adjusting entry at the end of each of the 10 years to amortize one-tenth of its cost. The $2,500 debit to Amortization Expense is on the income statement. The Accumulated Amortization—Patents account is a contra asset account to Patents.

Dec. 31	Amortization Expense—Patents.	2,500	
	Accumulated Amortization—Patents		2,500
	Amortize patent costs over its useful life.		

Assets = Liabilities + Equity
−2,500 −2,500

Copyrights

A **copyright** gives its owner the exclusive right to publish and sell a musical, literary, or artistic work during the life of the creator plus 70 years, although the useful life of most copyrights is much shorter. The costs of a copyright are amortized over its useful life. The only identifiable cost of many copyrights is the fee paid to the Copyright Office. Identifiable costs of a copyright are capitalized (recorded in an asset account) and amortized by debiting an account called Amortization Expense—Copyrights.

Franchises and Licenses

Franchises and **licenses** are rights that a company or government grants an entity to sell a product or service under specified conditions. Many organizations grant franchise and license rights—**Anytime Fitness, Firehouse Subs,** and **Major League Baseball** are just a few examples. The costs of franchises and licenses are debited to a Franchises and Licenses asset account and are amortized over the life of the agreement. If an agreement is for an indefinite time, those costs are not amortized.

Trademarks and Trade Names

A **trademark** or **trade (brand) name** is a symbol, name, phrase, or jingle identified with a company, product, or service. Examples are Nike Swoosh, Big Mac, Coca-Cola, and Corvette. Ownership and exclusive right to use a trademark or trade name often are granted to the company that used it first. Ownership is best established by registering a trademark or trade name with the government's Patent Office. The cost of developing, maintaining, or enhancing the value of a trademark or trade name (such as advertising) is charged to expense when incurred. If a trademark or trade name is purchased, however, its cost is debited to an asset account and then amortized over its expected life. If the company plans to renew indefinitely its right to the trademark or trade name, the cost is not amortized.

Point: McDonald's "golden arches" are one of the world's most valuable trademarks, yet this asset is not on McDonald's balance sheet.

Goodwill

Goodwill is the amount by which a company's value exceeds the value of its individual assets and liabilities. This implies that the company as a whole has certain valuable attributes not measured in assets and liabilities. These can include superior management, skilled workforce, good supplier or customer relations, quality products or services, good location, or other competitive advantages.

Goodwill is only recorded when an entire company or business segment is purchased. Purchased goodwill is computed as purchase price of the company minus the market value of net assets (excluding goodwill). **Google** paid $1.19 billion to acquire **YouTube**; about $1.13 of the $1.19 billion was for goodwill. Goodwill is recorded as an asset, and it is *not* amortized. Instead, goodwill is annually tested for impairment. (Details are in advanced courses.)

Right-of-Use Asset (Lease)

Property is rented under a contract called a **lease.** The property's owner, called the **lessor,** grants the lease. The one who secures the right to possess and use the property is called the **lessee.** A **leasehold** is the rights the lessor grants to the lessee under the terms of the lease.

Lease or Buy Some advantages of leasing an asset versus buying it are that

- Little or no up-front payment is normally required (making it more affordable).
- Lease terms often allow exchanges to trade up on leased assets (reducing obsolescence).

Leasehold Improvements A lessee sometimes pays for improvements to the leased property such as partitions, painting, and storefronts. These improvements are called **leasehold improvements,** and the lessee debits these costs to a Leasehold Improvements account. The lessee amortizes these costs over the life of the lease or the life of the improvements, whichever is shorter. The amortization entry *debits* Amortization Expense—Leasehold Improvements and *credits* Accumulated Amortization—Leasehold Improvements.

Other Intangibles There are other types of intangible assets such as software, noncompete covenants, customer lists, and so forth. Accounting for them is the same as for other intangibles.

Research and Development **Research and development costs** are expenditures to discover new products, new processes, or knowledge. Creating patents, copyrights, and innovative products and services requires research and development costs. **The costs of research and development are expensed when incurred** because it is difficult to predict the future benefits from research and development. GAAP does **not** include them as intangible assets.

Decision Insight

Yoshikazu Tsuno/AFP/Getty Images

Save Mickey **Walt Disney Company** successfully lobbied Congress to extend copyright protection from the life of the creator plus 50 years to the life of the creator plus 70 years. This extension allows the company to protect its characters for 20 additional years before the right to use them enters the public domain. Mickey Mouse is now protected by copyright law through start of 2024. The law is officially termed the Copyright Term Extension Act (CTEA), but it is also known as the Mickey Mouse Protection Act. ■

NEED-TO-KNOW 10-5

Accounting for Intangibles

P4

Do More: QS 10-15, QS 10-16, QS 10-17, QS 10-18, E 10-21, E 10-22, E 10-23

Part 1. A publisher purchases the copyright on a book for $1,000 on January 1 of this year. The copyright lasts five more years. The company plans to sell prints for seven years. Prepare entries to record the purchase of the copyright on January 1 and its annual amortization on December 31.

Part 2. On January 3 of this year, a retailer pays $9,000 to modernize its store. Improvements include lighting, partitions, and a sound system. These improvements are estimated to yield benefits for five years. The retailer leases its store and has three years remaining on its lease. Prepare the entry to record (a) the cost of modernization and (b) amortization at the end of this year.

Part 3. On January 6 of this year, a company pays $6,000 for a patent with a remaining 12-year legal life to produce a supplement expected to be marketable for 3 years. Prepare entries to record its acquisition and the December 31 amortization entry.

Solution—Part 1

Date	Account	Debit	Credit
Jan. 1	Copyright	1,000	
	Cash		1,000
	Record purchase of copyright.		

Date	Account	Debit	Credit
Dec. 31	Amortization Expense—Copyright	200	
	Accumulated Amortization—Copyright		200
	Record amortization ($1,000/5 years).		

Solution—Part 2

a.

Date	Account	Debit	Credit
Jan. 3	Leasehold Improvements	9,000	
	Cash		9,000
	Record leasehold improvements.		

b.

Date	Account	Debit	Credit
Dec. 31	Amortization Expense—Leasehold Improvements	3,000	
	Accumulated Amortization—Leasehold Improvements		3,000
	*Record amortization over remaining life.**		

*Amortization = $9,000/3-year lease term = $3,000 per year.

Solution—Part 3

Date	Account	Debit	Credit
Jan. 6	Patents	6,000	
	Cash		6,000
	Record purchase of patent.		

Date	Account	Debit	Credit
Dec. 31	Amortization Expense*	2,000	
	Accumulated Amortization— Patents		2,000
	Record amortization of patent.		
	**$6,000/3 years = $2,000*		

Total Asset Turnover  **Decision Analysis**

A1 Compute total asset turnover and apply it to analyze a company's use of assets.

One important measure of a company's ability to use its assets efficiently and effectively is **total asset turnover,** defined in Exhibit 10.18. Net sales is net amounts earned from the sale of products and services. Average total assets is (Current period-end total assets + Prior period-end total assets)/2. A higher total asset turnover means a company is generating more net sales for each dollar of assets. Management is evaluated on efficient and effective use of total assets by looking at total asset turnover.

EXHIBIT 10.18 Total Asset Turnover

$$\textbf{Total asset turnover} = \frac{\textbf{Net sales}}{\textbf{Average total assets}}$$

Let's look at total asset turnover in Exhibit 10.19 for two competing companies: **Starbucks** and **Jack in the Box.** To show how we use total asset turnover, let's look at Starbucks. We express Starbucks's use of assets in generating net sales by saying, "it turned its assets over 1.22 times during the current year." This means that each $1.00 of assets produced $1.22 of net sales.

EXHIBIT 10.19 Analysis Using Total Asset Turnover

Company	Figure ($ millions)	Current Year	1 Year Ago	2 Years Ago
Starbucks	Net sales..............	$26,509	$24,720	$22,387
	Average total assets......	$21,688	$19,261	$14,339
	Total asset turnover	**1.22**	**1.28**	**1.56**
Jack in the Box	Net sales..............	$950	$870	$1,097
	Average total assets......	$891	$1,029	$1,290
	Total asset turnover	**1.07**	**0.85**	**0.85**

Is a total asset turnover of 1.22 good or bad? All companies want a high total asset turnover. Interpreting the total asset turnover requires an understanding of company operations. Some operations are capital-intensive, meaning that a relatively large amount is invested in plant assets to generate sales. This results in a lower total asset turnover. Other companies' operations are labor-intensive, meaning that they generate sales using people instead of assets. In that case, we expect a higher total asset turnover.

Starbucks's turnover is higher than that for Jack in the Box. However, Starbucks's total asset turnover decreased over the last three years. To maintain a strong total asset turnover, Starbucks must grow sales at a rate equal to, or higher than, its total asset growth.

Decision Maker

Environmentalist A paper manufacturer claims it cannot afford more environmental controls. It points to its low total asset turnover of 1.9 and argues that it cannot compete with companies whose total asset turnover is much higher. Examples cited are food stores (5.5) and auto dealers (3.8). How do you respond? ■ *Answer:* The paper manufacturer's comparison of its total asset turnover with food stores and auto dealers is misdirected. You need to collect data from competitors in the paper industry to show that a 1.9 total asset turnover is about the norm for this industry.

NEED-TO-KNOW 10-6

COMPREHENSIVE

Acquisition, Cost Allocation, and Disposal of Tangible and Intangible Assets

On July 1, Year 1, Tulsa Company pays $600,000 to acquire a fully equipped factory. The purchase includes the following assets.

Asset	Appraised Value	Salvage Value	Useful Life	Depreciation Method
Land..................	$160,000			Not depreciated
Land improvements	80,000	$ 0	10 years	Straight-line
Building..............	320,000	100,000	10 years	Double-declining-balance
Machinery............	240,000	20,000	10,000 units	Units-of-production
Total..................	$800,000			

Required

1. Allocate the total $600,000 purchase cost among the separate assets in the table above.
2. Compute the Year 1 (six months) and Year 2 depreciation expense for each asset in the table above. The machinery produced 700 units in Year 1 and 1,800 units in Year 2.

3. Tulsa also discarded equipment at year-end that had been on its books for five years. The equipment's original cost was $12,000 (estimated life of five years) and its salvage value was $2,000. No depreciation had been recorded for the fifth year when the disposal occurred. Journalize the fifth year of depreciation (straight-line method) and the asset's disposal.
4. On January 1 of the current year, Tulsa purchased a patent for $100,000 cash. The company estimated the patent's useful life to be 10 years. Journalize the patent acquisition and its amortization for this year.
5. Tulsa also acquired an ore deposit for $600,000 cash. It added roads and built mine shafts for an additional cost of $80,000. Salvage value of the mine is estimated to be $20,000. The company estimated 330,000 tons of available ore. During the first year, Tulsa mined and sold 10,000 tons of ore. Journalize the mine's acquisition and its first year's depletion.

SOLUTION

1. Allocation of the total cost of $600,000 among the separate assets.

Asset	Appraised Value	Percent of Total Value	Apportioned Cost
Land	$160,000	20%	$120,000 ($600,000 × 20%)
Land improvements	80,000	10	60,000 ($600,000 × 10%)
Building	320,000	40	240,000 ($600,000 × 40%)
Machinery	240,000	30	180,000 ($600,000 × 30%)
Total	$800,000	100%	$ 600,000

2. Depreciation for each asset. (Land is not depreciated.)

Land Improvements

Cost	$ 60,000
Salvage value	0
Depreciable cost	$ 60,000
Useful life	10 years
Annual depreciation expense ($60,000/10 years)	$ 6,000
Year 1 depreciation ($6,000 × 6/12)	$ 3,000
Year 2 depreciation	$ 6,000

Building

Straight-line rate = 100%/10 years = 10%

Double-declining-balance rate = 10% × 2 = 20%

Year 1 depreciation ($240,000 × 20% × 6/12)	$ 24,000
Year 2 depreciation [($240,000 − $24,000) × 20%]	$ 43,200

Machinery

Cost	$180,000
Salvage value	20,000
Depreciable cost	$160,000
Total expected units of production	10,000 units
Depreciation per unit ($160,000/10,000 units)	$ 16
Year 1 depreciation ($16 × 700 units)	$ 11,200
Year 2 depreciation ($16 × 1,800 units)	$ 28,800

3. Record the depreciation up-to-date on the discarded asset.

Account	Debit	Credit
Depreciation Expense—Equipment	2,000	
Accumulated Depreciation—Equipment		2,000
Record depreciation on date of disposal: ($12,000 − $2,000)/5.		

Record the removal of discarded asset and its loss on disposal.

Account	Debit	Credit
Accumulated Depreciation—Equipment	10,000	
Loss on Disposal of Equipment	2,000	
Equipment		12,000
Record discarding of equipment with $2,000 book value.		

4.

Account	Debit	Credit
Patent	100,000	
Cash		100,000
Record patent acquisition.		

Account	Debit	Credit
Amortization Expense—Patent	10,000	
Accumulated Amortization—Patent		10,000
Record amortization expense: $100,000/10 years = $10,000.		

5.

Account	Debit	Credit
Ore Deposit	680,000	
Cash		680,000
Record ore deposit acquisition.		

Account	Debit	Credit
Depletion Expense—Ore Deposit	20,000	
Accumulated Depletion—Ore Deposit		20,000
Record depletion expense: ($680,000 − $20,000)/330,000 tons = $2 per ton. Depletion = $2 per ton × 10,000 tons mined and sold. = $20,000.		

APPENDIX

Exchanging Plant Assets

10A

P5 Account for asset exchanges.

Many plant assets such as machinery, automobiles, and equipment are exchanged for newer assets. In a typical exchange of plant assets, a *trade-in allowance* is received on the old asset and the balance is paid in cash. Accounting for the exchange of assets depends on whether the transaction has *commercial substance.* An exchange has commercial substance if the company's future cash flows change as a result of the exchange of one asset for another asset. If an asset exchange has commercial substance, a gain or loss is recorded based on the difference between the book value of the asset(s) given up and the market value of the asset(s) received. Because most exchanges have commercial substance, we cover gains and losses for only that situation. Advanced courses cover exchanges without commercial substance.

Exchange with Commercial Substance: A Loss A company acquires $42,000 in new equipment. In exchange, the company pays $33,000 cash and trades in old equipment. The old equipment originally cost $36,000 and has accumulated depreciation of $20,000, which implies a $16,000 book value at the time of exchange. This exchange has commercial substance and the old equipment has a trade-in allowance of $9,000. This exchange yields a loss, as computed in the middle (Loss) columns of Exhibit 10A.1; the loss is computed as Asset received − Assets given = $42,000 − $49,000 = $(7,000). We also can compute the loss as Trade-in allowance − Book value of assets given = $9,000 − $16,000 = $(7,000).

EXHIBIT 10A.1

Asset Exchange with Commercial Substance

Asset Exchange Has Commercial Substance	Loss		Gain	
Market value of asset received		$42,000		$42,000
Book value of assets given:				
Equipment ($36,000 − $20,000)	$16,000		$16,000	
Cash	33,000	49,000	23,000	39,000
Gain (loss) on exchange		$(7,000)		$ 3,000

The entry to record this asset exchange and the loss follows.

Jan. 3	Equipment **(new)**	42,000	
	Loss on Exchange of Assets	7,000	
	Accumulated Depreciation—Equipment **(old)**	20,000	
	Equipment **(old)**		36,000
	Cash		33,000
	Record exchange (with commercial substance) of old equipment and cash for new equipment.		

Assets	=	Liabilities	+	Equity
+42,000				−7,000
+20,000				
−36,000				
−33,000				

Point: "New" and "old" equipment are for illustration only. Both the debit and credit are to the same Equipment account.

Exchange with Commercial Substance: A Gain Let's assume the same facts as in the preceding asset exchange *except that the company pays $23,000 cash, not $33,000, with the trade-in.* This exchange has commercial substance and the old equipment has a trade-in allowance of $19,000. This exchange yields a gain, as computed in the right-most (Gain) columns of Exhibit 10A.1; the gain is computed as Asset received − Assets given = $42,000 − $39,000 = $3,000. We also can compute the gain as Trade-in allowance − Book value of assets given = $19,000 − $16,000 = $3,000. The entry to record this asset exchange and the gain follows.

Jan. 3	Equipment **(new)**	42,000	
	Accumulated Depreciation—Equipment **(old)**	20,000	
	Equipment **(old)**		36,000
	Cash		23,000
	Gain on Exchange of Assets		3,000
	Record exchange (with commercial substance) of old equipment and cash for new equipment.		

Assets	=	Liabilities	+	Equity
+42,000				+3,000
+20,000				
−36,000				
−23,000				

NEED-TO-KNOW 10-7

Asset Exchange

P5

Do More: QS 10-22, E 10-25, E 10-26

A company acquires $45,000 in new web servers. In exchange, the company trades in old web servers along with a cash payment. The old servers originally cost $30,000 and had accumulated depreciation of $23,400 at the time of the trade. Prepare entries to record the trade under two different assumptions where (a) the exchange has commercial substance and the old servers have a trade-in allowance of $3,000 and (b) the exchange has commercial substance and the old servers have a trade-in allowance of $7,000.

Solution

a.

Account	Debit	Credit
Equipment (new)	45,000	
Loss on Exchange of Assets	3,600	
Accumulated Depreciation—Equipment (old)	23,400	
Equipment (old)		30,000
Cash ($45,000 − $3,000)		42,000

b.

Account	Debit	Credit
Equipment (new)	45,000	
Accumulated Depreciation—Equipment (old)	23,400	
Equipment (old)		30,000
Cash ($45,000 − $7,000)		38,000
Gain on Exchange of Assets		400

Summary: Cheat Sheet

PLANT ASSETS

Cost of plant assets: Normal, reasonable, and necessary costs in preparing an asset for its intended use. If an asset is damaged during unpacking, the repairs are not added to its cost. Instead, they are charged to an expense account.

Machinery and equipment: Cost includes purchase price, taxes, transportation, insurance while in transit, installation, assembly, and testing.

Building: A purchased building's costs include its purchase price, real estate fees, taxes, title fees, and attorney fees. A constructed building's costs include construction costs and insurance during construction, but not insurance after it is completed.

Land improvements: Additions to land that have limited useful lives. Examples are parking lots, driveways, and lights.

Land: Has an indefinite (unlimited) life and costs include real estate commissions, clearing, grading, and draining.

Lump-sum purchase: Plant assets purchased as a group for a single lump-sum price. We allocate the cost to the assets acquired based on their relative market (or appraised) values.

	Appraised Value	Percent of Total	Apportioned Cost
Building	$ 60,000	60% ($60,000/$100,000)	$54,000 ($90,000 × 60%)
Land	40,000	40 ($40,000/$100,000)	36,000 ($90,000 × 40%)
Totals	$100,000	100%	$ 90,000

Entry for lump-sum cash purchase:

Account	Debit	Credit
Building	54,000	
Land	36,000	
Cash		90,000
Record costs of assets.		

Depreciation: Process of allocating the cost of a plant asset to expense while it is in use.

Salvage value: Estimate of the asset's value at the end of its useful life.

Useful life: Length of time a plant asset is to be used in operations.

Record depreciation expense:

Account	Debit	Credit
Depreciation Expense	1,800	
Accumulated Depreciation—"Asset Type"		1,800

Straight-line depreciation: Charges the same amount of depreciation expense in each period of the asset's useful life.

Straight-line depreciation formula:

$$\text{Depreciation expense} = \frac{\text{Cost} - \text{Salvage value}}{\text{Useful life in periods}}$$

Asset book value (or book value): Computed as the asset's total cost minus accumulated depreciation.

Units-of-production depreciation: Charges a varying amount for each period depending on an asset's usage.

Units-of-production formula:

Step 1 $\text{Depreciation per unit} = \frac{\text{Cost} - \text{Salvage value}}{\text{Total units of production}}$

Step 2 Depreciation expense = Depreciation per unit × Units produced in period

Double-declining-balance depreciation: Charges more depreciation in early years and less depreciation in later years.

Double-declining-balance formula:

Step 1 Straight-line rate = 100% ÷ Useful life

Step 2 Double-declining-balance rate = 2 × Straight-line rate

Step 3 Depreciation expense = Double-declining-balance rate × Beginning-period book value

Change in an accounting estimate: For plant assets, it is changing the estimate of useful life or salvage value. It only affects current and future depreciation expense. Do not go back and change prior years' depreciation.

Straight-line depreciation after change in accounting estimate:

$$\frac{\text{Book value} - \text{Revised salvage value}}{\text{Revised remaining useful life}}$$

Ordinary repairs (revenue expenditure): Expenditures to keep an asset in good operating condition. They do not increase useful life or productivity. Include cleaning, changing oil, and minor repairs.

Account	Debit	Credit
Repairs Expense	9,500	
Cash		9,500

Betterments (capital expenditure): Expenditures to make a plant asset more efficient or productive. Include upgrading components and adding additions onto plant assets.

Extraordinary repairs (capital expenditure): Expenditures that extend the asset's useful life beyond its original estimate.

Betterments and extraordinary repairs: These expenditures are "capitalized" by adding their costs to the plant asset.

Account	Debit	Credit
"Plant Asset"	1,800	
Cash		1,800

Before discarding, selling, or exchanging a plant asset: Must record depreciation up to that date.

Account	Debit	Credit
Depreciation Expense	500	
Accumulated Depreciation—Equipment		500

Discarding *fully* depreciated asset:

Accumulated Depreciation—Machinery	9,000	
Machinery		9,000

Discarding *partially* depreciated asset: Loss is the book value (Cost − Accumulated depreciation) of the asset when discarded.

Accumulated Depreciation—Equipment	6,500	
Loss on Disposal of Equipment	1,500	
Equipment		8,000

Sale of asset at book value: If sale price = book value, no gain or loss.

Cash	3,000	
Accumulated Depreciation—Equipment	13,000	
Equipment		16,000

Sale of asset *above* book value: If sale price > book value → gain.

Cash	7,000	
Accumulated Depreciation—Equipment	13,000	
Gain on Disposal of Equipment		4,000
Equipment		16,000

Sale of asset *below* book value: If sale price < book value → loss.

Cash	2,500	
Loss on Disposal of Equipment	500	
Accumulated Depreciation—Equipment	13,000	
Equipment		16,000

NATURAL RESOURCES

Natural resources: Assets that are physically consumed when used. Examples are standing timber, mineral deposits, and oil and gas fields.
Depletion: Process of allocating the cost of a natural resource.

Depletion formula:

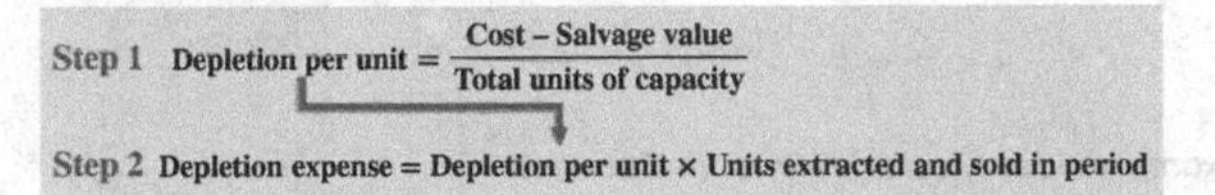

Step 1 Depletion per unit = Cost − Salvage value / Total units of capacity
Step 2 Depletion expense = Depletion per unit × Units extracted and sold in period

Depletion expense (when *all* units extracted are sold):

Depletion Expense—Mineral Deposit	170,000	
Accumulated Depletion—Mineral Deposit		170,000

Depletion expense (when *not all* units extracted are sold):

Depletion Expense—Mineral Deposit	140,000	
Ore Inventory	30,000	
Accumulated Depletion—Mineral Deposit		170,000

INTANGIBLES

Intangible assets: Nonphysical assets (used in operations) that give companies long-term rights, privileges, or competitive advantages.
Amortization: Intangible assets with limited useful lives require amortization. It is similar to depreciation and uses the shorter of the legal life or useful life of the intangible for straight-line amortization.

Amortization Expense—Patents	2,500	
Accumulated Amortization—Patents		2,500

Patent: Exclusive right to manufacture and sell a patented item or to use a process for 20 years.
Copyright: Exclusive right to publish and sell a musical, literary, or artistic work during the life of the creator plus 70 years.
Franchises or licenses: Rights to sell a product or service under specified conditions.
Trademark or trade (brand) name: A symbol, name, phrase, or jingle identified with a company, product, or service.
Goodwill: Amount by which a company's value exceeds the value of its individual assets and liabilities (net assets). Goodwill is only recorded when an entire company or business segment is purchased. Not amortized, but tested for impairment.
Right-of-use asset (lease): Rights the lessor grants to the lessee under terms of the lease.
Leasehold improvements: Improvements to a leased (rented) property such as partitions, painting, and storefronts. The lessee amortizes these costs over the life of the lease or the life of the improvements, whichever is shorter.

Key Terms

Accelerated depreciation method (362)
Amortization (370)
Asset book value (360)
Betterments (365)
Capital expenditures (365)
Change in an accounting estimate (363)
Copyright (371)
Cost (358)
Declining-balance method (362)
Depletion (368)
Depreciable cost (360)
Depreciation (368)
Extraordinary repairs (366)
Franchises (371)
Goodwill (371)
Impairment (370)
Inadequacy (360)
Indefinite life (370)
Intangible assets (370)
Land improvements (358)
Lease (371)
Leasehold (371)
Leasehold improvements (372)
Lessee (371)
Lessor (371)
Licenses (371)
Limited life (370)
Modified Accelerated Cost Recovery System (MACRS) (363)
Natural resources (368)
Obsolescence (360)
Ordinary repairs (365)
Patent (370)
Plant assets (357)
Research and development costs (372)
Revenue expenditures (365)
Salvage value (359)
Straight-line depreciation (360)
Total asset turnover (373)
Trademark or trade (brand) name (371)
Units-of-production depreciation (361)
Useful life (359)

Multiple Choice Quiz

1. A company paid $326,000 for property that included land, land improvements, and a building. The land was appraised at $175,000, the land improvements were appraised at $70,000, and the building was appraised at $105,000. What is the allocation of costs to the three assets?

a. Land, $150,000; Land Improvements, $60,000; Building, $90,000
b. Land, $163,000; Land Improvements, $65,200; Building, $97,800
c. Land, $150,000; Land Improvements, $61,600; Building, $92,400
d. Land, $159,000; Land Improvements, $65,200; Building, $95,400
e. Land, $175,000; Land Improvements, $70,000; Building, $105,000

2. A company purchased a truck for $35,000 on January 1, Year 1. The truck is estimated to have a useful life of four years and a salvage value of $1,000. Assuming that the company uses straight-line depreciation, what is depreciation expense for the year ended December 31, Year 2?

a. $8,750 **c.** $8,500 **e.** $25,500
b. $17,500 **d.** $17,000

3. A company purchased machinery for $10,800,000 on January 1, Year 1. The machinery has a useful life of 10 years and an estimated salvage value of $800,000. What is depreciation expense for the year ended December 31, Year 2, assuming that the double-declining-balance method is used?

a. $2,160,000 **c.** $1,728,000 **e.** $1,600,000
b. $3,888,000 **d.** $2,000,000

4. A company sold a machine that originally cost $250,000 for $120,000 when accumulated depreciation on the machine was $100,000. The gain or loss recorded on the sale is

a. $0 gain or loss. **c.** $30,000 loss. **e.** $150,000 loss.
b. $120,000 gain. **d.** $30,000 gain.

5. A company had average total assets of $500,000, gross sales of $575,000, and net sales of $550,000. The company's total asset turnover is

a. 1.15. **c.** 0.91. **e.** 1.05.
b. 1.10. **d.** 0.87.

ANSWERS TO MULTIPLE CHOICE QUIZ

1. b;

	Appraisal Value	%	Total Cost	Allocated
Land	$175,000	50%	$326,000	$163,000
Land improvements	70,000	20	326,000	65,200
Building	105,000	30	326,000	97,800
Totals	$350,000			$326,000

2. c; ($35,000 − $1,000)/4 years = $8,500 per year

3. c; Year 1: $10,800,000 × (2 × 10%) = $2,160,000
Year 2: ($10,800,000 − $2,160,000) × (2 × 10%) = $1,728,000

4. c;

Cost of machine	$250,000
Accumulated depreciation	100,000
Book value	150,000
Cash received	120,000
Loss on sale	$ 30,000

5. b; $550,000/$500,000 = 1.10

Superscript letter A denotes assignments based on Appendix 10A.

Select Quick Study and Exercise assignments feature Guided Example videos, called "Hints" in Connect. Hints use different numbers, and instructors can turn this feature on or off.

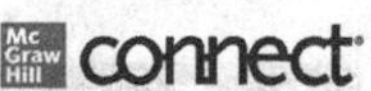

QUICK STUDY

QS 10-1
Cost of plant assets C1

Kegler Bowling buys scorekeeping equipment with an invoice cost of $190,000. The electrical work required for the installation costs $20,000. Additional costs are $4,000 for delivery and $13,700 for sales tax. During the installation, the equipment was damaged and the cost of repair was $1,850. What is the total recorded cost of the scorekeeping equipment?

QS 10-2
Assigning costs to plant assets
C1

Listed below are costs (or discounts) to purchase or construct new plant assets. (1) Indicate whether the costs should be *expensed* or *capitalized* (meaning they are included in the cost of the plant assets on the balance sheet). (2) For costs that should be capitalized, indicate in which category of plant assets (Equipment, Building, or Land) the related costs should be recorded on the balance sheet.

1. Wages paid to train employees to use new equipment.
2. Invoice cost paid for new equipment.
3. Early payment discount taken on the purchase of new equipment.
4. Realtor commissions incurred on land purchased.
5. Property taxes on land incurred a year after the land was purchased.
6. Costs of oil for the truck used to deliver new equipment.
7. Costs to lay foundation for a new building.
8. Insurance on a new building during its construction.

QS 10-3
Lump-sum purchase of assets C1

Diego Co. paid $180,000 cash to acquire a group of items consisting of land appraised at $50,000 and a building appraised at $150,000. Allocate total cost to these two assets and prepare an entry to record the purchase.

QS 10-4
Straight-line depreciation P1

On January 1, the Matthews Band pays $65,800 for sound equipment. The band estimates it will use this equipment for four years and perform 200 concerts. It estimates that after four years it can sell the equipment for $2,000. During the first year, the band performs 45 concerts.
Compute the first-year depreciation using the straight-line method.

QS 10-5
Units-of-production depreciation P1

On January 1, the Matthews Band pays $65,800 for sound equipment. The band estimates it will use this equipment for four years and perform 200 concerts. It estimates that after four years it can sell the equipment for $2,000. During the first year, the band performs 45 concerts.
Compute the first-year depreciation using the units-of-production method.

QS 10-6
Double-declining-balance method P1

A building is acquired on January 1 at a cost of $830,000 with an estimated useful life of eight years and salvage value of $75,000. Compute depreciation expense for the first three years using the double-declining-balance method.

QS 10-7
Computing depreciation under different methods P1

Equipment costing $13,000 with a 10-year useful life and an estimated $3,000 salvage value is acquired and started operating on January 1. The equipment is estimated to produce 2,000 units of product during its life. It produced 160 units in the first year. Compute depreciation for the first year under straight-line, units-of-production, and double-declining-balance.

QS 10-8
Recording depreciation journal entries P1

Refer to QS 10-7 and record the journal entries for equipment depreciation for the first year under straight-line, units-of-production, and double-declining-balance.

QS 10-9
Straight-line, partial-year depreciation C2

On October 1, Organic Farming purchases wind turbines for $140,000. The wind turbines are expected to last six years, have a salvage value of $20,000, and be depreciated using the straight-line method.

1. Compute depreciation expense for the last three months of the first year.
2. Compute depreciation expense for the second year.

QS 10-10
Computing revised depreciation C2

On January 1, the Matthews Band pays $65,800 for sound equipment. The band estimates it will use this equipment for four years and after four years it can sell the equipment for $2,000. Matthews Band uses straight-line depreciation but realizes at the start of the second year that this equipment will last only a total of three years. The salvage value is not changed.
Compute the revised depreciation for both the second and third years.

QS 10-11
Revenue and capital expenditures C3

1. Classify the following as either a revenue expenditure or a capital expenditure.
   a. Paid $40,000 cash to replace a motor on equipment that extends its useful life by four years.
   b. Paid $200 cash per truck for the cost of their annual tune-ups.
   c. Paid $175 for the monthly cost of replacement filters on an air-conditioning system.
   d. Completed an addition to a building for $225,000 cash.
2. Prepare the journal entries to record the four transactions from part 1.

QS 10-12
Disposal of assets P2

Garcia Co. owns equipment that cost $76,800, with accumulated depreciation of $40,800. Record the sale of the equipment under the following three separate cases assuming Garcia sells the equipment for (1) $47,000 cash, (2) $36,000 cash, and (3) $31,000 cash.

QS 10-13
Natural resources and depletion P3

Perez Company acquires an ore mine at a cost of $1,400,000. It incurs additional costs of $400,000 to access the mine, which is estimated to hold 1,000,000 tons of ore. The estimated value of the land after the ore is removed is $200,000.

1. Prepare the entry(ies) to record the cost of the ore mine.
2. Prepare the year-end adjusting entry if 180,000 tons of ore are mined and sold the first year.

QS 10-14
Classifying assets
P3 P4

Identify the following as intangible assets, natural resources, or some other asset.

a. Oil well	**d.** Gold mine	**g.** Franchise
b. Trademark	**e.** Building	**h.** Coal mine
c. Leasehold	**f.** Copyright	**i.** Salt mine

QS 10-15
Intangible assets and amortization P4

On January 1 of this year, Diaz Boutique pays $105,000 to modernize its store. Improvements include new floors, ceilings, wiring, and wall coverings. These improvements are estimated to yield benefits for 10 years. Diaz leases (does not own) its store and has eight years remaining on the lease. Prepare the entry to record (1) the cost of modernization and (2) amortization at the end of this current year.

QS 10-16
Reporting intangible assets
P4

Robotix Co. purchases a patent for $20,000 on January 1. The patent is good for 18 years, after which anyone can use the patent technology. However, Robotix plans to sell products using that patent technology for only 5 years. Prepare the intangible asset section of the year end balance sheet after amortization expense for the year is recorded.

QS 10-17
Computing goodwill P4

Baine Company purchased Vera Company at a price of $500,000. The fair value of the net assets purchased equals $420,000. Compute the amount of goodwill that Baine records at the purchase date.

QS 10-18
Identifying research and development expenses
P4

A&J Co. incurred the following expenses related to patented drugs.

1. Indicate costs that are reported as research and development expenses on the income statement.
2. Indicate costs that are capitalized and reported in the Patent account on the balance sheet.

Legal fees in successful patent defense	$20,000	Acquired a new patent.......	$50,000
Researcher salaries to develop drugs	85,000	Research lab rent expense	6,000

QS 10-19
Preparing an income statement
P1 P3 P4

Selected accounts from Westeros Co.'s adjusted trial balance for the year ended December 31 follow. Prepare its income statement.

Sales	$30,000	Depreciation expense	$ 5,000
Repairs expense............	500	Salaries expense	10,000
Depletion expense............	4,000	Amortization expense............	2,000

QS 10-20
Preparing assets section of a balance sheet
P1 P4

The asset accounts from Ridley Co.'s adjusted trial balance for its December 31 year-end follow. Prepare the assets section of its classified balance sheet.

Copyrights	$ 5,000	Trademarks	$20,000
Inventory	6,000	Cash............	8,000
Accumulated amortization—Copyrights	1,000	Buildings	90,000
Accumulated depreciation—Buildings	18,000	Land............	35,000

QS 10-21
Computing total asset turnover A1

Aneko Company reports the following: net sales of $14,800 for Year 2 and $13,990 for Year 1; end-of-year total assets of $19,100 for Year 2 and $17,900 for Year 1.

1. Compute total asset turnover for Year 2.
2. Aneko's competitor has a turnover of 2.0. Is Aneko performing better or worse than its competitor based on total asset turnover?

QS 10-22^A
Asset exchange
P5

Caleb Co. owns a machine that had cost $42,400 with accumulated depreciation of $18,400. Caleb exchanges the machine for a newer model that has a market value of $52,000.

1. Record the exchange assuming Caleb paid $30,000 cash and the exchange has commercial substance.
2. Record the exchange assuming Caleb paid $22,000 cash and the exchange has commercial substance.

Mc Graw Hill connect

EXERCISES

Exercise 10-1
Cost of plant assets C1

Rizio Co. purchases a machine for $12,500, terms 2/10, n/60, FOB shipping point. Rizio paid within the discount period and took the $250 discount. Transportation costs of $360 were paid by Rizio. The machine required mounting and power connections costing $895. Another $475 is paid to assemble the machine, and $40 of materials are used to get it into operation. During installation, the machine was damaged and $180 worth of repairs were made. Compute the cost recorded for this machine.

Exercise 10-2
Recording costs of assets
C1

Cala Manufacturing purchases land for $390,000 as part of its plans to build a new plant. The company pays $33,500 to tear down an old building on the lot and $47,000 to fill and level the lot. It also pays construction costs of $1,452,200 for the new building and $87,800 for lighting and paving a parking area. Prepare a single journal entry to record these costs incurred by Cala, all of which are paid in cash.

Exercise 10-3
Lump-sum purchase of plant assets C1

Rodriguez Company pays $395,380 for real estate with land, land improvements, and a building. Land is appraised at $157,040; land improvements are appraised at $58,890; and the building is appraised at $176,670. Allocate the total cost among the three assets and prepare the journal entry to record the purchase.

Exercise 10-4
Straight-line depreciation
P1

Ramirez Company installs a computerized manufacturing machine in its factory at the beginning of the year at a cost of $43,500. The machine's useful life is estimated at 10 years, or 385,000 units of product, with a $5,000 salvage value. During its second year, the machine produces 32,500 units of product. Determine the machine's second-year depreciation under the straight-line method.

Exercise 10-5
Units-of-production depreciation P1

Ramirez Company installs a computerized manufacturing machine in its factory at the beginning of the year at a cost of $43,500. The machine's useful life is estimated at 10 years, or 385,000 units of product, with a $5,000 salvage value. During its second year, the machine produces 32,500 units of product. Determine the machine's second-year depreciation using the units-of-production method.

Exercise 10-6
Double-declining-balance depreciation P1

Ramirez Company installs a computerized manufacturing machine in its factory at the beginning of the year at a cost of $43,500. The machine's useful life is estimated at 10 years, or 385,000 units of product, with a $5,000 salvage value. During its second year, the machine produces 32,500 units of product. Determine the machine's second-year depreciation using the double-declining-balance method.

Exercise 10-7
Straight-line depreciation
P1

NewTech purchases computer equipment for $154,000 to use in operating activities for the next four years. It estimates the equipment's salvage value at $25,000. Prepare a table showing depreciation and book value for each of the four years assuming straight-line depreciation.

Exercise 10-8
Double-declining-balance depreciation P1

NewTech purchases computer equipment for $154,000 to use in operating activities for the next four years. It estimates the equipment's salvage value at $25,000. Prepare a table showing depreciation and book value for each of the four years assuming double-declining-balance depreciation.

Exercise 10-9
Straight-line depreciation and income effects
P1

Tory Enterprises pays $238,400 for equipment that will last five years and have a $43,600 salvage value. By using the equipment in its operations for five years, the company expects to earn $88,500 annually, after deducting all expenses except depreciation. Prepare a table showing income before depreciation, depreciation expense, and net (pretax) income for each year and for the total five-year period, assuming straight-line depreciation is used.

Exercise 10-10
Double-declining-balance depreciation P1

Tory Enterprises pays $238,400 for equipment that will last five years and have a $43,600 salvage value. By using the equipment in its operations for five years, the company expects to earn $88,500 annually, after deducting all expenses except depreciation. Prepare a table showing income before depreciation, depreciation expense, and net (pretax) income for each year and for the total five-year period, assuming double-declining-balance depreciation is used.

Check Year 3 NI, $54,170

Exercise 10-11
Straight-line, partial-year depreciation C2

On April 1, Cyclone Co. purchases a trencher for $280,000. The machine is expected to last five years and have a salvage value of $40,000. Compute depreciation expense at December 31 for both the first year and second year assuming the company uses the straight-line method.

Exercise 10-12
Double-declining-balance, partial-year depreciation C2

On April 1, Cyclone Co. purchases a trencher for $280,000. The machine is expected to last five years and have a salvage value of $40,000. Compute depreciation expense at December 31 for both the first year and second year assuming the company uses the double-declining-balance method.

Exercise 10-13
Revising depreciation
C2

Apex Fitness Club uses straight-line depreciation for a machine costing $23,860, with an estimated four-year life and a $2,400 salvage value. At the beginning of the third year, Apex determines that the machine has three more years of remaining useful life, after which it will have an estimated $2,000 salvage value. Compute (1) the machine's book value at the end of its second year and (2) the amount of depreciation for each of the final three years given the revised estimates.

Check (2) $3,710

Exercise 10-14
Ordinary repairs, extraordinary repairs, and betterments
C3

Oki Company pays $264,000 for equipment expected to last four years and have a $29,000 salvage value. Prepare journal entries to record the following costs related to the equipment.

1. Paid $22,000 cash for a new component that increased the equipment's productivity.
2. Paid $6,250 cash for minor repairs necessary to keep the equipment working well.
3. Paid $14,870 cash for significant repairs to increase the useful life of the equipment from four to seven years.

Exercise 10-15
Extraordinary repairs; plant asset age
C3

Martinez Company owns a building that appears on its prior year-end balance sheet at its original $572,000 cost less $429,000 accumulated depreciation. The building is depreciated on a straight-line basis assuming a 20-year life and no salvage value. During the first week in January of the current calendar year, major structural repairs are completed on the building at a $68,350 cost. The repairs extend its useful life for 5 years beyond the 20 years originally estimated.

1. Determine the building's age (plant asset age) as of the prior year-end balance sheet date.
2. Prepare the entry to record the cost of the structural repairs that are paid in cash.
3. Determine the book value of the building immediately after the repairs are recorded.
4. Prepare the entry to record the current calendar year's depreciation.

Check (3) $211,350

Exercise 10-16
Financial statement impact of plant asset transactions
C3 P1

Analyze each of the following transactions by showing its effects on the accounting equation—specifically, identify the accounts and amounts (including + or −) for each transaction.

Jan. 1	Purchased equipment for $25,000 cash. Estimated useful life is six years and salvage value is $6,000.
Jan. 2	Paid $5,000 cash to install automated controls on equipment. This betterment did not impact useful life or salvage value.
Aug. 15	Paid $200 cash for minor repair costs to equipment.

Exercise 10-17
Disposal of assets
P2

Diaz Company owns a machine that cost $250,000 and has accumulated depreciation of $182,000. Prepare the entry to record the disposal of the machine on January 1 in each separate situation.

1. The machine needed extensive repairs and was not worth repairing. Diaz disposed of the machine, receiving nothing in return.
2. Diaz sold the machine for $35,000 cash.
3. Diaz sold the machine for $68,000 cash.
4. Diaz sold the machine for $80,000 cash.

Exercise 10-18
Partial-year depreciation; disposal of plant asset
P2

Rayya Co. purchases a machine for $105,000 on January 1, 2021. Straight-line depreciation is taken each year for four years assuming a seven-year life and no salvage value. The machine is sold on July 1, 2025, during its fifth year of service. Prepare entries to record the partial year's depreciation on July 1, 2025, and to record the sale under each separate situation.

1. The machine is sold for $45,500 cash.
2. The machine is sold for $25,000 cash.

Exercise 10-19
Depletion of natural resources
P3

Montana Mining Co. pays $3,721,000 for an ore deposit containing 1,525,000 tons. The company installs machinery in the mine costing $213,500. Both the ore and machinery will have no salvage value after the ore is completely mined. Montana mines and sells 166,200 tons of ore during the year. Prepare the December 31 year-end entries to record both the ore deposit depletion and the mining machinery depreciation. Mining machinery depreciation should be in proportion to the mine's depletion.

Exercise 10-20
Depletion of natural resources
P3

A company pays $760,000 cash to acquire an iron mine on January 1. At that same time, it incurs additional costs of $60,000 cash to access the mine, which is estimated to hold 100,000 tons of iron. The estimated value of the land after the iron is removed is $20,000.

1. Prepare the January 1 entry to record the cost of the iron mine.
2. Prepare the December 31 year-end adjusting entry if 20,000 tons of iron are mined but only 18,000 tons are sold this first year.

Exercise 10-21
Amortization of intangible assets P4

Milano Gallery purchases the copyright on a painting for $418,000 on January 1. The copyright is good for 10 more years, after which the copyright will expire and anyone can make prints. The company plans to sell prints for 11 years. Prepare entries to record the purchase of the copyright on January 1 and its annual amortization on December 31.

Exercise 10-22
Goodwill
P4

Robinson Company purchased Franklin Company at a price of $2,500,000. The fair market value of the net assets purchased equals $1,800,000.

1. What is the amount of goodwill that Robinson records at the purchase date?
2. Does Robinson amortize goodwill at year-end for financial reporting purposes? If so, over how many years is it amortized?
3. Robinson believes that its employees provide superior customer service, and through their efforts, Robinson believes it has created $900,000 of goodwill. Should Robinson Company record this goodwill?

Exercise 10-23
Preparing a balance sheet
P1 P3 P4

Selected accounts from Gregor Co.'s adjusted trial balance for the year ended December 31 follow. Prepare a classified balance sheet.

Gregor, Capital	$50,000	Accounts payable	$ 2,000
Patents	4,000	Accumulated depreciation—Equipment	13,000
Cash	6,000	Notes payable (due in 9 years)	11,000
Land	30,000	Goodwill	5,000
Equipment	20,000	Accumulated depletion—Silver mine	3,000
Silver mine	15,000	Accumulated amortization—Patents	1,000

Exercise 10-24
Computing and analyzing asset turnover **A1**

Lok Co. reports net sales of $5,856,480 for Year 2 and $8,679,690 for Year 3. End-of-year balances for total assets are Year 1, $1,686,000; Year 2, $1,800,000; and Year 3, $1,982,000. (*a*) Compute Lok's total asset turnover for Year 2 and Year 3. (*b*) Lok's competitor has a turnover of 3.0. Is Lok performing better or worse than its competitor on the basis of total asset turnover?

Exercise 10-25^A
Exchanging assets
P5

Gilly Construction trades in an old tractor for a new tractor, receiving a $29,000 trade-in allowance and paying the remaining $83,000 in cash. The old tractor had cost $96,000 and had accumulated depreciation of $52,500. Answer the following questions assuming the exchange has commercial substance.

1. What is the book value of the old tractor at the time of exchange?
2. What is the loss on this asset exchange?
3. What amount should be recorded (debited) in the asset account for the new tractor?

Check (2) $14,500

Exercise 10-26^A
Exchanging assets
P5

On January 2, Bering Co. disposes of a machine costing $44,000 with accumulated depreciation of $24,625. Prepare the entries to record the disposal under each separate situation.

1. The machine is sold for $18,250 cash.
2. The machine is traded in for a new machine having a $60,200 cash price. A $25,000 trade-in allowance is received, and the balance is paid in cash. Assume the asset exchange has commercial substance.
3. The machine is traded in for a new machine having a $60,200 cash price. A $15,000 trade-in allowance is received, and the balance is paid in cash. Assume the asset exchange has commercial substance.

Check (3) Dr. Loss on Exchange, $4,375

PROBLEM SET A

Problem 10-1A
Plant asset costs; depreciation methods
C1 P1

Timberly Construction makes a lump-sum purchase of several assets on January 1 at a total cash price of $900,000. The estimated market values of the purchased assets are building, $508,800; land, $297,600; land improvements, $28,800; and four vehicles, $124,800.

Required

1. Allocate the lump-sum purchase price to the separate assets purchased. Prepare the journal entry to record the purchase.
2. Compute the first-year depreciation expense on the building using the straight-line method, assuming a 15-year life and a $27,000 salvage value.
3. Compute the first-year depreciation expense on the land improvements assuming a five-year life and double-declining-balance depreciation.

Check (2) $30,000

(3) $10,800

Analysis Component

4. Compared to straight-line depreciation, does accelerated depreciation result in payment of less total taxes over the asset's life?

Problem 10-2A
Depreciation methods
P1

A machine costing $257,500 with a four-year life and an estimated $20,000 salvage value is installed in Luther Company's factory on January 1. The factory manager estimates the machine will produce 475,000 units of product during its life. It actually produces the following units: 220,000 in Year 1, 124,600 in Year 2, 121,800 in Year 3, and 15,200 in Year 4. The total number of units produced by the end of Year 4 exceeds the original estimate—this difference was not predicted. *Note:* The machine cannot be depreciated below its estimated salvage value.

Required

Check Year 4: units-of-production depreciation, $4,300; DDB depreciation, $12,187

Prepare a table with the following column headings and compute depreciation for each year (and total depreciation of all years combined) for the machine under each depreciation method.

Year	Straight-Line	Units-of-Production	Double-Declining-Balance

Problem 10-3A
Asset cost allocation; straight-line depreciation
C1 P1

On January 1, Mitzu Co. pays a lump-sum amount of $2,600,000 for land, Building 1, Building 2, and Land Improvements 1. Building 1 has no value and will be demolished. Building 2 will be an office and is appraised at $644,000, with a useful life of 20 years and a $60,000 salvage value. Land Improvements 1 is valued at $420,000 and is expected to last another 12 years with no salvage value. The land is valued at $1,736,000. The company also incurs the following additional costs.

Cost to demolish Building 1	$ 328,400	Cost of additional land grading	$175,400
Cost to construct Building 3, having a useful life of 25 years and a $392,000 salvage value. . . .	2,202,000	Cost of new Land Improvements 2, having a 20-year useful life and no salvage value	164,000

Required

Check (1) Land costs, $2,115,800; Building 2 costs, $598,000

(3) Depr.—Land Improv. 1 and 2, $32,500 and $8,200

1. Prepare a table with the following column headings: Land, Building 2, Building 3, Land Improvements 1, and Land Improvements 2. Allocate the costs incurred by Mitzu to the appropriate columns and total each column.
2. Prepare a single journal entry to record all the incurred costs assuming they are paid in cash on January 1.
3. Using the straight-line method, prepare the December 31 adjusting entries to record depreciation for the first year these assets were in use.

Problem 10-4A
Computing and revising depreciation; revenue and capital expenditures
C1 C2 C3

Champion Contractors completed the following transactions involving equipment.

Year 1

Jan. 1 Paid $287,600 cash plus $11,500 in sales tax and $1,500 in transportation (FOB shipping point) for a new loader. The loader is estimated to have a four-year life and a $20,600 salvage value. Loader costs are recorded in the Equipment account.

3 Paid $4,800 to install air-conditioning in the loader to enable operations under harsher conditions. This increased the estimated salvage value of the loader by another $1,400.

Dec. 31 Recorded annual straight-line depreciation on the loader.

Check Dec. 31, Year 1: Dr. Depr. Expense—Equip., $70,850

Year 2

Jan. 1 Paid $5,400 to overhaul the loader's engine, which increased the loader's estimated useful life by two years.

Feb. 17 Paid $820 for minor repairs to the loader after the operator backed it into a tree.

Dec. 31 Recorded annual straight-line depreciation on the loader.

Dec. 31, Year 2: Dr. Depr. Expense—Equip., $43,590

Required

Prepare journal entries to record these transactions and events.

Problem 10-5A
Computing and revising depreciation; selling plant assets
C2 P1 P2

Yoshi Company completed the following transactions and events involving its delivery trucks.

Year 1

Jan. 1 Paid $20,515 cash plus $1,485 in sales tax for a new delivery truck estimated to have a five-year life and a $2,000 salvage value. Delivery truck costs are recorded in the Trucks account.

Dec. 31 Recorded annual straight-line depreciation on the truck.

Year 2

Dec. 31 The truck's estimated useful life was changed from five to four years, and the estimated salvage value was increased to $2,400. Recorded annual straight-line depreciation on the truck.

Check Dec. 31, Year 2: Dr. Depr. Expense—Trucks, $5,200

Year 3

Dec. 31 Recorded annual straight-line depreciation on the truck.

31 Sold the truck for $5,300 cash.

Dec. 31, Year 3: Dr. Loss on Disposal of Trucks, $2,300

Required

Prepare journal entries to record these transactions and events.

Problem 10-6A
Disposal of plant assets
C1 P1 P2

Onslow Co. purchased a used machine for $178,000 cash on January 2. On January 3, Onslow paid $2,840 to wire electricity to the machine. Onslow paid an additional $1,160 on January 4 to secure the machine for operation. The machine will be used for six years and have a $14,000 salvage value. Straight-line depreciation is used. On December 31, at the end of its fifth year in operations, it is disposed of.

Required

1. Prepare journal entries to record the machine's purchase and the costs to ready it for use. Cash is paid for all costs incurred.
2. Prepare journal entries to record depreciation of the machine at December 31 of (*a*) its first year of operations and (*b*) the year of its disposal.
3. Prepare journal entries to record the machine's disposal under each separate situation: (*a*) it is sold for $15,000 cash and (*b*) it is sold for $50,000 cash.

Check (2*b*) Depr. Exp., $28,000

Problem 10-7A
Natural resources
P3

On July 23 of the current year, Dakota Mining Co. pays $4,715,000 for land estimated to contain 5,125,000 tons of recoverable ore. It installs and pays for machinery costing $410,000 on July 25. The company removes and sells 480,000 tons of ore during its first five months of operations ending on December 31. Depreciation of the machinery is in proportion to the mine's depletion as the machinery will be abandoned after the ore is mined.

Required

Prepare entries to record (*a*) the purchase of the land, (*b*) the cost and installation of machinery, (*c*) the first five months' depletion assuming the land has a net salvage value of zero after the ore is mined, and (*d*) the first five months' depreciation on the machinery.

Check (*c*) Depletion, $441,600
(*d*) Depreciation, $38,400

Analysis Component

(*e*) If the machine will be used at another site when extraction is complete, how would we depreciate this machine?

PROBLEM SET B

Problem 10-1B
Plant asset costs; depreciation methods
C1 P1

Nagy Company makes a lump-sum purchase of several assets on January 1 at a total cash price of $1,800,000. The estimated market values of the purchased assets are building, $890,000; land, $427,200; land improvements, $249,200; and five trucks, $213,600.

Required

1. Allocate the lump-sum purchase price to the separate assets purchased. Prepare the journal entry to record the purchase.
2. Compute the first-year depreciation expense on the building using the straight-line method, assuming a 12-year life and a $120,000 salvage value.
3. Compute the first-year depreciation expense on the land improvements assuming a 10-year life and double-declining-balance depreciation.

Check (2) $65,000

(3) $50,400

Analysis Component

4. Compared to straight-line depreciation, does accelerated depreciation result in payment of less total taxes over the asset's life?

Problem 10-2B
Depreciation methods
P1

On January 1, Manning Co. purchases and installs a new machine costing $324,000 with a five-year life and an estimated $30,000 salvage value. Management estimates the machine will produce 1,470,000 units of product during its life. Actual production of units is as follows: 355,600 in Year 1, 320,400 in Year 2, 317,000 in Year 3, 343,600 in Year 4, and 138,500 in Year 5. The total number of units produced by the end of Year 5 exceeds the original estimate—this difference was not predicted. *Note:* The machine cannot be depreciated below its estimated salvage value.

Required

Prepare a table with the following column headings and compute depreciation for each year (and total depreciation of all years combined) for the machine under each depreciation method.

Check DDB Depreciation, Year 3, $46,656; U-of-P Depreciation, Year 4, $68,720

Year	Straight-Line	Units-of-Production	Double-Declining-Balance

Problem 10-3B
Asset cost allocation; straight-line depreciation
C1 P1

On January 1, ProTech Co. pays a lump-sum amount of $1,550,000 for land, Building A, Building B, and Land Improvements B. Building A has no value and will be demolished. Building B will be an office and is appraised at $482,800, with a useful life of 15 years and a $99,500 salvage value. Land Improvements B is valued at $142,000 and is expected to last another five years with no salvage value. The land is valued at $795,200. The company also incurs the following additional costs.

Cost to demolish Building A	$ 122,000	Cost of additional land grading	$174,500
Cost to construct Building C, having a useful life of 20 years and a $258,000 salvage value	1,458,000	Cost of new Land Improvements C, having a 10-year useful life and no salvage value	103,500

Required

Check (1) Land costs, $1,164,500; Building B costs, $527,000

1. Prepare a table with the following column headings: Land, Building B, Building C, Land Improvements B, and Land Improvements C. Allocate the costs incurred by ProTech to the appropriate columns and total each column.
2. Prepare a single journal entry to record all incurred costs assuming they are paid in cash on January 1.
3. Using the straight-line method, prepare the December 31 adjusting entries to record depreciation for the first year these assets were in use.

(3) Depr.—Land Improv. B and C, $31,000 and $10,350

Problem 10-4B
Computing and revising depreciation; revenue and capital expenditures
C1 C2 C3

Mercury Delivery Service completed the following transactions involving equipment.

Year 1

Jan. 1 Paid $25,860 cash plus $1,810 in sales tax for a new delivery van that was estimated to have a five-year life and a $3,670 salvage value. Van costs are recorded in the Equipment account.
3 Paid $1,850 to install sorting racks in the van for more accurate and quicker delivery of packages. This increases the estimated salvage value of the van by another $230.
Dec. 31 Recorded annual straight-line depreciation on the van.

Check Dec. 31, Year 1: Dr. Depr. Expense—Equip., $5,124

Year 2

Jan. 1 Paid $2,064 to overhaul the van's engine, which increased the van's useful life by two years.
May 10 Paid $800 for minor repairs to the van after the driver backed it into a loading dock.
Dec. 31 Recorded annual straight-line depreciation on the van.

Dec. 31, Year 2: Dr. Depr. Expense—Equip., $3,760

Required

Prepare journal entries to record these transactions and events.

Problem 10-5B
Computing and revising depreciation; selling plant assets
C2 P1 P2

York Instruments completed the following transactions and events involving its machinery.

Year 1

Jan. 1 Paid $107,800 cash plus $6,470 in sales tax for a new machine. The machine is estimated to have a six-year life and a $9,720 salvage value.
Dec. 31 Recorded annual straight-line depreciation on the machinery.

Year 2

Dec. 31 The machine's estimated useful life was changed from six to four years, and the estimated salvage value was increased to $14,345. Recorded annual straight-line depreciation on the machinery.

Check Dec. 31, Year 2: Dr. Depr. Expense—Machinery, $27,500

Year 3

Dec. 31 Recorded annual straight-line depreciation on the machinery.
31 Sold the machine for $25,240 cash.

Dec. 31, Year 3: Dr. Loss on Disposal of Machinery, $16,605

Required

Prepare journal entries to record these transactions and events.

Problem 10-6B
Disposal of plant assets
C1 P1 P2

On January 1, Walker purchased a used machine for $150,000. On January 4, Walker paid $3,510 to wire electricity to the machine. Walker paid an additional $4,600 on January 5 to secure the machine for operation. The machine will be used for seven years and have an $18,110 salvage value. Straight-line depreciation is used. On December 31, at the end of its sixth year of use, the machine is disposed of.

Required

1. Prepare journal entries to record the machine's purchase and the costs to ready it for use. Cash is paid for all costs incurred.
2. Prepare journal entries to record depreciation of the machine at December 31 of (*a*) its first year of operations and (*b*) the year of its disposal.
3. Prepare journal entries to record the machine's disposal under each separate situation: (*a*) it is sold for $28,000 cash and (*b*) it is sold for $52,000 cash.

Check (2*b*) Depr. Exp., $20,000

Problem 10-7B
Natural resources
P3

On February 19 of the current year, Quartzite Co. pays $5,400,000 for land estimated to contain 4 million tons of recoverable ore. It installs and pays for machinery costing $400,000 on March 21. The company removes and sells 254,000 tons of ore during its first nine months of operations ending on December 31. Depreciation of the machinery is in proportion to the mine's depletion as the machinery will be abandoned after the ore is mined.

Required

Prepare entries to record (*a*) the purchase of the land, (*b*) the cost and installation of the machinery, (*c*) the first nine months' depletion assuming the land has a net salvage value of zero after the ore is mined, and (*d*) the first nine months' depreciation on the machinery.

Check (*c*) Depletion, $342,900
(*d*) Depreciation, $25,400

Analysis Component

(*e*) If the machine will be used at another site when extraction is complete, how would we depreciate this machine?

connect

SERIAL PROBLEM

Business Solutions
A1 P1

Serial problem began in Chapter 1. If previous chapter segments were not completed, the serial problem can begin at this point. It is available in **Connect** *with an algorithmic option.*

SP 10 Selected ledger account balances for **Business Solutions** follow.

	For Three Months Ended December 31, 2021	For Three Months Ended March 31, 2022
Office equipment	$ 8,000	$ 8,000
Accumulated depreciation—Office equipment	400	800
Computer equipment	20,000	20,000
Accumulated depreciation—Computer equipment	1,250	2,500
Total revenue	31,284	44,000
Total assets	83,460	120,268

Alexander Image/Shutterstock

Required

1. Assume that Business Solutions does not acquire additional office equipment or computer equipment in 2022. Compute amounts for *the year ended* December 31, 2022, for Depreciation Expense—Office Equipment and for Depreciation Expense—Computer Equipment (assume use of the straight-line method).
2. Given the assumptions in part 1, what is the book value of both the office equipment and the computer equipment as of December 31, 2022?
3. Compute the three-month total asset turnover for Business Solutions as of March 31, 2022. Use total revenue for the numerator and average the December 31, 2021, total assets and the March 31, 2022, total assets for the denominator. Interpret its total asset turnover if competitors average 2.5 for annual periods. (Round turnover to two decimals.)

Check (3) Three-month (annual) turnover = 0.43 (1.73 annual)

TABLEAU DASHBOARD ACTIVITIES

Tableau Dashboard Activities expose students to accounting analytics using visual displays. These assignments run in **Connect**. All are auto-gradable.

Tableau DA 10-1 Quick Study, Straight-line depreciation and book value, **P1**—similar to QS 10-4

Tableau DA 10-2 Exercise, Straight-line depreciation and sale of assets, **C2, P2**—similar to Exercises 10-13 and 10-17

Tableau DA 10-3 Mini-Case, Analyzing straight-line, units-of-production, and double-declining balance, **P1**—similar to Exercises 10-9 and 10-10

Accounting Analysis

connect

COMPANY ANALYSIS

A1

AA 10-1 Refer to **Apple**'s financial statements in Appendix A to answer the following.

1. What percent of the original cost of Apple's Property, Plant and Equipment account remains to be depreciated as of (*a*) September 28, 2019, and (*b*) September 29, 2018? Assume these assets have no salvage value and the entire account is depreciable. *Hint:* Accumulated Depreciation is listed under "Property, Plant and Equipment" in the notes to Apple's financial statements in Appendix A.
2. Much research and development are needed to create the next iPhone. Do companies capitalize and amortize research and development costs over the life of the product, or are research and development costs expensed as incurred?

3. Compute Apple's total asset turnover for the year ended (*a*) September 28, 2019, and (*b*) September 29, 2018. Total assets at September 30, 2017, are $375,319 ($ millions).

4. Using the results in part 3, is the change in Apple's asset turnover favorable or unfavorable?

COMPARATIVE ANALYSIS
A1

AA 10-2 Comparative figures for **Apple** and **Google** follow.

$ millions	Apple			Google		
	Current Year	One Year Prior	Two Years Prior	Current Year	One Year Prior	Two Years Prior
Total assets..........	$338,516	$365,725	$375,319	$275,909	$232,792	$197,295
Net sales..............	260,174	265,595	229,234	161,857	136,819	110,855

Required

1. Compute total asset turnover for the most recent two years for Apple and Google using the data shown.

2. In the current year, which company is more efficient in generating net sales given total assets?

3. Does asset turnover underperform or outperform the 0.5 industry asset turnover for (*a*) Apple and (*b*) Google?

EXTENDED ANALYSIS
A1

AA 10-3 Comparative figures for **Samsung**, **Apple**, and **Google** follow.

$ millions	Samsung			Apple		Google	
	Current Year	Prior Year	Two Years Prior	Current Year	Prior Year	Current Year	Prior Year
Total assets...	$302,511	$291,179	$274,268	$338,516	$365,725	$275,909	$232,792
Net sales.....	197,691	209,163	217,755	260,174	265,595	161,857	136,819

Required

1. Compute total asset turnover for the most recent two years for Samsung using the data shown.

2. Is the change in Samsung's asset turnover favorable or unfavorable?

3. For the current year, is Samsung's asset turnover better or worse than the asset turnover for (*a*) Apple and (*b*) Google?

Discussion Questions

1. What characteristics of a plant asset make it different from other assets?

2. What is the general rule for cost inclusion for plant assets?

3. What is different between land and land improvements?

4. Why is the cost of a lump-sum purchase allocated to the individual assets acquired?

5. Does the balance in the Accumulated Depreciation—Machinery account represent funds to replace the machinery when it wears out? If not, what does it represent?

6. Why is the Modified Accelerated Cost Recovery System not generally accepted for financial accounting purposes?

7. What is the difference between ordinary repairs and extraordinary repairs? How should each be recorded?

8. Identify events that might lead to disposal of a plant asset.

9. What is the process of allocating the cost of natural resources to expense as they are used?

10. Is the declining-balance method an acceptable way to compute depletion of natural resources? Explain.

11. What are the characteristics of an intangible asset?

12. What general procedures are applied in accounting for the acquisition and potential cost allocation of intangible assets?

13. When do we know that a company has goodwill? When can goodwill appear in a company's balance sheet?

14. Assume that a company buys another business and pays for its goodwill. If the company plans to incur costs each year to maintain the value of the goodwill, must it also amortize this goodwill?

15. How is total asset turnover computed? Why would a financial statement user be interested in total asset turnover?

16. Identify the main difference between (*a*) plant assets and current assets, (*b*) plant assets and inventory, and (*c*) plant assets and long-term investments.

Beyond the Numbers

ETHICS CHALLENGE
C1

BTN 10-1 Flo Choi owns a small business and manages its accounting. Her company just finished a year in which a large amount of borrowed funds was invested in a new building addition as well as in equipment and fixture additions. Choi's banker requires her to submit semiannual financial statements so he can monitor the financial health of her business. He has warned her that if profit margins erode, he might raise the interest rate on the borrowed funds to reflect the increased loan risk from the bank's point of view. Choi knows profit margin is likely to decline this year. As she prepares year-end adjusting entries, she decides to apply the following depreciation rule: All asset additions are considered to be in use on the first day of the following month. (The previous rule assumed assets are in use on the first day of the month nearest to the purchase date.)

Required

1. Identify decisions that managers like Choi must make in applying depreciation methods.
2. Is Choi's rule an ethical violation, or is it a legitimate decision in computing depreciation?
3. How will Choi's new depreciation rule affect the profit margin of her business?

COMMUNICATING IN PRACTICE
A1

BTN 10-2 Teams are to select an industry, and each team member is to select a different company in that industry. Each team member is to acquire the financial statements (Form 10-K) of the company selected—see the company's website or the SEC's EDGAR database (SEC.gov). Use the financial statements to compute total asset turnover. Communicate with teammates via a meeting, e-mail, or telephone to discuss the meaning of this ratio, how different companies compare to each other, and the industry norm. The team must prepare a one-page report that describes the ratios for each company and identifies the conclusions reached during the team's discussion.

TEAMWORK IN ACTION
P1

BTN 10-3 Each team member is to become an expert on one depreciation method to facilitate teammates' understanding of that method. Follow these procedures:

a. Each team member is to select an area of expertise from one of the following depreciation methods: straight-line, units-of-production, or double-declining-balance.

b. Expert teams are to be formed from those who have selected the same area of expertise. The instructor will identify the location where each expert team meets.

c. Using the following data, expert teams are to collaborate and develop a presentation answering the requirements. Expert team members must write the presentation in a format they can show to their learning teams.

Point: This activity can follow an overview of each method. Step *a* allows for three areas of expertise. Larger teams will have some duplication of areas, but the straight-line choice should not be duplicated. Expert teams can use the book and consult with the instructor.

Data and Requirements On January 8, 2020, Whitewater Riders purchases a van to transport rafters back to the point of departure at the conclusion of the rafting adventures. The cost of the van is $44,000. It has an estimated salvage value of $2,000 and is expected to be used for four years and driven 60,000 miles. The van is driven 12,000 miles in 2020; 18,000 miles in 2021; 21,000 miles in 2022; and 10,000 miles in 2023.

1. Compute the annual depreciation expense for each year of the van's estimated useful life.
2. Explain when and how annual depreciation is recorded.
3. Explain the impact on income of this depreciation method versus others over the van's life.
4. Identify the van's book value for each year of its life and illustrate the reporting of this amount for any one year.

d. Re-form original learning teams. In rotation, experts are to present to their teams the results from part *c*. Experts are to encourage and respond to questions.

ENTREPRENEURIAL DECISION
A1

BTN 10-4 Review the chapter's opening feature involving Elon Musk and SpaceX. Assume that the company currently has net sales of $8,000,000 and that it is planning an expansion that will increase net sales by $4,000,000. To accomplish this expansion, the company must increase its average total assets from $2,500,000 to $3,000,000.

Required

1. Compute the company's total asset turnover under (*a*) current conditions and (*b*) proposed conditions.
2. Evaluate and comment on the merits of the proposal given the analysis in part 1. Identify any concerns we would express about the proposal.

11 Current Liabilities and Payroll Accounting

Chapter Preview

KNOWN LIABILITIES	PAYROLL LIABILITIES	ESTIMATED LIABILITIES	CONTINGENCIES AND ANALYSIS
C1 Reporting liabilities	**P2** Employee payroll and deductions	**P4** Reporting for:	**C3** Accounting for contingencies:
C2 Sales taxes payable	**P3** Employer payroll taxes	Health and pension	Probable
Unearned revenues	Multi-period liabilities	Vacation benefits	Possible
P1 Short-term notes		Bonus plans	Remote
		Warranty liabilities	**A1** Times interest earned
NTK 11-1	**NTK 11-2**	**NTK 11-3**	**NTK 11-4**

Learning Objectives

CONCEPTUAL

C1 Describe current and long-term liabilities and their characteristics.

C2 Identify and describe known current liabilities.

C3 Explain how to account for contingent liabilities.

ANALYTICAL

A1 Compute the times interest earned ratio and use it to analyze liabilities.

PROCEDURAL

P1 Prepare entries to account for short-term notes payable.

P2 Compute and record *employee* payroll deductions and liabilities.

P3 Compute and record *employer* payroll expenses and liabilities.

P4 Account for estimated liabilities, including warranties and bonuses.

P5 *Appendix 11A*—Identify and describe the details of payroll reports, records, and procedures.

P6 *Appendix 11B*—Account for corporate income taxes.

Song and Dance

"Make people smile"—**Beto Perez**

HALLANDALE, FL—Beto Perez, the 16-year-old son of a single mother, took a job as a fitness instructor. When Beto accidentally forgot his aerobics notes at home, he made up a dance workout with Latin music. "They loved it," recalls Beto. He then, along with Alberto Perlman and Alberto Aghion, launched **Zumba** (**Zumba.com**), a fitness program combined with Latin music.

Success soon followed. Today, Zumba is in over 180 countries with more than 200,000 locations. Its Zumba Instructor Network has expanded Beto's reach. "I work hard to bring our instructors new rhythms, choreography, and a really good mix of music," declares Beto. "I want to create something [special]."

Yet, Zumba demands good business decisions. These include finding good employees and managing the payroll of a growing business. Zumba has more than 200 employees. Beto stresses that effective management of liabilities, especially payroll and employee benefits, is crucial to success.

Beto is optimistic. He is especially excited about potential uses of accounting analytics in predicting client purchasing preferences. "We're launching lots of new technology," explains Beto. He hopes that analytics can guide retail success based on client histories. Beto adds: "You can get 80% of your daily recommended steps in one Zumba class!"

Tiffany Rose/WireImage/Getty Images

Sources: *Zumba website*, January 2021; *Miami Herald*, August 2018; *Inc.*, August 2017; *CNBC.com*, September 2017; *Entrepreneur.wiki*, January 2020

KNOWN LIABILITIES

Characteristics of Liabilities

This section discusses characteristics of liabilities and how liabilities are classified.

C1 Describe current and long-term liabilities and their characteristics.

Defining Liabilities A *liability* is a probable future payment of assets or services that a company is presently obligated to make as a result of past transactions or events. This definition includes three elements that are shown in Exhibit 11.1. No liability is reported when one or more of those elements are missing. For example, companies expect to pay wages in future years, but these future payments are *not* liabilities because no past event such as employee work resulted in a present obligation. Instead, liabilities are recorded when employees perform work and earn wages.

EXHIBIT 11.1 Characteristics of a Liability

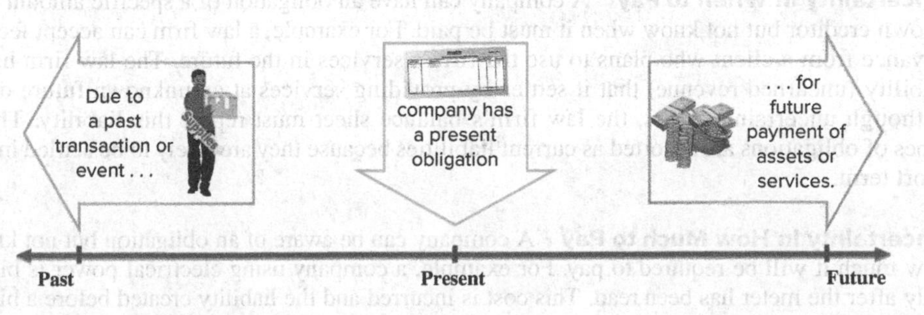

Due to a past transaction or event . . .
company has a present obligation
. . . for future payment of assets or services.
Past
Present
Future

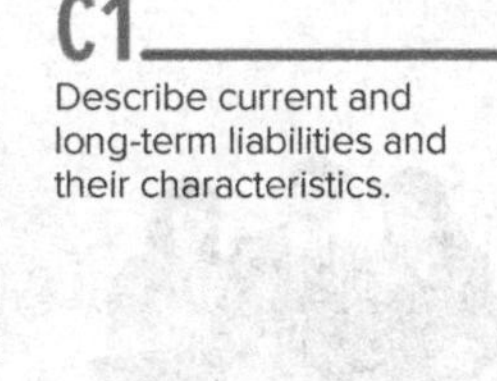

Point: Most liability accounts use *payable* or *unearned* in their titles.

Classifying Liabilities Liabilities are classified as either current or long term.

Current Liabilities **Current liabilities,** or *short-term liabilities,* **are liabilities due *within* one year** (or the company's operating cycle if longer). Most are paid using current assets or by creating other current liabilities. Common examples are accounts payable, short-term notes payable, wages payable, warranty liabilities, and taxes payable. Some liabilities do not have a fixed due date but instead are payable on the creditor's demand. These are reported as current liabilities because of the possibility of payment in the near term.

Current liabilities differ across companies because they depend on the type of company operations. For example, **MGM Resorts** reports casino outstanding chip liability. **Harley-Davidson** reports different current liabilities such as warranty, recall, and dealer incentive liabilities. Exhibit 11.2 shows current liabilities as a percentage of total liabilities for selected companies.

EXHIBIT 11.2

Current Liabilities as a Percentage of Total Liabilities

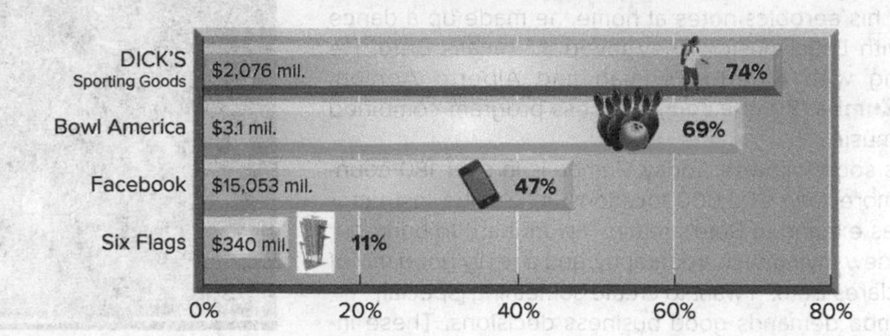

Long-Term Liabilities **Long-term liabilities** are obligations due *after* one year (or the company's operating cycle if longer). They include long-term notes payable, warranty liabilities, lease liabilities, and bonds payable. For example, **Domino's Pizza** reports long-term liabilities of $4,344 million. A single liability can be divided between the current and noncurrent sections if a company expects to make payments toward it in both the short and long term. Domino's reports long-term debt of $4,071 million and current portion of long-term debt of $43 million. The current portion is reported in current liabilities.

Uncertainty in Liabilities Accounting for liabilities involves answering three important questions: Whom to pay? When to pay? How much to pay? Answers are usually decided when a liability is incurred. For example, if a company has a $100 account payable to a firm, payable on March 15, the answers are clear. However, answers to one or more of these three questions are uncertain for some liabilities.

Uncertainty in Whom to Pay Liabilities can involve uncertainty in whom to pay. For example, a company can create a liability with a known amount when issuing a note that is payable to its holder. In this case, a specific amount is payable to the note's holder at a specified date, but the company does not know who the holder is until that date. Despite this uncertainty, the company reports this liability on its balance sheet.

Uncertainty in When to Pay A company can have an obligation of a specific amount to a known creditor but not know when it must be paid. For example, a law firm can accept fees in advance from a client who plans to use the firm's services in the future. The law firm has a liability (unearned revenue) that it settles by providing services at an unknown future date. Although uncertainty exists, the law firm's balance sheet must report this liability. These types of obligations are reported as current liabilities because they are likely to be settled in the short term.

Uncertainty in How Much to Pay A company can be aware of an obligation but not know how much it will be required to pay. For example, a company using electrical power is billed only after the meter has been read. This cost is incurred and the liability created before a bill is received. A liability to the power company is reported as an estimated amount if the balance sheet is prepared before a bill arrives.

Examples of Known Liabilities

C2 Identify and describe known current liabilities.

Known liabilities are measurable obligations arising from agreements, contracts, or laws. Known liabilities include accounts payable, notes payable, payroll obligations, sales taxes, and unearned revenues.

Accounts Payable

Accounts payable, or trade accounts payable, are amounts owed to suppliers for products or services purchased on credit. Accounts payable are a focus of the merchandising chapter.

Sales Taxes Payable

Nearly all states and many cities levy taxes on retail sales. Sales taxes are shown as a percent of selling prices. The seller collects sales taxes from customers when sales occur and sends these collections to the government. Because sellers currently owe these collections to the government, this amount is a current liability. If **Home Depot** sells materials on August 31 for $6,000 cash that are subject to a 5% sales tax, the revenue portion of this transaction is recorded as follows. Later, when Home Depot sends the $300 collected to the government, it debits Sales Taxes Payable and credits Cash.

Aug. 31	Cash	6,300	
	Sales		6,000
	Sales Taxes Payable ($6,000 × 0.05)		300
	*Record cash sales and 5% sales tax.**		
	*We also Dr. Cost of Sales and Cr. Inventory for cost of sales.		

Assets = Liabilities + Equity
+6,300 +300 +6,000

Unearned Revenues

Unearned revenues, or *deferred revenues,* are amounts received in advance from customers for future products or services. Unearned revenues arise with airline ticket sales, magazine subscriptions, construction projects, hotel reservations, gift card sales, and custom orders. Advance ticket sales for sporting events or concerts are other examples. If **Selena Gomez** sells $900,000 in tickets for three concerts, the entry is

Momcilog/iStock/Getty Images

June 30	Cash	900,000	
	Unearned Ticket Revenue		900,000
	Record sale of tickets for three concerts.		

Assets = Liabilities + Equity
+900,000 +900,000

Unearned Ticket Revenue is reported as a current liability. As each concert is played, 1/3 of the liability is satisfied and 1/3 of the revenue is recorded—this entry follows.

Oct. 31	Unearned Ticket Revenue	300,000	
	Ticket Revenue		300,000
	Record concert revenues ($900,000 × 1/3).		

Assets = Liabilities + Equity
−300,000 +300,000

Short-Term Notes Payable

P1 Prepare entries to account for short-term notes payable.

A **short-term note payable** is a written promise to pay a specified amount on a stated future date within one year. Notes can be sold or transferred. Most notes payable bear interest. The written documentation with notes is helpful in resolving legal disputes. We describe two transactions that create notes payable.

Note Given to Extend Credit Period A company can replace an account payable with a note payable. A common example is a creditor that requires an interest-bearing note for an overdue account payable. Assume that on August 23, Brady asks to extend its past-due $600 account payable to McGraw. After negotiations, McGraw agrees to accept $100 cash and a 60-day, 12%, $500 note payable to replace the account payable. Brady records the following.

Aug. 23	Accounts Payable—McGraw	600	
	Cash		100
	Notes Payable—McGraw		500
	Sent cash and a note for payment on account.		

Assets = Liabilities + Equity
−100 −600
+500

Point: Excel for accrued interest.

	A	B
1	Principal	$500
2	Rate	12%
3	Issue date	8/23
4	Days	60
5	Accrued interest	

=ACCRINTM(B3,B3+B4,B2,B1,2)=$10

Signing the note changes Brady's debt from an account payable to a note payable. McGraw prefers the note payable over the account payable because it earns interest and it is written documentation of the debt's existence, term, and amount. When the note comes due on its maturity date, Brady pays the note plus interest (called *maturity value*) to McGraw and records this entry.

Assets = Liabilities + Equity
−510 −500 −10

Oct. 22	Notes Payable—McGraw	500	
	Interest Expense	10	
	Cash		510
	Paid note with interest ($500 × 12% × 60/360).		

Point: Firms commonly compute interest using a 360-day year, called the *banker's rule.*

Interest expense is computed by multiplying the principal of the note ($500) by the annual interest rate (12%) for the fraction of the year the note is outstanding (60 days/360 days).

Note Given to Borrow from Bank A bank requires a borrower to sign a note when making a loan. When the note comes due, the borrower repays the note with an amount larger than the amount borrowed. The difference between the amount borrowed and the amount repaid is *interest*. The amount borrowed is called *principal* or *face value* of the note. Assume that a company borrows $2,000 from a bank at 12% annual interest. The loan is made on September 30, 2021, and is due in 60 days. The note says: *"I promise to pay $2,000 plus interest at 12% within 60 days after September 30."* The borrower records its receipt of cash and the new liability with this entry.

Assets = Liabilities + Equity
+2,000 +2,000

Sep. 30	Cash	2,000	
	Notes Payable		2,000
	Borrow $2,000 cash with 60-day, 12%, $2,000 note.		

Point: Excel for accrued interest.

	A	B
1	Principal	$2,000
2	Rate	12%
3	Issue date	9/30
4	Days	60
5	Accrued interest	

=ACCRINTM(B3,B3+B4,B2,B1,2)=$40

When principal and interest are paid, the borrower records payment with this entry.

Assets = Liabilities + Equity
−2,040 −2,000 −40

Nov. 29	Notes Payable	2,000	
	Interest Expense	40	
	Cash		2,040
	Paid note with interest ($2,000 × 12% × 60/360).		

When Note Extends over Two Periods When a note is issued in one period but paid in the next, interest expense is recorded in each period based on the number of days the note extends over each period. Assume a company borrows $2,000 cash on December 16, 2021, at 12% annual interest. This 60-day note matures on February 14, 2022, and the company's fiscal year ends on December 31. This means 15 of the 60 days are in 2021 and 45 of the 60 days are in 2022. Interest for these two periods is:

- 12/16/2021 to 12/31/2021 = 15 days. Interest expense = $2,000 × 12% × 15/360 = $10.
- 01/01/2022 to 02/14/2022 = 45 days. Interest expense = $2,000 × 12% × 45/360 = $30.

The borrower records the 2021 expense with the following adjusting entry.

Assets = Liabilities + Equity
+10 −10

Dec. 31, 2021	Interest Expense	10	
	Interest Payable		10
	Record accrued interest ($2,000 × 12% × 15/360).		

When this note is paid on February 14, the borrower records 45 days of interest expense in 2022 and removes the balances of the two liability accounts.

Feb. 14, 2022	Interest Expense*	30	
	Interest Payable	10	
	Notes Payable	2,000	
	Cash		2,040
	Paid note with interest. *$2,000 × 12% × 45/360		

Assets = Liabilities + Equity
−2,040 −10 −30
−2,000

Decision Insight

A High Note Franchisors such as **Pizza Hut** and **Domino's** use notes to help entrepreneurs acquire their own franchises, including notes to pay for the franchise fee and equipment. Payments on these notes are usually collected monthly and often are secured by the franchisees' assets. For example, a **McDonald's** franchise can cost from under $200,000 to over $2 million, depending on the type selected. ■

Oksana Mizina/Shutterstock

NEED-TO-KNOW 11-1

Accounting for Known Liabilities

C2 P1

Part 1. A retailer sells merchandise for $500 cash on June 30 (cost of merchandise is $300). The retailer collects 7% sales tax. Record the entry for the $500 sale and its applicable sales tax. Also record the entry that shows the taxes collected being sent to the government on July 15.

Part 2. A ticket agency receives $40,000 cash in advance ticket sales for Haim's upcoming four-date tour. Record the advance ticket sales on April 30. Record the revenue earned for the first concert date of May 15, assuming it represents one-fourth of the advance ticket sales.

Part 3. On November 25 of the current year, a company borrows $8,000 cash by signing a 90-day, 5% note payable with a face value of $8,000. (a) Compute the accrued interest payable on December 31 of the current year, (b) prepare the journal entry to record the accrued interest expense at December 31 of the current year, and (c) prepare the journal entry to record payment of the note at maturity.

Solution—Part 1

June 30	Cash	535	
	Sales		500
	Sales Taxes Payable		35
	Record cash sales and 7% sales tax.		
June 30	Cost of Goods Sold	300	
	Merchandise Inventory		300
	Record cost of June 30 sales.		
July 15	Sales Taxes Payable	35	
	Cash		35
	Record sales taxes sent to govt.		

Solution—Part 2

Apr. 30	Cash	40,000	
	Unearned Ticket Revenue		40,000
	Record sales in advance of concerts.		
May 15	Unearned Ticket Revenue	10,000	
	Ticket Revenue		10,000
	Record concert revenues ($40,000 × 1/4).		

Solution—Part 3

a.

Computation of interest payable at December 31:	
Days from November 25 to December 31	36 days
Accrued interest (5% × $8,000 × 36/360)	$40

Excel: Accrued interest, 11/25–12/31.

	A	B
1	Principal	$8,000
2	Rate	5%
3	Issue date	11/25
4	Days	36
5	Accrued interest	

=ACCRINTM(B3,B3+B4,B2,B1,2)=$40

b.

Dec. 31	Interest Expense	40	
	Interest Payable		40
	Record accrued interest (5% × $8,000 × 36/360).		

Excel: Accrued interest, 1/1–2/23.

	A	B
1	Principal	$8,000
2	Rate	5%
3	Issue date	11/25
4	Days	54
5	Accrued interest	

=ACCRINTM(B3,B3+B4,B2,B1,2)=$60

c.

Feb. 23	Interest Expense	60	
	Interest Payable	40	
	Notes Payable	8,000	
	Cash		8,100
	Record payment of note plus interest		
	(5% × $8,000 × 90/360 = $100 total interest)		
	(5% × $8,000 × 54/360 = $60 interest expense).		

Do More: QS 11-2, QS 11-3, QS 11-4, QS 11-5, E 11-2, E 11-3, E 11-4, E 11-5, E 11-6

PAYROLL LIABILITIES

Payroll liabilities are from salaries and wages, employee benefits, and payroll taxes levied on the employer. For example, **Boston Beer** reports current payroll liabilities of more than $14 million from accrued "employee wages, benefits and reimbursements."

P2 Compute and record *employee* payroll deductions and liabilities.

EMPLOYEE Payroll and Deductions

Gross pay is the total compensation an employee earns including wages, salaries, commissions, bonuses, and any compensation earned before deductions such as taxes. *Wages* usually refer to payments to employees at an hourly rate. *Salaries* usually refer to payments to employees at a monthly or yearly rate. **Net pay,** or *take-home pay,* is gross pay minus all deductions. **Payroll deductions,** or *withholdings,* are amounts withheld from an employee's gross pay, either required or voluntary. Required deductions result from laws and include income taxes and Social Security taxes. Voluntary deductions, at an employee's option, include pension and health contributions, health and life insurance premiums, union dues, and donations.

Exhibit 11.3 shows typical employee payroll deductions. The employer withholds payroll deductions from employees' pay and sends this money to the designated group or government. The employer records payroll deductions as current liabilities until these amounts are sent. This section covers major payroll deductions.

Point: Deductions at some companies, such as those for insurance coverage, are "required" under labor contracts.

EXHIBIT 11.3

Payroll Deductions

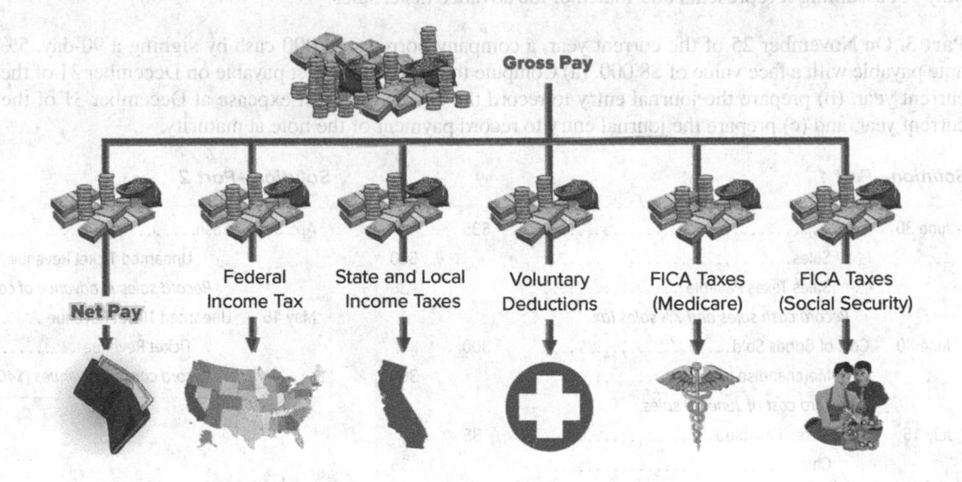

Employee FICA Taxes

Employers withhold **Federal Insurance Contributions Act (FICA) taxes** from employees' pay. Employers separate FICA taxes into two groups.

1. **Social Security taxes**—withholdings to cover retirement, disability, and survivorship.
2. **Medicare taxes**—withholdings to cover medical benefits.

Taxes for Social Security and Medicare are computed separately. For 2020, the amount withheld from each employee's pay for Social Security tax is 6.2% of the first $137,700 the employee earns in the calendar year. The Medicare tax is 1.45% of *all* amounts the employee earns; there is no maximum limit to Medicare tax. A 0.9% *Additional Medicare Tax* is imposed on the high-income employee for pay usually in excess of $200,000 (this additional tax is *not* imposed on the employer, whereas the others are). Until the taxes are sent to the Internal Revenue Service (IRS), they are included in employers' current liabilities. For any changes in rates or earnings levels, check **IRS.gov** or **SSA.gov**.

Point: Sources of U.S. tax receipts:
50% Personal income tax
35% FICA and FUTA taxes
10% Corporate income tax
5% Other taxes

Employee Income Tax

Most employers withhold federal income tax from each employee's paycheck. The amount withheld is computed using IRS tables. The amount depends on the employee's income and the number of *withholding allowances* the employee claims. Allowances reduce taxes owed to the government. Employees can claim allowances for themselves and their dependents. Until the government is paid, withholdings are reported as a current liability on the employer's balance sheet.

Employee Voluntary Deductions Voluntary deduction withholdings come from employee requests, contracts, unions, or other agreements. They include charitable giving, medical and life insurance premiums, pension contributions, and union dues. Until they are paid, voluntary withholdings are reported as part of employers' current liabilities.

Employee Payroll Recording Employers accrue payroll expenses and liabilities at the end of each pay period. Assume that an employee earns a salary of $2,000 per month. At the end of January, the employer's entry to accrue payroll expenses and liabilities for this employee is

Jan. 31	Salaries Expense	2,000	
	FICA—Social Security Taxes Payable (6.2%)		124
	FICA—Medicare Taxes Payable (1.45%)		29
	Employee Federal Income Taxes Payable*		213
	Employee Medical Insurance Payable*		85
	Employee Union Dues Payable*		25
	Salaries Payable		1,524
	Record accrued payroll for January.		

*Amounts taken from employer's accounting records.

Assets = Liabilities + Equity
+124 −2,000
+29
+213
+85
+25
+1,524

Salaries Expense shows that the employee earns a gross salary of $2,000. The first five payables show the liabilities the employer owes on behalf of this employee to cover FICA taxes, income taxes, medical insurance, and union dues. The Salaries Payable account records the $1,524 net pay the employee receives from the $2,000 gross pay earned. The February 1 entry to record cash payment to this employee is

Feb. 1	Salaries Payable	1,524	
	Cash		1,524
	Record payment of payroll.		

Assets = Liabilities + Equity
−1,524 −1,524

EMPLOYER Payroll Taxes

P3 Compute and record *employer* payroll expenses and liabilities.

Employers must pay payroll taxes in addition to those required of employees. Employer taxes include FICA and unemployment taxes.

Employer FICA Tax Employers must pay FICA taxes on their payroll. For 2020, the employer must pay Social Security tax of 6.2% on the first 137,700 earned by each employee and 1.45% Medicare tax on all earnings of each employee. An employer's tax is credited to the same FICA Taxes Payable accounts used to record the Social Security and Medicare taxes withheld from employees.

Point: A self-employed person must pay both the employee and employer FICA taxes.

Employer Unemployment Taxes The federal government works with states in a joint federal and state unemployment insurance program. Each state has its own program. These programs provide unemployment benefits to qualified workers.

Federal Unemployment Tax Act (FUTA) Employers must pay a federal unemployment tax on wages and salaries earned by their employees. For the recent year, employers were required to pay FUTA taxes of as much as 6.0% of the first $7,000 earned by each employee. This federal tax can be reduced by a credit of up to 5.4% for taxes paid to a state program. As a result, the net federal unemployment tax is often 0.6%.

State Unemployment Tax Act (SUTA) All states fund their unemployment insurance programs by placing a payroll tax on employers. (A few states require employees to make a contribution. In the book's assignments, we assume this tax is only levied on the employer.) In most states, the base rate for SUTA taxes is 5.4% of the first $7,000 earned by each employee (the dollar level varies by state). This base rate is adjusted according to an employer's merit rating. The state assigns a **merit rating** based on a company's stability in employing workers. A good rating reflects stability in employment and means an employer can pay less than the 5.4% base rate. A low rating means high turnover or seasonal hirings and layoffs.

Recording Employer Payroll Taxes Employer payroll taxes are an added expense beyond the wages and salaries earned by employees. These taxes are often recorded in an entry separate from the one recording payroll expenses and deductions. Assume that the $2,000 recorded salaries expense from the previous example is earned by an employee whose earnings have not yet reached $5,000 for the year. This means the entire salaries expense for this period is subject to tax because year-to-date pay is under $7,000. Consequently, the FICA portion of the employer's tax is $153, computed by multiplying both the 6.2% and 1.45% by the $2,000 gross pay. Assume that the federal unemployment tax rate is 0.6% and the state unemployment tax rate is 5.4%. This means state unemployment (SUTA) taxes are $108 (5.4% of the $2,000 gross pay) and federal unemployment (FUTA) taxes are $12 (0.6% of $2,000). The entry to record the employer's payroll tax expense and related liabilities is

Assets	= Liabilities	+ Equity
	+124	−273
	+29	
	+108	
	+12	

Jan. 31	Payroll Taxes Expense	273	
	FICA—Social Security Taxes Payable (6.2%)		124
	FICA—Medicare Taxes Payable (1.45%)		29
	State Unemployment Taxes Payable		108
	Federal Unemployment Taxes Payable		12
	Record employer payroll taxes.		

Employee and Employer Payroll Taxes Summary

Year-to-Date Pay Bracket (Set Yearly)	Employee Taxes	Employer Taxes
$0 to $7,000	FICA—Medicare FICA—Social Security State & Federal Income Tax	FICA—Medicare FICA—Social Security FUTA SUTA
$7,000 to $137,700	FICA—Medicare FICA—Social Security State & Federal Income Tax	FICA—Medicare FICA—Social Security
Above $137,700	FICA—Medicare State & Federal Income Tax	FICA—Medicare

Internal Control of Payroll

Internal controls are crucial for payroll because of a high risk of fraud and error. Exhibit 11.4 identifies and explains four key areas of payroll activities that we aim to *separate and monitor.*

EXHIBIT 11.4

Internal Controls in Payroll

Employee Hiring

Duty: Authorize, hire, and fire.
Aim: Keep fake workers off payroll.

Payroll Preparation

Duty: Verify tax rates and payroll amounts.
Aim: Rates updated and amounts accurate.

Timekeeping

Duty: Track and verify time worked.
Aim: Paid for time worked only.

Payroll Payment

Duty: Sign and issue prenumbered checks.
Aim: Checks valid, secured, and correct.

Multi-Period Known Liabilities

Many known liabilities extend over multiple periods. These often include unearned revenues and notes payable. For example, if **Sports Illustrated** sells a three-year digital magazine subscription, it records amounts received for this subscription in an Unearned Subscription Revenues account. Amounts in this account are liabilities, but are they current or long term? They are *both*. The portion of the Unearned Subscription Revenues account that will be fulfilled in the next year is reported as a current liability. The remaining portion is reported as a long-term liability.

The same analysis applies to notes payable. For example, a borrower reports a three-year note payable as a long-term liability in the first two years it is outstanding. In the third year, the borrower reclassifies this note as a current liability because it is due within one year. The **current portion of long-term debt** is that part of long-term debt due within one year. Long-term debt is reported under long-term liabilities, but the *current portion due* is reported under current liabilities. Assume that a $7,500 debt is paid in installments of $1,500 per year for five years. The $1,500 due within the year is reported as a current liability. We classify the amounts for debt as either current or long term when the balance sheet is prepared.

Ethical Risk

Dirty Work Probably the greatest number of frauds involve payroll. Controls include proper approvals and processes for employee additions, deletions, and pay rate changes. A common fraud is a manager adding a fictitious employee to the payroll and then cashing the fictitious employee's check. A study reports that 42% of employees in operations and service areas witnessed violations of employee wage, overtime, or benefit rules in the past year. Another 33% observed falsifying of time and expense reports (KPMG). ■

Ceridian Connection reports: **8.5%** of fraud is tied to payroll; **$72,000** is the median loss per payroll fraud; and **24 months** is the median time to uncover payroll fraud.

NEED-TO-KNOW 11-2

Payroll Liabilities

P2 P3

A company's first weekly pay period of the year ends on January 8. Sales employees earned $30,000 and office employees earned $20,000 in salaries. The employees are to have withheld from their salaries FICA Social Security taxes at the rate of 6.2%, FICA Medicare taxes at the rate of 1.45%, $9,000 of federal income taxes, $2,000 of medical insurance deductions, and $1,000 of pension contributions. No employee earned more than $7,000 in the first pay period.

Part 1. Prepare the journal entry to record the company's January 8 (employee) payroll expenses and liabilities.

Part 2. Prepare the journal entry to record the company's (employer) payroll taxes resulting from the January 8 payroll. Its state unemployment tax rate is 5.4% on the first $7,000 paid to each employee. The federal unemployment tax rate is 0.6%.

Solution—Part 1

Date	Account	Debit	Credit
Jan. 8	Sales Salaries Expense	30,000	
	Office Salaries Expense...............	20,000	
	FICA—Social Security Taxes Payable*		3,100
	FICA—Medicare Taxes Payable†		725
	Employee Fed. Income Taxes Payable		9,000
	Employee Med. Insurance Payable ..		2,000
	Employee Pensions Payable		1,000
	Salaries Payable		34,175
	Record payroll for period.		
	*$50,000 × 6.2% = $3,100		
	†$50,000 × 1.45% = $725		

Solution—Part 2

Date	Account	Debit	Credit
Jan. 8	Payroll Taxes Expense	6,825	
	FICA—Social Security Taxes Payable .		3,100
	FICA—Medicare Taxes Payable		725
	State Unemployment Taxes Payable*		2,700
	Federal Unemployment Taxes Payable†		300
	Record employer payroll taxes.		
	*$50,000 × 5.4% = $2,700		
	†$50,000 × 0.6% = $300		

Do More: QS 11-6, QS 11-7, QS 11-8, E 11-7, E 11-8, E 11-9, E 11-10, E 11-11

ESTIMATED LIABILITIES

P4 Account for estimated liabilities, including warranties and bonuses.

An **estimated liability** is a known obligation of an uncertain amount that can be reasonably estimated. Common examples are employee benefits such as pensions, health care, and vacation pay, and warranties offered by a seller.

Health and Pension Benefits

Many companies provide **employee benefits.** An employer often pays all or part of medical, dental, life, and disability insurance. Many employers also contribute to *pension plans,* which are agreements by employers to provide payments to employees after retirement. Many companies also provide medical care and insurance benefits to their retirees. Assume an employer agrees to (1) pay $8,000 for medical insurance and (2) contribute an additional 10% of the employees' $120,000 gross salaries to a retirement program. The entry to record these accrued benefits is

Assets = Liabilities + Equity
+8,000 −20,000
+12,000

Dec. 31	Employee Benefits Expense.	20,000	
	Employee Medical Insurance Payable		8,000
	Employee Retirement Program Payable		12,000
	Record costs of employee benefits.		

Vacation Benefits

Point: An *accrued expense* is an unpaid expense and is also called an *accrued liability.*

Many employers offer paid vacation benefits, or *paid absences.* Vacation benefits are estimated and expensed in the period when employees earn them. Assume that salaried employees earn 2 weeks' paid vacation per year. The year-end adjusting entry to record $3,200 of accrued vacation benefits follows.

Assets = Liabilities + Equity
+3,200 −3,200

Dec. 31	Vacation Benefits Expense	3,200	
	Vacation Benefits Payable		3,200
	Record vacation benefits accrued.		

Vacation Benefits Expense is an operating expense, and Vacation Benefits Payable is a current liability. When an employee takes a vacation, the employer reduces (debits) Vacation Benefits Payable and credits Cash.

Assets = Liabilities + Equity
−400 −400

Jan. 20	Vacation Benefits Payable........................	400	
	Cash..................................		400
	Record vacation benefits taken.		

Bonus Plans

Many companies offer bonuses to employees, and many of the bonuses depend on net income. Assume that an employer gives a bonus to its employees based on the company's annual net income (to be equally shared by all). The year-end adjusting entry to record a $10,000 bonus is

Assets = Liabilities + Equity
+10,000 −10,000

Dec. 31	Employee Bonus Expense	10,000	
	Bonus Payable		10,000
	Record expected bonus costs.		

Warranty Liabilities

A **warranty** is a seller's obligation to replace or fix a product or service that fails to perform as expected within a specified period. For example, a new **Jeep** is sold with a warranty covering parts for a specified period of time. The seller reports the expected warranty expense in the period when revenue from the sale of the product or service is reported. The seller reports this warranty liability, even though the existence, amount, payee, and date of future payments are uncertain. This is because warranty costs are probable and the amount can be estimated using past experience.

Assume a dealer sells a car for $16,000 on December 1, 2021, with a one-year or 12,000-mile warranty covering parts. Experience shows that warranty expense is 4% of a car's selling price, or $640 in this case ($16,000 × 4%). The dealer records the estimated expense and liability related to this sale with this end-of-period adjustment.

Dec. 31	Warranty Expense	640	
	Estimated Warranty Liability		640
	Record estimated warranty expense.		

Assets = Liabilities + Equity
+640 −640

This entry alternatively could be made at the time of sale. Either way, the estimated warranty expense is reported on the 2021 income statement and the warranty liability on the 2021 balance sheet. Continuing this example, assume the customer brings the car in for warranty repairs on January 9, 2022. The dealer fixes the car by replacing parts costing $200. The entry to record the repair is

Jan. 9	Estimated Warranty Liability	200	
	Parts Inventory		200
	Record costs of warranty repairs.		

Assets = Liabilities + Equity
−200 −200

This entry reduces the balance of the Estimated Warranty Liability account, but no expense is recorded in 2022 for the repair. Warranty expense was previously recorded in 2021, the year the car was sold with the warranty. Finally, what happens if total warranty expenses are more or less than the estimated 4%, or $640? The answer is that management should monitor actual warranty expenses to see if a 4% rate is accurate. If not, the rate is changed for future periods.

Multi-Period Estimated Liabilities

Estimated liabilities can be both current and long term. For example, pension liabilities to employees are long term to workers who will not retire within the next year. For employees who are retired or will retire within the next year, a portion of pension liabilities is current. Other examples include employee health benefits and warranties.

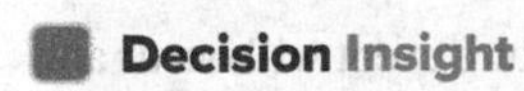
Decision Insight

Out of Play **Major League Baseball** was the first pro sport to set up a pension, originally up to $100 per month depending on years played. Many former players now take home six-figure pensions. Cal Ripken Jr.'s pension at age 62 is estimated at $180,000 per year (he played 21 seasons). The same applies to Ichiro Suzuki, who played 18 seasons—see photo. The requirement is 43 games for a full pension and just one game for full medical benefits for life. ■

Imac/Alamy Stock Photo

NEED-TO-KNOW 11-3

Estimated Liabilities

P4

Part 1. A company's salaried employees earn two weeks' vacation per year. The company estimated and must expense $9,000 of accrued vacation benefits for the year. (a) Prepare the December 31 year-end adjusting entry to record accrued vacation benefits. (b) Prepare the entry on May 1 of the next year when an employee takes a one-week vacation and is paid $450 cash for that week.

Part 2. For the current year ended December 31, a company has implemented an employee bonus program based on its net income, which employees share equally. Its bonus expense is $40,000. (a) Prepare the journal entry at December 31 of the current year to record the bonus due. (b) Prepare the journal entry at January 20 of the following year to record payment of that bonus to employees.

Part 3. On December 11 of the current year, a retailer sells a trimmer for $400 with a one-year warranty that covers parts. Warranty expense is estimated at 5% of sales. On March 24 of the next year, the trimmer is brought in for repairs covered under the warranty requiring $15 in materials taken from the Parts Inventory. Prepare the (a) December 11 entry to record the trimmer sale—ignore the cost of sales part of this sales entry, (b) December 31 adjusting entry for estimated warranty liability, and (c) March 24 entry to record warranty repairs.

[continued on next page]

[continued from previous page]

Solution—Part 1

a.

Dec. 31	Vacation Benefits Expense	9,000	
	Vacation Benefits Payable		9,000
	Record vacation benefits accrued.		

b.

May 1	Vacation Benefits Payable.......	450	
	Cash..................		450
	Record vacation benefits taken.		

Solution—Part 2

a.

Dec. 31	Employee Bonus Expense	40,000	
	Bonus Payable		40,000
	Record expected bonus costs.		

b.

Jan. 20	Bonus Payable	40,000	
	Cash.................		40,000
	Record payment of bonus.		

Solution—Part 3

Dec. 11	Cash	400	
	Sales		400
	Record trimmer sales.		
Dec. 31	Warranty Expense	20	
	Estimated Warranty Liability..................		20
	Record estimated warranty expense ($400 × 5%).		
Mar. 24	Estimated Warranty Liability	15	
	Parts Inventory............................		15
	Record cost of warranty repairs.		

Do More: QS 11-11 through QS 11-14, E 11-12, E 11-13, E 11-14, E 11-15, E 11-16

CONTINGENT LIABILITIES

C3 Explain how to account for contingent liabilities.

A **contingent liability** is a potential obligation that depends on a future event arising from a past transaction or event. An example is a pending lawsuit. Here, a past transaction or event leads to a lawsuit whose financial outcome depends on the result of the suit.

Accounting for Contingent Liabilities

Accounting for contingent liabilities depends on the likelihood that a future event will occur and the ability to estimate the future amount owed if this event occurs. Three different possibilities are shown in Exhibit 11.5: record liability with a journal entry, disclose in notes to financial statements, or no disclosure.

EXHIBIT 11.5

Contingent Liabilities

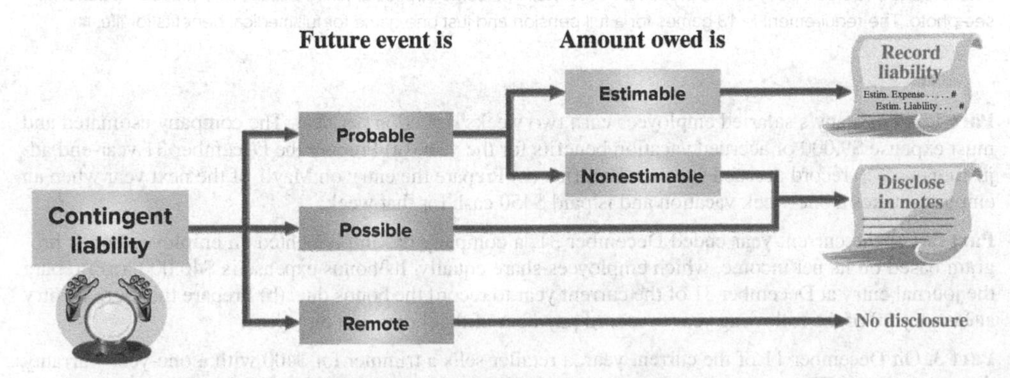

The conditions that determine each of these three possibilities follow.

1. **Record liability.** The future event is *probable* (likely) and the amount owed can be *reasonably estimated.* Examples are warranties, vacation pay, and income taxes.
2. **Disclose in notes.** The future event is *reasonably possible* (could occur).
3. **No disclosure.** The future event is *remote* (unlikely).

Point: A contingency is an *if.* Namely, *if* a future event occurs, then financial consequences are likely for the entity.

Applying Rules of Contingent Liabilities

This section covers common contingent liabilities.

Potential Legal Claims Many companies are sued or at risk of being sued. The accounting issue is whether the defendant records a liability or discloses a contingent liability in its notes while a lawsuit is outstanding and not yet settled. The answer is that a potential claim is recorded *only* if payment for damages is probable and the amount can be reasonably estimated. If the potential claim cannot be reasonably estimated but is reasonably possible, it is disclosed. For example, **Ford** includes the following note in its annual report: "Various legal actions, proceedings, and claims are pending . . . arising out of alleged defects in our products."

Debt Guarantees Sometimes a company guarantees the payment of debt owed by a supplier, customer, or another company. The guarantor usually discloses the guarantee in its financial statement notes as a contingent liability. If it is probable that the debtor will default, the guarantor reports the guarantee as a liability. The **Boston Celtics** report a unique guarantee: "Contracts provide for guaranteed payments which must be paid even if the employee [player] is injured or terminated."

Other Contingencies Other examples of contingencies include environmental damages, possible tax assessments, insurance losses, and government investigations. **Chevron**, for example, reports that it "is subject to loss contingencies . . . related to environmental matters. . . . The amount of additional future costs are not fully determinable." Many of Chevron's contingencies are revealed only in notes.

Uncertainties That Are Not Contingencies

All organizations face uncertainties from future events such as natural disasters and new technologies. These uncertainties are not contingent liabilities because they are future events *not* arising from past transactions. Accordingly, they are not disclosed.

Decision Insight

On the Safe Side When we purchase a new laptop at **Best Buy**, a sales clerk commonly asks: *"Do you want the Geek Squad Protection Plan?"* Best Buy earns about a 60% profit margin on such warranty contracts, and those contracts are a large part of its profit—see table (*BusinessWeek*). ■

Warranties as a percent of sales	4%
Warranties as a percent of operating profit. . . .	45%

NEED-TO-KNOW 11-4

Contingent Liabilities

C3

The following legal claims exist for a company. Identify the accounting treatment for each claim as either (a) a liability that is recorded or (b) an item described in notes to its financial statements.

1. The company (defendant) estimates that a pending lawsuit could result in damages of $500,000; it is reasonably possible that the plaintiff will win the case.
2. The company faces a probable loss on a pending lawsuit; the amount is not reasonably estimable.
3. The company estimates environmental damages in a pending case at $900,000 with a high probability of losing the case.

Solution

1. (b); reason—is reasonably estimated but not a probable loss.
2. (b); reason—probable loss but cannot be reasonably estimated.
3. (a); reason—can be reasonably estimated and loss is probable.

Do More: QS 11-15, E 11-17

Times Interest Earned Ratio  **Decision Analysis**

A1 Compute the times interest earned ratio and use it to analyze liabilities.

Interest expense is often called a *fixed expense* because it usually does not vary due to short-term changes in sales or other operating activities. While fixed expenses can be good when a company is growing, they create risk. The risk is that a company might be unable to pay fixed expenses if sales decline. Consider Diego Co.'s results for 2021 and two possible outcomes for year 2022 in Exhibit 11.6. Expenses excluding interest are expected to remain at 75% of sales. Expenses that change with sales volume are *variable expenses*. Interest expense is fixed at $60 per year.

EXHIBIT 11.6

Actual and Projected Results

$ millions	2021	2022 Projections: Sales Increase	2022 Projections: Sales Decrease
Sales	$600	$900	$300
Expenses (75% of sales)	450	675	225
Income before interest	150	225	75
Interest expense (fixed)	60	60	60
Net income	$ 90	$165	$ 15

The Sales Increase column of Exhibit 11.6 shows that Diego's net income increases by 83% to $165 if sales increase by 50% to $900. The Sales Decrease column shows that net income decreases by 83% if sales decline by 50%. These results show that the amount of fixed interest expense affects a company's risk of its ability to pay interest. One measure of "ability to pay" is the **times interest earned** ratio in Exhibit 11.7.

EXHIBIT 11.7

Times Interest Earned

$$\textbf{Times interest earned} = \frac{\textbf{Income before interest expense and income taxes}}{\textbf{Interest expense}}$$

For 2021, Diego's times interest earned is computed as $150/$60, or 2.5 times. This ratio means that Diego has low to moderate risk because its sales must decline sharply before it is unable to pay its interest expenses. If times interest earned falls below around 1.5, a company will likely be at risk of not being able to pay its liabilities.

Decision Maker

Entrepreneur You wish to invest in a franchise for either one of two national chains. Each franchise has an expected annual net income *after* interest and taxes of $100,000. Net income for the first franchise includes a regular fixed interest charge of $200,000. The fixed interest charge for the second franchise is $40,000. Which franchise is riskier to you if sales forecasts are not met? ■ *Answer:* Times interest earned for the first franchise is 1.5 [($100,000 + $200,000)/$200,000], whereas it is 3.5 for the second [($100,000 + $40,000)/$40,000]. This shows the first franchise is more at risk of incurring a loss if its sales decline.

NEED-TO-KNOW 11-5

COMPREHENSIVE

Accounting for Current Liabilities Including Warranties, Notes, Contingencies, Payroll, and Income Taxes

The following transactions took place at Kern Co. during its recent calendar-year reporting period.

a. In September, Kern sold $140,000 of merchandise covered by a 180-day warranty. Prior experience shows that costs of the warranty equal 5% of sales. Compute September's warranty expense and prepare the adjusting journal entry for the warranty liability as recorded at September 30. Also prepare the journal entry on October 8 to record a $300 cash payment to provide warranty service on an item sold in September.

b. On October 12, Kern replaced an overdue $10,000 account payable by paying $2,500 cash and signing a note for $7,500. The note matures in 90 days and has a 12% interest rate. Prepare the entries recorded on October 12, December 31, and January 10.

c. In late December, Kern is facing a product liability suit filed by an unhappy customer. Kern's lawyer says it will probably suffer a loss from the lawsuit, but the amount is impossible to estimate.

d. Sally Bline works for Kern. For the pay period ended November 30, her gross earnings are $3,000. Bline has $800 deducted for federal income taxes and $200 for state income taxes from each paycheck. Additionally, a $35 premium for health insurance and a $10 donation to United Way are deducted. Bline pays FICA Social Security taxes at a rate of 6.2% and FICA Medicare taxes at a rate of 1.45%. She has not earned enough this year to be exempt from any FICA taxes. Journalize the accrual of salaries expense for Bline by Kern.

e. On November 1, Kern borrows $5,000 cash from a bank in return for a 60-day, 12%, $5,000 note. Record the note's issuance on November 1 and its repayment with interest on December 31.

f[B] *(Part f covers Appendix 11B.)* Kern has estimated and recorded its quarterly income tax payments. In reviewing its year-end tax adjustments, it identifies an additional $5,000 of income taxes expense that should be recorded. A portion of this additional expense, $1,000, is deferred to future years. Record this year-end income taxes expense adjusting entry.

SOLUTION

a. Warranty expense = 5% × $140,000 = $7,000

Date	Account	Debit	Credit
Sep. 30	Warranty Expense	7,000	
	Estimated Warranty Liability		7,000
	Record warranty expense.		
Oct. 8	Estimated Warranty Liability	300	
	Cash		300
	Record cost of warranty service.		

b. Interest expense for current year = 12% × $7,500 × 80/360 = $200
Interest expense for following year = 12% × $7,500 × 10/360 = $25

Date	Account	Debit	Credit
Oct. 12	Accounts Payable	10,000	
	Notes Payable		7,500
	Cash		2,500
	Paid $2,500 cash and gave a 90-day, 12% note to extend due date on the account.		
Dec. 31	Interest Expense	200	
	Interest Payable		200
	Accrue interest on note payable.		
Jan. 10	Interest Expense	25	
	Interest Payable	200	
	Notes Payable	7,500	
	Cash		7,725
	Paid note with interest, including accrued interest payable.		

c. Disclose the pending lawsuit in the financial statement notes. Although the loss is probable, no liability is accrued because the loss cannot be reasonably estimated.

d.

Date	Account	Debit	Credit
Nov. 30	Salaries Expense	3,000.00	
	FICA—Social Security Taxes Payable (6.2%)		186.00
	FICA—Medicare Taxes Payable (1.45%)		43.50
	Employee Federal Income Taxes Payable		800.00
	Employee State Income Taxes Payable		200.00
	Employee Medical Insurance Payable		35.00
	Employee United Way Payable		10.00
	Salaries Payable		1,725.50
	Record Bline's accrued payroll.		

e.

Date	Account	Debit	Credit
Nov. 1	Cash	5,000	
	Notes Payable		5,000
	Borrowed cash with a 60-day, 12% note.		

When the note and interest are paid 60 days later, Kern Co. records this entry.

Date	Account	Debit	Credit
Dec. 31	Notes Payable	5,000	
	Interest Expense	100	
	Cash		5,100
	Paid note with interest ($5,000 × 12% × 60/360).		

f.[B]

Date	Account	Debit	Credit
Dec. 31	Income Taxes Expense	5,000	
	Income Taxes Payable		4,000
	Deferred Income Tax Liability		1,000
	Record added income taxes expense and the deferred tax liability.		

APPENDIX

11A Payroll Reports, Records, and Procedures

P5 Identify and describe the details of payroll reports, records, and procedures.

This appendix focuses on payroll accounting reports, records, and procedures.

Payroll Reports

Most employees and employers are required to pay local, state, and federal payroll taxes. Payroll expenses are liabilities to individual employees, to federal and state governments, and to other organizations such as insurance companies. Employers are required to prepare and submit reports explaining how they computed these payments.

Reporting FICA Taxes and Income Taxes The Federal Insurance Contributions Act (FICA) requires each employer to file an Internal Revenue Service (IRS) **Form 941,** the *Employer's Quarterly Federal Tax Return,* within one month after the end of each calendar quarter. A sample Form 941 is shown in Exhibit 11A.1 for Phoenix Sales & Service, a landscape design company. Accounting information and software are helpful in tracking payroll transactions and reporting the accumulated information on Form 941. Specifically, the employer reports total wages subject to income tax withholding on line 2 of Form 941. (For simplicity, this appendix uses *wages* to refer to both wages and salaries.) The income tax withheld is reported on line 3. The combined amount of employee and employer FICA (Social Security)

Point: Line 5a shows the matching nature of FICA tax as 6.2% × 2, or 12.4%, which is shown as 0.124.

Point: Auditors rely on the four 941 Forms filed during a year when auditing a company's annual wages and salaries expense account.

EXHIBIT 11A.1

Form 941

Form **941** **Employer's QUARTERLY Federal Tax Return**
Department of the Treasury — Internal Revenue Service

(EIN) Employer identification number: 8 6 – 3 2 1 4 5 8 7
Name (not your trade name): Phoenix Sales & Service
Trade name (if any):
Address: 1214 Mill Road
Number Street Suite or room number
Phoenix AZ 85621
City State ZIP code

Report for this Quarter ... (Check one.)
☐ 1: January, February, March
☐ 2: April, May, June
☐ 3: July, August, September
☒ 4: October, November, December

Part 1: Answer these questions for this quarter.

1 Number of employees who received wages, tips, or other compensation for the pay period including: *Mar. 12* (Quarter 1), *June 12* (Quarter 2), *Sept. 12* (Quarter 3), *Dec. 12* (Quarter 4)		1	2
2 Wages, tips, and other compensation		2	36,599.00
3 Federal income tax withheld from wages, tips, and other compensation		3	3,056.47
4 If no wages, tips, and other compensation are subject to social security or Medicare tax		☐	Check and go to line 6.

	Column 1		Column 2
5a Taxable social security wages	36,599.00	× .124 =	4,538.28
5b Taxable social security tips	.	× .124 =	.
5c Taxable Medicare wages & tips	36,599.00	× .029 =	1,061.37
5d Taxable wages & tips subject to Additional Medicare Tax withholding	.	× 0.009 =	.

5e Add Column 2 from lines 5a, 5b, 5c, and 5d	5e	5,599.65
5f Section 3121(q) Notice and Demand–Tax due to unreported tips (see instructions)	5f	.
6 Total taxes before adjustments. Add lines 3, 5e, and 5f	6	8,656.12
7 Current quarter's adjustment for fractions of cents	7	.
8 Current quarter's adjustment for sick pay	8	.
9 Current quarter's adjustments for tips and group-term life insurance	9	.
10 Total taxes after adjustments. Combine lines 6 through 9	10	8,656.12
11 Qualified small business payroll tax credit for increasing research activities. Attach Form 8974.	11	.
12 Total taxes after adjustments and credits. Subtract line 11 from line 10	12	8,656.12
13 Total deposits for this quarter, including overpayment applied from a prior quarter and overpayments applied from Form 941-X, 941-X (PR), 944-X, or 944-X (SP) filed in the current quarter	13	8,656.12
14 Balance due. If line 12 is more than line 13, enter the difference and see instructions	14	0.00

15 **Overpayment.** If line 13 is more than line 12, enter the difference [.] Check one: ☐ Apply to next return. ☐ Send a refund.

Part 2: Tell us about your deposit schedule and tax liability for this quarter.

If you are unsure about whether you are a monthly schedule depositor or a semiweekly schedule depositor, see section 11 of Pub. 15.

16 Check one: ☐ **Line 12 on this return is less than $2,500 or line 12 on the return for the prior quarter was less than $2,500, and you didn't incur a $100,000 next-day deposit obligation during the current quarter.** If line 12 for the prior quarter was less than $2,500 but line 12 on this reutm is $100,000 or more, you must provide a record of your federal tax liability. If you are a monthly schedule depositor, complete the deposit schedule below; if you are a semiweekly schedule depositor, attach Schedule B (Form 941). Go to Part 3.

☒ **You were a monthly schedule depositor for the entire quarter. Enter your tax liability for each month and total liability for the quarter,** then go to Part 3.

Tax liability:	
Month 1	3,079.11
Month 2	2,049.77
Month 3	3,527.24
Total liability for quarter	8,656.12

Total must equal line 12.

☐ **You were a semiweekly schedule depositor for any part of this quarter.** Complete *Schedule B (Form 941): Report of Tax Liability for Semiweekly Schedule Depositors,* and attach it to Form 941.

Part 3: Tell us about your business. If a question does NOT apply to your business, leave it blank.

17 **If your business has closed or you stopped paying wages** ☐ Check here, and enter the final date you paid wages [/ /].

18 **If you are a seasonal employer and you do not have to file a return for every quarter of the year** ☐ Check here.

Part 4: May we speak with your third-party designee?

Do you want to allow an employee, a paid tax preparer, or another person to discuss this return with the IRS? See the instructions for details.

☐ Yes. Designee's name and phone number

Select a 5-digit Personal Identification Number (PIN) to use when talking to the IRS.

☒ No.

Part 5: Sign here. You MUST complete both pages of Form 941 and SIGN it.

Under penalties of perjury, I declare that I have examined this return, including accompanying schedules and statements, and to the best of my knowledge and belief, it is true, correct, and complete. Declaration of preparer (other than taxpayer) is based on all information of which preparer has any knowledge.

✗ Sign your name here | Print your name here | Print your title here

Date [/ /] | Best daytime phone

taxes for Phoenix Sales & Service is reported on line 5a (taxable Social Security wages, $36,599 × 12.4% = $4,538.28). The 12.4% is the sum of the Social Security tax withheld, computed as 6.2% tax withheld from the employee wages for the quarter, plus the 6.2% tax levied on the employer. The combined amount of employee Medicare wages is reported on line 5c. The 2.9% is the sum of 1.45% withheld from employee wages for the quarter plus 1.45% tax levied on the employer. Total FICA taxes are reported on line 5e and are added to the total income taxes withheld of $3,056.47 to yield a total of $8,656.12. For this year, assume that income up to $137,700 is subject to Social Security tax. There is no income limit on amounts subject to Medicare tax. Congress sets rates owed for Social Security tax (and it typically changes each year).

Federal depository banks are authorized to accept deposits of amounts payable to the federal government. Deposit requirements depend on the amount of tax owed. For example, when the sum of FICA taxes plus the employee income taxes is less than $2,500 for a quarter, the taxes can be paid when Form 941 is filed.

Reporting FUTA Taxes and SUTA Taxes An employer's federal unemployment taxes (FUTA) are reported on an annual basis by filing an *Annual Federal Unemployment Tax Return,* IRS **Form 940.** It must be mailed on or before January 31 following the end of each tax year. Ten more days are allowed if all required tax deposits are filed on a timely basis and the full amount of tax is paid on or before January 31. FUTA payments are made quarterly to a federal depository bank if the total amount due exceeds $500. If $500 or less is due, the taxes are remitted annually. Requirements for paying and reporting state unemployment taxes (SUTA) vary depending on the laws of each state. Most states require quarterly payments and reports.

Reporting Wages and Salaries Employers are required to give each employee an annual report of his or her wages subject to FICA and federal income taxes along with the amounts of these taxes withheld. This report is called a *Wage and Tax Statement,* or **Form W-2.** It must be given to employees before January 31 following the year covered by the report. Exhibit 11A.2 shows Form W-2 for one of the employees at Phoenix Sales & Service. Copies of Form W-2 must be sent to the Social Security Administration, where the amount of the employee's wages subject to FICA taxes and FICA taxes withheld are posted to each employee's Social Security account. These posted amounts become the basis for determining an employee's retirement and survivors' benefits. The Social Security Administration also transmits to the IRS the amount of each employee's wages subject to federal income taxes and the amount of taxes withheld.

EXHIBIT 11A.2

Form W-2

Form **W-2** Wage and Tax Statement — Department of Treasury—Internal Revenue Service
Copy 1—For State, City, or Local Tax Department

22222 — a Employee's social security number: 333-22-9999 — OMB No. 1545-0008

b Employer identification number (EIN)	86-3214587	1 Wages, tips, other compensation	4,910.00
		2 Federal income tax withheld	333.37
c Employer's name, address and ZIP code	Phoenix Sales & Service, 1214 Mill Road, Phoenix, AZ 85621	3 Social security wages	4,910.00
		4 Social security tax withheld	304.42
		5 Medicare wages and tips	4,910.00
		6 Medicare tax withheld	71.20
		7 Social security tips	
		8 Allocated tips	
d Control number	AR101	9	
		10 Dependent care benefits	
e Employee's first name and initial	Robert J.	11 Nonqualified plans	
Last name	Austin	12a Code	
f Employee's address and ZIP code	18 Roosevelt Blvd., Apt. C, Tempe, AZ 86322	13 Statutory employee / Retirement plan / Third-party sick pay	
		12b Code	
		14 Other	
		12c Code	

15 State	Employer's state ID number	16 State wages, tips, etc.	17 State income tax	18 Local wages, tips, etc.	19 Local income tax	20 Locality name
AZ	13-902319	4,910.00	26.68			

Payroll Records Employers must keep payroll records in addition to reporting and paying taxes. These records usually include a payroll register and an individual earnings report for each employee.

Payroll Register A **payroll register** usually shows the pay period dates, hours worked, gross pay, deductions, and net pay of each employee for each pay period. Exhibit 11A.3 shows a payroll register for Phoenix Sales & Service. It is organized into nine columns:

Col. A Employee Identification (ID); Employee name; Social Security number (SS No.); Reference (check number); and Date (date check issued)
Col. B Pay Type (regular and overtime)
Col. C Pay Hours (number of hours worked as regular and overtime)
Col. D Gross Pay (amount of gross pay)
Col. E FIT (federal income taxes withheld); FUTA (federal unemployment taxes)
Col. F SIT (state income taxes withheld); SUTA (state unemployment taxes)
Col. G FICA-SS_EE (Social Security taxes withheld, employee); FICA-SS_ER (Social Security taxes, employer)
Col. H FICA-Med_EE (Medicare tax withheld, employee); FICA-Med_ER (Medicare tax, employer)
Col. I Net Pay (gross pay less amounts withheld from employees)

Net pay for each employee is computed as gross pay minus the items on the first line of columns E through H. The employer's payroll tax for each employee is computed as the sum of items on the third line of columns E through H. A payroll register includes all data necessary to record payroll. In some software programs, the entries to record payroll are made in a special *payroll journal.*

EXHIBIT 11A.3

Payroll Register

A	B	C	D	E	F	G	H	I
Phoenix Sales & Service Payroll Register For Week Ended Jan. 8, 2021								
Employee ID	Gross Pay			FIT	SIT	FICA-SS_EE	FICA-Med_EE	
Employee				[blank]	[blank]	[blank]	[blank]	
SS No. Refer., Date	Pay Type	Pay Hours	Gross Pay	FUTA	SUTA	FICA-SS_ER	FICA-Med_ER	Net Pay
AR101	Regular	40.00	400.00	-28.99	-2.32	-24.80	-5.80	338.09
Robert Austin	Overtime	0.00	0.00					
333-22-9999			400.00	-2.40	-10.80	-24.80	-5.80	
9001, 1/8/21								
CJ102	Regular	40.00	560.00	-52.97	-4.24	-36.02	-8.42	479.35
Judy Cross	Overtime	1.00	21.00					
299-11-9201			581.00	-3.49	-15.69	-36.02	-8.42	
9002, 1/8/21								
DJ103	Regular	40.00	560.00	-48.33	-3.87	-37.32	-8.73	503.75
John Diaz	Overtime	2.00	42.00					
444-11-9090			602.00	-3.61	-16.25	-37.32	-8.73	
9003, 1/8/21								
KK104	Regular	40.00	560.00	-68.57	-5.49	-34.72	-8.12	443.10
Kay Keife	Overtime	0.00	0.00					
909-11-3344			560.00	-3.36	-15.12	-34.72	-8.12	
9004, 1/8/21								
ML105	Regular	40.00	560.00	-34.24	-2.74	-34.72	-8.12	480.18
Lee Miller	Overtime	0.00	0.00					
444-56-3211			560.00	-3.36	-15.12	-34.72	-8.12	
9005, 1/8/21								
SD106	Regular	40.00	560.00	-68.57	-5.49	-34.72	-8.12	443.10
Dale Sears	Overtime	0.00	0.00					
909-33-1234			560.00	-3.36	-15.12	-34.72	-8.12	
9006, 1/8/21								
Totals	Regular	240.00	3,200.00	-301.67	-24.15	-202.30	-47.31	2,687.57
	Overtime	3.00	63.00					
			3,263.00	-19.58	-88.10	-202.30	-47.31	

Point: Gross Pay column shows regular hours worked on the first line multiplied by regular pay rate. Overtime hours multiplied by the overtime premium rate equals overtime pay on the second line. For this company, workers earn 150% of their regular rate for hours in excess of 40 per week.

Payroll Check Payment of payroll is usually done by check or electronic funds transfer. Exhibit 11A.4 shows a *payroll check* for a Phoenix employee. This check includes a detachable *statement of earnings* (at top) showing gross pay, deductions, and net pay.

EXHIBIT 11A.4

Check and Statement of Earnings

EMPLOYEE NO.	EMPLOYEE NAME	SOCIAL SECURITY NO.	PAY PERIOD END	CHECK DATE
AR101	Robert Austin	333-22-9999	1/8/21	1/8/21

ITEM	RATE	HOURS	TOTAL	ITEM	THIS CHECK	YEAR TO DATE
Regular	10.00	40.00	400.00	Gross	400.00	400.00
Overtime	15.00			Fed. Income tax	-28.99	-28.99
				FICA-Soc. Sec.	-24.80	-24.80
				FICA-Medicare	-5.80	-5.80
				State Income tax	-2.32	-2.32

HOURS WORKED	GROSS THIS PERIOD	GROSS YEAR TO DATE	NET CHECK	CHECK NO.
40.00	400.00	400.00	$338.09	9001

(Detach and retain for your records)

PHOENIX SALES & SERVICE
1214 Mill Road
Phoenix, AZ 85621
602-555-8900

Phoenix Bank and Trust
Phoenix, AZ 85621
3312-87044

No. 9001

DATE January 8, 20 21

Check No. 9001

Amount Three Hundred Thirty-Eight and 91/100 Dollars

$ **************$338.09

Pay to the order of
Robert Austin
18 Roosevelt Blvd., Apt C
Tempe, AZ 86322

Mary Wills
AUTHORIZED SIGNATURE

Employee Earnings Report An **employee earnings report** is a cumulative record of an employee's hours worked, gross earnings, deductions, and net pay. Payroll information on this report is taken from the payroll register. The employee earnings report for R. Austin at Phoenix Sales & Service is shown in Exhibit 11A.5. An employee earnings report accumulates information that can show when an employee's earnings reach the tax-exempt points for FICA, FUTA, and SUTA taxes. It also gives data an employer needs to prepare Form W-2.

EXHIBIT 11A.5

Employee Earnings Report

Phoenix Sales & Service
Employee Earnings Report
For Month Ended Dec. 31, 2021

Employee ID Employee SS No.	Date Reference	Gross Pay	FIT [blank] FUTA	SIT [blank] SUTA	FICA-SS_EE [blank] FICA-SS_ER	FICA-Med_EE [blank] FICA-Med_ER	Net Pay
Beginning balance for Robert Austin	11/26/21 (balance)	2,910.00	−188.42	−15.08	−180.42	−42.20	2,483.88
			−17.46	−78.57	−180.42	−42.20	
AR101 Robert Austin 333-22-9999	12/03/21 9049	400.00	−28.99	−2.32	−24.80	−5.80	338.09
			−2.40	−10.80	−24.80	−5.80	
AR101 Robert Austin 333-22-9999	12/10/21 9055	400.00	−28.99	−2.32	−24.80	−5.80	338.09
			−2.40	−10.80	−24.80	−5.80	
AR101 Robert Austin 333-22-9999	12/17/21 9061	400.00	−28.99	−2.32	−24.80	−5.80	338.09
			−2.40	−10.80	−24.80	−5.80	
AR101 Robert Austin 333-22-9999	12/24/21 9067	400.00	−28.99	−2.32	−24.80	−5.80	338.09
			−2.40	−10.80	−24.80	−5.80	
AR101 Robert Austin 333-22-9999	12/31/21 9073	400.00	−28.99	−2.32	−24.80	−5.80	338.09
			−2.40	−10.80	−24.80	−5.80	
Total 5-wk month thru 12/31/21		2,000.00	−144.95	−11.60	−124.00	−29.00	1,690.45
			−12.00	−54.00	−124.00	−29.00	
Year-to-date total for Robert Austin	12/31/21 (balance)	4,910.00	−333.37	−26.68	−304.42	−71.20	4,174.33
			−29.46	−132.57	−304.42	−71.20	

Point: Year-end balances agree with W-2.

Payroll Procedures Employers must be able to compute federal income tax for payroll purposes. This section explains how we compute this tax and how to use a payroll bank account.

Computing Federal Income Taxes To compute the amount of taxes withheld from each employee's wages, we need to determine both the employee's wages earned and the employee's number of *withholding allowances.* Each employee records the number of withholding allowances claimed on a withholding allowance certificate, **Form W-4,** filed with the employer. When the number of withholding allowances increases, the amount of income taxes withheld decreases.

Form **W-4** — **Employee's Withholding Certificate** — OMB No. 1545–0074 — 20__

Department of the Treasury
Internal Revenue Service

▶ Complete Form W-4 so that your employer can withhold the correct federal income tax from your pay.
▶ Give Form W-4 to your employer.
▶ Your withholding is subject to review by the IRS.

Step 1: Enter Personal Information
(a) First name and middle initial: *Robert J.* Last name: *Austin*
(b) Social security number: *333-22-9999*
Address: *18 Roosevelt Blvd., Apt. C*
City or town, state, and ZIP code: *Tempe, AZ 86322*
▶ **Does your name match the name on your social security card?** If not, to ensure you get credit for your earnings, contact SSA at 800-772-1213 or go to *www.ssa.gov.*
(c) ☒ **Single or Married filing separately** ☐ **Married filing jointly** (or Qualifying widow(er))
☐ **Head of household** (Check only if you're unmarried and pay more than half the costs of keeping up a home for yourself and a qualifying individual.)

Complete Steps 2–4 ONLY if they apply to you; otherwise, skip to Step 5. See page 2 for more information on each step, who can claim exemption from withholding, when to use the online estimator, and privacy.

Step 2: Multiple Jobs or Spouse Works
Complete this step if you (1) hold more than one job at a time, or (2) are married filing jointly and your spouse also works. The correct amount of withholding depends on income earned from all of these jobs.
Do **only one** of the following.
(a) Use the estimator at *www.irs.gov/W4App* for most accurate withholding for this step (and Steps 3–4); **or**
(b) Use the Multiple Jobs Worksheet on page 3 and enter the result in Step 4(c) below for roughly accurate withholding; **or**
(c) If there are only two jobs total, you may check this box. Do the same on Form W-4 for the other job. This option is accurate for jobs with similar pay; otherwise, more tax than necessary may be withheld .... ▶ ☐
TIP: To be accurate, submit a Form W-4 for all other jobs. If you (or your spouse) have self-employment income, including as an independent contractor, use the estimator.

Complete Steps 3–4(b) on Form W-4 for only ONE of these jobs. Leave those steps blank for the other jobs. (Your withholding will be most accurate if you complete Steps 3–4(b) on the Form W-4 for the highest paying job.)

Step 3: Claim Dependents
If your income will be $200,000 or less ($400,000 or less if married filing jointly):
Multiply the number of qualifying children under age 17 by $2,000 ▶ $
Multiply the number of other dependents by $500 .... ▶ $
Add the amounts above and enter the total here .... 3 $

Step 4: (optional): Other Adjustments
(a) Other income (not from jobs). If you want tax withheld for other income you expect this year that won't have withholding, enter the amount of other income here. This may include interest, dividends, and retirement income .... 4(a) $
(b) Deductions. If you expect to claim deductions other than the standard deduction and want to reduce your withholding, use the Deductions Worksheet on page 3 and enter the result here .... 4(b) $
(b) Extra withholding. Enter any additional tax you want withheld each pay period .... 4(b) $

Step 5: Sign Here
Under penalties of perjury, I declare that this certificate, to the best of my knowledge and belief, is true, correct, and complete.
▶ *Robert J. Austin* — **Employee's signature** (This form is not valid unless you sign it.) ▶ **Date** *January 1*

Employers Only
Employer's name and address: *Phoenix Sales & Service, 1214 Mill Rd, Phoenix, AZ 85621*
First date of employment
Employer identification number (EIN): *86-3214587*

For Privacy Act and Paperwork Reduction Act Notice, see page 3. Cat. No. 10220Q Form **W-4**

Employers often use a **wage bracket withholding table** similar to the one shown in Exhibit 11A.6 to compute the **federal income taxes withheld** from each employee's gross pay. The table in Exhibit 11A.6 is for a single employee paid weekly. Tables also are provided for married employees and for biweekly, semimonthly, and monthly pay periods (most payroll software includes these tables). When using a wage bracket withholding table to compute federal income tax withheld from an employee's gross wages, we need to locate an employee's wage bracket within the first two columns. We then find the amount withheld by looking in the withholding allowance column for that employee.

EXHIBIT 11A.6

Wage Bracket Withholding Table

SINGLE Persons—WEEKLY Payroll Period

If the wages are—		And the number of withholding allowances claimed is—										
At least	But less than	0	1	2	3	4	5	6	7	8	9	10
		The amount of income tax to be withheld is—										
$600	$610	$76	$67	$58	$49	$39	$30	$21	$12	$6	$0	$0
610	620	79	69	59	50	41	32	22	13	7	1	0
620	630	81	70	61	52	42	33	24	15	8	2	0
630	640	84	72	62	53	44	35	25	16	9	3	0
640	650	86	73	64	55	45	36	27	18	10	4	0
650	660	89	75	65	56	47	38	28	19	11	5	0
660	670	91	76	67	58	48	39	30	21	12	6	0
670	680	94	78	68	59	50	41	31	22	13	7	1
680	690	96	81	70	61	51	42	33	24	14	8	2
690	700	99	83	71	62	53	44	34	25	16	9	3
700	710	101	86	73	64	54	45	35	27	17	10	4
710	720	104	88	74	65	56	47	37	28	19	11	5
720	730	106	91	76	67	57	48	39	30	20	12	6
730	740	109	93	78	68	59	50	40	31	22	13	7
740	750	111	96	80	70	60	51	42	33	23	14	8

Payroll Bank Account Companies with few employees often pay them with checks drawn on the company's regular bank account. Companies with many employees often use a special **payroll bank account** to pay employees. When this account is used, a company either (1) draws one check for total payroll on the regular bank account and deposits it in the payroll bank account or (2) executes an *electronic funds transfer* to the payroll bank account. Individual payroll checks are then drawn on this payroll bank account. Because only one check for the total payroll is drawn on the regular bank account each payday, use of a special payroll bank account helps with internal control. It also helps in reconciling the regular bank account. When companies use a payroll bank account, they usually include check numbers in the payroll register. The payroll register in Exhibit 11A.3 shows check numbers in column A. For instance, Check No. 9001 is issued to Robert Austin. With this information, the payroll register serves as a supplementary record of wages earned by and paid to employees.

Who Pays What Payroll Taxes and Benefits We conclude this appendix with the following table identifying who pays which payroll taxes and which common employee benefits such as medical, disability, pension, charitable, and union costs. Who pays which employee benefits, and what portion, is subject to agreements between companies and their workers. Also, self-employed workers must pay both the employer and employee FICA taxes for Social Security and Medicare.

Employer Payroll Taxes and Costs	Employee Payroll Deductions
• FICA—Social Security taxes	• FICA—Social Security taxes
• FICA—Medicare taxes	• FICA—Medicare taxes
• FUTA (federal unemployment taxes)	• Federal income taxes
• SUTA (state unemployment taxes)	• State and local income taxes
• Share of medical coverage, if any	• Share of medical coverage, if any
• Share of pension coverage, if any	• Share of pension coverage, if any
• Share of other benefits, if any	• Share of other benefits, if any

APPENDIX

Corporate Income Taxes

11B

This appendix covers current liabilities for income taxes of C corporations. Income tax on sole proprietorships, partnerships, S corporations, and LLCs is computed on their owner's tax filings and is not covered here.

P6 Account for corporate income taxes.

Income Tax Liabilities Corporations are subject to income taxes and must estimate their income tax liability when preparing financial statements. Because income tax expense is created by earning income, a liability is incurred when income is earned. This tax must be paid quarterly. Consider a corporation that prepares monthly financial statements. Based on its income in January, this corporation estimates that it owes income taxes of $12,100. The following adjusting entry records this estimate.

		Debit	Credit
Jan. 31	Income Taxes Expense	12,100	
	Income Taxes Payable		12,100
	Accrue January income taxes.		

Assets = Liabilities + Equity
+12,100 −12,100

The tax liability is recorded each month until the first quarterly payment is made. If the company's estimated taxes for this first quarter total $30,000, the entry to record its payment is

		Debit	Credit
Apr. 10	Income Taxes Payable	30,000	
	Cash		30,000
	Paid estimated first-quarter income taxes.		

Assets = Liabilities + Equity
−30,000 −30,000

This process of accruing and then paying estimated income taxes continues through the year. When annual financial statements are prepared at year-end, the corporation knows its actual total income and the actual amount of income taxes it must pay. This information allows it to accurately record income taxes expense for the fourth quarter so that the total of the four quarters' expense amounts equals the actual taxes paid to the government.

Deferred Income Tax Liabilities An income tax liability for corporations can arise when the amount of income before taxes that the corporation reports on its income statement is not the same as the amount of income reported on its income tax return. This difference occurs because income tax laws and GAAP measure income differently. Differences between tax laws and GAAP arise because Congress uses tax laws to generate receipts, stimulate the economy, and influence behavior, whereas GAAP is intended to provide financial information useful for business decisions. Also, tax accounting often follows the cash basis, whereas GAAP follows the accrual basis.

Some differences between tax laws and GAAP are temporary. *Temporary differences* arise when the tax return and the income statement report a revenue or expense in different years. As an example, companies are often able to deduct higher amounts of depreciation in the early years of an asset's life and smaller amounts in later years for tax reporting in comparison to GAAP. This means that in the early years, depreciation for tax reporting is often more than depreciation on the income statement. In later years, depreciation for tax reporting is often less than depreciation on the income statement. When temporary differences exist between taxable income on the tax return and the income before taxes on the income statement, corporations compute income taxes expense based on the income reported on the income statement. The result is that income taxes expense reported in the income statement is often different from the amount of income taxes payable to the government. This difference is the **deferred income tax liability.**

Point: For a temporary difference, if GAAP income exceeds taxable income, a deferred tax liability is created. If GAAP income is initially less than taxable income, a deferred tax asset is created.

Assume that in recording its usual quarterly income tax payments, a corporation computes $25,000 of income taxes expense. It also determines that only $21,000 is currently due and $4,000 is deferred to future years (a timing difference). The entry to record this end-of-period adjustment is

Assets	= Liabilities	+ Equity
	+21,000	−25,000
	+4,000	

Dec. 31	Income Taxes Expense	25,000	
	Income Taxes Payable		21,000
	Deferred Income Tax Liability		4,000
	Record tax expense and deferred tax liability.		

The credit to Income Taxes Payable is the amount currently due to be paid. The credit to Deferred Income Tax Liability is tax payments deferred until future years when the temporary difference reverses.

Deferred Income Tax Assets Temporary differences also can cause a company to pay income taxes *before* they are reported on the income statement. If so, the company reports a *Deferred Income Tax Asset* on its balance sheet.

Summary: Cheat Sheet

KNOWN LIABILITIES

Current liabilities (or short-term liabilities): Liabilities due *within* one year.
Long-term liabilities: Liabilities due *after* one year.

Sales tax collection:

Cash	6,300	
Sales		6,000
Sales Taxes Payable		300

Unearned revenues (or deferred revenues): Amount received in advance from customers for future products or services; to record cash received in advance.

Cash	900,000	
Unearned Revenue		900,000

Unearned revenue is earned: To record service or product delivered.

Unearned Revenue	300,000	
Revenue		300,000

Short-term note payable: A written promise to pay a specified amount on a stated future date within one year.

Note given to replace accounts payable (partial cash paid):

Accounts Payable	600	
Cash		100
Notes Payable		500

Note given to borrow cash:

Cash	2,000	
Notes Payable		2,000

Note and interest paid:

Notes Payable	500	
Interest Expense	10	
Cash		510

Interest expense incurred but not yet paid:

Interest Expense	10	
Interest Payable		10

Interest formula (year assumed to have 360 days):

Principal of the note × Annual interest rate × Time expressed in fraction of year = Interest

PAYROLL LIABILITIES

Gross pay: Total compensation an employee earns before deductions such as taxes.

Payroll deductions (or withholdings): Amounts withheld from an employee's gross pay, either required or voluntary.

FICA—Social Security taxes payable: Withholdings to cover retirement, disability, and survivorship. Social Security tax is 6.2% of the first $137,700 the employee earns for the year.

FICA—Medicare taxes payable: Withholdings to cover medical benefits. The Medicare tax is 1.45% of all amounts the employee earns; there is no maximum limit to Medicare tax.

Employee federal income taxes payable: Federal income tax withheld from each employee's paycheck.

Employee voluntary deductions: Voluntary withholdings for things such as union dues, charitable giving, and health insurance.

Employee payroll taxes:

Account	Debit	Credit
Salaries Expense	2,000	
FICA—Social Security Taxes Payable (6.2%)		124
FICA—Medicare Taxes Payable (1.45%)		29
Employee Federal Income Taxes Payable		213
Employee Medical Insurance Payable		85
Employee Union Dues Payable		25
Salaries Payable		1,524

Payment of salary to employees:

Account	Debit	Credit
Salaries Payable	1,524	
Cash		1,524

Federal Unemployment Tax Act (FUTA): Employers pay a federal unemployment tax on wages and salaries earned by their employees. FUTA taxes are between 0.6% and 6.0% of the first $7,000 earned by each employee.

State Unemployment Tax Act (SUTA): Employers pay a state unemployment tax on wages and salaries earned by their employees. SUTA taxes are up to 5.4% of the first $7,000 earned by each employee.

Employer payroll taxes expense:

Account	Debit	Credit
Payroll Taxes Expense	273	
FICA—Social Security Taxes Payable (6.2%)		124
FICA—Medicare Taxes Payable (1.45%)		29
State Unemployment Taxes Payable		108
Federal Unemployment Taxes Payable		12

ESTIMATED LIABILITIES

Health and pension benefits:

Account	Debit	Credit
Employee Benefits Expense	20,000	
Employee Medical Insurance Payable		8,000
Employee Retirement Program Payable		12,000

Accrual of vacation benefits (also called *paid absences*):

Account	Debit	Credit
Vacation Benefits Expense	3,200	
Vacation Benefits Payable		3,200

Vacation benefits are used:

Account	Debit	Credit
Vacation Benefits Payable	400	
Cash		400

Bonus plan accrued:

Account	Debit	Credit
Employee Bonus Expense	10,000	
Bonus Payable		10,000

Warranty: A seller's obligation to replace or fix a product or service that fails to perform as expected within a specified period. Warranty expense is recorded in the period when revenue from the sale of the product or service is reported.

Warranty expense accrued:

Account	Debit	Credit
Warranty Expense	640	
Estimated Warranty Liability		640

Warranty repairs and replacements:

Account	Debit	Credit
Estimated Warranty Liability	200	
Parts Inventory		200

CONTINGENCIES AND ANALYSIS

Contingent liability: A potential liability that depends on a future event arising from a past transaction or event. An example is a pending lawsuit.

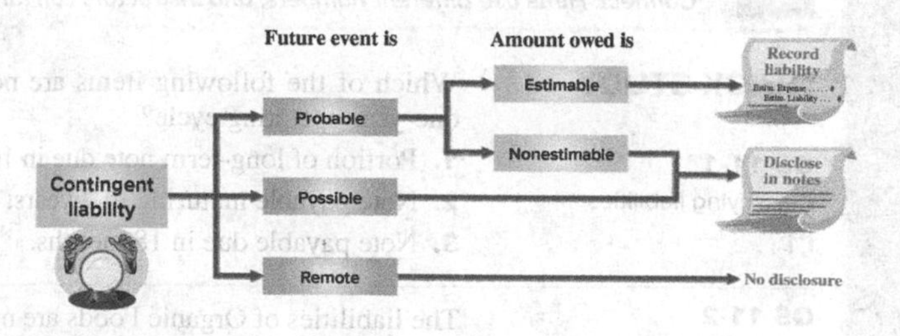

Key Terms

Contingent liability (402)
Current liabilities (391)
Current portion of long-term debt (399)
Deferred income tax liability (412)
Employee benefits (400)
Employee earnings report (409)
Estimated liability (399)
Federal depository bank (407)
Federal income taxes withheld (410)
Federal Insurance Contributions Act (FICA) taxes (396)
Federal Unemployment Tax Act (FUTA) (397)
Form 940 (407)
Form 941 (406)
Form W-2 (407)
Form W-4 (410)
Gross pay (396)
Known liabilities (392)
Long-term liabilities (392)
Merit rating (398)
Net pay (396)
Payroll bank account (410)
Payroll deductions (396)
Payroll register (408)
Short-term note payable (393)
State Unemployment Tax Act (SUTA) (397)
Times interest earned (404)
Wage bracket withholding table (410)
Warranty (400)

Multiple Choice Quiz

1. On December 1, a company signed a $6,000, 90-day, 5% note payable, with principal plus interest due on March 1 of the following year. What amount of interest expense should be accrued at December 31 on the note?

a. $300 **c.** $100 **e.** $0
b. $25 **d.** $75

2. An employee earned $50,000 during the year. FICA tax for Social Security is 6.2% and FICA tax for Medicare is 1.45%. The employer's share of FICA taxes is

a. $0; employee pay exceeds FICA limit. **d.** $725.
b. $0; FICA is not an employer tax. **e.** $3,825.
c. $3,100.

3. Assume the FUTA tax rate is 0.6% and the SUTA tax rate is 5.4%. Both taxes are applied to the first $7,000 of an employee's pay. What is the total unemployment tax an employer must pay on an employee's annual wages of $40,000?

a. $2,400
b. $420
c. $42
d. $378
e. $0; employee's wages exceed the $7,000 maximum.

4. A company sold 10,000 TVs in July and estimates warranty expense for these TVs to be $25,000. During July, 80 TVs were serviced under warranty at a cost of $18,000. The credit balance in the Estimated Warranty Liability account at July 1 was $26,000. What is the company's warranty expense for the month of July?

a. $51,000 **c.** $25,000 **e.** $18,000
b. $1,000 **d.** $33,000

5. AXE Co. is the defendant in a lawsuit. AXE reasonably estimates that this pending lawsuit will result in damages of $99,000. It is probable that AXE will lose the case. What should AXE do?

a. Record a liability **c.** Have no disclosure
b. Disclose in notes

ANSWERS TO MULTIPLE CHOICE QUIZ

1. b; $\$6,000 \times 0.05 \times 30/360 = \$25$
2. e; $\$50,000 \times (0.062 + 0.0145) = \$3,825$
3. b; $\$7,000 \times (0.006 + 0.054) = \$420$
4. c; $25,000
5. a; Reason—it is reasonably estimated and is a probable loss. AXE would record an estimated legal expense and liability.

Superscript letter A or B denotes assignments based on Appendix 11A or 11B.

Select Quick Study and Exercise assignments feature Guided Example videos, called "Hints" in Connect. Hints use different numbers, and instructors can turn this feature on or off.

QUICK STUDY

QS 11-1
Classifying liabilities
C1

Which of the following items are normally classified as current liabilities for a company that has a one-year operating cycle?

1. Portion of long-term note due in 10 months.
2. Note payable maturing in 2 years.
3. Note payable due in 18 months.
4. Accounts payable due in 11 months.
5. FICA taxes payable.
6. Salaries payable.

QS 11-2
Reporting current portion of long-term debt C1

The liabilities of Organic Foods are made up of $60,000 in notes payable as of its December 31 year-end. For those notes payable, $3,000 is due within the next year. Prepare the liabilities section of Organic Foods's December 31 year-end balance sheet.

QS 11-3
Accounting for sales taxes C2

Dextra Computing sells merchandise for $6,000 cash on September 30 (cost of merchandise is $3,900). Dextra collects 5% sales tax. (1) Record the entry for the $6,000 sale and its sales tax. (2) Record the entry that shows Dextra sending the sales tax on this sale to the government on October 15.

QS 11-4
Unearned revenue C2

Ticketsales, Inc., receives $5,000,000 cash in advance ticket sales for a four-date tour of Bon Jovi. Record the advance ticket sales on October 31. Record the revenue earned for the first concert date of November 5, assuming it represents one-fourth of the advance ticket sales.

QS 11-5
Interest-bearing note transactions P1

On November 7, Mura Company borrows $160,000 cash by signing a 90-day, 8%, $160,000 note payable. (1) Compute the accrued interest payable on December 31; (2) prepare the journal entry to record the accrued interest expense at December 31; and (3) prepare the journal entry to record payment of the note at maturity on February 5.

QS 11-6
Computing net pay
P2

At the end of the first pay period of the year, Sofia earned $4,000 of salary. Withholdings from Sofia's salary include FICA Social Security taxes at the rate of 6.2%, FICA Medicare taxes at the rate of 1.45%, $500 of federal income taxes, $160 of medical insurance deductions, and $10 of life insurance deductions. Compute Sofia's net pay for this first pay period.

QS 11-7
Recording employee payroll taxes P2

During the month of January, an employee earned $4,000 of salary. Withholdings from the employee's salary consist of FICA Social Security taxes of $248, FICA Medicare taxes of $58, federal income taxes of $426, and medical insurance deductions of $170. Prepare the journal entry to record the employer's salaries expense and related liabilities assuming these wages will be paid in early February.

QS 11-8
Recording employee payroll taxes P2

On January 15, the end of the first pay period of the year, North Company's employees earned $35,000 of sales salaries. Withholdings from the employees' salaries include FICA Social Security taxes at the rate of 6.2%, FICA Medicare taxes at the rate of 1.45%, $6,500 of federal income taxes, $772.50 of medical insurance deductions, and $120 of union dues. No employee earned more than $7,000 in this first period. Prepare the journal entry to record North Company's January 15 salaries expense and related liabilities. (Round amounts to cents.)

QS 11-9
Recording employer payroll taxes P3

During the month of January, an employer incurred the following payroll taxes: FICA Social Security taxes of $372, FICA Medicare taxes of $87, FUTA taxes of $36, and SUTA taxes of $324. Prepare the journal entry to record the employer's payroll tax expense assuming these wages will be paid in early February.

QS 11-10
Recording employer payroll taxes P3

Merger Co. has 10 employees, each of whom earns $2,000 per month and has been employed since January 1. FICA Social Security taxes are 6.2% of the first $137,700 paid to each employee, and FICA Medicare taxes are 1.45% of gross pay. FUTA taxes are 0.6% and SUTA taxes are 5.4% of the first $7,000 paid to each employee. Prepare the March 31 journal entry to record the March payroll taxes expense.

QS 11-11
Accounting for bonuses P4

Noura Company offers an annual bonus to employees (to be shared equally) if the company meets certain net income goals. Prepare the journal entry to record a $15,000 bonus owed (but not yet paid) to its workers at calendar year-end.

QS 11-12
Accounting for vacations P4

Chavez Co.'s salaried employees earn four weeks' vacation per year. Chavez estimated and must expense $8,000 of accrued vacation benefits for the year. (*a*) Prepare the December 31 year-end adjusting entry for accrued vacation benefits. (*b*) Prepare the entry on April 1 of the next year when an employee takes a one-week vacation and is paid $500 cash for that week.

QS 11-13
Recording warranty repairs P4

On December 1, Home Store sells a mower (that costs $200) for $500 cash with a one-year warranty that covers parts. Warranty expense is estimated at 8% of sales. On January 24 of the following year, the mower is brought in for repairs covered under the warranty requiring $35 in materials taken from the Parts Inventory. Prepare the December 1 entry to record the mower sale (and cost of sale), the December 31 adjusting entry for estimated warranty liability, and the January 24 entry to record the warranty repairs.

QS 11-14
Accounting for health and pension benefits P4

Riverrun Co. provides medical care and insurance benefits to its retirees. In the current year, Riverrun agrees to pay $5,500 for medical insurance and contribute an additional $9,000 to a retirement program. Record the entry for these accrued (but unpaid) benefits on December 31.

QS 11-15
Accounting for contingent liabilities C3

Huprey Co. is the defendant in the following legal claims. For each of the following separate claims, indicate whether Huprey should (*a*) record a liability, (*b*) disclose in notes, or (*c*) have no disclosure.

1. Huprey can reasonably estimate that a pending lawsuit will result in damages of $1,250,000. It is probable that Huprey will lose the case.
2. It is reasonably possible that Huprey will lose a pending lawsuit. The loss cannot be estimated.
3. Huprey is being sued for damages of $2,000,000. It is very unlikely (remote) that Huprey will lose the case.

QS 11-16
Preparing liabilities section of balance sheet C1 P2 P3

Selected accounts from Russel Co.'s adjusted trial balance for the year ended December 31 follow. Prepare the liabilities section of its classified balance sheet.

FICA—Social Security taxes payable	$1,600	Sales tax payable (due in 1 week)	$ 150
State unemployment taxes payable	800	Salaries payable	17,000
Current portion of long-term debt	2,000	Notes payable (due in 4 years)	6,000
Employee federal income taxes payable	5,000	FICA—Medicare taxes payable	300
Federal unemployment taxes payable	100	Accounts payable	2,600

QS 11-17
Times interest earned A1

Park Company reports interest expense of $145,000 and income before interest expense and income taxes of $1,885,000. (1) Compute its times interest earned. (2) Park's competitor's times interest earned is 4.0. Is Park in a better or worse position than its competitor to make interest payments if the economy turns bad?

QS 11-18A
Federal income tax withholdings
P5

Organic Farmers Co-Op has three employees and pays them weekly. Using the withholding bracket table in Exhibit 11A.6, determine each employee's federal income tax withholding.

1. Maria earns $735 per week and claims three withholding allowances.
2. Jeff earns $607 per week and claims five withholding allowances.
3. Alicia earns $704 per week and does not claim any withholding allowances.

QS 11-19A
Net pay and tax computations
P5

The payroll records of Speedy Software show the following information about Marsha Gottschalk, an employee, for the weekly pay period ending September 30. Gottschalk is single and claims one allowance. Compute her Social Security tax (6.2%), Medicare tax (1.45%), federal income tax withholding (use the withholding table in Exhibit 11A.6), state income tax (1.0%), and net pay for the current pay period. Round tax amounts to the nearest cent.

Check Net pay, $579.99

Total (gross) earnings for current pay period	$740	Cumulative earnings of previous pay periods	$9,700

QS 11-20B
Recording deferred income tax liability P6

Sera Corporation has made and recorded its quarterly income tax payments. After a final review of taxes for the year, the company identifies an additional $40,000 of income tax expense that should be recorded. A portion of this additional expense, $6,000, is deferred for payment in future years. Record Sera's year-end adjusting entry for income tax expense.

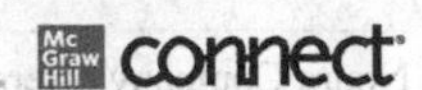

EXERCISES

Exercise 11-1
Classifying liabilities
C1

The following items appear on the balance sheet of a company with a one-year operating cycle. Identify each item as a current liability, a long-term liability, or not a liability.

1. Notes payable (due in 13 to 24 months).
2. Notes payable (due in 6 to 11 months).
3. Notes payable (mature in five years).
4. Current portion of long-term debt.
5. Notes payable (due in 120 days).
6. FUTA taxes payable.
7. Accounts receivable.
8. Sales taxes payable.
9. Salaries payable.
10. Wages payable.

Exercise 11-2
Recording known current liabilities
C2

1. On July 15, Piper Co. sold $10,000 of merchandise (costing $5,000) for cash. The sales tax rate is 4%. On August 1, Piper sent the sales tax collected from the sale to the government. Record entries for the July 15 and August 1 transactions.
2. On November 3, the **Milwaukee Bucks** sold a six-game pack of advance tickets for $300 cash. On November 20, the Bucks played the first game of the six-game pack (this represented one-sixth of the advance ticket sales). Record the entries for the November 3 and November 20 transactions.

Exercise 11-3
Financial statement impact of current liability transactions C2

Analyze each separate transaction from Exercise 11-2 by showing its effects on the accounting equation—specifically, identify the accounts and amounts (including + or –) for each transaction.

Exercise 11-4
Accounting for note payable P1

Sylvestor Systems borrows $110,000 cash on May 15 by signing a 60-day, 12%, $110,000 note.

1. On what date does this note mature?
2. Prepare the entries to record (*a*) issuance of the note and (*b*) payment of the note at maturity.

Exercise 11-5
Interest-bearing notes payable with year-end adjustments P1

Check (2) $3,000
(3) $1,500

Keesha Co. borrows $200,000 cash on November 1 of the current year by signing a 90-day, 9%, $200,000 note.

1. On what date does this note mature?
2. How much interest expense is recorded in the current year? (Assume a 360-day year.)
3. How much interest expense is recorded in the following year? (Assume a 360-day year.)
4. Prepare journal entries to record (*a*) issuance of the note, (*b*) accrual of interest on December 31, and (*c*) payment of the note at maturity.

Exercise 11-6
Note given to extend credit period P1

On March 1, LGE asks to extend its past-due $1,200 account payable to Tyson. Tyson agrees to accept $200 cash and a 180-day, 8%, $1,000 note payable to replace the account payable. (1) Prepare the March 1 entry for LGE. (2) Prepare the September 27 entry for LGE when it pays the note and interest to Tyson.

Exercise 11-7
Computing payroll taxes
P2 P3

BMX Company has one employee. FICA Social Security taxes are 6.2% of the first $137,700 paid to its employee, and FICA Medicare taxes are 1.45% of gross pay. For BMX, its FUTA taxes are 0.6% and SUTA taxes are 5.4% of the first $7,000 paid to its employee. Compute BMX's amounts for each of these four taxes as applied to the employee's gross earnings for September under each of three separate situations (*a*), (*b*), and (*c*). Round amounts to cents.

	Gross Pay through August 31	Gross Pay for September
a.	$ 6,400	$ 800
b.	2,000	2,100
c.	131,400	8,000

Check (*a*) FUTA, $3.60; SUTA, $32.40

Exercise 11-8
Payroll-related journal entries P2

Using the data in *situation* (*a*) of Exercise 11-7, prepare the employer's September 30 journal entry to record salary expense and its related payroll liabilities for this employee. The employee's federal income taxes withheld by the employer are $80 for this pay period. Round amounts to cents.

Exercise 11-9
Payroll-related journal entries P3

Using the data in *situation* (*a*) of Exercise 11-7, prepare the employer's September 30 journal entry to record the *employer's* payroll taxes expense and its related liabilities. Round amounts to cents.

Exercise 11-10
Recording payroll
P2 P3

The following monthly data are taken from Ramirez Company at July 31: sales salaries, $200,000; office salaries, $160,000; federal income taxes withheld, $90,000; state income taxes withheld, $20,000; Social Security taxes withheld, $22,320; Medicare taxes withheld, $5,220; medical insurance premiums, $7,000; life insurance premiums, $4,000; union dues deducted, $1,000; and salaries subject to unemployment taxes, $50,000. The employee pays 40% of medical and life insurance premiums.

Prepare journal entries to record (1) accrued payroll, including employee deductions, for July; (2) cash payment of the net payroll (salaries payable) for July; (3) accrued employer payroll taxes, and other related employment expenses, for July—assume that FICA taxes are identical to those on employees and that SUTA taxes are 5.4% and FUTA taxes are 0.6%; and (4) cash payment of all liabilities related to the July payroll.

Exercise 11-11
Computing payroll taxes
P2 P3

Mest Company has nine employees. FICA Social Security taxes are 6.2% of the first $137,700 paid to each employee, and FICA Medicare taxes are 1.45% of gross pay. FUTA taxes are 0.6% and SUTA taxes are 5.4% of the first $7,000 paid to each employee. Cumulative pay for the current year for each of its employees follows.

Employee	Cumulative Pay	Employee	Cumulative Pay	Employee	Cumulative Pay
Ken S.	$ 6,000	Julie W.	$143,500	Christina S.	$140,200
Tim V.	40,400	Michael M.	106,900	Kitty O.	36,900
Steve S.	87,000	Zach R.	137,700	John W.	4,000

a. Prepare a table with the following six column headings. Compute the amounts in this table for each employee and then total the numerical columns.

Employee	Cumulative Pay	Pay Subject to FICA Social Security	Pay Subject to FICA Medicare	Pay Subject to FUTA Taxes	Pay Subject to SUTA Taxes

b. For the company, compute each total for FICA Social Security taxes, FICA Medicare taxes, FUTA taxes, and SUTA taxes. *Hint:* Remember to include in those totals any employee share of taxes that the company must collect. Round amounts to cents.

Exercise 11-12
Warranty expense and liability computations and entries
P4

Hitzu Co. sold a copier (that costs $4,800) for $6,000 cash with a two-year parts warranty to a customer on August 16 of Year 1. Hitzu expects warranty costs to be 4% of dollar sales. It records warranty expense with an adjusting entry on December 31. On January 5 of Year 2, the copier requires on-site repairs that are completed the same day. The repairs cost $209 for materials taken from the parts inventory. These are the only repairs required in Year 2 for this copier.

1. How much warranty expense does the company report for this copier in Year 1?
2. How much is the estimated warranty liability for this copier as of December 31 of Year 1?
3. How much is the estimated warranty liability for this copier as of December 31 of Year 2?
4. Prepare journal entries to record (*a*) the copier's sale; (*b*) the adjustment to recognize the warranty expense on December 31 of Year 1; and (*c*) the repairs that occur on January 5 of Year 2.

Check (1) $240

(3) $31

Exercise 11-13
Financial statement impact of warranty transactions P4

Analyze each of the following transactions from Exercise 11-12: (*a*) the copier's sale; (*b*) the adjustment to recognize the warranty expense on December 31 of Year 1; and (*c*) the repairs that occur on January 5 of Year 2. Show each transaction's effect on the accounting equation—specifically, identify the accounts and amounts (including + or −) for each.

Exercise 11-14
Recording bonuses
P4

For the year ended December 31, Lopez Company implements an employee bonus program based on company net income, which the employees share equally. Lopez's bonus expense is computed as $14,563.

1. Prepare the journal entry at December 31 to record the bonus due the employees.
2. Prepare the later journal entry at January 19 to record payment of the bonus to employees.

Exercise 11-15
Accounting for estimated liabilities
P4

Prepare adjusting entries at December 31 for Maxum Company's year-end financial statements for each of the following separate transactions.

1. Employees earn vacation pay at a rate of one day per month. Maxum estimated and must expense $13,000 of accrued vacation benefits for the year.
2. During December, Maxum Company sold 12,000 units of a product that carries a 60-day warranty. December sales for this product total $460,000. The company expects 10% of the units to need warranty repairs, and it estimates the average repair cost per unit will be $15.

Exercise 11-16
Accounting for health and pension benefits
P4

Vander Co. provides medical care and insurance benefits to its retirees. In the current year, Vander agrees to pay $9,500 for medical insurance and contribute an additional 5% of the employees' $200,000 gross salaries to a retirement program. (1) Record the entry for these accrued (but unpaid) benefits on December 31. (2) Assuming $5,000 of the retirement benefits are not to be paid for five years, how should this amount be reported on the current balance sheet?

Exercise 11-17
Accounting for contingent liabilities
C3

For each separate situation, indicate whether Cruz Company should (*a*) record a liability, (*b*) disclose in notes, or (*c*) have no disclosure.

1. Cruz Company guarantees the $100,000 debt of a supplier. It is not probable that the supplier will default on the debt.
2. A disgruntled employee is suing Cruz Company. Legal advisers believe that the company will likely need to pay damages, but the amount cannot be reasonably estimated.

Exercise 11-18
Preparing a balance sheet
C1 P2 P3

Selected accounts from Lue Co.'s adjusted trial balance for the year ended December 31 follow. Prepare a classified balance sheet.

Total equity	$30,000	Employee federal income taxes payable	$9,000
Equipment	40,000	Federal unemployment taxes payable	200
Salaries payable	34,000	FICA—Medicare taxes payable	725
Accounts receivable	5,100	FICA—Social Security taxes payable	3,100
Cash	50,000	Employee medical insurance payable	2,000
Current portion of long-term debt	4,000	State unemployment taxes payable	1,800
Notes payable (due in 6 years)	10,000	Sales tax payable (due in 2 weeks)	275

Exercise 11-19
Computing and interpreting times interest earned
A1

Check (*b*) 11.0

Use the following information from separate companies *a* through *d* to compute times interest earned. Which company indicates the strongest ability to pay interest expense as it comes due?

	Net Income (Loss)	Interest Expense	Income Taxes
a.	$119,000	$44,000	$35,000
b.	135,000	16,000	25,000
c.	138,000	12,000	30,000
d.	314,000	14,000	50,000

Exercise 11-20A
Computing gross and net pay P5

Lenny Florita, an unmarried employee, works 48 hours in the week ended January 12. His pay rate is $14 per hour, and his wages have deductions for FICA Social Security, FICA Medicare, and federal income taxes. He claims two withholding allowances.

Compute his regular pay, overtime pay (Lenny earns $21 per hour for each hour over 40 per week), and gross pay. Then compute his FICA tax deduction (6.2% for the Social Security portion and 1.45% for the

Medicare portion), income tax deduction (use the wage bracket withholding table from Exhibit 11A.6), total deductions, and net pay. Round tax amounts to the nearest cent.

Check Net pay, $596.30

Exercise 11-21^A^
Preparing payroll register and related entries
P5

Stark Company has five employees. Employees paid by the hour earn $10 per hour for the regular 40-hour workweek and $15 per hour beyond the 40 hours per week. Hourly employees are paid every two weeks, but salaried employees are paid monthly on the last biweekly payday of each month. FICA Social Security taxes are 6.2% of the first $137,700 paid to each employee, and FICA Medicare taxes are 1.45% of gross pay. FUTA taxes are 0.6% and SUTA taxes are 5.4% of the first $7,000 paid to each employee. The company has a benefits plan that includes medical insurance, life insurance, and retirement funding for employees. Under this plan, employees must contribute 5% of their gross income as a payroll withholding, which the company matches with *double* the amount. Following is the partially completed payroll register for the biweekly period ending August 31, which is the last payday of August.

Employee	Cumulative Pay (Excludes Current Period)	Current-Period Gross Pay: Pay Type	Pay Hours	Gross Pay	FIT / SIT	FUTA / SUTA	FICA-SS_EE / FICA-SS_ER	FICA-Med_EE / FICA-Med_ER	EE-Ben_Plan Withholding / ER-Ben_Plan Expense	Employee Net Pay (Current Period)
Kathleen	$135,900.00	Salary	—	$7,000.00	$2,000.00					
					300.00					
Anthony	6,800.00	Salary	—	500.00	80.00				25.00	
					20.00				50.00	
Nichole	25,800.00	Regular	80		110.00					
		Overtime	8		25.00					
Zoey	6,500.00	Regular	80		100.00					
		Overtime	4		22.00					
Gracie	5,000.00	Regular	74	740.00	90.00					
		Overtime	0	0.00	21.00					
Totals	$180,000.00				2,380.00					
					388.00					

Note: Table abbreviations follow those in Exhibit 11A.3; "Ben_Plan" refers to employee (EE) withholding or the employer (ER) expense for the benefits plan.

a. Complete this payroll register by filling in all cells for the pay period ended August 31. *Hint:* See Exhibit 11A.5 for guidance. Round amounts to cents.

b. Prepare the August 31 journal entry to record the accrued biweekly payroll and related liabilities for deductions.

c. Prepare the August 31 journal entry to record the employer's cash payment of the net payroll of part *b*.

d. Prepare the August 31 journal entry to record the employer's payroll taxes including the contribution to the benefits plan.

e. Prepare the August 31 journal entry to pay all liabilities (except for the net payroll in part *c*) for this biweekly period.

Exercise 11-22^B^
Accounting for income taxes **P6**

Nishi Corporation prepares financial statements for each month-end. As part of its accounting process, estimated income taxes are accrued each month for 30% of the current month's net income. The income taxes are paid in the first month of each quarter for the amount accrued for the prior quarter. The following information is available for the fourth quarter of the year just ended. When tax computations are completed on January 20 of the following year, Nishi determines that the quarter's Income Taxes Payable account balance should be $28,300 on December 31 of the year just ended (its unadjusted balance is $24,690).

October net income $28,600	November net income..... $19,100	December net income $34,600

1. Determine the amount of the accounting adjustment (dated as of December 31) to get the correct ending balance in the Income Taxes Payable account.

2. Prepare journal entries to record (*a*) the December 31 adjustment to the Income Taxes Payable account and (*b*) the later January 20 payment of the fourth-quarter taxes.

Check (1) $3,610

PROBLEM SET A

Problem 11-1A
Short-term notes payable transactions and entries
P1

Tyrell Co. entered into the following transactions involving short-term liabilities.

Year 1

Apr. 20 Purchased $40,250 of merchandise on credit from Locust, terms n/30.
May 19 Replaced the April 20 account payable to Locust with a 90-day, 10%, $35,000 note payable along with paying $5,250 in cash.
July 8 Borrowed $80,000 cash from NBR Bank by signing a 120-day, 9%, $80,000 note payable.
__?__ Paid the amount due on the note to Locust at the maturity date.
__?__ Paid the amount due on the note to NBR Bank at the maturity date.
Nov. 28 Borrowed $42,000 cash from Fargo Bank by signing a 60-day, 8%, $42,000 note payable.
Dec. 31 Recorded an adjusting entry for accrued interest on the note to Fargo Bank.

Year 2

__?__ Paid the amount due on the note to Fargo Bank at the maturity date.

Required

1. Determine the maturity date for each of the three notes described.

2. Determine the interest due at maturity for each of the three notes. Assume a 360-day year.

3. Determine the interest expense recorded in the adjusting entry at the end of Year 1.

4. Determine the interest expense recorded in Year 2.

5. Prepare journal entries for all the preceding transactions and events.

Check (2) Locust, $875
(3) $308
(4) $252

Problem 11-2A
Entries for payroll transactions
P2 P3

On January 8, the end of the first weekly pay period of the year, Regis Company's employees earned $22,760 of office salaries and $65,840 of sales salaries. Withholdings from the employees' salaries include FICA Social Security taxes at the rate of 6.2%, FICA Medicare taxes at the rate of 1.45%, $12,860 of federal income taxes, $1,340 of medical insurance deductions, and $840 of union dues. No employee earned more than $7,000 in this first period.

Required

1. Calculate FICA Social Security taxes payable and FICA Medicare taxes payable. Prepare the journal entry to record Regis Company's January 8 *employee* payroll expenses and liabilities. Round amounts to cents.

2. Prepare the journal entry to record Regis's *employer* payroll taxes resulting from the January 8 payroll. Regis's state unemployment tax rate is 5.4% of the first $7,000 paid to each employee. The federal unemployment tax rate is 0.6%. Round amounts to cents.

Check (1) Cr. Salaries Payable, $66,782.10
(2) Dr. Payroll Taxes Expense, $12,093.90

Problem 11-3A
Payroll expenses, withholdings, and taxes
P2 P3

Paloma Co. has four employees. FICA Social Security taxes are 6.2% of the first $137,700 paid to each employee, and FICA Medicare taxes are 1.45% of gross pay. Also, for the first $7,000 paid to each employee, the company's FUTA taxes are 0.6% and SUTA taxes are 5.4%. The company is preparing its payroll calculations for the week ended August 25. Payroll records show the following information for the company's four employees.

	A	B	C	D
1		Gross Pay	Current Week	
2	Name	through Aug. 18	Gross Pay	Income Tax Withholding
3	Dali	$136,600	$2,000	$284
4	Trey	136,800	900	145
5	Kiesha	6,900	450	39
6	Chee	1,250	400	30

In addition to gross pay, the company must pay two-thirds of the $60 per employee weekly health insurance; each employee pays the remaining one-third. The company also contributes an extra 8% of each employee's gross pay (at no cost to employees) to a pension fund.

Required

Compute the following for the week ended August 25 (round amounts to the nearest cent):

1. Each employee's FICA withholdings for Social Security.

2. Each employee's FICA withholdings for Medicare.

3. Employer's FICA taxes for Social Security.

Check (3) $176.70

4. Employer's FICA taxes for Medicare.
5. Employer's FUTA taxes.
6. Employer's SUTA taxes.
7. Each employee's net (take-home) pay.
8. Employer's total payroll-related expense for each employee.

(4) $54.38
(5) $3.00
(7) Total net pay, $2,940.92

Problem 11-4A
Estimating warranty expense and liability
P4

On October 29, Lobo Co. began operations by purchasing razors for resale. The razors have a 90-day warranty. When a razor is returned, the company discards it and mails a new one from merchandise inventory to the customer. The company's cost per new razor is $20 and its retail selling price is $75. The company expects warranty costs to equal 8% of dollar sales. The following transactions occurred.

Nov.	11	Sold 105 razors for $7,875 cash.
	30	Recognized warranty expense related to November sales with an adjusting entry.
Dec.	9	Replaced 15 razors that were returned under the warranty.
	16	Sold 220 razors for $16,500 cash.
	29	Replaced 30 razors that were returned under the warranty.
	31	Recognized warranty expense related to December sales with an adjusting entry.
Jan.	5	Sold 150 razors for $11,250 cash.
	17	Replaced 50 razors that were returned under the warranty.
	31	Recognized warranty expense related to January sales with an adjusting entry.

Required

1. Prepare journal entries to record these transactions and adjustments.
2. How much warranty expense is reported for November and for December?
3. How much warranty expense is reported for January?
4. What is the balance of the Estimated Warranty Liability account as of December 31?
5. What is the balance of the Estimated Warranty Liability account as of January 31?

Check (3) $900
(4) $1,050 Cr.
(5) $950 Cr.

Problem 11-5A
Computing and analyzing times interest earned
A1

Shown here are condensed income statements for two different companies (assume no income taxes).

Miller Company	
Sales	$1,000,000
Variable expenses (80%)	800,000
Income before interest	200,000
Interest expense (fixed)	60,000
Net income	$ 140,000

Weaver Company	
Sales	$1,000,000
Variable expenses (60%)	600,000
Income before interest	400,000
Interest expense (fixed)	260,000
Net income	$ 140,000

Required

1. Compute times interest earned for Miller Company and for Weaver Company.
2. What happens to each company's net income if sales increase by 30%?
3. What happens to each company's net income if sales increase by 50%?
4. What happens to each company's net income if sales decrease by 10%?
5. What happens to each company's net income if sales decrease by 40%?

Check (2) Miller net income, $200,000 (43% increase)
(4) Weaver net income, $100,000 (29% decrease)

Analysis Component

6. Which company would have a greater ability to pay interest expense if sales were to decrease?

Problem 11-6A^A
Entries for payroll transactions
P5

Francisco Company has 10 employees, each of whom earns $2,800 per month and is paid on the last day of each month. All 10 have been employed continuously at this amount since January 1. On March 1, the following accounts and balances exist in its general ledger.

a. FICA—Social Security Taxes Payable, $3,472; FICA—Medicare Taxes Payable, $812. (The balances of these accounts represent total liabilities for *both* the employer's and employees' FICA taxes for the February payroll only.)
b. Employees' Federal Income Taxes Payable, $4,000 (liability for February only).
c. Federal Unemployment Taxes Payable, $336 (liability for January and February together).
d. State Unemployment Taxes Payable, $3,024 (liability for January and February together).

[continued on next page]

[continued from previous page]

The company had the following payroll transactions.

Mar. 15 Issued check payable to Swift Bank, a federal depository bank authorized to accept employers' payments of FICA taxes and employee income tax withholdings. The $8,284 check is in payment of the February FICA and employee income taxes.

31 Recorded the journal entry for the March salaries payable. Then recorded the cash payment of the March payroll (the company issued checks payable to each employee in payment of the March payroll). The payroll register shows the following summary totals for the March pay period.

Check March 31: Salaries Payable, $21,858

Salaries				Federal	
Office Salaries	Shop Salaries	Gross Pay	FICA Taxes*	Income Taxes	Net Pay
$11,200	$16,800	$28,000	$1,736 $ 406	$4,000	$21,858

*FICA taxes are Social Security and Medicare, respectively.

March 31: Dr. Payroll Taxes Expense, $2,982

31 Recorded the employer's payroll taxes resulting from the March payroll. The company has a state unemployment tax rate of 5.4% on the first $7,000 paid to each employee. The federal rate is 0.6%.

April 15: Cr. Cash, $8,284 (Swift Bank)

Apr. 15 Issued check to Swift Bank in payment of the March FICA and employee income taxes.

15 Issued check to the State Tax Commission for the January, February, and March state unemployment taxes. Filed the check and the first-quarter tax return with the Commission.

30 Issued check payable to Swift Bank in payment of the employer's FUTA taxes for the first quarter of the year.

30 Filed Form 941 with the IRS, reporting the FICA taxes and the employees' federal income tax withholdings for the first quarter.

Required

Prepare journal entries to record these transactions and events.

PROBLEM SET B

Problem 11-1B
Short-term notes payable transactions and entries
P1

Warner Co. entered into the following transactions involving short-term liabilities.

Year 1

Apr. 22 Purchased $5,000 of merchandise on credit from Fox-Pro, terms n/30.

May 23 Replaced the April 22 account payable to Fox-Pro with a 60-day, 15%, $4,600 note payable along with paying $400 in cash.

July 15 Borrowed $12,000 cash from Spring Bank by signing a 120-day, 10%, $12,000 note payable.

___?___ Paid the amount due on the note to Fox-Pro at maturity.

___?___ Paid the amount due on the note to Spring Bank at maturity.

Dec. 6 Borrowed $8,000 cash from City Bank by signing a 45-day, 9%, $8,000 note payable.

31 Recorded an adjusting entry for accrued interest on the note to City Bank.

Year 2

___?___ Paid the amount due on the note to City Bank at maturity.

Required

1. Determine the maturity date for each of the three notes described.
2. Determine the interest due at maturity for each of the three notes. Assume a 360-day year.
3. Determine the interest expense recorded in the adjusting entry at the end of Year 1.
4. Determine the interest expense recorded in Year 2.
5. Prepare journal entries for all the preceding transactions and events.

Check (2) Fox-Pro, $115
(3) $50
(4) $40

Problem 11-2B
Entries for payroll transactions
P2 P3

Tavella Company's first weekly pay period of the year ends on January 8. On that date, Tavella's sales employees earned $34,745, office employees earned $21,225, and delivery employees earned $1,030 in salaries. The employees are to have withheld from their salaries FICA Social Security taxes at the rate of 6.2%, FICA Medicare taxes at the rate of 1.45%, $8,625 of federal income taxes, $1,160 of medical insurance deductions, and $138 of union dues. No employee earned more than $7,000 in the first pay period.

Required

1. Calculate FICA Social Security taxes payable and FICA Medicare taxes payable. Prepare the journal entry to record Tavella Company's January 8 *employee* payroll expenses and liabilities. Round amounts to cents.
2. Prepare the journal entry to record Tavella's *employer* payroll taxes resulting from the January 8 payroll. Tavella's state unemployment tax rate is 5.4% of the first $7,000 paid to each employee. The federal unemployment tax rate is 0.6%. Round amounts to cents.

Check (1) Cr. Salaries Payable, $42,716.50

(2) Dr. Payroll Taxes Expense, $7,780.50

Problem 11-3B
Payroll expenses, withholdings, and taxes
P2 P3

Fishing Guides Co. has four employees. FICA Social Security taxes are 6.2% of the first $137,700 paid to each employee, and FICA Medicare taxes are 1.45% of gross pay. Also, for the first $7,000 paid to each employee, the company's FUTA taxes are 0.6% and SUTA taxes are 5.4%. The company is preparing its payroll calculations for the week ended September 30. Payroll records show the following information for the company's four employees.

	A	B	C	D
1		Gross Pay	Current Week	
2	Name	through Sep. 23	Gross Pay	Income Tax Withholding
3	Ahmed	$136,100	$2,500	$198
4	Carlos	136,185	1,515	182
5	Jun	6,650	475	32
6	Marie	23,700	1,000	68

In addition to gross pay, the company must pay 60% of the $50 per employee weekly health insurance; each employee pays the remaining 40%. The company also contributes an extra 5% of each employee's gross pay (at no cost to employees) to a pension fund.

Required

Compute the following for the week ended September 30 (round amounts to the nearest cent):

1. Each employee's FICA withholdings for Social Security.
2. Each employee's FICA withholdings for Medicare.
3. Employer's FICA taxes for Social Security.
4. Employer's FICA taxes for Medicare.
5. Employer's FUTA taxes.
6. Employer's SUTA taxes.
7. Each employee's net (take-home) pay.
8. Employer's total payroll-related expense for each employee.

Check (3) $284.58

(4) $79.61

(5) $2.10

(7) Total net pay, $4,565.81

Problem 11-4B
Estimating warranty expense and liability
P4

On November 10, Lee Co. began operations by purchasing coffee grinders for resale. The grinders have a 60-day warranty. When a grinder is returned, the company discards it and mails a new one from merchandise inventory to the customer. The company's cost per new grinder is $24 and its retail selling price is $50. The company expects warranty costs to equal 10% of dollar sales. The following transactions occurred.

Nov.	16	Sold 50 grinders for $2,500 cash.
	30	Recognized warranty expense related to November sales with an adjusting entry.
Dec.	12	Replaced six grinders that were returned under the warranty.
	18	Sold 200 grinders for $10,000 cash.
	28	Replaced 17 grinders that were returned under the warranty.
	31	Recognized warranty expense related to December sales with an adjusting entry.
Jan.	7	Sold 40 grinders for $2,000 cash.
	21	Replaced 36 grinders that were returned under the warranty.
	31	Recognized warranty expense related to January sales with an adjusting entry.

Required

1. Prepare journal entries to record these transactions and adjustments.
2. How much warranty expense is reported for November and for December?
3. How much warranty expense is reported for January?
4. What is the balance of the Estimated Warranty Liability account as of December 31?
5. What is the balance of the Estimated Warranty Liability account as of January 31?

Check (3) $200

(4) $698 Cr.

(5) $34 Cr.

Problem 11-5B
Computing and analyzing times interest earned
A1

Shown here are condensed income statements for two different companies (assume no income taxes).

Ellis Company		Seidel Company	
Sales	$240,000	Sales	$240,000
Variable expenses (50%)	120,000	Variable expenses (75%)	180,000
Income before interest	120,000	Income before interest	60,000
Interest expense (fixed)	90,000	Interest expense (fixed)	30,000
Net income	$ 30,000	Net income	$ 30,000

Required

1. Compute times interest earned for Ellis Company and for Seidel Company.
2. What happens to each company's net income if sales increase by 10%?
3. What happens to each company's net income if sales increase by 40%?
4. What happens to each company's net income if sales decrease by 20%?
5. What happens to each company's net income if sales decrease by 50%?

Check (3) Ellis net income, $78,000 (160% increase)
(4) Seidel net income, $18,000 (40% decrease)

Analysis Component

6. Which company would have a greater ability to pay interest expense if sales were to decrease?

Problem 11-6B^A
Entries for payroll transactions
P5

MLS Company has five employees, each of whom earns $1,600 per month and is paid on the last day of each month. All five have been employed continuously at this amount since January 1. On June 1, the following accounts and balances exist in its general ledger.

a. FICA—Social Security Taxes Payable, $992; FICA—Medicare Taxes Payable, $232. (The balances of these accounts represent total liabilities for *both* the employer's and employees' FICA taxes for the May payroll only.)
b. Employees' Federal Income Taxes Payable, $1,050 (liability for May only).
c. Federal Unemployment Taxes Payable, $66 (liability for April and May together).
d. State Unemployment Taxes Payable, $594 (liability for April and May together).

The company had the following payroll transactions.

June 15 Issued check payable to Security Bank, a federal depository bank authorized to accept employers' payments of FICA taxes and employee income tax withholdings. The $2,274 check is in payment of the May FICA and employee income taxes.

30 Recorded the journal entry for the June salaries payable. Then recorded the cash payment of the June payroll (the company issued checks payable to each employee in payment of the June payroll). The payroll register shows the following summary totals for the June pay period.

Check June 30: Cr. Salaries Payable, $6,338

Salaries				Federal	
Office Salaries	Shop Salaries	Gross Pay	FICA Taxes*	Income Taxes	Net Pay
$3,800	$4,200	$8,000	$496 $116	$1,050	$6,338

*FICA taxes are Social Security and Medicare, respectively.

30 Recorded the employer's payroll taxes resulting from the June payroll. The company has a state unemployment tax rate of 5.4% on the first $7,000 paid to each employee. The federal rate is 0.6%.

July 15 Issued check payable to Security Bank in payment of the June FICA and employee income taxes.

15 Issued check to the State Tax Commission for the April, May, and June state unemployment taxes. Filed the check and the second-quarter tax return with the State Tax Commission.

31 Issued check payable to Security Bank in payment of the employer's FUTA taxes for the first quarter of the year.

31 Filed Form 941 with the IRS, reporting the FICA taxes and the employees' federal income tax withholdings for the second quarter.

Check June 30: Dr. Payroll Taxes Expense, $612
July 15: Cr. Cash, $2,274 (Security Bank)

Required

Prepare journal entries to record the transactions and events.

connect

*Serial problem began in Chapter 1. If previous chapter segments were not completed, the serial problem can begin at this point. It is available in **Connect** with an algorithmic option.*

SERIAL PROBLEM

Business Solutions

C2 P2 P3

SP 11 Review the February 26 and March 25 transactions for **Business Solutions** (SP 5) from Chapter 5.

Feb. 26 The company paid cash to Lyn Addie for eight days' work at $125 per day.

Mar. 25 The company sold merchandise with a $2,002 cost for $2,800 on credit to Wildcat Services, invoice dated March 25.

Alexander Image/Shutterstock

Required

1. Assume that Lyn Addie is an unmarried employee. Her $1,000 of wages have deductions for FICA Social Security taxes, FICA Medicare taxes, and federal income taxes. Her federal income taxes for this pay period total $159. Compute her net pay for the eight days' work paid on February 26. Round amounts to the nearest cent.
2. Record the journal entry to reflect the payroll payment to Lyn Addie as computed in part 1.
3. Record the journal entry to reflect the (employer) payroll tax expenses for the February 26 payroll payment. Assume Lyn Addie has not met earnings limits for FUTA and SUTA (the FUTA rate is 0.6% and the SUTA rate is 5.4% for the company). Round amounts to the nearest cent.
4. Record the entry(ies) for the merchandise sold on March 25 if a 4% sales tax rate applies.

connect

***Comprehensive Problem** is available in **Connect** with an algorithmic option.*

COMPREHENSIVE PROBLEM

Bug-Off Exterminators

(Review of Chapters 1–11)

CP 11 **Bug-Off Exterminators** provides pest control services and sells extermination products manufactured by other companies. The following six-column table contains the company's unadjusted trial balance as of December 31, 2021.

December 31, 2021	Unadjusted Trial Balance		Adjustments		Adjusted Trial Balance	
Cash	$ 17,000					
Accounts receivable	4,000					
Allowance for doubtful accounts		$ 828				
Merchandise inventory	11,700					
Trucks	32,000					
Accum. depreciation—Trucks		0				
Equipment	45,000					
Accum. depreciation—Equipment		12,200				
Accounts payable		5,000				
Estimated warranty liability		1,400				
Unearned services revenue		0				
Interest payable		0				
Long-term notes payable		15,000				
D. Buggs, Capital		59,700				
D. Buggs, Withdrawals	10,000					
Extermination services revenue		60,000				
Interest revenue		872				
Sales (of merchandise)		71,026				
Cost of goods sold	46,300					
Depreciation expense—Trucks	0					
Depreciation expense—Equipment	0					
Wages expense	35,000					
Interest expense	0					
Rent expense	9,000					
Bad debts expense	0					
Miscellaneous expense	1,226					
Repairs expense	8,000					
Utilities expense	6,800					
Warranty expense	0					
Totals	$226,026	$226,026				

[continued on next page]

[continued from previous page]

The following information in *a* through *h* applies to the company at the end of the current year.

a. The bank reconciliation as of December 31, 2021, includes the following facts.

Cash balance per bank	$15,100	Deposit in transit	$2,450
Cash balance per books	17,000	Interest earned (on bank account)	52
Outstanding checks	1,800	Bank service charges (miscellaneous expense)	15

Reported on the bank statement is a canceled check that the company failed to record. (Information from the bank reconciliation allows you to determine the amount of this check, which is a payment on an account payable.)

b. An examination of customers' accounts shows that accounts totaling $679 should be written off as uncollectible. Using an aging of receivables, the company determines that the ending balance of the Allowance for Doubtful Accounts should be $700.

c. A truck is purchased and placed in service on January 1, 2021. Its cost is being depreciated with the straight-line method using the following facts and estimates.

Original cost	$32,000	Expected salvage value	$8,000	Useful life (years)	4

d. Two items of equipment (a sprayer and an injector) were purchased and put into service in early January 2019. They are being depreciated with the straight-line method using these facts and estimates.

	Sprayer	Injector
Original cost	$27,000	$18,000
Expected salvage value	$ 3,000	$ 2,500
Useful life (years)	8	5

e. On August 1, 2021, the company is paid $3,840 cash in advance to provide monthly service for an apartment complex for one year. The company began providing the services in August. When the cash was received, the full amount was credited to the Extermination Services Revenue account.

f. The company offers a warranty for the services it sells. The expected cost of providing warranty service is 2.5% of the extermination services revenue of $57,760 for 2021. No warranty expense has been recorded for 2021. All costs of servicing warranties in 2021 were properly debited to the Estimated Warranty Liability account.

g. The $15,000 long-term note is an 8%, five-year, interest-bearing note with interest payable annually on December 31. The note was signed with First National Bank on December 31, 2021.

h. The ending inventory of merchandise is counted and determined to have a cost of $11,700. Bug-Off uses a perpetual inventory system.

Required

1. Use the preceding information to determine amounts for the following items.

a. Correct (reconciled) ending balance of Cash; and the amount of the omitted check.

b. Adjustment needed to obtain the correct ending balance of the Allowance for Doubtful Accounts.

c. Depreciation expense for the truck used during year 2021.

d. Depreciation expense for the two items of equipment used during year 2021.

e. The adjusted 2021 ending balances of the Extermination Services Revenue and Unearned Services Revenue accounts.

f. The adjusted 2021 ending balances of the Warranty Expense and the Estimated Warranty Liability accounts.

g. The adjusted 2021 ending balances of the Interest Expense and the Interest Payable accounts. (Round amounts to nearest whole dollar.)

2. Use the results of part 1 to complete the six-column table by first entering the appropriate adjustments for items *a* through *g* and then completing the Adjusted Trial Balance columns. *Hint:* Item *b* requires two adjustments.

3. Prepare journal entries to record the adjustments entered on the six-column table. Assume Bug-Off's adjusted balance for Merchandise Inventory matches the year-end physical count.

4. Prepare a single-step income statement, a statement of owner's equity (cash withdrawals during 2021 were $10,000 and owner investments were $0), and a classified balance sheet.

Check (1*a*) Reconciled cash bal., $15,750
(1*b*) $551 credit

(1*f*) Estimated Warranty Liability, $2,844 Cr.

(2) Adjusted trial balance totals, $238,207

(4) Net income, $9,274; Total assets, $82,771

connect

TABLEAU DASHBOARD ACTIVITIES

Tableau Dashboard Activities expose students to accounting analytics using visual displays. These assignments run in **Connect**. All are auto-gradable.

Tableau DA 11-1 Quick Study, Computing warranty expense, **P4**—similar to QS 11-13

Tableau DA 11-2 Exercise, Warranty expense and liability computations and entries, **P4**—similar to Exercise 11-12

Tableau DA 11-3 Mini-Case, Analyzing warranty liabilities, **P4**—similar to Exercise 11-13

GENERAL LEDGER

General Ledger (GL) Assignments expose students to general ledger software similar to that in practice. GL is part of **Connect**, and GL assignments are auto-gradable and have algorithmic options.

GL 11-1 focuses on transactions related to accounts and notes payable; it highlights the impact each transaction has on interest expense, if any.

Accounting Analysis

connect

COMPANY ANALYSIS

A1 P4

AA 11-1 Use the table below and **Apple**'s financial statements in Appendix A to answer the following.

$ millions	2019	2018	2017
Interest expense.........	$3,576	$3,240	$2,323

1. Compute times interest earned for each of the three years shown.
2. Is Apple in a good or bad position to pay interest obligations? Assume an industry average of 10.

COMPARATIVE ANALYSIS

A1

AA 11-2 Key figures for **Apple** and **Google** follow.

	Apple			Google		
$ millions	Current Year	One Year Prior	Two Years Prior	Current Year	One Year Prior	Two Years Prior
Net income........	$55,256	$59,531	$48,351	$34,343	$30,736	$12,662
Income taxes.......	10,481	13,372	15,738	5,282	4,177	14,531
Interest expense....	3,576	3,240	2,323	100	114	109

Required

1. Compute times interest earned for the three years' data shown for each company.
2. In the current year, and using times interest earned, which company appears better able to pay interest obligations?
3. In the current year, and using times interest earned, is the company in a good or bad position to pay interest obligations for (*a*) Apple and (*b*) Google? Assume an industry average of 10.

EXTENDED ANALYSIS

A1

AA 11-3 Comparative figures for **Samsung**, **Apple**, and **Google** follow.

	Samsung		Apple		Google	
In millions	Current Year	Prior Year	Current Year	Prior Year	Current Year	Prior Year
Net Income	$18,653	$38,049	$55,256	$59,531	$34,343	$30,736
Income taxes.............	7,459	14,428	10,481	13,372	5,282	4,177
Interest expense..........	577	567	3,576	3,240	100	114

Required

1. Compute the times interest earned ratio for the most recent two years for Samsung using the data shown.
2. Is the change in Samsung's times interest earned ratio favorable or unfavorable?
3. In the current year, is Samsung's times interest earned ratio better or worse than the same ratio for (*a*) Apple and (*b*) Google?

Discussion Questions

1. What is the difference between a current and a long-term liability?
2. What is an estimated liability?
3. What are the three important questions concerning the uncertainty of liabilities?
4. What is the combined amount (in percent) of the employee and employer Social Security tax rate? (Assume wages do not exceed $137,700 per year.)
5. What is the current Medicare tax rate? This rate is applied to what maximum level of salary and wages?
6. Which payroll taxes are the employee's responsibility and which are the employer's responsibility?
7. What determines the amount deducted from an employee's wages for federal income taxes?
8. What is an employer's unemployment merit rating? How are these ratings assigned to employers?
9. Why are warranty liabilities usually recognized on the balance sheet as liabilities even when they are uncertain?
10. Suppose a company has a facility located where disastrous weather conditions often occur. Should it report a probable loss from a future disaster as a liability on its balance sheet? Explain.
11.[A] What is a wage bracket withholding table?
12.[A] What amount of income tax is withheld from the salary of an employee who is single with two withholding allowances and earns $725 per week? What if the employee earns $625 and has no withholding allowances? (Use Exhibit 11A.6.)

Beyond the Numbers

ETHICS CHALLENGE

P4

BTN 11-1 Cameron Bly is a sales manager for an automobile dealership. He earns a bonus each year based on revenue from the number of autos sold in the year less related warranty expenses. Actual warranty expenses have varied over the prior 10 years from a low of 3% of an automobile's selling price to a high of 10%. In the past, Bly has tended to estimate warranty expenses on the high end to be conservative. He must work with the dealership's accountant at year-end to arrive at the warranty expense accrual for cars sold each year.

1. Does the warranty accrual decision create any ethical dilemma for Bly?
2. Because warranty expenses vary, what percent do you think Bly should choose for the current year? Justify your response.

COMMUNICATING IN PRACTICE

C3

BTN 11-2 Dusty Johnson is the accounting and finance manager for a manufacturer. At year-end, he must determine how to account for the company's contingencies. His manager, Tom Pretti, objects to Johnson's proposal to recognize an expense and a liability for warranty service on units of a new product introduced in the fourth quarter. Pretti comments, "There's no way we can estimate this warranty cost. We don't owe anyone anything until a product fails and it is returned. Let's report an expense if and when we do any warranty work."

Required

Prepare a one-page memorandum for Johnson to send to Pretti defending his proposal.

TAKING IT TO THE NET

C1 A1

BTN 11-3 Access the February 22, 2019, filing of the December 31, 2018, annual 10-K report of **McDonald's Corporation** (ticker: MCD), which is available from SEC.gov.

Required

1. Identify the current liabilities on McDonald's balance sheet as of December 31, 2018.
2. Use the consolidated statement of income for the year ended December 31, 2018, to compute McDonald's times interest earned ratio. Comment on the result. Assume an industry average of 5.0.

TEAMWORK IN ACTION

C2 P1

BTN 11-4 Assume that your team is in business and you must borrow $6,000 cash for short-term needs. You have been shopping banks for a loan, and you have the following two options.

A. Sign a $6,000, 90-day, 10% interest-bearing note dated June 1.
B. Sign a $6,000, 120-day, 8% interest-bearing note dated June 1.

Required

1. Discuss these two options and determine the better choice. Ensure that all teammates concur with the decision and understand the rationale.
2. Each member of the team is to prepare *one* of the following journal entries.
   a. Option A—at date of issuance.
   b. Option B—at date of issuance.
   c. Option A—at maturity date.
   d. Option B—at maturity date.
3. In rotation, each member is to explain to the team the entry he or she prepared in part 2. Ensure that all team members concur with and understand the entries.
4. Assume that the funds are borrowed on December 1 (instead of June 1) and your business operates on a calendar-year reporting period. Each member of the team is to prepare *one* of the following entries.
   a. Option A—the year-end adjustment.
   b. Option B—the year-end adjustment.
   c. Option A—at maturity date.
   d. Option B—at maturity date.
5. In rotation, each member is to explain to the team the entry he or she prepared in part 4. Ensure that all team members concur with and understand the entries.

ENTREPRENEURIAL DECISION

A1

BTN 11-5 Review the chapter's opening feature about Beto Perez and **Zumba**. Assume the company is considering expanding to Europe and that the current abbreviated income statement appears as follows.

Income Statement For Year Ended December 31	
Sales	$1,000,000
Operating expenses (55%)	550,000
Net income	$ 450,000

Assume also that the company currently has no interest-bearing debt. If it expands to Europe, it will require a $300,000 loan. The company has found a bank that will loan it the money on a 7% note payable. The company believes that, at least for the first few years, sales in Europe will equal $250,000 and that all expenses at both locations will continue to equal 55% of sales.

Required

1. Prepare an income statement (showing three separate columns for current operations, European, and total) for the company assuming that it borrows the funds and expands to Europe. Annual revenues for current operations are expected to remain at $1,000,000.
2. Compute the company's times interest earned under the expansion assumptions in part 1.
3. Assume sales in Europe are $400,000. Prepare an income statement (with columns for current operations, European, and total) for the company and compute times interest earned.
4. Assume sales in Europe are $100,000. Prepare an income statement (with columns for current operations, European, and total) for the company and compute times interest earned.
5. Comment on your results from parts 1 through 4.

appendix A

Financial Statement Information

This appendix includes financial information for (1) **Apple**, (2) **Google**, and (3) **Samsung**. Apple states that it designs, manufactures and markets smartphones, personal computers, tablets, wearables, and accessories, and sells a variety of related services. It competes with both Google and Samsung in the United States and globally. The information in this appendix is taken from annual 10-K reports (or annual report for Samsung) filed with the SEC or other regulatory agency. An **annual report** is a summary of a company's financial results for the year along with its current financial condition and future plans. This report is directed to external users of financial information, but it also affects the actions and decisions of internal users.

A company often uses an annual report to showcase itself and its products. Many annual reports include photos, diagrams, and illustrations related to the company. The primary objective of annual reports, however, is the financial section, which communicates much information about a company, with most data drawn from the accounting information system. The content of a typical annual report's financial section follows:

- Letter to Shareholders
- Financial History and Highlights
- Quantitative and Qualitative Disclosures about Risk Factors
- Management Discussion and Analysis
- Management's Report on Financial Statements and on Internal Controls
- Report of Independent Accountants (Auditor's Report) and on Internal Controls
- Financial Statements
- Notes to Financial Statements
- Directors, Officers, and Corporate Governance
- Executive Compensation
- Accounting Fees and Services

This appendix provides the financial statements for Apple (plus selected notes), Google, and Samsung. (Note: Google is part of **Alphabet**; we refer to Alphabet as "Google" because of its global familiarity and because Google makes up 99% of Alphabet's revenues.) The appendix is organized as follows:

APPLE
GOOGLE
Samsung

- **Apple A-1** through **A-8**
- **Google A-9** through **A-12**
- **Samsung A-13** through **A-16**

Many assignments at the end of each chapter refer to information in this appendix. We encourage readers to spend time with these assignments; they are especially useful in showing the relevance and diversity of accounting and reporting.

Special note: The SEC maintains the EDGAR (**E**lectronic **D**ata **G**athering, **A**nalysis, and **R**etrieval) database at **SEC.gov** for U.S. filers. The **Form 10-K** is the annual report form for most companies. It provides electronically accessible information. The **Form 10-KSB** is the annual report form filed by small businesses. It requires slightly less information than the Form 10-K. One of these forms must be filed within 90 days after the company's fiscal year-end. (Forms 10-K405, 10-KT, 10-KT405, and 10-KSB405 are slight variations of the usual form due to certain regulations or rules.)

Apple Inc.
CONSOLIDATED BALANCE SHEETS
(In millions, except number of shares which are reflected in thousands and par value)

	September 28, 2019	September 29, 2018
ASSETS		
Current assets		
Cash and cash equivalents	$ 48,844	$ 25,913
Marketable securities	51,713	40,388
Accounts receivable, net	22,926	23,186
Inventories	4,106	3,956
Vendor non-trade receivables	22,878	25,809
Other current assets	12,352	12,087
Total current assets	162,819	131,339
Non-current assets		
Marketable securities	105,341	170,799
Property, plant and equipment, net	37,378	41,304
Other non-current assets	32,978	22,283
Total non-current assets	175,697	234,386
Total assets	$ 338,516	$ 365,725
LIABILITIES AND SHAREHOLDERS' EQUITY		
Current liabilities		
Accounts payable	$ 46,236	$ 55,888
Other current liabilities	37,720	33,327
Deferred revenue	5,522	5,966
Commercial paper	5,980	11,964
Term debt	10,260	8,784
Total current liabilities	105,718	115,929
Non-current liabilities		
Term debt	91,807	93,735
Other non-current liabilities	50,503	48,914
Total non-current liabilities	142,310	142,649
Total liabilities	248,028	258,578
Commitments and contingencies		
Shareholders' equity		
Common stock and additional paid-in capital, $0.00001 par value: 12,600,000 shares authorized; 4,443,236 and 4,754,986 shares issued and outstanding, respectively	45,174	40,201
Retained earnings	45,898	70,400
Accumulated other comprehensive income (loss)	(584)	(3,454)
Total shareholders' equity	90,488	107,147
Total liabilities and shareholders' equity	$ 338,516	$ 365,725

See accompanying Notes to Consolidated Financial Statements.

Apple Inc.
CONSOLIDATED STATEMENTS OF OPERATIONS
(In millions, except number of shares which are reflected in thousands and per share amounts)

Years ended	September 28, 2019	September 29, 2018	September 30, 2017
Net sales:			
Products	$ 213,883	$ 225,847	$ 196,534
Services	46,291	39,748	32,700
Total net sales	260,174	265,595	229,234
Cost of sales:			
Products	144,996	148,164	126,337
Services	16,786	15,592	14,711
Total cost of sales	161,782	163,756	141,048
Gross margin	98,392	101,839	88,186
Operating expenses:			
Research and development	16,217	14,236	11,581
Selling, general and administrative	18,245	16,705	15,261
Total operating expenses	34,462	30,941	26,842
Operating income	63,930	70,898	61,344
Other income (expense), net	1,807	2,005	2,745
Income before provision for income taxes	65,737	72,903	64,089
Provision for income taxes	10,481	13,372	15,738
Net income	$ 55,256	$ 59,531	$ 48,351
Earnings per share:			
Basic	$ 11.97	$ 12.01	$ 9.27
Diluted	$ 11.89	$ 11.91	$ 9.21
Shares used in computing earnings per share:			
Basic	4,617,834	4,955,377	5,217,242
Diluted	4,648,913	5,000,109	5,251,692

See accompanying Notes to Consolidated Financial Statements.

Apple Inc.
CONSOLIDATED STATEMENTS OF COMPREHENSIVE INCOME
(In millions)

Years ended	September 28, 2019	September 29, 2018	September 30, 2017
Net income	$ 55,256	$ 59,531	$ 48,351
Other comprehensive income (loss):			
Change in foreign currency translation, net of tax	(408)	(525)	224
Change in unrealized gains/losses on derivative instruments, net of tax:			
Change in fair value of derivatives	(661)	523	1,315
Adjustment for net (gains) losses realized and included in net income	23	382	(1,477)
Total change in unrealized gains/losses on derivative instruments	(638)	905	(162)
Change in unrealized gains/losses on marketable securities, net of tax:			
Change in fair value of marketable securities	3,802	(3,407)	(782)
Adjustment for net (gains) losses realized and included in net income	25	1	(64)
Total change in unrealized gains/losses on marketable securities	3,827	(3,406)	(846)
Total other comprehensive income (loss)	2,781	(3,026)	(784)
Total comprehensive income	$ 58,037	$ 56,505	$ 47,567

See accompanying Notes to Consolidated Financial Statements.

Apple Inc.
CONSOLIDATED STATEMENTS OF SHAREHOLDERS' EQUITY
(In millions)

Years ended	September 28, 2019	September 29, 2018	September 30, 2017
Total shareholders' equity, beginning balances	$ 107,147	$ 134,047	$ 128,249
Common stock and additional paid-in capital			
Beginning balances	40,201	35,867	31,251
Common stock issued	781	669	555
Common stock withheld related to net share settlement of equity awards	(2,002)	(1,778)	(1,468)
Share-based compensation	6,194	5,443	4,909
Tax benefit from equity awards, including transfer pricing adjustments	—	—	620
Ending balances	45,174	40,201	35,867
Retained earnings			
Beginning balances	70,400	98,330	96,364
Net income	55,256	59,531	48,351
Dividends and dividend equivalents declared	(14,129)	(13,735)	(12,803)
Common stock withheld related to net share settlement of equity awards	(1,029)	(948)	(581)
Common stock repurchased	(67,101)	(73,056)	(33,001)
Cumulative effects of changes in accounting principles	2,501	278	—
Ending balances	45,898	70,400	98,330
Accumulated other comprehensive income (loss)			
Beginning balances	(3,454)	(150)	634
Other comprehensive income (loss)	2,781	(3,026)	(784)
Cumulative effects of changes in accounting principles	89	(278)	—
Ending balances	(584)	(3,454)	(150)
Total shareholders' equity, ending balances	$ 90,488	$ 107,147	$ 134,047

See accompanying Notes to Consolidated Financial Statements.

Apple Inc.
CONSOLIDATED STATEMENTS OF CASH FLOWS
(In millions)

Years ended	**September 28, 2019**	**September 29, 2018**	**September 30, 2017**
Cash, cash equivalents and restricted cash, beginning balances	$ 25,913	$ 20,289	$ 20,484
Operating activities			
Net income	55,256	59,531	48,351
Adjustments to reconcile net income to cash generated by operating activities:			
Depreciation and amortization	12,547	10,903	10,157
Share-based compensation expense	6,068	5,340	4,840
Deferred income tax expense (benefit)	(340)	(32,590)	5,966
Other	(652)	(444)	(166)
Changes in operating assets and liabilities:			
Accounts receivable, net	245	(5,322)	(2,093)
Inventories	(289)	828	(2,723)
Vendor non-trade receivables	2,931	(8,010)	(4,254)
Other current and non-current assets	873	(423)	(5,318)
Accounts payable	(1,923)	9,175	8,966
Deferred revenue	(625)	(3)	(593)
Other current and non-current liabilities	(4,700)	38,449	1,092
Cash generated by operating activities	69,391	77,434	64,225
Investing activities			
Purchases of marketable securities	(39,630)	(71,356)	(159,486)
Proceeds from maturities of marketable securities	40,102	55,881	31,775
Proceeds from sales of marketable securities	56,988	47,838	94,564
Payments for acquisition of property, plant and equipment	(10,495)	(13,313)	(12,451)
Payments made in connection with business acquisitions, net	(624)	(721)	(329)
Purchases of non-marketable securities	(1,001)	(1,871)	(521)
Proceeds from non-marketable securities	1,634	353	126
Other	(1,078)	(745)	(124)
Cash generated by (used in) investing activities	45,896	16,066	(46,446)
Financing activities			
Proceeds from issuance of common stock	781	669	555
Payments for taxes related to net share settlement of equity awards	(2,817)	(2,527)	(1,874)
Payments for dividends and dividend equivalents	(14,119)	(13,712)	(12,769)
Repurchases of common stock	(66,897)	(72,738)	(32,900)
Proceeds from issuance of term debt, net	6,963	6,969	28,662
Repayments of term debt	(8,805)	(6,500)	(3,500)
Proceeds from (Repayments of) commercial paper, net	(5,977)	(37)	3,852
Other	(105)	—	—
Cash used in financing activities	(90,976)	(87,876)	(17,974)
Increase (decrease) in cash, cash equivalents and restricted cash	24,311	5,624	(195)
Cash, cash equivalents and restricted cash, ending balances	$ 50,224	$ 25,913	$ 20,289
Supplemental cash flow disclosure:			
Cash paid for income taxes, net	$ 15,263	$ 10,417	$ 11,591
Cash paid for interest	$ 3,423	$ 3,022	$ 2,092

See accompanying Notes to Consolidated Financial Statements.

APPLE INC.
SELECTED NOTES TO CONSOLIDATED FINANCIAL STATEMENTS

Basis of Presentation and Preparation

In the opinion of the Company's management, the consolidated financial statements reflect all adjustments, which are normal and recurring in nature, necessary for fair financial statement presentation. The preparation of these consolidated financial statements and accompanying notes in conformity with U.S. generally accepted accounting principles requires management to make estimates and assumptions that affect the amounts reported.

The Company's fiscal year is the 52- or 53-week period that ends on the last Saturday of September. The Company's fiscal years 2019 and 2018 spanned 52 weeks each, whereas fiscal year 2017 included 53 weeks. A 14th week was included in the first fiscal quarter of 2017, as is done every five or six years, to realign the Company's fiscal quarters with calendar quarters. Unless otherwise stated, references to particular years, quarters, months and periods refer to the Company's fiscal years ended in September and the associated quarters, months and periods of those fiscal years.

Revenue Recognition

Net sales consist of revenue from the sale of iPhone, Mac, iPad, Services and other products. The Company recognizes revenue at the amount to which it expects to be entitled when control of the products or services is transferred to its customers. Control is generally transferred when the Company has a present right to payment and title and the significant risks and rewards of ownership of products or services are transferred to its customers. For most of the Company's Products net sales, control transfers when products are shipped. For the Company's Services net sales, control transfers over time as services are delivered. Payment for Products and Services net sales is collected within a short period following transfer of control or commencement of delivery of services, as applicable.

The Company records reductions to Products net sales related to future product returns, price protection and other customer incentive programs based on the Company's expectations and historical experience.

For arrangements with multiple performance obligations, which represent promises within an arrangement that are capable of being distinct, the Company allocates revenue to all distinct performance obligations based on their relative stand-alone selling prices ("SSPs"). When available, the Company uses observable prices to determine SSPs. When observable prices are not available, SSPs are established that reflect the Company's best estimates of what the selling prices of the performance obligations would be if they were sold regularly on a stand-alone basis.

The Company has identified up to three performance obligations regularly included in arrangements involving the sale of iPhone, Mac, iPad and certain other products. The first performance obligation, which represents the substantial portion of the allocated sales price, is the hardware and bundled software delivered at the time of sale. The second performance obligation is the right to receive certain product-related bundled services, which include iCloud, Siri and Maps. The third performance obligation is the right to receive, on a when-and-if-available basis, future unspecified software upgrades relating to the software bundled with each device. The Company allocates revenue and any related discounts to these performance obligations based on their relative SSPs. Because the Company lacks observable prices for the undelivered performance obligations, the allocation of revenue is based on the Company's estimated SSPs. Revenue allocated to the delivered hardware and bundled software is recognized when control has transferred to the customer, which generally occurs when the product is shipped. Revenue allocated to the product-related bundled services and unspecified software upgrade rights is deferred and recognized on a straight-line basis over the estimated period they are expected to be provided. Cost of sales related to delivered hardware and bundled software, including estimated warranty costs, are recognized at the time of sale. Costs incurred to provide product-related bundled services and unspecified software upgrade rights are recognized as cost of sales as incurred.

For the sale of third-party products where the Company obtains control of the product before transferring it to the customer, the Company recognizes revenue based on the gross amount billed to customers. The Company considers multiple factors when determining whether it obtains control of third-party products including, but not limited to, evaluating if it can establish the price of the product, retains inventory risk for tangible products or has the responsibility for ensuring acceptability of the product. For thirdparty applications sold through the App Store, Mac App Store, TV App Store and Watch App Store and certain digital content sold through the Company's other digital content stores, the Company does not obtain control of the product before transferring it to the customer. Therefore, the Company accounts for such sales on a net basis by recognizing in Services net sales only the commission it retains.

The Company has elected to record revenue net of taxes collected from customers that are remitted to governmental authorities, with the collected taxes recorded within other current liabilities until remitted to the relevant government authority.

Deferred Revenue As of September 28, 2019 and September 29, 2018, the Company had total deferred revenue of $8.1 billion and $8.8 billion, respectively. As of September 28, 2019, the Company expects 68% of total deferred revenue to be realized in less than a year, 25% within one-to-two years, 6% within two-to-three years and 1% in greater than three years.

Advertising Costs

Advertising costs are expensed as incurred and included in selling, general and administrative expenses.

Apple Inc. Notes—continued

Other Income and Expense

$ millions	2019	2018	2017
Interest and dividend income	$ 4,961	$ 5,686	$ 5,201
Interest expense	(3,576)	(3,240)	(2,323)
Other income (expense), net	422	(441)	(133)
Total other income (expense), net	$ 1,807	$ 2,005	$ 2,745

Cash Equivalents and Marketable Securities

All highly liquid investments with maturities of three months or less at the date of purchase are classified as cash equivalents. The Company's investments in marketable debt securities have been classified and accounted for as available-for-sale. The Company classifies its marketable debt securities as either short-term or long-term based on each instrument's underlying contractual maturity date. Unrealized gains and losses on marketable debt securities classified as available-for-sale are recognized in other comprehensive income/(loss) ("OCI").

The Company's investments in marketable equity securities are classified based on the nature of the securities and their availability for use in current operations. The Company's marketable equity securities are measured at fair value with gains and losses recognized in other income/(expense), net ("OI&E"). The cost of securities sold is determined using the specific identification method.

Restricted Cash and Restricted Marketable Securities

The Company considers cash and marketable securities to be restricted when withdrawal or general use is legally restricted. The Company records restricted cash as other assets in the Consolidated Balance Sheets, and determines current or non-current classification based on the expected duration of the restriction. The Company records restricted marketable securities as current or non-current marketable securities in the Consolidated Balance Sheets based on the classification of the underlying securities.

The Company's restricted cash primarily consisted of cash required to be on deposit under a contractual agreement with a bank to support the Company's iPhone Upgrade Program.

Accounts Receivable (Trade Receivables)

The Company has considerable trade receivables outstanding with its third-party cellular network carriers, wholesalers, retailers, resellers, small and mid-sized businesses and education, enterprise and government customers.

As of September 28, 2019, the Company had no customers that individually represented 10% or more of total trade receivables. As of September 29, 2018, the Company had one customer that represented 10% or more of total trade receivables, which accounted for 10%. The Company's cellular network carriers accounted for 51% and 59% of total trade receivables as of September 28, 2019 and September 29, 2018, respectively.

Inventories

Inventories are measured using the first-in, first-out method.

Property, Plant and Equipment

Depreciation on property, plant and equipment is recognized on a straight-line basis over the estimated useful lives of the assets, which for buildings is the lesser of 30 years or the remaining life of the underlying building; between one and five years for machinery and equipment, including product tooling and manufacturing process equipment; and the shorter of lease term or useful life for leasehold improvements. Capitalized costs related to internal-use software are amortized on a straight-line basis over the estimated useful lives of the assets, which range from three to five years. Depreciation and amortization expense on property and equipment was $11.3 billion, $9.3 billion and $8.2 billion during 2019, 2018 and 2017, respectively.

$ millions	2019	2018
Land and buildings	$17,085	$16,216
Machinery, equipment and internal-use software	69,797	65,982
Leasehold improvements	9,075	8,205
Gross property, plant and equipment	95,957	90,403
Accumulated depreciation and amortization	(58,579)	(49,099)
Total property, plant and equipment, net	$37,378	$41,304

Fair Value Measurements

The fair values of the Company's money market funds and certain marketable equity securities are based on quoted prices in active markets for identical assets. The valuation techniques used to measure the fair value of the Company's debt instruments and all other financial instruments, which generally have counterparties with high credit ratings, are based on quoted market prices or model-driven valuations using significant inputs derived from or corroborated by observable market data.

Financial Instruments

The Company typically invests in highly rated securities, with the primary objective of minimizing the potential risk of principal loss. The Company's investment policy generally requires securities to be investment grade and limits the amount of credit exposure to any one issuer. Fair values were determined for each individual security in the investment portfolio.

Accrued Warranty and Guarantees

The following table shows changes in the Company's accrued warranties and related costs for 2019 and 2018:

$ millions	2019	2018
Beginning accrued warranty and related costs	$ 3,692	$ 3,834
Cost of warranty claims	(3,857)	(4,115)
Accruals for product warranty	3,735	3,973
Ending accrued warranty and related costs	$ 3,570	$ 3,692

Apple Inc. Notes—continued

Other Non-Current Liabilities

$ millions	2019	2018
Long-term taxes payable	$29,545	$33,589
Other non-current liabilities	20,958	15,325
Total other non-current liabilities	$50,503	$48,914

Term Debt

As of September 28, 2019, the Company had outstanding floating- and fixed-rate notes with varying maturities for an aggregate principal amount of $101.7 billion (collectively the "Notes"). The Notes are senior unsecured obligations and interest is payable in arrears.

The Company recognized $3.2 billion, $3.0 billion and $2.2 billion of interest cost on its term debt for 2019, 2018 and 2017, respectively.

The future principal payments for the Company's Notes as of September 28, 2019 are as follows (in millions):

2020	$ 10,270
2021	8,750
2022	9,528
2023	9,290
2024	10,039
Thereafter	53,802
Total term debt	$101,679

As of September 28, 2019 and September 29, 2018, the fair value of the Company's Notes, based on Level 2 inputs, was $107.5 billion and $103.2 billion, respectively.

Share Repurchase Program

On April 30, 2019, the Company announced the Board of Directors increased the current share repurchase program authorization from $100 billion to $175 billion of the Company's common stock, of which $96.1 billion had been utilized as of September 28, 2019. During 2019, the Company repurchased 345.2 million shares of its common stock for $67.1 billion, including 62.0 million shares delivered under a $12.0 billion accelerated share repurchase arrangement dated February 2019, which settled in August 2019. The Company's share repurchase program does not obligate it to acquire any specific number of shares.

Contingencies

The Company is subject to various legal proceedings and claims that have arisen in the ordinary course of business and that have not been fully resolved. The outcome of litigation is inherently uncertain. If one or more legal matters were resolved against the Company in a reporting period for amounts above management's expectations, the Company's financial condition and operating results for that reporting period could be materially adversely affected. In the opinion of management, there was not at least a reasonable possibility the Company may have incurred a material loss, or a material loss greater than a recorded accrual, concerning loss contingencies for asserted legal and other claims, except for the following matters:

- VirnetX
- Qualcomm
- iOS Performance Management Cases
- French Competition Authority

Disaggregated Revenue by Significant Products and Services

Net sales (mil.)	2019	2018	2017
iPhone	$142,381	$164,888	$139,337
Mac	25,740	25,198	25,569
iPad	21,280	18,380	18,802
Wearables, Home and Accessories	24,482	17,381	12,826
Services	46,291	39,748	32,700
Total net sales	$260,174	$265,595	$229,234

Reportable segment (mil.)	2019	2018	2017
Americas:			
Net sales	$116,914	$112,093	$96,600
Operating income	$ 35,099	$ 34,864	$30,684
Europe:			
Net sales	$ 60,288	$ 62,420	$54,938
Operating income	$ 19,195	$ 19,955	$16,514
Greater China:			
Net sales	$ 43,678	$ 51,942	$44,764
Operating income	$ 16,232	$ 19,742	$17,032
Japan:			
Net sales	$ 21,506	$ 21,733	$17,733
Operating income	$ 9,369	$ 9,500	$ 8,097
Rest of Asia Pacific:			
Net sales	$ 17,788	$ 17,407	$15,199
Operating income	$ 6,055	$ 6,181	$ 5,304

A reconciliation of the Company's segment operating income to the Consolidated Statements of Operations for 2019, 2018 and 2017 is as follows:

$ millions	2019	2018	2017
Segment operating income	$ 85,950	$ 90,242	$77,631
Research and development expense	(16,217)	(14,236)	(11,581)
Other corporate expenses, net	(5,803)	(5,108)	(4,706)
Total operating income	$ 63,930	$ 70,898	$61,344

APPLE

Apple Inc. Notes—continued

Selected Financial Data

(in millions, except number of shares, which are reflected in thousands, and per share amounts).

	2019	2018	2017	2016	2015
Total net sales	$ 260,174	$ 265,595	$ 229,234	$ 215,639	$ 233,715
Net income	$ 55,256	$ 59,531	$ 48,351	$ 45,687	$ 53,394
Earnings per share:					
Basic	$ 11.97	$ 12.01	$ 9.27	$ 8.35	$ 9.28
Diluted	$ 11.89	$ 11.91	$ 9.21	$ 8.31	$ 9.22
Cash dividends declared per share	$ 3.00	$ 2.72	$ 2.40	$ 2.18	$ 1.98
Shares used in computing earnings per share:					
Basic	4,617,834	4,955,377	5,217,242	5,470,820	5,753,421
Diluted	4,648,913	5,000,109	5,251,692	5,500,281	5,793,069
Total cash, cash equivalents and marketable securities	$ 205,898	$ 237,100	$ 268,895	$ 237,585	$ 205,666
Total assets	$ 338,516	$ 365,725	$ 375,319	$ 321,686	$ 290,345
Non-current portion of term debt	$ 91,807	$ 93,735	$ 97,207	$ 75,427	$ 53,329
Other non-current liabilities	$ 50,503	$ 48,914	$ 44,212	$ 39,986	$ 38,104

Company Background

The Company designs, manufactures and markets smartphones, personal computers, tablets, wearables and accessories, and sells a variety of related services. The Company's fiscal year is the 52- or 53-week period that ends on the last Saturday of September. The Company is a California corporation established in 1977.

Products

iPhone iPhone® is the Company's line of smartphones based on its iOS operating system. In September 2019, the Company introduced three new iPhones: iPhone 11, iPhone 11 Pro and iPhone 11 Pro Max.

Mac Mac® is the Company's line of personal computers based on its macOS® operating system. During 2019, the Company released a new version of MacBook Air® and a new Mac mini®, and introduced an updated Mac Pro®, which is expected to be available in the fall of 2019.

iPad iPad® is the Company's line of multi-purpose tablets. iPad is based on the Company's iPadOS™ operating system, which was introduced during 2019. Also during 2019, the Company released two new versions of iPad Pro®, an iPad Air®, an updated iPad mini® and a new 10.2-inch iPad.

Wearables, Home and Accessories Wearables, Home and Accessories includes AirPods®, Apple TV®, Apple Watch®, Beats® products, HomePod™, iPod touch® and other Apple-branded and third-party accessories. AirPods are the Company's wireless headphones that interact with Siri. In October 2019, the Company introduced AirPods Pro™. Apple Watch is a personal electronic device that combines the watchOS® user interface and other technologies created specifically for a smaller device. In September 2019, the Company introduced Apple Watch Series 5.

Services

Digital Content Stores and Streaming Services The Company operates various platforms that allow customers to discover and download applications and digital content, such as books, music, video, games and podcasts. These platforms include the App Store®, available for iPhone and iPad, the Mac App Store, the TV App Store and the Watch App Store.

The Company also offers subscription-based digital content streaming services, including Apple Music®, which offers users a curated listening experience with on-demand radio stations, and Apple TV+, which offers exclusive original content, and is expected to be available in November 2019.

AppleCare AppleCare® includes AppleCare+ ("AC+") and the AppleCare Protection Plan, which are fee-based services that extend the coverage of phone support eligibility and hardware repairs. AC+ offers additional coverage for instances of accidental damage and is available in certain countries for certain products. Additionally, AC+ with theft and loss protection is available for iPhone in the U.S.

iCloud iCloud® is the Company's cloud service, which stores music, photos, contacts, calendars, mail, documents and more, keeping them up-to-date and available across multiple Apple devices and Windows personal computers.

Licensing The Company licenses the use of certain of its intellectual property, and provides other related services.

Other Services The Company delivers a variety of other services available in certain countries, including Apple Arcade™, a game subscription service; Apple Card™, a co-branded credit card; Apple News+, a subscription news and magazine service; and Apple Pay, a cashless payment service.

Markets and Distribution

The Company's customers are primarily in the consumer, small and mid-sized business, education, enterprise and government markets. The Company sells its products and resells third-party products in most of its major markets directly to consumers, small and mid-sized businesses, and education, enterprise and government customers through its retail and online stores and its direct sales force. The Company also employs a variety of indirect distribution channels, such as third-party cellular network carriers, wholesalers, retailers and resellers. During 2019, the Company's net sales through its direct and indirect distribution channels accounted for 31% and 69%, respectively, of total net sales.

Employees

As of September 28, 2019, the Company had approximately 137,000 full-time equivalent employees.

Google Inc. (Alphabet Inc.)[a]
CONSOLIDATED BALANCE SHEETS
(In millions, except share amounts which are reflected in thousands, and par value per share amounts)

	December 31, 2018	December 31, 2019
Assets		
Current assets		
Cash and cash equivalents	$ 16,701	$ 18,498
Marketable securities	92,439	101,177
Total cash, cash equivalents, and marketable securities	109,140	119,675
Accounts receivable, net of allowance of $729 and $753	20,838	25,326
Income taxes receivable, net	355	2,166
Inventory	1,107	999
Other current assets	4,236	4,412
Total current assets	135,676	152,578
Non-marketable investments	13,859	13,078
Deferred income taxes	737	721
Property and equipment, net	59,719	73,646
Operating lease assets	0	10,941
Intangible assets, net	2,220	1,979
Goodwill	17,888	20,624
Other non-current assets	2,693	2,342
Total assets	$ 232,792	$ 275,909
Liabilities and Stockholders' Equity		
Current liabilities		
Accounts payable	$ 4,378	$ 5,561
Accrued compensation and benefits	6,839	8,495
Accrued expenses and other current liabilities	16,958	23,067
Accrued revenue share	4,592	5,916
Deferred revenue	1,784	1,908
Income taxes payable, net	69	274
Total current liabilities	34,620	45,221
Long-term debt	4,012	4,554
Deferred revenue, non-current	396	358
Income taxes payable, non-current	11,327	9,885
Deferred income taxes	1,264	1,701
Operating lease liabilities	0	10,214
Other long-term liabilities	3,545	2,534
Total liabilities	55,164	74,467
Commitments and Contingencies		
Stockholders' equity		
Convertible preferred stock, $0.001 par value per share, 100,000 shares authorized; no shares issued and outstanding	0	0
Class A and Class B common stock, and Class C capital stock and additional paid-in capital, $0.001 par value per share: 15,000,000 shares authorized (Class A 9,000,000, Class B 3,000,000, Class C 3,000,000); 695,556 (Class A 299,242, Class B 46,636, Class C 349,678) and 688,335 (Class A 299,828, Class B 46,441, Class C 342,066) shares issued and outstanding	45,049	50,552
Accumulated other comprehensive loss	(2,306)	(1,232)
Retained earnings	134,885	152,122
Total stockholders' equity	177,628	201,442
Total liabilities and stockholders' equity	$ 232,792	$ 275,909

[a]Google is part of Alphabet, but we loosely refer to Alphabet as "Google" because of its global familiarity and because Google provides 99% of Alphabet's $161,857 billion in revenues.

See accompanying notes.

Google Inc. (Alphabet Inc.)[a]
CONSOLIDATED STATEMENTS OF INCOME
(In millions)

Year Ended December 31	2017	2018	2019
Revenues	$ 110,855	$ 136,819	$ 161,857
Costs and expenses			
Cost of revenues	45,583	59,549	71,896
Research and development	16,625	21,419	26,018
Sales and marketing	12,893	16,333	18,464
General and administrative	6,840	6,923	9,551
European Commission fines	2,736	5,071	1,697
Total costs and expenses	84,677	109,295	127,626
Income from operations	26,178	27,524	34,231
Other income (expense), net	1,015	7,389	5,394
Income before income taxes	27,193	34,913	39,625
Provision for income taxes	14,531	4,177	5,282
Net income	$ 12,662	$ 30,736	$ 34,343

[a]Google is part of Alphabet, but we loosely refer to Alphabet as "Google" because of its global familiarity and because Google provides 99% of Alphabet's $161,857 billion in revenues.

See accompanying notes.

Google Inc. (Alphabet Inc.)[a]
CONSOLIDATED STATEMENTS OF COMPREHENSIVE INCOME
(In millions)

Year Ended December 31	2017	2018	2019
Net income	$ 12,662	$ 30,736	$ 34,343
Other comprehensive income (loss):			
Change in foreign currency translation adjustment	1,543	(781)	(119)
Available-for-sale investments:			
Change in net unrealized gains (losses)	307	88	1,611
Less: reclassification adjustment for net (gains) losses included in net income	105	(911)	(111)
Net change (net of tax effect of $0, $156, and $221)	412	(823)	1,500
Cash flow hedges:			
Change in net unrealized gains (losses)	(638)	290	22
Less: reclassification adjustment for net (gains) losses included in net income	93	98	(299)
Net change (net of tax effect of $247, $103, and $42)	(545)	388	(277)
Other comprehensive income (loss)	1,410	(1,216)	1,104
Comprehensive income	$ 14,072	$ 29,520	$ 35,447

[a]Google is part of Alphabet, but we loosely refer to Alphabet as "Google" because of its global familiarity and because Google provides 99% of Alphabet's $161,857 billion in revenues.

See accompanying notes.

Google Inc. (Alphabet Inc.)[a]
CONSOLIDATED STATEMENTS OF STOCKHOLDERS' EQUITY
(In millions, except share amounts which are reflected in thousands)

	Class A and Class B Common Stock, Class C Capital Stock and Additional Paid-In Capital		Accumulated Other Comprehensive Income (Loss)	Retained Earnings	Total Stockholders' Equity
	Shares	Amount			
Balance as of December 31, 2016	691,293	$ 36,307	$ (2,402)	$ 105,131	$ 139,036
Cumulative effect of accounting change	0	0	0	(15)	(15)
Common and capital stock issued	8,652	212	0	0	212
Stock-based compensation expense	0	7,694	0	0	7,694
Tax withholding related to vesting of restricted stock units	0	(4,373)	0	0	(4,373)
Repurchases of capital stock	(5,162)	(315)	0	(4,531)	(4,846)
Sale of interest in consolidated entities	0	722	0	0	722
Net income	0	0	0	12,662	12,662
Other comprehensive income	0	0	1,410	0	1,410
Balance as of December 31, 2017	694,783	40,247	(992)	113,247	152,502
Cumulative effect of accounting change	0	0	(98)	(599)	(697)
Common and capital stock issued	8,975	148	0	0	148
Stock-based compensation expense	0	9,353	0	0	9,353
Tax withholding related to vesting of restricted stock units and other	0	(4,782)	0	0	(4,782)
Repurchases of capital stock	(8,202)	(576)	0	(8,499)	(9,075)
Sale of interest in consolidated entities	0	659	0	0	659
Net income	0	0	0	30,736	30,736
Other comprehensive loss	0	0	(1,216)	0	(1,216)
Balance as of December 31, 2018	695,556	45,049	(2,306)	134,885	177,628
Cumulative effect of accounting change	0	0	(30)	(4)	(34)
Common and capital stock issued	8,120	202	0	0	202
Stock-based compensation expense	0	10,890	0	0	10,890
Tax withholding related to vesting of restricted stock units and other	0	(4,455)	0	0	(4,455)
Repurchases of capital stock	(15,341)	(1,294)	0	(17,102)	(18,396)
Sale of interest in consolidated entities	0	160	0	0	160
Net income	0	0	0	34,343	34,343
Other comprehensive income (loss)	0	0	1,104	0	1,104
Balance as of December 31, 2019	688,335	$ 50,552	$ (1,232)	$ 152,122	$ 201,442

[a]Google is part of Alphabet, but we loosely refer to Alphabet as "Google" because of its global familiarity and because Google provides 99% of Alphabet's $161,857 billion in revenues.

See accompanying notes.

GOOGLE

Google Inc. (Alphabet Inc.)[a]
CONSOLIDATED STATEMENTS OF CASH FLOWS
(In millions)

Year Ended December 31	2017	2018	2019
Operating activities			
Net income	$ 12,662	$ 30,736	$ 34,343
Adjustments:			
Depreciation and impairment of property and equipment	6,103	8,164	10,856
Amortization and impairment of intangible assets	812	871	925
Stock-based compensation expense	7,679	9,353	10,794
Deferred income taxes	258	778	173
(Gain) loss on debt and equity securities, net	37	(6,650)	(2,798)
Other	294	(189)	(592)
Changes in assets and liabilities, net of effects of acquisitions:			
Accounts receivable	(3,768)	(2,169)	(4,340)
Income taxes, net	8,211	(2,251)	(3,128)
Other assets	(2,164)	(1,207)	(621)
Accounts payable	731	1,067	428
Accrued expenses and other liabilities	4,891	8,614	7,170
Accrued revenue share	955	483	1,273
Deferred revenue	390	371	37
Net cash provided by operating activities	37,091	47,971	54,520
Investing activities			
Purchases of property and equipment	(13,184)	(25,139)	(23,548)
Purchases of marketable securities	(92,195)	(50,158)	(100,315)
Maturities and sales of marketable securities	73,959	48,507	97,825
Purchases of non-marketable investments	(1,745)	(2,073)	(1,932)
Maturities and sales of non-marketable investments	533	1,752	405
Acquisitions, net of cash acquired, and purchases of intangible assets	(287)	(1,491)	(2,515)
Proceeds from collection of notes receivable	1,419	0	0
Other investing activities	99	98	589
Net cash used in investing activities	(31,401)	(28,504)	(29,491)
Financing activities			
Net payments related to stock-based award activities	(4,166)	(4,993)	(4,765)
Repurchases of capital stock	(4,846)	(9,075)	(18,396)
Proceeds from issuance of debt, net of costs	4,291	6,766	317
Repayments of debt	(4,377)	(6,827)	(585)
Proceeds from sale of interest in consolidated entities	800	950	220
Net cash used in financing activities	(8,298)	(13,179)	(23,209)
Effect of exchange rate changes on cash and cash equivalents	405	(302)	(23)
Net increase (decrease) in cash and cash equivalents	(2,203)	5,986	1,797
Cash and cash equivalents at beginning of period	12,918	10,715	16,701
Cash and cash equivalents at end of period	$ 10,715	$ 16,701	$ 18,498
Supplemental disclosures of cash flow information			
Cash paid for taxes, net of refunds	$ 6,191	$ 5,671	$ 8,203

[a]Google is part of Alphabet, but we loosely refer to Alphabet as "Google" because of its global familiarity and because Google provides 99% of Alphabet's $161,857 billion in revenues.

See accompanying notes.

GOOGLE

Samsung Electronics Co., Ltd. and Subsidiaries
CONSOLIDATED STATEMENTS OF FINANCIAL POSITION

In thousands of US dollars	**December 31, 2019**	**December 31, 2018**
Assets		
Current assets		
Cash and cash equivalents	$ 23,069,002	$ 26,033,073
Short-term financial instruments	65,426,571	56,538,875
Short-term financial assets at amortized cost	3,358,516	2,319,851
Short-term financial assets at fair value through profit or loss	1,482,192	1,717,732
Trade receivables	30,143,757	29,059,541
Non-trade receivables	3,585,812	2,643,362
Advance payments	1,224,266	1,168,472
Prepaid expenses	2,064,610	3,548,957
Inventories	22,966,437	24,869,754
Other current assets	2,312,887	1,996,067
Total current assets	**155,634,050**	**149,895,684**
Non-current assets		
Financial assets at amortized cost	—	204,476
Financial assets at fair value through other comprehensive income	7,654,241	6,264,780
Financial assets at fair value through profit or loss	900,077	665,340
Investment in associates and joint ventures	6,513,833	6,274,952
Property, plant and equipment	102,813,888	99,031,047
Intangible assets	17,764,234	12,777,442
Net defined benefit assets	506,094	482,518
Deferred income tax assets	3,865,469	4,691,711
Other non-current assets	6,859,137	10,890,850
Total assets	**$302,511,023**	**$291,178,800**
Liabilities and Equity		
Current liabilities		
Trade payables	$ 7,480,499	$ 7,276,025
Short-term borrowings	12,350,032	11,657,766
Other payables	10,298,520	9,190,823
Advances received	919,862	703,812
Withholdings	769,958	816,205
Accrued expenses	16,611,144	17,452,068
Current income tax liabilities	1,190,751	7,482,067
Current portion of long-term liabilities	725,971	28,646
Provisions	3,491,005	3,761,637
Other current liabilities	889,802	904,980
Total current liabilities	**54,727,544**	**59,274,029**
Non-current liabilities		
Debentures	836,835	825,401
Long-term borrowings	1,885,248	73,006
Long-term other payables	1,874,152	2,740,586
Net defined benefit liabilities	403,944	432,502
Deferred income tax liabilities	14,632,684	13,009,904
Long-term provisions	524,342	569,405
Other non-current liabilities	2,066,906	1,674,233
Total liabilities	**76,951,655**	**78,599,066**
Equity attributable to owners of the parent company		
Preference shares	102,506	102,506
Ordinary shares	667,588	667,588
Share premium	3,778,674	3,778,674
Retained earnings	218,439,838	208,243,059
Other components of equity	(4,263,406)	(6,805,356)
	218,725,200	**205,986,471**
Non-controlling interests	6,834,168	6,593,263
Total equity	**225,559,368**	**212,579,734**
Total liabilities and equity	**$302,511,023**	**$291,178,800**

The above consolidated statement of financial position should be read in conjunction with the accompanying notes.

SAMSUNG

Samsung Electronics Co., Ltd. and Subsidiaries
CONSOLIDATED STATEMENTS OF PROFIT OR LOSS

For the year ended December 31	2019	2018
In thousands of US dollars		
Revenue	$197,690,938	$209,163,262
Cost of sales	126,335,995	113,598,417
Gross profit	**71,354,943**	**95,564,845**
Selling and administrative expenses	47,528,721	45,038,298
Operating profit	**23,826,222**	**50,526,547**
Other non-operating income	1,526,149	1,274,207
Other non-operating expense	1,213,861	979,886
Share of net profit of associates and joint ventures	354,332	463,203
Financial income	8,718,988	8,579,720
Financial expense	7,100,090	7,386,694
Profit before income tax	**26,111,740**	**52,477,097**
Income tax expense	7,459,135	14,427,866
Profit for the year	**$ 18,652,605**	**$ 38,049,231**
Profit attributable to owners of the parent company	$ 18,451,988	$ 37,659,703
Profit attributable to non-controlling interests	$ 200,617	$ 389,528
Earnings per share (in US dollars)		
—Basic	$ 2.72	$ 5.54
—Diluted	2.72	5.54

The above consolidated statement of financial position should be read in conjunction with the accompanying notes.

Samsung Electronics Co., Ltd. and Subsidiaries
CONSOLIDATED STATEMENTS OF COMPREHENSIVE INCOME

For the year ended December 31	2019	2018
In thousands of US dollars		
Profit for the year	**$18,652,605**	**$38,049,231**
Other comprehensive income (loss)		
Items that will not be reclassified to profit or loss subsequently:		
Gain (loss) on valuation of financial assets at fair value through other comprehensive income, net of tax	983,817	(202,380)
Share of other comprehensive loss of associates and joint ventures, net of tax	(14,497)	(9,122)
Remeasurement of net defined benefit liabilities (assets), net of tax	(1,012,877)	(351,922)
Items that may be reclassified to profit or loss subsequently:		
Share of other comprehensive income of associates and joint ventures, net of tax	41,742	5,739
Foreign currency translation, net of tax	2,588,248	506,786
Gain on valuation of cash flow hedge derivatives	1,553	40,395
Other comprehensive income (loss) for the year, net of tax	**2,587,986**	**(10,504)**
Total comprehensive income for the year	**$21,240,591**	**$38,038,727**
Comprehensive income attributable to:		
Owners of the parent company	$20,993,415	$37,652,492
Non-controlling interests	$ 247,176	$ 386,235

The above consolidated statement of financial position should be read in conjunction with the accompanying notes.

SAMSUNG

Samsung Electronics Co., Ltd. and Subsidiaries
CONSOLIDATED STATEMENTS OF CHANGES IN EQUITY
(In thousands of US dollars)

	Preference shares	Ordinary shares	Share premium	Retained earnings	Other components of equity	Equity attributable to owners of the parent company	Non-controlling interests	Total
Balance as of January 1, 2018	**102,506**	**667,588**	**$3,778,674**	**$185,172,550**	**$(11,925,927)**	**$177,795,391**	**$6,244,755**	**$184,040,146**
Cumulative effect of changes in accounting policies	—	—	—	211,529	(224,576)	(13,047)		(13,047)
Restated total equity at the beginning of the financial year	**102,506**	**667,588**	**3,778,674**	**185,384,079**	**(12,150,503)**	**177,782,344**	**6,244,755**	**184,027,099**
Profit for the year	—	—	—	37,659,703	—	37,659,703	389,528	38,049,231
Gain (loss) on valuation of financial assets at fair value through other comprehensive income, net of tax	—	—	—	(2,581)	(202,789)	(205,370)	2,990	(202,380)
Share of other comprehensive income (loss) of associates and joint ventures, net of tax	—	—	—	—	(3,463)	(3,463)	80	(3,383)
Foreign currency translation, net of tax	—	—	—	—	497,023	497,023	9,763	506,786
Remeasurement of net defined benefit liabilities (assets), net of tax	—	—	—	—	(335,796)	(335,796)	(16,126)	(351,922)
Gain on valuation of cash flow hedge derivatives	—	—	—	—	40,395	40,395	—	40,395
Total comprehensive income (loss)	—	—	—	**37,657,122**	**(4,630)**	**37,652,492**	**386,235**	**38,038,727**
Dividends	—	—	—	(8,703,297)	—	(8,703,297)	(43,465)	(8,746,762)
Capital transaction under common control	—	—	—	—	1,474	1,474	6,856	8,330
Changes in consolidated entities	—	—	—	—	—	—	35	35
Acquisition of treasury shares	—	—	—	—	(750,872)	(750,872)	—	(750,872)
Retirement of treasury shares	—	—	—	(6,094,845)	6,094,845	—	—	—
Other	—	—	—	—	4,330	4,330	(1,153)	3,177
Total transactions with owners	—	—	—	**(14,798,142)**	**5,349,777**	**(9,448,365)**	**(37,727)**	**(9,486,092)**
Balance as of December 31, 2018	**102,506**	**667,588**	**3,778,674**	**208,243,059**	**(6,805,356)**	**205,986,471**	**6,593,263**	**212,579,734**
Balance as of January 1, 2019	**102,506**	**667,588**	**3,778,674**	**208,243,059**	**(6,805,356)**	**205,986,471**	**6,593,263**	**212,579,734**
Profit for the year	—	—	—	18,451,988		18,451,988	200,617	18,652,605
Gain (loss) on valuation of financial assets at fair value through other comprehensive income, net of tax	—	—	—	(1,085)	953,498	952,413	31,404	983,817
Share of other comprehensive income (loss) of associates and joint ventures, net of tax	—	—	—	(522)	27,009	26,487	758	27,245
Foreign currency translation, net of tax	—	—	—	—	2,545,753	2,545,753	42,495	2,588,248
Remeasurement of net defined benefit liabilities (assets), net of tax	—	—	—	—	(984,779)	(984,779)	(28,098)	(1,012,877)
Gain on valuation of cash flow hedge derivatives	—	—	—	—	1,553	1,553	—	1,553
Total comprehensive income	—	—	—	**18,450,381**	**2,543,034**	**20,993,415**	**247,176**	**21,240,591**
Dividends	—	—	—	(8,253,602)	—	(8,253,602)	(18,327)	(8,271,929)
Capital transaction under common control	—	—	—	—	(73)	(73)	6,312	6,239
Changes in consolidated entities	—	—	—	—	—	—	4,917	4,917
Other	—	—	—	—	(1,011)	(1,011)	827	(184)
Total transactions with owners	—	—	—	**(8,253,602)**	**(1,084)**	**(8,254,686)**	**(6,271)**	**(8,260,957)**
Balance as of December 31, 2019	**102,506**	**667,588**	**$3,778,674**	**$218,439,838**	**$(4,263,406)**	**$218,725,200**	**$6,834,168**	**$225,559,368**

The above consolidated statement of financial position should be read in conjunction with the accompanying notes.

SAMSUNG

Samsung Electronics Co., Ltd. and Subsidiaries
CONSOLIDATED STATEMENTS OF CASH FLOWS

For the year ended December 31	2019	2018
In thousands of US dollars		
Cash flows from operating activities		
Profit for the year	$18,652,605	$38,049,231
Adjustments	32,126,956	37,414,045
Changes in assets and liabilities arising from operating activities	(2,184,336)	(8,515,406)
Cash generated from operations	**48,595,225**	**66,947,870**
Interest received	1,978,962	1,534,604
Interest paid	(497,640)	(470,434)
Dividends received	207,473	185,328
Income tax paid	(11,344,104)	(10,681,998)
Net cash inflow from operating activities	**38,939,916**	**57,515,370**
Cash flows from investing activities		
Net increase in short-term financial instruments	(1,742,585)	(10,612,375)
Net increase in short-term financial assets at amortized cost	(701,945)	(1,232,856)
Net decrease (increase) in short-term financial assets at fair value through profit or loss	321,746	(119,839)
Disposal of long-term financial instruments	3,935,450	219,527
Acquisition of long-term financial instruments	(10,918,835)	(6,588,518)
Disposal of financial assets at amortized cost	595,974	—
Acquisition of financial assets at amortized cost	(707,898)	(136,183)
Disposal of financial assets at fair value through other comprehensive income	1,351	13,910
Acquisition of financial assets at fair value through other comprehensive income	(54,719)	(391,377)
Disposal of financial assets at fair value through profit or loss	55,189	68,761
Acquisition of financial assets at fair value through profit or loss	(116,543)	(166,327)
Disposal of investment in associates and joint ventures	10,424	127
Acquisition of investment in associates and joint ventures	(10,964)	(43,953)
Disposal of property, plant and equipment	440,397	477,900
Acquisition of property, plant and equipment	(21,766,303)	(25,360,292)
Disposal of intangible assets	6,213	10,241
Acquisition of intangible assets	(2,788,525)	(875,635)
Cash outflow from business combinations	(874,680)	(85,038)
Cash inflow (outflow) from other investing activities	39,512	(1,965)
Net cash outflow from investing activities	**(34,276,741)**	**(44,823,892)**
Cash flows from financing activities		
Net increase (decrease) in short-term borrowings	742,876	(1,755,933)
Acquisition of treasury shares	—	(750,872)
Proceeds from long-term borrowings	—	3,072
Repayment of debentures and long-term borrowings	(608,687)	(1,704,560)
Dividends paid	(8,270,727)	(8,746,499)
Net increase (decrease) in non-controlling interests	(1,459)	6,924
Net cash outflow from financing activities	**(8,137,997)**	**(12,947,868)**
Effect of exchange rate changes on cash and cash equivalents	510,751	80,816
Net decrease in cash and cash equivalents	**(2,964,071)**	**(175,574)**
Cash and cash equivalents		
Beginning of the year	**26,033,073**	**26,208,647**
End of the year	**$23,069,002**	**$26,033,073**

The above consolidated statements of cash flows should be read in conjunction with the accompanying notes.

SAMSUNG

B Time Value of Money

Appendix Preview

PRESENT AND FUTURE VALUE CONCEPTS	VALUE OF A SINGLE AMOUNT	VALUE OF AN ANNUITY
C1 Time is money Concept of interest	**P1** Present value of a single amount **P2** Future value of a single amount NTK B-1, B-2	**P3** Present value of an annuity **P4** Future value of an annuity NTK B-3, B-4

Learning Objectives

CONCEPTUAL

C1 Describe the earning of interest and the concepts of present and future values.

PROCEDURAL

P1 Apply present value concepts to a single amount by using interest tables.

P2 Apply future value concepts to a single amount by using interest tables.

P3 Apply present value concepts to an annuity by using interest tables.

P4 Apply future value concepts to an annuity by using interest tables.

PRESENT AND FUTURE VALUE CONCEPTS

C1 Describe the earning of interest and the concepts of present and future values.

The old saying "Time is money" means that as time passes, the values of assets and liabilities change. This change is due to *interest,* which is a borrower's payment to the owner of an asset for its use. The most common example of interest is a savings account. Cash in the account earns interest paid by the financial institution. An example of a liability is a car loan. As we carry the balance of the loan, we accumulate interest costs on it. We must ultimately repay this loan with interest.

Present and future value computations enable us to measure or estimate the interest component of holding assets or liabilities over time. The present value computation is used to compute the value of future-day assets *today.* The future value computation is used to compute the value of present-day assets *at a future date.* The first section focuses on the present value of a single amount. The second section focuses on the future value of a single amount. Then both the present and future values of a series of amounts (called an *annuity*) are defined and explained.

Decision Insight

What's Five Million Worth? Robert Miles, a maintenance worker, purchased a scratch-off ticket that won him a $5 million jackpot. The $5 million payout was offered to Miles as a $250,000 annuity for 20 years **or** as a lump-sum payment of $3,210,000, which is about $2,124,378 after taxes. ■

PRESENT VALUE OF A SINGLE AMOUNT

Graph of PV of a Single Amount We graphically express the present value, called *p*, of a single future amount, called *f*, that is received or paid at a future date in Exhibit B.1.

EXHIBIT B.1

Present Value of a Single Amount Diagram

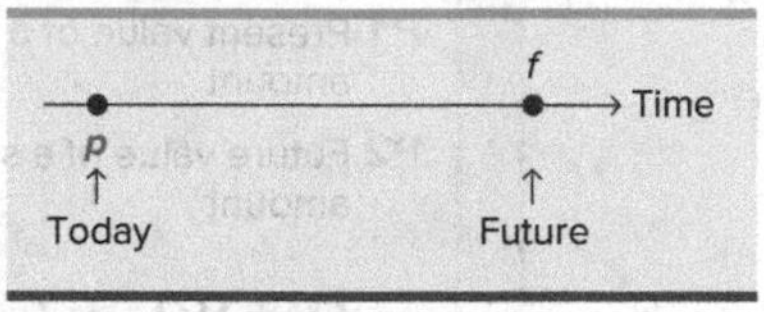

p ↑ Today — f ↑ Future → Time

P1 Apply present value concepts to a single amount by using interest tables.

Formula of PV of a Single Amount The formula to compute the present value of a single amount is shown in Exhibit B.2, where p = present value (PV); f = future value (FV); i = rate of interest per period; and n = number of periods. (Interest is also called the *discount,* and interest rate is also called the *discount rate.*)

EXHIBIT B.2

Present Value of a Single Amount Formula

$$p = \frac{f}{(1 + i)^n}$$

Illustration of PV of a Single Amount for One Period To illustrate present value concepts, assume that we need $220 one period from today. We want to know how much we must invest now, for one period, at an interest rate of 10% to provide for this $220. For this illustration, the *p*, or present value, is the unknown amount—the specifics are shown graphically as follows.

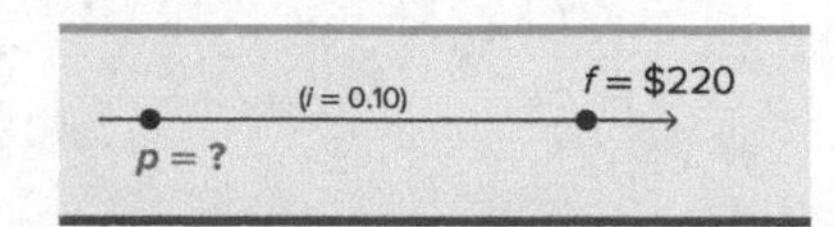

Conceptually, we know *p* must be less than $220. This is clear from the answer to: Would we rather have $220 today or $220 at some future date? If we had $220 today, we could invest it and see it grow to something more than $220 in the future. Therefore, we would prefer the $220 today. This means that if we were promised $220 in the future, we would take less than $220 today. But how much less? To answer that question, we compute an estimate of the present value of the $220 to be received one period from now using the formula in Exhibit B.2 as follows.

$$p = \frac{f}{(1+i)^n} = \frac{\$220}{(1+0.10)^1} = \$200$$

We interpret this result to say that given an interest rate of 10%, we are indifferent between $200 today or $220 at the end of one period.

Illustration of PV of a Single Amount for Multiple Periods We can use this formula to compute the present value for *any number of periods.* To illustrate, consider a payment of $242 at the end of two periods at 10% interest. The present value of this $242 to be received two periods from now is computed as follows.

$$p = \frac{f}{(1+i)^n} = \frac{\$242}{(1+0.10)^2} = \$200$$

Point: Excel for PV.

	A	B
1	Future value	$242
2	Periods	2
3	Period int. rate	10%
4	Present value	

=−PV(B3,B2,0,B1) = $200

Together, these results tell us we are indifferent between $200 today, or $220 one period from today, or $242 two periods from today given a 10% interest rate per period.

The number of periods (*n*) in the present value formula does not have to be expressed in years. Any period of time such as a day, a month, a quarter, or a year can be used. Whatever period is used, the interest rate (*i*) must be compounded for the same period. This means that if a situation expresses *n* in months and *i* equals 12% per year, then *i* is transformed into interest earned per month (or 1%). In this case, interest is said to be *compounded monthly.* For example, the present value of $1 when *n* is 12 months and *i* is 12% compounded monthly follows.

I will pay your allowance at the end of the month. Do you want to wait or receive its present value today?

$$p = \frac{1}{(1+0.01)^{12}} = \$0.8874$$

Using Present Value Table to Compute PV of a Single Amount A present value table helps us with present value computations. It gives us present values (factors) for a variety of both interest rates (*i*) and periods (*n*). Each present value in a present value table assumes that the future value (*f*) equals 1. When the future value (*f*) is different from 1, we simply multiply the present value (*p*) from the table by that future value to give us the estimate. The formula used to construct a table of present values for a single future amount of 1 is shown in Exhibit B.3.

$$p = \frac{1}{(1+i)^n}$$

EXHIBIT B.3

Present Value of 1 Formula

This formula is identical to that in Exhibit B.2 except that *f* equals 1. **Table B.1** at the end of this appendix is such a present value table. It is often called a **present value of 1 table.** A present value table has three factors: *p*, *i*, and *n*. Knowing two of these three factors allows us to compute the third. (A fourth is *f*, but, as already explained, we need only multiply the 1 used in the formula by *f*.) To illustrate the use of a present value table, consider three cases.

Case 1 **Solve for *p* when knowing *i* and *n*.** To show how we use a present value table, let's look again at how we estimate the present value of $220 (the *f* value) at the end of one period ($n = 1$) where the interest rate (*i*) is 10%. To solve this case, we go to the present value table (Table B.1) and look in the row for one period and in the column for 10% interest. Here we find a present value (*p*) of 0.9091 based on a future value of 1. This means, for instance, that $1 to be received one period from today at 10% interest is worth $0.9091 today. Because the future value in this case is not $1 but $220, we multiply the 0.9091 by $220 to get an answer of $200.

Case 2 **Solve for *n* when knowing *p* and *i*.** To illustrate, assume a $100,000 future value (*f*) that is worth $13,000 today (*p*) using an interest rate of 12% (*i*) but where *n* is unknown. In particular, we want to know how many periods (*n*) there are between the present value and the future value. To put this in context, it would fit a situation in which we want to retire with $100,000 but currently have only $13,000 that is earning a 12% return and we are unable to save additional money. How long will it be before we can retire? To answer this, we go to Table B.1

and look in the 12% interest column. Here we find a column of present values (p) based on a future value of 1. To use the present value table for this solution, we must divide $13,000 ($p$) by $100,000 ($f$), which equals 0.1300. This is necessary because *a present value table defines* f *equal to 1, and* p *as a fraction of 1.* We look for a value nearest to 0.1300 (p), which we find in the row for 18 periods (n). This means that the present value of $100,000 at the end of 18 periods at 12% interest is $13,000; alternatively stated, we must work 18 more years.

Case 3 Solve for i when knowing p and n. In this case, we have, say, a $120,000 future value ($f$) worth $60,000 today ($p$) when there are nine periods (n) between the present and future values, but the interest rate is unknown. As an example, suppose we want to retire with $120,000 in nine years, but we have only $60,000 and we are unable to save additional money. What interest rate must we earn to retire with $120,000 in nine years? To answer this, we go to the present value table (Table B.1) and look in the row for nine periods. To use the present value table, we must divide $60,000 ($p$) by $120,000 ($f$), which equals 0.5000. Recall that this step is necessary because a present value table defines f equal to 1 and p as a fraction of 1. We look for a value in the row for nine periods that is nearest to 0.5000 (p), which we find in the column for 8% interest (i). This means that the present value of $120,000 at the end of nine periods at 8% interest is $60,000 or, in our example, we must earn 8% annual interest to retire in nine years.

NEED-TO-KNOW B-1

Present Value of a Single Amount

P1

A company is considering an investment expected to yield $70,000 after six years. If this company demands an 8% return, how much is it willing to pay for this investment today?

Solution

Today's value = $70,000 × 0.6302 = $44,114 (using PV factor from Table B.1, i = 8%, n = 6)

FUTURE VALUE OF A SINGLE AMOUNT

P2

Apply future value concepts to a single amount by using interest tables.

Formula of FV of a Single Amount

We must modify the formula for the present value of a single amount to obtain the formula for the future value of a single amount. In particular, we multiply both sides of the equation in Exhibit B.2 by $(1 + i)^n$ to get the result shown in Exhibit B.4.

EXHIBIT B.4

Future Value of a Single Amount Formula

$$f = p \times (1 \times i)^n$$

Illustration of FV of a Single Amount for One Period

The future value (f) is defined in terms of p, i, and n. We can use this formula to determine that $200 ($p$) invested for one period (n) at an interest rate of 10% (i) yields a future value of $220 as follows.

$$\begin{aligned} f &= p \times (1 + i)^n \\ &= \$200 \times (1 + 0.10)^1 \\ &= \$220 \end{aligned}$$

Illustration of FV of a Single Amount for Multiple Periods

This formula can be used to compute the future value of an amount for *any number of periods* into the future. To illustrate, assume that $200 is invested for three periods at 10%. The future value of this $200 is $266.20, computed as follows.

Point: The FV factor in Table B.2 when n = 3 and i = 10% is 1.3310.

$$\begin{aligned} f &= p \times (1 + i)^n \\ &= \$200 \times (1 + 0.10)^3 \\ &= \$200 \times 1.3310 \\ &= \$266.20 \end{aligned}$$

Point: Excel for FV.

	A	B
1	Present value	$200
2	Periods	3
3	Period int. rate	10%
4	Future value	

=-FV(B3,B2,0,B1) = $266.20

Using Future Value Table to Compute FV of a Single Amount

A future value table makes it easier for us to compute future values (f) for many different combinations of interest rates (i) and time periods (n). Each future value in a future value table assumes the present value (p)

is 1. If the future amount is something other than 1, we multiply our answer by that amount. The formula used to construct a table of future values (factors) for a single amount of 1 is in Exhibit B.5.

$$f = (1 + i)^n$$

EXHIBIT B.5

Future Value of 1 Formula

Table B.2 at the end of this appendix shows a table of future values for a current amount of 1. This type of table is called a **future value of 1 table.**

There are some important relations between Tables B.1 and B.2. In Table B.2, for the row where $n = 0$, the future value is 1 for each interest rate. This is because no interest is earned when time does not pass. We also see that Tables B.1 and B.2 report the same information but in a different manner. In particular, one table is simply the *reciprocal* of the other. To illustrate this inverse relation, let's say we invest $100 for a period of five years at 12% per year. How much do we expect to have after five years? We can answer this question using Table B.2 by finding the future value (f) of 1, for five periods from now, compounded at 12%. From that table we find $f = 1.7623$. If we start with $100, the amount it accumulates to after five years is $176.23 ($100 × 1.7623). We can alternatively use Table B.1. Here we find that the present value (p) of 1, discounted five periods at 12%, is 0.5674. Recall the inverse relation between present value and future value. This means that $p = 1/f$ (or equivalently, $f = 1/p$). We can compute the future value of $100 invested for five periods at 12% as follows: f = $100 × (1/0.5674) = $176.24 (which equals the $176.23 just computed, except for a 1 cent rounding difference).

Point: 1/PV factor = FV factor. 1/FV factor = PV factor.

Point: The FV factor when $n = 2$ and $i = 10\%$ is 1.2100. Its reciprocal, 0.8264, is the PV factor when $n = 2$ and $i = 10\%$.

A future value table has three factors: f, i, and n. Knowing two of these three factors allows us to compute the third. To illustrate, consider three possible cases.

Case 1 Solve for f when knowing i and n. Our preceding example fits this case. We found that $100 invested for five periods at 12% interest accumulates to $176.24.

Case 2 Solve for n when knowing f and i. In this case, we have, say, $2,000 ($p$) and we want to know how many periods (n) it will take to accumulate to $3,000 ($f$) at 7% interest ($i$). To answer this, we go to the future value table (Table B.2) and look in the 7% interest column. Here we find a column of future values (f) based on a present value of 1. To use a future value table, we must divide $3,000 ($f$) by $2,000 ($p$), which equals 1.500. This is necessary because *a future value table defines* p *equal to 1, and* f *as a multiple of 1.* We look for a value nearest to 1.50 (f), which we find in the row for six periods (n). This means that $2,000 invested for six periods at 7% interest accumulates to $3,000.

Case 3 Solve for i when knowing f and n. In this case, we have, say, $2,001 ($p$) today, and in nine years (n) we want to have $4,000 ($f$). What rate of interest must we earn to accomplish this? To answer that, we go to Table B.2 and search in the row for nine periods. To use a future value table, we must divide $4,000 ($f$) by $2,001 ($p$), which equals 1.9990. Recall that this is necessary because a future value table defines p equal to 1 and f as a multiple of 1. We look for a value nearest to 1.9990 (f), which we find in the column for 8% interest (i). This means that $2,001 invested for nine periods at 8% interest accumulates to $4,000.

Decision Maker

Entrepreneur You are a retailer planning a sale on a security system that requires no payments for two years. At the end of two years, buyers must pay the full amount. The system's suggested retail price is $4,100, but you are willing to sell it today for $3,000 cash. What is your sale price if payment will not occur for two years and the market interest rate is 10%? ■ *Answer:* This is a present value question. The interest rate (10%) and present value ($3,000) are known, but the payment required two years later is unknown. The two-year-later price of $3,630 is computed as $3,000 × 1.10 × 1.10. The $3,630 two years from today is equivalent to $3,000 today.

NEED-TO-KNOW B-2

Future Value of a Single Amount

P2

Assume that you win a $150,000 cash sweepstakes today. You decide to deposit this cash in an account earning 8% annual interest, and you plan to quit your job when the account equals $555,000. How many years will it be before you can quit working?

Solution

Future value factor = $555,000/$150,000 = 3.7000

Searching for 3.7 in the 8% column of Table B.2 shows you cannot quit working for 17 years if your deposit earns 8% interest.

PRESENT VALUE OF AN ANNUITY

P3 Apply present value concepts to an annuity by using interest tables.

Graph of PV of an Annuity

An *annuity* is a series of equal payments occurring at equal intervals. One example is a series of three annual payments of $100 each. An *ordinary annuity* is defined as equal end-of-period payments at equal intervals. An ordinary annuity of $100 for three periods and its present value (p) are illustrated in Exhibit B.6.

EXHIBIT B.6

Present Value of an Ordinary Annuity Diagram

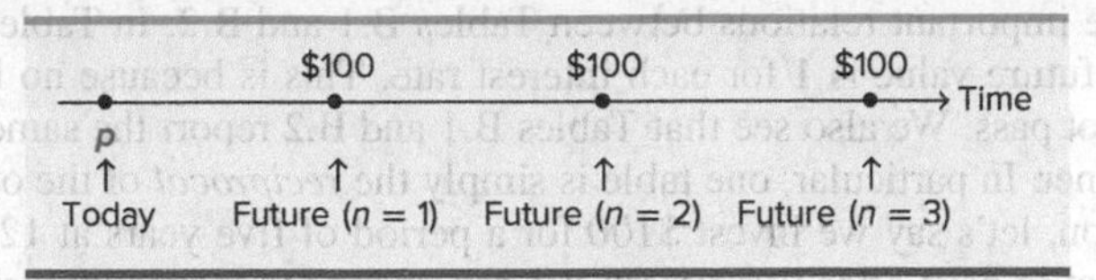

Formula and Illustration of PV of an Annuity

One way to compute the present value of an ordinary annuity is to find the present value of each payment using our present value formula from Exhibit B.3. We then add each of the three present values. To illustrate, let's look at three $100 payments at the end of each of the next three periods with an interest rate of 15%. Our present value computations are

$$p = \frac{\$100}{(1+0.15)^1} + \frac{\$100}{(1+0.15)^2} + \frac{\$100}{(1+0.15)^3} = \$228.32$$

Using Present Value Table to Compute PV of an Annuity

This computation is identical to computing the present value of each payment (from Table B.1) and taking their sum or, alternatively, adding the values from Table B.1 for each of the three payments and multiplying their sum by the $100 annuity payment.

A more direct way is to use a present value of annuity table. **Table B.3** at the end of this appendix is one such table. This table is called a **present value of an annuity of 1 table.** If we look at Table B.3 where $n = 3$ and $i = 15\%$, we see the present value is 2.2832. This means that the present value of an annuity of 1 for three periods, with a 15% interest rate, equals 2.2832.

A present value of an annuity formula is used to construct Table B.3. It also can be constructed by adding the amounts in a present value of 1 table. To illustrate, we use Tables B.1 and B.3 to confirm this relation for the prior example.

From Table B.1		From Table B.3	
$i = 15\%, n = 1$	0.8696		
$i = 15\%, n = 2$	0.7561		
$i = 15\%, n = 3$	0.6575		
Total....................	2.2832	$i = 15\%, n = 3$..........	2.2832

Point: Excel for PV annuity.

	A	B
1	Payment	$100
2	Periods	3
3	Period int. rate	15%
4	Present value	

=–PV(B3,B2,B1) = $228.32

We also can use business calculators or spreadsheet programs to find the present value of an annuity.

Decision Insight

Count Your Blessings "I don't have good luck—I'm blessed," proclaimed Andrew "Jack" Whittaker, a sewage treatment contractor, after winning the largest ever undivided jackpot in a U.S. lottery. Whittaker had to choose between $315 million in 30 annual installments or $170 million in one lump sum ($112 million after taxes). ■

NEED-TO-KNOW B-3

Present Value of an Annuity

P3

A company is considering an investment that would produce payments of $10,000 every six months for three years. The first payment would be received in six months. If this company requires an 8% annual return, what is the maximum amount it is willing to pay for this investment today?

Solution

Maximum paid = $10,000 × 5.2421 = $52,421 (using PV of annuity factor from Table B.3, $i = 4\%$, $n = 6$)

FUTURE VALUE OF AN ANNUITY

P4 Apply future value concepts to an annuity by using interest tables.

Graph of FV of an Annuity The future value of an *ordinary annuity* is the accumulated value of each annuity payment with interest as of the date of the final payment. To illustrate, let's consider the earlier annuity of three annual payments of $100. Exhibit B.7 shows the point in time for the future value (f). The first payment is made two periods prior to the point when future value is determined, and the final payment occurs on the future value date.

EXHIBIT B.7

Future Value of an Ordinary Annuity Diagram

	$100	$100	$100 → Time ($f$)
Today	Future (n = 1)	Future (n = 2)	Future (n = 3)

Formula and Illustration of FV of an Annuity One way to compute the future value of an annuity is to use the formula to find the future value of *each* payment and add them. If we assume an interest rate of 15%, our calculation is

Point: An ordinary annuity is a series of equal cash flows, with the payment at the *end* of each period.

$$f = \$100 \times (1 + 0.15)^2 + \$100 \times (1 + 0.15)^1 + \$100 \times (1 + 0.15)^0 = \$347.25$$

This is identical to using Table B.2 and summing the future values of each payment, or adding the future values of the three payments of 1 and multiplying the sum by $100.

Using Future Value Table to Compute FV of an Annuity A more direct way is to use a table showing future values of annuities. Such a table is called a **future value of an annuity of 1 table. Table B.4** at the end of this appendix is one such table. Note that in Table B.4 when $n = 1$, the future values equal 1 ($f = 1$) for all rates of interest. This is because such an annuity consists of only one payment, and the future value is determined on the date of that payment—no time passes between the payment and its future value. The future value of an annuity formula is used to construct Table B.4. We also can construct it by adding the amounts from a future value of 1 table. To illustrate, we use Tables B.2 and B.4 to confirm this relation for the prior example.

From Table B.2		From Table B.4	
i = 15%, n = 0	1.0000		
i = 15%, n = 1	1.1500		
i = 15%, n = 2	1.3225		
Total....................	3.4725	i = 15%, n = 3..........	3.4725

Point: Excel for FV annuity.

	A	B
1	Payment	$100
2	Periods	3
3	Period int. rate	15%
4	Future value	

=–FV(B3,B2,B1) = $347.25

Note that the future value in Table B.2 is 1.0000 when $n = 0$, but the future value in Table B.4 is 1.0000 when $n = 1$. Is this a contradiction? No. When $n = 0$ in Table B.2, the future value is determined on the date when a single payment occurs. This means that no interest is earned because no time has passed, and the future value equals the payment. Table B.4 describes annuities with equal payments occurring at the end of each period. When $n = 1$, the annuity has one payment, and its future value equals 1 on the date of its final and only payment. Again, no time passes between the payment and its future value date.

NEED-TO-KNOW B-4

Future Value of an Annuity

P4

A company invests $45,000 per year for five years at 12% annual interest. Compute the value of this annuity investment at the end of five years.

Solution

Future value = $45,000 × 6.3528 = $285,876 (using FV of annuity factor from Table B.4, i = 12%, n = 5)

Summary: Cheat Sheet

PV OF A SINGLE AMOUNT

$p = \frac{f}{(1+i)^n}$ where p = present value (PV); f = future value (FV); i = rate of interest per period; and n = number of periods. Excel follows:

Point: Excel for PV.

	A	B
1	Future value	$242
2	Periods	2
3	Period int. rate	10%
4	Present value	

=−PV(B3,B2,0,B1) = $200

PV OF AN ANNUITY

$p = f \times \left[1 - \frac{1}{(1+i)^n}\right]/i$ where p = present value (PV); f = future value (FV); i = rate of interest per period; and n = number of periods. Excel follows:

Point: Excel for PV annuity.

	A	B
1	Payment	$100
2	Periods	3
3	Period int. rate	15%
4	Present value	

=−PV(B3,B2,B1) = $228.32

FV OF A SINGLE AMOUNT

$f = p \times (1+i)^n$ where p = present value (PV); f = future value (FV); i = rate of interest per period; and n = number of periods. Excel follows:

Point: Excel for FV.

	A	B
1	Present value	$200
2	Periods	2
3	Period int. rate	10%
4	Future value	

=−FV(B3,B2,0,B1) = $266.20

FV OF AN ANNUITY

$f = p \times [(1+i)^n - 1]/i$ where p = present value (PV); f = future value (FV); i = rate of interest per period; and n = number of periods. Excel follows:

Point: Excel for FV annuity.

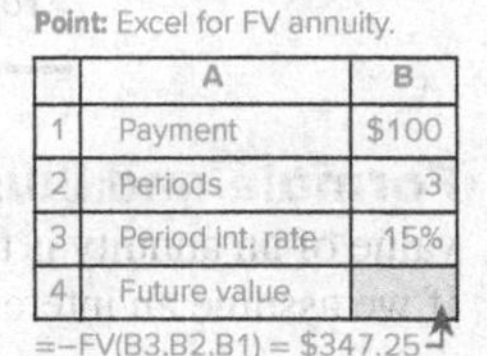

	A	B
1	Payment	$100
2	Periods	3
3	Period int. rate	15%
4	Future value	

=−FV(B3,B2,B1) = $347.25

Select Quick Study and Exercise assignments feature Guided Example videos, called "Hints" in Connect. Hints use different numbers, and instructors can turn this feature on or off.

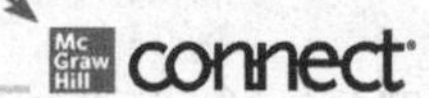

QUICK STUDY

QS B-1
Identifying interest rates in tables
C1

Assume that you must estimate what the future value will be two years from today using the *future value of 1 table* (Table B.2). Which interest rate column *and* number-of-periods row do you use when working with the following rates?

1. 12% annual rate, compounded annually
2. 6% annual rate, compounded semiannually
3. 8% annual rate, compounded quarterly
4. 12% annual rate, compounded monthly (the answer for number-of-periods in part 4 is not shown in Table B.2)

QS B-2
Interest rate on an investment P1

Ken Francis is offered the possibility of investing $2,745 today; in return, he would receive $10,000 after 15 years. What is the annual rate of interest for this investment? (Use Table B.1.)

QS B-3
Number of periods of an investment P1

Megan Brink is offered the possibility of investing $6,651 today at 6% interest per year in a desire to accumulate $10,000. How many years must Brink wait to accumulate $10,000? (Use Table B.1.)

QS B-4
Present value of an amount P1

Flaherty is considering an investment that, if paid for immediately, is expected to return $140,000 five years from now. If Flaherty demands a 9% return, how much is she willing to pay for this investment?

QS B-5
Future value of an amount P2

CII, Inc., invests $630,000 in a project expected to earn a 12% annual rate of return. The earnings will be reinvested in the project each year until the entire investment is liquidated 10 years later. What will the cash proceeds be when the project is liquidated?

QS B-6
Present value of an annuity P3

Beene Distributing is considering a project that will return $150,000 annually at the end of each year for the next six years. If Beene demands an annual return of 7% and pays for the project immediately, how much is it willing to pay for the project?

QS B-7
Future value of an annuity P4

Claire Fitch is planning to begin an individual retirement program in which she will invest $1,500 at the end of each year. Fitch plans to retire after making 30 annual investments in the program earning a return of 10%. What is the value of the program on the date of the last payment (30 years from the present)?

connect

EXERCISES

Exercise B-1
Present value of an amount P1

Mike Derr Company expects to earn 10% per year on an investment that will pay $606,773 six years from now. Use Table B.1 to compute the present value of this investment. (Round the amount to the nearest dollar.)

Exercise B-2
Present value of an amount P1

On January 1, a company agrees to pay $20,000 in three years. If the annual interest rate is 10%, determine how much cash the company can borrow with this agreement.

Exercise B-3
Number of periods of an investment P2

Tom Thompson expects to invest $10,000 at 12% and, at the end of a certain period, receive $96,463. How many years will it be before Thompson receives the payment? (Use Table B.2.)

Exercise B-4
Interest rate on an investment P2

Bill Padley expects to invest $10,000 for 25 years, after which he wants to receive $108,347. What rate of interest must Padley earn? (Use Table B.2.)

Exercise B-5
Future value of an amount P2

Mark Welsch deposits $7,200 in an account that earns interest at an annual rate of 8%, compounded quarterly. The $7,200 plus earned interest must remain in the account 10 years before it can be withdrawn. How much money will be in the account at the end of 10 years?

Exercise B-6
Future value of an amount P2

Catten, Inc., invests $163,170 today earning 7% per year for nine years. Use Table B.2 to compute the future value of the investment nine years from now. (Round the amount to the nearest dollar.)

Exercise B-7
Interest rate on an investment P3

Jones expects an immediate investment of $57,466 to return $10,000 annually for eight years, with the first payment to be received one year from now. What rate of interest must Jones earn? (Use Table B.3.)

Exercise B-8
Number of periods of an investment P3

Keith Riggins expects an investment of $82,014 to return $10,000 annually for several years. If Riggins earns a return of 10%, how many annual payments will he receive? (Use Table B.3.)

Exercise B-9
Present value of an annuity P3

Dave Krug finances a new automobile by paying $6,500 cash and agreeing to make 40 monthly payments of $500 each, the first payment to be made one month after the purchase. The loan bears interest at an annual rate of 12%. What is the cost of the automobile?

Exercise B-10
Present values of annuities P3

C&H Ski Club recently borrowed money and agreed to pay it back with a series of six annual payments of $5,000 each. C&H subsequently borrows more money and agrees to pay it back with a series of four annual payments of $7,500 each. The annual interest rate for both loans is 6%.

1. Use Table B.1 to find the present value of these two separate annuities. (Round amounts to the nearest dollar.)
2. Use Table B.3 to find the present value of these two separate annuities. (Round amounts to the nearest dollar.)

Exercise B-11
Present value with semiannual compounding C1 P3

Otto Co. borrows money on January 1 and promises to pay it back in four semiannual payments of $13,000 each on June 30 and December 31 of both this year and next year.

1. How much money is Otto able to borrow if the interest rate is 8%, compounded semiannually?
2. How much money is Otto able to borrow if the interest rate is 12%, compounded semiannually?
3. How much money is Otto able to borrow if the interest rate is 16%, compounded semiannually?

Exercise B-12
Present value of bonds P1 P3

Spiller Corp. plans to issue 10%, 15-year, $500,000 par value bonds payable that pay interest semiannually on June 30 and December 31. The bonds are dated January 1 of the current year and are issued on that date. If the market rate of interest for the bonds is 8% on the date of issue, what will be the total cash proceeds from the bond issue?

Exercise B-13
Present value of an amount and of an annuity
P1 P3

Compute the amount that can be borrowed under each of the following circumstances:

1. A promise to repay $90,000 seven years from now at an interest rate of 6%.
2. An agreement to make three separate annual payments of $20,000, with the first payment occurring 1 year from now. The annual interest rate is 10%.

Exercise B-14
Interest rate on an investment P4

Algoe expects to invest $1,000 annually for 40 years to yield an accumulated value of $154,762 on the date of the last investment. For this to occur, what rate of interest must Algoe earn? (Use Table B.4.)

Exercise B-15
Number of periods of an investment P4

Steffi Derr expects to invest $10,000 annually that will earn 8%. How many annual investments must Derr make to accumulate $303,243 on the date of the last investment? (Use Table B.4.)

Exercise B-16
Future value of an annuity P4

Kelly Malone plans to have $50 withheld from her monthly paycheck and deposited in a savings account that earns 12% annually, compounded monthly. If Malone continues with her plan for two and one-half years, how much will be accumulated in the account on the date of the last deposit?

Exercise B-17
Future value of an amount plus an annuity
P2 P4

Starr Company decides to establish a fund that it will use 10 years from now to replace an aging production facility. The company will make a $100,000 initial contribution to the fund and plans to make quarterly contributions of $50,000 beginning in three months. The fund earns 12%, compounded quarterly. What will be the value of the fund 10 years from now?

Exercise B-18
Practical applications of the time value of money
P1 P2 P3 P4

a. How much would you have to deposit today if you wanted to have $60,000 in four years? Annual interest rate is 9%.

b. Assume that you are saving up for a trip around the world when you graduate in two years. If you can earn 8% on your investments, how much would you have to deposit today to have $15,000 when you graduate?

c. Would you rather have $463 now or $1,000 ten years from now? Assume that you can earn 9% on your investments.

d. Assume that a college parking sticker today costs $90. If the cost of parking is increasing at the rate of 5% per year, how much will the college parking sticker cost in eight years?

e. Assume that the average price of a new home is $158,500. If the cost of a new home is increasing at a rate of 10% per year, how much will a new home cost in eight years?

f. An investment will pay you $10,000 in 10 years *and* it also will pay you $400 at the end of *each* of the next 10 years (Years 1 through 10). If the annual interest rate is 6%, how much would you be willing to pay today for this type of investment?

g. A college student is reported in the newspaper as having won $10,000,000 in the Kansas State Lottery. However, as is often the custom with lotteries, she does *not* actually receive the entire $10 million now. Instead she will receive $500,000 at the end of the year for *each* of the next 20 years. If the annual interest rate is 6%, what is the present value (today's amount) that she won? (Ignore taxes.)

Exercise B-19
Using present and future value tables
C1 P1 P2 P3 P4

For each of the following situations, identify (1) the case as either (*a*) a present or a future value and (*b*) a single amount or an annuity, (2) the table you would use in your computations (but do not solve the problem), and (3) the interest rate and time periods you would use.

a. You need to accumulate $10,000 for a trip you wish to take in four years. You are able to earn 8% compounded semiannually on your savings. You plan to make only one deposit and let the money accumulate for four years. How would you determine the amount of the one-time deposit?

b. Assume the same facts as in part (*a*) except that you will make semiannual deposits to your savings account.

c. You want to retire after working 40 years with savings in excess of $1,000,000. You expect to save $4,000 a year for 40 years and earn an annual rate of interest of 8%. Will you be able to retire with more than $1,000,000 in 40 years? Explain.

d. A sweepstakes agency names you a grand prize winner. You can take $225,000 immediately or elect to receive annual installments of $30,000 for 20 years. You can earn 10% annually on any investments you make. Which prize do you choose to receive?

$p = 1/(1+i)^n$

TABLE B.1*

Present Value of 1

Periods	1%	2%	3%	4%	5%	6%	7%	8%	9%	10%	12%	15%	Periods
						Rate							
1	0.9901	0.9804	0.9709	0.9615	0.9524	0.9434	0.9346	0.9259	0.9174	0.9091	0.8929	0.8696	1
2	0.9803	0.9612	0.9426	0.9246	0.9070	0.8900	0.8734	0.8573	0.8417	0.8264	0.7972	0.7561	2
3	0.9706	0.9423	0.9151	0.8890	0.8638	0.8396	0.8163	0.7938	0.7722	0.7513	0.7118	0.6575	3
4	0.9610	0.9238	0.8885	0.8548	0.8227	0.7921	0.7629	0.7350	0.7084	0.6830	0.6355	0.5718	4
5	0.9515	0.9057	0.8626	0.8219	0.7835	0.7473	0.7130	0.6806	0.6499	0.6209	0.5674	0.4972	5
6	0.9420	0.8880	0.8375	0.7903	0.7462	0.7050	0.6663	0.6302	0.5963	0.5645	0.5066	0.4323	6
7	0.9327	0.8706	0.8131	0.7599	0.7107	0.6651	0.6227	0.5835	0.5470	0.5132	0.4523	0.3759	7
8	0.9235	0.8535	0.7894	0.7307	0.6768	0.6274	0.5820	0.5403	0.5019	0.4665	0.4039	0.3269	8
9	0.9143	0.8368	0.7664	0.7026	0.6446	0.5919	0.5439	0.5002	0.4604	0.4241	0.3606	0.2843	9
10	0.9053	0.8203	0.7441	0.6756	0.6139	0.5584	0.5083	0.4632	0.4224	0.3855	0.3220	0.2472	10
11	0.8963	0.8043	0.7224	0.6496	0.5847	0.5268	0.4751	0.4289	0.3875	0.3505	0.2875	0.2149	11
12	0.8874	0.7885	0.7014	0.6246	0.5568	0.4970	0.4440	0.3971	0.3555	0.3186	0.2567	0.1869	12
13	0.8787	0.7730	0.6810	0.6006	0.5303	0.4688	0.4150	0.3677	0.3262	0.2897	0.2292	0.1625	13
14	0.8700	0.7579	0.6611	0.5775	0.5051	0.4423	0.3878	0.3405	0.2992	0.2633	0.2046	0.1413	14
15	0.8613	0.7430	0.6419	0.5553	0.4810	0.4173	0.3624	0.3152	0.2745	0.2394	0.1827	0.1229	15
16	0.8528	0.7284	0.6232	0.5339	0.4581	0.3936	0.3387	0.2919	0.2519	0.2176	0.1631	0.1069	16
17	0.8444	0.7142	0.6050	0.5134	0.4363	0.3714	0.3166	0.2703	0.2311	0.1978	0.1456	0.0929	17
18	0.8360	0.7002	0.5874	0.4936	0.4155	0.3503	0.2959	0.2502	0.2120	0.1799	0.1300	0.0808	18
19	0.8277	0.6864	0.5703	0.4746	0.3957	0.3305	0.2765	0.2317	0.1945	0.1635	0.1161	0.0703	19
20	0.8195	0.6730	0.5537	0.4564	0.3769	0.3118	0.2584	0.2145	0.1784	0.1486	0.1037	0.0611	20
25	0.7798	0.6095	0.4776	0.3751	0.2953	0.2330	0.1842	0.1460	0.1160	0.0923	0.0588	0.0304	25
30	0.7419	0.5521	0.4120	0.3083	0.2314	0.1741	0.1314	0.0994	0.0754	0.0573	0.0334	0.0151	30
35	0.7059	0.5000	0.3554	0.2534	0.1813	0.1301	0.0937	0.0676	0.0490	0.0356	0.0189	0.0075	35
40	0.6717	0.4529	0.3066	0.2083	0.1420	0.0972	0.0668	0.0460	0.0318	0.0221	0.0107	0.0037	40

*Used to compute the present value of a known future amount. For example: How much would you need to invest today at 10% compounded semiannually to accumulate $5,000 in 6 years from today? Using the factors of $n = 12$ and $i = 5\%$ (12 semiannual periods and a semiannual rate of 5%), the factor is 0.5568. You would need to invest $2,784 today ($5,000 × 0.5568).

$f = (1+i)^n$

TABLE B.2†

Future Value of 1

Periods	1%	2%	3%	4%	5%	6%	7%	8%	9%	10%	12%	15%	Periods
						Rate							
0	1.0000	1.0000	1.0000	1.0000	1.0000	1.0000	1.0000	1.0000	1.0000	1.0000	1.0000	1.0000	0
1	1.0100	1.0200	1.0300	1.0400	1.0500	1.0600	1.0700	1.0800	1.0900	1.1000	1.1200	1.1500	1
2	1.0201	1.0404	1.0609	1.0816	1.1025	1.1236	1.1449	1.1664	1.1881	1.2100	1.2544	1.3225	2
3	1.0303	1.0612	1.0927	1.1249	1.1576	1.1910	1.2250	1.2597	1.2950	1.3310	1.4049	1.5209	3
4	1.0406	1.0824	1.1255	1.1699	1.2155	1.2625	1.3108	1.3605	1.4116	1.4641	1.5735	1.7490	4
5	1.0510	1.1041	1.1593	1.2167	1.2763	1.3382	1.4026	1.4693	1.5386	1.6105	1.7623	2.0114	5
6	1.0615	1.1262	1.1941	1.2653	1.3401	1.4185	1.5007	1.5869	1.6771	1.7716	1.9738	2.3131	6
7	1.0721	1.1487	1.2299	1.3159	1.4071	1.5036	1.6058	1.7138	1.8280	1.9487	2.2107	2.6600	7
8	1.0829	1.1717	1.2668	1.3686	1.4775	1.5938	1.7182	1.8509	1.9926	2.1436	2.4760	3.0590	8
9	1.0937	1.1951	1.3048	1.4233	1.5513	1.6895	1.8385	1.9990	2.1719	2.3579	2.7731	3.5179	9
10	1.1046	1.2190	1.3439	1.4802	1.6289	1.7908	1.9672	2.1589	2.3674	2.5937	3.1058	4.0456	10
11	1.1157	1.2434	1.3842	1.5395	1.7103	1.8983	2.1049	2.3316	2.5804	2.8531	3.4785	4.6524	11
12	1.1268	1.2682	1.4258	1.6010	1.7959	2.0122	2.2522	2.5182	2.8127	3.1384	3.8960	5.3503	12
13	1.1381	1.2936	1.4685	1.6651	1.8856	2.1329	2.4098	2.7196	3.0658	3.4523	4.3635	6.1528	13
14	1.1495	1.3195	1.5126	1.7317	1.9799	2.2609	2.5785	2.9372	3.3417	3.7975	4.8871	7.0757	14
15	1.1610	1.3459	1.5580	1.8009	2.0789	2.3966	2.7590	3.1722	3.6425	4.1772	5.4736	8.1371	15
16	1.1726	1.3728	1.6047	1.8730	2.1829	2.5404	2.9522	3.4259	3.9703	4.5950	6.1304	9.3576	16
17	1.1843	1.4002	1.6528	1.9479	2.2920	2.6928	3.1588	3.7000	4.3276	5.0545	6.8660	10.7613	17
18	1.1961	1.4282	1.7024	2.0258	2.4066	2.8543	3.3799	3.9960	4.7171	5.5599	7.6900	12.3755	18
19	1.2081	1.4568	1.7535	2.1068	2.5270	3.0256	3.6165	4.3157	5.1417	6.1159	8.6128	14.2318	19
20	1.2202	1.4859	1.8061	2.1911	2.6533	3.2071	3.8697	4.6610	5.6044	6.7275	9.6463	16.3665	20
25	1.2824	1.6406	2.0938	2.6658	3.3864	4.2919	5.4274	6.8485	8.6231	10.8347	17.0001	32.9190	25
30	1.3478	1.8114	2.4273	3.2434	4.3219	5.7435	7.6123	10.0627	13.2677	17.4494	29.9599	66.2118	30
35	1.4166	1.9999	2.8139	3.9461	5.5160	7.6861	10.6766	14.7853	20.4140	28.1024	52.7996	133.1755	35
40	1.4889	2.2080	3.2620	4.8010	7.0400	10.2857	14.9745	21.7245	31.4094	45.2593	93.0510	267.8635	40

†Used to compute the future value of a known present amount. For example: What is the accumulated value of $3,000 invested today at 8% compounded quarterly for 5 years? Using the factors of $n = 20$ and $i = 2\%$ (20 quarterly periods and a quarterly interest rate of 2%), the factor is 1.4859. The accumulated value is $4,457.70 ($3,000 × 1.4859).

TABLE B.3[‡]

Present Value of an Annuity of 1

$$p = \left[1 - \frac{1}{(1+i)^n}\right] / i$$

Periods	1%	2%	3%	4%	5%	6%	7%	8%	9%	10%	12%	15%	Periods
	Rate												
1	0.9901	0.9804	0.9709	0.9615	0.9524	0.9434	0.9346	0.9259	0.9174	0.9091	0.8929	0.8696	1
2	1.9704	1.9416	1.9135	1.8861	1.8594	1.8334	1.8080	1.7833	1.7591	1.7355	1.6901	1.6257	2
3	2.9410	2.8839	2.8286	2.7751	2.7232	2.6730	2.6243	2.5771	2.5313	2.4869	2.4018	2.2832	3
4	3.9020	3.8077	3.7171	3.6299	3.5460	3.4651	3.3872	3.3121	3.2397	3.1699	3.0373	2.8550	4
5	4.8534	4.7135	4.5797	4.4518	4.3295	4.2124	4.1002	3.9927	3.8897	3.7908	3.6048	3.3522	5
6	5.7955	5.6014	5.4172	5.2421	5.0757	4.9173	4.7665	4.6229	4.4859	4.3553	4.1114	3.7845	6
7	6.7282	6.4720	6.2303	6.0021	5.7864	5.5824	5.3893	5.2064	5.0330	4.8684	4.5638	4.1604	7
8	7.6517	7.3255	7.0197	6.7327	6.4632	6.2098	5.9713	5.7466	5.5348	5.3349	4.9676	4.4873	8
9	8.5660	8.1622	7.7861	7.4353	7.1078	6.8017	6.5152	6.2469	5.9952	5.7590	5.3282	4.7716	9
10	9.4713	8.9826	8.5302	8.1109	7.7217	7.3601	7.0236	6.7101	6.4177	6.1446	5.6502	5.0188	10
11	10.3676	9.7868	9.2526	8.7605	8.3064	7.8869	7.4987	7.1390	6.8052	6.4951	5.9377	5.2337	11
12	11.2551	10.5753	9.9540	9.3851	8.8633	8.3838	7.9427	7.5361	7.1607	6.8137	6.1944	5.4206	12
13	12.1337	11.3484	10.6350	9.9856	9.3936	8.8527	8.3577	7.9038	7.4869	7.1034	6.4235	5.5831	13
14	13.0037	12.1062	11.2961	10.5631	9.8986	9.2950	8.7455	8.2442	7.7862	7.3667	6.6282	5.7245	14
15	13.8651	12.8493	11.9379	11.1184	10.3797	9.7122	9.1079	8.5595	8.0607	7.6061	6.8109	5.8474	15
16	14.7179	13.5777	12.5611	11.6523	10.8378	10.1059	9.4466	8.8514	8.3126	7.8237	6.9740	5.9542	16
17	15.5623	14.2919	13.1661	12.1657	11.2741	10.4773	9.7632	9.1216	8.5436	8.0216	7.1196	6.0472	17
18	16.3983	14.9920	13.7535	12.6593	11.6896	10.8276	10.0591	9.3719	8.7556	8.2014	7.2497	6.1280	18
19	17.2260	15.6785	14.3238	13.1339	12.0853	11.1581	10.3356	9.6036	8.9501	8.3649	7.3658	6.1982	19
20	18.0456	16.3514	14.8775	13.5903	12.4622	11.4699	10.5940	9.8181	9.1285	8.5136	7.4694	6.2593	20
25	22.0232	19.5235	17.4131	15.6221	14.0939	12.7834	11.6536	10.6748	9.8226	9.0770	7.8431	6.4641	25
30	25.8077	22.3965	19.6004	17.2920	15.3725	13.7648	12.4090	11.2578	10.2737	9.4269	8.0552	6.5660	30
35	29.4086	24.9986	21.4872	18.6646	16.3742	14.4982	12.9477	11.6546	10.5668	9.6442	8.1755	6.6166	35
40	32.8347	27.3555	23.1148	19.7928	17.1591	15.0463	13.3317	11.9246	10.7574	9.7791	8.2438	6.6418	40

[‡]Used to calculate the present value of a series of equal payments made at the end of each period. For example: What is the present value of \$2,000 per year for 10 years assuming an annual interest rate of 9%? For ($n = 10$, $i = 9\%$), the PV factor is 6.4177. \$2,000 per year for 10 years is the equivalent of \$12,835 today (\$2,000 × 6.4177).

TABLE B.4[§]

Future Value of an Annuity of 1

$$f = [(1+i)^n - 1]/i$$

Periods	1%	2%	3%	4%	5%	6%	7%	8%	9%	10%	12%	15%	Periods
	Rate												
1	1.0000	1.0000	1.0000	1.0000	1.0000	1.0000	1.0000	1.0000	1.0000	1.0000	1.0000	1.0000	1
2	2.0100	2.0200	2.0300	2.0400	2.0500	2.0600	2.0700	2.0800	2.0900	2.1000	2.1200	2.1500	2
3	3.0301	3.0604	3.0909	3.1216	3.1525	3.1836	3.2149	3.2464	3.2781	3.3100	3.3744	3.4725	3
4	4.0604	4.1216	4.1836	4.2465	4.3101	4.3746	4.4399	4.5061	4.5731	4.6410	4.7793	4.9934	4
5	5.1010	5.2040	5.3091	5.4163	5.5256	5.6371	5.7507	5.8666	5.9847	6.1051	6.3528	6.7424	5
6	6.1520	6.3081	6.4684	6.6330	6.8019	6.9753	7.1533	7.3359	7.5233	7.7156	8.1152	8.7537	6
7	7.2135	7.4343	7.6625	7.8983	8.1420	8.3938	8.6540	8.9228	9.2004	9.4872	10.0890	11.0668	7
8	8.2857	8.5830	8.8923	9.2142	9.5491	9.8975	10.2598	10.6366	11.0285	11.4359	12.2997	13.7268	8
9	9.3685	9.7546	10.1591	10.5828	11.0266	11.4913	11.9780	12.4876	13.0210	13.5795	14.7757	16.7858	9
10	10.4622	10.9497	11.4639	12.0061	12.5779	13.1808	13.8164	14.4866	15.1929	15.9374	17.5487	20.3037	10
11	11.5668	12.1687	12.8078	13.4864	14.2068	14.9716	15.7836	16.6455	17.5603	18.5312	20.6546	24.3493	11
12	12.6825	13.4121	14.1920	15.0258	15.9171	16.8699	17.8885	18.9771	20.1407	21.3843	24.1331	29.0017	12
13	13.8093	14.6803	15.6178	16.6268	17.7130	18.8821	20.1406	21.4953	22.9534	24.5227	28.0291	34.3519	13
14	14.9474	15.9739	17.0863	18.2919	19.5986	21.0151	22.5505	24.2149	26.0192	27.9750	32.3926	40.5047	14
15	16.0969	17.2934	18.5989	20.0236	21.5786	23.2760	25.1290	27.1521	29.3609	31.7725	37.2797	47.5804	15
16	17.2579	18.6393	20.1569	21.8245	23.6575	25.6725	27.8881	30.3243	33.0034	35.9497	42.7533	55.7175	16
17	18.4304	20.0121	21.7616	23.6975	25.8404	28.2129	30.8402	33.7502	36.9737	40.5447	48.8837	65.0751	17
18	19.6147	21.4123	23.4144	25.6454	28.1324	30.9057	33.9990	37.4502	41.3013	45.5992	55.7497	75.8364	18
19	20.8109	22.8406	25.1169	27.6712	30.5390	33.7600	37.3790	41.4463	46.0185	51.1591	63.4397	88.2118	19
20	22.0190	24.2974	26.8704	29.7781	33.0660	36.7856	40.9955	45.7620	51.1601	57.2750	72.0524	102.4436	20
25	28.2432	32.0303	36.4593	41.6459	47.7271	54.8645	63.2490	73.1059	84.7009	98.3471	133.3339	212.7930	25
30	34.7849	40.5681	47.5754	56.0849	66.4388	79.0582	94.4608	113.2832	136.3075	164.4940	241.3327	434.7451	30
35	41.6603	49.9945	60.4621	73.6522	90.3203	111.4348	138.2369	172.3168	215.7108	271.0244	431.6635	881.1702	35
40	48.8864	60.4020	75.4013	95.0255	120.7998	154.7620	199.6351	259.0565	337.8824	442.5926	767.0914	1,779.0903	40

[§]Used to calculate the future value of a series of equal payments made at the end of each period. For example: What is the future value of \$4,000 per year for 6 years assuming an annual interest rate of 8%? For ($n = 6$, $i = 8\%$), the FV factor is 7.3359. \$4,000 per year for 6 years accumulates to \$29,343.60 (\$4,000 × 7.3359).

C Activity-Based Costing

Appendix Preview

PLANTWIDE OVERHEAD RATE METHOD	ACTIVITY-BASED COSTING
P1 Plantwide rate	**P2** Three-step method
Allocated cost	Activity rate and allocation
Illustration	Illustration
NTK C-1	**NTK C-2**

Learning Objectives

PROCEDURAL

P1 Allocate overhead costs using the plantwide overhead rate method.

P2 Allocate overhead costs using activity-based costing.

PLANTWIDE OVERHEAD RATE METHOD

P1

Allocate overhead costs using the plantwide overhead rate method.

The *single plantwide overhead rate method,* or *plantwide overhead rate method,* uses one overhead rate to allocate overhead costs. The target of the cost assignment, or **cost object,** is the unit of product—see Exhibit C.1. The rate is determined using volume-related measures such as direct labor hours or machine hours.

EXHIBIT C.1

Plantwide Overhead Rate Method

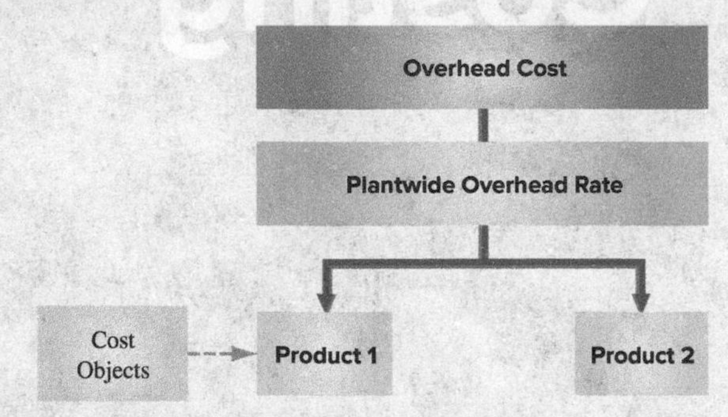

Applying Plantwide Overhead Rate Method

Under the plantwide overhead rate method, total budgeted overhead costs are divided by the allocation base, such as total budgeted direct labor hours, to get the plantwide overhead rate. This rate is used to allocate overhead costs to products based on the actual amount of allocation base used.

To illustrate, consider data from KartCo, a go-kart manufacturer that produces both standard and custom go-karts for amusement parks. The standard go-kart is a basic model sold primarily to amusement parks that service county and state fairs. Custom go-karts are produced for theme parks that need unique go-karts to fit their themes. KartCo allocates overhead using direct labor hours and reports the following budgeted overhead cost and direct labor hours for this year.

Total budgeted overhead cost	$4,800,000
Total budgeted direct labor hours..............	100,000 hours

The two go-karts' total budgeted direct labor hours are in Exhibit C.2.

EXHIBIT C.2

KartCo's Budgeted Production and Direct Labor Hours

	Number of Units	Direct Labor Hours per Unit	Direct Labor Hours
Standard go-kart.....	5,000	15	75,000
Custom go-kart......	1,000	25	25,000
Total..............			100,000

The single plantwide overhead rate is computed as follows.

$$\textbf{Plantwide overhead rate} = \frac{\textbf{Total budgeted overhead cost}}{\textbf{Total budgeted allocation base}} = \frac{\$4{,}800{,}000}{100{,}000\text{ DLH}} = \$48\text{ per DLH}$$

This plantwide overhead rate is then used to allocate overhead cost to products based on the actual number of direct labor hours used to produce each unit as follows.

Allocated cost per unit = Plantwide overhead rate × DLH used

For KartCo, overhead cost is allocated to its two products as follows (on a per unit basis).

Allocated Overhead Cost per Unit
Standard go-kart: $48 per DLH × 15 DLH per unit = $ 720 per unit
Custom go-kart: $48 per DLH × 25 DLH per unit = $1,200 per unit

Exhibit C.3 summarizes overhead allocation for KartCo using the plantwide method.

EXHIBIT C.3

Plantwide Method—KartCo

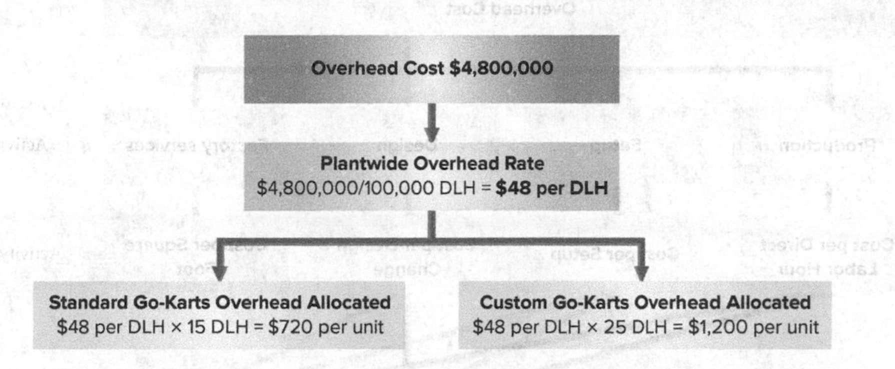

KartCo uses per unit overhead costs to compute the product cost per unit as follows. Direct materials and direct labor costs per unit are taken from its cost records.

Product Cost per Unit Using the Plantwide Rate Method				
	Direct Materials	Direct Labor	Overhead	Product Cost per Unit
Standard go-kart.	$400	$350	$ 720	$1,470
Custom go-kart.	600	500	1,200	2,300

NEED-TO-KNOW C-1

Plantwide Overhead Rate Method

P1

HMS Mfg. budgets total overhead costs of $2,480,000. HMS allocates overhead based on 125,000 budgeted direct labor hours.

1. Compute the single plantwide overhead rate based on budgeted direct labor hours.
2. The company's standard model requires 10 direct labor hours per unit and its deluxe model requires 15 direct labor hours per unit. Compute the overhead cost per unit allocated to these two products.

Solution

1. Plantwide overhead rate = Total budgeted overhead cost/Total budgeted direct labor hours
   = $2,480,000/125,000 = $19.84 per direct labor hour

2.

Allocated Overhead Cost per Unit
Standard: $19.84 per DLH × 10 DLH per unit = $198.40 per unit
Deluxe: $19.84 per DLH × 15 DLH per unit = $297.60 per unit

Do More: QS C-1, QS C-2, QS C-3, QS C-4, E C-1, E C-2, E C-3

ACTIVITY-BASED COSTING

P2 Allocate overhead costs using activity-based costing.

Activity-based costing (ABC) allocates overhead costs by focusing on activities. Unlike the plantwide rate method, ABC uses more than one rate. The basic idea underlying activity-based costing is that an **activity,** which is a task, operation, or procedure, is what causes overhead costs to be incurred. Examples of activities are production setups, machine usage, fabrication, design, assembly, and inspections. Activity-based costing follows three steps—see Exhibit C.4.

1 Identify activities and assign budgeted costs to activity cost pools.

2 Compute overhead activity rates.

3 Allocate overhead costs to cost objects (products).

EXHIBIT C.4
Activity-Based Costing

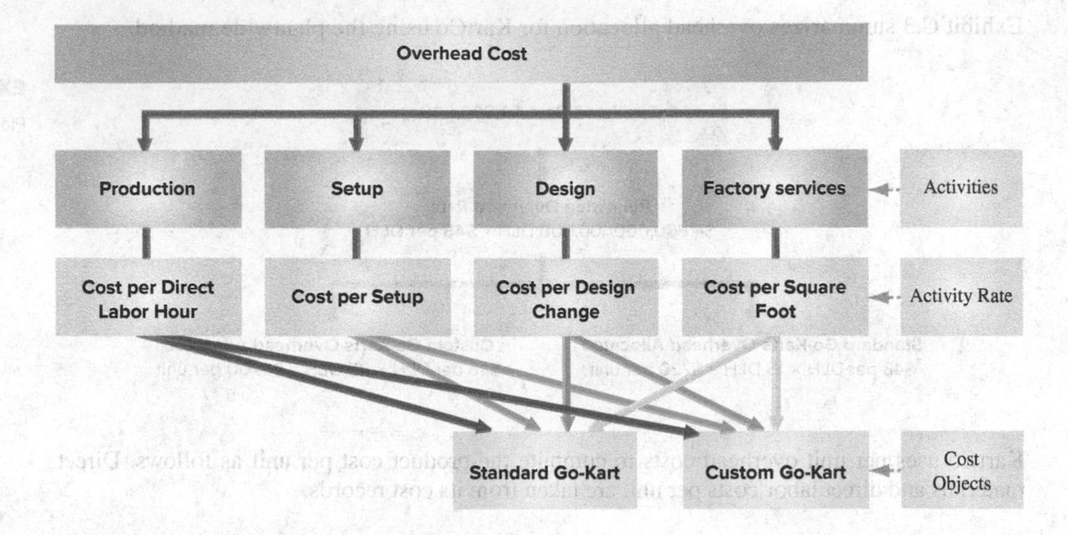

Applying Activity-Based Costing

1 Step 1 identifies individual activities, which are grouped into *cost pools.* An **activity cost pool** is a group of costs that are related to the same activity. An **activity cost driver,** or *cost driver,* is a factor that causes the cost of an activity to go up or down. For example, factory maintenance, cleaning, and utilities can be grouped into a "factory services" activity cost pool because they are related to square feet of space. KartCo applies step 1 below.

Activity	Budgeted Cost	Activity Cost Driver	Budgeted Activity Usage
Production..........	$ 600,000	Direct labor hours	100,000 labor hours
Setup..............	2,000,000	Number of setups	200 setups
Design.............	1,200,000	Number of design changes	10 changes
Factory services	1,000,000	Square feet	20,000 sq. feet
Total...............	$4,800,000		

2 Step 2 computes an **activity rate** for each activity cost pool. KartCo collects the following information for this purpose.

	Activity Usage		
Activity Cost Driver	Standard Model	Custom Model	Total
Direct labor hours......	75,000	25,000	100,000
Setups..............	40	160	200
Design changes	0	10	10
Square feet...........	12,000	8,000	20,000

Each activity rate is computed as follows.

$$\textbf{Activity rate} = \frac{\textbf{Budgeted activity cost}}{\textbf{Budgeted activity usage}}$$

Activity rates for KartCo are computed and shown in Exhibit C.5.

EXHIBIT C.5

Computing Activity Rates

Activity	Budgeted Cost	÷	Budgeted Activity Usage	=	Activity Rate
Production	$ 600,000	÷	100,000 direct labor hours	=	$6 per direct labor hour
Setup	2,000,000	÷	200 setups	=	$10,000 per setup
Design	1,200,000	÷	10 design changes	=	$120,000 per change
Factory services	1,000,000	÷	20,000 square feet	=	$50 per square foot

3 Step 3 allocates overhead costs to products using activity rates and the *actual* amount of the cost driver used as shown in Exhibit C.6. We multiply a product's actual activity usage by the activity rate as follows to get the overhead cost allocated to each activity.

Allocated cost = Actual activity usage × Activity rate

For each product, the allocated activity costs are added together and divided by the number of units to compute the overhead cost per unit.

EXHIBIT C.6

Overhead Cost Allocation Using Activity-Based Costing

	Standard Go-kart					Custom Go-kart				
Activity	Activity Usage	×	Activity Rate	=	Allocated Cost	Activity Usage	×	Activity Rate	=	Allocated Cost
Production	75,000 DLH	×	$6 per DLH	=	$ 450,000	25,000 DLH	×	$6 per DLH	=	$ 150,000
Setup	40 setups	×	$10,000 per setup	=	400,000	160 setups	×	$10,000 per setup	=	1,600,000
Design	0 changes	×	$120,000 per change	=	0	10 changes	×	$120,000 per change	=	1,200,000
Factory services	12,000 sq. ft.	×	$50 per square foot	=	600,000	8,000 sq. ft.	×	$50 per square foot	=	400,000
Total allocated cost					$1,450,000					$3,350,000
Units produced					÷ 5,000					÷ 1,000
Overhead cost per unit					= $290					= $3,350

Standard go-karts used 75,000 direct labor hours, so we allocate $450,000 (75,000 × $6 per DLH) of production costs to that product. Custom go-karts used 25,000 direct labor hours, so we allocate $150,000 (25,000 DLH × $6 per DLH) of production costs to that product. We similarly allocate the setup, design, and factory services costs to each type of go-kart. KartCo assigned no design costs to standard go-karts because standard go-karts are sold as "off-the-shelf" items.

Using ABC, $1,450,000 of overhead costs is allocated to standard go-karts and $3,350,000 is allocated to custom go-karts. While the total cost allocated of $4,800,000 is the same as under the plantwide method, the amounts allocated to the two product lines differ.

Overhead cost per unit is computed by dividing total overhead cost allocated to each product by the number of product units. KartCo's overhead cost per unit is $290 for its standard and $3,350 for its custom go-karts. Exhibit C.7 summarizes the overhead cost per unit calculations using ABC.

Total product cost per unit for KartCo using ABC follows. Direct materials and direct labor cost per unit are taken from its cost records.

	Direct Materials	+	Direct Labor	+	Overhead	=	Product Cost per Unit
Standard go-kart	$400		$350		$ 290		$1,040
Custom go-kart	600		500		3,350		4,450

EXHIBIT C.7

Overhead Allocated to Go-Karts

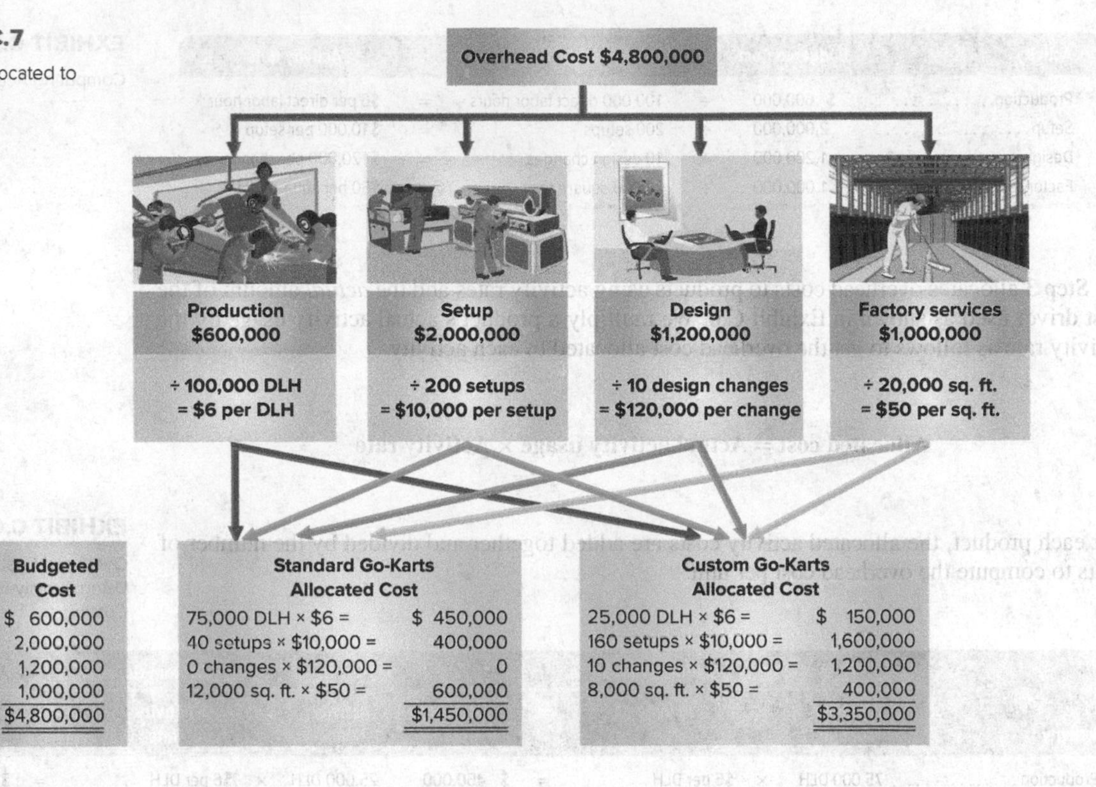

Comparing ABC with Plantwide Rate and for Business Decisions We compare total product cost per unit for standard and custom go-karts using either the plantwide or activity-based costing methods as follows.

Product Cost per Unit	Standard	Custom
Plantwide rate method.	$1,470	$2,300
Activity-based costing	1,040	4,450

Sergey Ryzhov/123RF

Compared to the plantwide rate method, product cost per unit is lower for the standard model and higher for the custom model under activity-based costing. Overhead cost allocated to custom go-karts is much higher under ABC. This is because the custom model uses more of the activities that drive overhead costs. ABC emphasizes *activities* and their costs, and arguably better reflects how overhead costs are used in making products. A single plantwide rate does not capture the products' different uses of these activities and often distorts product costs. *With the plantwide rate method, low-volume complex products are often undercosted, and high-volume simpler products are often overcosted.*

More accurate overhead allocation helps managers make better product pricing and product mix decisions. Looking at standard go-karts, what are the implications if standard go-karts sell for $1,200 per unit? Using the plantwide method, KartCo would not make standard go-karts as their product cost per unit ($1,470) would exceed the selling price. Using activity-based costing, however, the standard go-kart is profitable as its product cost per unit of $1,040 is below the price of $1,200 per unit. Looking at custom go-karts, and if their selling price is $3,500 per unit, the plantwide method shows it is profitable to produce custom go-karts. Selling price minus product cost is $1,200 ($3,500 – $2,300). Selling price minus product cost is $950 using ABC ($3,500 – $4,450), which shows a loss for each custom go-kart.

A manufacturer makes two types of snowmobiles, Basic and Deluxe, and reports the following. The company budgets production of 6,000 Basic snowmobiles and 2,000 Deluxe snowmobiles.

NEED-TO-KNOW C-2

Activity-Based Costing

P2

Activity	Budgeted Cost	Activity Cost Driver	Budgeted Activity Usage: Basic	Budgeted Activity Usage: Deluxe
Machine setup	$ 150,000	Number of setups	200 setups	300 setups
Materials handling........	250,000	Number of parts	60,000 parts	40,000 parts
Machine depreciation......	720,000	Machine hours (MH)	6,000 MH	3,000 MH
Total	$1,120,000			

1. Compute an overhead activity rate for each activity using activity-based costing (ABC).
2. Compute the overhead cost per unit for each of the two product lines using ABC.

Solution

1.

Activity	Budgeted Cost	÷	Budgeted Activity Usage	=	Activity Rate
Machine setup	$150,000	÷	500 setups	=	$300 per setup
Materials handling	250,000	÷	100,000 parts	=	$2.50 per part
Machine depreciation.....	720,000	÷	9,000 machine hours	=	$80 per machine hour

2.

	Basic Snowmobile					Deluxe Snowmobile				
Activity	Activity Usage	×	Activity Rate	=	Allocated Cost	Activity Usage	×	Activity Rate	=	Allocated Cost
Machine setup..........	200 setups	×	$300 per setup	=	$ 60,000	300 setups	×	$300 per setup	=	$ 90,000
Materials handling.......	60,000 parts	×	$2.50 per part	=	150,000	40,000 parts	×	$2.50 per part	=	100,000
Machine depreciation....	6,000 MH	×	$80 per machine hour	=	480,000	3,000 MH	×	$80 per machine hour	=	240,000
Total allocated cost					$690,000					$430,000
Units produced					÷ 6,000					÷ 2,000
Overhead cost per unit ...					= $115					= $215

Do More: QS C-5, QS C-6, QS C-7, QS C-8, E C-6, E C-7, E C-8

Summary: Cheat Sheet

PLANTWIDE RATE METHOD

Plantwide rate method: Uses one overhead rate.

$$\text{Overhead rate} = \frac{\text{Total budgeted overhead cost}}{\text{Total budgeted amount of allocation base}}$$

Example: Budgeted overhead = $4,800,000; Budgeted DLH = 100,000.

$$\text{Plantwide rate} = \frac{\$4{,}800{,}000}{100{,}000} = \$48 \text{ per DLH}$$

Allocated cost = Plantwide rate × DLH per unit

Example: Product uses 15 DLH per unit.
Allocated cost = $48 × 15 DLH per unit = $720 per unit.

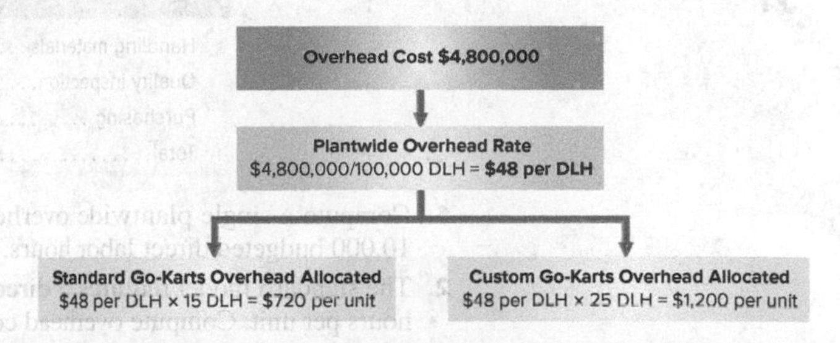

ACTIVITY-BASED COSTING

Activity cost pool: Group of costs related to same activity.
Activity cost driver: Activity that causes costs to go up or down.
Three Steps to Activity-Based Costing:

1. Identify activities and assign budgeted costs to activity cost pools.
2. Compute overhead activity rates.

$$\text{Activity rate} = \frac{\text{Budgeted activity cost}}{\text{Budgeted activity usage}}$$

3. Allocate overhead costs to cost objects (products).

$$\text{Allocated cost} = \text{Actual activity usage} \times \text{Activity rate}$$

Computing Overhead Activity Rates

Activity	Budgeted Cost	÷	Budgeted Activity Usage	=	Activity Rate
Production.	$ 600,000	÷	100,000 direct labor hours	=	$6 per direct labor hour
Setup.	2,000,000	÷	200 setups	=	$10,000 per setup
Design.	1,200,000	÷	10 design changes	=	$120,000 per change
Factory services	1,000,000	÷	20,000 square feet	=	$50 per square foot

Overhead Allocation with Activity-Based Costing

	Standard Go-Kart					Custom Go-Kart				
Activity	Activity Usage	×	Activity Rate	=	Allocated Cost	Activity Usage	×	Activity Rate	=	Allocated Cost
Production	75,000 DLH	×	$6 per DLH	=	$ 450,000	25,000 DLH	×	$6 per DLH	=	$ 150,000
Setup	40 setups	×	$10,000 per setup	=	400,000	160 setups	×	$10,000 per setup	=	1,600,000
Design	0 changes	×	$120,000 per change	=	0	10 changes	×	$120,000 per change	=	1,200,000
Factory services.	12,000 sq. ft.	×	$50 per square foot	=	600,000	8,000 sq. ft.	×	$50 per square foot	=	400,000
Total allocated cost					$1,450,000					$3,350,000
Units produced					÷ 5,000					÷ 1,000
Overhead cost per unit . . .					= $290					= $3,350

Key Terms

Activity-based costing (ABC) (C-3)
Activity cost driver (C-4)
Activity cost pool (C-4)
Activity rate (C-4)
Cost object (C-2)

QUICK STUDY

QS C-1
Computing plantwide overhead rate P1

Shaw Co. budgets total overhead of $1,800,000. The company allocates overhead based on 100,000 budgeted direct labor hours. Compute the single plantwide overhead rate.

QS C-2
Allocating overhead—plantwide rate P1

Neal Co. allocates overhead using a single plantwide overhead rate of $20 per direct labor hour. Each product unit requires three direct labor hours. Compute the overhead cost per unit.

QS C-3
Allocating overhead—plantwide rate P1

A manufacturer uses machine hours to allocate overhead costs to products. Budgeted information for the current year follows. (*a*) Compute the plantwide overhead rate based on machine hours. (*b*) How much overhead cost is allocated to Job A2, which uses 4 machine hours?

Budgeted overhead cost.	$54,400
Budgeted machine hours	640 machine hours

QS C-4
Computing plantwide overhead rate P1

Chan Company identified the following activities, costs, and activity drivers for this year. The company manufactures two types of scooters: standard and fast.

Activity	Budgeted Costs	Budgeted Activity
Handling materials	$625,000	100,000 parts
Quality inspection.	90,000	1,500 inspections
Purchasing	25,000	1,000 orders
Total.	$740,000	

1. Compute a single plantwide overhead rate assuming that the company allocates overhead based on 10,000 budgeted direct labor hours.
2. The standard model requires 5 direct labor hours per unit, and the fast model requires 10 direct labor hours per unit. Compute overhead cost per unit for each model.

Refer to the information in QS C-4. Compute the overhead activity rate for each activity assuming the company uses activity-based costing.

QS C-5
Computing overhead rates using ABC **P2**

Qinto Company sells two types of products: basic and deluxe. The company provides technical support for its products at a budgeted cost of $250,000 per year. The company allocates technical support costs based on 10,000 budgeted technical support calls per year.

1. Compute the activity rate for technical support using activity-based costing.
2. During January, Qinto received 650 calls on its deluxe model and 150 calls on its basic model. Allocate technical support costs to each model.

QS C-6
Allocating costs using ABC for a service company
P2

A company sells two types of products: standard and deluxe. It prepares the following analysis showing budgeted cost and cost driver activity for each of its three activity cost pools. Compute an activity rate for each cost pool using activity-based costing.

QS C-7
Computing activity rates using ABC
P2

		Budgeted Activity of Cost Driver		
Activity (Cost driver)	Budgeted Cost	Standard	Deluxe	Total
Factory services (square feet)	$87,000	3,000	2,800	5,800
Setup (number of setups)..............	10,000	300	200	500
Quality (number of units inspected).....	93,000	2,500	5,250	7,750

Mia Co. uses activity-based costing and reports the following. The company budgets 2,000 machine hours and 6,000 direct labor hours for the year. (*a*) Compute an overhead activity rate for each activity using activity-based costing. (*b*) Allocate overhead costs to a product that used 20 machine hours and 15 direct labor hours.

QS C-8
Activity-based costing and overhead cost allocation
P2

Activity (Cost driver)	Budgeted Cost
Cutting (machine hours)..........	$14,000
Assembly (direct labor hours)	60,000
Total..........................	$74,000

Rand Co. computed the following activity rates using activity-based costing.

QS C-9
Allocating overhead cost using activity-based costing
P2

Activity	Activity Rate
Setup................	$1,000 per setup
Materials handling	$50 per materials requisition
Inspection............	$2 per unit inspected

The company's deluxe model used the following activities to produce 1,000 units. Compute the overhead cost per unit for the deluxe model using activity-based costing.

Activity	Activity Usage
Setup...............	3 setups
Materials handling	25 materials requisitions
Inspection............	1,000 units inspected

QS C-10
Activity-based costing for services
P2

Data Insights provides accounting services. The company computed the following activity rates using activity-based costing. The forensic accounting department has 10 employees, occupies 1,500 square feet, and completed 40 jobs. Compute overhead cost per job for the forensic accounting department.

Activity	Activity Rate
Clerical support.	$600 per employee
Building.	$50 per sq. foot
Supplies.	$80 per job

QS C-11
Computing activity rate and allocating cost
P2

Chen Co. uses activity-based costing. It budgets $825,000 to sustainably dispose of 3,300 tons of hazardous waste.

a. Compute the activity rate for hazardous waste disposal based on tons of hazardous waste.
b. The company disposed of 5 tons of hazardous waste in completing Job 125. Allocate hazardous waste disposal cost to Job 125 using activity-based costing.

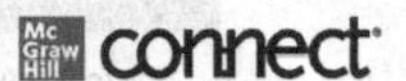

EXERCISES

Exercise C-1
Using plantwide overhead rate to allocate overhead
P1

Shakti Co. budgets overhead of $72,000 for the year. The company reports the following for its two products.

Cost per Unit	Standard	Deluxe
Direct materials	$12	$23
Direct labor.	18	27

1. Compute a single plantwide overhead rate assuming the company allocates overhead based on 6,000 direct labor hours.
2. The standard model uses 2 direct labor hours per unit and the deluxe model uses 3 direct labor hours per unit. Compute overhead cost per unit for each model.
3. Compute the total product cost per unit for both products.

Exercise C-2
Computing plantwide overhead rate
P1

Hydro Sports budgets overhead of $420,000 for the year. The company manufactures two types of jet skis: standard and deluxe. The standard model requires 8 direct labor hours and the deluxe model requires 12 direct labor hours. The company budgets production of 100 units of the standard model and 100 units of the deluxe model for the year.

1. Compute the total number of budgeted direct labor hours for the year.
2. Compute the plantwide overhead rate using direct labor hours.
3. Compute overhead cost per unit for each model using the plantwide overhead rate.

Exercise C-3
Computing plantwide overhead rate
P1

Dade Metals manufactures patio furniture. The company budgets overhead of $400,000 for the year. It also budgets 20,000 machine hours and 5,000 direct labor hours for the year.

1. Compute the plantwide overhead rate, assuming the company allocates overhead based on (a) machine hours and (b) direct labor hours.
2. Job 121 uses 100 machine hours and 50 direct labor hours. Allocate overhead to Job 121 assuming overhead is allocated based on (a) machine hours—use answer from part 1a, and (b) direct labor hours—use answer from part 1b.

Exercise C-4
Plantwide rate for a service
P1

Health Co-op is an outpatient surgical clinic. It budgets $540,000 of overhead costs for the year. The two main surgical units and their data follow.

Service	Budgeted Patients
General surgery	400
Orthopedic surgery............	200

1. Compute a single plantwide rate, assuming the company allocates overhead based on 600 budgeted patients.
2. In May of this year, the company performed 20 general surgeries and 14 orthopedic surgeries. Allocate overhead to each type of surgery using the single plantwide overhead rate.

Exercise C-5
Product mix and plantwide rate versus ABC
P1 P2

Wess Co. has limited capacity and can produce either its standard product or its deluxe product. Additional information follows.

Per Unit	Standard	Deluxe
Selling price	$60	$90
Direct materials..........	30	35
Direct labor	20	25

1. Using a single plantwide rate, the company computes overhead per unit of $15 for the standard model and $20 for the deluxe model. Which model should the company produce?
   Hint: Compute product cost per unit and compare that with selling price to get profit per unit.
2. Using activity-based costing, the company computes overhead per unit of $5 for the standard model and $40 for the deluxe model. Which model should the company produce?
   Hint: Compute product cost per unit and compare that with selling price to get profit per unit.

Exercise C-6
Allocating overhead costs to jobs using activity-based costing
P2

Pro-CraftCo. computed the following activity rates to allocate overhead for the year.

Activity	Activity Rate
Materials handling	$50 per materials requisition
Quality inspection......	$40 per inspection
Utilities	$5 per machine hour

During January, the company produced the following two jobs. Allocate overhead costs to each job using the activity rates.

	Activity Usage	
Cost Driver	Job A	Job B
Materials requisitions.....	5	3
Inspections	8	4
Machine hours	300	200

Exercise C-7
Computing activity rates
P2

Lucern Co. reports the following for its overhead costs for the year.

Activity	Budgeted Cost	Budgeted Activity Driver
Engineering support.....	$24,500	70 design changes
Electricity.............	34,000	3,400 machine hours
Setup..................	52,500	350 setups

1. Compute the activity rate for each activity cost pool using activity-based costing.
2. The company's Pro model used these activities to produce 1,200 units during the year: 2 design changes, 140 machine hours, and 12 setups. Allocate overhead costs to the Pro model and compute overhead cost per unit using activity-based costing.

Exercise C-8
Allocating overhead costs using activity-based costing
P2

Trax Co. manufactures 75 stationary bikes and 100 rowing machines. Activity cost pools and activity rates to produce these products follow.

Activity	Activity Rate
Assembly.......	$20 per direct labor hour
Purchasing	$10 per purchase order
Inspection	$25 per inspection

Activity usage for each product follows. Compute the overhead cost per unit for the stationary bikes and the rowing machines.

	Activity Usage	
Cost Driver	Stationary Bikes	Rowing Machines
Direct labor hours............	300	500
Purchase orders	12	18
Inspections	15	20

Exercise C-9
Using ABC in a service company
P2

Singh and Danzin is an architectural firm that provides services for residential construction projects. The following data are from the current period.

Activity	Budgeted Costs	Budgeted Activity
Client consultation	$270,000	1,500 contact hours
Drawings........	115,000	2,000 design hours

1. Compute an activity rate for each activity using activity-based costing.
2. Allocate costs to a job that requires 45 contact hours and 340 design hours.

Exercise C-10
Activity-based costing
P2

Northwest Company produces two types of glass shelving: rounded edge and squared edge. The company reports the following.

	Rounded Edge	Squared Edge	Total
Direct materials	$31,200	$ 44,800	$ 76,000
Direct labor..........................	12,200	23,800	36,000
Overhead (using plantwide rate).....	36,600	71,400	108,000
Total product cost....................	$80,000	$140,000	$220,000
Units produced	10,000	14,000	
Product cost per unit..............	$ 8.00	$ 10.00	

Northwest's controller wants to apply activity-based costing to allocate the $108,000 of overhead costs to the two products to see whether product cost per unit would change markedly from that above. The following information is collected.

			Activity Usage		
Activity	Budgeted Cost	Activity Driver	Rounded Edge	Squared Edge	Total
Purchasing	$ 5,400	Purchase orders	109 orders	431 orders	540 orders
Depreciation of machinery......	56,600	Machine hours	500 hours	1,500 hours	2,000 hours
Setup........................	46,000	Setups	40 setups	210 setups	250 setups
Total overhead	$108,000				

Required

1. Compute an activity rate for each activity using activity-based costing.
2. Compute overhead cost per unit for each of the two products using activity-based costing.
3. Determine product cost per unit for each of the two products using activity-based costing.

Exercise C-11
Using ABC to assess profitability
P2

Ice Cool produces two different models of air conditioners. The activities, costs, and cost drivers associated with the two manufacturing processes and the support process follow.

Process	Activity	Budgeted Cost	Cost Driver	Budgeted Activity Usage
Assembly	Machining	$279,000	Machine hours (MH)	6,000
	Setups	24,000	Number of setups	120
		$303,000		
Finishing	Inspection	$210,000	Number of inspections	700
Support	Purchasing	$135,000	Purchase orders	450

Additional production information concerning its two models follows.

Units and Activities	Model X	Model Z
Units produced	1,724	3,463
Machine hours	1,800	4,200
Setups	40	80
Inspections	400	300
Purchase orders	300	150

Per Unit	Model X	Model Z
Selling price per unit	$420	$400
Direct materials cost per unit. . .	100	90
Direct labor cost per unit	150	160

1. Compute the activity rate for each activity using activity-based costing.
2. Using activity-based costing, compute the overhead cost per unit for each model.
3. Compute the total product cost per unit for each model.
4. For each model, compute the selling price per unit minus product cost per unit.

Exercise C-12
Computing product cost per unit using plantwide method and ABC
P1 P2

Consider the following data for two products of Vigano Manufacturing.

Activity	Budgeted Cost (Activity Driver)
Machine setup	$121,000 (22 machine setups)
Parts handling	48,000 (16,000 parts)
Quality inspections	80,000 (250 inspections)
Total budgeted overhead . .	$249,000

Unit Information	Product A	Product B
Units produced.	1,000 units	200 units
Direct materials cost . .	$20 per unit	$30 per unit
Direct labor cost.	$40 per unit	$50 per unit
Direct labor hours	2 DLH per unit	2.5 DLH per unit

1. Using a plantwide overhead rate based on 2,500 direct labor hours, compute the total product cost per unit for each product.
2. Consider the following additional information about these two products. If activity-based costing is used for allocating overhead costs to products, what is the product cost per unit for each product?

Activity Driver Usage	Product A	Product B
Setups	10	12
Parts	10,000	6,000
Inspections	40	210

PROBLEM SET A

Problem C-1A
Comparing plantwide rate method and activity-based costing
P1 P2

Craftmore Machining reports the following for this year.

Activity	Budgeted Cost	Activity Cost Driver	Budgeted Activity Usage
Assembly.	$390,000	Direct labor hours	13,000
Product design	60,000	Engineering hours	1,000
Electricity.	20,000	Machine hours	10,000
Setup.	50,000	Setups	400
Total.	$520,000		

Required

1. Compute a single plantwide overhead rate assuming the company allocates overhead based on 13,000 direct labor hours.
2. Job 31 used 200 direct labor hours and Job 42 used 480 direct labor hours. Allocate overhead costs to each job using the single plantwide overhead rate from part 1.

	Activity Usage	
Activity Cost Driver	Job 31	Job 42
Direct labor hours......	200	480
Engineering hours	26	32
Machine hours	50	60
Setups..............	4	6

3. Compute an activity rate for each activity using activity-based costing.
4. Allocate overhead costs to the following jobs using activity-based costing.

Problem C-2A
Pricing analysis with plantwide overhead rate
P1

Tent Master produces Pup tents and Pop-up tents. The company budgets $252,000 of overhead costs and 42,000 direct labor hours for this year. Additional information follows.

Per Unit	Selling Price	Direct Materials	Direct Labor
Pup tent	$78	$20	$45
Pop-up tent.....	73	25	30

Required

1. Compute a single plantwide overhead rate assuming the company allocates overhead based on 42,000 direct labor hours.
2. Pup tents require 3 direct labor hours per unit and Pop-up tents require 2 direct labor hours per unit. Compute the overhead cost per unit for each product.
3. Compute the product cost per unit for each product.
4. For each product, compute the selling price per unit minus the product cost per unit.

Problem C-3A
Pricing analysis with activity-based costing
P2

Refer to the information in Problem C-2A. Additional information on overhead costs follows.

Activity	Budgeted Cost	Activity Cost Driver	Budgeted Activity Usage
Assembly..............	$168,000	Direct labor hours	42,000
Electricity............	24,000	Machine hours	10,000
Materials purchasing	60,000	Purchase orders	400
Total..................	$252,000		

Required

1. Compute an activity rate for each activity using activity-based costing.
2. The company used the activities below to produce 10,000 Pup tents and 6,000 Pop-up tents. Allocate overhead costs to Pup tents and to Pop-up tents and compute overhead cost per unit for each.

	Activity Usage	
Activity Cost Driver	Pup tents	Pop-up tents
Direct labor hours.....	30,000	12,000
Machine hours	4,000	6,000
Purchase orders......	150	250

3. Compute product cost per unit for Pup tents and for Pop-up tents.
4. For each product, compute the selling price per unit minus the product cost per unit.

Problem C-4A
Activity-based costing for a service company
P2

Optimal Health is an outpatient surgical clinic. The clinic's three activity cost pools and their cost drivers follow.

Activity	Budgeted Cost	Activity Cost Driver	Budgeted Activity Usage
Supplies.	$200,000	Surgical hours	10,000
Patient services.	37,500	Number of patients	500
Building cost	300,000	Square feet	2,000

The two main surgical units and their actual cost driver usage follow.

	Actual Cost Driver Usage		
Service	Hours	Patients	Square Feet
General surgery	2,500	400	720
Orthopedic surgery.	7,500	100	1,280

Required

1. Compute activity rates using activity-based costing.
2. Allocate overhead costs to both the general surgery and the orthopedic surgery units. Compute total overhead cost and average overhead cost per patient for both surgery units.

SERIAL PROBLEM
Business Solutions
P1 P2

Alexander Image/Shutterstock

This serial problem began in Chapter 1 and continues through most of the book. If previous chapter segments were not completed, the serial problem can begin at this point.

SP C After reading an article about activity-based costing, Santana Rey decides to analyze overhead costs at **Business Solutions**. In a recent month, she found that setup costs, inspection costs, and utility costs made up most of the company's overhead. Additional information follows.

Activity	Budgeted Cost	Budgeted Activity Driver
Setup.	$20,000	25 setups
Inspection	7,500	5,000 inspected
Utilities	10,000	5,000 machine hours
Total.	$37,500	

The following data pertain to Job 615.

Direct materials	$2,500	Setups.	2 setups
Direct labor.	$3,500	Parts inspected.	400 parts inspected
Overhead	$____	Machine hours	600 machine hours

Required

1. What is the total product cost of Job 615 if Business Solutions allocates overhead using a plantwide rate based on 5,000 machine hours?
2. What is the total product cost of Job 615 if Business Solutions uses activity-based costing?

Discussion Questions

1. Why are overhead costs allocated to products and not traced to products as direct materials and direct labor are?
2. How are overhead costs allocated to products with the single plantwide rate method?
3. What is a cost object?
4. What is activity-based costing? What is its goal?
5. What is an activity cost driver?

Index

Note: **Bold** entries indicate defined terms.

Chart of Accounts

Following is a typical chart of accounts, which is used in many assignments. Each company has its own unique set of accounts and numbering system.
*An asterisk denotes a contra account.

Assets

Current Assets

101 Cash
102 Petty cash
103 Cash equivalents
104 Short-term investments
105 Fair value adjustment–______ (ST)
106 Accounts receivable
107 Allowance for doubtful accounts*
108 Allowance for sales discounts*
109 Interest receivable
110 Rent receivable
111 Notes receivable
112 Legal fees receivable
119 Merchandise inventory (or Inventory)
120 ______ inventory
121 Inventory returns estimated
124 Office supplies
125 Store supplies
126 ______ supplies (or Supplies)
128 Prepaid insurance
129 Prepaid interest
131 Prepaid rent
132 Raw materials inventory
133 Work in process inventory, ______
134 Work in process inventory, ______
135 Finished goods inventory
136 Debt investments–Trading (ST)
137 Debt investments–Held-to-maturity (ST)
138 Debt investments–Available-for-sale (ST)
139 Stock investments (ST)

Long-Term Investments

141 Long-term investments
142 Fair value adjustment–______ (LT)
144 Investment in ______
145 Bond sinking fund
146 Debt investments–Held-to-maturity (LT)
147 Debt investments–Available-for-sale (LT)
148 Stock investments (LT)
149 Equity method investments

Plant Assets (Property, Plant, & Equipment)

151 Automobiles
152 Accumulated depreciation–Automobiles*
153 Trucks
154 Accumulated depreciation–Trucks*
155 Boats
156 Accumulated depreciation–Boats*
157 Professional library
158 Accumulated depreciation–Professional library*
159 Law library
160 Accumulated depreciation–Law library*
161 Furniture
162 Accumulated depreciation–Furniture*
163 Office equipment
164 Accumulated depreciation–Office equipment*
165 Store equipment
166 Accumulated depreciation–Store equipment*
167 ______ equipment
168 Accumulated depreciation–______ equipment*
169 Machinery
170 Accumulated depreciation–Machinery*
173 Building ______
174 Accumulated depreciation–Building ______*
175 Building ______
176 Accumulated depreciation–Building ______*
179 Land improvements ______
180 Accumulated depreciation–Land improvements ______*
181 Land improvements ______
182 Accumulated depreciation–Land improvements ______*
183 Land

Natural Resources

185 Mineral deposit
186 Accumulated depletion–Mineral deposit*

Intangible Assets

191 Patents
192 Leasehold
193 Franchise
194 Copyrights
195 Leasehold improvements
196 Licenses
197 Right-of-use asset
198 Accumulated amortization–______*
199 Goodwill

Liabilities

Current Liabilities

201 Accounts payable
202 Insurance payable
203 Interest payable
204 Legal fees payable
207 Office salaries payable
208 Rent payable
209 Salaries payable
210 Wages payable
211 Accrued payroll payable
212 Factory wages payable
214 Estimated warranty liability
215 Income taxes payable
216 Common dividend payable
217 Preferred dividend payable
218 State unemployment taxes payable
219 Employee federal income taxes payable
221 Employee medical insurance payable
222 Employee retirement program payable
223 Employee union dues payable
224 Federal unemployment taxes payable
225 FICA taxes payable
226 Estimated vacation pay liability
227 Sales refund payable
228 Loan payable
229 Current portion of long-term debt

Unearned Revenues

230 Unearned consulting fees (or revenue)
231 Unearned legal fees (or revenue)
232 Unearned property management fees
233 Unearned ______ fees
234 Unearned ______ fees
235 Unearned janitorial revenue
236 Unearned ______ revenue
238 Unearned rent

Notes Payable

240 Short-term notes payable
241 Discount on short-term notes payable*
244 Current portion of long-term notes payable
245 Notes payable
251 Long-term notes payable
252 Discount on long-term notes payable*

Long-Term Liabilities

253 Lease liability
255 Bonds payable
256 Discount on bonds payable*
257 Premium on bonds payable
258 Deferred income tax liability

Equity

Owner's Equity

301 ______, Capital
302 ______, Withdrawals
303 ______, Capital
304 ______, Withdrawals
305 ______, Capital
306 ______, Withdrawals

Paid-In Capital

307 Common stock, $ ______ par value
308 Common stock, no-par value
309 Common stock, $ ______ stated value

310 Common stock dividend distributable
311 Paid-in capital in excess of par value, Common stock
312 Paid-in capital in excess of stated value, No-par common stock
313 Paid-in capital from retirement of common stock
314 Paid-in capital, Treasury stock
315 Preferred stock
316 Paid-in capital in excess of par value, Preferred stock

Retained Earnings

318 Retained earnings
319 Cash dividends (or Dividends)
320 Stock dividends

Other Equity Accounts

321 Treasury stock, Common*
322 Unrealized gain–Equity
323 Unrealized loss–Equity

Revenues

401 __________ fees earned
402 __________ revenues
403 __________ revenue
404 Revenues
405 Commissions revenue (or earned)
406 Rent revenue (or Rent earned)
407 Dividends revenue (or Dividends earned)
408 Earnings from investment in ______
409 Interest revenue (or Interest earned)
410 Sinking fund earnings
413 Sales
414 Sales returns and allowances*
415 Sales discounts*
420 Earnings from equity method investments

Cost of Sales

Cost of Goods Sold

502 Cost of goods sold
505 Purchases
506 Purchases returns and allowances*
507 Purchases discounts*
508 Transportation-in

Manufacturing

520 Raw materials purchases
521 Freight-in on raw materials
530 Direct labor
541 Indirect materials
542 Indirect labor
543 Factory insurance expired
544 Factory supervision
545 Factory supplies used
546 Factory utilities
547 Miscellaneous production costs
548 Property taxes on factory building
549 Property taxes on factory equipment
550 Rent on factory building
551 Repairs, factory equipment
552 Small tools written off
560 Depreciation of factory equipment
561 Depreciation of factory building
570 Conversion costs

Standard Cost Variances

580 Direct material quantity variance
581 Direct material price variance
582 Direct labor efficiency variance
583 Direct labor rate variance
584 Volume variance
585 Controllable variance

Expenses

Amortization, Depletion, and Depreciation

601 Amortization expense–______
602 Amortization expense–______
603 Depletion expense–______
604 Depreciation expense–Boats
605 Depreciation expense–Automobiles
606 Depreciation expense–Building ______
607 Depreciation expense–Building ______
608 Depreciation expense–Land improvements ______
609 Depreciation expense–Land improvements ______
610 Depreciation expense–Law library
611 Depreciation expense–Trucks
612 Depreciation expense–______ equipment
613 Depreciation expense–______ equipment
614 Depreciation expense–______
615 Depreciation expense–______

Employee-Related Expenses

620 Office salaries expense
621 Sales salaries expense
622 Salaries expense
623 ______ wages expense
624 Employee benefits expense
625 Payroll taxes expense

Financial Expenses

630 Cash over and short
631 Discounts lost
632 Factoring fee expense
633 Interest expense

Insurance Expenses

635 Insurance expense–Delivery equipment
636 Insurance expense–Office equipment
637 Insurance expense–______

Rental Expenses

640 Rent (or Rental) expense
641 Rent expense–Office space
642 Rent expense–Selling space
643 Press rental expense
644 Truck rental expense
645 ______ rental expense

Supplies Expenses

650 Office supplies expense
651 Store supplies expense
652 ______ supplies expense
653 ______ supplies expense

Miscellaneous Expenses

655 Advertising expense
656 Bad debts expense
657 Blueprinting expense
658 Boat expense
659 Collection expense
661 Concessions expense
662 Credit card expense
663 Delivery expense
664 Dumping expense
667 Equipment expense
668 Food and drinks expense
671 Gas and oil expense
672 General and administrative expense
673 Janitorial expense
674 Legal fees expense
676 Mileage expense
677 Miscellaneous expenses
678 Mower and tools expense
679 Operating expense
680 Organization expense
681 Permits expense
682 Postage expense
683 Property taxes expense
684 Repairs expense–______
685 Repairs expense–______
687 Selling expense
688 Telephone expense
689 Travel and entertainment expense
690 Utilities expense
691 Warranty expense
692 ______ expense
695 Income tax expense

Gains and Losses

701 Gain on retirement of bonds
702 Gain on sale of machinery
703 Gain on sale of investments
704 Gain on sale of trucks
705 Gain on ______
706 Foreign exchange gain or loss
801 Loss on disposal of machinery
802 Loss on exchange of equipment
803 Loss on exchange of ______
804 Loss on sale of notes
805 Loss on retirement of bonds
806 Loss on sale of investments
807 Loss on sale of machinery
808 Loss on ______
809 Unrealized gain–Income
810 Unrealized loss–Income
811 Impairment gain
812 Impairment loss
815 Gain on sale of debt investments
816 Loss on sale of debt investments
817 Gain on sale of stock investments
818 Loss on sale of stock investments

Clearing Accounts

901 Income summary
902 Factory overhead

BRIEF REVIEW: MANAGERIAL ANALYSES AND REPORTS

① Cost Types

Variable costs:	Total cost changes in proportion to volume of activity.
Fixed costs:	Total cost does not change in proportion to volume of activity.
Mixed costs:	Cost consists of both a variable and a fixed element.

② Product Costs

Direct materials:	Raw materials costs directly linked to finished product.
Direct labor:	Employee costs directly linked to finished product.
Overhead:	Production costs indirectly linked to finished product.

③ Costing Systems

Job order costing:	Costs assigned to each unique unit or batch of units.
Process costing:	Costs assigned to similar products that are mass-produced in a continuous manner.

④ Costing Ratios

Contribution margin ratio = (Sales − Variable costs)/Sales
Predetermined overhead rate = Estimated overhead costs/Estimated activity base
Break-even point in units = Total fixed costs/Contribution margin per unit

⑤ Planning and Control Metrics

Cost variance = Actual cost − Standard (budgeted) cost
Sales (revenue) variance = Actual sales − Standard (budgeted) sales

⑥ Capital Budgeting

Payback period = Time expected to recover initial investment cost
Accounting rate of return = Annual income/Average investment
Net present value (NPV) = PV of future cash flows − Initial investment cost

NPV rule: 1. Compute net present value (NPV in $).
2. If NPV > 0, then accept project; If NPV < 0, then reject project.

Internal rate of return rule: 1. Compute internal rate of return (IRR in %).
2. If IRR > hurdle rate, accept project; If IRR < hurdle rate, reject project.

⑦ Costing Terminology

Relevant range:	Organization's normal range of operating activity.
Direct cost:	Cost incurred for the benefit of one cost object.
Indirect cost:	Cost incurred for the benefit of more than one cost object.
Product cost:	Cost that is necessary and integral to finished products.
Period cost:	Cost identified more with a time period than with finished products.
Overhead cost:	Cost not separately or directly traceable to a cost object.
Relevant cost:	Cost that is pertinent to a decision.
Opportunity cost:	Benefit lost by choosing an action from two or more alternatives.
Sunk cost:	Cost already incurred that cannot be avoided or changed.
Out-of-pocket cost:	Requires a future outlay of cash.
Avoidable cost:	Can be eliminated by choosing one alternative over another.
Standard cost:	Cost computed using standard price and standard quantity.
Budget:	Formal statement of an organization's plans in monetary terms.
Break-even point:	Sales level at which an organization earns zero profit.
Incremental revenue:	Revenue earned if the organization takes a certain action.
Incremental cost:	Cost incurred only if the organization undertakes a certain action.
Incremental income:	Incremental revenue minus incremental cost.
Transfer price:	Price on transaction between divisions within a company.

⑧ Standard Cost Variances

Total materials variance = Materials price variance + Materials quantity variance

Total labor variance = Labor rate variance + Labor efficiency variance

Standard overhead rate = Flexible overhead budget at predicted activity level / Standard allocation base at predicted activity level

Standard overhead applied = Actual production × Standard amount of allocation base × Standard overhead rate

Total overhead variance = Actual total overhead − Standard overhead applied
or = Overhead contollable variance + Overhead volume variance

Controllable variance = Actual total overhead − Budgeted (flexible) overhead at units produced

Volume variance = Budgeted (flexible) overhead at units produced − Standard overhead applied

Materials price variance	= [AQ × AP] − [AQ × SP]
Materials quantity variance	= [AQ × SP] − [SQ × SP]
Labor rate variance	= [AH × AR] − [AH × SR]
Labor efficiency variance	= [AH × SR] − [SH × SR]

where AQ is Actual Quantity of materials; AP is Actual Price of materials; AH is Actual Hours of labor; AR is Actual Rate of wages; AVR is Actual Variable Rate of overhead; SQ is Standard Quantity of materials; SP is Standard Price of materials; SH is Standard Hours of labor; SR is Standard Rate of labor; SVR is Standard Variable Rate of overhead.

⑨ Sales Variances

Sales price variance	= [AS × AP] − [AS × BP]
Sales volume variance	= [AS × BP] − [BS × BP]

where AS = Actual Sales units; AP = Actual sales Price;
BP = Budgeted sales Price; BS = Budgeted Sales units (fixed budget).

Schedule of Cost of Goods Manufactured
For *period* Ended *date*

Direct materials	
Raw materials inventory, beginning	$ #
Raw materials purchases	#
Raw materials available for use	#
Less raw materials inventory, ending	(#)
Direct materials used	#
Direct labor	#
Factory overhead (applied)	#
Total manufacturing costs	#
Add work in process inventory, beginning	#
Total cost of work in process	#
Less work in process inventory, ending	(#)
Cost of goods manufactured	$ #

Contribution Margin Income Statement
For *period* Ended *date*

Sales	$ #
Variable costs	#
Contribution margin	#
Fixed costs	#
Income	$ #

Flexible Budget
For *period* Ended *date*

	Variable Amount per Unit	Total Fixed Cost	Flexible Budget for Unit Sales of #
Sales	$ #		$ #
Variable costs			
Examples: Direct materials, Direct labor, Delivery costs, Sales commissions	#		#
Total variable costs	#		#
Contribution margin	$ #		#
Fixed costs			
Examples: Depreciation, Property taxes, Supervisory salaries, Administrative salaries, Insurance		$ #	#
		#	#
Total fixed costs		$ #	#
Income			$ #

Total flexible budget costs = Total fixed costs + (Total variable costs per unit × Units of activity level)

Budget variance* = Budget amount − Actual amount
*Applies to both flexible and fixed budgets. *F* = Favorable variance; *U* = Unfavorable variance.

Budget Performance Report*
For *period* Ended *date*

	Budget	Actual Results	Variances†
Sales (in units)	#	#	
Sales (in dollars)	$ #	$ #	$ # *F* or *U*
Variable costs			
Direct materials	#	#	# *F* or *U*
Direct labor	#	#	# *F* or *U*
Indirect materials	#	#	# *F* or *U*
Others: Sales commissions	#	#	# *F* or *U*
Contribution margin	#	#	# *F* or *U*
Fixed costs			
Examples: Depreciation, Insurance	#	#	# *F* or *U*
Total fixed costs	$ #	$ #	$ # *F* or *U*
Income	$ #	$ #	$ # *F* or *U*

*Applies to both flexible and fixed budgets. †*F* = Favorable variance; *U* = Unfavorable variance.

Master Budget Sequence

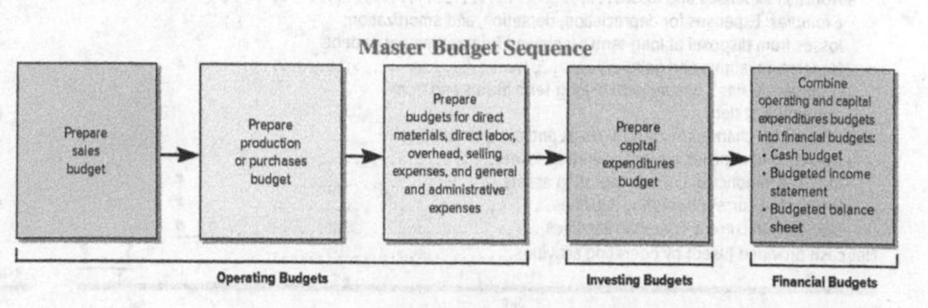

Prepare sales budget
Prepare production or purchases budget
Prepare budgets for direct materials, direct labor, overhead, selling expenses, and general and administrative expenses
Prepare capital expenditures budget
Combine operating and capital expenditures budgets into financial budgets:
• Cash budget
• Budgeted income statement
• Budgeted balance sheet
Operating Budgets
Investing Budgets
Financial Budgets

BRIEF REVIEW: FINANCIAL REPORTS AND TABLES

Income Statement*
For *period* Ended *date*

Net sales (revenues)		$ #
Cost of goods sold (cost of sales)		#
Gross margin (gross profit)		#
Operating expenses		
Examples: depreciation, salaries, wages, rent, utilities,	$ #	
interest, amortization, advertising, insurance,	#	
taxes, selling, general and administrative	#	
Total operating expenses		#
Nonoperating gains and losses (unusual and/or infrequent)		#
Net income (net profit or earnings)		$ #

*A typical chart of accounts is at the end of the text and classifies all accounts by financial statement categories.

Balance Sheet
Date

ASSETS

Current assets		
Examples: cash, cash equivalents, short-term investments,	$ #	
accounts receivable, current portion of notes receivable,	#	
inventory, inventory returns estimated, prepaid expenses	#	
Total current assets		$ #
Long-term investments		
Examples: investment in stock, investment in bonds,	#	
land for expansion	#	
Total long-term investments		#
Plant assets		
Examples: equipment, machinery, buildings, land	#	
Total plant assets, net of depreciation		#
Intangibles		
Examples: patent, trademark, copyright, license, right-of-use, goodwill	#	
Total intangible assets, net of amortization		#
Total assets		$ #

LIABILITIES AND EQUITY

Current liabilities		
Examples: accounts payable, wages payable, salaries payable,	$ #	
current notes payable, taxes payable, interest payable,	#	
unearned revenues, current portion of debt, sales refund payable	#	
Total current liabilities		$ #
Long-term liabilities		
Examples: notes payable, bonds payable, lease liability	#	
Total long-term liabilities		#
Total liabilities		#
Equity*		
Owner, capital		#
Total liabilities and equity		$ #

*A corporation's equity consists of: paid-in capital and retained earnings (less any treasury stock).

Statement of Cash Flows
For *period* Ended *date*

Cash flows from operating activities	
[Prepared using the indirect (see below)† or direct method]	
Net cash provided (used) by operating activities	$ #
Cash flows from investing activities	
[List of individual investing inflows and outflows]	
Net cash provided (used) by investing activities	#
Cash flows from financing activities	
[List of individual financing inflows and outflows]	
Net cash provided (used) by financing activities	#
Net increase (decrease) in cash	$ #
Cash (and equivalents) balance at beginning of period	#
Cash (and equivalents) balance at end of period	$ #

Separate schedule or note disclosure of any "Noncash investing and financing transactions" is required.

†Indirect Method: Cash Flows from Operating Activities

Cash flows from operating activities		
Net income		$ #
Adjustments for operating items not providing or using cash		
+Noncash expenses and losses	$ #	
Examples: Expenses for depreciation, depletion, and amortization; losses from disposal of long-term assets and from retirement of debt		
−Noncash revenues and gains	#	
Examples: Gains from disposal of long-term assets and from retirement of debt		
Adjustments for changes in current assets and current liabilities		
+Decrease in noncash current operating assets	#	
−Increase in noncash current operating assets	#	
+Increase in current operating liabilities	#	
−Decrease in current operating liabilities	#	
Net cash provided (used) by operating activities		$ #

Statement of Owner's Equity
For *period* Ended *date*

Owner, Capital, beginning		$ #
Add: Investments by owner	$ #	
Net income	#	#
		#
Less: Withdrawals by owner		#
Net loss (if exists)		#
Owner, Capital, ending		$ #

Statement of Retained Earnings (CORPORATION only)
For *period* Ended *date*

Retained earnings, beginning	$ #
Add: Net income	#
	#
Less: Dividends declared	#
Net loss (if exists)	#
Retained earnings, ending	$ #

Premium Bond Amortization (Straight-Line) Table*

Semiannual Period-End	Unamortized Bond Premium†	Bond Carrying Value‡
Bond life-start	$#	$ #
⋮	⋮	⋮
Bond life-end	0	par

*Bond carrying value is adjusted downward to par and its amortized premium downward to zero over the bond life (carrying value less unamortized bond premium equals par).
†Equals total bond premium less its accumulated amortization.
‡Equals bond par value plus its unamortized bond premium.

Discount Bond Amortization (Straight-Line) Table*

Semiannual Period-End	Unamortized Bond Discount†	Bond Carrying Value‡
Bond life-start	$#	$ #
⋮	⋮	⋮
Bond life-end	0	par

*Bond carrying value is adjusted upward to par and its amortized discount downward to zero over the bond life (unamortized bond discount plus carrying value equals par).
†Equals total bond discount less its accumulated amortization.
‡Equals bond par value less its unamortized bond discount.

Effective Interest Amortization Table for Bonds with Semiannual Interest Payment

Semiannual Interest Period-End	Cash Interest Paid[A]	Bond Interest Expense[B]	Discount or Premium Amortization[C]	Unamortized Discount or Premium[D]	Carrying Value[E]
#	#	#	#	#	#
⋮	⋮	⋮	⋮	⋮	⋮

[A]Par value multiplied by the semiannual contract rate.
[B]Prior period's carrying value multiplied by the semiannual market rate.
[C]The difference between interest paid and bond interest expense.
[D]Prior period's unamortized discount or premium less the current period's discount or premium amortization.
[E]Par value less unamortized discount or plus unamortized premium.

Installment Notes Payment Table

		Payments					
		Debit		*Debit*		*Credit*	
Period Ending Date	Beginning Balance	Interest Expense	+	Notes Payable	=	Cash	Ending Balance
#	#	#		#		#	#
⋮	⋮	⋮		⋮		⋮	⋮

Bank Reconciliation
Date

Bank statement balance	$#	Book balance	$#
Add: Deposits in transit	#	Add: Interest earned & unrecorded cash receipts	#
Bank errors understating the balance	#	Book errors understating the balance	#
Less: Outstanding checks	#	Less: Bank fees & NSF checks	#
Bank errors overstating the balance	#	Book errors overstating the balance	#
Adjusted bank balance	$#	**Adjusted book balance**	$#

Balances are equal (reconciled)

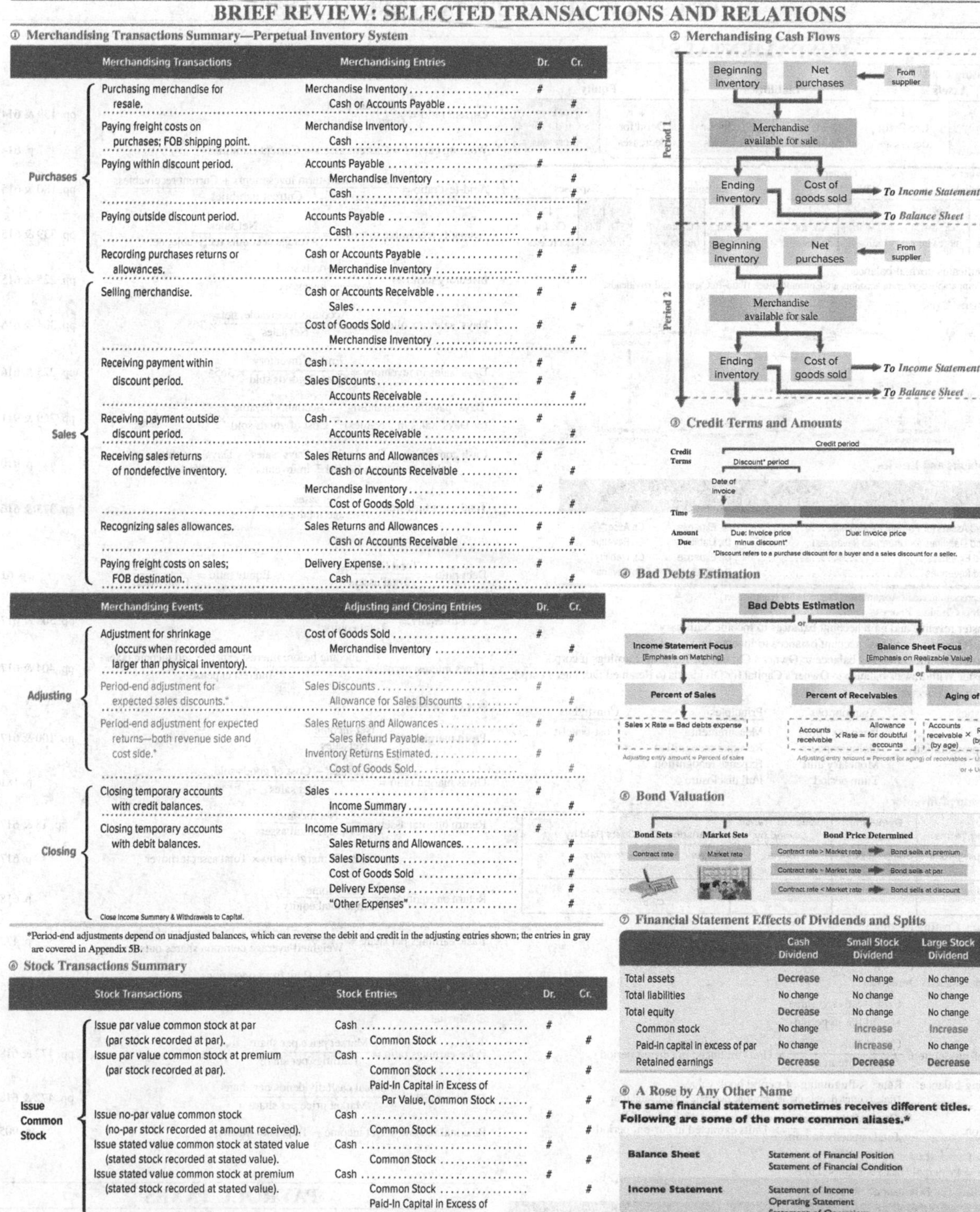

BRIEF REVIEW: SELECTED TRANSACTIONS AND RELATIONS

① Merchandising Transactions Summary—Perpetual Inventory System

	Merchandising Transactions	Merchandising Entries	Dr.	Cr.
Purchases	Purchasing merchandise for resale.	Merchandise Inventory	#	
		Cash or Accounts Payable		#
	Paying freight costs on purchases; FOB shipping point.	Merchandise Inventory	#	
		Cash		#
	Paying within discount period.	Accounts Payable	#	
		Merchandise Inventory		#
		Cash		#
	Paying outside discount period.	Accounts Payable	#	
		Cash		#
	Recording purchases returns or allowances.	Cash or Accounts Payable	#	
		Merchandise Inventory		#
Sales	Selling merchandise.	Cash or Accounts Receivable	#	
		Sales		#
		Cost of Goods Sold	#	
		Merchandise Inventory		#
	Receiving payment within discount period.	Cash	#	
		Sales Discounts	#	
		Accounts Receivable		#
	Receiving payment outside discount period.	Cash	#	
		Accounts Receivable		#
	Receiving sales returns of nondefective inventory.	Sales Returns and Allowances	#	
		Cash or Accounts Receivable		#
		Merchandise Inventory	#	
		Cost of Goods Sold		#
	Recognizing sales allowances.	Sales Returns and Allowances	#	
		Cash or Accounts Receivable		#
	Paying freight costs on sales; FOB destination.	Delivery Expense	#	
		Cash		#

	Merchandising Events	Adjusting and Closing Entries	Dr.	Cr.
Adjusting	Adjustment for shrinkage (occurs when recorded amount larger than physical inventory).	Cost of Goods Sold	#	
		Merchandise Inventory		#
	Period-end adjustment for expected sales discounts.*	Sales Discounts	#	
		Allowance for Sales Discounts		#
	Period-end adjustment for expected returns—both revenue side and cost side.*	Sales Returns and Allowances	#	
		Sales Refund Payable		#
		Inventory Returns Estimated	#	
		Cost of Goods Sold		#
Closing	Closing temporary accounts with credit balances.	Sales	#	
		Income Summary		#
	Closing temporary accounts with debit balances.	Income Summary	#	
		Sales Returns and Allowances		#
		Sales Discounts		#
		Cost of Goods Sold		#
		Delivery Expense		#
		"Other Expenses"		#
	Close Income Summary & Withdrawals to Capital.			

*Period-end adjustments depend on unadjusted balances, which can reverse the debit and credit in the adjusting entries shown; the entries in gray are covered in Appendix 5B.

② Merchandising Cash Flows

③ Credit Terms and Amounts

*Discount refers to a purchase discount for a buyer and a sales discount for a seller.

④ Bad Debts Estimation

⑤ Bond Valuation

⑥ Stock Transactions Summary

	Stock Transactions	Stock Entries	Dr.	Cr.
Issue Common Stock	Issue par value common stock at par (par stock recorded at par).	Cash	#	
		Common Stock		#
	Issue par value common stock at premium (par stock recorded at par).	Cash	#	
		Common Stock		#
		Paid-In Capital in Excess of Par Value, Common Stock		#
	Issue no-par value common stock (no-par stock recorded at amount received).	Cash	#	
		Common Stock		#
	Issue stated value common stock at stated value (stated stock recorded at stated value).	Cash	#	
		Common Stock		#
	Issue stated value common stock at premium (stated stock recorded at stated value).	Cash	#	
		Common Stock		#
		Paid-In Capital in Excess of Stated Value, Common Stock		#
Issue Preferred Stock	Issue par value preferred stock at par (par stock recorded at par).	Cash	#	
		Preferred Stock		#
	Issue par value preferred stock at premium (par stock recorded at par).	Cash	#	
		Preferred Stock		#
		Paid-In Capital in Excess of Par Value, Preferred Stock		#
Reacquire Common Stock	Reacquire its own common stock (treasury stock recorded at cost).	Treasury Stock, Common	#	
		Cash		#
Reissue Common Stock	Reissue its treasury stock at cost (treasury stock removed at cost).	Cash	#	
		Treasury Stock, Common		#
	Reissue its treasury stock above cost (treasury stock removed at cost).	Cash	#	
		Treasury Stock, Common		#
		Paid-In Capital, Treasury		#
	Reissue its treasury stock below cost (treasury stock removed at cost).	Cash	#	
		Paid-In Capital, Treasury	#	
		Treasury Stock, Common		#

⑦ Financial Statement Effects of Dividends and Splits

	Cash Dividend	Small Stock Dividend	Large Stock Dividend	Stock Split
Total assets	Decrease	No change	No change	No change
Total liabilities	No change	No change	No change	No change
Total equity	Decrease	No change	No change	No change
Common stock	No change	Increase	Increase	No change
Paid-in capital in excess of par	No change	Increase	No change	No change
Retained earnings	Decrease	Decrease	Decrease	No change

⑧ A Rose by Any Other Name

The same financial statement sometimes receives different titles. Following are some of the more common aliases.*

Balance Sheet	Statement of Financial Position Statement of Financial Condition
Income Statement	Statement of Income Operating Statement Statement of Operations Statement of Operating Activity Earnings Statement Statement of Earnings Profit and Loss (P&L) Statement
Statement of Cash Flows	Statement of Cash Flow Cash Flows Statement Statement of Changes in Cash Position Statement of Changes in Financial Position
Statement of Owner's Equity	Statement of Changes in Owner's Equity Statement of Changes in Owner's Capital Statement of Shareholders' Equity† Statement of Changes in Shareholders' Equity† Statement of Stockholders' Equity and Comprehensive Income† Statement of Changes in Capital Accounts†

*The term **Consolidated** often precedes or follows these statement titles to reflect the combination of different entities, such as a parent company and its subsidiaries.
† Corporation only

BRIEF REVIEW: FUNDAMENTALS AND ANALYSES

FUNDAMENTALS

① Accounting Equation

Assets		=	Liabilities		+	Equity	
↑ Debit for increases	↓ Credit for decreases		↓ Debit for decreases	↑ Credit for increases		↓ Debit for decreases	↑ Credit for increases

Owner's Capital*		−	Owner's Withdrawals*		+	Revenues		−	Expenses	
↓ Dr. for decreases	↑ Cr. for increases		↑ Dr. for increases	↓ Cr. for decreases		↓ Dr. for decreases	↑ Cr. for increases		↑ Dr. for increases	↓ Cr. for decreases

■ Indicates normal balance.

*Comparable corporate accounts are Common Stock (Paid-In Capital) and Dividends.

② Accounting Cycle

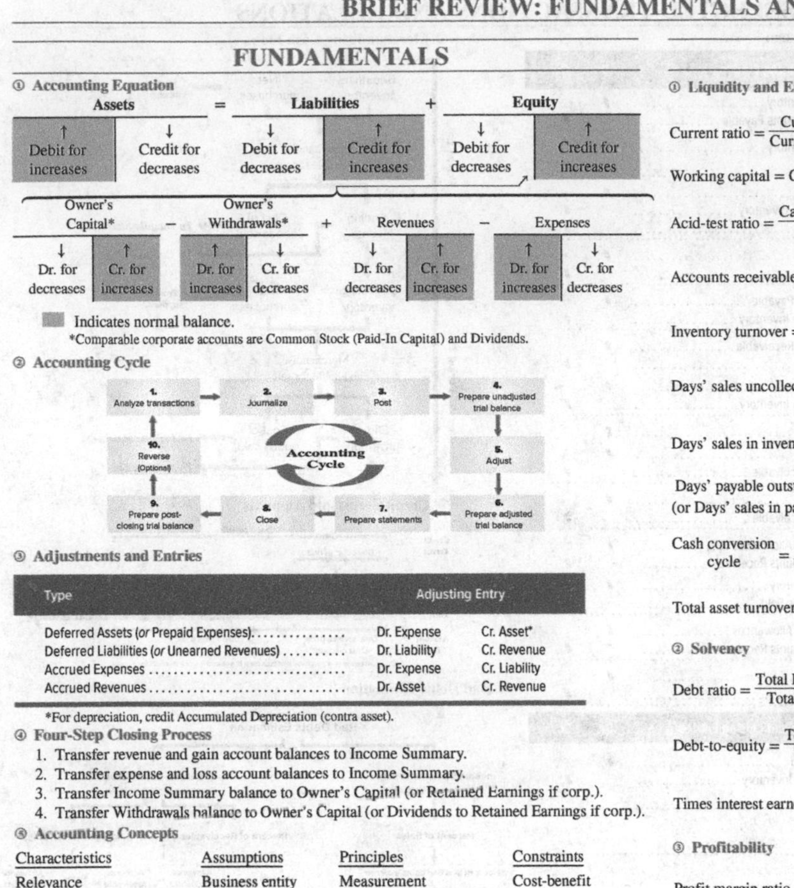

③ Adjustments and Entries

Type	Adjusting Entry	
Deferred Assets (or Prepaid Expenses)	Dr. Expense	Cr. Asset*
Deferred Liabilities (or Unearned Revenues)	Dr. Liability	Cr. Revenue
Accrued Expenses	Dr. Expense	Cr. Liability
Accrued Revenues	Dr. Asset	Cr. Revenue

*For depreciation, credit Accumulated Depreciation (contra asset).

④ Four-Step Closing Process

1. Transfer revenue and gain account balances to Income Summary.
2. Transfer expense and loss account balances to Income Summary.
3. Transfer Income Summary balance to Owner's Capital (or Retained Earnings if corp.).
4. Transfer Withdrawals balance to Owner's Capital (or Dividends to Retained Earnings if corp.).

⑤ Accounting Concepts

Characteristics	Assumptions	Principles	Constraints
Relevance	Business entity	Measurement	Cost-benefit
Faithful representation	Going concern	Revenue recognition	
	Monetary unit	Expense recognition	
	Time period	Full disclosure	

⑥ Ownership of Inventory

Shipping Terms	Ownership Transfers at	Goods in Transit Owned by	Transportation Costs Paid by	
FOB shipping point	Shipping point	Buyer	Buyer	Merchandise Inventory ... # Cash ... #
FOB destination	Destination	Seller	Seller	Delivery Expense ... # Cash ... #

⑦ Inventory Costing Methods

- Specific identification (SI)
- First-in, first-out (FIFO)
- Weighted-average (WA)
- Last-in, first-out (LIFO)

⑧ Depreciation and Depletion

Straight-line: $\dfrac{\text{Cost} - \text{Salvage value}}{\text{Useful life in periods}}$

Units-of-production: $\dfrac{\text{Cost} - \text{Salvage value}}{\text{Useful life in units}} \times \text{Units produced in current period}$

Declining-balance: Rate* × Beginning-of-period book value

*Rate is often double the straight-line rate, or 2 × (1/Useful life)

Depletion: $\dfrac{\text{Cost} - \text{Salvage value}}{\text{Total capacity in units}} \times \text{Units extracted in current period}$

⑨ Interest Computation

Interest = Principal (face) × Rate × Time

⑩ Accounting for Investment Securities

Classification	Investments Account Reported at
Short-Term Investment in Securities	
Debt Investments—Held-to-Maturity	Cost (without any discount or premium amortization)
Debt Investments—Trading	Fair value (with fair value adjustment to income)
Debt Investments—Available-for-Sale	Fair value (with fair value adjustment to equity)
Stock Investments—insignificant influence	Fair value (with fair value adjustment to income)
Long-Term Investment in Securities	
Debt Investments—Held-to-Maturity	Cost (with any discount or premium amortization)
Debt Investments—Available-for-Sale	Fair value (with fair value adjustment to equity)
Stock Investments—insignificant influence	Fair value (with fair value adjustment to income)
Equity Method Investments—significant influence	Equity method (no fair value adjustment)
Consolidated Investments—controlling influence	Consolidation method (no fair value adjustment)

ANALYSES

① Liquidity and Efficiency

Current ratio $= \dfrac{\text{Current assets}}{\text{Current liabilities}}$ — pp. 139 & 614

Working capital = Current assets − Current liabilities — p. 614

Acid-test ratio $= \dfrac{\text{Cash} + \text{Short-term investments} + \text{Current receivables}}{\text{Current liabilities}}$ — pp. 180 & 615

Accounts receivable turnover $= \dfrac{\text{Net sales}}{\text{Average accounts receivable, net}}$ — pp. 339 & 615

Inventory turnover $= \dfrac{\text{Cost of goods sold}}{\text{Average inventory}}$ — pp. 225 & 615

Days' sales uncollected $= \dfrac{\text{Accounts receivable, net}}{\text{Net sales}} \times 365$ — pp. 304 & 616

Days' sales in inventory $= \dfrac{\text{Ending inventory}}{\text{Cost of goods sold}} \times 365$ — pp. 225 & 616

Days' payable outstanding (or Days' sales in payables) $= \dfrac{\text{Accounts payable}}{\text{Cost of goods sold}} \times 365$ — pp. 269 & 911

Cash conversion cycle = Days' sales uncollected + Days' sales in inventory − Days' payable outstanding — p. 910

Total asset turnover $= \dfrac{\text{Net sales}}{\text{Average total assets}}$ — pp. 373 & 616

② Solvency

Debt ratio $= \dfrac{\text{Total liabilities}}{\text{Total assets}}$ Equity ratio $= \dfrac{\text{Total equity}}{\text{Total assets}}$ — p. 61

Debt-to-equity $= \dfrac{\text{Total liabilities}}{\text{Total equity}}$ — pp. 505 & 617

Times interest earned $= \dfrac{\text{Income before interest expense and income taxes}}{\text{Interest expense}}$ — pp. 404 & 617

③ Profitability

Profit margin ratio $= \dfrac{\text{Net income}}{\text{Net sales}}$ — pp. 100 & 617

Gross margin ratio $= \dfrac{\text{Net sales} - \text{Cost of goods sold}}{\text{Net sales}}$ — p. 181

Return on total assets $= \dfrac{\text{Net income}}{\text{Average total assets}}$ — pp. 18 & 617

= Profit margin ratio × Total asset turnover — p. 617

Return on equity $= \dfrac{\text{Net income}}{\text{Average total equity}}$ — p. 618

Basic earnings per share $= \dfrac{\text{Net income} - \text{Preferred dividends}}{\text{Weighted-average common shares outstanding}}$ — p. 472

Cash flow on total assets $= \dfrac{\text{Cash flow from operations}}{\text{Average total assets}}$ — p. 575

④ Market

Price-earnings ratio $= \dfrac{\text{Market price per share}}{\text{Earnings per share}}$ — pp. 472 & 618

Dividend yield $= \dfrac{\text{Annual cash dividends per share}}{\text{Market price per share}}$ — pp. 472 & 618

Residual income = Net income − Target net income — p. 905

PAYROLL TAXES

Year-to-Date Pay Bracket (Set Yearly)	Employee Taxes	Employer Taxes
$0 to $7,000	FICA—Medicare FICA—Social Security State & Federal Income Tax	FICA—Medicare FICA—Social Security FUTA SUTA
$7,000 to $137,700	FICA—Medicare FICA—Social Security State & Federal Income Tax	FICA—Medicare FICA—Social Security
Above $137,700	FICA—Medicare State & Federal Income Tax	FICA—Medicare

Credits

1. Accounting in Business: *Chapter 1 from Fundamental Accounting Principles, 25th Edition by Wild, Shaw, 2021* 2
2. Analyzing and Recording Transactions: *Chapter 2 from Fundamental Accounting Principles, 25th Edition by Wild, Shaw, 2021* 44
3. Adjusting Accounts for Financial Statements: *Chapter 3 from Fundamental Accounting Principles, 25th Edition by Wild, Shaw, 2021* 84
4. Completing the Accounting Cycle: *Chapter 4 from Fundamental Accounting Principles, 25th Edition by Wild, Shaw, 2021* 126
5. Accounting for Merchandising Operations: *Chapter 5 from Fundamental Accounting Principles, 25th Edition by Wild, Shaw, 2021* 164
6. Inventories and Cost of Sales: *Chapter 6 from Fundamental Accounting Principles, 25th Edition by Wild, Shaw, 2021* 212
7. Accounting Information Systems: *Chapter 7 from Fundamental Accounting Principles, 25th Edition by Wild, Shaw, 2021* 256
8. Cash, Fraud, and Internal Control: *Chapter 8 from Fundamental Accounting Principles, 25th Edition by Wild, Shaw, 2021* 288
9. Accounting for Receivables: *Chapter 9 from Fundamental Accounting Principles, 25th Edition by Wild, Shaw, 2021* 324
10. Plant Assets, Natural Resources, and Intangibles: *Chapter 10 from Fundamental Accounting Principles, 25th Edition by Wild, Shaw, 2021* 356
11. Current Liabilities and Payroll Accounting: *Chapter 11 from Fundamental Accounting Principles, 25th Edition by Wild, Shaw, 2021* 390

Appendix: Financial Statement Information: *Appendix A from Fundamental Accounting Principles, 25th Edition by Wild, Shaw, 2021* A

Appendix: Time Value of Money: *Appendix B from Fundamental Accounting Principles, 25th Edition by Wild, Shaw, 2021* B-1

Appendix: Activity-Based Costing: *Appendix C from Fundamental Accounting Principles, 25th Edition by Wild, Shaw, 2021* C-1

Index: *Chapter from Fundamental Accounting Principles, 25th Edition by Wild, Shaw, 2021* IND-1

Chart of Accounts: *Chapter from Fundamental Accounting Principles, 25th Edition by Wild, Shaw, 2021* CA-1

Brief Review: *Chapter from Fundamental Accounting Principles, 25th Edition by Wild, Shaw, 2021* BR-1

Online Supplements

Connect 180 Day Access for Fundamental Accounting Principles, 25th Edition: *Media by Wild* 504

Access Code for the Online Supplements 505

Online Supplements

Connect 180 Day Access for Fundamental Accounting Principles, 25th Edition

McGraw-Hill Connect is a digital teaching and learning environment that improves performance over a variety of critical outcomes. With Connect, instructors can deliver assignments, quizzes and tests easily online. Students can practice important skills at their own pace and on their own schedule.

HOW TO REGISTER

Using a Print Book?
To register and activate your Connect account, simply follow these easy steps:

1. **Go to the Connect course web address provided by your instructor or visit the Connect link set up on your instructor's course within your campus learning management system.**
2. **Click on the link to register.**
3. **When prompted, enter the Connect code found on the inside back cover of your book and click Submit. Complete the brief registration form that follows to begin using Connect.**

Using an eBook?
To register and activate your Connect account, simply follow these easy steps:

1. **Upon purchase of your eBook, you will be granted automatic access to Connect.**
2. **Go to the Connect course web address provided by your instructor or visit the Connect link set up on your instructor's course within your campus learning management system.**
3. **Sign in using the same email address and password you used to register on the eBookstore. Complete your registration and begin using Connect.**

**Note: Access Code is for one use only. If you did not purchase this book new, the access code included in this book is no longer valid.*

Need help? Visit mhhe.com/support